The Bloomsbury Companion to Locke

Bloomsbury Companions

The *Bloomsbury Companions* series is a major series of single volume companions to key research fields in the humanities aimed at postgraduate students, scholars and libraries. Each companion offers a comprehensive reference resource giving an overview of key topics, research areas, new directions and a manageable guide to beginning or developing research in the field. A distinctive feature of the series is that each companion provides practical guidance on advanced study and research in the field, including research methods and subject-specific resources.

Titles currently available in the series:

Aesthetics, edited by Anna Christina Ribeiro

Analytic Philosophy, edited by Barry Dainton and Howard Robinson

Aristotle, edited by Claudia Baracchi

Continental Philosophy, edited by John Mullarkey and Beth Lord

Epistemology, edited by Andrew Cullison

Ethics, edited by Christian Miller

Existentialism, edited by Jack Reynolds, Felicity Joseph and Ashley Woodward

Hegel, edited by Allegra de Laurentiis and Jeffrey Edwards

Heidegger, edited by Francois Raffoul and Eric Sean Nelson

Hobbes, edited by S.A. Lloyd

Hume, edited by Alan Bailey and Dan O'Brien

Kant, edited by Gary Banham, Dennis Schulting and Nigel Hems

Leibniz, edited by Brendan Look

Metaphysics, edited by Robert W. Barnard and Neil A. Manson

Philosophy of Language, edited by Manuel García-Carpintero and Max Kölbel

Philosophy of Mind, edited by James Garvey

Philosophy of Science, edited by Steven French and Juha Saatsi

Plato, edited by Gerald A. Press

Pragmatism, edited by Sami Pihlström

Socrates, edited by John Bussanich and Nicholas D. Smith

Spinoza, edited by Wiep van Bunge

THE BLOOMSBURY COMPANION TO LOCKE

GENERAL EDITORS

S.-J. Savonius-Wroth
Paul Schuurman
Jonathan Walmsley

B L O O M S B U R Y
LONDON · NEW DELHI · NEW YORK · SYDNEY

Bloomsbury Academic

An imprint of Bloomsbury Publishing Plc

50 Bedford Square	1385 Broadway
London	New York
WC1B 3DP	NY 10018
UK	USA

www.bloomsbury.com

Bloomsbury is a registered trade mark of Bloomsbury Publishing Plc

First published in paperback 2014

First published as *The Continuum Companion to Locke* 2010

© S.-J. Savonius-Wroth, Paul Schuurman,
Jonathan Walmsley and Contributors 2014

S.-J. Savonius-Wroth, Paul Schuurman and Jonathan Walmsley have asserted
their rights under the Copyright, Designs and Patents Act, 1988, to
be identified as the Editors of this work.

British Library Cataloguing-in-Publication Data
A catalogue record for this book is available from the British Library.

ISBN: PB:	978-1-47252-844-5
ePDF:	978-1-47252-494-2
ePub:	978-1-47252-416-4

Library of Congress Cataloging-in-Publication Data
A catalog record for this book is available from the Library of Congress.

Typeset by Newgen Knowledge Works (P) Ltd., Chennai, India
Printed and bound in Great Britain

CONTENTS

Introduction   ix
Acknowledgements   xiii
Abbreviations   xv
List of Contributors   xvii

1. LIFE   1
  The Life of John Locke   *Mark Goldie*   1
  A Chronology of Locke's Life   *Mark Goldie*   37
  A Summary Bibliography of Locke's Works   *Mark Goldie*   42

2. SOURCES AND CONTEMPORARIES   47
  Robert Boyle (1627–91)   *James Hill*   47
  Catherine Cockburn (1679–1749)   *Patricia Sheridan*   51
  René Descartes (1596–1650)   *Paul Schuurman*   53
  Robert Filmer (c. 1588–1653)   *Ian Harris*   57
  Thomas Hobbes (1588–1679)   *Jon Parkin*   61
  Philippus van Limborch (1633–1712)   *Luisa Simonutti*   65
  Nicolas Malebranche (1638–1715)   *Andrew Pyle*   68
  Damaris Masham (1658–1708)   *Sarah Hutton*   72
  Isaac Newton (1643–1727)   *G.A.J. Rogers*   76
  The First Earl of Shaftesbury (1621–83)   *J.R. Milton*   80
  Thomas Sydenham (1624–89)   *Jonathan Walmsley*   84

3. EARLY CRITICS   89
  George Berkeley (1685–1753)   *Jonathan Walmsley*   89
  Thomas Burnet (c.1635–1715)   *Laurent Jaffro*   93
  John Edwards (1637–16)   *John C. Higgins-Biddle*   95
  Gottfried Wilhelm Leibniz (1646–1716)   *Pauline Phemister*   97
  John Milner (1628–1702)   *J.K. Numao*   100
  John Norris (1657–1712)   *Paul Schuurman*   103

CONTENTS

Jonas Proast (c.1642–1710)   *Jean-Fabien Spitz*   105
John Sergeant (1623–1707)   *Jasper Reid*   107
The Third Earl of Shaftesbury (1671–1713)   *J.R. Milton*   109
Edward Stillingfleet (1635–99)   *Neil Fairlamb*   113
Richard Willis (1664–1734)   *J.K. Numao*   117

4. CONCEPTS   119
Absolutism   *Clare Jackson*   119
Abstraction, Universals and Species   *Jonathan Walmsley*   122
Ancient Constitutionalism   *Clare Jackson*   124
Association of Ideas   *John P. Wright*   127
Coinage   *Richard Boyd*   129
Consent and Social Contract   *R.E.R. Bunce*   131
Curriculum, The   *Sorana Corneanu*   133
Deism   *Victor Nuovo*   135
Education and Its Methods   *Sorana Corneanu*   137
Education and Its Role in Civil Society   *S.-J. Savonius-Wroth*   139
Enthusiasm   *Victor Nuovo*   141
Essences, Real and Nominal   *Margaret Atherton*   143
Faculties   *Paul Schuurman*   145
Faith, Reason and Opinion   *Benjamin Hill*   147
Free Will and Volition   *Gideon Yaffe*   150
God   *G.A.J. Rogers*   153
Hedonism   *Andrew Starkie*   156
Hypothesis and Analogy   *Jonathan Walmsley*   157
Ideas   *Keith Allen*   159
Innateness   *Daniel Carey*   165
Intuition and Demonstration   *Benjamin Hill*   169
Knowledge   *Benjamin Hill*   170
Logic   *Paul Schuurman*   174
Meaning and Signification   *Hannah Dawson*   175
Modes   *Benjamin Hill*   177
Molyneux Problem, The   *Marjolein Degenaar and Gert-Jan Lokhorst*   179
Morality and Its Demonstration   *John Colman*   183
Names   *Hannah Dawson*   184
Natural History   *Jonathan Walmsley*   186
Natural Law   *Kari Saastamoinen*   188
Number and Infinity   *Yasuhiko Tomida*   191
Obligation, Moral   *R.E.R. Bunce*   193
Perception   *Keith Allen*   194
Personal Identity   *Udo Theil*   196

Primary and Secondary Qualities   *James Hill*   199
Property   *Koen Stapelbroek*   201
Rate of Interest   *Richard Boyd*   204
Republicanism   *Markku Peltonen*   206
Resistance and Revolution   *S.-J. Savonius-Wroth*   209
Scholasticism   *James Hill*   211
Socinianism   *John Marshall*   213
Space and Time   *Benjamin Hill*   215
State of Nature, The   *Kari Saastamoinen*   216
Substance   *Michael Ayers*   218
Toleration   *Andrew Starkie*   224
Truth and Falsity   *Benjamin Hill*   228
Value and Wealth   *Koen Stapelbroek*   230
Words, Their Imperfections and Abuses   *Hannah Dawson*   232

5. SYNOPSES OF KEY WRITINGS   234
An Essay concerning Human Understanding   *Jonathan Walmsley*   234
Two Treatises of Government   *S.-J. Savonius-Wroth*   249
Letters concerning Toleration   *Timothy Stanton*   257
Some Thoughts concerning Education   *Sorana Corneanu*   265
The Reasonableness of Christianity and its Vindications   *John C. Higgins-Biddle*   269
Papers on Money   *Koen Stapelbroek*   273
Of the Conduct of the Understanding   *Paul Schuurman*   275
A Paraphrase and Notes on the Epistles of St Paul   *Victor Nuovo*   277

6. INFLUENCE   281
The Influence of Locke's Philosophy in the Eighteenth Century: Epistemology and Politics   *G.A.J.Rogers*   281
The Reception of Locke in England in the Early Eighteenth Century: Metaphysics, Religion and the State   *Timothy Stanton*   292
Locke's Civil Philosophy in the Early Eighteenth-century *République des Lettres*: An Important Footnote   *Petter Korkman*   302
Contemporary Locke Scholarship   *Roger Woolhouse and Timothy Stanton*   314

Index of Locke's Works   321
Index of Names   323
Index of Topics   327

INTRODUCTION

To go about explaining any of John Locke's works, after so great a train of expositors and commentators, might seem an attempt at vanity, censurable for its needlessness, were there not three good reasons to justify it. First of these is the current health and vigour of Locke scholarship. For almost 250 years after Locke's death scholars generally had to content themselves with the study of his published works and the occasional volume of letters or manuscripts that might find its way into print. Locke's papers were preserved by the Earls of Lovelace, descendants of Locke's relatives, and the Lovelace Collection, as it was known, was secured for posterity by the Bodleian Library in 1947. From this point forward scholars found themselves with access to notebooks, drafts, letters and records from the entirety of Locke's career. They have busied themselves in cataloguing, researching and publishing interesting findings from the collection, showing it to be rich, deep and revealing. Important works, previously known only through oblique references, have come to light – for example *The Essays on the Law of Nature*. Dates of key events in Locke's career have been definitively established, often with surprising consequences – in particular, Peter Laslett's research concerning the *Two Treatises of Government* cast this work in an entirely new light. Even now, more than sixty years after the collection was acquired by the Bodleian, substantial texts remain unpublished – for example, Locke's 'Critical Notes' on Stillingfleet's *The Mischief of Separation* (1680) and *The Unreasonableness of Separation* (1681). Locke's journals, which he kept for much of his adult life, are still only partly available in print. Important new discoveries are still being made – for example, an accurate chronology of the extant drafts of the *Essay concerning Human Understanding* has only recently been established. Looking beyond the Lovelace Collection, significant stretches of Locke's career have yet to be fully researched – Dutch records concerning his exile in Holland, for instance, have not yet been fully explored and exploited.

Capitalizing on all this scholarly activity, the Oxford University Press, aiming to produce the first comprehensive critical publication of the Lockean canon, has sponsored the *Clarendon Edition of the Works of John Locke*. This has already resulted in Nidditch's edition of the *Essay*, and De Beer's *Correspondence*, not to mention editions of *St. Paul*, the *Reasonableness*, *Some Thoughts Concerning Education*, the *Papers on Money* and, most recently, Locke's early work on *Toleration*. Scholars still have much to look forward to – a complete edition of the *Drafts of the Essay*, the Stillingfleet Correspondence, the *Letters on Toleration*, the *Two Treatises*, the journals, and several other volumes. So while much research has been completed, a great deal more remains to be undertaken. It is likely that there are more interesting scholarly discoveries yet to be made. There has, in short, never been a better time to be a Locke scholar.

If the health and vigour of Locke scholarship provides the first good reason for a fresh consideration of Locke's work, the changing tenor of this scholarship provides the second. We do not expect historians of science to be practising scientists, or historians of art, artists. The history of philosophy is something of an exception to this rule. Contemporary philosophers often act as custodians of their subject's past – taking the work of their predecessors as their starting point, and using it for their own ends. Thinkers such as Locke set the terms of modern philosophical debate. But contemporary philosophers sometimes forget that both the terms and the debate have evolved radically over the last 300 years. Philosophers today can all too easily overlook the historical context in which their predecessors worked and treat them as if they were engaged in current philosophical disputes. This can impose categories and concerns on their work, of which they had no conception.

In Locke's case, thanks to the recent wave of scholarly activity, such an ahistorical attitude is no longer tenable. Locke must now be read as very much a man of his times, whose considerations and conclusions were stimulated by the era in which he lived, and whose views cannot be properly understood outside it. Locke scholarship today is much more likely to be about the circumstances in which Locke made a certain remark, and what it might mean in that context, than about whether his views can immediately solve today's pressing philosophical problems. Indeed, the former is necessary for the latter to be possible.

A third good reason for re-examining Locke's work is the expanding scope of Locke studies. If contemporary philosophers have sometimes been remiss in the way they have studied Locke's work, they have also been somewhat partial in what they have studied. Locke has been viewed as the writer of the *Essay*, the *Two Treatises* and (sometimes) the *Letters on Toleration*. These texts have been taken to define his intellectual interests, and consideration of his life and work has been largely confined to these alone. Examining some current summaries of his thinking, readers might have no idea that Locke wrote a seminal work on education, helped draft the constitution for one of England's North American colonies, produced two significant works of biblical scholarship, published papers on economic theory and wrote several reports on a variety of government affairs. They would not know that he trained to be a doctor, was a diplomat and a civil servant, worked with some of the keenest political minds of his generation and went into exile under suspicion of sedition. He was much more than what we would today consider a 'philosopher'. Contemporary philosophers often lack the training in intellectual history that would help them appreciate the full spectrum of Locke's work and, as a consequence, the breadth and depth of his thinking has been neglected. The recent proliferation of Locke scholarship, and the broader consideration of the context of his work, has led to a much wider appreciation of his diverse intellectual interests, and the interconnections between them.

Given these three reasons then, this *Companion* aims to present a rounded view of the whole of Locke's work, and to offer interpretations where detailed historical research informs rigorous conceptual analysis. Rather than present a small number of lengthy essays on purely 'philosophical' topics, this *Companion* provides a large number of concise accounts embracing all areas of Locke's thinking. The core of the book comprises fifty or so succinct essays on the key concepts of his work in epistemology, theology, education, economics, politics and ethics. This 'dictionary' of Lockean concepts is complemented by synopses of his most important publications. These include his most famous works, the *Essay concerning Human Understanding*, the *Two Treatises of Government* and the *Letters on Toleration*, but also encompass outlines of his *Reasonableness of Christianity*, the *Paraphrase and Notes on the Epistles of St. Paul*, *Some Thoughts concerning Education*, his papers on economics, and the posthumously published *Of Conduct of the Understanding*. These two sections will thus present the important elements of Locke's thought, with an overview of the works in which this thinking was presented.

To place Locke's work in its biographical context, a substantial 'Life' is provided. In addition, a number of essays are devoted to Locke's contemporaries and influences, showing how certain thinkers stimulated his views and helped shape the works for which he is now renowned. Likewise, a similar number of essays is devoted to his early critics, illustrating the various disputes, publications and rebuttals they occasioned. To conclude, four longer essays furnish an overview of Locke's influence and the reception of his work. The first of these presents a broad review of Locke's long-standing influence in the fields of epistemology and politics. The next deals with the reception of Locke's works in early eighteenth-century England, bringing into focus his impact on the debate regarding the relations between Church and state. The third shows how the continental audience became aware of his civil philosophy, and how Locke's became a voice of the European Enlightenment. The last provides an overview of the state of contemporary Locke scholarship.

There will be areas of overlap. A topic with its own essay may also be touched on in essays dealing with related subjects, and in the description of the work in which it first appeared. Locke's treatment of the issue may have drawn inspiration from one of his contemporaries, and provoked the ire of another. The reader will thus be able to see the same subject from a variety of different perspectives, giving them a deeper sense of the matter at hand, an impression of how the various areas of Locke's work are connected, and a sense of how different scholars regard the same question. This should allow the reader requiring a quick overview of an area immediately to attain it, but also give those with a more sustained interest the chance to gain a better understanding of the context and content of Locke's thinking. There should be much of interest for the beginner and the dedicated scholar alike.

Authors for each of the essays have been selected for their subject-matter expertise, but also for their differing perspectives on Locke's work and their diverse backgrounds. Each writer has been encouraged, within the broadly historical approach of the work as a whole, to provide their personal view of the subjects that they are covering. Contributors work in a variety of disciplines – history, philosophy, theology, economics and politics. Several of the editors of the Clarendon Edition have made contributions. Authors hail from Australia, Canada, the Czech Republic, Finland, France, Germany, Great Britain, Italy, Japan, the Republic of Ireland, the Netherlands, Romania and the United States of America. This kaleidoscope of opinions, multiplicity of view points and diversity of subject matter should create a uniquely rounded view of Locke, providing a comprehensive portrait of the man, his life and times, his contemporaries and critics, his work and enduring influence.

ACKNOWLEDGEMENTS

The editors would like to thank the Continuum International Publishing Group for supporting this project, and the several members of staff there who have assisted in the production of this volume: Rudi Thoemmes, Anthony Haynes, Evander Lomke, David Barker, Sarah Campbell and Merilyn Holme.

The editors would also like to thank Bloomsbury Publishing for supporting this project and producing the paperback edition of the book – in particular Camilla Erskine, Liza Thompson and Rachel Eisenhauer.

The editors would like to thank Bart Leeuwenburgh for his invaluable editorial assistance. Thanks are also due to J.R. Milton and G.A.J. Rogers for their helpful advice on the overall direction of this *Companion* and their specific comments on certain of the essays.

The editors would also like to thank each of the contributors for their work on this project: Keith Allen, Margaret Atherton, Michael Ayers, Richard Boyd, Robin Bunce, Daniel Carey, John Colman, Sorana Corneanu, Hannah Dawson, Marjolein Degenaar, Neil Fairlamb, Mark Goldie, Ian Harris, John Higgins-Biddle, Benjamin Hill, James Hill, Sarah Hutton, Clare Jackson, Laurent Jaffro, Petter Korkman, Gert-Jan Lockhorst, John Marshall, J.R. Milton, Kei Numao, Victor Nuovo, Jon Parkin, Markku Peltonen, Pauline Phemister, Andrew Pyle, Jasper Reid, G.A.J. Rogers, Kari Saastamoinen, Patricia Sheridan, Luisa Simonutti, J.F. Spitz, Tim Stanton, Koen Stapelbroek, Andrew Starkie, Udo Thiel, Yasuhiko Tomida, Roger Woolhouse, John Wright and Gideon Yaffe.

For their help, and for countless acts of friendship, Sami Savonius-Wroth is deeply grateful to Paul Schuurman and Jonathan Walmsley.

Paul Schuurman would like to thank G.A.J. Rogers, Bart Leeuwenburgh and Wiep van Bunge for their support, his incomparable fellow editors Craig and Sami for sharing his burdens as an Under-Labourer, and Mark Brummel for his company and his cigarettes.

Jonathan Walmsley would like to thank his wife Kate, his Mum and Dad, Paul, for inviting him to participate in this project, Sami for his editorial acumen, and J.R. Milton for introducing him to Dr Locke.

ABBREVIATIONS

In this work the following abbreviations are used:

Corr.   Locke, John, *The Correspondence of John Locke*, 8 vols to date, ed. E.S. de Beer (Oxford, 1976–).

Draft A or B   Locke, John, *Drafts for the Essay concerning Human Understanding and Other Philosophical Writings, vol. I: Drafts A and B*, ed. Peter H. Nidditch and G.A.J. Rogers (Oxford, 1990).
                 Citations are by Draft, section, and page number from this edition.

Draft C   Locke, John, 'An Essay Concerning humane understanding in fower books 1685', Pierpont Morgan Library, New York, Shelfmark MA 998.
                 Citations are by book, chapter and section.

E   Locke, John, *An Essay concerning Human Understanding*, ed. Peter H. Nidditch (Oxford, 1975).
                 Citations are by book, chapter, section and page number from this edition.

EdT   Locke, John, *Epistola de Tolerantia: A Letter on Toleration*, ed. Raymond Klibansky and J.W. Gough (Oxford, 1968).

ELN   Locke, John, *Essays on the Law of Nature*, ed. W. von Leyden (Oxford, 1954).

ETol.   Locke, John, *An Essay concerning Toleration and Other Writings on Law and Politics, 1667–1683*, ed. J.R. Milton and Philip Milton (Oxford, 2006).

LoM   Locke, John, *Locke on Money*, 2 vols, ed. Patrick Hyde Kelly (Oxford, 1991).

ABBREVIATIONS

ParN   Locke, John, *A Paraphrase and Notes on the Epistles of St Paul to the Galatians, 1 and 2 Corinthians, Romans, Ephesians*, 2 vols, ed. Arthur W. Wainwright (Oxford, 1987).

RCh.   Locke, John, *The Reasonableness of Christianity: As delivered in the Scriptures*, ed. John C. Higgins-Biddle (Oxford, 1999).

STE   Locke, John, *Some Thoughts concerning Education*, ed. John W. and Jean S. Yolton (Oxford, 1989).

TTG   Locke, John, *Two Treatises of Government*, ed. Peter Laslett (Student edn, Cambridge, 1988).
              Citations are by treatise and section number.

W   Locke, John, *The Works of John Locke: A New Edition, Corrected*, 10 vols (Aalen, 1963, repr. of London, 1823).

LIST OF CONTRIBUTORS

Keith Allen
Lecturer
Department of Philosophy
University of York
UK

Margaret Atherton
Distinguished Professor
Department of Philosophy
University of Wisconsin-Milwaukee
USA

Michael Ayers
Professor
Wadham College
University of Oxford
UK

Richard Boyd
Associate Professor of Government
Georgetown University, Washington
USA

R.E.R. Bunce
Bye-Fellow
St Edmund's College
University of Cambridge
UK

Daniel Carey
Senior Lecturer
School of Humanities
National University of Ireland, Galway
Ireland

John Colman
Honorary Research Associate
University of Tasmania
Australia

Sorana Corneanu
Lecturer in English
University of Bucharest
Romania

Hannah Dawson
Lecturer in the History of Ideas
School of History, Classics and
Archaeology
University of Edinburgh
UK

Marjolein Degenaar
Teacher
Erasmiaans Gymnasium Rotterdam
The Netherlands

Neil Fairlamb
Rector of Beaumaris
The Church in Wales
UK

LIST OF CONTRIBUTORS

Mark Goldie
Reader in British Intellectual History
Faculty of History
University of Cambridge
UK

Ian Harris
Lecturer
University of Leicester
UK

John C. Higgins-Biddle
Assistant Professor (Retired)
University of Connecticut School of
Medicine
USA

Benjamin Hill
Assistant Professor of History of Early
Modern Philosophy
Department of Philosophy
University of Western Ontario
Canada

James Hill
Charles University
Prague
Czech Republic

Sarah Hutton
Professor
Department of English and Creative
Writing
University of Aberystwyth
UK

Clare Jackson
Trinity Hall
University of Cambridge
UK

Laurent Jaffro
Professor of Moral Philosophy
Department of Philosophy
Université de Paris 1 Panthéon-
Sorbonne
France

Petter Korkman
Helsinki Collegium
University of Helsinki
Finland

Gert-Jan Lokhorst
Assistant Professor
Department of Philosophy
Delft University of Technology
The Netherlands

John Marshall
Professor
Department of History
Johns Hopkins University, Baltimore
USA

J.R. Milton
Professor of the History of Philosophy
Department of Philosophy
King's College London
UK

J.K. Numao
Part-time Lecturer
Faculty of Law
Keio University
Japan

Victor Nuovo
Charles A. Dana Professor of
Philosophy Emeritus and Senior
Research Fellow
Middlebury College, Vermont
USA

Jon Parkin
Senior Lecturer
Department of Politics
University of York
UK

Markku Peltonen
University of Helsinki
Finland

Pauline Phemister
Reader in Philosophy
University of Edinburgh
UK

Andrew Pyle
Reader in Modern Philosophy
University of Bristol
UK

Jasper Reid
Lecturer in Philosophy
King's College London
UK

G.A.J. Rogers
Emeritus Professor of the History of
Philosophy
Keele University
UK

Kari Saastamoinen
University of Helsinki
Finland

S.-J. Savonius-Wroth
Fellow, Helsinki Collegium
University of Helsinki
Finland

Paul Schuurman
Assistant Professor in the History of
Philosophy
Faculty of Philosophy
Erasmus University Rotterdam
The Netherlands

Patricia Sheridan
Associate Professor
Department of Philosophy
University of Guelph
Canada

Luisa Simonutti
Professor
L'Istituto per la Storia del Pensiero
Filosofico e Scientifico Moderno
Consiglio Nazionale delle Ricerche
ISPF-Milano/Università degli studi di
Ferrara
Italy

Jean-Fabien Spitz
Professor of Political Philosophy
Department of Philosophy
Université de Paris 1 Panthéon-
Sorbonne and Institut Universitaire de
France
France

Timothy Stanton
Lecturer in Political Philosophy
Department of Politics
University of York
UK

Koen Stapelbroek
Erasmus University Rotterdam and
Helsinki Collegium for Advanced
Studies, University of Helsinki
The Netherlands and Finland

LIST OF CONTRIBUTORS

Andrew Starkie
Vicar
St Gabriel's
Middleton Junction, Manchester
UK

Udo Thiel
Professor
Institut für Philosophie
University of Graz
Austria

Yasuhiko Tomida
Professor
Graduate School of Human and
Environmental Studies
Kyoto University
Japan

Jonathan Walmsley
London
UK

Roger Woolhouse
Emeritus Professor
Department of Philosophy
University of York
UK

John Prentice Wright
Professor of Philosophy
Department of Philosophy and Religion
Central Michigan University
USA

Gideon Yaffe
Associate Professor of Philosophy and
Law
University of Southern California
USA

1

LIFE

THE LIFE OF JOHN LOCKE

Locke was a child of the late Reformation and a parent of the early Enlightenment. He was born when universities renewed their study of Aristotle and died when universities were trying to understand NEWTON's *Principia*. He was born when England was weak in European reckoning and died when it had become a global imperial power. He was born when court masques lauded the divinity of kingship and died when journalists celebrated parliamentary liberty. More than most of his contemporaries, Locke helped facilitate these transitions. Such a claim is of course sententious and perilously close to elevating individual human agency, and intellectual agency at that, too far above the deeper structures of historical change. It is also apt to be tautological, since concepts like 'Enlightenment' are abstractions we construct from the thought of individuals such as Locke. The name 'Locke' is in danger of serving as a signifier of schematic categories, soon detaching him from historical and textual specificity. Nonetheless, such general claims help to provide a compass as we enter the contingencies of an individual life of prodigious intellectual energy as well as energetic public engagement. What follows is a narrative of Locke's life, but one that pauses to pursue themes beyond immediate moments. It avoids litanies of precise dates and accordingly is supplemented by appendices providing more exact chronologies of his life and publications.

Early Life and Education

John Locke's father was not quite a gentleman. He ranked with the 'parish gentry' but not with the county gentry. His own father had been a prosperous clothier and his wife, Agnes Keene, was a tanner's daughter; one of his brothers was a brewer and a nephew was a pewterer. He suffered financially during the Civil Wars, but was able to bequeath to his son a small estate with a few tenants. His son thereby became familiar with the vicissitudes of the rural economy, though in later life he would be an absentee landlord, keeping up with his native West Country at second hand, via reports from stewards. Locke's conception of justice was to lead him to instruct a steward to be tough with able-bodied tenants – 'I have sent you a warrant for distraining ... I believe Pensford is not without a bailiff' – while at the same time urging charity to ease the deserving indigent – 'about Christmas lay out twenty shillings in bread to be distributed to the poor of Pensford, especially those that are old and cannot work and those who have a numerous family ... preferring the honest and industrious to those that are or have been lazy and vicious' (*Corr.*, vol. viii, pp. 23–4). The duty to be 'honest and industrious' was fundamental to Locke's moral universe.

Pensford is a village six miles south of Bristol. The economic prosperity of the region depended upon the textile trade. There were many stages in turning wool into cloth, involving a high degree of division of labour. 'Labour,' Locke averred, 'puts the difference of value on everything.' Rightly ordered

1

economies, he judged, exhibited a progressive intensification in the application of labour to land. Land that was left to nature, 'that hath no improvement of pasturage, tillage, or planting, is ... waste'. There was, he believed, scarcely a greater offence against God than waste. In his *Two Treatises of Government* (1689), Locke was to cite the West Country as paradigmatic of a virtuously productive agrarian economy (*TTG* II.40, 42, 37).

John Locke senior's principal avocation was as an attorney and he served as clerk to the justices of the peace for the county of Somerset. His surviving notebook is largely concerned with magistratical duties, such as the disciplining of tavern keepers, vagrants and the begetters of bastards (British Library, London (BL), Add. MS 28273). Locke later recalled that his father kept him 'much in awe, and at a distance whilst he was a boy, but relaxing ... by degrees of that severity as he grew up ... till ... he lived perfectly with him as a friend'. His mother he described as 'a very pious woman and ... affectionate' (*The Early Lives of John Locke* (*EL*): Masham).

When Locke was ten, the Civil Wars broke out. His father fought in the Parliamentarian army. Locke thus grew up among those who made war against King Charles I. Yet they were not fighting against kingship, as most Parliamentarians aimed to limit rather than destroy the crown, and believed in a 'mixed' polity in which king, lords and commons provided mutual counterbalances. The Parliamentarian leaders repeatedly negotiated with Charles, but were outmanoeuvred by their own increasingly radical army. The regicide of 1649 appalled them, and most of those who had fought against Charles welcomed the restoration of his son to the throne in 1660 after the collapse of Oliver Cromwell's republic.

In religion, Locke grew up among Puritans. Yet these were not enemies of a disciplined national church. Most Puritans believed in the Church of England, for which they sought 'further reformation' and the purging of remnants of 'popery'. They repudiated a cere-monialism which seemed to accent the superstitions of the altar over the preaching of the Word; they deplored the theology of Arminianism, which, in emphasizing human moral effort, seemed to weaken God's omnipotence and Christ's atonement for sin; and they resented episcopal authoritarianism. They took for granted the desirability of a church with a common worship and creed under a single ecclesiastical discipline, and were appalled by the emergence of radical sects and outlandish heresies. They were Presbyterians, though the term is inexact, since few were fully committed to Calvinism. Characteristic of the people who surrounded the young Locke was Samuel Crooke, the minister who baptized him. Before the War, Crooke ignored those rubrics of the Book of Common Prayer to which he objected, and survived the wrath of his bishop. Typical too were Locke's grandfather, who bequeathed money for a weekly Bible lecture, and his father, who wondered if bowing to the altar and kneeling to receive communion were impious, and whether 'the voice of the people', rather than the mandate of bishops, should determine the choice of parish ministers (BL, Add. MS 28273, p. 136).

Little evidence from Locke's first quarter-century helps to establish his own religious convictions with any precision. We cannot, for instance, find any expression of the Calvinist doctrine of divine predestination. In a letter of 1661 Locke implied scepticism about a preacher who insisted 'that the elect could not fall from grace, let devils do and men say what they would' (*Corr.*, vol. i, p. 171). We should avoid the venerable error of supposing that Puritanism predisposed Locke to religious, or any other kind of, 'liberalism'. Even the Independents, champions of religious TOLERA-TION, drew a line at the sects. We can be confident that Locke deprecated the sects, notably the Quakers, of whose 'ENTHUSIASM' he was suspicious, their notion of an 'inner light' through God's direct and immediate inspiration, and penchant for forms of religious experience given to ecstasy and mystical reverie

(*Corr.*, vol. i, pp. 43–4, 82–4, 122–4). Locke's personal piety was sober and dry, even anaemic: his papers are not suggestive of prayerfulness, spiritual introspection or passionate communion with the divine. 'We cannot be all devotion, all praises and hallelujahs and perpetually in the vision of things above.' Religion was a matter of considered belief and the pragmatics of dutiful worldly living, the 'management of ... temporal affairs' that puts us in 'a condition of doing that good and performing those offices required ... in [our] station' (*Corr.*, vol. i, p. 649). Though he later became a defender of religious toleration, trenchantly insisting on the rights of separatist denominations, he remained a uniformitarian by inclination, not because he thought the rituals and governance of the Church of England were directly given by God, but, on the contrary, since they were manmade, he deemed it unduly scrupulous and spiritually precious to object to conventional norms. Accordingly, Locke conformed to the public worship of the Cromwellian Church and then to the public worship of the re-established Anglican Church. Whatever sympathy Locke came to have for Dissenters, and whatever anticlerical vehemence he was to show against oppressive church hierarchies, he never evinced any desire to become a Dissenter himself. So far as we can tell, after re-establishment, he attended Anglican parish worship and took the Anglican Eucharist until his dying day. In 1673 he stepped into a government post vacated by a Dissenter who scrupled to take the Anglican sacrament required to qualify him for office.

Locke attended Westminster School in London. Seventeenth-century English education was not as socially exclusive as it was to become during the ensuing two centuries. A talented boy of modest background could go to a good school and to university, if he had a patron. Locke's patron was Colonel Alexander Popham, Member of Parliament for Bath, under whom his father served both in the army and as steward of estates. During the war, Popham's troops smashed the 'superstitious'

windows, organ and bishop's throne in Wells Cathedral, and Popham became an elder in the (largely abortive) Presbyterian Church that rose from the ashes of episcopacy. His politics and religion epitomize those adumbrated above. By the time of the Restoration, Popham, now retreating from the radicalism he had unwittingly unleashed, was in touch with royalist agents. That he served in parliament and local office after the Restoration is a measure both of Puritan rapprochement with Stuart monarchy and of Charles II's skill in appeasing his father's enemies. The young Locke, in gratitude for benefits received, sent Popham a letter, a conventional exercise in panegyric to a Maecenas: 'The greatest advantage I demand of my studies is an ability to serve you ... best patron ... If then I have made any acquisitions in learning 'tis fit I dedicate them to you as their first author.' In also remarking that 'the whole nation looks on you as a defender of their laws and liberties', Locke implied his alignment with Popham's politics (*Corr.*, vol. i, p. 145).

Westminster School under the revered but severe Richard Busby was the finest school in England. Locke's fellow pupils included John Dryden, Robert Hooke and Christopher Wren, as well as William Godolphin, brother of Sidney to whom Thomas HOBBES dedicated *Leviathan* (1651). At such schools the mainstay of the CURRICULUM was classics. Like his learned contemporaries, Locke acquired a deep familiarity with classical philosophy and Latin literature. Composing and conversing in Latin was the scholarly norm. However, Locke's mature work shared in a cultural shift towards the vernacular and he took care in his *Essay concerning Human Understanding* (1689) to write in a plain, easy, discursive style, eschewing the heaviness of recondite scholastic and Latinate erudition. Of his mature works, only the *Epistola de Tolerantia* (*Letter concerning Toleration*, 1689) was written in Latin, since it was primarily intended for a continental audience. The *Epistola* is a good instance of Locke's assumption that his gentlemanly audience appreciated allusions to Latin literature, for it contains references to Cicero, Horace, Ovid, Tacitus and Virgil. Godly, scriptural Protestants were generally remarkably absorptive of pagan learning and rarely resisted the pervasive culture of classical humanism. Late in life, Locke recommended the New Testament and Cicero's *On Duties* as the two best works of moral teaching (Locke, 1997, p. 377; *Corr.*, vol. viii, p. 57).

Oxford University

A few yards from Locke's school, Charles I was executed in 1649. England became a republic, governed by the 'Rump' Parliament and Cromwell's army. Among institutions purged were the two universities, which, having already lost their Anglican royalists, now lost their Presbyterian royalists. The college of Christ Church, Oxford, which Locke entered in 1652, was now headed by John Owen, nicknamed 'Cromwell's pope'. A religious Independent, Owen was Calvinist in his doctrine of salvation, but anti-Presbyterian and congregationalist in his doctrine of ecclesiastical polity. Locke's tutor was William Cole, also an Independent, who was later to reject the Restoration Church and become a Dissenting minister. The high Tory biographer Anthony Wood was to remark that Locke had had a 'fanatical tutor', but men of Wood's ilk called all varieties of Puritan 'fanatics' (*EL*: Wood).

As the richest and socially weightiest in Oxford, Christ Church was an unusual college. In unrevolutionary times it was a principal engine for generating the Church of England's hierarchy, counting many bishops among its alumni. Before and after the Wars and the Republic, its chapel had been and would again be a cathedral, that of the bishop of Oxford. It did not have Fellows; rather, it was governed by the dean and canons of the cathedral, distinct from its main body of academic staff who were called 'students'. The students began as undergraduates and proceeded as bachelors and masters. They were required to pass a number of hurdles, involving residence, the taking of degrees, ordination to the clerical ministry and

the avoidance of marriage. In common with other colleges, the teaching staff were generally young, as college tutoring was normally superseded by acquiring a parish and a wife. Since their pupils were also young, often matriculating in their mid-teens, the role of tutors was pastoral as well as pedagogic. Most teaching was collegiate; the wider university had a limited role and there were few posts of university professor. One whom Locke admired was Edward Pococke, professor of Arabic and Hebrew, whose son he tutored and about whom he wrote an affectionate memoir (*Corr.*, vol. viii, pp. 37–42).

The universities inherited the medieval practices of lecturing by means of exposition of classical and patristic authorities, and of public disputation, in which forensic skills were honed by challenges and responses to hypotheses. Locke later denounced the fatuity of these scholastic methods and the backward curriculum. He wrote that he 'never loved the trade of disputing in the schools, but was always wont to declaim against it as being rather invented for wrangling or ostentation than to discover truth', and that he 'lost a great deal of time ... because the only philosophy then known at Oxford was the peripatetic [the Aristotelian], perplexed with obscure terms and stuffed with useless questions' (*EL*: Masham, Le Clerc). He contemptuously called disputation 'hogshearing', from a proverb: 'a great cry and little wool, quoth the devil when he sheared the hog' (*Corr.*, vol. viii, p. 230; cf. i, pp. 253–5; iv, pp. 623–8). According to Damaris MASHAM's memoir, Locke attributed his philosophical awakening to independent reading of DESCARTES, though it is easier to document his encounter with Descartes's natural philosophy than with his metaphysics (*EL*: Masham).

Locke can barely be said to have had a frivolous phase of youth, though it is reported that his intellectual irritation expressed itself in reading plays and romances, the composition of witty letters in the spirit of the French stylist Vincent Voiture, and the cultivation of a characteristic rhetorical facility of the age, 'raillery', ironic wordplay that hovered on the edge of offensive sarcasm. He was to caution that raillery was 'the nicest [trickiest] part of conversation' because of its 'dangerous consequence, if not well managed' (*EL*: Masham). In maturity, Locke's means of expressing anger was by the sharpness of his tongue; he needed neither passion nor a raised voice to inflict a crushing rebuke, and his correspondence is littered with the injured remonstrations of his victims. In youth, the playful, yet also archly artificial, style of some of his letters is exemplified in a series exchanged with a circle of young women at Black Hall in Oxford. He was perhaps in love with Elinor Parry, though it is difficult to decode his mannered Platonic tropes. 'My fair Urania', he called her: Plato had turned Aphrodite, goddess of sexual love, into Urania, goddess of intellectual or heavenly love (*Corr.*, vol. i, pp. 103–5).

At the restoration of the monarchy in 1660, the universities were purged again. Christ Church acquired a new dean, John Fell, who was later also vice-chancellor and Bishop of Oxford, and who dominated the college for the next quarter-century. There is no sign that Locke had difficulty accepting the new order and he soon received a certificate of orthodoxy signed by Fell. During the first half of the 1660s Locke was an assiduous college teacher. He was appointed successively to the posts of praelector in Greek and rhetoric, censor in moral philosophy, and tutor. He lectured in the college hall, and, as a tutor, took charge of pupils, *in loco parentis*, overseeing their expenditure and corresponding with their parents. Conventionally enough, a couple of former pupils became members of parliament, a couple scholars, others clergymen (Milton, 1994).

Shortly after the Restoration, Locke wrote, but did not publish, two works which mark his first sustained reflection on religious, philosophical, moral and political matters. The first is now known as the *Two Tracts on Government*, a title it acquired when first published in 1967, and which scarcely reveals that these are disquisitions on ecclesiology: the gov-

ernance of religion. Locke addressed an urgent topical matter. For many months after the Restoration, the future character of the national Church remained in contention. Politically, the Restoration was a compromise between Anglican and Presbyterian royalists. Former Parliamentarians joined the king's privy council and received peerages, and it seemed that, in parallel, a compromise church settlement might be achieved. In the event, the Act of Uniformity of 1662 proved dogmatically narrow in its Anglicanism, but in the meantime the matter remained open. Much heat was generated over ceremonies, because of what they symbolized. Puritans objected to kneeling to receive the Eucharist, since it betokened a popish veneration of the body of Christ, and they objected to ministers wearing white surplices instead of black 'Geneva gowns'. At Christ Church, the national argument was played out in microcosm, as rival groups of students seized white and black vestments and dumped them in the river. Some argued that such matters ought not to be rigidly stipulated, but that the state should tolerate different practices according to preference. In this view, these matters were 'things indifferent' to salvation, or 'adiaphora'; that is, they were not required by Scripture and hence were not 'things necessary' to salvation. One who argued this case was Edward Bagshaw, Locke's colleague at Christ Church, in his *Great Question concerning Things Indifferent in Religious Worship* (1660). In replying to Bagshaw, Locke accepted that there was a sphere of things 'indifferent', but took the line that it was nonetheless right for the state to impose conformity in matters indifferent, for the sake of unity, decency and public safety.

The *Tracts* were not primarily works of political theory, but they reflect Locke at his most conservative. They are deeply Augustinian in emphasizing the necessity of magistracy as the rod of discipline over sinful and violent humankind. This mood is palpable in letters Locke wrote at the time of the collapse of the republic into months of chaos before the return of monarchy. 'This great Bedlam England'; 'Oh for a pilot that would steer the tossed ship of this state to the haven of happiness!'; ''Tis the great misery of this shattered and giddy nation that wars have produced nothing but wars'; it is a land of 'tyrants such as are the promisers of liberty' (*Corr.*, vol. i, pp. 124–5, 136–7).

Locke's second early piece of writing is now known as the *Essays on the Law of Nature*, again from its first edition of 1954. The *Essays* are more accurately termed 'Disquisitions' or 'Questions', since they follow the format of scholastic disputations, in which points of difficulty are posed as propositions and then sustained or refuted. While Locke probably planned to publish the *Tracts*, the *Essays* were designed as pedagogic exercises. The eight essays explore possible grounds for holding that there is a binding law of nature. Locke doubts that there are any innate moral intuitions: there is no universal judgement of humankind about ethical values, and there is abundant anthropological evidence of the remarkable cultural diversity of moral beliefs. This does not rule out rational investigation of the moral law and the fourth essay is called 'Can reason attain to the knowledge of NATURAL LAW through sense experience?', to which the answer is affirmative. The empirical character of Locke's mature epistemology and moral philosophy is already visible here.

During the 1660s Locke developed a new range of interests in what today would be called 'science' but is less anachronistically termed 'natural philosophy'. He became acquainted with Robert BOYLE, whose laboratory he probably attended, took classes on chemistry with Peter Stahl and medicine with Thomas Willis, and participated in anatomical dissections. He absorbed the new mechanical philosophy, expressed in such works as Boyle's *New Essays Physico-Mechanical* (1660). 'Physick' became Locke's principal interest and he was especially curious about respiration and the circulation of the blood. In London he befriended the influential physician Thomas SYDENHAM, endorsing the latter's observational approach to the investigation of epidemic fevers. Under Sydenham's aegis, Locke composed two tracts, 'De arte medica' and 'Anatomia', which are profoundly sceptical of medical theorizing and urge careful practical observation. The second edition of Sydenham's *Methodus curandi febres* (1668) included an admiring poem by Locke; the complement was returned in the dedication to the third edition (1676), where Sydenham wrote that Locke was 'a man whom, in the acuteness of his intellect, in the steadiness of his judgement, in the simplicity, that is, in the excellence of his manners, I confidently declare to have, amongst the men of our time, few equals'. In due course, Locke took a medical degree, and became an occasional practitioner for the rest of his life, often styled 'Dr Locke'. His notebooks contain extensive extracts from medical treatises and numerous recipes for remedies. As was the custom, he frequently diagnosed by correspondence, furnishing friends and acquaintances with medical advice.

Locke's scientific interests were confirmed by election as a Fellow of the Royal Society in 1668. Though he occasionally attended meetings and submitted short papers for publication in the Society's *Transactions*, he was never an active member. Of his submissions, the most significant is an extract from his weather observations, having begun to keep such a record in 1666 and continuing at first intermittently and then very regularly in the 1690s. It is one of the earliest efforts at systematic meteorological observation. Another extract appeared in Boyle's posthumously published *General History of the Air* (1692), which Locke saw through the press.

The Earl of Shaftesbury's Household

By the middle of the 1660s Locke had become dissatisfied with the trajectory of his Oxford life. The most tangible sign of this was his reluctance to seek ordination to the priesthood, which was required by his studentship and which he could no longer evade. The reasons for his reluctance are unclear, though the poverty of country parsons and the demeaning search for preferment may have weighed (*Corr.*, vol. i, pp. 215, 303–4). Yet ordination need not have entailed parish responsibilities – it was possible to become a household chaplain to the great or to take up a prestigious cathedral post – and he was not a reluctant adherent of the Church. It is evident that Locke wished to retain his studentship, whether or not he continued to reside in Oxford and undertake college duties, and he achieved his aim by a striking device. He successfully obtained a royal dispensation, suspending the statutory requirement of ordination. It was common for the crown to use the royal prerogative to evade university statutes in order to award favoured individuals with fellowships or degrees, and sometimes college authorities themselves requested royal mandates to circumvent inconvenient rules. Mostly the practice was uncontroversial, notwithstanding some irritation at the crown's profligate use of mandates. Under James II, however, the practice was to become hugely provocative, when it was ruthlessly deployed to force upon the universities Roman Catholic fellows and heads of colleges. The fact is that Locke was prepared to take advantage of a royal edict to override local statute, an exercise of arbitrary royal power, albeit in microcosm. There would always be ambiguity in Locke's relationship to the power of the state. As for his unorthodox retention of his studentship, he later regularized his position by securing election to a 'faculty' studentship in medicine, which did not require ordination.

Locke now considered a career as a servant of the state, which is what he became during a significant proportion of his ensuing life. This may seem surprising, given that our prevailing image of his political identity is as the revolutionary author of the *Two Treatises of Government* (1689) and as someone engaged in seditious conspiracy against the Stuart crown in the 1680s (Ashcraft, 1986). Yet Locke's alienation from the regime was highly contingent; it is characteristic neither of his younger period during the first fifteen years of Charles II's reign nor of his post-Revolution life in the 1690s, after the second overthrow of the House of Stuart. Moreover, we need to be wary of a modern romantic miasma that surrounds Locke, and renders him a cynosure of radicalism and resistance. The rebel Locke was also a courtier and civil servant.

One motive the crown had for the use of mandates was to recruit able university men for royal service. Locke's mandate has the look of this. He may be compared with his fellow student, John Ellis, who also received a dispensation, and became a secretary to diplomats and ministers, in which role he would later receive intelligence reports on Locke's suspicious political activities. In 1665 Locke accepted an offer to serve as secretary to the English envoy to the city of Cleves (Kleve) in a province of the Elector of Brandenburg, close to the Dutch border, at a time when Charles II was seeking benign neutrality from the Elector during the Second Dutch War. On his return from Cleves, Locke was offered a similar post, to Spain, but declined.

Cleves was a revelation to him. It was one of the German cities which had achieved toleration for rival Christian confessions, as part of the Treaty of Westphalia which settled the religious conflicts of the Thirty Years War. Not only were Calvinists and Lutherans at liberty, but also Catholics. In few places in Europe was it possible to spend a Sunday watching Protestants and Catholics openly and peaceably going to church a few streets away from one other. Locke became a confessional tourist, agog. He dropped in on Catholics ('bad Latin and worse pronunciation') and Lutherans ('merrily singing with their hats on') and Calvinists ('no pictures at all'), and marvelled that 'they quietly permit one another to choose their own way to heaven, for I cannot observe any quarrels or animosities amongst them upon the account of religion' (*Corr.*, vol. i, pp. 235–7, 228). The experience taught Locke the important lesson that toleration of a plurality of faiths was feasible. This was, however, a thought that hardly dared speak its name in Restoration England. Locke came to accept that, whatever the spiritual merits of permitting rival religions, as a matter of 'reason of state' confessional diversity need not inevitably be a source of fratricidal violence. Most religious groups, when not provoked by harassment, had no motive to be disruptive. Such thoughts permanently altered Locke's opinions on religious toleration.

In 1666 Locke met the most important man in his life. By happenstance, he was deputed to fetch spa water for Anthony Ashley Cooper, Lord Ashley, future Earl of SHAFTESBURY, a member of the king's council and Chancellor of the Exchequer. Locke served Shaftesbury for most of the rest of the earl's life: he died in exile in Holland in 1683. Early memoirs of Locke are almost embarrassingly fulsome about the immediate rapport and mutual regard between the two men. It is plain that Locke himself, late in life, waxed lyrical about Shaftesbury. Locke's relationship with Shaftesbury was transformative, rendering him a more obviously political creature, both philosophically and governmentally. It also made him metropolitan, for he moved to London, and, when in England, London remained his principal residence until his own flight to Holland in 1683. To what extent Locke's opinions were shaped by Shaftesbury, and vice versa, is hard to judge. Contemporary attributions of influence, in both directions, do not always convince. Lady Mordaunt, for instance, attributed Locke's competency to write a 'scheme of government' to his 'having been infected by that great man Lord Shaftesbury' (*Corr.*, vol. iii, p. 538), whilst Robert Ferguson, conversely, alleged that the earl, on his deathbed, proved shockingly infected by anti-Trinitarian heresy acquired from reading Locke's unpublished *Essay* (Ouvry, 1874, p. 9). Whatever the case, Locke had, by his visit to Cleves, already broken his Oxford mould before his crucial encounter with Shaftesbury; his new circumstances accelerated the changes in him.

It is difficult to calibrate the precise terms of Locke's relationship with Shaftesbury, both practically and intellectually. Hindsight is apt unduly to elevate Locke's position, involving an erroneous assumption that intellectual acumen brought parity of social status. This matter is of increasing importance in contemporary scholarship, since it has become common to inflate Locke's influence in Shaftesbury's colonial enterprises, with a view to hardening the connections between philosophy and empire. In worldly reputation, Locke was not renowned before the 1690s; on the contrary, he was obscure. Early memoirs stress that Shaftesbury insisted on friendship, which denoted a suspension of deference, and Locke, it seems, felt free on occasion to be tartly sardonic. A story is told of the earl settling to card games and chitchat with fellow noblemen, during which Locke pointedly had his notebook open ready to record their *aperçus*; his failing to write anything down attracted their attention, and he, remarking on his impatience to learn from the 'most ingenious men of the age', embarrassed them into serious conversation (*EL*: Le Clerc).

In one crucial episode in Shaftesbury's life, Locke's role may be exaggerated. Memoirs tell us that Locke saved Shaftesbury's life. The earl suffered from a ruptured cyst on his liver, and a decision was taken to operate, which, in an age without anaesthetics or antisepsis, was traumatic and risky. A silver pipe to drain the abscess was successfully inserted. Although Locke himself said that the earl believed 'he owed his life to my care', he had not wielded the knife – no physician would engage in surgery – and he had not been the sole nor perhaps the chief adviser (*Corr.*, vol. ii, p. 662). The pipe would later become a source of punning mockery among the earl's political enemies: Shaftesbury, whose family name was Cooper, had literally become a barrel with a pipe: he was 'Count Tapski'.

Against a modern tendency to elevate Locke, it is worth stressing his junior position. Shaftesbury was a great and wealthy magnate, with a household entourage of forty. One document specified that Locke should dine among the senior servants at the steward's table (National Archives, MS PRO 30/24/4/236). In official processions between Exeter House in the Strand and Whitehall, Locke walked beside his lordship's coach. Documents from the 1680s describe Locke as Shaftesbury's 'secretary', though Locke himself denied he ever had that 'business or title' (BL, Add. MS 41810, fol. 187; *EL*: Le Clerc). He was what contemporaries termed a 'domestic', meaning of the *domus*, or member of the household. Given the anti-patriarchalism of Locke's *Two Treatises*, it is striking that Locke was both described and described himself as being 'of Shaftesbury's family', again denoting the household, since 'family' and 'household' were largely synonymous (*Corr.*, vol. i, p. 662; *EL*: Shaftesbury). The Aristotelian idea of the *oikos*, the household-family as the fundamental unit of society, remained commonplace.

At the higher social levels, England was a confederation of gentry households, within which the senior 'domestics' were commonly on terms of friendship with the heads. A household chaplain might be a bishop in the making, a tutor of the children, or a future head of an Oxbridge college. From the Renaissance to the eighteenth century, philosophers commonly served households rather than holding university posts. Magnates needed well-educated factotums. Hobbes, for example, served the earls of Devonshire. In the household of Lord Holles there served Roger Morrice, an almost exact contemporary of Locke's. Nominally chaplain – he was an ejected Puritan minister – Morrice undertook a variety of tasks, buying books for the library, drafting memoranda, operating as an 'intelligencer' with eyes and ears open in coffee houses, Westminster Hall and the Royal Exchange, acting as electoral agent on behalf of like-minded MPs, distributing charitable donations, and negotiating matches in the elaborate marriage market (Goldie, 2007). Locke performed practically all these roles for Shaftesbury. He went to Belvoir Castle in Leicestershire to arrange the marriage of the future second earl of Shaftesbury to the daughter of the Earl of Rutland, was present at the birth of the future third earl, and assumed

responsibility for the child's education. He took a charitable interest in the welfare of a Dissenting schoolmaster and his daughter: like Holles, Shaftesbury was sympathetic to Dissent and, through his servant, provided protection for Puritan clergy (*Corr.*, vol. i, p. 418; ii, p. 154). Locke also arranged accommodation for Shaftesbury's entourage when Charles II summoned parliament to meet at Oxford in 1681, which was not straightforward in a university hostile to the earl's Whig party. He bought books for Shaftesbury's library, on politics and religion, husbandry and horsemanship. To what extent Locke drafted political memoranda and pamphlets is a more difficult question to which we shall return.

It was during Locke's period with Shaftesbury that it is most likely that he encountered the aged Hobbes. Our witness is John Aubrey, in a letter that captures the role of individuals like Hobbes and Locke, functioning as intellectual advisers to statesmen and monarchs. Aubrey recommended that Locke visit Hobbes's publisher's shop and take a look at two of his unpublished treatises, the *Dialogue of the Common Laws*, which 'speaks highly for the king's prerogative', which 'if your lord saw it he would like it' (and, being concise, is 'the fitter for your reading, being so full of business'); and *Behemoth*, Hobbes's history of the Civil Wars, which the king 'likes extremely, but ... dares not licence for fear of displeasing the bishops'. Aubrey closed with a request that 'if you see' the 'old gent', please convey his regards (*Corr.*, vol. i, pp. 375–6).

Shaftesbury was not the only nobleman whom Locke served. He was a visitor at Northumberland House, one of many aristocratic palaces in the Strand, and he accompanied the earl and countess of Northumberland to Paris. In the 1670s Locke was *au fait* with other colleagues of Shaftesbury: Lord Holles, the Earl of Salisbury, and the Duke of Buckingham. At the time of the Revolution of 1688 Locke was to belong to the entourage of Lord Mordaunt, and in the 1690s he was close to Lord Chancellor Somers. All these men were active in Parliament, though, as noblemen, they sat in the House of Lords. Locke also knew many elected members of the Commons, yet his experience of English politics, and of its social system, was as much aristocratic as gentry-democratic. In one sense it was wholly aristo-cratic, for gentlemen were of the *noblesse*, of which titled nobles were a subset. One historian called early-modern England a 'one-class society': gentlemen and the rest (Laslett, 1965). In his preface to *Some Thoughts concerning Education* (1693), Locke indicated that his book was 'suited to our English gentry ... for if those of that rank are by their education once set right, they will quickly bring all the rest into order'. Near the end of his life, Locke offered some 'thoughts concerning reading', designed for 'a gentleman, whose proper calling is the service of his country; and so is most properly concerned in moral, and political knowledge; and thus the studies which more immediately belong to his calling, are those which treat of virtues and vices, of civil society, and the arts of government' (Locke, 1997, p. 350). For Locke, the 'arts of government' were the special concern of the five per cent of families who belonged to the gentlemanly class.

It might be thought that Locke was a poor judge of his patrons. Although Shaftesbury was undoubtedly charismatic, charming and clever, he was also regarded, admittedly chiefly by his enemies, as mercurial, facile, ambitious, hypo-critical and opportunistic. As Shaftesbury's servant, Locke was involved in his master's support for a series of royal policies, during the period 1667 to 1673, which in later historical writing has produced a charge sheet against Charles II as an arbitrary and absolutist monarch. Shaftesbury backed religious tolera-tion, but since parliament had imposed a coercive system of religious uniformity, achiev-ing toleration entailed using the royal prerog-ative, and in 1672 Charles suspended the penal laws by his Declaration of Indulgence, which parliament duly condemned as unlawful. Among the earl's papers are memoranda, some-times erroneously attributed to Locke, which promoted a strongly Erastian position, desig-nating the king as independent governor of the Church entitled to evade the authority of both bishops and parliament (National Archives, PRO 30/24/6/427–30). Furthermore, with dubious legality, Shaftesbury issued writs to fill vacant seats in the House of Commons.

Above all, the earl supported the Third Dutch War, fought in alliance with Catholic France against the Protestant Dutch Republic. Contemporary commentators quickly regarded this war as a catastrophic connivance with the Continent's growing geopolitical threat: Louis XIV. In the meantime, although unbeknownst to Shaftesbury, Charles II had agreed secret clauses in the Treaty of Dover with Louis XIV, which held out the possibility of returning England to Catholicism, in return for which Louis paid subsidies to Charles so that he could avoid parliament. Until the great foreign policy reversal at the Revolution in 1688, England would be a client state of France. The apogee of Shaftesbury's commitment to Charles was his notorious 'Delenda est Carthago' speech of February 1673, in which he echoed Cato's saying that 'Carthage [meaning Holland] must be destroyed'. The speech became the blackest mark against Shaftesbury's reputation, not least when he was later obliged to seek political refuge in 'Carthage' itself. The third Earl of SHAFTESBURY's memoir claims that Locke liter-ally stood behind Shaftesbury to help him through the speech. Whilst it is scarcely likely that Locke would have been admitted to the Lords' chamber, the third earl evidently did not doubt Locke's involvement in the speech. He strove to excuse his grandfather by insisting that, as Lord Chancellor, he had had no choice but to be a royal mouthpiece, and that in reality he was already an enemy of the king's Catholicizing inclinations and in collusion with the king's opponents (*EL*: Shaftesbury). Certainly, within months of this speech, seeing the imminent collapse of royal policies in the face of parliamentary objections, Shaftesbury scuttled towards the opposition. The king dis-missed him as Chancellor, and he launched himself on a new career of implacable opposition to both Charles and his brother and heir, the future James II, a convert to Catholicism. Locke followed Shaftesbury into opposition, but quite how he interpreted his master's tergiversations is opaque. Whatever the case, Locke had served a chief minister of a king who was engaged in exerting royal power in unpopular ways.

There are further aspects to Locke's public engagements between 1667 and 1673. To serve a minister of the crown was to inhabit an amphibious position in the pre-modern state, for the role was both private and public. Governance was gradually becoming professionalized, in the sense of salaried state employment. Yet much English governance remained essentially amateur, an avocation of gentlemen who were independent as well as being agents of the crown. In serving an earl who was also Chancellor of the Exchequer and then Lord Chancellor, Locke simultaneously served an aristocratic household and the king's court. When Shaftesbury became Lord Chancellor, Locke acquired formal posts as a salaried official. He was made secretary for clerical appointments, charged with recommending clergy to fill incumbencies that belonged to the patronage of the crown. Among his nominees was an old friend, and one of the earl's chaplains, Nathaniel Hodges. Radical Puritans profoundly objected to such state imposition of clergy upon congregations.

More importantly, Locke served as secretary to the Council for Trade and Plantations, with onerous responsibilities as the conduit of official correspondence with England's burgeoning colonial empire in the Americas. This turn in Locke's life is immensely significant because the relationship between his political philosophy and colonialism and slavery has come to loom large in recent scholarship. Not only is the *Two Treatises* the first canonical classic of political thought to refer extensively to America, but Locke was also personally involved in English imperial activity, both as a servant of the Council and through private

investment. The stimulus seems to have been wholly Shaftesbury's.

For a short period Locke held stock in the Africa Company, which supplied slaves to the West Indies and the North American mainland. In 1672 he became a founding 'adventurer' – the term for those who risked their capital in overseas trade – of the Bahamas Company. He invested £200, and attended company meetings, one of which was held on board the *Bahama Merchant* in London's docks (BL, Add. MS 15640). Locke's connection with slaving continued. When he served on the Board of Trade in the 1690s, he signed a memorandum expressing concern about policies that might 'prejudice us in the West Indies, especially Jamaica' in respect of England's 'advantage of commerce ... for negroes and European commodities' (Huntington Library, MS BL6).

Locke also played a significant role as Shaftesbury's aide in the affairs of the Carolina Company, in which Shaftesbury was the principal Lord Proprietor. The Proprietors' domain extended over most of present-day North and South Carolina and Georgia, though settlement had scarcely penetrated inland. The town of Charleston was named after the king; it stands on the Ashley River, named after Shaftesbury (when Lord Ashley); an offshore island was named Locke Island (today Edisto Island); and Locke was appointed a 'landgrave', one of the putative new nobility of the plantation. In later years Carolina would often recur in Locke's thoughts, whether as a fantasy place of imagined retreat from tribulation, or as a practical place of exile for his master. In 1681 he was involved in transmitting the earl's desperate message to Charles II, offering to retire to America if the king would agree to drop the charge of treason against him (*Corr.*, vol. ii, p. 32; Morrice, 2007, p. 296).

Locke's extra-European connections provided inspiration for his growing curiosity about the diversity of the natural and human world. Arguably, he saw empire as having a providential purpose, in allowing humankind the opportunity gradually to recover the original perfection of Adam's prelapsarian knowledge of the world and of God's designs, the *prisca theologia*. Just as the Fall had required humankind industriously to labour for its bread, so it also required intellectual labour for its knowledge (Irving, 2008). Locke constantly sought reports on botanical flora and fauna from travellers to Asia and the Americas, while his anthropological interests were fed by reports of native practices, rites and skills. He was interested in whether Indian 'arithmetic turns at ten as ours does', in the 'ceremonies of the Hindus', and in the pearls, incense, spices, precious metals, textiles and ceramics traded at Amoy in China (*Corr.*, vol. ii, pp. 591–3; vii, pp. 471, 509–11). Locke's library contained scores of travel books, especially those of early Spanish and French explorers in the Americas. In the *Two Treatises* he cited José de Acosta's *Natural and Moral History of the Indies* (1604) and Garcilaso de la Vega's *History of the Incas* (1633), while in the *Essay* a series of such works was drawn upon, including Jean de Léry's *Voyage to Brazil* (1578) and Domingo Navarrette's *Account of the Monarchy of China* (1676).

The early years of Locke's immersion in Shaftesbury's affairs yielded three tracts. He certainly authored two of these, though neither was published at the time, while the extent of his involvement in the third, which was published, remains uncertain. 'Some of the Consequences that are Like to Follow upon Lessening of Interest to Four Per Cent' (1668) was later redeployed in *Some Considerations of the Consequences of the Lowering of Interest* (1692). Addressing Josiah Child's proposal that the legal interest rate should be lowered from six per cent to four, Locke's response was twofold: a lesser rate would adversely affect trade, by insufficiently compensating the risk of lending; but, more largely, there should not be a statutory rate at all, for the market rate should prevail. Locke's interest in economics was aroused and he now turned to read such books as Thomas Mun's *England's Treasure by Foreign Trade* (1664).

Locke's 'Essay concerning Toleration' (1667) marked a decisive shift in his thinking on that subject, many of its claims later resurfacing in his published *Letter concerning Toleration* (1689). Locke now adopted a radical distinction between the purposes of a church and a civil commonwealth, and hence the absolute impropriety of the latter enforcing membership of the former. Purely speculative opinions, modes of worshipping God, and even moral virtues and vices, were no business of the state, so long as they were not inimical to public peace, PROPERTY and the 'preservation of mankind'. Quite simply, 'the magistrate hath nothing to do with the good of men's souls', but only with 'the quiet and comfortable living of men in society' (*ETol.*, pp. 281–2).

In respect of the Lockean canon, the third tract is more problematic. The *Fundamental Constitutions of Carolina*, first published in 1670, is a curious document. It was a blueprint for the governance of Carolina and although many of its provisions never took effect, it was nominally in place until the colonists rejected it in the 1720s. It elaborately reconstructs in the New World the institutions of English local self-government, and in this respect it implies a republican regime, in the sense of citizen self-rule, encompassing intensive obligations of officeholding. In the higher echelons of government, the *Constitutions* establishes an aristocratic republic, in which the crown's suzerainty is only nominally present and the Proprietors form the ruling caste, under whom there is a hereditary landed nobility, composed rather fancifully of 'landgraves' and 'caciques'. The preamble is explicit about seeking to 'avoid erecting a numerous democracy'. Among more than 100 clauses, several are striking. There is to be religious toleration for any kind of theist, and public office is to be open to members of any church. Native Americans are not to be coerced into Christian observance, and slaves are to be admitted to whichever church they please (Locke, 1997, pp. 162, 178–9).

Locke's role in drafting the *Fundamental Constitutions* is ambiguous. One manuscript starts in his hand and is then turned over to a scribe. This establishes his secretarial presence, but not his authorship. Plainly the text cannot be a purely personal act of political imagination, since it was created for, and approved by, the Proprietors. Nor was it claimed by Locke when he listed his anonymous works in his will and neither did it appear in the first edition of his collected *Works* in 1714. Its first attribution to Locke came with its inclusion in Pierre Des Maizeaux's *Collection of Several Pieces of Mr John Locke* in 1720. Des Maizeaux offered a couple of specifics, such as that Locke was hostile to the inclusion of a clause requiring an Anglican establishment, implying that he approved other provisions. Moreover, a colleague of Locke remarked on 'that excellent form of government in the composure of which you had so great a hand' (*Corr.*, vol. i, p. 395); whilst Locke's patent as landgrave commended 'his great prudence, learning, and industry ... in settling the form of government'. Recent research draws Locke even closer to the *Constitutions*: not only did he retain and distribute copies over a long period, but also, crucially, he revised it in 1682. These revisions enhance his authorial presence, and the timing is significant, since it coincided with his drafting of the second of the *Two Treatises*. This makes it more difficult to presume that Locke had put aside the aristocratic and colonial assumptions of the *Constitutions* when he came to write his major political work (Armitage, 2004).

As well as these writings, Locke also embarked on what was to become the *Essay concerning Human Understanding*, the earliest surviving draft of which is dated 1671. Locke's later Epistle to the Reader explained that the work began in a conversation with 'five or six friends, meeting in my chamber and discoursing on a subject very remote from this', which led him to 'examine our own abilities, and see what objects our understandings were or were not fitted to deal with' (*E*, p. 7). In his own copy of the *Essay*, James Tyrrell recorded: 'This was in winter 1673 as I remember being myself one of those that then met there when the discourse began about the principles of morality and revealed religion' (BL, C.122.f.14). Although Tyrrell's date is mistaken, the interest of his remark lies in the conversation's subject. For, what the modern philosophical tradition has come to regard as the cardinal text of empiricist epistemology was evidently rooted elsewhere, in questions of moral philosophy and the certitude of religious truth. Our knowledge of Locke's early *Essays on the Law of Nature* enhances the view that his empiricism derived from doubts about a body of contemporary literature that grounded the moral law in innate moral intuitions. The greatest shock to contemporary readers of the *Essay*, initially at least, was its comprehensive attack on innate IDEAS in Book I. It was here that ethics and epistemology met.

English Opposition, French Sojourn

By the mid-1670s a 'Country party' had developed in parliament, disturbed by the changing character of Charles II's rule. Reconciliation achieved at the Restoration now gave way to a narrowly exclusive regime, dominated by former Cavalier royalists and ecclesiastical hardliners. From an early stage, the Restoration had been narrow in its religious settlement, in seeking to suppress Puritan nonconformity, but now it also threatened narrowness in public office, in excluding former Parliamentarians and Puritan-inclined laity from office at court and in the localities. It was feared that the House of Commons was increasingly manipulated by the crown, through the device of 'placemen': the award of salaried offices to those who ought to represent constituents rather than serve government interests. Attacks on 'placemen' were combined with condemnation of the king's 'standing army' – a professional royal army, as opposed to a citizen militia, was held to be inimical to liberty. These critiques prompted an enduring tradition of 'Country' aspiration that the legislature should be rendered independent of the executive. Nor was this all: the king's pro-French foreign policy was denounced as culpable in the face of Louis XIV's aggrandizing ambitions.

A comprehensive indictment of these developments appeared in 1675, entitled *A Letter from a Person of Quality to his Friend in the Country*. It was the manifesto of the future Whig movement. Although anonymous, the tract certainly issued from Shaftesbury's circle; the precise role Locke played in its composition is unknown. The case for Locke's involvement rests on the tract's inclusion in Des Maizeaux's *Collection of Several Pieces*, buttressed by a remark of the third Earl of Shaftesbury that the first earl made use of Locke's 'assistant pen'. Whatever the case, Locke surely shared the tract's sentiments. It catalogued the statutes by which the Cavalier party and the Church hierarchy had steadily entrenched their positions, and concluded that in England now, 'priest and prince [must] be worshipped together as divine in the same temple'. This was a classic formulation of the charge that priests were apt to preach up the divine right of kings as a *quid pro quo* for being granted coercive power over the Church. In an addendum to his 'Essay concerning Toleration', Locke, remarking on the overweening power of clergies, who persuade secular rulers to lend them temporal power, observed that the clergy 'for thus doing their drudgery ... have (whenever princes have been serviceable to their ends) been careful to preach up monarchy *jure divino* [by divine right]' (*ETol.*, p. 314, 376; Locke, 1997, p. 234, 365).

A striking feature of the *Letter* and of other Country party tracts is their emphasis on the aristocracy's role as the 'balance' of the constitution. What now re-emerged was the classic doctrine of Civil War Parliamentarianism: that the polity was not a 'pure' but a 'mixed' monarchy, comprising elements of monarchy, aristocracy and democracy. Locke's *Two Treatises* subsequently said little about the institutions of particular polities, but it took for granted the 'supposal' of a legislature made of 'three distinct persons', which included 'a single hereditary person' and 'an assembly of hered-

itary nobility' (*TTG* II.213). Locke did not doubt the virtue of England's tripartite regime of king, lords and commons, and he adhered to a pervasive classical conception of the mixing of the three elemental forms of polity. Since no type of polity was ordained by God, civil societies may choose any type they deemed best, yet a strong implication was that, abstract right notwithstanding, prudence dictated that the English should choose their 'ancient constitution'. Towards the end of his life, Locke recommended several 'mixed monarchy' treatises such as Sir Thomas Smith's *De Republica Anglorum* (1583), John Sadler's *Rights of the Kingdom* (1649), and James Tyrrell's *History of England* (1697–1700). If, he wrote, Samuel Pufendorf's *On the Duty of Man and Citizen* (1673) and his own *Two Treatises* addressed 'the ground and nature of civil society', these other treatises give 'insight into the particular constitution [of our] own country' (*Corr.*, vol. viii, p. 58; Locke, 1997, p. 377). It was remarked earlier that after the Civil War Parliamentarians had been outflanked by republicans; after 1660 they were outflanked by absolutists; the Revolution of 1688 would, however, reinstate the tripartite doctrine. During the Restoration, the Country and Whig movements embodied the tenets of Civil War Parliamentarians: these movements were not, in the main, republican or Leveller. True to his Parliamentarian roots, Locke, writing in 1690, was even-handed in his vehemence against politicized clergies who used the pulpits to preach either 'absolute monarchy' or 'antimonarchical principles', 'as the one or other have been in vogue' (*W*, vol. vi, p. 86). Although Locke grounded the legitimacy of polities in the consent of all, and issued a clarion call for resistance against tyrants, he was neither a democrat nor a republican. The aristocratic *art* or *practice* of government remained distinct from a universalist grounding of the *legitimacy* of government.

The House of Lords condemned the 1675 *Letter* as seditious. Shortly afterwards, Locke travelled to France, where he remained for four years. It is uncertain if the storm over the *Letter* prompted his decision to leave England; his ostensible reason was ill health. By now he was suffering from respiratory afflictions – asthma and bronchitis – which plagued him for the rest of his life. He was prone to anxiety about his health and, as Sydenham detected, was apt to drive himself to nervous exhaustion (*Corr.*, vol. i, p. 415).

Although Locke primarily resided at Montpellier in southern France, he travelled extensively and spent time in Paris, where he attended the sickbed of the Countess of Northumberland, now married to the English ambassador. He undertook a characteristic task for one of his class, serving as tutor and companion to the son of a wealthy East India Company merchant and government financier, Sir John Banks. He encountered a circle of Parisian *virtuosi*, whose interests encompassed astronomy, metrology, mechanical invention and scriptural hermeneutics. Locke thereafter maintained a correspondence with Nicolas Toinard, discussing the comet of 1682 (Halley's), microscopy, hygrometry, phonetic orthography and ancient chronology. Other friendships included the librarian Henri Justel and the physician and traveller François Bernier. Locke became absorbed in Jansenist moral philosophy, rigorist in its asceticism and concerned, in the tradition of Montaigne, with moral psychology and the relationship of virtue to the passions. He prepared an English translation of three of Pierre Nicole's *Essais de morale* (1671–8), which he later presented to the Countess of Shaftesbury. Through learning French, he gained access to a rich fund of recent philosophical writing in the Cartesian tradition, unavailable in Latin or English, notably Nicolas MALEBRANCHE's *De la recherche de la vérité* (*Search after Truth*, 1674–5).

Locke started to keep a journal, which offers the reader a meld of acute, often sardonic, observations on French mores and institutions, together with abundant exemplars of his kaleidoscopic scientific curiosities, intermingled with memoranda and reflections indicating that he continued to work on the *Essay* (Locke, 1953; cf. *Corr.*, vol. i, pp. 366–8, 439–44). His wry remark on the uncomfortableness of sabots, the wooden clogs worn by French peasants, and his determination 'never [to] make choice of a country ... where they are in fashion', allusively indicts absolute monarchy, in a manner soon to become a commonplace in an English political slogan that damned 'popery and wooden shoes' (*Corr.*, vol. i, p. 441). In June 1677 Locke witnessed Louis XIV himself, the king pointing with his cane across the baroque splendour of the gardens of the Palace of Versailles (Locke, 1953, p. 152).

Locke's attitude to the duties and quotidian practices of life are revealed in a series of lengthy advisory letters he sent to an unhappy and importunate Denis Grenville, an English clergymen who befriended him in Montpellier. Locke shows himself an enemy of undue scrupulosity, where moral doubt serves to inhibit action. We should 'do our duties [and] need not perplex ourselves with too scrupulous an enquiry into the precise bounds of them'. He is suspicious of spiritual narcissism and religious melancholy, for private communion with the divine should not excuse us from our principal godly duty to attend to worldly business. 'God delights not to have us miserable [and] having given us all things richly and to enjoy we cannot imagine that in our recreations we should be denied delight'. He warns against the pathology of obsessive studiousness and stresses the importance of recreation. Everyone ought to engage in a manual skill and in physical exercise, advice he was to repeat in his *Thoughts concerning Education*: he himself gardened and cultivated fruit trees, and was a keen horse rider. He respected practical skills, deprecating the idle fatuity of the fashionable rich and the labourious pedantry of scholars. Memoirists remarked on his constant curiosity about manual skills and his cross-questioning of artisans and tradesmen. 'He always kept the useful in his eye in all his disquisitions' (*EL*: Coste; *Corr.*, vol. i, p. 473; cf. pp. 556–9, 646–50).

The Whig Movement

Locke was abroad when Charles II's regime met its crisis in 1678. He returned to witness a nation which, until 1682, was in danger of meltdown. The king was challenged by what now became known as the 'Whig' party. The spark was the revelation of a 'Popish Plot' to destroy the Protestant polity, which, in turn, provoked a Whig demand for the removal from the royal succession of the king's brother, James, Duke of York, whose Catholicism was held to be incompatible with English Protestant liberties. The Whigs introduced a bill of exclusion in three successive parliaments, but despite their electoral success in viciously partisan general elections, Charles, holding the constitutional trump cards, outmanoeuvred them. In one parliament, the Lords, which included a solid phalanx of courtier bishops, termed the 'dead weight' by the Whigs, voted exclusion down. In two parliaments, Charles used his prerogative of dissolution, spectacularly at the Oxford Parliament in 1681 which was dismissed after one week. He never called another parliament for the remainder of his reign. During his last years, the early 1680s, the king and his supporters, now termed 'Tories', went on the offensive in a ferocious purge of civil society. They set about destroying their Whig opponents, together with the Puritan Dissenters, whom they deemed republicans and fanatical revivers of the Civil War. Charges of sedition and treason were brought against Whig dissidents and prosecutions for religious nonconformity peaked: hundreds died in jail. Deprived of a parliamentary forum for opposition, some Whigs turned to conspiracy and rebellion; they failed, and suffered the consequences. In 1681 Shaftesbury was charged with treason and held in the Tower of London, and although a Whig grand jury declared he had no case to answer, Charles soon secured control over the appointment of London juries, prompting Shaftesbury to flee the country.

Conclusive evidence for Locke's practical role in the Exclusion Crisis is surprisingly fragmentary, and he may well have destroyed some of his papers. It seems that he was, in this second period of association with Shaftesbury from 1679 to 1682, less tied to the earl. He spent a substantial amount of time in Oxford rather than London. It has been claimed that he was an active agitator and conspirator, leaning towards the radical wing of the Whigs, revivers of the Leveller cause, and that he mingled with seditious tradesmen and shopkeepers in the newly fashionable coffee houses (Ashcraft, 1986). The evidence is, however, largely circumstantial or ambiguous, or depends on guilt by association. Locke was certainly a committed Whig, close to many activists, and undertook political business for the earl; but, temperamentally, he preferred the study and the pen to the tavern and the barricade. Commitment was married to caution, and only occasional evidence pinpoints direct engagement. In 1681 he arranged accommodation for Shaftesbury's entourage at the Oxford parliament, and was in contact with one of the lawyers defending Stephen College, a Whig agitator executed at Oxford (BL, Add. MS 28929, fol. 110). When Shaftesbury was in the Tower, he investigated the king's powers over the appointment of juries (*ETol.*, pp. 118–36).

One incident of personal activism has recently come to light. After the second parliamentary election of 1679, Charles refused to allow the new parliament to meet and by repeated prorogations held it at bay for a year. The Whigs mounted a campaign of mass petitioning demanding that parliament assemble, while the crown's defenders responded with declarations of abhorrence of such seditious barracking of the king. In London a Whig 'monster petition' was collected, containing thousands of names. On the forty-first sheet Locke's signature is unmistakable. The petition pronounced that there was 'a most damnable and hellish popish plot ... against your majesty's most sacred person, the Protestant religion, and the well established government of your realm', that cried out for investigation and redress by parliament. The tone was still studiously loyal, but the people's *right* to a parliament was strongly asserted (Huntington Library, MS HM68; Knights, 1993).

The anti-popery of the 'monster' petition is manifest, underlining the importance of avoiding an anachronistically secular understanding of Whig politics. Shaftesbury's movement depended on a national belief in a palpable Catholic threat. While the Whigs rode high, they themselves used the law courts to their own advantage, sending three dozen Catholics to their deaths on dubious charges of treason or under Elizabethan statutes that made being a Catholic priest a capital offence. Victorian liberals tried to detach Locke from Shaftesbury's anti-popery, but Locke was deeply hostile to Catholicism. His library contained such Whig classics as Andrew Marvell's *Account of the Growth of Popery and Arbitrary Power in England* (1677) and Charles Blount's *Appeal from the Country ... for the Preservation of ... the Protestant Religion* (1679). His unpublished papers include essays against the Catholic doctrine of infallibility, and his French journals comment scathingly on popery. In the *Letter concerning Toleration*, Locke debarred Catholics. It is true that he was careful to say that it was not the absurdity or superstitiousness of their theology that justified their exclusion. Rather, it was that certain Catholic beliefs were inconsistent with the safety and welfare of the polity. Locke shared his fellow Protestants' catalogue of the doctrines that made Catholicism uncivil: that 'dominion is founded in grace', namely that political rule belongs to true believers, and hence that the pope could authorize the deposition of heretical rulers; and that 'faith need not be kept with heretics', namely that Catholics could break their promises. Furthermore, it was held that Catholics, given the opportunity of power, would inevitably unleash expropriation, incarceration, torture and death against 'heretics'. Locke later took a keen interest in his friend Philip van LIMBORCH's edition of the records of the Inquisition, the *Historia Inquisitionis* (1692). Catholics, in sum, could not be loyal citizens unless they abandoned doctrines that were apparently fundamental to them.

Locke vindicated the Whig cause chiefly with his pen. Some time during the Exclusion Crisis he composed the *Two Treatises*. When published after the Revolution in 1689, it contained a preface which misleadingly encouraged the notion that the book had been written to defend the legitimacy – 'in the consent of the people' – of the new king, William III. Yet it is certain that Locke wrote the book several years earlier. To have published it before 1689 would have been suicidal, for it was a call to arms to overthrow a tyrannical monarch. The First Treatise was probably prepared around 1680, and comprises a refutation of the principles of patriarchal kingship contained in Sir Robert FILMER's *Patriarcha, Or the Natural Power of Kings* (1680). Filmer was a Royalist who had published tracts defending Charles I during the Civil Wars, and who died in 1653, and his *éclat* was posthumous. His hitherto unpublished masterwork, written around 1630, was now launched as an ideological flagship for the Tory cause. Whereas the First Treatise is a minute and relentless dissection of his opponent's text, the Second is a systematic and abstract statement of Locke's cardinal principles concerning natural right, liberty, consent, property and arbitrary power. The present scholarly consensus is that the Second Treatise was probably composed after the dissolution of the Oxford Parliament in March 1681, rather than earlier, since a call to arms seems inappropriate at a time when the Whigs were winning elections within the framework of parliamentary politics. The charge of treason against Shaftesbury and the king's coup against the City of London and its juries in 1682 may have been the final provocation.

The *Two Treatises* was not Locke's only sustained piece of writing at this time. With the help of his friend James Tyrrell, and largely at the latter's home near Oxford, Locke composed a long treatise defending religious toleration in refutation of Edward STILLINGFLEET's sermon *The Mischief of Separation* (1680), and its expanded version, *The Unreasonableness of Separation* (1681). Locke's critique remains a substantial 'black hole' in Lockean textual scholarship, as there is no published edition, and only a few pages are readily accessible (meanwhile, see Stanton, 2003).

As a member of Shaftesbury's circle, Locke was a marked man. During the early 1680s he was spied upon and the government received intelligence concerning his activities. The informants included a fellow student at Christ Church, Humphrey Prideaux, and a lawyer, Richard Holloway. Locke was rumoured to have written *No Protestant Plot* (1681), which was in fact authored by an incendiary Dissenting clergyman, Robert Ferguson (BL, Add. MS 28929, fol. 77). Locke, however, was a master of discretion and, to the frustration of his observers, never incriminated himself. He 'lives a very cunning unintelligible life'; 'lives very quietly with us and not a word ever drops from his mouth that discovers anything of his heart within'. Aware he was being watched, he supplied his friend Edward Clarke with a note assigning numbers to the names of friends, saying 'there may possibly be some occasion for this following cypher' (BL, Add. MS 28929, fos. 77, 95, 100; *Corr.*, vol. i, p. 603).

Exile in Holland

The Whig movement reached its nadir with the uncovering of the Rye House Plot in the summer of 1683. Many arrests were made. Algernon Sidney and Lord William Russell were executed for treason, and the Earl of Essex, awaiting trial in the Tower, cut his own throat, though Whigs suspected murder. Over dinner at Christ Church, Locke was visibly shaken to hear that one of his acquaintances, the Whig lawyer Robert West, had been arrested, and he now 'thought it time to shift for himself' (BL, Add. MS 28929, fol. 110). Accordingly, he was observed removing 'baskets of papers' from his college rooms and lodging them with Tyrrell and a Whig former mayor of Oxford, Robert Pawling. A report to Whitehall urged that 'it may conduce to his

majesty's service' to 'search Mr Locke's chamber', as well as the homes of Tyrrell and Pawling (*Calendar of State Papers, Domestic, 1683*, pp. 109–10). Late in the summer Locke fled to Holland, where he was to spend the next five and a half years in exile, only returning in the aftermath of the Revolution. Even in exile, he could not feel secure given that, for instance, the Whig activist Sir Thomas Armstrong was abducted on the streets of Amsterdam and taken back to England for execution. Modern historians have been as unsuccessful as Charles II's government in pinning treasonable conspiracy on Locke, though he evidently knew and mingled with conspirators, and was reported to be consorting with Ferguson and the Whig grandee Lord Grey (*EL*: Wood; Milton, 2000).

Locke could still be victimized *in absentia*. In 1684 the crown ordered Christ Church to expel him from his studentship. At first Dean Fell demurred, indicating that Locke had been carefully watched, but had revealed nothing incriminatory; he intended to summon Locke to answer for himself. The government's response, a peremptory demand for immediate expulsion, was, however, obeyed. The provocation for the crown's action was probably the suspicion that Locke was author of a tract which offered evidence that Charles and his brother had been responsible for the Earl of Essex's murder (*EL*: Wood; BL, Add. MS 28929, fol. 112; 41810, fols 187–8). The allegation could hardly be more offensive, since nothing so fulfilled the classical character of a tyrant than that he should be a murderer of his own subjects: no crime more negated just rule and reduced the ruler to a beast who preyed on his own people, and no crime more fully justified a right of self-defence and tyrannicide. The third Earl of Shaftesbury, writing after Locke's death in the blithe glow of 'Revolution principles', blandly stated that the expulsion was because Locke had 'become the great assertor of the rights of the people'. By his expulsion, Locke had, as one spy put it, become a 'brother sufferer' with the Whigs, and would not now be so reckless as to 'venture his neck by coming any more within reach of the king's justice' (BL, Add. MS 28929, fol. 110). Locke's expulsion was welcomed by high Tories such as Anthony Wood, who was nevertheless angry that, when Locke fled, his rooms had not been 'ransacked' for incriminating evidence; Locke was 'a man of a turbulent spirit, clamorous and never contented'. The English envoy in the Netherlands remarked that studentships of Christ Church were 'never intended for the maintenance and support of such as seek to overthrow the government and to bring the king's sacred person into contempt and even into horror with all men as if he were the worst of tyrants' (*EL*: Wood; BL, Add. MS 41810, fols 187–8).

Shortly after his expulsion from Christ Church, Locke wrote a remarkable letter to Thomas Herbert, Earl of Pembroke, whom he had met in France in the 1670s. He protested that he had not shown the least sign of being 'undutiful against the government', nor of 'turbulency, faction, or sedition', nor was he ever 'of any suspected clubs or cabals'. Furthermore, 'I here solemnly protest in the presence of God, that I am not the author, not only of any libel, but not of any pamphlet or treatise whatsoever in print good, bad, or indifferent'. Locke's statement seems disingenuous, but forgivably so in his dire circumstances, and the phrase 'in print' is perhaps the saving clause (*Corr.*, vol. ii, pp. 663–4).

Controversy surrounds the degree of Locke's involvement in the rebellion staged in 1685 by the Duke of Monmouth, Charles II's illegitimate but Protestant son and hero-mascot of the Whig cause. Having landed from Holland in the West Country with only eighty men, Monmouth hoped to spearhead a spontaneous national uprising at the outset of the reign of his Catholic uncle, James II. He declared himself king, and raised 3,000 men, untrained and ill-equipped, mostly weavers, artisans and farmers; the gentry, cowed or sceptical, conspicuously avoided him. His followers were slaughtered at Sedgemoor in Somerset in the last pitched battle fought on English soil; the survivors were tried at the 'Bloody Assize' and hanged or transported into slavery in the West Indies; Monmouth himself was executed. For his part, Locke can be convicted of nothing more than association in Holland with some of those involved. Although he banked money with Monmouth's paymaster, Thomas Dare, the 'Locke' cited in some of the records as a financial contributor to Monmouth's cause was a London tobacconist, Joshua Locke. In his memoir, Le Clerc wrote that Locke 'had not such high thoughts, as to expect anything from his [Monmouth's] undertaking'; besides, he was 'rather fearful, than courageous'. Nonetheless, Locke's name was included among a list of eighty-four exiles whose extradition the English envoy requested that autumn, obliging Locke to go into temporary hiding under the assumed name of Dr van der Linden.

James II's reign proved, however, deeply paradoxical. The king sought to advance Catholicism and, finding no support from his traditional Tory and Anglican allies, tried instead to construct an unlikely alliance of all their opponents, by offering religious toleration to Protestant Dissenters and political amnesty to Whigs. By 1687 the political climate had transformed so dramatically that Tyrrell deemed it propitious for Locke to publish on toleration. As a Whig whose associates had endured the fury of the Tory reaction, Tyrrell welcomed the pressure now placed on the Anglican hierarchy by James II (*Corr.*, vol. iii, pp. 191–3; Goldie, 1992). One result of these new circumstances was an offer by the Quaker leader William Penn, the king's most ardent Dissenting supporter, to secure a pardon for Locke, although Locke angrily responded that he had done nothing to require a pardon (*EL*: Masham; cf. *Corr.*, vol. ii, p. 729).

Locke travelled a good deal during his Dutch exile, residing in Amsterdam, Leiden, Utrecht and Rotterdam, and also returning to Cleves. He visited the utopian community of a sect called the Labadists, who 'live all in common' (Locke, 1997, pp. 293–6). Among his Dutch hosts were the physicians Egbertus Veen and

Pieter Guenellon, and a Quaker merchant, Benjamin Furly. The Furly warehouse in Rotterdam housed an extraordinary library, containing some of the most freethinking books of the age, not least a notorious tract that circulated in manuscript, the 'Treatise of the Three Imposters' (Moses, Christ and Muhammad). Within the Furly circle, it is possible to identify two incipient strands of the early Enlightenment: a moderate, latitudinarian, Christian element, of which Locke was a part, and a radically sceptical element, espoused by Furly and, among his later visitors, John Toland and Anthony Collins, the latter of whom put the word 'freethinker' into the language. Through the Furly circle, Locke encountered thinkers who displayed a deistic indifference to Christian revelation, a circumstance that offers a means to calibrate his own religious heterodoxy.

Locke's exile allowed him to return to scholarship, philosophy and a growing interest in theology. He encountered Remonstrants and Huguenots. 'Remonstrant' was the name given to the Arminian wing of the Dutch Reformed Church, heirs to the early seventeenth-century anti-Calvinist Jacob Arminius, who had broken the prevailing predestinarian consensus. In their soteriology, the Remonstrants' emphasis on 'moralism' and natural virtue opened them to charges of undermining Christ's divinity, since Christ's salvific role could be judged superfluous if humanity can achieve salvation through its own moral efforts. Denounced as 'Socinian' heretics by Calvinists, the Remonstrants defended toleration for theological speculation. They echoed the concern for 'rational Christianity' expressed by the English latitudinarians and Cambridge Platonists, with whom they shared many literary contacts. Locke became a lifelong friend and correspondent of Philip van Limborch, Remonstrant professor of theology at Amsterdam, and author of an Arminian compendium, the *Theologia Christiana* (1686).

Before and after Louis XIV's Revocation of the Edict of Nantes in 1685, thousands of French Protestants, the Huguenots, fled France and thereby put a new word into the English language, 'refugee'. Holland and latterly England were the largest recipients of these exiles, and, for the remainder of his life, Locke was to be enmeshed in the Huguenot community. He befriended Jean Le Clerc, philosopher, theologian and journalist, editor of the *Bibliothèque Universelle*, one of the new genre of literary journals which reviewed the latest works of scholarship and controversy, and whose burgeoning success rendered the Netherlands the capital of the 'Republic of Letters'. Strictly, Le Clerc was not a Huguenot, being Genevan, but he was the centre of a network of refugees, anxious for intelligent employment. Le Clerc assiduously disseminated summaries of Locke's works in his journals, and authored the most influential memoir of Locke: the *Eloge*, translated as *The Life and Character of Mr John Locke* (1706). Locke sought posts for Huguenots in England, and his own literary legacy in the francophone world would depend on Huguenot scholars. Pierre Coste resided with Locke during the last years of his life and produced translations into French of *Some Thoughts concerning Education*, *The Reasonableness of Christianity* and the *Essay concerning Human Understanding*. Another Huguenot, David Mazel, published a French translation of the second of the *Two Treatises* in 1691, which Locke deemed unsatisfactory, later inviting Coste to prepare a new one, though the project was aborted at Locke's death (Milton, 2008; Savonius, 2004).

Le Clerc drew Locke into the world of jobbing literary journalism, commissioning from him a series of reviews of new books for the *Bibliothèque Universelle*. The reviews appeared anonymously, but we can be certain that Locke was responsible for an assessment of Newton's *Principia Mathematica* (1687). Another minor literary venture was the 'New Method of a Commonplace Book', which appeared in the same journal in 1686. Nevertheless, it is important to acknowledge that, by the end of 1688, the sum total of Locke's publications (at least for which his authorship is certain) was very small indeed: three occasional poems in university collections, another poem in praise of Sydenham, a letter in the *Philosophical Transactions*, and recent contributions to Le Clerc's journal.

The Revocation and the plight of the Huguenots were the immediate impetuses for Locke's *Epistola de Tolerantia*, penned in the closing weeks of 1685. It was published in Gouda by Limborch in 1689 and soon after in London in William Popple's English translation. It is a short pamphlet, plangent in demanding toleration for all peaceable religious practice, not only Christian, but also any theistic, including Islamic, Jewish or Native American. The defence of toleration had plenty of precedents in England, including Roger Williams, William Walwyn and William Penn, as well as contemporary Huguenot voices in Holland, such as Noël Aubert de Versé, Henri Basnage, Charles Le Cène, and Isaac Papin, alongside Limborch and Le Clerc. Indeed, on publication, Locke's tract was suspected to be the work of a Huguenot, Jacques Bernard. Yet the intellectual defence of toleration needed restatement. In France by Catholics, in England by Anglicans, in Holland by Calvinists, coercion in religion was not only cruelly practised but also philosophically defended. Religious minorities were deemed intolerable because politically subversive, ecclesiastically schismatic and theologically heretical. Pulpits invoked Christ's injunction in St Luke's Gospel to 'compel them to come in', the classic text for religious persecution since its first deployment by St Augustine. The injunction '*compelle intrare*' explains the title of the most important work for toleration contemporary with Locke's, another by a Huguenot exile, Pierre Bayle's *Philosophical Commentary on These Words of the Gospel, Luke 14:23, 'Compel them to Come In*' (1686). Locke's chief ground for toleration lay in a radical separation of Church and state: the civil magistrate is concerned only with temporal welfare and not the salvation of souls. In agreeing to erect government, we could not rationally consent to licence coercion of our consciences. This was an extrapolation of the principles of the *Two Treatises*. In common with most contemporary tracts for toleration, Locke's *Epistola* remained within the premise of Christian evangelism, since he did not deny the Christian duty of persuading people of the saving truth of Christ's teaching: he does not ground toleration on sceptical doubts about Christianity. Rather, his case is that coercion is not the proper means: it is not Christ-like, nor pertinent to the state, nor instrumentally useful, since force cannot procure belief and can only produce hypocrites or martyrs. By contrast, Bayle and the Dutch Jew Benedict de Spinoza were more radical in their arguments for toleration, both as to their premises and the catholicity of its scope.

In Holland, Locke finally completed the *Essay concerning Human Understanding*, which he dedicated to the Earl of Pembroke. In preparing to publish the whole work, he drafted a short summary which he published as the 'Extrait' in Le Clerc's journal and which, as the *Abrégé*, was separately printed for private distribution and sent to such friends as Pembroke, Boyle and Lady Guise.

In this productive period, Locke also embarked on a new subject, education. He began a series of extended letters to his West Country friend Edward Clarke on the upbringing of Clarke's son, which later formed the basis of *Thoughts concerning Education*. Only partially concerned with academic curricula, Locke's advice was principally directed to nurture, character and parenting. He encouraged the rearing of young people who had stoical self-control, were conversable and sociable, and did not disdain practical, manual and scientific knowledge. During the eighteenth century, of all Locke's books, it was this one that ran through more editions than any other, a parents' handbook for Enlightenment civility.

The Revolution
In the autumn of 1688 a Dutch army invaded England. The English prefer to call this event a 'Revolution'. William of Orange was welcomed

and offered the crown, but the overthrow of James II could not have been achieved without a large foreign army, for the military and fiscal infrastructure of the later Stuart state was remarkably robust. William sought a transformation of English foreign policy and he needed England's resources to save the Dutch republic from destruction by Louis XIV's France. He got what he wanted, for the Nine Years War ensued, and the new king spent much of his reign commanding armies on the Continent. It was a war on many fronts, for although William secured England peacefully, military operations were required to defeat forces in Scotland and Ireland loyal to the Stuarts, the 'Jacobites'. The 'bloodless' English Revolution was accomplished by the reconquest of Ireland at the Battle of the Boyne in 1690, thereby thwarting a Jacobite Ireland perceived to be a client of France. Accordingly, the 'Revolution' needs to be construed geopolitically as well as constitutionally, a dimension of which Locke was acutely aware.

Domestically, the overthrow of James brought in its wake the Bill of Rights, a document later apotheosized as a cardinal link in a chain extending from the Magna Carta to modern universal declarations of rights. Historians wince at such teleologies, but there is a good case for holding that the Revolution, rather than the Civil Wars of the 1640s, marked the foundation of the modern British constitution. That constitution has, however, been marked not only by doctrines of civil rights embodied in law, but also by strong doctrines of parliamentary sovereignty and executive supremacy which would often prove inimical to the freedoms of civil society, as well as of subordinate nations within and beyond the British Isles. This has bearing on our understanding of Locke's Two Treatises, since scholars have not resolved whether that book was conservative in its endorsement of the Revolution, or radical in its scepticism about the limited character of that event.

It is probable that Locke was an early supporter of William's plan to intervene in England, on account of his personal closeness to Charles, Lord Mordaunt, future Earl of Monmouth and Peterborough. As in the case of Shaftesbury, Locke's taste in patrons can seem odd. Mordaunt, too, was charismatic, a scion of the hardline Whig cause, but he was so mercurial and highhanded that William's consort Queen Mary thought him unstable. A member of the exile community in Holland, Mordaunt was an early advocate of William's invasion. At the Revolution, Locke returned to England when summoned by Mordaunt, and thereafter Locke frequented the Mordaunts' home at Putney, played courtier to the flirtatious Lady Mordaunt, sent and received packages to and from Holland aboard Mordaunt's yacht, and was offered government posts through Mordaunt's patronage. There are further signs that, during Locke's Dutch exile, others who were 'in the Prince's inner counsels', Hans Willem Bentinck, future Earl of Portland, and Everard van Dijkveld, William's personal negotiator, intervened to ensure that Locke would be at 'no further risk' in Holland from James II's envoys (Corr., vol. iii, pp. 390–1).

What Locke precisely thought of the Revolution is difficult to discern. Naturally he thought the removal of James a triumph and, writing to Mordaunt, he styled William 'our great deliverer' (Corr., vol. iii, p. 574). A conundrum lies in Locke's attitude to the Convention that assembled in January 1689 to make a settlement. This Convention was a parliament in all but name, but the fact that it was not a parliament was crucial, since it could be construed as a body that transcended parliaments with a capacity to act foundationally. At the close of the Two Treatises, Locke argued that when governments are dissolved, power 'reverts to the society and the people have a right to act as supreme', either to erect a new form of government or to place the old form in new hands, 'as they think good' (TTG II.243). In this view, the Convention could create any sort of polity it chose. For their part, the Tories were anxious for continuity; they held that James had 'abdicated' by his flight from England and that all that remained was to install his heir, his daughter Mary, as queen. They achieved as much, but they had to swallow the co-monarchy of her husband. Within a few days of the Convention's opening, the crown was offered jointly to William and Mary. A small group of radical Whigs argued, however, that the regality should be delayed, urging that the dissolution of government provided a unique opportunity for a fundamental overhaul, a Leveller-like devolution of power, perhaps even the creation of a republic.

Locke's position was paradoxical. It is probable that he regarded the Convention as an embodiment of the political community, free to act at the moment of dissolution: it was *not* a parliament. The preface to the *Two Treatises*, published a few months later, pointedly did not mention Mary, or parliament, and grounded William's claim 'in the consent of the people', an implicit repudiation of both hereditary right and parliamentary continuity. Writing to Locke, Lady Mordaunt asserted that the collapse of James's regime 'has given us by this Convention an occasion not of amending the government, but of melting it down and mak[ing] all new', and in this she was Locke's pupil (*Corr.*, vol. iii, p. 538). Yet equally, like William, Locke was in a constitutional hurry. As we have seen, he approved of the 'ancient constitution', the tripartite polity; the Convention, free to choose any polity, ought to adopt precisely the old polity. Present geopolitical imperatives powerfully reinforced 'ancient prudence'. To delay, to destabilize England and risk Holland in the face of the French onslaught, would be catastrophic. This is the right way to understand Locke's letter to Clarke of 29 January 1689. The Convention should not 'think of themselves as a parliament' but as 'something of another nature', a convention, which has 'an opportunity offered to ... set up a constitution ... for the security of civil rights and the liberty and property of all the subjects of the nation'. Yet this can 'no way so well be done as by restoring our ancient government, the best possibly that ever was ...

in its original constitution'. Settlement must be reached quickly, for, 'if they consider foreign affairs, I wonder any of them can sleep, till they see the nation ... putting itself in a posture of defence and support of the common interest of Europe. The spring comes on apace, and if we be [idle], France will not be'. While, therefore, it was possible for radicals to invoke a Lockean thesis of 'dissolution' to advocate a prolonged period of radical constitutional reconstruction, Locke himself regarded such a course as disastrous. For Locke, the Revolution was fundamentally restorative, for if, by princely tyranny, the 'original constitution' had 'not been invaded, men have done very ill to complain' (*Corr.*, vol. iii, pp. 545–6).

Of the legislative achievements of the Revolution, it was not the Bill of Rights that attracted Locke's attention, but the Toleration Act, which, he believed, was 'not perhaps so wide in scope as might be wished for ... Still, it is something to have progressed so far'. In the same breath he referred to the recent publication of his own *Letter concerning Toleration* (*Corr.*, vol. iii, p. 633; cf. pp. 583–4, 689). Under the Act, Protestants, but not Catholics, were free to worship as they chose, although Dissenters remained excluded from public office. Again, a question arises as to how the principles of the *Letter* square with the Revolution settlement. During the coming century the tract would, on the one hand and rather complacently, be regarded as an endorsement of the settlement's partial restriction of the Anglican hegemony, and, on the other, as a clarion call for a more perfect separation of Church and state.

Within days of the Revolution, Locke was, through Mordaunt, offered an ambassadorship, probably to Brandenburg. He graciously declined, remarking, *inter alia*, that he could not handle drink the way diplomats must, but also making clear the role he sought: 'to serve his majesty [with] some little knowledge I perhaps may have in the constitutions of my country, the temper of my countrymen, and the divisions and interests amongst [them]'

(*Corr.*, vol. iii, p. 576). Mordaunt became first Lord of the Treasury, and Locke agreed to accept a non-onerous post as commissioner for excise appeals, on a salary of £200 per annum. Rumours a few months later that Locke had been appointed Secretary for War were false, but indicative of the extent to which he was regarded as a favoured man in the new administration (*EL*: Wood).

The new king was scarcely less protective of monarchical power than his predecessors, and was insistent on appeasing the Tories. From a Whig point of view, the new regime should have been exclusively Whig. Locke's commitment to Mordaunt entailed a stance of ferocious hostility to the Tory cohorts of James II's discredited regime and their conciliation by William. The Tories and the Anglican hierarchy, although advocates of the rights of Stuart monarchy, had become profoundly alienated by James's aggressively Catholicizing policies, and it was prudent of William to seek their loyalty as they struggled to come to terms with the Revolution. Yet the Whigs found it deeply shocking that William should take into government leading agents of Stuart tyranny and to insist on an amnesty for them. The Whigs devoted an inordinate amount of parliamentary time in 1689–90 to exposing the culprits behind the anti-Whig purges of the preceding decade and to exonerating Whig 'martyrs'. Locke's own minor martyrdom, his expulsion from Christ Church, figured here, as he attempted to secure a restitution of his studentship, though he soon abandoned the attempt. Another indication of his stance is the presence in his papers of memoranda claiming that the Earl of Essex had been murdered, upon which a parliamentary enquiry now ensued (MS Locke b.4, fol. 59). The clearest evidence of Locke's militancy is his vehement opposition to the doctrine of *de facto* allegiance which the Tories concocted to assuage their consciences in ditching their sacred oath of allegiance to James and taking the new oath to William and Mary. To accommodate them, the new oath omitted the traditional promise to uphold the monarch as 'rightful and lawful', but Locke and hardline Whigs demanded restoration of the clause. For Locke, the only honest ground for the Revolution was that of the *Two Treatises*, and its publication was partly intended to serve as an 'allegiance tract' amid scores published at this time. His position was further outlined in a paper of 1690, during debates on the amnesty bill, and in a critical commentary on the *de facto* theory articulated in William Sherlock's *Case of Allegiance* (1691). For Locke, for Tories to persist with the notion that the crown was 'established *jure divino* [by divine right] ... carries an irreconcilable opposition to ... [the] establishment of our present constitution' (Locke, 1997, p. 309). However, once William insisted on amnesty, and the Tories proved successful in the 1690 general election, Locke evidently resolved that it was no longer practical to press the cause of Whig retribution. Nonetheless, the principles of the *Two Treatises* soon began to be used as a standing refutation of Tory allegiance theory. Locke's friend Furly had 'pleasant sport' with 'a scrupulous Cambridge scholar' who could not see his way to renouncing his solemn oath to King James and who remained wedded to Filmer's doctrines; while William Atwood, in publishing the first citation of the *Two Treatises*, recommended the reading of Locke's book ('every morning some pages') as an exercise in intellectual hygiene, to clear away the rubbish of Tory doctrine: 'an effectual catholicon against nonsense and absurdities' (*Corr.*, vol. iii, pp. 638–9; Goldie, ed., *The Reception of Locke's Politics* (*RLP*), 1999, vol. i, p. 39). When the 'rightful and lawful' clause was finally restored in the 1696 Association Oath, Locke took the oath, as Whigs readily did, whilst those who did not subscribe were marked out as crypto-Jacobites and enemies of 'Revolution principles'.

William was a monarch who vetoed parliamentary bills, suspended *habeas corpus*, and did not stop at having a Jacobite suspect interrogated under torture. Some Whigs became so disillusioned with Williamite authoritarianism that they embarked on a career of 'Country' Whiggery, resolutely hostile to executive power and its baleful influence over parliament. A few even turned Jacobite and denounced the new Dutch tyranny, among them the firebrand of the 1680s, Robert Ferguson. Locke, by contrast, offered no critical commentary hostile to the Williamite polity. Far from becoming alienated from the Revolution regime, he became one of its grandees: he became a Court Whig.

Publications and Vindications

The Revolution was the pivot on which Locke's public life turned. He was fifty-six, hitherto had published virtually nothing, and was unknown. During the remaining fifteen years of his life he became a renowned public figure. This was overwhelmingly because of the rapid acclaim and notoriety accorded to his *Essay concerning Human Understanding*, which went through four editions before his death. Locke's fame arose also because he became a leading public servant. It is readily overlooked that his greatest impact on the daily lives of his contemporaries was as a result of his role in the national recoinage undertaken in the mid-1690s. This led in turn to his membership of the Board of Trade, where he operated at the heart of English imperial, commercial and social policy. It was not the *Two Treatises* that brought Locke into the public eye, despite occasional citations of it. That book appeared anonymously and Locke strove to conceal his authorship, only admitting it when he wrote his will. Despite persistent rumours of his authorship, the book had little *éclat* during its first decade in print. Only in 1703 was the epithet 'the great Locke' attached to the author of the *Two Treatises* and then by a savage Tory opponent. In the meantime, when the author of *Decus et Tutamen* (1696) praised Locke's 'excellent ... political maxims', he was not thinking of the *Two Treatises* but of Locke's writings on the currency (*RLP*, vol. vi, p. 61). It is, furthermore, worth noting that whereas the *Essay* was published in folio, the format

designed for major works for the library, the *Two Treatises* came out in octavo, a format commonly used for ephemeral pamphlets.

Locke's great quartet of books, the *Essay*, *Two Treatises*, *Toleration* and *Education*, had all been long in gestation, nearly twenty years in the case of the *Essay*. All had been drafted before the Revolution but not published until afterwards, three appearing in 1689, followed by *Education* in 1693. Similarly, Locke's tract on economics was drafted in 1668 but only appeared, as *Some Considerations of the Consequences of the Lowering of Interest*, in 1692. The cautious author, who voiced conventional tropes of reluctance to take up the pen and of finding public controversy distasteful, now became a profligate author, capable of sustaining punishing marathons of polemic. He published new work, notably his *Reasonableness of Christianity* (1695) and a series of tracts on the recoinage (1695–6). Moreover, in the years between 1690 and 1699 he published no fewer than seven books that were vindications of earlier work, which amount to 1,275 pages in the nineteenth-century edition of his collected *Works*. He defended the *Letter concerning Toleration*, in both a second and an immensely long third *Letter*, against an Oxford clergyman Jonas PROAST, who argued a case for the practicability and desirability of religious coercion. He defended the *Essay* against his old adversary Edward Stillingfleet, now Bishop of Worcester, who denounced him for the dubiety of his position on the doctrine of the Trinity. And he justified the *Reasonableness* against a Cambridge clergyman, John EDWARDS.

It was Locke's own intention that the *Essay* should secure his reputation. For the second edition he commissioned a portrait engraving for the frontispiece, his auto-icon. There were new editions in 1694, 1695, 1700 and (posthumously) 1706, each amended by him, and, in the case of the second and fourth, having new chapters, in the former on 'Identity' and in the latter on the 'Association of Ideas' and 'Enthusiasm'. Locke encouraged the preparation of an abridgement of the *Essay* by John Wynne (1696), a translation into French by Coste (1700) and into Latin by Ezekiel Burridge (1701). The *Essay* found allies in tracts by Samuel Bold, Richard Burthogge and Catherine Trotter, and in Latin textbooks prepared by Le Clerc, entitled *Logica*, *Ontologia* and *Pneumatologia* (1692–7). The *Essay* also brought Locke his most fruitful philosophical friendship, with William Molyneux of Dublin, a relationship pursued by correspondence, for they met only once, just before Molyneux's sudden death in 1698. Their correspondence enabled Locke to hone the *Essay* in its successive revisions. The two men rehearsed topics that proved of enduring interest to future interpreters, such as Locke's notorious suggestion that 'matter might think', a groundwork for materialism; the relationship of freedom of the will to the causal determinacy of bodily SUB-STANCE in a mechanical world; and the nature of PERSONAL IDENTITY and consciousness. What became known as 'MOLYNEUX'S PROBLEM' was posed: it concerns a blind person's capacity to connect what has been learned by touch with what would be seen were sight to be acquired: psychologists as well as philosophers have pursued this question ever since (*Corr.*, vol. iv, p. 651; *E*, II.ix.8, pp. 145–6).

Attacks on the *Essay* fell into two distinct phases. In the early 1690s objections chiefly related to the book's moral philosophy and focused on the first book, the critique of innate IDEAS. The denial of innate knowledge was held to jeopardize moral intuitions. Locke's constant citation of the strange multiplicity of human ethical beliefs and practices in divergent cultures implied a capitulation to conventionalism, in other words to the notion that moral standards are merely local, cultural and customary, and lacked any universal standard. Soon after the *Essay*'s publication, Tyrrell reported that 'some thinking men in Oxford', perhaps including Thomas Creech and Sir George Mackenzie of Rosehaugh, were 'dissatisfied with what you have said concerning the law of nature', because, in rejecting 'an innate law', Locke's

argument 'resolved all virtue and vice ... out[side] of a commonwealth and abstracted from divine revelation, into the praise or dispraise that men give to certain actions in several ... societies'. In other words, Locke had endorsed 'the law of fashion ... which seems to come very near what is so much cried out upon in Mr Hobbes' (*Corr.*, vol. iv, pp. 101–2; cf. pp. 108–9). Isaac Newton, writing to Locke from the Bull Tavern in Shoreditch, apologized for his initial misapprehension that the *Essay* so 'struck at the root of morality' that 'I took you for a Hobbist' (*Corr.*, vol. iv, p. 727). The *Essay*'s lack of scriptural support for the moral law rendered the subject particularly problematic, and Locke protested in vain that the *Essay* was an investigation of what reason could know rather than what revelation could teach (*Corr.*, vol. iv, pp. 110–13). Nowhere did Lord Ashley, the future third Earl of Shaftesbury, in his friendly and meandering correspondence with his former tutor, indicate the savage critique he would later make, after Locke's death, against the *Essay* as a 'selfish' system: hedonic, Hobbist, and Epicurean. Even so, the *Essay* did make positive headway. Its critique of innatism was favourably pursued in the pulpit by Richard Bentley in his Boyle Lectures in 1692 and by William Whiston in his *New Theory of the Earth* (1696).

A new phase of critique opened in the mid-1690s when Stillingfleet began to find theological fault and charged Locke with SOCINIANISM. In 1697 Locke recorded that William Sherlock 'has been pleased to declare against my doctrine ... from the pulpit ... and ... charged it with little less than atheism'. He continued, dolefully, 'my book crept into the world about six or seven years ago, without any opposition, and has since passed amongst some for useful, and, the least favourable, for innocent. But ... it is agreed by some men that it should no longer do so' (*Corr.*, vol. vi, pp. 5–6). Whilst Locke exaggerated the earlier lack of criticism, he was correct that it now came thick and fast, and on grounds of heresy.

Locke was necessarily selective in replying to his critics. Besides published vindications, he drafted short responses to others, not published until after his death. One was directed against the Cartesian Malebranche's dictum of 'seeing all things in God', a phrase which summarized the 'occasionalist' doctrine that only the constant action of God explained the interaction of two kinds of SUBSTANCE, material and immaterial, that apparently cannot causally act on one another. Another was a critique of the English neo-Platonist John NORRIS. Locke's work in revising the *Essay* also prompted a remarkable little treatise, originally intended for inclusion but appearing separately as *The Conduct of the Understanding* (1706), an epitome of many of Locke's characteristic philosophical positions, which deserves to be read more widely. He also wrote a short tract for children, *The Elements of Natural Philosophy* (1720).

By the mid-1690s, defences of the *Essay* became embroiled with reaction to Locke's new work, *The Reasonableness of Christianity*, which argued that to be a Christian was to believe no more than that Jesus was the Messiah and Son of God. Christian doctrine was not to be darkened by theological abstruseness beyond the capacity of the illiterate multitude. Locke's doctrinal minimalism exposed him to charges of disregarding the doctrines of the Trinity and the Incarnation. What rendered the book more dangerous was its extrapolation in John Toland's *Christianity not Mysterious* (1696). An Irishman of quick wit and ready pen, Toland built a dazzling and provocative career publishing works of heresy, anticlericalism and neo-republican Whiggery. Locke was not alone in being initially beguiled by the young Toland, who was a past master at persuading influential people to sponsor him. Although Locke's *Reasonableness* was rooted in divine revelation, it came to be suspected of encouraging DEISM, and the Middlesex grand jury accordingly condemned the *Reasonableness* alongside Toland's book, while the Irish Parliament ordered the latter to be burnt. There were evidently still those who 'make our civil courts judges of religious doctrines' (*Corr.*, vol. vi, p. 163). One of Locke's admirers, Elizabeth Berkeley, urged him to be 'more cautious' of his dubious fans, 'proud of every shadow of authority to believe as little as they can' (*Corr.*, vol. v, p. 664). The tarring of Locke with Toland's brush again raises the question of Locke's relationship with the 'radical Enlightenment'. It would be mistaken to trace a direct lineage from Locke to deism; indeed, William Popple's hope was that the *Reasonableness* would arrest the growth of deism. Popple summed up deism as the denial of immaterial beings, the rejection of revelation in favour of natural religion, and the derivation of morality from natural virtue; and he feared that the age was 'running from one extreme to another. Atheism, or, (if that word be too harsh), even irreligion is a sad sanctuary from the mischiefs of superstition. ... Is there no medium?' (*Corr.*, vol. v, p. 519).

Locke's own doubts about the Trinity are notoriously difficult to pin down. Whilst he certainly became familiar with the corpus of Socinian writings by followers of the Italian anti-Trinitarian Faustus Socinus, he judiciously avoided public discussion of the subject. One clue may lie in the membership of Locke's 'Dry Club', a discussion group dedicated to theological subjects in a spirit of liberty for 'speculative opinions', which included the unitarians Popple and Henry Hedworth (*Corr.*, vol. iv, p. 581). Liberty to speculate mattered: Locke was particularly sensitive to incurring charges of heresy, not least because the lapse of the Licensing Act in 1695 was blamed by orthodox theologians for unleashing a flood of irreligious publications. In 1697 Locke took a keen interest in the trial and hanging of an Edinburgh university student Thomas Aikenhead, the last capital punishment for blasphemy exacted in Britain. As Locke's Scottish correspondent reported, the Scottish law of blasphemy still made the 'denying ... any of the persons of the Trinity ... punishable with death' (*Corr.*, vol. vi, p. 18; Hunter, 1992).

One characteristic of the religious sensibility of the 1690s was a vociferous anticlericalism. The new word 'priestcraft' became fashionable, connoting a propensity towards clerical ambition and the manipulation of religious belief to serve clerical power, and attributable to all organized priesthoods, Protestant as well as papist, Christian as well as pagan. Locke used the term just once, in the *Reasonableness*; his colleagues more often, when characterizing his thought. It is no surprise that the Quaker Furly should be fond of the term. He suspected that, long after overcoming the 'intolerable yoke of Romish slavery' in the Reformation, we might still be forced to 'bow our necks to the same pretences among their successors' (*Corr.*, vol. v, p. 63). Popple remarked that modern youth were 'disgusted' with 'clerical fard [sham]' (*Corr.*, vol. v, p. 519). The matter of priestcraft could be quotidian: Locke received an unsolicited fan letter from a reader of *Thoughts concerning Education* who was 'loathe to have my children tutored by any of the clergy, for most of them have still a hankering after *jure divino* and passive obedience principles, and are over-tenacious as to indifferent ceremonies, and very fond of niceties in religion, which are matters I would have none of my children trouble their heads about' (*Corr.*, vol. v, p. 11).

One book that Locke never defended was the *Two Treatises*. Although the book certainly endangered his life before the Revolution, this is not the case thereafter, and the reasons for his obsessive secrecy are elusive. There can, however, be little doubt that his authorship was soon widely known and long before Molyneux was the first to moot it in print in 1698. Within months of publication in 1689, Tyrrell reported that there were people in Oxford who 'make you ... author', while in 1695 an Oxford undergraduate informed his father, 'here is a book writ by Mr Locke which makes a great noise. The title is *Two Treatises of Government*' (*Corr.*, vol. iv, p. 36; MacGrath, 1924, pp. 193–4). In the latter year the Advocates Library in Edinburgh accessioned a copy of 'Locke on Government'. Contemporary awareness of Locke's authorship renders more puzzling the book's lack of impact, since, as we shall see, it failed to generate a controversial reception until the opening of the new century.

The Masham Manor and the Court Whigs

For nearly two years after his return to England in 1689, Locke lodged in London, at first with Rabsy Smithsby and subsequently with Robert Pawling. Thereafter he moved to Oates, a manor house in Essex twenty miles north of London, where he lived for the remainder of his life, returning to spend summer weeks in London. Oates was the home of a remarkable woman, Damaris Masham. The daughter of the Cambridge Platonist and Master of Christ's College, Ralph Cudworth, she was well educated, and just twenty-two when Locke first met her around 1681. He had been immediately struck by her acuity and forthrightness. She insisted on defending the Platonists, their version of innatism and their aspiration to mystical communion with the divine, and she debated with him John Smith's *Select Discourses* (1660). Locke probably fell in love with her but lacked the courage or inclination to act on his feelings. He was, in any case, soon in exile abroad, from where he received her abrupt announcement that she had married Sir Francis Masham. There is little sign that the match was passionate; Sir Francis was a nondescript, complaisant gentleman of standing, soon to become Whig MP for Essex. He had ten children from his previous marriage, and his new wife brought one further child, Francis. Lady Masham chafed at the duties of household management, memorably complaining to Locke that 'household affairs are the opium of the soul' and that conversation among country ladies did not rise above 'sublime ideas of goose pie', but that, nonetheless, in her chamber, among the clutter of account books, medicinal remedies and spinning wheel, she had copies of Abraham Cowley's *Poems*, Marcus Aurelius' *Meditations*, and Descartes's *Principles of Philosophy* (*Corr.*, vol. ii, pp. 757–9).

The household at Oates once Locke arrived is intriguing, since it gives the impression of being governed by Locke and Damaris Masham. Locke took great care over the upbringing of Francis, to whom he later bequeathed half his wealth. In a household containing more than a dozen servants, and to which scandal only once attached, the relationship between the two of them must have been chaste. In 1697 John Edwards outraged them by a published reference to 'the seraglio at Oates', and a retraction was extracted from the Cambridge vice-chancellor who had authorized the book (*Corr.*, vol. vi, pp. 210–11). Of Damaris Masham, Locke wrote that she was 'much occupied with study and reflection on theological and philosophical matters ... I know few men capable of discussing with such insight the most abstruse subjects, such as are beyond the grasp, I do not say of women, but even of most educated men' (*Corr.*, vol. iv, p. 237). She published, anonymously, two works of philosophy, *A Discourse concerning the Love of God* (1695), against John Norris and Mary Astell, who assumed it was written by Locke, and *Occasional Thoughts in Reference to a Virtuous or Christian Life* (1705), both issued by Locke's publisher Awnsham Churchill. She also exchanged letters with Limborch in Holland and LEIBNIZ in Germany.

Oates allowed Locke the seclusion he sought to think and write, and gave him clean air, as the London smog left him gasping for breath and fearful for his life. He drew a stream of visitors to this secluded manor house, including Newton, Lord Ashley, the cabbalist physician Francis Mercury van Helmont, and the painter Sir Godfrey Kneller. Evidence from the local parish records of High Laver provides vignettes of Locke's life there. When the vicar made regular collections for charitable causes, such as for Irish and Huguenot refugees, or towns ravaged by fire, Locke's donation was, in one instance, the second largest in the parish, largesse being one way in which social rank was registered. When the Association Oath was imposed in 1696, the entire male population of the village signed, and Locke's signature appears at the top, just under Sir Francis's. Of some sixty-five signatories, more than half were illiterate, signing with their marks (Essex Record Office, D/P/111/1/1; Q/RRO/2/1).

Rural seclusion notwithstanding, Locke more fully entered the political arena in the mid-1690s. He advised on the recoinage. The currency was in disarray; there was a shortage of coin for everyday transactions; clipping, the fraudulent practice of paring away the precious metal, was rife. Some precautions, such as the use of new technology for milled edges, were readily agreed, but controversy arose about the optimum monetary system to adopt. A treasury official, William Lowndes, did not believe it necessary for the face value of a coin to be underpinned by an equivalent value of precious metal, thereby anticipating the modern system of nominal valuation. This approach would facilitate the issue of sufficient COINAGE for cash transactions without draining the government's bullion stock. Although Lowndes argued that public valuation of coinage depended on trust and on the probity of the government and the banks, rather than on metal content, Locke disagreed, repudiating devaluation and insisting that the monetary standard be maintained. A series of memoranda were commissioned, involving consultation with, *inter alia*, Newton and Christopher Wren. Locke won his case. But the recoinage was ineptly handled: the Mint was unable to produce new coins fast enough, and would not fully honour demonetized clipped coins, to the detriment especially of the poor. One critic protested that Locke had 'done more mischief by his ... folly' than 10,000 copies of his *Essay* could compensate for (Anon., 1696, p. 6).

Locke was also involved in securing the abolition of censorship of the press. After 1695 books were no longer required to carry a pre-publication licence from officials of state or church. Through his 'College' of like-minded MPs, principally Clarke, Locke brought his influence to bear. Although Clarke's bill for 'regulating the press' bore a reassuring title, it was in fact designed to free the press, and was opposed by bishops, Tories and the Stationers' Company. Clarke was 'attacked on all sides' by Anglicans and Dissenters, who thought that 'more care might be taken of the church and the truth' (*Corr.*, vol. v, pp. 482–3). Locke's memoranda did not offer sonorous Miltonic appeals for liberty of expression, though he certainly expressed worries about liberty of theological speculation. He dwelt chiefly on the damage wreaked by the Stationers' Company's printing monopolies on scholarship and the intellectual property rights of authors (*Corr.*, vol. v, pp. 785–96; Locke, 1997, pp. 329–39; Astbury, 1978).

In 1696 a Board of Trade and Plantations was created to which Locke was appointed one of eight commissioners on a substantial annual salary of £1000. The role was onerous and Locke was assiduous, remarking to Masham's stepdaughter Esther that 'my head ... belongs now to a man of trade and is thwacked with sea coal and fuller's earth' (*Corr.*, vol. v, p. 693). Locke's best-known Board document is his *Essay on the Poor Law* (1697), a scheme to invigorate the Poor Law by providing workhouses for the able-bodied and subsistence for the deserving weak. Though disciplinarian as to the necessity that fit people must labour and not be 'begging drones', Locke equally held that, one way or another, 'everyone must have meat, drink, clothing, and firing' (Locke, 1997, pp. 184, 189). Besides this solely authored memorandum, Locke appended his name alongside those of his colleagues to numerous position papers and official letters. In 1698 he co-authored a report on Virginia, analysing its economic problems and maladministration: the governor was sacked and replaced with Locke's favoured candidate. One policy that Locke supported, in the teeth of Tory xenophobia, was legislation for a general naturalization of foreign immigrants. The case was demographic and economic: there was a widespread view that England was underpopulated and that skilled migrants were an economic boon. A correspondent urging this policy on Locke argued that tyrannies were apt to weaken themselves through 'dispeopling': by contrast, free nations with open borders were rich nations (*Corr.*, vol. vi, pp. 14–17).

In 1698 Locke clashed, at a remove, with his friend Molyneux. The Board's policy, strongly encouraged by West Country textile interests in parliament, was to protect the English woollen industry from external competition. The Board proposed that Ireland be forbidden to export woollens and instead encouraged to develop linen manufacture. The Irish parliament objected, and Molyneux published a provocative tract, *The Case of Ireland*, extrapolating a general case for Ireland's autonomy as an independent kingdom under the crown, a kingdom collateral with, rather than subordinate to, England. Denying thereby that the Westminster parliament had legislative authority over Ireland, Molyneux cited the *Two Treatises*, 'said to be written by my excellent friend, John Locke', to endorse the proposition that the Irish had not consented to be governed by England (*RLP*, vol. i, p. 225). This was the first time that colonial nationalism expressed itself through Locke's *Two Treatises*, and, decades later, *The Case of Ireland* would be cited in colonial America during the era of Independence. It should be noted, however, that Molyneux's 'nationalism' was of the 'Protestant Ascendancy': he represented the small minority of Anglo-Irish who dominated an otherwise Catholic island. Locke made no public comment, but government pamphleteers denied that the *Two Treatises* was pertinent to the Irish case (*RLP*, vol. i, pp. 282–4; cf. *Corr.*, vol. vi, pp. 366–8 and 376–8).

In 1701 the *Two Treatises* was cited in an American context for the first time, again in a manner uncomfortable for its author. The case was rather parallel to that of Molyneux and Ireland, as Locke's book was used to defend English settlers in the province of New York from the high-handedness of the colonial governor, Lord Bellomont, who was a friend and ally of Locke. Bellomont told Locke that the New York assembly had, under his direction, revoked injudicious land grants, which had provoked protest from injured grantees, led by a 'great knave'. The protest had produced a pamphlet that cited the *Two Treatises* in defence of the fundamental obligation of government to protect, rather than invade, private property rights; it pointedly noted that its author was a member of the offending Board of

Trade. Once again, Locke's book offered ideological possibilities that conflicted with his own policy positions (*Corr.*, vol. vi, p. 676; Montague, 1701).

Politically, Locke was close to the 'Junto' Whigs who dominated William's administration for most of the 1690s; he was particularly close to Lord Somers, who became Lord Chancellor in 1697, and was the dedicatee of two of Locke's economic tracts. During that decade, English governance underwent a transformation. A paradox of the Revolution is that it overthrew Stuart royal ABSOLUTISM but installed a more powerful state apparatus in its place. The personal rule of a princely court yielded to the bureaucratic rule of a parliamentary state, the infrastructure of which rapidly expanded, owing to foreign war fought on an unprecedented scale. Thus the 'fiscal-military state' emerged. War entailed high taxes and high taxes entailed intrusive officialdom. The state's ability to levy tax was enhanced by legislative consent, supplied by parliament, which now sat every year. Although parliament demanded accountability from the executive, that executive skilfully engineered parliamentary consent, not least through 'placemen', against which the Country party had vigorously protested in the 1670s. The cost of war also brought fiscal innovation, in land taxes and expanded excise duties, and in deficit financing, through the creation of the Bank of England to manage a national debt. Prosperous citizens invested in government stock and became rentiers of the state. War furthermore ensured that a substantial portion of private entrepreneurship depended on state contracts, to build ships, victual and clothe armies, and supply munitions. The symbolic birth of the modern fiscal state occurred in 1698 with parliament's creation of the 'civil list', by which the monarch himself became a salaried official: the state ceased to be identical with the royal household. It becomes possible to speak non-anachronistically of a 'civil service', as distinct from 'courtiers' of the royal household, although the process of disaggregation was gradual.

In William's reign this process was largely managed by Whigs. To many contemporaries, both Tories and 'Country' Whigs, such developments were dubious, even pernicious, prompting polemic against 'corruption', 'placemen' and 'standing armies'. Anxiety was expressed about overweening executive power and the unfreedom of living under a government of salaried officials rather than citizen-officeholders, as well as about the inauthenticity of bankers' wealth as against landed wealth. The Whig cause fractured. Those, variously called 'Country', 'true', 'real' or 'commonwealth' Whigs, denounced the Court or 'Junto' Whigs for betraying Whig principles which had been hostile to central power. The classic denunciation of the new order came from a Tory pamphleteer, Charles Davenant, in his *True Picture of a Modern Whig* (1701), an imaginary dialogue at Garraway's coffee house between 'Mr Whiglove' and the egregious 'Tom Double', the very model of a modern Whig apparatchik.

Such is the flexibility of Locke's *Two Treatises* that during the eighteenth century it was destined to be deployed by both friends and enemies of the Court Whig vision. It is clear where Locke personally stood: he was unmistakably a Court Whig. As commissioner of excise appeals, itself a salaried state position, his task was to adjudicate excise disputes; the excise was a recent and burgeoning fiscal instrument. The Board of Trade, on which Locke sat, was created after a protracted dispute over its control, which Junto Whigs won against Country opposition. Locke's 'College' colleague Edward Clarke was a skilful and energetic manager of legislation on behalf of the Court; Locke's notions were voiced in Clarke's parliamentary speeches. Clarke was Auditor-General to the queen and an excise commissioner. In 1695 a Country opposition polemicist drew up a list of grasping 'placemen', which included the names of Locke's West Country friend Sir Walter Yonge, one of his bankers, Sir Stephen Evance, and three fellow members of the commission for excise appeals;

the only reason Locke's name was not among them is that the list was confined to Members of Parliament (Bodleian Library, MS Rawlinson D846, fols 1–5). In 1701 a hostile tract entitled *The Taunton Dean Letter* appeared, whose very title points to Locke's closest parliamentary ally, Clarke, MP for Taunton. It is a catalogue of Court Whig sleaze, of corrupt practices by revenue commissioners, military contractors and electoral manipulators. Furthermore, a broadside published shortly after Locke's death directly charged Locke with publishing in defence of high interest rates because he himself had been a 'trader in money', who got rich by money-lending, and asserted that it was 'well known' that Locke had died wealthy, and that he and his 'skilful friends' epitomized 'the new man with money' (*RLP*, vol. vi, pp. 163–7).

The Country party objected to the machinery of state patronage, but Locke was assiduous in the exercise of such patronage. When he joined the Board of Trade, the translator of the *Letter concerning Toleration*, William Popple, was appointed its secretary. When a tax was imposed on legal documents, Locke's London landlord and close friend, Robert Pawling, became Comptroller of the Stamp Office. Whereas Popple and Pawling had formerly been merchants, they now became state officials. Locke's secretary Sylvester Brounower moved to become Popple's clerk at the Board. Locke frequently received letters craving his patronage: Lady Eyre sought his influence in securing a place for her son in the treasury, customs or admiralty (*Corr.*, vol. vii, p. 552; cf. p. 717). The Locke who remains to many modern readers a totemic theorist of the minimal state and of libertarian hostility to 'big government' was an active engineer of England's burgeoning executive and fiscal apparatus. Around 1698 Locke added a passage in the margin of his copy of the *Two Treatises* applauding the 'wise and godlike' prince who directs the manpower and resources of the commonwealth, this being 'the great art of government' (*TTG* II.42).

Recessional

Ill health forced Locke's retirement from the Board in 1700, after which he rarely left Oates. There were, however, two late proxy encounters with politics. In 1700 the Whigs lost office and Somers was impeached. The Tories, now in command, procrastinated over renewal of war against France. A temporary peace had been achieved by the Treaty of Ryswick in 1698, but now the appalling prospect opened of Spain and its empire falling to the French Bourbon dynasty. Worse, on the death of the deposed James II, Louis XIV recognized his son, the 'Pretender', as king of England, Scotland and Ireland. Locke's correspondence shared the Whigs' campaign for war. 'I wonder how anyone of the House can sleep till he sees England in a better state of defence', a striking echo of what he had urged on the Convention in 1689 (*Corr.*, vol. vii, pp. 261–2; cf. p. 209). His letters are littered with remarks on the 'liberties of Europe', the 'Protestant interest' and the 'balance of power', and he raged against Tory appeasement of the European dictator. Locke strongly believed that the first obligation of the post-Revolution state was to galvanize its powers to crush France. When a group of Whig Kentish citizens petitioned the Commons for war, demanding that it listen to the 'voice of the people', Lord Somers published a tract in their defence, citing the *Two Treatises* on the right of the people to remonstrate on behalf of their grievances. In a unique polemical conjunction, Locke was momentarily joined with the great publicists Daniel Defoe and Jonathan Swift, collectively pressing the cause of a (presumptively Whiggish) 'people' against a reluctant Tory parliament. For the first time, the *Two Treatises* was prominently deployed as a populist work within the frame of parliamentary politics. Hence the high Tory Charles Leslie denounced the 'great Locke' as an ideological ally of Somers, Defoe and Swift, and the *Two Treatises* began to enter the canon of major political texts.

Locke's final proxy intervention in current politics was in the furore over 'occasional conformity'. The Tories and high Anglican churchmen profoundly objected to the practice whereby Dissenters nominally qualified themselves for public office by taking the Anglican sacrament once a year, and then worshipping in their own chapels for the rest of the year. As a campaign for legislation to suppress this practice gathered pace, two leading spokesmen for the Dissenters made overt use of Locke's *Letter concerning Toleration* to vindicate the civil rights of religious minorities: John Shute Barrington in *The Interest of England* (1703) and Edmund Calamy in *A Defence of Moderate Nonconformity* (1704). Locke befriended Shute and sent Calamy a letter expressing approval of his book. Shute flattered Locke as the author of both the *Two Treatises*, which 'baffled the boldest champion of slavery' (Filmer), and the *Letter concerning Toleration*, which 'exposed the sophistry of a ... refined scheme of persecution' (Proast's), and he thought it a natural corollary that Locke should 'once more resume your pen, and vindicate the liberty of occasional communion' (*Corr.*, vol. viii, pp. 133–4). The ailing Locke demurred and urged Shute to write a tract, although he himself did commence a fourth letter on toleration, a final sally against Proast, left unfinished at his death. At this juncture, the Dissenters decisively sought to capture Locke for their cause, laying a foundation for a close association during the coming century between Lockean principles and 'Rational Dissent'.

Locke's last substantial scholarly project was a commentary on the epistles of St Paul, published shortly after his death. Locke's interest in the Bible had increased during the 1680s. He was a literalist, like most of his contemporaries, and he helped to establish the eighteenth century's preoccupation with the forensic analysis of Scripture as historical evidence. The Bible was treated as a historical rather than an imaginative work, a source of narrative fact and empirical demonstration of Christian claims, rather than as a resource for allegory, metaphor, poetic truth or meditation. Locke's friend Toinard had long laboured to perfect an authoritative 'harmony' of the gospels, to render their chronologies coherent. Other chronologers strove to reconcile biblical history with non-Christian narratives. Locke recommended Aegidius Strauch's *Chronology* (1657), which judiciously evaluated various attempts to determine the age of the world, the consensus placing it around 4000 BC. He commented on Thomas BURNET'S *Theory of the Earth* (1684–90), an influential attempt to provide scientific explanations for Old Testament phenomena. He corresponded with Newton on Trinitarian passages apparently interpolated in the New Testament and discussed with him the prophetic books of Daniel and Revelation (*Corr.*, vol. iv, pp. 164–5, 197). As an exegete of the New Testament, Locke offered a general essay on hermeneutics, in his prefatial 'Essay for the Understanding of St Paul's Epistles'. He stressed the need to understand Scripture contextually, having regard to authorial intention, and he deplored the practice of breaking Scripture into 'atoms', decontextualized verses that too readily became an arbitrary ammunition of 'proofs'. Scripture did provide proofs, but not if read naïvely.

Locke's lengthy commentaries on the Pauline epistles are today the least studied of his substantial works. His exegetical prowess tempted opportunist publishers to attribute to him such works as *A Commonplace Book to the Holy Bible*, nineteenth-century editions of which still carried his name. One immediate impact of his elucidations was among contemporary feminists. In explaining 1 Corinthians 11:2–16, he commented on women's role in the Church, in remarks that could lend themselves to both feminist and anti-feminist constructions. Quaker defenders of female preaching (a shocking innovation of the time) took courage from Locke, and he was cited by those who wished to defend this practice against detractors. On the other hand, Locke's remark about the 'natural subjection' of women outraged Mary Astell, who is sometimes called 'the first English feminist'. Her preface to *Reflections upon Marriage* in 1706, which contained the eloquent query upon which rests her feminist credentials today, 'If all men are born free, how is that all women are born slaves?', proceeded to quote and denounce Locke's commentary (*RLP*, vol. ii, pp. 107–26; vi, pp. 129–42).

During his final years, Locke was supported by a coterie of friends who screened him from the consequences of fame. They bought books, summarized them and wrote rejoinders. Among this circle were Locke's bookseller Awnsham Churchill, the clergyman Samuel Bold, for whom Locke prepared 'Some Thoughts concerning Reading and Study for a Gentleman', and two new acolytes, the deist Anthony Collins, and Locke's cousin, a lawyer, MP and future Lord Chancellor, Peter King. Locke's correspondence with Collins is a model, probably contrived so, of the ethos of 'politeness', full of gracious apostrophes on friendship, which levels hierarchy, the pursuit of truth, which overcomes self-serving dogma, and the love of conversation, which nurtures human sympathies (*Corr.*, vol. viii, pp. 97–8).

Locke died at Oates on 28 October 1704, shortly after listening to Damaris Masham read to him from the Psalms. He was buried at High Laver parish church, where his epitaph urges that we should 'learn from his writings, which will tell you whatever there is to be said about him more faithfully than the dubious eulogies of an epitaph'. Sitting in the garden at Oates, he had unwittingly proposed another apt epitaph, when recollecting a passage in Horace's *Epistles*:

When the milder sun brings you a larger audience, you will tell them about me: that I was a freedman's son, and amid slender means spread wings too wide for my nest, thus adding to my merits what you take from my birth; that I found favour, both in war and peace, with the foremost in the state; of small stature, grey before my time, fond of the sun, quick in temper, yet so as to be easily appeased (*EL*: Coste).

Locke left £12,000, enough to count him a wealthy man, for we should multiply by about 100 to equate with modern values. His inherited means were modest and his West Country rents never amounted to much. In the mid-1660s his income from all sources had been about £100 *per annum*, which put him, like his father, on the margins of gentility. During the years that Shaftesbury was in government, he gained additional official income, though Charles II was an erratic paymaster, and also subventions from the earl himself. His most lucrative acquisition was his purchase from Shaftesbury, on favourable terms, of a lifetime annuity that yielded £100. His background compelled him to be financially anxious: in 1684 he worried that the loss of his Christ Church studentship was critical financially, apart from the hazard to his reputation and personal security. It was only after the Revolution that his capital grew rapidly, partly from state service, but mainly from investment. He traded stock in the Bank of England and the East India Company. By his will, the two principal beneficiaries of his wealth and books were Peter King, through whose descendants, the earls of Lovelace, the capacious Locke archive in the Bodleian Library derives, and Damaris Masham's son, Francis, who pursued an unremarkable career in the law, and whose share of Locke's books and *objets* were lost.

Locke's ambiguous philosophical reputation at the time of his death is captured by the contrariness of Oxford University. Whilst some heads of colleges sought to ban 'the new philosophy which was too much read; and in particular your book', others deprecated such a move as likely to incur ridicule, as if the university 'went about to forbid the reading of all philosophy save that of Aristotle' (*Corr.*, vol. viii, pp. 269–70). At the same time, the university librarian sought to acquire copies of all Locke's works, of which Locke duly made a gift, including, at last, those whose authorship he had hitherto striven to hide. His admirers were convinced that this body of work was destined to 'abridge the empire of darkness' (*Corr.*, vol. vi, p. 38). With such phrases was the Enlightenment made.

BIBLIOGRAPHY

Unpublished Sources
Bodleian Library, Oxford:
    MS Locke b.4, fol. 59, Depositions concerning the Earl of Essex.
    MS Rawlinson D846, fols 1–5, Samuel Grascome's list of placemen.
British Library, London (=BL):
    Add. MS 15640, Minutes of the Bahama Islands Adventurers.
    Add. MS 28273, Notebook of John Locke, senior.
    Add. MS 28929, Correspondence of Humphrey Prideaux.
    Add. MS 41810, Despatches of Thomas Chudleigh.
Essex Record Office, Chelmsford:
    D/P/111/1/1, High Laver Parish Register.
    Q/RRO/2/1, Essex Association Oath Roll, 1696.
Huntington Library, San Marino, California:
    MS BL 6, William Blathwayt papers.
    MS HM 68, London 'monster petition' of 1680.
National Archives, London:
    MS PRO 30/24/4/236, Shaftesbury's household in 1672.
    MS PRO 30/24/6/427–30, Memoranda on ecclesiastical government.

Printed Primary Sources
Anon., *A Letter Humbly Offer'd to the Consideration of all Gentlemen* (1696).
Goldie, Mark (ed.), *The Reception of Locke's Politics*, 6 vols (London, 1999) (=*RLP*).
——, and Delphine Soulard (eds), *The Early Lives of John Locke* (Oxford, forthcoming) (=*EL*). [The principal early memoirs are those of Pierre Coste, Pierre Des Maizeaux, Jean Le Clerc, Damaris Masham, the third Earl of Shaftesbury and Anthony Wood.]
Locke, John, *Locke's Travels in France, 1675–1679*, ed. John Lough (Cambridge, 1953).
——, *Political Essays*, ed. Mark Goldie (Cambridge, 1997).

MacGrath, J. (ed.), *The Flemings in Oxford*, vol. iii (Oxford, 1924).
Montague, John, *Arguments Offer'd to the Right Honourable the Lords Commissioners for Trade and Plantation Relating to Some Acts of Assembly Past at New-York in America* (New York, 1701).
Morrice, Roger, *The Entring Book of Roger Morrice*, vol. ii, ed. John Spurr (Woodbridge, Suffolk, 2007).
Ouvry, Frederic (ed.), *Letters Addressed to Thomas Hearne* (London, 1874).

Secondary Literature
Armitage, David, 'John Locke, Carolina, and the *Two Treatises of Government*', *Political Theory*, vol. xxxii (2004), pp. 602–27.
Arneil, Barbara, *John Locke and America* (Oxford, 1996).
Ashcraft, Richard, *Revolutionary Politics and Locke's 'Two Treatises of Government'* (Princeton, 1986).
Astbury, Raymond, 'The Renewal of the Licensing Act in 1693 and its Lapse in 1695', *The Library*, vol. xxxiii (1978), pp. 296–322.
Bourne, H.R. Fox, *The Life of John Locke*, 2 vols (London, 1876).
Cranston, Maurice, *John Locke: A Biography* (Oxford, 1957).
Goldie, Mark, 'John Locke's Circle and James II', *Historical Journal*, vol. xxxv (1992), pp. 557–86.
——, *Roger Morrice and the Puritan Whigs*, vol. i of *The Entring Book of Roger Morrice* (Woodbridge, Suffolk, 6 vols, 2007).
Harris, Ian, *The Mind of John Locke* (Cambridge, 1994).
Hunter, Michael, 'Aikenhead the Atheist: The Context and Consequences of Articulate Irreligion in the Late Seventeenth Century', in Michael Hunter and David Wootton (eds), *Atheism from the Reformation to the Enlightenment* (Oxford, 1992).

Irving, Sarah, *Natural Science and the Origins of the British Empire* (London, 2008).

Knights, Mark, 'Petitioning and the Political Theorists: John Locke, Algernon Sidney, and London's "Monster" Petition of 1680', *Past and Present*, vol. cxxxviii (1993), pp. 94–111.

Laslett, Peter, *The World We Have Lost* (London, 1965).

Marshall, John, *John Locke: Resistance, Religion, and Responsibility* (Cambridge, 1994).

Milton, J.R., 'Locke at Oxford', in G.A.J. Rogers (ed.), *Locke's Philosophy: Context and Content* (Oxford, 1994).

——, 'John Locke', in *The Oxford Dictionary of National Biography* (Oxford, 2004).

——, 'Pierre Coste, John Locke, and the Third Earl of Shaftesbury', in Sarah Hutton and Paul Schuurman (eds), *Studies on Locke: Sources, Contemporaries, and Legacy* (Dordrecht, 2008).

Milton, Philip, 'John Locke and the Rye House Plot', *Historical Journal*, vol. xliii (2000), pp. 647–68.

——, 'John Locke's Expulsion from Christ Church in 1689', *Eighteenth-Century Thought*, vol. iv (2009), pp. 29–65.

Savonius, S.-J., 'Locke in French: the *Du gouvernement civil* of 1691 and its Readers', *Historical Journal*, vol. xlvii (2004), pp. 47–79.

Stanton, Timothy, 'John Locke, Edward Stillingfleet, and Toleration' (PhD thesis, Leicester, 2003). [Vol. 2 contains a transcript of Locke's critique of Stillingfleet.]

Woolhouse, Roger, *Locke: A Biography* (Cambridge, 2007).

Yolton, Jean, *John Locke: A Descriptive Bibliography* (Bristol, 1998).

Notes

Quotations from primary sources have been modernized.

There are three full-length biographies: Bourne, 1876, Cranston, 1957, and Woolhouse, 2007; also valuable is Milton, 2004. Four recent studies have a considerable biographical aspect: Arneil, 1996, Ashcraft, 1986, Harris, 1994, and Marshall, 1994. In preparing the present essay I am indebted to Clare Jackson, Dmitri Levitin, John Milton and Sami Savonius-Wroth.

Mark Goldie

CHRONOLOGY OF LOCKE'S LIFE

1632	Born in Wrington, Somerset, 29 August
1637	René Descartes, *Discourse on Method*
1642	Outbreak of the Civil Wars
1643	Troops of Colonel Popham, Locke's future patron, despoil Wells Cathedral
1645	Defeat of Charles I at Naseby by Oliver Cromwell
1647	Admitted to Westminster School, London
1648	Treaty of Westphalia ends European wars of religion
1649	Execution of Charles I; England a republic
1651	Thomas Hobbes, *Leviathan*
1652	Elected a Student of Christ Church, Oxford
1652–67	Usually resident in Oxford
1656	Graduates Bachelor of Arts James Harrington, *Oceana*
1658	Graduates Master of Arts Death of Lord Protector Oliver Cromwell
1660	Restoration of monarchy under Charles II
1660–2	Writes first political essays, *Two Tracts on Government*, against religious toleration (pub. 1967)
1661–4	Lecturer in Greek, rhetoric and moral philosophy
1662	Act of Uniformity reimposes Anglicanism; Dissenting worship illegal Antoine Arnauld and Pierre Nicole, *La Logique ou L'Art de penser*
1663	Attends chemical and medical classes
1663–4	Writes *Essays on the Law of Nature* (pub. 1954)
1665	First extant correspondence with Robert Boyle
1665–6	Secretary to an embassy to the Elector of Brandenburg at Cleves

1666	Licensed to practise medicine Granted dispensation to retain studentship without taking holy orders Begins to record meteorological observations Great Fire of London
1667	Joins Lord Ashley's household; usually resident in London until 1675 Writes *Essay concerning Toleration*
1668	Oversees life-saving operation on Ashley Elected a Fellow of the Royal Society Composes tract on the lowering of interest (pub. 1691)
1669	Negotiates marriage of Ashley's son to Lady Dorothy Manners Helps draft *The Fundamental Constitutions of Carolina* Composes critique of Samuel Parker's *Ecclesiastical Politie*
1670	Baruch Spinoza, *Tractatus Theologico-Politicus*
1671	Secretary to the Lords Proprietors of Carolina (until 1675) First drafts of *An Essay concerning Human Understanding* Granted title of Landgrave of Carolina
1672	First visit to France Ashley created Earl of Shaftesbury and Lord Chancellor Appointed Secretary for Ecclesiastical Presentations (to 1673) Samuel Pufendorf, *De Jure Naturae et Gentium* (*On the Law of Nature and Nations*)
1673	Secretary and Treasurer of the Council of Trade and Plantations (to 1674) Joins Bahamas Adventurers The king's brother and heir, James, Duke of York, converts to

Catholicism
Shaftesbury ousted from office; begins to lead opposition
Samuel Pufendorf, *De Officio Hominis et Civis* (*On the Duty of Man and Citizen*)

1674 Invests in Royal African Company
Nicolas Malebranche, *De la Recherche de la Vérité* (*Search after Truth*)

1675 Shaftesburian manifesto, *A Letter from a Person of Quality*
Graduates Bachelor of Medicine
To France; chiefly resident at Montpellier until 1677; then mainly Paris
Begins to keep a journal, continuing to the end of his life

1676 Translates parts of Pierre Nicole's *Essais de Morale* (pub. 1712)

1677 First extant correspondence with James Tyrrell, Whig author
Marriage of Prince William of Orange to Princess Mary of England
Repeal of writ *de haeretico comburendo*, abolishing burning for heresy
Andrew Marvell, *An Account of the Growth of Popery*

1678 Sole extant correspondence with Samuel Pepys and Robert Hooke
First extant correspondence with Nicolas Toinard, French polymath
The Popish Plot revealed; executions of Catholics follow (to 1681)
Ralph Cudworth, *True Intellectual System of the Universe*

1679–81 Exclusion Crisis; Whigs seek to exclude Catholic heir from the throne
Whig victory in three general elections; but Whigs outmanoeuvred

1679 Returns to England
Habeas Corpus Act

1680 Signs London's 'monster petition'

demanding sitting of parliament
Robert Filmer, *Patriarcha, or The Natural Power of Kings* (posthumous)

1679–83 Resides in Oxford, London, and Oakley (James Tyrrell's home)
Writes *Two Treatises of Government*

1681 Writes a defence of toleration against Edward Stillingfleet
Rumoured to be author of (Robert Ferguson's) *No Protestant Plot*
Assists Shaftesbury at the Oxford Parliament
Oxford Parliament dismissed; Charles summons no more parliaments
Beginning of Tory backlash against Whigs and Dissenters
Shaftesbury charged with treason; charge dismissed by a Whig grand jury
Whig satirist Stephen College executed for treason
Scottish Succession Act declares hereditary succession inviolable
William Petty, *Political Arithmetic*

1682 First extant correspondence with Damaris Cudworth (later Lady Masham)
First extant correspondence with Edward Clarke, Whig politician
Court coup against Whig leadership of the City of London
Flight of Shaftesbury to Holland

1683 Death of Shaftesbury in Holland; Locke attends funeral in Dorset
Whig Rye House Plot to assassinate the king exposed
Execution of Lord William Russell and Algernon Sidney
Earl of Essex's suicide in the Tower; Whigs suspect state murder
Judgment and Decree of Oxford University against seditious doctrines

38

1683–9	Exile in Holland; lives mainly in Utrecht, Amsterdam and Rotterdam	
1684	Rumoured to be author of tracts on the 'murder' of Essex Expelled *in absentia* from studentship of Christ Church Begins correspondence with Edward Clarke concerning education First extant correspondence with Philip van Limborch, Dutch Remonstrant	
1685	Death of Charles II; accession of James II and VII Abortive rebellion of the Whig Duke of Monmouth; his execution Louis XIV revokes Edict of Nantes; persecution of Huguenots English envoy seeks Locke's extradition; in hiding in Amsterdam Writes *Epistola de Tolerantia (Letter concerning Toleration)* Marriage of Damaris Cudworth to Sir Francis Masham	
1686	*An Essay concerning Human Understanding* substantially finished First extant correspondence with Jean Le Clerc, Amsterdam publicist Publishes 'Method of Commonplacing' in the *Bibliothèque Universelle et Historique* Pierre Bayle, *Commentaire philosophique sur ces paroles … Contrain-les d'éntrer (Philosophical Commentary* on Jesus' injunction 'Compel them to come in')	
1687	James issues Declaration of Indulgence (edict of toleration) Catholics and Protestant Dissenters free to worship James II seeks to woo Dissenters and Whigs	

Reviews books for Le Clerc's *Bibliothèque Universelle et Historique*
Isaac Newton, *Principia Mathematica* (which Locke reviews)
First extant correspondence with Benjamin Furly, Quaker of Rotterdam
And with Anthony Ashley Cooper, future third Earl of Shaftesbury

1688	Culmination of resistance to James II's Catholicizing policies 'Glorious Revolution': invasion of England by William of Orange James II flees to France: 'abdication' or 'deposition'? Publishes *Abregé* (summary) of the *Essay* in Le Clerc's *Bibliothèque*
1689	National Convention installs King William III and Queen Mary II Nine Years War against Louis XIV begins Toleration Act: freedom of worship for Protestant Dissenters Returns to England in February; client of Lord Mordaunt Declines an ambassadorship Appointed Commissioner of Appeals in Excise Publication of *Epistola de Tolerantia / A Letter concerning Toleration* Publication of *Two Treatises of Government* Publication of *An Essay concerning Human Understanding* First extant correspondence with John Somers, future Whig leader
1690	Battle of the Boyne: William defeats Jacobites in Ireland *Letter concerning Toleration* attacked by Jonas Proast Publication of *A Second Letter concerning Toleration* First extant correspondence with Isaac Newton

1691	Settles at Oates in Essex in Damaris Masham's household Publication of *Some Considerations of the ... Lowering of Interest*		Pierre Coste, Huguenot translator Damaris Masham, *Discourse concerning the Love of God*
1692	Publication of *A Third Letter for Toleration* Prepares Robert Boyle's *General History of the Air* for publication First extant correspondence with William Molyneux, Dublin philosopher Memorandum on the general naturalisation of immigrants William Popple reports new members of the Dry Club	1696	Appointed a member of the Board of Trade and Plantations The *Essay* attacked by Bishop Edward Stillingfleet John Toland, *Christianity not Mysterious* Pierre Bayle, *Dictionnaire historique et critique* (*Historical and Critical Dictionary*)
1693	Publication of *Some Thoughts concerning Education* Composes 'Examination of Malebranche's Opinion' (pub. 1706)	1697	Treaty of Ryswick: temporary peace with France Publication of *Second Vindication of the Reasonableness of Christianity* Publication of two replies to Stillingfleet in defence of the *Essay* Composes *An Essay on the Poor Law* (pub. 1789)
1694	Founding of the Bank of England; invests £500 First letter in 'College' series, advising Whig Members of Parliament First extant correspondence with Hans Sloane of the Royal Society Triennial Act: regular parliamentary elections Mary Astell, *Serious Proposal to the Ladies*		Composes report on the government of Virginia Composes *The Conduct of the Understanding* (pub. 1706) Pierre Coste settles at Oates, to translate Locke's books First extant correspondence with Peter King, politician, cousin, co-heir Hanging of Thomas Aikenhead for blasphemy in Edinburgh
1695	Advises on the ending of press censorship and the recoinage Sermon preached in Oxford against the *Two Treatises* Publication of *The Reasonableness of Christianity* The *Reasonableness* attacked by John Edwards; publishes *Vindication* Publication of *Further Considerations concerning ... Money* Composes 'Remarks upon some of Mr Norris's Books' (pub. 1720) First extant correspondence with	1698	Molyneux's *Case of Ireland* cites *Two Treatises* in defence of Ireland Algernon Sidney, *Discourses concerning Government* (posthumous)
		1699	Publishes third and final reply to Stillingfleet in defence of the *Essay* François Fénelon, *Les aventures de Télémaque* (*Telemachus*)
		1700	Composes 'Some Thoughts on Reading and Study' (pub. 1720) Pierre Coste's French translation of the *Essay* published Resigns from the Board of Trade
		1701	Act of Settlement, ensuring

	Protestant (Hanoverian) succession		Gottfried Wilhelm Leibniz, *Essais*
	Ezekiel Burridge's Latin translation		*de Théodicée* (*Theodicy*)
	of the *Essay* published	1711	Earl of Shaftesbury, *Characteristics*
	Renewal of war against France		*of Men, Manners, Opinions,*
1702	Final visit to London		*Times*
	Composes *A Discourse on*	1713	Treaty of Utrecht ends war with
	Miracles (pub. 1706)		France
	First extant correspondence with		Anthony Collins, *Discourse of*
	Jean Barbeyrac, Huguenot jurist		*Freethinking*
	Death of William III; accession of	1714	Publication of the first edition of
	Queen Anne		the *Works of John Locke*
	World's first daily newspaper, in		Hanoverian succession: accession
	London		of George I
1703	Sends interlineary *Aesop's Fables*	1720	Publication of *A Collection of*
	to press		*Several Pieces of Mr John Locke*
	Oxford College heads discourage		
	study of the *Essay*		Mark Goldie
	First major published critique of		
	Two Treatises, by Charles Leslie		
	First extant correspondence with		
	Anthony Collins, 'freethinker'		
1704	Battle of Blenheim: Marlborough's		
	victory over France		
	Completion of *A Paraphrase and*		
	Notes on the Epistles of St Paul		
	Dies at Oates, 28 October; buried		
	in High Laver churchyard, Essex		
	Edward Hyde, Earl of Clarendon,		
	History of the Rebellion (posthu-		
	mous)		
	Samuel Clarke, *Demonstration of*		
	the Being and Attributes of God		
	Isaac Newton, *Opticks*		
1705	Damaris Masham, *Occasional*		
	Thoughts		
1705–7	Publication of *A Paraphrase and*		
	Notes on the Epistles of St Paul		
1706	Publication of *Posthumous Works*		
	of Mr John Locke		
1707	Treaty of Union between England		
	and Scotland		
1708	Publication of *Some Familiar*		
	Letters between Mr Locke ...		
1709	George Berkeley, *New Theory of*		
	Vision		
1710	Publication of *Oeuvres diverses de*		
	Monsieur Jean Locke		

LOCKE'S WORKS

Listing Locke's works chronologically by date of *publication* is salutary, since today we know many more of his *compositions* than his contemporaries did; by 1688 he had written a great deal but had published little, and several early writings remained in manuscript until the twentieth century. In this list, all items appearing in Locke's lifetime were anonymous unless otherwise stated; all were published in London unless otherwise stated; the notes mention later editions during his lifetime, and posthumous editions if they contained his editorial contributions. The list omits minor publications, such as poems, contributions to the *Philosophical Transactions of the Royal Society*, book reviews in the *Bibliothèque Universelle*, and medical essays. The section for the twentieth century gives only the most important editions of writings newly recovered from Locke's archive. Publication of the Clarendon Edition of the Works of John Locke began in 1975; seventeen volumes have so far appeared and seventeen more are due; volumes already available are cited below. The most substantial writings remaining unpublished are the critique of Stillingfleet in defence of toleration (but see Stanton, 2003), and the journals (but see King, 1829; Aaron and Gibb, 1936; Locke, 1953).

1689–1704

Epistola de Tolerantia (1689) / *A Letter concerning Toleration* (1689). Written, 1685; Latin edition, Gouda, 1689, dedicated to Philip van Limborch; English edition, 1689, translated by William Popple; 2nd edition, 'corrected', London, 1690; Dutch edition, 1689, of which no copies survive.

Two Treatises of Government (1689). Title page gives '1690', but available by November 1689. Title page continues: *In the Former, the False Principles, and Foundation of Sir Robert Filmer, and his Followers, are Detected and Overthrown. The Latter is an Essay concerning the True Original, Extent, and End of Civil Government*; 2nd edition, 'corrected', 1694; 3rd edition, 1698; 4th edition, 1713, containing Locke's corrections to the 1698 edition, and now with his name on the title page; French edition of the Second Treatise, Amsterdam, 1691, translated by David Mazel; the authoritative modern edition is by Peter Laslett (Cambridge, 1960).

An Essay concerning Human Understanding (1689). Title page gives '1690', but available by December 1689; dedicated to Thomas Herbert, earl of Pembroke; dedication signed 'John Locke'; 2nd edition, 'with large additions', 1694, with a new chapter, 'Of Identity and Diversity'; now with author's name on the title page, and portrait; 3rd edition, 1695; 4th edition, 1700, with two new chapters, 'Of the Association of Ideas' and 'Of Enthusiasm'; posthumous 5th edition, 1706, with further authorial amendments; French edition, Amsterdam, 1700, *Essai philosophique concernant l'entendement humain*, translated by Pierre Coste; Latin edition, 1701, *De intellectu humano*, translated by Ezekiel Burridge; abridged edition, 1696, *An Abridgment of Mr Locke's Essay concerning Human Understanding*, dedicated to Locke by the abridger, John Wynne; 2nd abridged edition, 1700; before the appearance of the *Essay*, Locke had published a brief 'Extrait' in the *Bibliothèque Universelle et Historique* (1688), also separately as the *Abrégé* (Amsterdam, 1688); Locke began to draft the *Essay* in 1671; Clarendon Edition, edited by Peter H. Nidditch (Oxford,1975); and of the *Drafts for the Essay concerning Human Understanding*, edited by Peter H. Nidditch and G.A.J. Rogers, vol. i (of iii) (Oxford,1990).

A Second Letter concerning Toleration (1690). A reply to Jonas Proast, *The Argument of the Letter concerning Toleration, Briefly Consider'd and Answer'd* (Oxford, 1690).

Some Considerations of the Consequences of the Lowering of Interest, and Raising the Value of Money, in a Letter to a Member of Parliament (1691). Title page gives '1692', but available by December 1691; perhaps addressed to John Somers, though he is not named and the dedication is addressed 'Sir'; 2nd edition, 'corrected', 1696, postscript signed 'John Lock', included in *Several Papers*; drafted in 1668.

A Third Letter for Toleration (1692). Title continues: *To the Author of the Third Letter concerning Toleration*; signed 'Philanthropus'; a reply to Jonas Proast, *A Third Letter concerning Toleration: In Defence of the Argument of the Letter concerning Toleration* (Oxford, 1691).

Some Thoughts concerning Education (1693). Two editions, 1693, dedicated to Edward Clarke; 3rd edition, 'enlarged', 1695, new material added and paragraphs renumbered; dedication now signed by Locke; 4th edition, 'enlarged', 1699; 5th edition, 'enlarged', 1705, Locke's name now on title page; French edition, Amsterdam, 1695, *De l'éducation des enfans*, translated by Pierre Coste; French (pirated) edition, 'Amsterdam' (really Geneva?), 1699, *Nouvelles instructions pour l'éducation des enfans*; Dutch edition, Rotterdam, 1698, *Verhandeling over de opvoeding der kinderen*, by 'Dr Johannes Lock'; Clarendon Edition, edited by John W. and Jean S. Yolton, 1989.

The Reasonableness of Christianity, as Delivered in the Scriptures (1695). 2nd edition, '1696' (available by October 1695), *To Which is Added, A Vindication of the Same, from Mr. Edwards's Exceptions* (see below); French edition, Amsterdam, 1696, *Que la réligion chrétienne est très-raisonnable telle qu'elle nous est représentée dans l'Écriture sainte*, translated by Pierre Coste ; a 'Seconde partie', Amsterdam, 1703, containing a condensation of Locke's two *Vindications*; French edition, Amsterdam, 1715, revised by Coste under Locke's direction, and retitled *Le Christianisme raisonable*; Clarendon Edition, edited by John C. Higgins-Biddle, 1999.

A Vindication of the Reasonableness of Christianity, &c. From Mr Edwards's Reflections (1695). A reply to John Edwards, *Some Thoughts concerning the Several Causes and Occasions of Atheism, Especially in the Present Age* (1695); for French abridged translation, see preceding item; Clarendon Edition, edited by Victor Nuovo, 2012.

Short Observations on a Printed Paper, Intituled, For Encouraging the Coining Silver Money in England, and After for Keeping it Here (1695). 2nd edition, 1696, included in *Several Papers*.

Further Considerations concerning Raising the Value of Money. Wherein Mr. Lowndes's Arguments for it in his Late Report concerning An Essay for the Amendment of the Silver Coins, are Particularly Examined (1696). Dedicated to Sir John Somers, and signed John Locke; a reply to William Lowndes, *A Short Report Containing an Essay for the Amendment of the Silver Coins* (1695); 2nd edition, 1695; 3rd, but called 'second', edition, 1696, included in *Several Papers*.

Several Papers Relating to Money, Interest and Trade, &c. Writ upon Several Occasions, and Published at Different Times (1696). A collective title page for *Some Considerations*, *Short Observations*, and *Further Considerations* (as above); the Term Catalogue gives this as 'by Mr John Locke'; Clarendon Edition, *Locke on Money*, edited by Patrick Hyde Kelly, 2 vols, 1991.

A Letter to [the Right Reverend] Edward Ld Bishop of Worcester, concerning Some Passages Relating to Mr Locke's Essay of Humane Understanding: In a Late Discourse of his Lordships, in Vindication of the Trinity (1697). Two issues, the phrase in square brackets occurring in the second; author's name on title page ('John Locke, Gent.'). A reply to Edward Stillingfleet, *A Discourse in Vindication of the Doctrine of the Trinity; with an Answer to the late Socinian Objections against it from Scripture, Antiquity and Reason* (1696).

A Second Vindication of the Reasonableness of Christianity, &c. (1697). A reply to John Edwards, *Some Thoughts concerning the Several Causes and Occasions of Atheism, Especially in the Present Age; with Some Brief Reflections on Socinianism, and on a Late Book Entituled The Reasonableness of Christianity* (1695). For French abridged edition see under *Reasonableness*; Clarendon Edition, edited by Victor Nuovo, 2012.

Mr Locke's Reply to the Right Reverend the Lord Bishop of Worcester's Answer to his Letter, concerning some Passages Relating to Mr Locke's Essay of Humane Understanding: In a Late Discourse of his Lordships, In Vindication of the Trinity (1697). The second reply to Stillingfleet; this one to *The Bishop of Worcester's Answer to Mr Locke's Letter* (1697); the 'Remarks' at the end reply to Thomas Burnet, *Remarks upon An Essay concerning Human Understanding* (1697); the Term Catalogue gives author's name.

Mr Locke's Reply to the Right Reverend the Lord Bishop of Worcester's Answer to his Second Letter: Wherein, besides other Incident Matters, what his Lordship has said concerning Certainty by Reason, Certainty by Ideas, and Certainty of Faith. The Resurrection of the same Body. The Immateriality of the Soul. The Inconsistency of Mr Locke's Notions with the Articles of the Christian Faith, and their Tendency to Sceptism, is Examined (1699). The third and final reply to Stillingfleet, this one to *The Bishop of Worcester's Answer to Mr Locke's Second Letter: Wherein his Notion of Ideas is Prov'd to be Inconsistent with itself and with the Articles of the Christian Faith* (1698).

Posthumous, 1705–20

Posthumous Works of Mr John Locke (1706). Comprises: 'Of the Conduct of the Understanding', 'An Examination of P. Malebranche's Opinion of Seeing all Things in God', 'A Discourse of Miracles', 'Part of a Fourth Letter for Toleration', 'Memoirs Relating to the Life of Anthony First Earl of Shaftesbury', and 'New Method of a Commonplace Book'. The life of Shaftesbury first appeared in *Bibliothèque Choisie* (1705); and the 'New Method' in French in the *Bibliothèque Universelle et Historique* (1686).

A Paraphrase and Notes on the Epistles of St Paul to the Galatians, Corinthians, Romans, and Ephesians, to which is Prefix'd, An Essay for the Understanding of St Paul's Epistles, by Consulting St. Paul Himself (1707). This is a collective title for the set of commentaries separately published, 1705–7: Galatians (1705), First Corinthians (1706), Second Corinthians (1706), Romans (1707), Ephesians (1707), and the prefatory 'Essay' (1707). Clarendon Edition, edited by Arthur W. Wainright, 2 vols, 1987.

Some Familiar Letters between Mr Locke, and Several of his Friends (1708). Mainly correspondence with William Molyneux and Philip van Limborch.

Œuvres diverses de Monsieur Jean Locke (1710). Rotterdam. Comprises (in French): Le Clerc's 'Elegy' on Locke, *Letter concerning Toleration*, 'Conduct of the Understanding', 'Discourse of Miracles', 'New Method of a Commonplace Book', 'Life of Shaftesbury'

Discourses on the Being of God, and the Immortality of the Soul; of the Weakness of Man; and concerning the Way of Preserving Peace with Men: Being some of the Essays Written in French by Messieurs du Port Royal. Render'd into English by the Late John Lock, Gent. (1712). Locke's translation (1676) of three of Pierre Nicole's *Essais de morale*, dedicated to the countess of Shaftesbury.

The Works of John Locke, Esq., 3 vols (1714). Vol. i: *Essay, Reply, and Second Reply to Stillingfleet*; vol. ii: *Some Considerations, Short Observations, Further Considerations, Two Treatises, Letters concerning Toleration, Reasonableness of Christianity, Vindication, Second Vindication*; vol. iii: *Education, Paraphrase and Notes, Posthumous Works, Some Familiar Letters.* There would be twelve further editions of the *Works* down to 1824, reaching to ten volumes.

The Remains of John Locke Esq. (1714). Comprises: 'Some Memoirs of the Life and Character of Dr Edward Pococke', 'Instructions for the Conduct of Young Gentlemen, as to Religion and Government', 'The Best Method of Studying, and Interpreting the Scriptures', and 'Sentiments concerning the Society for Promoting Christian Knowledge'; in fact, five letters dressed up as 'works' by an opportunist publisher.

A Collection of Several Pieces of Mr John Locke, Never Before Printed, or Not Extant in his Works (1720). Edited by Pierre De Maizeaux. Comprises: 'The Fundamental Constitutions of Carolina', 'A Letter from a Person of Quality', 'Remarks upon Some of Mr Norris's Books', 'Elements of Natural Philosophy', 'Some Thoughts concerning Reading and Study for a Gentleman', and 'Rules of a Society', together with Pierre Coste's 'Character of Mr Locke'. Locke's authorial contribution to the 'Constitutions' (1669) and the 'Letter' (1675) remain controversial.

Late Eighteenth Century

Observations upon the Growth and Culture of Vines and Olives (1766). Written c. 1675–7. MS in National Archives.

An Essay on the Poor Law (1789). This tract, which in the manuscript in the National Archives is entitled 'Draft of a Representation, Containing [a] Scheme of Methods for the Employment of the Poor', was written for the Board of Trade in 1697, and was first printed in *An Account of the Origin, Proceedings, and Intentions of the Society for the Promotion of Industry* (Louth, Lincolnshire), at pp. 101–49.

Nineteenth Century

Extracts from Locke's journals and commonplace books, poorly edited, appeared in Lord King's *Life of John Locke* (1829) and one version of the *Essay concerning Toleration* (1668) appeared in H.R.F. Bourne's *Life of John Locke* (1876).

Twentieth Century

An Early Draft of Locke's Essay, Together with Excerpts from his Journals (1936). Edited by R.I. Aaron and Jocelyn Gibb (Oxford). Written 1670s–80s.

Locke's Travels in France, 1675–1679 (1953). Edited by John Lough (Cambridge). Extracted from the journals.

Essays on the Law of Nature (1954). Edited by W. von Leyden (Oxford). Written 1663–4.

Two Tracts on Government (1967). Edited by Philip Abrams (Cambridge). Written 1660–2.

The Correspondence of John Locke, 8 vols (1976–89). Clarendon Edition, edited by E.S. de Beer. A ninth volume containing index and addenda is in preparation.

Critique of Edward Stillingfleet (2003). A transcription in vol. ii of Timothy Stanton, 'John Locke, Edward Stillingfleet, and Toleration' (PhD thesis, Leicester University). Written 1681.

An Essay concerning Toleration and Other Writings on Law and Politics, 1667–1683 (2006). Clarendon Edition, edited by J.R. Milton and Philip Milton. The 'Essay' was written in 1667. Includes the Shaftesburian *Letter from a Person of Quality* (1675).

Mark Goldie

2

SOURCES
AND CONTEMPORARIES

BOYLE, Robert (1627–91)

In a well-known passage of the *Essay*, Locke describes Robert Boyle, along with SYDENHAM, Huyghens and NEWTON, as 'Master-builders', who 'will leave lasting Monuments to the Admiration of Posterity' (*E*, p. 9). The influence of Huyghens and Newton on the *Essay* was slight at best. The influence of Sydenham is still the object of debate. But Locke's intellectual debt to Boyle has been amply demonstrated. Boyle helped shape Locke's views on PRIMARY AND SECONDARY QUALITIES, on matter and its cohesion, on the notion of real essence and on the role of ANALOGY. Boyle is perhaps the thinker who had the greatest positive influence on Locke's *Essay*.

Robert Boyle, son of the first Earl of Cork, led a life devoted to science, supported by his inherited means. He was, in his day, most famous for his experimental work on air, and now he is best remembered for 'Boyle's Law' which states that, where temperature is constant, the pressure of an enclosed gas is in inverse proportion to its volume. In fact, Boyle made significant contributions to experimental chemistry across the board, and he is sometimes known as 'the father of chemistry'.

Chemistry, in so far as it existed as a discipline in the seventeenth century, was dominated by the inheritors of the alchemist tradition. These chemists (often referred to as 'chymists') were avid experimenters, devoted to their furnaces, and Boyle made no secret of the fact that he was inspired by the 'Practicall Art'

of their investigations (Boyle, 1999–2000, vol. v, p. 301). But the chemists also advanced a speculative theory – their doctrine of the 'hypostatical principles' – which, in one common version, claimed that the material world was constituted by the *tria prima* of mercury, sulphur and salt. Boyle's attitude to chemical theory is still a matter of debate, with some scholars (e.g. Principe, 1994 and Clericuzio, 1994) holding that Boyle was influenced by it, and that he even accepted the possibility of alchemical transmutation of metals into gold (Principe, 1994, pp. 92–3). There is no debate, however, that generally speaking Boyle thought chemical theory was extravagant and obscure.

A different approach to natural philosophy prevailed within the walls of academia. SCHOLASTICISM, usually eschewing practical investigation, sought to understand the natural world in a broadly Aristotelian framework. Nature was ultimately constituted by the elements of fire, air, water and earth. It was divided into species of things (for example, metals and minerals) thanks to the presence of a 'substantial form', which informed a piece of matter, imbuing it with specific qualities and powers. In practice, scholastics often had resort to 'occult qualities', which were known only through their effects. The circularity of the appeal to occult qualities and the general obscurity of substantial forms were particular targets of Boyle's criticism.

Boyle's own approach to natural philosophy displayed two principal features. Firstly, he sought to develop and extend the experimentation of the chemists in a new spirit of responsibility and openness in keeping with the empirical method of Francis Bacon. In his own private laboratories, first in a family manor in Dorset, then in Oxford and London, Boyle, with the help of assistants, made many thousands of experiments. He recorded his findings and presented them to the public in the form of 'experimental histories' – systematic collections of observational data 'upon which a Theory, to be Solid and Usefull, must be Built' (Boyle, 1999–2000, vol. v, p. 299).

The second feature of Boyle's approach to natural philosophy was his advocacy of the corpuscularian HYPOTHESIS. This explained physical phenomena by the mechanical interaction of imperceptible corpuscles, characterized only by motion, size and shape. This hypothesis was to take the place of both the chemists' hypostatical principles and the scholastics' elements and substantial forms. The corpuscular hypothesis was notable, in contrast to these approaches, for its simplicity and intuitiveness and for its rejection of occult qualities.

Boyle sought to supply a corpuscular understanding of what the underlying 'nature' of a species consisted in, to replace the doctrine of substantial forms. In elucidating the properties and powers of gold, for example, he proposed a mechanical nature, which did not stem from the particular character of the corpuscles constituting gold, but from the 'posture' and 'order' in which they were combined. There was a 'Contrivance of Parts', 'which we may call the *Texture* of it' (Boyle, 1999–2000, vol. v, pp. 316). It is this texture which gave rise to the distinguishing qualities and powers of gold, known to goldsmiths and refiners, such as its solubility in aqua regia and insolubility in aqua fortis (Boyle, 1999–2000, vol. v, pp. 310–11). Textures had the distinct advantage over substantial forms of being conceivable independently of the qualities to which they gave rise.

Boyle's corpuscularianism is often treated as a revival of the atomist tradition. While it is undoubtedly true that he was influenced by the work of Gassendi and by the ancient Epicureans – particularly Lucretius – such a characterization can be misleading. Boyle strenuously avoided either advocating or denying the existence of atoms, and he coined the term 'corpuscularianism' precisely so as to remain noncommittal on indivisibles (*corpuscula* are just 'small bodies' in Latin). Corpuscles were stable concretions of the more mysterious *prima naturalia*, but as Boyle clearly stated in *The Origin of Forms and Qualities* (1666), none of his arguments are 'either grounded on, *or* suppose, Indivisible Corpuscles, call'd *Atoms*' (Boyle, 1999–2000, vol. v, p. 292).

Boyle wished to overcome the sectarianism in the mechanical philosophy and unite the opposing parties of Gassendists and Cartesians who were 'for' and 'against' the atoms respectively. He also, like Locke, abhorred the atheist associations of ancient atomism. But we should not forget that Boyle's experimental, Baconian background led him to be satisfied with a more cautious and undogmatic version of mechanism than was common on the Continent.

Boyle's importance for Locke is evident in the generous representation he had in Locke's library, which contained sixty-two titles by Boyle, more than by any other author (Harrison and Laslett, 1965, entries 413–73). From 1660 Locke was in the habit of making notes from Boyle's books soon after they came out (Milton, 1994, p. 37). Ten letters from Locke to Boyle survive, some of which refer to their scientific collaboration and all of which bear witness to a respectful friendship. In one letter, Locke reports back to Boyle on a trip he made to the Mendips with one of Boyle's barometers to measure the atmospheric pressure in a mine (Locke to Boyle, 5.5.1666, *Corr.* vol. i, pp. 273–6). Boyle dedicated his *Memoirs for the Natural History of Humane Blood* (1684), a project in which Locke had taken an active role, to 'the very Ingenious and Learned Doctor JL'. Boyle also sought help from the 'Learned Doctor' in compiling his *General History of the Air*, with Locke providing examples, taking responsibility for editing, and seeing the work through the press. Boyle's trust in Locke was such that he appointed him to help take posthumous care of his papers.

It was Locke's interest in Boyle's experimental work, especially as it was relevant to medicine, that probably first drew the two men together in Oxford, their acquaintance beginning no later than 1660. Their shared appetite for practical investigation is evident in the scores of experimental notes, including direct instructions from Boyle, that Locke took down in his notebooks (see, for example, Oxford, Bodleian Library MS Locke f.25). It is unlikely, however, that the experimental and historical character of Boyle's work gave a wholly new impulse to Locke's thinking, although it undoubtedly reinforced its tendency. Bacon was already widely influential among British practitioners of the new science, and Locke's devotion to the observation of nature would be equally evident in his collaboration with Sydenham in the late 1660s, particularly in 'De Arte Medica' and 'Anatomia'.

It was Boyle's corpuscularian hypothesis that probably had the most significant impact on Locke's work. Locke's adoption of corpuscularianism was actually somewhat slow, and it was arguably not until 1671, more than ten years after his first meeting with Boyle, that we first see him fully persuaded of its advantage over other theories of nature (Walmsley, 2003). By the time the *Essay* was published, the influence of the corpuscularian hypothesis is evident in many areas of Locke's thought. Most famously, it plays a significant role in the distinction between 'primary' and 'secondary qualities' (*E*, II.viii, pp. 132–43). Boyle had come close to this terminology of Locke's, talking of the 'primary affections' of body, and Locke's lists of PRIMARY QUALITIES and his references to 'texture' show the mark of Boyle. Locke made extensive use of the corpuscularian hypothesis to illustrate how primary qualities alone can explain the physical process of PERCEPTION (*E*, II.viii.12–14, pp. 136–7), thereby supporting his claim that only these qualities belong to bodies categorically.

The corpuscularian hypothesis also shaped Locke's thinking about ESSENCES. Boyle's textures offered Locke a framework within which he could make a systematic distinction between the 'real' and 'nominal' essences of substances. The nominal essence involves observable qualities and powers, known by observation and experiment, while the real essence is 'the constitution of the insensible parts', on which the observable qualities depend (*E*, III.vi.2, p. 439). Following Boyle, Locke postulated that this constitution was a 'Texture of parts' (*E*, III.vi.9, p. 444).

Locke was also influenced by Boyle's awareness of the limits of mechanical explanation. In *The History of Fluidity and Firmness* (1661), Boyle had noted that explanations of the cohesion ('firmness') of bodies always presuppose cohesion in smaller insensible particles. No non-circular mechanical explanation of cohesion was ultimately forthcoming. In particular, Boyle rejected the atomist explanation claiming that the smallest particles cohere because they have no vacuity within – it was not clear, he thought, *how* an internal plenitude might cause cohesion (Boyle, 1999–2000, vol. ii, pp. 164–5). This discussion has much in common with Locke's own treatment of the question in the *Essay* (*E*, II.xxiii.23–7, pp. 308–11; cf. Hill, 2006), in which he rejects the various explanations of cohesion offered by his contemporaries as begging the question. He asserts that we have no way of explaining the ultimate binding of the smallest bodies and concludes that material cohesion is an unfathomable mystery. For Locke this has a wider epistemological significance than for Boyle, reinforcing his conviction that 'the SUBSTANCE of Body' itself, like the substance of spirit, is 'unknown to us' (*E*, II.xxiii.30, p. 313).

Boyle and Locke were both sensitive to the charge that the corpuscular hypothesis went beyond the warrant of empirical experimentation. The imperceptible micromechanisms had, of course, never been observed. To bridge the gap between his Baconian experimental work and his assertion of the corpuscularian hypothesis, Boyle made frequent use of analogies from everyday observations. For example, in discussing a corpuscular theory of colour, Boyle points to how the grinding of glass into powder renders it white – but the only change has been caused to the number and size of the granular parts which now, because of 'the multitude of their surfaces', reflect light (Boyle, 1999–2000, vol. vi, p. 281). Another example offered is the bruising of an apple. The impact on the fruit can have only changed the texture of the bruised part, which then comes to have a different 'Colour, Tast, Smell and Consistence' (Boyle, 1999-2000, vol. v, p. 327).

In the *Essay*, Locke likewise commends 'a wary Reasoning from ANALOGY' in speculating about matters beyond perception (*E*, IV.xvi.12, pp. 665–7). He cites, for example, how the rubbing together of bodies produces heat, evidence for the corpuscularian view that 'what we call Heat and Fire consists in a violent agitation of the imperceptible minute parts of the burning matter' (*E*, IV.xvi.12, p. 666). And elsewhere he gives the example of how pounding an almond alters its colour and taste, when the impact of the pestle can only directly affect the texture of the nut – the implication being that colour and taste are the causal products of texture (*E*, II.viii.20, p. 139). The overall role of analogy in Locke's thinking, however, remains relatively minor. Indeed, he had serious reservations about any kind of hypotheses that go beyond observation (Anstey, 2003), and generally his support for the corpuscularian hypothesis was never as robust as Boyle's.

What most impressed Locke was the comprehensibility of corpuscularianism in comparison with its chemical and scholastic rivals, and he joined in Boyle's appreciation of the 'intelligibleness and clearness of Mechanical principles and explications' (Stewart, 1991, p. 139). Locke writes in the *Essay*:

I have here instanced in the corpuscularian Hypothesis, as that which is thought to go farthest in an intelligible Explication of the Qualities of Bodies; and I fear the

Weakness of humane Understanding is scarce able to substitute another, which will afford us a fuller and clearer discovery of the necessary Connexion, and *Co-existence*, of the Powers, which are to be observed united in several sorts of them (*E*, IV.iii.16, pp. 547–8).

Neither Boyle nor Locke explained this intelligibility by the application of mathematics or geometry, as the Cartesian mechanists were wont to do. Instead they were more inspired by the craftsman's understanding of the working of his machines. Boyle compared the powers of chemicals to modify metals, with the capacity of certain keys to open certain locks on account of their size, shape and movement (Boyle, 1999–2000, vol. v, pp. 309–10). Locke surmised that: 'Did we know the Mechanical affections of the Particles of ... *Opium*, and a *Man*, as a Watchmaker does those of a Watch', we could comprehend 'before Hand' why '*Opium* make[s] a Man sleep; as well as a Watch-maker can, that a little piece of Paper laid on the Balance, will keep the Watch from going, till it be removed...' (*E*, IV.iii.25, p. 556). Both men treated the humble mechanic – a figure ignored or looked down upon by the scholastics (*E*, III.x.9, p. 495) – as having an insight into how things work that might be treated as the ideal of intelligibility in natural philosophy.

BIBLIOGRAPHY
Primary Sources
Boyle, Robert, *The Works of Robert Boyle*, 14 vols, ed. Michael Hunter and Edward B. Davis (London, 1999–2000).
Stewart, M.A. (ed.), *Selected Philosophical Papers of Robert Boyle* (Cambridge, 1991).

Secondary Literature
Anstey, P.R., 'Locke on Method in Natural Philosophy', in P.R. Anstey (ed.) *The Philosophy of John Locke: New Perspectives* (London, 2003), pp. 26–42.

COCKBURN

Clericuzio, Antonio, 'Carneades and the
Chemists', in Michael Hunter (ed.), *Robert Boyle Reconsidered* (Cambridge, 1994), pp. 79–89.

Harrison, John, and Peter Laslett, *The Library of John Locke* (Oxford, 1965).

Hill, James, 'Locke's Account of Cohesion and its Philosophical Significance', in Peter Anstey (ed.), *John Locke: Critical Assessments*, II (Oxford, 2006), vol. iii, pp. 145–65.

Hunter, Michael (ed.), *Robert Boyle Reconsidered* (Cambridge, 1994).

Milton, John, 'Locke at Oxford', in G.A.J. Rogers (ed.), *Locke's Philosophy: Content and Context* (Oxford, 1994).

Principe, Lawrence M., 'Boyle's Alchemical Pursuits', in Michael Hunter (ed.), *Robert Boyle Reconsidered* (Cambridge, 1994), pp. 91–105.

Walmsley, Jonathan, 'The Development of Locke's Mechanism in the Drafts of the *Essay*', *British Journal for the History of Philosophy*, vol. xi (2003), pp. 417–49.

James Hill

COCKBURN, Catherine (née Trotter)
(1679–1749)

Catherine Cockburn was a philosopher and playwright, whose best-known philosophical work, *A Defence of Mr. Locke's Essay of Human Understanding* (1702), defends Locke's moral and religious principles against one of his most persistent critics, Thomas BURNET. Cockburn's work so impressed Locke that he formally thanked her and expressed his admiration of the 'strength and clearness' of her reasoning. Cockburn went on to write two further works in defence of Locke's moral and religious views, two works in defence of Samuel Clarke, a famous moralist of the period, as well as two lengthy works defending Locke against one of his theological critics, Dr Winch Holdsworth (*Letter to Dr. Holdsworth Occasioned by his Sermon* (1726) and *A Vindication of Mr. Locke's Principles* (1751)). Cockburn was unusually prolific for a woman of her time, adding plays and a voluminous correspondence to her philosophical and theological writings. Near the end of her life, her reputation was such that the well-known historian and biographer Thomas Birch approached her with an interest in compiling an edition of her collected works and correspondence. She agreed to help him with this project, which was eventually published in 1751, two years after her death.

Cockburn was born in London on 16 August 1679. In her youth, she taught herself to write, and became proficient in French, Latin and LOGIC. She completed her first play, *Agnes de Castro*, in 1695 at the age of sixteen, and her second, *Fatal Friendship*, in 1698. Both plays were staged and, soon after, printed. Cockburn continued to write plays over the following few years, but her intellectual interests soon moved into more philosophical directions. In her late teens, Cockburn began studying John Locke's enormously influential work, *An Essay concerning Human Understanding*. She was so inspired by the ideas she found in Locke's writing, that she penned a response to Thomas BURNET's three critical pamphlets the *First-, Second-, and Third Remarks upon An Essay concerning Humane Understanding* (1697, 1697, 1699, respectively).

Not long after this, Cockburn's philosophical career was put on hold for several years, during which time her husband was forced into penurious circumstances as a result of his refusal to acknowledge the king's rightful claim to the crown. Cockburn was forced to put aside her writing to attend to her children and the upkeep of the household, until her husband finally came back into the king's good graces in the mid-1720s. Cockburn quickly resumed her intellectual work and correspondence, completing her two replies to Holdsworth as well

51

as her works in defence of Clarke. She had, by the end of her life, earned a considerable reputation amongst her intellectual contemporaries. Despite failing eyesight, she continued writing and working with Birch on her collected works, until her death in 1749.

Cockburn's *Defence of Mr. Locke's Essay* addresses concerns raised by Burnet regarding the adequacy of Locke's empiricism in accounting for the origins of our concepts of moral good and evil, of the soul's nature, and of God's veracity. Burnet articulates the central problem when he declares, 'I do not find that my Eyes, Ears, Nostrils, or any other outward Senses, make any Distinction of [good and evil] as they do of Sounds, Colours, Scents, or other outward Objects' (Burnet, 1984, p. 5). Cockburn's *Defence* speaks mainly to Burnet's worries about morality. In her response she seeks to explicate Locke's epistemological principles and show how they provide adequate foundations for our knowledge of moral ideas and principles. Cockburn emphasizes Locke's notion of *reflection* – i.e. the faculty by which we acquire knowledge of our own mental operations – as the key to explaining the origin of these ideas, arguing that it is impossible to know what *right* is without first engaging in *reflection* upon our own natures and the operations of our minds. Since we cannot know the nature of God to be good without reflecting first upon our own natures, it stands to reason, she argues, that the notion of goodness itself can only be understood in relation to our natures. In this way, ideas about human nature become the basis for our moral, and religious, ideas.

Cockburn's discussion of the nature of the soul takes up the question of its immateriality. She explains that Locke's principles may limit what we can claim with certainty, but that we can, using Locke's principles, conclude the soul's immateriality with high probability. This, she concludes, is all we need for the purposes of appreciating the concepts of divine retribution and our future state in the afterlife.

Cockburn concludes with a consideration of *conscience* as a source of moral motivation.

Her arguments on the issue seek to respond to the innatism which Burnet had opposed to Locke's empiricism. Confronting Burnet's contention that conscience is the source of innate moral concepts of good and evil, Cockburn counters that conscience cannot be a *source* of moral knowledge. It is, more properly speaking, a 'sudden affection' of the mind, which approves whatever reason determines to be right. Conscience, for Cockburn, is the source of benevolent feelings and thus of the motivation to act according to the dictates of reason. This view of natural benevolence and moral motivation becomes much more pronounced in Cockburn's later writing in defence of Samuel Clarke's moral fitness view. In the works *Remarks upon some Writers* (1743) and *Remarks upon the Principles and Reasonings of Dr. Rutherforth's* Essay (1747), Cockburn defends Clarke's view that morality is grounded in, and a proper expression of, human nature. Clarke's notion of *fitness* was meant to capture the idea that morally good behaviour is achieved by attending to the dictates of our divinely authored human natures. Cockburn takes Clarke's concept of human nature to include the natural affections, arguing that our natural benevolent affections motivate the achievement of fit and proper relations with other people and with God. It is by acting in accordance with our rational and affective natures that we are properly guided in our moral duties. With her emphasis on our affective natures, Cockburn combines Clarkean moral theory with a theory of moral psychology not developed by Clarke himself. Cockburn develops the idea of benevolent affections into what she terms a 'moral sense', which was a term later made famous by the eighteenth-century moralists SHAFTESBURY and Hutcheson.

BIBILOGRAPHY
Primary Sources
Burnet, Thomas, John Locke and Noah Porter, *Remarks Upon an Essay concerning Humane Understanding, Five Tracts* (New York, 1984).

Cockburn, Catharine, *The Works of Mrs. Catharine Cockburn, Theological, Moral, Dramatic, and Poetical. In Two Volumes* (London, 1992, repr. of London, 1751).
——, *Catharine Trotter Cockburn: Philosophical Writings*, ed. Patricia Sheridan, (Peterborough, Canada, 2006).
Clarke, Samuel, *A Demonstration of the Being and Attributes of God and Other Writings*, ed. Ezio Vailati (Cambridge, 1998).

Secondary Sources
Bolton, Martha Brandt, 'Some Aspects of the Philosophical Work of Catharine Trotter Cockburn', in *Hypatia's Daughters: Fifteen Hundred Years of Women Philosophers*, ed. Linda Lopez McAlister (Bloomington, 1996), pp. 139–64.
Broad, Jacqueline, *Women Philosophers of the Seventeenth Century* (Cambridge, 2003).
Kelley, Anne, *Catharine Trotter: An Early Modern Writer in the Vanguard of Feminism* (Aldershot, 2002).
Sheridan, Patricia, 'Reflection, Nature and Moral Law: The Extent of Cockburn's Lockeanism in her Defence of Mr. Locke's Essay', in *Hypatia*, vol. xxiii, no. 1 (Summer 2007).
Waithe, Mary Ellen, 'Catharine Trotter Cockburn', in Mary Ellen Waithe (ed.), *A History of Women Philosophers: Modern Women Philosophers, 1600–1900* (Dordrecht, 1991).

Patricia Sheridan

DESCARTES, René (1596–1650)

Over the last decades modern scholarship has tended to soften the traditional picture of a stark divide between Descartes the rationalist and Locke the anti-Cartesian empiricist. The picture that is presently arising is of a rather more complicated nature and takes into account not only the undeniable differences but also the fundamental resemblances between these towering geniuses of the seventeenth century.

Locke himself had been the first to pay tribute to the importance of Descartes in his development as a philosopher. In her letter of 12 January 1705, containing biographical information about Locke that Jean le Clerc was to use for his 'Eloge du feu M. Locke', Lady MASHAM wrote 'The first Books (as *Mr Locke* himself has told me) which gave him a relish of Philosophical Studys were those of *Descartes*' (MS Amsterdam University Library R.K.-J 57a). There is indeed clear proof of Locke's interest in Descartes's philosophy, especially his natural philosophy. Locke possessed the principal works of Descartes as well as an edition of his correspondence. Evidence from Locke's notebooks indicates that during his years in Oxford he embarked on a programme of systematic reading of the mechanicist philosophers from 1660 onwards, starting with BOYLE and continuing with Descartes's *Opera Philosophica* (Amsterdam, 1656). His immersion in the works of Descartes started with the *Principia philosophiae* and continued with the *Discours de la méthode* and its *Essais*, the *Dioptrique* and the *Meteores*. He also acquainted himself with the *Meditationes*, including the *Objections* and *Replies*, and the *Passions de l'âme* (Milton, 1984, pp. 37–8). He read these works in Latin, which is not surprising, since at this time he knew little French. This was to change during his visit to France from 1675 to 1679. During this long stay he read the works of Jacques Rohault, Pierre-Sylvain Régis, Gérauld de Cordemoy, Louis de la Forge and other Cartesian philosophers. On 7 March 1678 he made a note in his Journal, in French, giving (or copying) a 'Methode pour bien etudier la doctrine de Mr de Cartes', that advises readers to start with the *Discours de la méthode*, while also giving the works of Descartes's followers (Locke, 1936, p. 108).

In spite of Locke's interest in Descartes's works, there are obvious differences between their philosophies. In epistemology, there is of course Locke's famous attack against innate IDEAS in the first book of the *Essay*. He may have reacted partly against Herbert of Cherbury and the Cambridge Platonists, but his main target was probably the innatism of Descartes. Major differences are also present between Locke's epistemological agnosticism and Descartes's apodictic knowledge claim about substances. Whereas Descartes was certain that extension is the essence of matter and thinking the essence of the soul, Locke denied the possibility of knowledge about the essence of any SUBSTANCE whatsoever (already present in Draft A, sect. 1, p. 2) and hence he saw no evidence that rules out the very un-Cartesian possibility of thinking matter (*E*, IV. iii. 6, pp. 539–43). Other differences include Locke's opposition to Descartes's positive formulation of the idea of the infinite (*E*, II. xvii. 14–16, pp. 217–19), and also appear in the field of natural philosophy (defence of vacuum against Cartesian plenism, *E*, II. xiii. 21 [*bis*], pp. 176–7) and their views on method (Locke's distrust of hypotheses, letter to Molyneux, 15 June 1697, *Corr.*, vol. vi, p. 144).

Yet there are vital similarities between Locke and Descartes; perhaps one of the most important is a shared LOGIC of ideas. Descartes's derision of the empty verbal character of traditional logic, including the complaint that syllogisms fail to produce new knowledge since they are not the source but only the result of previous discoveries, his confidence that man is able to reach truth by using his mental FACULTIES, and the importance that he attached in the *Regulae* to INTUITION as 'the conception of a clear and attentive mind, which is so easy and distinct that there can be no room for doubt about what we are understanding' (Descartes, 1984, vol. i, p. 14) are all echoed by Locke, who gave a similar definition of our 'native rustick Reason'. This faculty provides us with knowledge that is '... irresistible, and like the bright Sun-shine, forces it self immediately to be perceived, as soon as ever the Mind turns its view that way ...' (*E*, IV. ii. 1, pp. 530–1). The *Regulae* were not published in the Latin version in which they were originally written until 1701, but Locke may well have had access to this work while he was working on the *Essay* during his exile in the Dutch Republic. Manuscript copies of the *Regulae* are known to have circulated in the Netherlands and France and a Dutch translation was already published in 1684; Locke read Dutch (Bonno, 1955, p. 236). In addition, the Second Edition (and subsequent editions) of the *Logique* of Port-Royal (1664) contained substantial passages based on this work. Locke owed the Paris 1674 reissue of the fourth edition of 1671 of the *Logique* (Harrison and Laslett, 1965, p. 178, no. 1803).

While much of the *Essay* shows Cartesian influences, Locke knew at the same time how to use Descartes's concepts for his own epistemological agenda. A fascinating example is found in Locke's usage of the terminology of 'clear and distinct ideas'. Although use of concepts as a third element, in addition to words and objects existing outside us, was by no means new in the history of philosophy, the use of the term 'idea' in the seventeenth century can in most cases be traced back to its (re-)introduction by Descartes. The term 'clear and distinct' is even more unmistakably Cartesian. In the *Meditations*, Descartes lays down his famous 'general rule that whatever I perceive very clearly and distinctly is true' (Descartes, 1984, vol. ii, p. 24). According to this dictum the criterion of truth for perceptions is their clarity and distinctness. The most complete definition of 'clear' and 'distinct' can be found in the *Principia philosophiae*: 'I call a PERCEPTION "clear" when it is present and accessible to the attentive mind – just as we say that we see something clearly when it is present to the eye's gaze and stimulates it with a sufficient degree of strength and accessibility. I call a perception "distinct" if, as well as being clear, it is so sharply separated from all other perceptions that it contains within itself only what is clear' (Descartes, 1984, vol. i, pp. 207–8). When Descartes uses the terms 'clarity' and 'distinctness', he tries to dispel scepticism about the existence of external objects. Clear and distinct perceptions enable us to bridge the gap between what we think and what exists outside our mind. In Descartes's epistemology, clarity and distinction are doing a job that cannot be left to the senses. Instead of setting his stakes on 'the fluctuating testimony of the senses', he confides in 'the indubitable conception of a clear and attentive mind which proceeds solely from the light of reason' (*Regulae*, Descartes, 1984, vol. i, p. 14).

In Locke's *Essay*, clarity and distinctness play again an important role in providing us with truth. Moreover, his definition of these concepts echoes Descartes. Clarity again pertains to the relation between ideas in our mind and external objects, while distinctness again concerns the relation between any one idea and all other ideas: 'As a *clear Idea* is that whereof the Mind has such a full and evident perception, as it does receive from an outward Object operating duly on a well-disposed Organ, so a *distinct Idea* is that wherein the Mind perceives a difference from all other [ideas]' (*E*, II. xxix. 4, p. 364).

Although Locke's definition of clarity and distinction is influenced by Descartes, there are differences. Firstly, there is a difference of a predominantly technical nature. After Descartes had formulated his rule 'that whatever I perceive very clearly and distinctly is true' in the *Meditations*, he explained in *Principia* part I, article 48 that the objects of these perceptions can be things, the affectations of things, or eternal truths (Descartes, 1984, vol. i, p. 208). Eternal truths have a propositional character. Perceptions of 'things' or their affectations, on the other hand, have a non-propositional character. These perceptions of non-propositional things are called 'ideas'. Things are the objects of which ideas are 'like pictures, or images' (Descartes 1984, vol 2, p. 29). The upshot of Descartes's use of clarity and distinctness is that not only propositions, but also ideas can be

true or false. By contrast, Locke's 'way of ideas' consists of two sharply separated stages that seem to preclude any such direct connection between ideas and truth or falsity. In the first stage of this way of ideas, we must take care that each of our ideas is clear and distinct. In the second stage these ideas are compared. The first stage is restricted to individual ideas, while the second stage involves at least two ideas. Locke's very definition of truth is rigorously tied up with this second stage. Truth is 'nothing but *the joining or separating of Signs, as the Things signified by them, do agree or disagree one with another*' (*E*, IV. v. 2, p. 574). These signs can be either ideas or words. In both cases, 'The *joining* or *separating* of signs here meant is what by another name, we call Proposition' (ibid.). When the signs that are joined or separated are ideas, they form a *mental* proposition. When the signs are words, the result is a *verbal* proposition. From these clear-cut divisions it follows that truth is always a property of propositions and never of ideas. Yet Locke himself frequently slips into the use of the term true and false ideas, for which he gives the following rather lame explanation: 'what Words are there, that are not used with great Latitude, and with some deviation from their strict and proper Significations?' (*E*, II. xxxii. 1, p. 384). So, for both Locke and Descartes, clarity and distinction is intimately connected with truth. However, whereas for Descartes the clarity and distinctness of *perceptions* is the criterion of their truth of falsity, for Locke the clarity and distinctness of individual ideas is, strictly speaking, a necessary precondition for the subsequent activity of correctly joining or separating these ideas, but not a criterion of truth in itself.

Secondly, there is a difference that is related to the different epistemological views of Descartes and Locke. The latter does not think that the clarity and distinctness of an idea can be used as a bridge to the existence of things, nor does he think that he needs such a link. He assumes that the ontological relation between our natural FACULTIES (including our senses) and the things in nature that are perceived by these faculties, guarantees an epistemological fit between natural subject and natural object. Although Locke is sceptical about attempts at grasping the *essence* of substances, his robust and confident empiricism rules out Cartesian worries about the certainty of our knowledge of the *existence* of substances (*E*, IV. xi. 8, pp. 634–5). Since he never takes this kind of scepticism seriously he does not need Descartes's *cogito* as a basis of all subsequent knowledge (although he does presents a version of the *cogito* in *E*, IV. ix. 3, pp. 618–19). Locke has his own worries, and these are prompted not so much by ideas that lack clarity, i.e. ideas that are obscure, as by ideas that lack distinctness, i.e. ideas that are confused. Locke remarks that, strictly speaking, confusion is an unlikely state of mind, insofar as most men are perfectly able to see that different ideas are not the same and that the same ideas are not different (*E*, II. xxix. 5, p. 364). Error lurks elsewhere. We give NAMES to our ideas and we should not forget that every idea, whether simple or complex, should have a precise name and every name should refer only to this idea and not to another idea. The problem is that human beings have great difficulty in adhering to this fundamental law and this gives wide scope for confusion: 'Now every *Idea* a man has, being visibly what it is, and distinct from all other *Ideas* but it self, that which makes it *confused* is, when it is such, that it may as well be called by another Name, as that which it is expressed by' (*E*, II. xxix. 6, p. 364). This means that confusion is not really a property of the relation between ideas, but rather of the relation between words on the one hand and ideas on the other.

So, although Locke takes over the words 'clear' and 'distinct' from Descartes, they attach different weights to these terms. Descartes's worries about the relation between ideas and external objects can be expressed in terms of obscurity or the absence of *clarity*, and Locke's obsession with the relation between words and ideas can be formulated in terms of confusion or the absence of *distinctness*. Instead of using clarity and distinctness for a Cartesian attempt at bridging the divide between ideas in our mind and objects in the external world, Locke uses clarity and distinction to draw attention to the problematic relation between words and ideas. This marks a shift in focus that would have a profound impact on the future development of Western philosophy: a shift away from the relation between ideas and *things*, towards the relation between ideas and *words*.

BIBLIOGRAPHY
Manuscript Sources
Amsterdam University Library, MS R.K. - J 57a (published in Jean le Clerc, *Epistolario*, 4 vols, ed. Mario Sina, Florence, 1987–97).

Primary Sources
[Arnauld, Antoine and Pierre Nicole], *La logique ou l'art de penser* (2nd edn, Paris, 1664).
Clerc, Jean le, 'Eloge de feu M. Locke', *Bibliothèque choisie*, vol. vi (1705), pp. 342–411.
Descartes, René, *Opera Philosophica* (Amsterdam, 1656).
——, *The Philosophical Writings of Descartes*, 3 vols, trans. John Cottingham, Robert Stoothoff, Dugald Murdoch and (vol. 3) Anthony Kenny (Cambridge, 1984–91).
——, *Regulæ ad directionem ingenii (1701)*, ed. Giovanni Crapuli (The Hague, 1966).
Locke, John, *An Early Draft of Locke's Essay together with Excerpts from his Journal*, ed. R.I. Aaron and Jocelyn Gibb (Oxford, 1936).

Secondary Literature
Bonno, Gabriel, *Les relations intellectuelles de Locke avec la France*, University of California Publications in Modern Philosophy, vol. xxxviii, no. 2 (Berkeley and Los Angeles, 1955), pp. 37–264.
Harrison, John, and Peter Laslett, *The Library of John Locke* (Oxford, 1965).

Milton, J.R., 'Locke at Oxford', in G.A.J. Rogers (ed.), *Locke's Philosophy. Content and Context* (Oxford, 1994), pp. 29–47.

Schuurman, Paul, *Ideas, Mental Faculties and Method. The Logic of Ideas of Descartes and Locke and Its Reception in the Dutch Republic, 1630–1750* (Leiden, 2004).

Paul Schuurman

FILMER, Robert (c. 1588–1653)

Robert Filmer has two claims to appear here: as the author of political works diametrically opposed to Locke's in their metaphysical origins and practical implications, and as the object of Locke's direct and extended attack in the first of *Two Treatises of Government*, an attack conducted in a way that supplied content to the agenda of the second.

Filmer's most basic intellectual assumptions were the existence of God and the normative authority of the Bible in relation to conduct. For instance, *Quaestio quodlibetica*, probably written in the later 1620s, defended interest payments as compatible with scriptural practice. Scripture plays a fundamental role in the last work Filmer published, *An Advertisement to the Jury-Men of England, Touching Witches* (1653), which argued that it did not support claims that witchcraft implied a pact with the Devil. Between these two works, Filmer published a number of political pamphlets, which assumed the conclusions of *Patriarcha*, which he wrote during and after the 1620s, but did not publish. It is for *Patriarcha*, which appeared posthumously, and for the political tracts which Filmer himself issued from 1648 to 1652, that he is best known, and which were the objects of Locke's critique.

Patriarcha and Filmer's other writings about politics assumed the validity of his theological postulates, and used these in company with Aristotelian views about causality and nature as postulates for the political authority of Adam and of monarchs, whom he identified as Adam's proper successors in an absolute authority over the ruled. The essence which supported this position was a combination of biblical statements of fact with LOGIC and biology, both of Aristotelian character. The biblical claim that there is one God, who is omnipotent, makes him the universal cause. To this factual claim, Filmer added the scholastic maxim that the cause is greater than the caused: and this causal superiority implied authority when it was found along with eminent intelligence and goodness in a person. The person in whom power, wisdom and goodness are united to the greatest degree is God, so that he has universal authority. He exercised it to create the first man, Adam, and from Adam the first woman, Eve. Adam was Eve's superior, as her cause, but also he caused the whole human race, for Aristotelian conceptions of causality and of biology implied as much. Aristotle had distinguished four types of cause – formal, final, material and efficient. The most important of these was the formal (or model), in which both final (end in view) and efficient (immediate occasioning) were implied. The least important was material, for this was merely the content on which formal and efficient cause worked to realize final cause. This conception of causality by itself implied nothing about Adam's causal role, but Aristotelian embryology located the formal and efficient cause of procreation in the motion of male characteristics, and understood the female merely as the material receptacle in which male force was matured into an infant. Thus Adam turned out to be, in the more important senses of the word, the cause of the whole human race. As its cause, and so greater than what he caused, and as the pre-eminent human repository of goodness and intelligence, Adam was also its superior. So God and Nature determined terrestrial authority.

Filmer thus wove together biblical facts with Aristotelian thinking. He was not unusual amongst his contemporaries in combining sacred history and peripatetic philosophy: where he distinguished himself was in developing his combination of them into a distinctive form, which comprised both positive assertions about political superiority and searching criticisms of other views of it.

The assertions had both explanatory and practical force. The explanatory force in *Patriarcha* was to use nature as Filmer understood it. Adam's authority was natural, by virtue of his procreative role and other characteristics. Filmer interpreted paternal authority over children as political authority, and therefore presented Adam as lord paramount over his descendants, that is to say the whole human race. This dominion, further, was not only political but also proprietoral, for Filmer used *Genesis* 1, 28 to argue that God had granted Adam the fullest PROPERTY in the world and all its creatures. The ejection of Adam and Eve from Eden, and their consequent mortality, raised the question of what happened to Adam's superiority after his death. Filmer answered that it devolved to his male descendants. Hence all the kings now on earth were supposed to be the next heirs to their Adamic progenitor in their realm. Their authority, just as it was inclusive in scope, was total in degree, for Adam was its lord in the fullest sense. It followed that monarchical authority, as the sole sort authorized by God, was the only acceptable sort; that it was complete; and that it did not arise from the people. The latter, moreover, could not in their nature be free from a superior, precisely because of Adam, and therefore there was no natural equality of status.

The practical force of *Patriarcha*, when drafted, was to argue for the claims of monarchs against the contrasting claim of Rome and Geneva, and to look askance at some parliamentary claims. The church-states constituted by the Papacy and by Calvin's Swiss hierocracy rested on claims about their own directly divine origin, and complemented these by arguing that the authority of monarchs came

via the people. So civil authority was subordinate to clerical. This conclusion was not congenial in England, which was a state-church, and pundits, including King James, argued *per contra* that political authority resided in monarchs, not peoples, and came directly from God. It was therefore absolute, not to be controlled or circumscribed by non-monarchical men, including churchmen. These claims suited monarchical convenience, in that they implied that nobles and representative assemblies did not have the status to oppose royal policy: an opposition with which James was even more familiar as James VI of Scotland (1567–1625) than as James I of England (1603–25). His successor, Charles I, experienced these difficulties as king (1625–49) with infinitely greater intensity, including two civil wars (1642–6, 1648), and died on the scaffold in 1649.

The practical force of Filmer's publications of 1648 was directed to their situation. The first civil war had ended with royal defeat and captivity: but monarchy still persisted. Filmer pointed first, in *The Freeholder's Grand Inquest* of February, to the fact that parliaments were summoned by royal writ, which limited their activity to advice from the Lords and information from the Commons, and was altogether subordinate to the monarch, who was the only source of law. Next, in April, Filmer added, in *The Anarchy of a Limited or Mixed Monarchy*, that all government implied an unlimited legislative authority. He also attacked the alternative views of Henry Parker, and, especially, Philip Hunton. Finally, August saw *The Necessity of the Absolute Power of all Kings*, which reinforced the preceding arguments by carefully culled extracts from Jean Bodin. Filmer thus urged a complementary range of positions: absolute monarchy implied legislative ABSOLUTISM and the subordination of parliament to kings. If these three pamphlets urged a common perspective on a constitutional question, other royalists took a more direct route. The risings known as the Second Civil War included one in Kent, and, though Filmer is not known to have participated in this, it is improbable that he was ignorant of or out of sympathy with royalist conspiracy.

Conspiracy failed, and the sequel to the execution of the king was the abolition of the monarchy. The next heir, Charles II, attempted to defeat the English army with Scottish assistance but failed totally in 1651. The questions Filmer asked in 1652 were about the proper grounds of authority and how to conduct oneself under the rule of a usurper. *Observations concerning the Originall of Government* examined critically the non-patriarchal accounts of political authority given recently by HOBBES and Milton in order to point towards a monarchical conclusion. *Observations concerning Aristotle's Politiques* examined older arguments in order to demonstrate that these, along with Scripture, proved that patriarchally generated monarchy was the only proper and successful form of government. This conclusion looked to better times, and implied that they would return. Meanwhile, the appended *Directions for Obedience to Governours in dangerous and doubtfull times* examined how far usurpers should be tolerated and identified how they should perform the role to which they were not entitled.

All Filmer's political pamphlets assumed but scarcely expounded fully his biblical and philosophical assumptions. *The Freeholder's Grand Inquest* was preoccupied wholly with parliament, and where the other pamphlets used Adamic arguments they did so hypothetically and briefly. These emphasized the problems of anti-royal or Aristotelian political arguments in order to deliver the conclusion of absolute monarchy. Such reserve about general assumptions was doubtless prudent in conducting polemics for the benefit of an ancient monarchy, and also allowed Filmer to devote his energies to incisive critiques of its opponents. But this same procedure made his works appear as those of a highly intelligent pamphleteer rather than someone with a positive argument about political authority: only a vocal cock on the dung heap of controversy.

The publication of *Patriarcha* in 1680 disclosed a very different reality, one of political argument proceeding from assumptions about nature understood in terms of Aristotelian metaphysics. This was a reality that was of crucial importance to the controversy that overtook the restored monarchy of Charles II (1660–85) in 1679–81. The king had been seriously ill, and had no Protestant heir: his younger brother, James, Duke of York, being a Catholic convert. Protestant England was carried by hysteria about an alleged Jesuit plot to murder the king into the Exclusion Crisis, in which those who feared a Catholic ruler or exploited fear sought to change the succession or limit the monarchy. Any change in the character of the monarchy, given Charles's unwillingness to weaken his position or his brother's, implied that the Lords and Commons had an authority superior to the monarch's. So it was necessary to move from constitutional custom and law to general argument in order to determine the causal source of political authority. In this place *Patriarcha* was a gift to the monarchy, for it used the *natural* character of the power of kings to trump all possible alternatives, and thus excluded the possibility of the legislator being anyone other than the monarch. Filmer stood revealed as a most significant and strikingly relevant figure, one who had got to the intellectual bottom of the practical problem preoccupying the nation. Anyone in doubt about his significance was enlightened by the frontispiece portrait of Charles II in *Patriarcha* when it was published in 1680.

Filmer therefore claimed the sustained attention of those who favoured the other side of the question, so that Algernon Sidney and James Tyrrell responded to him in books considerably longer than *Patriarcha*. The response of greatest importance, however, came from Locke in *Two Treatises of Government*.

Locke, who knew the Bible as well as Filmer had done, began from a different metaphysical and natural philosophy. He had rejected an Aristotelian account of causality, considering that the only type of causality was efficient.

His conception of motion and its source was also non-Aristotelian. Everything was in a condition of continuing dependence on God as their author and upholder: and God, because the source of all power, originated all matter and motion. As the efficient cause of everything, he could hardly be taken to play second fiddle to Adam in procreation, and, given that there was no category of material causality, there could be no conceptual reason to suppose that Eve played a lesser part than Adam in producing the human race. The Aristotelian metaphysics and biology that to Filmer was a firm foundation for political thought was liable to Lockean subsidence.

If Locke considered Filmer philosophically and scientifically weak, he knew that *Patriarcha* and the related works had a contemporary constituency, and (still worse) situated the features of civil life that the English valued – household order and legislative authority, besides civil liberty and private property – in terms of absolute monarchy. It was therefore necessary to achieve two objectives. One was to shred Filmer's arguments, the other to replace them with explanations of civil life that connected it firmly with a non-absolute polity. *Two Treatises* performs these tasks. The tasks, in fact, were complementary, in that dismembering the Filmerian body politic provided means to generate the Lockean one.

The dismembering provided body parts, and the instrument for extracting them was Filmer's own method. Locke drew from that intellectual corpus what he wanted – exactly the procedure Filmer had used on others. Locke distinguished the relations of father, property-owner and sovereign that Filmer had colligated, and, by doing so, modified their content and changed their purpose. Thus, having discounted Filmer's reading of *Genesis* as a warrant for Adam's sovereignty and his property in the world, Locke understood it to establish a property common to all mankind, given in order to preserve life and raise children; and parental duty was discovered to be the end of Scripture and nature, not absolute paternal authority,

because God, not people, created children and he made them for a purpose. That was disclosed by *Genesis*: in fact, God there issued a 'great Design' for mankind to multiply, subdue the earth and improve human life: procreation, child-rearing and property were alike part of his purpose. These moves of Locke's placed social relations in a new perspective. There was also a change in political relations. Locke supposed that if Filmer was wrong about Adamic sovereignty, people would be 'left again to the old way', i.e. natural freedom, via consent, being their means to establish a government. Locke therefore took care to criticize Filmer's argument about political authority in order to provide a route to freedom and equality. In short, the project of the first of *Two Treatises* was to distinguish the relations of fatherhood, sovereignty and property, to establish that Filmer had not disproved natural freedom and equality, to provide elements for alternative readings of these relations, and to suggest a divine purpose that was incumbent on man.

The second of the *Two Treatises* begins with the postulates of natural freedom and equality, a sense that relations need to be considered anew and a sense of divine purpose. From these results of his critical reading of Filmer, Locke constituted a wholly different account of society and government. Once one assumed that people were by nature free and equal, and once Locke added that divine purpose precluded voluntary slavery to absolute rulers, the way was open to argue that people could and did constitute a government by consent, limited to the purposes for which they consented. Those purposes were the preservation of themselves and others, and Locke explained the relations of private property and parenthood as contributions to those ends, and to the improvement of life, i.e. as contributions to God's 'great Design' in ways that established them independently of government – which was no absolute sovereign but constituted a means to an end, in which the legislative was superior to the executive. Locke thus owed a significant debt to Filmer, though there is no reason to suppose that Filmer would have wished this.

Filmer would not have enjoyed the sequel. NEWTON's *Principia* made conceptions of matter, motion and divine action like Locke's the norm for natural philosophy. The Glorious Revolution, and its sequels, established that parliament, not the monarch alone, was the effective sovereign of England. Locke's *Essay* disseminated a post-Aristotelian view of metaphysics throughout the world. *Two Treatises* achieved popularity as the work of 'the great Mr. Locke', became a convenient instrument for the American Revolution, and continues to be a strong intellectual currency in the universities of the world's democracies. Filmerian thinking has been displaced both intellectually and practically. It had to wait until the twentieth century for scholarly curiosity: and that curiosity treats Filmer mostly as an interesting royalist with biblical interests, rather than also as one who turned philosophical assumptions to political use, and who, by an exquisite irony, played a role in generating Locke's *Two Treatises*.

BIBLIOGRAPHY
Primary Sources
Filmer, Robert, *Patriarcha and Other Writings*, ed. J.P. Sommerville (Cambridge, 1991).

Ian Harris

HOBBES, Thomas (1588–1679)

The relationship between Locke and Hobbes constitutes one of the most enduring puzzles of early-modern intellectual history. The two thinkers shared many fundamental philosophical positions, from foundational interests in empirical epistemology and mechanical explanation through to common beliefs about the liberty and equality of all men. These views put both philosophers in the ranks of a rela-

tively small intellectual *avant-garde*. And not only were they close intellectually, they were also, for several years, near neighbours. During the later 1660s and early 1670s they lived in London, just opposite each other on the Strand (Rogers, 1998, p. 61). The surviving evidence suggests that they moved in interrelated social circles (e.g. Aubrey to Locke, 11 February 1673, *Corr.*, vol. i, pp. 375–7). This intellectual, social and physical proximity might lead us to expect that there would be plentiful evidence of an intellectual relationship, but when one examines Locke's works there is only a handful of explicit references to Hobbes and, to date, only two quotations from Hobbes have been found in Locke's extensive manuscripts (*TTG*, 74n; *RCh.*, p. lxxvii, n. 1). This apparent disinterest appears to be supported by Locke's own account in the 1690s of his relationship with Hobbes: he repeatedly claimed that he simply did not know about Hobbes's views (e.g. W, vol. vii, pp. 420–1). The fact that Locke's library ultimately contained only three works by Hobbes (*Leviathan*, 1651, the scientific work *Problemata Physica*, 1662 and the pastoral poem *De mirabilibus pecci*, 1666; Harrison and Laslett, 1965, p. 155) seems to support Locke's claim that he was 'not so well read' in Hobbes (W, vol. iv, p. 477).

Can it really be the case that Locke simply had little interest in, or intellectual relationship to, one of the most infamous and important thinkers of his age? This thought was just as difficult for Locke's contemporaries as it is for us today. When his work was first published in the 1690s, critics (including Isaac NEWTON) were quick to accuse him of Hobbism, a charge that elicited his strident denials, but one that would haunt him for the rest of his life (Edwards, 1699, p. 27; Newton, 1961, vol. iii p. 280). The thought that Locke in fact owed more to Hobbes than he was admitting has persisted in modern scholarship (e.g. Strauss, 1953, pp. 202–51). Other scholars have been more prepared to take Locke at his word. Peter Laslett, in his edition of the *Two Treatises*, suggests that Locke's mature political theory was not a response to Hobbes, nor an engagement with him (*TTG*, pp. 67–92). Commentary in this, largely contextualist, vein tends to downplay Locke's interest in Hobbes's ideas beyond the contingent moments at which their political agendas appeared to overlap (Marshall, 1994; Tuck, 1990, pp. 153–71). The same sceptical approach has been applied to their scientific interests (Rogers, 1998).

But even if we might doubt that Locke is simply a closet Hobbist, there are reasons to suppose that his relative silence about Hobbes conceals a more substantive interaction with Hobbes's ideas. Firstly, it seems likely that Locke had a greater familiarity with Hobbes's works than his slim library holdings would suggest. For example, a lengthy quotation recorded in one of his interleaved Bibles shows that he had encountered Hobbes's writings on liberty and necessity (*RCh.*, p. lxxvii, n. 1). His notebook from 1669 records that he bought the recently published edition of Hobbes's works in Latin (British Library, Add. MS 46470 f. 19r, see also f. 50v). Locke also possessed a large number of works that discussed Hobbes in considerable detail (*TTG*, p. 75), including critiques by George Lawson, Thomas Tenison, Samuel Pufendorf, John Templer, the Earl of Clarendon and Ralph Cudworth. In addition he possessed all Robert BOYLE's attacks upon Hobbes's scientific work (Harrison and Laslett, 1965, pp. 92–3). Even if Locke did not have Hobbes's books to hand (and much has been made of the fact that his own copy of *Leviathan* was unavailable to him between 1674 and 1691), he did not need them to have access to all Hobbes's most notorious passages, which were often reproduced *verbatim* by his critics.

Secondly, although Locke does not explicitly mention Hobbes very often, he does more regularly allude to him in a variety of subtle ways. Although this sort of evidence is difficult to gauge, context and a careful reading of Locke's arguments do reveal some of this hidden dialogue. Hobbes did have an important role to play, most obviously as a negative stimulus to the development of Locke's ideas. Hobbes and

Locke may have shared theoretical concepts but Hobbes offered an unacceptably reductive account of the relationships between them. Following Laslett, we might also say that Locke could sometimes feel the gravitational pull of Hobbesian solutions upon his own materials. But it was a force that Locke consistently sought to resist in his struggle to formulate an alternative and opposed system from the same elements. That said, the very difficulty of the struggle might have been one of the reasons why Locke sought to deflect attention from it.

Although Locke leaves few clues about his knowledge of Hobbes, there can be little doubt that from an early stage in his career he knew about the debate over Hobbist ideas. From 1654 onwards Locke's Oxford was the epicentre of the controversy over Hobbes's work (Parkin, 2007, chap. 3). If Oxonians such as John Wallis and Seth Ward sought to demolish Hobbes's project, he was defended by others such as Locke's colleague Henry Stubbe. Indeed, sympathy for Hobbes within Christ Church made it the most congenial environment for the consideration of Hobbes's theories within the university. Locke appears to have read *Leviathan* together with commentary upon it during this period (for example, the work of Lawson and Wren; Harrison and Laslett, 1965, pp. 170, 266).

In this environment, it is perhaps no surprise to find Locke deploying suggestively Hobbesian rhetoric in his unpublished *Tracts on Government*. Justifying the magistrate's imposition of religious *adiaphora*, Locke discussed the inconveniences of the STATE OF NATURE (Locke, 1997, p. 37) and the necessarily absolutist character of political authority (Locke, 1997, p. 11), recalling distinctive Hobbesian formulae. However, we should not assume that these passages indicate that Locke was a disciple of Hobbes. Firstly, Anglican arguments about the state's authority over religious practice could *sound* Hobbesian. Secondly, the use of Hobbesian rhetoric may also be connected with the fact that Locke was addressing Hobbesian sympathizers such as Bagshaw and

Stubbe. Lastly, there is no doubt that Hobbes's undoubted gift for trenchant utterances made his rhetoric attractive even to those who rejected his larger theory. That Locke might have fallen into this category is indicated by his theoretical position in the *Tracts*. His discussion appears to be carefully configured to avoid what Locke took to be distinctive about Hobbism. This was specifically the manner in which Hobbes deliberately sought to collapse political and religious obligation in the artificial person of a sovereign, whose authority was derived from the self-preserving instincts of individuals. It is striking that whenever Locke alludes to Hobbism, it is usually to draw attention to the inadequacies of this reductive foundation for moral and political duties (e.g. Locke, 1997, p. 371; *E*, I.iii.5, p. 68). Locke was careful to insulate the arguments of the *Tracts* from this suggestion by stressing God's role as the source of natural obligation (Locke, 1997, pp. 10–11), a position foundational to his arguments. A few years later, in his *Essays on the Law of Nature*, Locke would again highlight explicitly anti-Hobbesian arguments: the insufficiency of self-interest and self-preservation as a basis for NATURAL LAW (*ELN*, pp. 181, 205).

It should also be noted that it did not require Locke to focus exclusively on Hobbes's work for the Hobbesian *reductio* to arise as a distinctive issue. Restoration Anglican discourse tended in a distinctively Hobbesian direction. This was particularly the case with the controversy over Samuel Parker's *Discourse of Ecclesiastical Polity* (1669). Parker pressed the power of the sovereign over religious doctrine and was widely accused of Hobbism. The accusation was echoed by Locke when he was moved to ask in his manuscript notes 'how far is this short of Mr Hobbes's doctrine?' (*ETol.*, p. 326). Hobbism here represented the fatal terminus of Anglican attempts to rationalize political and religious authority; the resulting debate over Hobbes would produce a number of critiques that Locke owned (for example those by Tenison and Templer). It is also striking that this phase of the debate over

Hobbism also encouraged some Anglican thinkers to rearticulate the epistemological basis of their moral theory (for example, Richard Cumberland's *De legibus naturae*), and it may not be entirely fanciful to suggest that Locke's early attempts to do the same thing in the drafts of the *Essay concerning Human Understanding* may well have been prompted by similar background concerns.

By the end of the 1670s, the anti-Hobbesian thrust of Locke's arguments in ecclesiology and politics can be discerned more clearly. The Hobbesian implications of the Anglican position resurfaced in Edward STILLINGFLEET's polemical writings against dissenters, to which Locke offered a decisive response in his 'Defence of Nonconformity' (Bodleian Library, MS Locke c.34). Here Locke distinguished secular and ecclesiastical forms of association where Hobbes had characteristically sought to make them identical. Locke's passing remarks on Hobbes here make it clear that he was rejecting this Hobbesian feature of the Anglican project (MS Locke c.34, p. 40). There can also be little doubt that anti-Hobbism played a minor but distinctive role in Locke's *Two Treatises* (Parkin, 2007, pp. 365–8). The danger of *Leviathan*-style ABSOLUTISM was a common theme of Whig propaganda and Locke's work, although noticeably less explicit in this regard, is both allusively and structurally anti-Hobbesian. For example, Locke subtly rejects a Hobbesian account of the state of nature when he denies that the state of nature is a state of war (*TTG*, II.19). He also rejects the peculiar asymmetry of the Hobbesian contract and its resulting absolutism (*TTG*, II.93). His own theory depends upon the subordination of political authority to an independently obligatory natural law. Again, there are signs that Locke was drawing upon anti-Hobbesian literature in making these distinctions, with a view to ruling out Hobbism (*TTG*, p. 75). The shadowy character of Locke's engagement with Hobbes is somewhat puzzling in the light of the fact that other Whigs were quite happy to attack the author of *Leviathan*, but Locke's stance may simply reflect a prudent attempt to avoid trouble. Hobbes was routinely bracketed *with* Whig writers because of the allegedly seditious implications of their contractualism. As many writers had discovered, noisy attempts to refute Hobbes could often attract damaging counter-charges of Hobbism. By quietly deflecting Hobbesian views at important moments, Locke advertised his anti-Hobbesian stance without drawing unnecessary attention to the issue of Hobbism. Locke may not have written the *Two Treatises* against Hobbes, but we can detect Hobbes's presence in the debates of the 1680s shaping Locke's targets, his fears, and perhaps even elements of his anti-absolutist theory.

Locke's most bruising association with Hobbes nevertheless occurred in the 1690s, when the publication of his work elicited widespread allegations of Hobbism. Locke's *sotto voce* anti-Hobbism, when put in the context of broader generic similarities between the thinkers, proved difficult for his contemporaries to appreciate. His reluctance to discuss the mechanics of natural MORAL OBLIGATION in the *Essay* prompted critics to suspect that his own position implied Hobbism; his friend James Tyrrell reported the suspicion of 'thinking men' in Oxford that Locke's formula came 'very near what is so much cried out upon in Mr: Hobbs' (30 June 1690, *Corr.*, vol. iv, p. 102). Newton levelled the charge of Hobbism more directly because Locke had appeared to strike at 'ye root of morality' (Newton, 1961, vol. iii, p. 280). The critics were quick to identify the resemblances between Hobbes and Locke, but were less effective at identifying Locke's implicitly anti-Hobbesian account of an obligation to the laws of a purposive God that did not rely upon earthly authorities.

Arguably his most decisive response to the Hobbesian *reductio* was to reinforce the authority of the divine, but ironically this move was ultimately to mire him further in accusations of Hobbism. If *The Reasonableness of Christianity's* argument was that belief in Jesus Christ was the only knowledge required for salvation, critics soon identified that it was also a central tenet of Hobbes's theology (Parkin, 2008, pp. 397–402). Here again a superficial similarity concealed a substantial theoretical difference. For Hobbes, the point of making mere belief in Christ the sole condition of salvation was to ensure that Christian doctrine could never challenge the authority of the sovereign. For Locke, by contrast, Christ's role was to complete and underwrite natural law, to guarantee the independent obligation of that divinely ordained legislation (Stanton, 2008). Here, as in so many other places, Locke was almost diametrically opposed to Hobbes, supporting a different view of the relationship between religious and political authority with more or less the same conceptual resources.

Locke's way of dealing with the accusations was to deny all knowledge of Hobbes's opinions in these matters, a prudent strategy of avoidance in an atmosphere where the accusation of Hobbism could have dangerous consequences. But, as the evidence suggests, it seems very likely that Locke was only too aware of the moments when he was sharing intellectual territory with the most notorious philosopher in England. It can also be no accident that Locke's arguments, when considered carefully, more often than not turn out to be completely opposed to Hobbism. The Hobbesian *reductio* threatened most of Locke's core beliefs with ideas that they had in common. As John Dunn has remarked, Hobbes's arguments were not simply an intellectual challenge, still less an intellectual seduction. They constituted in a very real sense an intellectual nightmare (Dunn, 1969, p. 81). To that extent, the development of Locke's work was shaped around the rejection of that distinctive vision and the struggle to create a viable alternative.

BIBLIOGRAPHY
Manuscript Sources
Bodleian Library MS Locke c.34 'Defence of Nonconformity'.
British Library Add. MS 46470.

Primary Sources

Edwards, Jonathan, *The Eternal and Intrinsick Reasons of Good and Evil* (London, 1699).

Locke, John, *Political Essays*, ed. Mark Goldie (Cambridge, 1997).

Newton, Isaac, *The Correspondence of Isaac Newton*, ed. H.W. Turnbull, 7 vols (Cambridge, 1959–).

Secondary Sources

Dunn, J., *The Political Thought of John Locke: An Historical Account of the Argument of the 'Two Treatises of Government'* (Cambridge, 1969).

Harrison, John, and Peter Laslett, *The Library of John Locke* (Oxford, 1965).

Marshall, J., *John Locke: Resistance, Religion, Responsibility* (Cambridge, 1994).

Parkin, J., *Taming the Leviathan: The Reception of the Political and Religious Ideas of Thomas Hobbes in England 1640–1700* (Cambridge, 2008).

Rogers, G.A.J., 'The Intellectual Relationship between Hobbes and Locke – A Reappraisal', in G.A.J. Rogers (ed.), *Locke's Enlightenment: Aspects of the Origin, Nature and Impact of his Philosophy* (Hildesheim, 1998), pp. 61–77.

Stanton, T., 'Hobbes and Locke on Natural Law and Jesus Christ', *History of Political Thought*, vol. xxix, no. 1 (2008), pp. 65–88.

Strauss, L., *Natural Right and History* (Chicago, 1953).

Tuck, R., 'Hobbes and Locke on Toleration' in M. Dietz (ed.), *Thomas Hobbes and Political Theory* (Lawrence, 1990), pp. 153–71.

Jon Parkin

LIMBORCH, Philippus van (1633–1712)

Philippus van Limborch was the leading Remonstrant in the seventeenth century. Through his friendship with Jean Le Clerc (1657–1736) and his intellectual partnership with Locke, he secured a position right at the centre of intellectual life in the Dutch Republic. He was born in Amsterdam on 19 June 1633 and died in the same town on 30 April 1712. He was the son of Frans van Limborch, a merchant and a lawyer, and of Gertrud (Geertruida) Bisschop, a niece of the major Remonstrant theologian Simon Episcopius (Simon Bisschop). Philippus received his education in Amsterdam (under the guidance of Gerard Vossius, Gaspar Barlaeus, Arnold Senguerd and Etienne de Courcelles) and in Utrecht. He became a pastor in Gouda in 1657, and he was transferred to Amsterdam in 1668, where the office of professor of theology was added to his pastoral charge at the Remonstrant Church. Limborch was a productive writer, mainly in the field of theology. His most important works include the *Epistolae theologicae* (1660), a collection of letters from the main Arminian thinkers, a selection from the correspondence of the English ambassadors at the Synod of Dordrecht (1618), and a brief history of the Dutch controversy on predestination between the Arminians and the Gomarists.

In January 1684 Limborch met Locke, who had just found refuge in the Netherlands. After Locke's death, Limborch was to describe to Lady Damaris MASHAM his first meeting with Locke:

The onlookers included Locke who had learnt from Guenellon that I held a tenure as a professor of philosophy at the Remonstrant seminary, and he introduced himself to me, and afterwards we had many conversations about religion, in which he acknowledged that he had long attributed to the Remonstrants certain doctrines very different from those which they held, and now that he understood what they really were, he was surprised to find how closely they agreed with many of his own opinions (Simonutti, 1999, p. 321).

Stimulated by the conversation with Limborch, Locke started reading the works of the main Remonstrant thinkers and other Dutch theologians.

Limborch was of the same age as Locke, and at this time he was reaching a peak in his intellectual activities. After assembling his earlier considerations on TOLERATION against the Calvinist Sceperus, and upon completing the history of the Synod of Dordrecht, he completed the first edition of the *Epistolae Ecclesiasticae et Theologicae* of Arminius and other key representatives of Arminianism. He also edited the works of Episcopius and Courcelles. These Remonstrants all preferred a rational, non-fanatical and non-tyrannical path towards Christianity. They shared this attitude with the Socinians, the British Platonists and Latitudinarians, and the French Protestants.

When Locke finished his *Epistola de tolerantia* in the second half of 1685 in Cleves, he may have perused two manuscripts on which Limborch was still working at that time: the *Theologia Christiana* and the *De veritate Religionis Christianae amica collatio cum erudito judaeo*. Limborch had started the draft of the *Theologia Christiana* in 1681–2 (Simonutti, 1984, pp. 81–2), at the request of many; there had been no previous theoretical and practical exposition of the Remonstrant doctrine, notwithstanding the wealth of works and teachings by the Arminian forefathers. In the last two chapters of this work Limborch expounded his concept of toleration based upon rational consensus, and a minimal creed that is accessible for all. He forged these elements into an effective plea for peaceful coexistence between different confessions, as an instrument that guarantees the 'libertas prophetandi' and prevents the propagation of conflict and confusion.

While he is keen to pass judgement upon idolaters and those who deny the principles of religion, he wants to guarantee freedom of conscience for dissenters, and mutual tolerance among Christians. Judges should have no jurisdiction on religious matters, and should focus only on civilian society. Whenever this distinction is lost, conscience suffers undue constraints, and religious persecutions will follow in its wake. The separation between the two powers guarantees a form of justice that is free from malice and in accordance with reason.

From a doctrinal point of view, Limborch differentiates between fundamental dogmas aimed at the salvation of the soul and non-fundamental dogmas that are meant to promote Christian *pietas*. While the violation of fundamental dogmas – limited in number and clearly identified in Scripture – results in an alienation from the religious community, dissent from non-fundamental dogmas should be allowed. According to Limborch, tolerance does not lead to scepticism and indifference, and it implies no danger to the 'libertas prophetandi', to religion or to the Church. He pointed out that the truth of this point has been corroborated by the responsible behaviour of the Remonstrants (Limborch, 1686, pp. 914–15). According to Limborch, a peaceful, free, orderly and tolerant society can be achieved only through the demarcation of clear boundaries between state and Church, a pursuit of the moral objectives of religion, and the rule of reason.

These views on toleration formed the background for the question raised by Locke in his first *Epistola de tolerantia*: 'Since you are pleased to inquire what are my thoughts about the mutual toleration of Christians in their different professions of religion, I must needs answer you freely, that I esteem that toleration to be the chief characteristic mark of the true church' (*W*, vol. vi, p. 5). The *Epistola*, recommended by and dedicated to Limborch, included a number of references to the Remonstrant environment (Locke, 1983, pp. 147–173). The theoretical framework and the objectives of the *Theologia* and the *Epistola de tolerantia* as formulated in the last chapters of the two works are different; the former concentrates on theological and the latter on civilian issues. Yet they both offered a definition of the rational conditions necessary to achieve tolerance.

Locke and Limborch shared the same analysis of the meaning and the implications of the concept of indifference, both in politics and in the foundations of their theory of tolerance, but they had disagreements on the complicated matter of our FREE WILL. Limborch placed liberty in an indifference antecedent to the determination of the will (Limborch to Locke, 8/18 July 1701, *Corr.*, vol. vii, pp. 369–70). Locke's final view on this matter was that this notion of antecedent difference 'seems to me to place Liberty in a state of darkness, wherein we can neither see nor say any thing of it; at least it places it in a subject incapable of it, no Agent being allowed capable of Liberty, but in consequence of Thought and Judgment' (*E*, II.xxi.71, p. 283; see also Simonutti, 2001, pp. 135–75).

Limborch's work on the edition of the *Historia Inquisitionis* (1692) formed another impetus for his intellectual partnership with Locke. John Locke had been attracted by a rare manuscript, the *Sententiarum Inquisitionis Tholosanae*. He had convinced Benjamin Furly, a wealthy merchant in Rotterdam, to buy it, and then Limborch to take care of its edition. Rather than focusing on easy polemic comments and conventional religious hagiography, Limborch used the plain sharp words of the apograph to describe both the procedures that led to the capital sentence, and the heinous execution of the prisoners. He linked the archival documentation to its context through a detailed and extended history of the French, Spanish, Italian and Central European medieval Inquisition, along with a detailed description of the role of the vicars, notaries, inquisitional judges, etc., along with the relationship between secular and ecclesiastical magistrates. In the *Historia Inquisitionis* Limborch linked his interest in the ancient and the modern sacred historiography with the philological attention typical of both a modern scholar and a historian. In this work he

tried to complete his analysis of the concepts of heresy and tolerance that he started at the end of the *Theologia Christiana*. The *Historia Inquisitionis* secured Limborch's fame. Although it was placed on the Index of the Holy Office in May 1694, it achieved a wide circulation in Europe, Italy included.

After Locke's return to England in 1689, the friends remained in contact, and Limborch became a keen reader of the successive replies to Jonas PROAST (c.1642–1710), of the writings concerning the Christian religion and the new editions of the *Essay*. The intellectual *rapport* between the two authors was maintained after Locke's return to England, in spite of a growing divergence between Locke's ethical and religious interests and Limborch's philosophical and gnoseological views.

BIBLIOGRAPHY
Primary Sources
Clerc, Jean le, *An Account of the Life and Writings of Mr. John Locke* (2nd edn, London, 1713).
Limborch, Philippus van, *Historia Inquisitionis, cui subjungitur Liber sententiarum Inquisitionis Tholosanae ab anno Christi 1307 ad annum 1323* (Amsterdam, 1692).
——, *Theologia Christiana, ad praxin pietatis ac promotionem pacis christianae unice directa* (Amsterdam, 1686).
Locke, John, *Epistola de Tolerantia*, in *On Toleration and the Unity of God*, ed. M. Montuori (Amsterdam, 1983).
Præstantium ac eruditorum virorum Epistolæ ecclesiasticæ et theologicæ varii argumenti interquas eminent eæ quæ a J. Arminio, C. Vorstio, S. Episcopio, H. Grotio, C. Barlæo conscriptæ sunt, ed. Christian Hartsoeker and P. van Limborch (Amsterdam, 1660; 2nd edn, 1684).

Secondary Literature
Berg, J. van den, 'John Locke en Philippus van Limborch' in H.J. Adriaanse et al. (eds), *Voorbeeldige vriendschap: vrienden en*

vriendinnen in theologie en cultuur: aange-
boden aan prof. dr. E.J. Kuiper t.g.v. zijn
afscheid als hoogleraar van het Seminarium
der Remonstranten (Groningen, 1993), pp.
57–66.

Barnouw, Pieter, *Philippus van Limborch* (The
Hague, 1963).

Schepper, R.M. de, 'Liberty in Willing. Van
Limborch's Influence on Locke's *Essay*',
Geschiedenis van de Wijsbegeerte in
Nederland, vol. iv (1993), pp. 127–146.

Simonutti, Luisa, *Arminianesimo e tolleranza*
nel Seicento olandese. Il carteggio Ph. van
Limborch- J. Le Clerc (Florence, 1984).

——, 'Religion, Philosophy and Science:
Locke and the Limborch's Circle', in J.E.
Force and D.S. Katz (eds), *Everything*
Connects: In Conference with Richard H.
Popkin (Leiden, 1999), pp. 295–324.

——, 'Limborch's *Historia Inquisitionis*: An
Episode in the Pursuit of Toleration', in
Allison P. Coudert, Sarah Hutton and
Richard H. Popkin (eds), *Judaeo-Christian*
Intellectual Culture in the Seventeenth
Century (Dordrecht, 1999).

——, 'Necessità, indifferenza, libertà. I
Rimostranti e Locke', in Luisa Simonutti
(ed.), *Dal necessario al possibile.*
Determinismo e libertà nel pensiero anglo-
olandese del XVII secolo (Milano, 2001),
pp. 135–175.

——, 'Between History and Politics:
Limborch's *Historia Inquisitionis*', in J.C.
Laursen (ed.), *Histories of Heresy,*
1600–1800 (New York, 2002), pp.
101–117.

——, 'Resistance, Obedience and Toleration.
Przypkowski and Limborch', in Martin
Mulsow and Jan Rohls (eds), *Socinianism*
and Arminianism. Antitrinitarians,
Calvinists and Cultural Exchange in
Seventeenth-Century Europe (Leiden,
2005), pp. 187–206.

Luisa Simonutti

MALEBRANCHE, Nicolas (1638–1715)

In 1693 and 1695 Locke found himself in correspondence with his Irish friend William
Molyneux (1656–98), concerning possible
additions to the second (1694) and third (1695)
editions of the *Essay*. Locke informs Molyneux
on 23 March 1693 that he has composed some
critical comments on Malebranche's 'hypothesis' of seeing all things in God, and wonders
whether they should be included (*Corr.*, vol. iv,
p. 665). Molyneux replies on 18 April, noting
Locke's reluctance to enter into 'philosophick
controversy', but urging him to do so in this
case, suggesting that Malebranche's notions
are 'perfectly unintelligible', the fruits of mere
'ENTHUSIASM' rather than serious study of
nature (*Corr.*, vol. iv, p. 668). On 8 March
1695 Locke writes again, saying that he has
examined Malebranche's opinion, and 'to my
own satisfaction, laid open the vanity, and
inconsistency, and unintelligibleness of that
way of explaining humane understanding', but
doubts whether he will even finish – let alone
publish – the critique (*Corr.*, vol. v, p. 287).
Urged once more by Molyneux to publish,
Locke replies in the following terms on 26
April: 'What I have writ concerning seeing all
things in God, would make a little treatise of it
self. But I have not quite gone through it, for
fear I should by somebody or other be tempted
to print it. For I love not controversies, and
have a personal kindness for the author' (*Corr.*,
vol. v, pp. 352–3).

Locke's allusion here to a 'personal kindness'
for Malebranche has led to suggestions that
the two men met during one of Locke's
extended visits to Paris in 1678 and 1679.
There is, however, no positive evidence for any
such meeting: we have no entries in Locke's
journal, no allusion in Locke's reading notes,
no reports by other witnesses, and no resulting
correspondence. We must remember, in
addition, two other significant facts.
Malebranche had published the *Recherche*
anonymously, so Locke could scarcely have
deliberately sought him out. And

Malebranche's superiors at the Oratory disapproved strongly of his taste for rationalist (Cartesian) philosophy, so he was suffering, at this period, from official censure. Only much later would Malebranche become a celebrity in the world of learning, and visiting scholars and dignitaries make a point of paying a courtesy call to his humble cell. Although the supposition of an actual meeting cannot be decisively refuted, the balance of the evidence is against it.

When Locke speaks of Malebranche's philosophy, it is almost invariably the *Recherche* that he has in mind. We know from the work of Gabriel Bonno that he acquired the original two-volume version (without the *Eclaircissements*) at Montpellier in 1676, and we must presume that he read it at that time, although we have only his reading notes from a second perusal, made in Holland in 1684. A glance at the contents of Locke's library, as compiled by Harrison and Laslett, confirms that he owned no fewer than three copies of various editions of the *Recherche* (first edition, Paris, 1674). Not surprisingly, given Locke's theological interests and concerns, he also owned the *Traité de la Nature et de la Grace* (Amsterdam, 1680). More surprising is the absence of Malebranche's later works, particularly the *Entretiens sur la Métaphysique et sur la Religion* (Rotterdam, 1688), which provides the most luminous statement of Malebranche's mature philosophy. The library also contains Arnauld's attack on Malebranche's theory of IDEAS, *Des Vraies et Fausses Idées* (Cologne, 1683), but not Malebranche's *Réponse* (Rotterdam, 1684), nor the ensuing polemical exchanges, which occupy volumes 6 to 9 of Robinet's edition of the *Oeuvres Complètes*. Locke could have followed the debate by means of the *comptes rendus* of Pierre Bayle, but he does not seem to have studied the later developments in Malebranche's philosophy in any depth or detail.

Locke's reactions to the *Recherche* belong in the context of his response to Cartesianism. We know that he made a close but critical study of DESCARTES, accepting much of the theory of ideas, but deeply sceptical regarding some of Descartes's more controversial claims such as innate ideas, the *bête-machine*, and the a priori argument for a plenum. In addition to the works of Descartes himself, he also acquired works of second-generation Cartesians such as Cordemoy and La Forge, and of course the famous Port-Royal *Logic* of Arnauld and Nicole. In this context he would have seen the *Recherche* as making a significant contribution both to our understanding of the sources of human error (Books 1–5) and to the articulation of a proper method for making judgements based on clear ideas, and thus avoiding error (Book 6). Paul Schuurman has suggested that the *Recherche*, along with the Port-Royal *Logic*, the famous *Art de Penser*, may have contributed to Locke's conception of a new LOGIC, based on the theory of ideas, and intended to replace the Aristotelian syllogistic of the schools.

If Locke was sympathetic to Cartesian views about the search for clear and distinct ideas, the same cannot be said about his response to Malebranche's two distinctive and characteristic theses, namely occasionalism and the Vision in God. His objections to occasionalism can be found in his unpublished *Remarks upon some of Mr Norris's Books*, in which he replies – in rather acerbic manner – to the *Cursory Reflections* on Locke's *Essay* that John NORRIS had appended to his *Christian Blessedness* (1690). If God is omnipotent, Locke asks, surely he can give powers to creatures: 'The infinite eternal God is certainly the cause of all things, the fountain of all being and power. But, because all being was from him, can there be nothing but God himself? Or, because all power was originally in him, can there be nothing of it communicated to creatures? This is to set very narrow limits to the power of God, and, by pretending to extend it, takes it away' (*W*, vol. ix, p. 255).

If God causes our sensory ideas directly, he objects, then all the delicate contrivances of the eye and the ear, so much admired by anatomists, become entirely redundant:

'Farther, if light striking upon the eyes be but the occasional cause of seeing: God, in making the eyes of so curious a structure, operates not by the simplest ways; for God could have produced visible ideas upon the occasion of light upon the eye-lids or forehead' (W, vol. ix, p. 254). Worse still, occasionalism undermines the very foundations of morality by making men entirely passive both in thinking and in willing: 'A man cannot move his arm or his tongue; he has no power; only upon occasion, the man willing it, God moves it. The man wills, he doth something; or else God, upon the occasion of something, which he himself did before, produced this will, and this action in him. This is the HYPOTHESIS that clears doubts, and brings us at last to the religion of HOBBES and Spinoza, by resolving all, even the thoughts and will of men, into an irresistible fatal necessity' (W, vol. ix, p. 255–6).

None of these objections is remotely original: Malebranche had explicitly addressed them all in the Eclaircissements added to the Recherche in 1678. To the delegated powers objection Malebranche replied with his doctrine of continuous creation (no creature can have the power of creation); to the objection from the complex design of the sense organs he replied with his insistence on the simplicité des voies (God's operating in accordance with universal laws, including the established laws of mechanism and of apparent mind-body interaction); to the 'fatal necessity' objection he replied that our second-order acts of consent or dissent to first-order motivations remain within our power, and provide a sufficient basis for agency and responsibility. Locke could not have been ignorant of the broad outlines of these responses. By repeating those objections here he is presumably indicating his judgement that Malebranche's replies fail to rebut the objections.

In the Examination of Père Malebranche's Opinion of Seeing all Things in God, published posthumously by Peter King in 1706, the Vision in God is dismissed as in itself unintelligible, and at best only feebly supported by the eliminative argument offered in its support in Book

Three of the Recherche. Malebranche insists that material things cannot be 'united' to the human soul in such a way as to be the true causes of its perceptions, but, Locke objects, he nowhere explains the nature of this metaphysical 'union', nor how God can be so united with our souls when bodies cannot. If he invokes rational principles of intelligibility to bolster his arguments, they will backfire against him, since his own account cannot satisfy the demands of the understanding. Malebranche tells us that only the SUBSTANCE of God is 'perfectly intelligible'; Locke protests that this leaves him entirely in the dark, 'having no notion at all of the "substance of God"; nor being able to conceive how he is more intelligible than any other substance' (W, vol. x, p. 214).

What, Locke asks, is wrong with the familiar corpuscular account of PERCEPTION, combined with a modest agnosticism about the underlying metaphysics? 'Impressions made on the retina by rays of light, I think I understand; and motions from thence continued to the brain may be conceived, and that these produce ideas in our minds, I am persuaded, but in a manner to me incomprehensible. This I can resolve only into the good pleasure of God, whose ways are past finding out' (W, vol. x, p. 217).

As for the argument by elimination, any argument of this form 'loses all its force as soon as we consider the weakness of our minds, and the narrowness of our capacities' (W, vol. x, p. 212). God can do many things in ways that surpass our understanding, so even if Malebranche can show that the Vision in God is the best of the five accounts of perception he is considering, this will prove nothing: 'To say that there can be no other, because we conceive of no other, does not, I confess, much instruct' (W, vol. x, p. 215).

Had Locke published the Examination in 1695, he might have found himself accused of misrepresentation based on inadequate and outdated reading. Locke takes the statement of the Vision in God directly from the Recherche, without considering the modifications required to meet Arnauld's objections, or

Malebranche's definitive statement of his mature metaphysics in the *Entretiens* of 1688. In this later work, the eliminative argument for the Vision in God plays an increasingly marginal role, with greater emphasis being placed instead on the argument from properties and from the very possibility of objective thought. Ideas, Malebranche insists in his replies to Arnauld, cannot simply be identified with perceptions, which are modifications of the soul of the perceiver. Ideas are necessary, eternal, immutable and universal; perceptions are contingent, fleeting, changeable and particular, confined to the individual mind that experiences them. Given these incompatible lists of properties, to identify ideas with perceptions is to commit a metaphysical category mistake. And if ideas are merely perceptions, Malebranche continues, how is the Cartesian to escape from subjective scepticism? Each mind will make judgements, based on its own ideas, about the world *as it represents it*; the very notion of a shared objective world will be deeply problematic. On the other hand, if ideas are the divine archetypes, on the basis of which all things were (and are) created, all minds will have access to the same intelligible realm. If the idea of intelligible extension (*étendue intelligible*) represents extension as infinitely divisible, then I can know a priori that all matter (which has been created in accordance with that archetype) is infinitely divisible. Without the assurance provided by the Vision in God, Malebranche argues, such objective thought would be impossible.

Whether Locke took sides in the famous dispute between Malebranche and Arnauld continues to divide the commentators. John Yolton has argued that Locke's position is very close to that of Arnauld, which identifies ideas with perceptions. On this theory, an idea has two aspects: in its intrinsic or 'formal' reality, it is a modification of the mind of the perceiver; in its representative or 'objective' reality, it represents some object or other. What Arnauld explicitly denies is the existence of any 'representative beings distinct from perceptions' that would serve as a veil of ideas cutting off the mind from access to the world. Michael Ayers warns that Locke's attack on Malebranche does not automatically place him in the same camp as Arnauld, and cites passages from the *Essay* that seem to require a stronger reading of 'idea'. At *Essay* IV.xxi.4, for example, Locke argues as follows: 'For, since the things the mind contemplates are none of them, besides itself, present to the understanding, it is necessary that something else, as a sign or representation of the thing it considers, should be present to it: and these are *Ideas*' (*E*, IV.xxi.4, p. 721) This passage, Ayers argues, would reduce to a tautology on Arnauld's reading of ideas as mere contents of perceptions, but Locke clearly intends the claim to be informative rather than trivial. Locke seems to need a notion of 'idea' that is more robust than Arnauld's, but less metaphysically extravagant than Malebranche's. On this difficult and contentious issue, however, Locke does little to help us, insisting on the virtues of his 'plain historical method' and on the immediate – and perfectly adequate – knowledge we all have of our own ideas through introspection.

As Locke's works began to appear in French translation, Malebranche began to launch his own counter-blasts. A French *Abrégé* of the *Essay* was published in Amsterdam in 1688, followed in 1700 by Pierre Coste's widely read translation of the whole work. In Malebranche's later writings, he shows his awareness of the *Essay*, and his sense that it is sceptical in its implications. In the *Avertissement* to his *Reply to Arnauld's Third Letter* (Amsterdam, 1704), Malebranche insists both on the importance of the topic (the nature of ideas) and of the dangers of Locke's growing reputation. The esteem in which both Locke and his *Essay* are held has provided him with a new reason to publish his *Reply*, 'with the intention of disabusing those readers who might allow themselves to be taken in by sentiments which seem to me to establish Pyrrhonism' (Malebranche, 1958, vol. ix, p. 899).

In the *Entretien d'un Philosophe Chrétien et d'un Philosophe Chinois* (Paris, 1708), the same accusation is again levelled against Locke's theory of ideas. If ideas are divine archetypes, Malebranche repeats, we can reason safely from ideas to things, because we know that all things must conform to their divine archetypes; if ideas are mere perceptions we have no escape from Pyrrhonism (Malebranche, 1958, vol. xv, p. 51). Locke tells us, for example, that 'morality is capable of demonstration' (*E*, III.xi.16, pp. 516–17), but he also tells us that moral ideas are complex ideas of the kind that he calls 'mixed MODES', and are thus not intended to copy some independent reality. Malebranche objects that the possibility of a demonstrative science of ethics rests on the existence of an objective archetype of order that is common to all minds, and plays the same role in ethics that the archetype of matter (intelligible extension) plays in geometry. Without this objective archetype, Malebranche argues, the composition of simple ideas in any given complex idea will be ultimately subjective and hence dangerously arbitrary.

BIBLIOGRAPHY
Primary Sources
Locke, John, *An Examination of Pere Malebranche's Opinion of Seeing all Things in God,* in *W*, vol. ix.
——, *Remarks upon some of Mr Norris' Books,* in *W*, vol. x.
Malebranche, Nicolas, *Oeuvres Complètes,* ed. André Robinet, 20 vols (Paris, 1958–78).

Secondary Literature
Ayers, Michael, *Locke: Epistemology and Ontology* (London and New York, 1991).
Bonno, Gabriel, *Les relations intellectuelles de Locke avec la France,* University of California Publications in Modern Philology, vol. xxxviii, no. 2, pp. 37–264.
Harrison, John, and Peter Laslett, *The Library of John Locke* (Oxford, 1971).
Schuurman, Paul, 'Locke's Logic of Ideas in Context: Content and Structure', *British Journal for the History of Philosophy,* vol. ix (2001), pp. 439–65.
Yolton, John, *Perceptual Acquaintance from Descartes to Reid* (Minneapolis, 1984).
Woolhouse, Roger, *Locke: A Biography* (Cambridge, 2007).

Andrew Pyle

MASHAM, Damaris (née Cudworth) (1658–1708)

Lady Damaris Masham was Locke's closest female friend and a philosopher in her own right. She was the daughter of Ralph Cudworth, Master of Christ's College Cambridge, and leading philosopher of the Cambridge Platonists. She met Locke sometime during the 1680s, probably through their mutual friend, Edward Clark. In their early friendship she inspired Locke to write pastoral love poetry (under the *nom de plume* 'Philander'), but in 1685, shortly after Locke went into voluntary exile in Holland, she married Sir Francis Masham, a gentleman widower and the father of nine children. Locke and Lady Masham nevertheless maintained a correspondence with one another during his exile and resumed acquaintance after his return to England in 1689. Locke was first visitor, and subsequently lodger (Sir Francis required him to pay rent) at the Masham home at the manor of Oates, near High Laver in the county of Essex. It was here, in the presence of Lady Masham, that Locke died, in 1704. In his will, Locke left a substantial legacy to her son, Francis Cudworth Masham. She subsequently wrote a memoir of Locke (Woolhouse, 2003), which was used as a source by Locke's earliest biographers, Le Clerc (Le Clerc, 1705) and Moreri (Moreri, 1717).

Lady Masham's early letters to Locke indicate that her interest in philosophy developed in the context of the Cambridge Platonist environment in which she grew up. She was also familiar with Cartesianism. Her Platonist background is evident in early letters to Locke which discuss the work of the Cambridge Platonist, John Smith, and from the admiration accorded her by John NORRIS, who dedicated his *Reflections upon the Conduct of Human Life* (1690) to her. The little evidence available is insufficient for establishing her early philosophical position unequivocally. But she certainly was receptive to Locke's philosophical views and it was apparently with his encouragement that she published two works of moral philosophy: *A Discourse concerning the Love of God* (1696) and *Occasional Thoughts in Reference to a Vertuous or Christian Life* (1705), both of which were printed anonymously. Her philosophical views can also be gauged from her letters to Locke and her brief correspondence with LEIBNIZ. It was a contemporary debate that provided the occasion for both her books: John Norris's correspondence with Mary Astell, which Norris published as *Letters concerning the Love of God* (1695). Although not intended as a polemical work, or as a specifically Lockean response, Masham's *A Discourse concerning the Love of God* (1696) is directed at Nicolas MALEBRANCHE and his foremost English admirer, Norris. It was Mary Astell's riposte, *The Christian Religion as Professed by a Daughter of the Church* (1705) that gave a polemical edge to the discussion, Astell having taken *A Discourse* to be by Locke. Lady Masham's *Occasional Thoughts* is in part, an answer to Mary Astell's intervention.

Lady Masham's writings on moral philosophy offer an optimistic view of human beings as rational and social creatures motivated by desire for happiness. At issue in *A Discourse concerning the Love of God* are the nature of love, happiness and moral conduct. According to Lady Masham, happiness consists of the enjoyment of pleasure, guided by the exercise of reason towards the greatest happiness, that is, God. The pleasure we take in the created

world leads us to love the creator. Norris had articulated an occasionalist position, in which he maintained that created things are merely the occasional causes of pleasing effects in us. The immediate cause of pleasure for us is God, who is, therefore, the sole and proper object of our love. By contrast, our love of creatures is inferior and secondary to our love of God. Lady Masham denies a distinction between the love of God and the love we bear for created beings. She argues that our love of God is something we learn from observing the world around us, not from a divinely instilled idea of God in our minds. The love of creatures is therefore not a secondary form of love, but an essential means for generating love of God: 'if we lov'd not the Creatures, it is not conceivable how we should love God' (Masham, 1705, p. 62). Masham objects that, by denigrating Gods works, Norris's occasionalism undermines the basis of morality and hence the bonds of human society and the foundation of religion itself. By contrast with Norris, she emphasizes the importance of practical morality, arguing that it is an integral part of religion. *A Discourse* was translated into French by Pierre Coste, Locke's French translator, who had been appointed tutor to Francis Cudworth Masham in 1697.

The *Occasional Thoughts in Reference to a Vertuous or Christian Life* (1705) is also concerned with virtuous conduct, or practical morality. Presented as a discussion of the foundational principles of religious belief, the book deals with several interconnected topics: the role of reason in religion and in ethics, practical morality, and the education of women. Lady Masham emphasizes the moral and practical aspect of religion, rather than its doctrinal content. She argues that moral conduct is central to religious practice and that virtuous living is more important than religious ceremonial. Morality and religion should not, therefore, be separated in religious instruction. Although moral principles exist independently as part of the nature of things, virtuous conduct is something that must be learned. Education is therefore the key means to inculcate virtue, which is to be acquired not through precept but by developing a rational understanding of moral principles. Furthermore, civil and religious liberties are necessary for the exercise of virtue. There are clear echoes of Locke in *Occasional Thoughts*, for example her definition of love as 'complaisance', and in her account of the process of reason – for example her distinction between IDEAS formed by sensation and reflection and between simple and complex ideas. But Lady Masham goes beyond Locke in her treatment of ethics and education: unlike Locke, the focus of her thoughts on education is the education of women. This arises logically from the emphasis she places on the key role that mothers play in the early education of their children, especially in laying the foundations of morality through what they teach them.

Between 1704 and 1705–6, Lady Masham corresponded with Leibniz, at his instigation, perhaps because he hoped initially to have contact with Locke through her. The letters were an opportunity for her to discuss Leibniz's philosophy as well as the philosophy of her father, Ralph Cudworth. Lady Masham knew Leibniz's philosophy only indirectly from the *Journal des sçavans* of 1695, and Bayle's article 'Rorarius' in the first edition of his *Dictionnaire*. The themes of their discussion are connected to the concerns of her other writings. She takes issue with Leibniz on a number of points, particularly his theory of pre-established harmony which she argues is no more than a HYPOTHESIS. She objects that since pre-established harmony does not require soul-body interaction, the structure and organization of bodies are rendered superfluous. In this respect it is open to the same objection that can be brought against occasionalism. She also objects that in its very conception pre-established harmony excludes FREE WILL. Another topic discussed in the letters is her father's doctrine of 'plastic nature', which she defends in response to Pierre Bayle's critique of Cudworth in his *Oeuvres diverses*.

It does no justice to Lady Masham's standing as a philosopher to characterize her thought solely in terms of her philosophical mentors and interlocutors. In the present volume, however, it is relevant to focus on her relationship to Locke, especially since she certainly came under his influence in her later writings – so much so that her books were mistaken as works of his. Her receptivity to Locke's philosophy may be attributed to her Cambridge Platonist background since the areas where she is most in agreement with Locke entail no sacrifice of Cudworthian principles, in particular the foundation of morality in reason and the freedom to act, the view that the end of ethics is human happiness, and that the exercise of virtue requires a right disposition of mind. Common to all three was a firm commitment to religious TOLERATION. Although a sympathetic student of Locke, she did not enter into the debates ensuing upon the publication of Locke's *Essay* – notwithstanding John Norris's attack on it in his *Cursory Reflections upon a Book Call'd Essay concerning Human Understanding* (1690). In this respect her receptivity to Locke is rather different from Catharine Trotter COCKBURN's. The question of Lady Masham's debt to Locke is perhaps easier to answer than the question of his debt to her. There is no doubt that he considered her an intellectual peer, whom he held in the highest esteem. He told Philip van LIMBORCH, 'Her judgement is singularly keen, and I know of few men capable of discussing with such insight the most abstruse subjects ... and of resolving the difficulties they present' (13 March 1691, *Corr.* 1375, vol. iv, p. 237). For her part, Lady Masham regarded Locke as an 'Extraordinarie friend, as well as Extraordinarie Man' (Leibniz, 1875–90, vol. iii p. 315). Locke's references to her in *Some Thoughts concerning Education* indicate that she must have played some role in its final production (though it is Edward Clark who is normally credited). Another area where she may have had some influence may have been revisions and additions to later versions of the *Essay*. But these are questions that remain to be explored.

BIBLIOGRAPHY
Unpublished Sources
Amsterdam University Library, MS M31c.
  Three letters from Lady Masham to Philip
  van Limborch.
Amsterdam University Library, Remonstrants
  MSS J. 57a. Memoir of Locke which forms
  the basis of the 'Eloge de feu Mr. Locke' by
  Jean Le Clerc. For a shortened version of
  this see the entry on Locke in Moreri
  (1717).
London, National Archives, PRO 30/24/20,
  fols 266–7 & 273–4. Letters to
  Shaftesbury.

Primary Sources
Le Clerc, Jean, 'Eloge de feu Mr. Locke',
  *Bibliothèque choisie, pour servir de suite à
  la Bibliothèque universelle*, vol. vi (1705),
  pp. 342–411.
Leibniz, G.W., *Die Philosophischen Schriften
  von Gottfried Wilhelm Leibniz*, ed. C.I.
  Gerhardt, 7 vols (Berlin, 1875–90), vol. iii,
  p. 372.
[Masham, Damaris], *A Discourse concern-
  ing the Love of God*. French translation:
  Discours sur l'Amour Divin (Amsterdam,
  1705).
———, *Occasional Thoughts in Reference to
  a Vertuous or Christian Life* (1705, 2nd
  printing, misattributed to Locke, with title,
  Thoughts on a Christian Life, 1747).
———, *The Philosophical Works of Damaris,
  Lady Masham*, with an introduction by
  James G. Buickerood (Bristol, 2004).
Moreri, Louis, *Le grand dictionaire his-
  torique*, 3 vols (Amsterdam, 1717).

Secondary Sources
Broad, Jacqueline, *Women Philosophers of
  the Seventeenth Century* (Cambridge,
  2003a).
———, 'Adversaries or Allies? Occasional
  Thoughts on the Masham-Astell
  Exchange', *Eighteenth Century Thought*
  (2003b), pp. 123–49.
———, 'A Woman's Influence? John Locke
  and Damaris Masham on Moral
  Accountability', *Journal of the History of
  Ideas*, vol. lxvii (2006), pp. 489–510.
Buickerood, James G., 'Masham, Damaris',
  in Andrew Pyle (ed.), *The Dictionary of
  Seventeenth-Century Philosophy*, 2 vols
  (Bristol, 2000), vol. ii pp. 559–62.
Frankel, Lois, 'Damaris Cudworth Masham,
  a Seventeenth-Century Feminist
  Philosopher', *Hypatia*, vol. iv (1989), pp.
  80–90.
Goldie, Mark, 'John Locke and the Mashams
  at Oates' (Cambridge, 2004).
Hill, Bridget, 'Masham (née Cudworth)
  Damaris', *Oxford Dictionary of National
  Biography*, s.v. Masham (Oxford, 2004).
Hutton, Sarah, 'Damaris Cudworth, Lady
  Masham: Between Platonism and
  Enlightenment', *British Journal for the
  History of Philosophy*, vol. i (1993), pp.
  29–54.
———. 'Lady Damaris Masham', *Stanford
  Enclycopedia of Philosophy*,
  http://plato.stanford.edu/entries/lady-
  masham/.
Laslett, Peter, 'Masham of Oates', *History
  Today*, vol. iii (1953), pp. 535–43.
Phemister, Pauline, '"All the time and every-
  where, everything's the same as here": the
  Principle of Uniformity in Leibniz's
  Correspondence with Lady Masham', in
  Paul Lodge (ed.), *Leibniz and his
  Correspondents* (Cambridge, 2004), pp.
  193–213.
———, and Justin Smith, 'Leibniz and the
  Cambridge Platonists and the Debate over
  Plastic Natures', in Pauline Phemister and
  Stuart Brown (eds), *Leibniz's Philosophy
  and the English-Speaking World*
  (Dordrecht, 2007), pp. 95–110.
Ready, Kathryn, 'Damaris Cudworth
  Masham, Catharine Trotter Cockburn,
  and the Feminist Legacy of Locke's Theory
  of Personal Identity', *Eighteenth-Century
  Studies*, vol. xxxv (2002), pp. 563–76.
Simonutti, Luisa, 'Damaris Cudworth
  Masham: una Lady della Repubblica delle

Lettere', *Studi in Onore di Eugenio Garin* (Pisa, 1987), pp. 141–65.

Sleigh, Robert C., 'Reflections on the Masham Correspondence', in Christia Mercer and Eileen O'Neill (eds), *Early Modern Philosophy: Mind, Matter, and Metaphysics* (Oxford, 2005), pp. 119–27.

Widmaier, Rita, 'Korrespondenten von G.W. Leibniz. 8. Damaris Masham, geb. Cudworth', *Studia Leibnitiana*, vol. xviii (1986), pp. 211–27.

Wilson, Catherine, 'Love of God and Love of Creatures: The Astell-Masham Debate', *History of Philosophy Quarterly*, vol. xxi (2004), pp. 281–98.

Woolhouse, Roger, 'Lady Masham's Account of Locke', *Locke Studies*, vol. iii (2003), pp. 167–93.

Sarah Hutton

NEWTON, Isaac (1642–1727)

Isaac Newton was the outstanding natural philosopher of his, and some would say, of any age. He was born in Woolsthorpe, near Grantham, Lincolnshire, on Christmas Day 1642, his father having died before he was born. His mother remarried when he was three and left him in the care of her parents. He was educated in Grantham and in 1661 he entered Trinity College, Cambridge, where he graduated BA in 1665. He was elected to a fellowship in 1668, which was recognition of his ability, confirmed in the following year by his election to the Lucasian chair of mathematics. Even at this young age, Newton was already beginning to make some of his most important discoveries. When in 1665 plague caused the closure of the university, Newton retreated to Woolsthorpe. It was there, as he tells us, that 'I was in the prime of my age for invention & minded Mathematicks & Philosophy more

than at any time since' (cf. Westfall, p. 143). He was elected a Fellow of the Royal Society in 1675 and met Robert BOYLE there. Locke had been elected a Fellow in 1668 but there is no evidence that they actually met until 1689, which is not so surprising when we remember that Newton was rarely in London before 1688 and Locke was often abroad in the intervening years. In the meantime Newton was engaged in a variety of branches of natural philosophy and in mathematics, including his invention of the infinitesimal calculus. His supposition of the earth's gravity extending to the moon caused him to engage in a substantial body of mathematical physics which was, under the encouragement of Edmund Halley especially, to emerge in 1687 as the *Philosophiae Naturalis Principia Mathematica*, the *Principia*, that was to revolutionize our understanding of the universe. In 1687 Locke was in Holland, where he had retreated in 1683, and it was there that he read Newton's work and wrote a review of it for Le Clerc's *Bibliothèque universelle* in 1688 (cf. Axtell, 1965b and Milton, forthcoming).

The *Principia* made Newton famous in England and he was soon to be acknowledged more widely elsewhere. But in its first edition, especially, it is philosophically an austere work giving few clues as to Newton's methodological assumptions or his ontology. However, his manuscript notebooks, his correspondence and his later works, including the second and third editions of the *Principia*, allow us to see further into his philosophy. Through them we can see Newton moving from the philosophy of the Cambridge Platonists to a Lockean empiricism. To appreciate this we must remember that, when Newton went to Cambridge, the major philosophers in the university were Ralph Cudworth, then Master of Christ's College, and Henry More, also of Christ's – both leading members of the Cambridge Platonists. As the name implies, they argued a philosophical position which owed much to the thought of Plato, a version of Christian Platonism, and thus a commitment to innate ideas in epistemology combined with a strong dualism which owed much to DESCARTES. But whilst Descartes had held that mind was essentially not extended but active, both More and Cudworth believed that mind was extended but, unlike matter, was not solid. Matter, on the other hand, was passive. In so far as nature was active it was because of the presence of active spirit as a causal agent, and its presence was witnessed by gravitation and magnetism, and by human action.

More, like Newton, came from Grantham and they came to know each other in Cambridge and to discuss theology (cf. Westfall, pp. 348–9). Further, as a young man Newton made extensive notes from More's *The Immortality of the Soul* (1659), which are preserved in one of his undergraduate notebooks (University of Cambridge, Library MS. Add. 3996; cf. McGuire and Tamny, 1983; Rogers, 1979). More's influence on Newton is now widely accepted, especially in his account of absolute space (cf., for example, Power, 1970). But it is less clear how much else he took from More's wider philosophy, for the simple reason that Newton left comparatively few traces of his wider philosophical commitments. This lack of a paper trail suggests that his primary interests were not narrowly philosophical but were rooted in his wider concern with natural philosophy and especially in mathematical physics, optics and mathematics. But it is not unreasonable to suppose a link between More's account of spirit and Newton's commitment to active and passive principles in nature.

Another philosopher whose works Newton did read with consideration and attention was Descartes and in many ways it was reading Descartes's works that set the agenda for much of his work in natural philosophy. Through his study of Descartes's geometry and other mathematical works he soon revealed himself to be a mathematician of the highest quality, which led to his chair appointment in 1669. But Newton also read the works of many other contemporary thinkers including Robert Boyle,

Kenelm Digby, Joseph Glanvill, Galileo, Thomas HOBBES, Pierre Gassendi and Walter Charleton. In about 1668 Newton added another scientific interest to his enquiries: chemistry, a discipline in anything like its modern form only just then taking shape as it gradually broke free of the alchemical theory and practice in which it had substantially been buried.

As we have noted, there is no reason to believe that Newton and Locke became personally acquainted until Locke's return from Holland in early 1689, probably at Lord Pembroke's London salon. But already the Royal Society was a common factor and leading fellows such as Robert Boyle were mutual friends. It was not long before they were exchanging ideas in an atmosphere of mutual respect that developed into a real and strong friendship. That Newton and Locke should be attracted towards each other is no surprise. By the end of 1689 each was the author of a work that was to be regarded as paradigmatic in its respective sphere for well over a century, but they were at that stage only beginning to make their wider mark on the intellectual world in Europe and beyond. As we have seen, Locke had already read the *Principia* in Holland and his regard for its author was to be found in the Epistle to the Reader of his own great work where he had written of himself as the under-labourer for the masterbuilders, BOYLE, SYDENHAM, Huygens and 'the incomparable Mr Newton' (*E*, p. 10). Newton was the recipient of a presentation copy of the *Essay* which is still extant and shows clear evidence of having been read by its owner, which is also confirmed by their correspondence. It is worth noting what has often been ignored by commentators, that Locke only ever saw the first edition of the *Principia*, though the copy he owned was given him by Newton with the latter's hand corrections of minor printing errors, showing Newton's personal commitment to the recipient (cf. Harrison, 1965, p. 195). In March 1690 Newton sent Locke a substantial manuscript of about 2,500 words, 'A Demonstration That the Planets, by their gravity towards the Sun, may move in Ellipses' (Newton, 1959, vol. iii, pp. 71–7), which strongly suggests that the content of the *Principia* had early been a subject of mutual conversation. We shall return to the epistemological content of Newton's philosophy later. We need first to follow through the personal relationship between the two men as it was to develop in the remaining years of Locke's life.

The first extant letter from Newton to Locke of October 1690 alludes to common interest in theological questions which no doubt had been the subject of either earlier exchanges or conversation in London in the year since they had met. Newton's theology was not orthodox and he shared with Locke more than a suspicion that the usual texts cited to establish the Trinitarian doctrine were corrupt and later interpolations into Scripture. According to his biographer, they were views he had not dared share with anyone else (Westfall, 1980, p. 490). Both Newton and Locke were well aware that there was danger in holding publicly such positions. That they were prepared to exchange opinions itself implies a considerable mutual confidence of trust. Newton sent Locke a long manuscript of some 19,000 words on the texts of I John 5:7 and I Timothy 3.16 in which he argued their corruption towards a Trinitarian reading. He sent it so that Locke could pass it on anonymously to Jean Le Clerc in Holland for translation into French and possible publication. He soon changed his mind about publication and Locke was able to stop it appearing (cf. *Correspondence*, no. 1465, 4, p. 387–8; Westfall, p. 491). When Locke moved to Oates as his home in December 1690, Newton was evidently keen for their conversation to continue for in February 1691 he paid Locke a visit. Newton hoped he had not overstayed (Newton, 1959, vol. iv, p. 197).

Other matters of mutual interest also held their attention. In June Newton indicated that Locke was involved in attempting to obtain a post at the London Mint for him. Newton's letter of June refers to this and to visual experiments and the continuing theological enquiries.

Locke's support was also later crucial for Newton's appointment as Warden of the Mint in 1696. In 1692 there was an exchange on alchemical, or perhaps more correctly called chemical, interests, which resulted in Locke sending Newton some 'red earth' that was connected with experiments that had been conducted by Robert Boyle. Locke had been appointed by Boyle in his will to carry out 'the inspection of his papers' (Newton, 1959, vol. iv, p. 485) and Locke sent copies of two of these to Newton. He visited Newton in Cambridge at the latter's invitation. Later, in April 1693, Locke apparently invited Newton (and Newton's young friend, the sickly Fatio de Duillier) to settle with the MASHAM household at Oates (Newton, 1959, vol. iv, p. 391).

We come now to the strangest incident in the relationship between Locke and Newton. It seems that it is beyond question that in the summer of 1693 Newton had something approaching a mental breakdown. He wrote disturbed letters to both Samuel Pepys and Locke and there is plenty of independent evidence of his state of mind. In his letter of 16 September 1693 Newton apologized for having thought that Locke intended 'to embroil [him] with weomen … I beg your pardon for having hard thoughts of you … and for representing that you struck at the root of morality in a principle you laid down in your book of Ideas and designed to pursue in another book and that I took you for a Hobbist …' (*Corr.* vol. iv p. 727). Aside from the implausibility of Locke trying to engage Newton with dubious female companionship, the philosophical interest of the letter is that it seems to suggest that at this stage Newton was still willing to cite the standard Cambridge view that our knowledge of right and wrong derived from innate ideas and it was the rejection of this position that he found unacceptable in Locke's work. His accusation that Locke was a Hobbist might well derive from the fact that at certain points in the *Essay* Locke appears to identify, in a Hobbist fashion, good and evil with pleasure and pain (e.g. *E*, II. xxviii. 5, p. 351), a passage to which

Newton appears to have drawn attention in his own copy (cf. Rogers, 1979, pp. 199–200). Locke's response to Newton's admission and apology was warm and forgiving, and their friendship continued without further eruptions.

We now make the promised return to the epistemological content of Newton's *Principia* through its three editions. It is for our purposes an important fact that the epistemological content of the first edition is considerably less than that of the two later ones, published long after Locke's death. Thus the *Regulae Philosophandi* of Book 3 of the *Principia* only appear in that form in the second edition. In the first edition under the generic title 'Hypotheses' are listed two of the later rules and a series of phenomena. But it is only in the third edition of 1726, not long before Newton's death, that the full methodological force of the four *regulae philosophandi* can be seen. A draft projected Rule 5 in Newton's hand also exists, which sets out an unambiguously Lockean epistemology. This arises as part of Newton's rejection of hypotheses in natural philosophy and the draft rule contains the following: 'Whatever is not derived from things themselves, whether by the eternal senses or by the sensation of internal thoughts, is to be taken for a HYPOTHESIS. Thus I sense that I am thinking, which could not happen unless at the same time I were to sense that I am. But I do not sense that any idea whatever may be innate ...' (Koyré, 1965, p. 272). That Newton never published this draft Rule is probably because he did not wish to become embroiled in philosophical dispute. But it is an important fact that it strongly implies that by the end of his life he was philosophically a Lockean. His rejection of innate ideas can scarcely be given any other reading, especially, as we have already seen, that at the time of his mental difficulties in 1693 he was almost certainly a believer in innate ideas.

The *Principia* was not Newton's only major work in natural philosophy. His other was the *Opticks* of 1704, published only months before Locke's death. A presentation copy was in Locke's final library and they had from time to time discussed optical matters in their correspondence and, doubtless, also at their meetings. There is no doubt that Locke accepted Newton's work and Newton's account of light and the mechanics of the *Principia* are incorporated in his *Elements of Natural Philosophy* (W, vol. iii, pp. 303–30), an elementary and brief educational text, written towards the end of his life, whose contents he may well have discussed with Newton (Axtell, 1965a). As with the *Principia*, Locke saw only the first edition of the *Opticks* but, and again paralleling the *Principia*, it was in the later editions of 1717, and 1730 especially, that Newton, in the Queries added at the end of the work, expanded on philosophical themes. It is perhaps significant that in the closing paragraphs Newton describes what he understood as the correct method to be followed in natural philosophy: 'This consists ... in making Experiments and Observations, and in drawing general Conclusions from them by Induction, and admitting of no Objections against the Conclusions, but such as are taken from Experiments or other certain Truths. For Hypotheses are not to be regarded in experimental Philosophy ...' (Newton, 1952, p. 404). Locke would have been very happy to endorse these sentiments of his friend.

BIBLIOGRAPHY
Primary Sources
Newton, Isaac, *Philosophiae Naturalis Principia Mathematica* (1687; 2nd edn, 1713; 3rd edn, 1726; trans. as *Mathematical Principles of Natural Philosophy*, 2 vols, 1729). See also *The Principia. A New Translation*, by I. Bernard Cohen and Anne Whitman (Berkeley, 1999).
——, *Opticks*, (1704; 2nd edn, 1717; 4th edn, 1730; modern Dover edn, 1952).
——, *The Correspondence of Isaac Newton*, ed. H.W. Turnbull et al., 7 vols (Cambridge, 1959–77).
——, *Certain Philosophical Questions. Newton's Trinity Notebook*, ed. J.E.

McGuire and Martin Tamny (Cambridge, 1983).

Secondary Sources

Axtell, James, 'Locke, Newton and the 'Elements of Natural Philosophy,' *Paedagogica Europaea*, vol. i (1965a), pp. 235–45.

——, 'Locke's Review of the *Principia*,' *Notes and Records of the Royal Society*, vol. xx (1965b), pp. 152–61.

Harrison, John, and Peter Laslett, *The Library of John Locke* (Oxford, 1965).

Koyré, Alexandre, *Newtonian Studies* (Chicago, 1965).

Milton, J.R., 'Locke's Contributions to the *Bibliothèque universelle et historique*', *British Journal for the History of Philosophy* (forthcoming).

Power, E., 'Henry More and Isaac Newton on Absolute Space', *Journal of the History of Ideas*, vol. xxxi (1970), pp. 289–96.

Rogers, G.A.J., 'Locke's *Essay* and Newton's *Principia*,' *Journal of the History of Ideas*, vol. xxxix (1978), pp. 217–32.

——, 'Locke, Newton, and the Cambridge Platonists on Innate Ideas', *Journal of the History of Ideas*, vol. xl (1979), pp. 191–206.

Westfall, Richard S., *Never at Rest. A Biography of Isaac Newton* (Cambridge, 1980).

Manuscript Holdings

University of Cambridge, Library MS Add. 3996, Isaac Newton: Undergraduate Notebook.

G.A.J. Rogers

SHAFTESBURY, First Earl of (1621–83)

Anthony Ashley Cooper inherited his father's baronetcy at the age of nine, was raised to the peerage as Lord Ashley in 1661, and became first Earl of Shaftesbury in 1672. He first met Locke – quite by chance – in the summer of 1666, while visiting Oxford, and subsequently invited him to join his household in London. Locke lived with his new patron at Exeter House, in the Strand, from May 1667 until November 1675, when he departed for France. On his return to England at the end of April 1679 he resumed contact with the household, now at Thanet House, in Aldersgate Street, though he was much less closely involved with Shaftesbury's affairs.

Shaftesbury seems to have been regarded by his contemporaries as able, versatile and slippery – it was not for nothing that he was known as the Dorsetshire Eel (Haley, 1968, p. 742) – and even a brief survey of his earlier career can explain why. In the Civil War he began by fighting for the king, and then defected to parliament. Never a fanatic, he played no part in the trial and condemnation of Charles I, but after his death took the oath of engagement to the new regime, re-entering public life as an MP in the Barebones Parliament and a member of Cromwell's Council of State (1653–4), though he subsequently fell out of favour with the Lord Protector. He was never trusted by either the hard-line republicans or the leaders of the army, but it was not until the spring of 1660, when the restoration of the monarchy had become inevitable, that he moved visibly and decisively into the royalist camp. His reward was a place in the Privy Council and subsequently a seat in the House of Lords, as Baron Ashley of Wimborne St Giles, the family seat in Dorset.

Ashley's ministerial career in the 1660s – as Chancellor of the Exchequer, then a second-rank post – was uneventful. He was not trusted by the king – though Charles was not much inclined to trust anyone – and was not regarded with favour by his most powerful minister, the

Earl of Clarendon. After Clarendon's fall in 1667 the ministry became known to contemporaries (and to posterity) as the 'Cabal', after the names of its main members – Clifford, Arlington, Buckingham, Ashley and Lauderdale – but Ashley's inclusion in the group had perhaps more to do with the need to complete the acronym than his actual influence at the centre of government. For a long time his health had been poor, and in 1668 he underwent a novel and extremely dangerous operation to drain a cyst on his liver. Locke seems to have recommended the operation, though he certainly did not perform it himself, and – according to Locke at least – Ashley subsequently acknowledged that he owed his life to Locke's care (Locke to Pembroke, 28 November 1684, *Corr.*, vol. ii, p. 662).

In April 1672 Ashley was created Earl of Shaftesbury, and in November appointed Lord Chancellor, an office he held for just less than a year. It was the pinnacle of his ministerial career. By virtue of his office he became publicly linked with a set of royal policies that were widely unpopular – the Stop of the Exchequer in January 1672, when the government suspended payments to its creditors, the Declaration of Indulgence two months later, when TOLERATION was granted to both Catholics and Protestant dissenters by royal prerogative, and above all the third Dutch War (1672–4), when England appeared to be betraying her own interest by helping Louis XIV extinguish one of the main bastions of the Protestant cause in Europe, the Dutch republic. After Shaftesbury was dismissed in November 1673, he moved rapidly into opposition. The most public manifestation of his alienation from the new government, headed by the Earl of Danby, was in the spring of 1675, when he led the opposition in the House of Lords to a new Test Bill instigated by Danby that would have required all office holders to take an oath promising not to propose or support any alterations in government in either Church or state. The bill never became law, but November saw the publication of an anonymous pamphlet, *A Letter from a Person of Quality to his Friend in the Country*, which attacked in violent terms Danby's bill and its supporters, and (by implication) the whole course of royal policy since the Restoration. As contemporary observers at once recognized, Shaftesbury was behind its publication, and there are grounds – albeit less secure ones – for supposing that Locke was also involved. Locke left for a three-year visit to France a few days after the *Letter*'s publication, though as this had been arranged some time previously there is no reason to suppose he was trying to escape from the searches being undertaken for those responsible (*ETol.*, pp. 99–101).

Shaftesbury remained in England, and spent a year in prison in the Tower of London (February 1677–February 1678) for having claimed that Charles's failure to summon parliament meant that legally it had been dissolved. It was eventually dissolved in January 1679, and its successor met in March, nearly two months before Locke's return from France: Shaftesbury and his associates in the nascent Whig party had a comfortable majority in the House of Commons, though their control of the Lords was less secure.

The years from 1679 to 1683 are among the most turbulent of English political history. Shaftesbury, who had never quite been in the front rank of Charles's ministers when in office, was now clearly the most capable, most resourceful and most dangerous of his opponents. The chief political issue was Exclusion: the ultimately unsuccessful attempt by Shaftesbury and his allies to force through parliament a bill that would exclude the Duke of York from the succession to the throne. The last parliament of Charles's reign – the last indeed ever to meet anywhere except Westminster – was called in Oxford in March 1681; Locke attended to much of the business of finding accommodation for Shaftesbury and his associates. The parliament was dissolved after sitting for a week. In July Shaftesbury was arrested and sent to the Tower of London, charged with treason; he was to remain there until the end of November, when a grand jury packed with his supporters declined to indict him, and he had to be released. Locke's main contribution to his defence was to write a short tract on the legal principles involved in the selection of members of grand juries; it was not printed, and remained unnoticed among the Shaftesbury Papers until it was published in 1997 (*ETol.*, pp. 118–36, 377–82). Shaftesbury's grand jury had been selected by the sheriffs of the City of London, who were staunch Whigs, and when the shrieval elections in the following summer produced two Tories, he was no longer safe. After the new sheriffs took up their posts in the autumn he went into hiding and then fled to Holland, where he died in January 1683.

Some aspects of Locke's involvement in Shaftesbury's affairs are very well documented, while others are much more obscure. One thing beyond doubt is that Locke regarded his former patron with unstinted admiration. In the words of the epitaph Locke wrote for him, probably a short time before his own death, Shaftesbury was praised as a vigorous and unwearied defender of civil and religious liberty: 'In courtesy, sharpness of understanding, persuasiveness, judgement, courage, perseverance, faithfulness, you will scarcely find an equal anywhere, and nowhere a superior' (translated from *W*, vol. ix, p. 281). Similar praise was recorded by both of Locke's earliest biographers, Jean Le Clerc and Pierre Coste. How Shaftesbury regarded Locke is much less clear, but there is little reason to assent to Richard Ashcraft's description of Locke as Shaftesbury's 'most intimate friend' (Ashcraft, 1986, p. 83), or to suppose that he was his confidential political adviser. When Shaftesbury dined at Exeter House, Locke was not even on the same table (National Archives, PRO 30/24/4/236; PRO 30/24/5/264/2), and when he died, Locke was left nothing in his will.

There is, however, no doubt that Locke undertook a very large amount of secretarial and administrative work for his patron, almost all of it during his first period as a member of Shaftesbury's household, at Exeter House. To judge from the surviving records in the Shaftesbury Papers and elsewhere, a considerable part of it was concerned with Shaftesbury's colonial interests in Carolina, but Locke was also closely involved with ecclesiastical patronage when Shaftesbury was Lord Chancellor, and with parliamentary business. After 1679, when Shaftesbury was at Thanet House, there is far less material in Locke's hand: Shaftesbury had a new secretary – Samuel Wilson – and Locke spent an increasingly large part of his time away from London, mostly either in Oxford or staying nearby in Oakley with James Tyrrell.

Two works that were certainly written for Shaftesbury were attributed to Locke by Pierre Des Maizeaux (Locke, 1720): the *Fundamental Constitutions of Carolina* and the *Letter from a Person of Quality*. Locke certainly had a hand in the composition of the first of these, and perhaps of the second also, though it is likely that both are composite works. However, even if Locke was acting as Shaftesbury's 'assistant pen' – to use the phrase of the third Earl (Shaftesbury to Le Clerc, 8 Feb. 1705, Barrell, 1989, p. 86) – neither work can safely be used as a source of Locke's own opinions, whether on slavery, government or any other matter.

How much Shaftesbury knew about Locke's own compositions can only be a matter of speculation. The *Essay concerning Toleration* that Locke began soon after arriving at Exeter House may have been started as a result of discussions between Locke and his new patron, but it may also have been a purely private investigation initiated by Locke himself. The same is true of the paper on rates of interest begun in 1668. The discussions with the five or six friends meeting at Locke's chamber that led to the writing of the *Essay concerning Human Understanding* probably took place at Exeter House, but there is no reason to suppose that Shaftesbury was present, or that he had any interest in the project.

The work whose possible connection with Shaftesbury has attracted most comment is the *Two Treatises of Government*. As a result of the investigations undertaken by Peter Laslett, it is now generally agreed that both parts of this were written between April 1679, when Locke returned from France, and August 1683, when he fled into exile in the Netherlands, with only minor changes being made before publication at the end of 1689. Locke and Shaftesbury shared a common political outlook, and it is tempting to embed the *Two Treatises* in its putative political context by trying to relate it to Shaftesbury's own campaigns and projects during these years. There are, however, serious problems in doing this. Until the failure of the Oxford Parliament in the spring of 1681 Shaftesbury's main concern was Exclusion: persuading (or rather coercing) the king into allowing parliament to meet, and then forcing through a bill to exclude the Duke of York from the throne. There is little or nothing in either the First or the Second Treatise that bears directly on this, and it is striking that the issue that had generated the whole crisis – James's conversion and very public adherence to Catholicism – was not discussed at all, even in the most general terms. In the summer and autumn of 1681 Shaftesbury was in the Tower, and it is clear that his main concern was to avoid a trial for high treason that would almost certainly have resulted in his conviction and execution. There is some reason for supposing that Locke was thinking hard about the foundations of government during these months, but it is unlikely that his patron was: he had other matters on his mind.

In 1682, after the failure of the Exclusion project had become apparent, Shaftesbury's thoughts turned towards armed resistance. Whether Locke knew much about these projects is very doubtful: he was never named by any of the conspirators, and was not even in London in the autumn of 1682, when the final planning for the abortive insurrection was taking place. This is a period of Shaftesbury's life when even his closest associates feared that his hitherto excellent judgement of men and affairs had started to break down, with his wild talk of 10,000 'brisk boys' from Wapping who would join in an insurrection, and his fan-

tasies of 'dy[ing]' at the head of the People of England fighting for their Libertyes and in their Cause' (National Archives, PRO 30/24/17/18, fol. 34v.). Locke was a very cautious man indeed: if he knew anything about what was being planned – and it is not clear that he did – he would almost certainly have wished to distance himself from it in any way that he could manage.

There are some parallels between Shaftesbury's plotting and the later chapters of the Second Treatise, especially those on Tyranny and on the Dissolution of Government. It is, however, very unlikely that either of these chapters – or indeed any other part of the Second Treatise – was written as a manifesto for an insurrection: Locke's aim, here as elsewhere, was not to spur men into action, but to change the way they thought about fundamental principles.

When Shaftesbury was slowly dying in Amsterdam in January 1683, it is unlikely that he thought much about his former secretary. He would undoubtedly have recognized Locke as a man of considerable, even exceptional ability, but it is not at all certain that he cared much – or even knew much – about the incomplete and unpublished writings that Locke kept carefully locked away in his desk, or in the various boxes and chests in his room. He would certainly have had no intimations whatever that Locke's fame would eventually surpass his own.

BIBLIOGRAPHY
Unpublished Sources
National Archives, Kew, Shaftesbury Papers, PRO 30/24/4/236; PRO 30/24/5/264/2; PRO 30/24/17/18.

Primary Sources
Barrell, Rex A. (ed.), *Anthony Ashley Cooper Earl of Shaftesbury (1671–1713) and 'Le Refuge Français'-Correspondence* (Lewiston, New York, 1989).
Locke, John, *A Collection of Several Pieces of Mr. John Locke* (London, 1720).

Secondary Literature

Ashcraft, Richard, *Revolutionary Politics & Locke's Two Treatises of Government* (Princeton, 1986).

Haley, K.H.D., *The First Earl of Shaftesbury* (Oxford, 1968).

Milton, J.R., 'The Unscholastic Statesman: Locke and the Earl of Shaftesbury', in John Spurr (ed.), *Anthony Ashley Cooper, First Earl of Shaftesbury 1621–1683* (Farnham, 2011).

Milton, Philip, 'John Locke and the Rye House Plot', *Historical Journal*, vol. xliii (2000), pp. 647–68.

J.R. Milton

SYDENHAM, Thomas (1624–89)

If Anthony Ashley Cooper, first Earl of SHAFTESBURY, had the greatest impact on Locke's life and politics, Thomas Sydenham had the greatest impact on his philosophy. Sydenham's studies at Oxford in the early 1640s were interrupted by the Civil War. From a staunchly parliamentarian family, Sydenham served alongside his brothers Francis, John and William in the parliamentary army. Returning to college in 1646 after fighting had ceased, Sydenham travelled to London with the physician Thomas Coxe, who was then treating one of Sydenham's brothers. Coxe, a member of Samuel Hartlib's circle, interested Sydenham in medicine, and gave some direction to what was, up to that point, Sydenham's undistinguished academic career (Sydenham, 1848–50, vol. i, p. 3). Parliament wished to have oversight of the universities and, upon returning to Oxford in 1647, Sydenham was appointed as delegate to Wadham College. He there oversaw the expulsion of some twenty-two members of staff for failing to take the 'Negative Oath' – an oath not to support the king. Perhaps as a reward for his service, Sydenham was awarded a medical baccalaureate on the final day of expulsions.

Fighting resumed intermittently and, on 21 April 1651, Sydenham accepted a commission as captain of a cavalry regiment. More heavy combat likely followed and, Sydenham later reported, he was once left for dead on the battlefield. The war over, Sydenham appears to have resumed his medical studies in Oxford, though details of the development of his methodology are sketchy. Researchers were then working on a wide range of problems – for example, the application of chemistry to medicine, the circulation of the blood, the purpose of respiration, and DESCARTES's mechanical philosophy. There is, however, no record of Sydenham taking part in such researches. It is easy to imagine academic pursuits taxing the patience of a battle-hardened veteran. When asked in later life what books should be read to prepare for medical practice, Sydenham replied, 'Read Don Quixot, it is a very good Book, I read it still' (Meynell, 1988, p. 71).

It is not clear when he first began treating patients, but his move to London in 1655 may have been decisive. His practice there was never fashionable, and the bulk of his patients were from middling professions – though he also treated the poor, who were daily callers at his home in Pall Mall. One of his neighbours, Lady Ranelagh, was the sister of Robert BOYLE. Boyle stayed with his sister when in London, and this may have occasioned the first acquaintance between the two men. The Restoration dashed any hopes Sydenham might have had for additional preferment, and it was around this time that, under Boyle's 'persuasion and recommendation', he began systematically compiling empirical observations of different disease types, and their most effective means of cure (Sydenham, 1987, p. 5; I.KJ).

This compilation was eventually to lead, in 1666, to Sydenham's first publication – *Thomae Sydenham Methodus curandi febres, propriis observationibus superstructa* – 'Thomas Sydenham's method of curing fevers based on his own observations'. Sydenham held that nature was often its own best defence, and that doctors should try to assist natural processes, rather than fight them. His book presented only a minimal theoretical structure, rejecting hypotheses about the nature of the body or disease. He was adamant that it was impossible to determine the causes of illness: 'Aetiology is a difficult, and, perhaps, an inexplicable affair; and I choose to keep my hands clear of it' (op. cit., p. 103). It was nonetheless clear that there were 'species of fever' which acted in a systematic way: 'Nature here as elsewhere, moves in a regular and orderly manner' (ibid.). But as to the essence of these disease species

if any one, I say, requires an answer upon all these points, I am ready to confess my ignorance. No one, that I know of, has hitherto gone far enough in such matters to flatter himself for having solved these problems of Nature. For my own part, I am not ambitious of the name of a Philosopher, and those who think themselves so, may, perhaps, consider me blameable on the score of my not having attempted to pierce these mysteries (op. cit., p. 101).

As such, experience was the sole touchstone of effective therapy: 'To some it may appear that the method which I adopt is based upon insecure foundations. I am, however, on my part, fully convinced, and I truly affirm, that it [is] altogether proved by a manifest experience (op. cit., p. 9). This unconventional approach was clearest in his management of smallpox. Contemporary physicians saw the speedy expulsion of the morbific matter as imperative – the sooner it was expelled, the sooner the patient would recover. Thus, to hasten matters, they would warm the patient. Sydenham let nature take its course, and found, through careful and continued observation, that light cooling was a more effective treatment. Such unorthodoxy provoked indignation from the established medical community, who were simply not prepared to accept the advice of an

upstart 'empirick' of limited training, dubious credentials and questionable politics.

In the spring of 1667 Locke moved to London to take up residence in Ashley's household. At Oxford, Locke had been one of those engaged in cutting-edge natural philosophical research. He had read widely, taken copious notes, tried experimental chemistry, written his own speculative theory of disease and put forward hypotheses on the nature of respiration. He had never treated a patient. He was, in short, precisely the sort of academic physician Sydenham had in mind when he lamented that 'one had as good send a man to Oxford to learn shoemaking as practising physick' (Meynell, 1988, p. 68). Locke's 'empiricism' had been expressed clearly in the *Essays on the Law of Nature* from the mid-1660s, and he was very much a 'modern' in outlook. He worked closely with some of the most talented thinkers of his day – Hooke, Willis, Lower and Boyle – and favoured the Helmontian HYPOTHESIS in natural philosophy. But the character of his empiricism and the nature of his modernism were to undergo a radical transformation at Sydenham's hand.

Boyle was the dedicatee of the *Methodus*, and may have recommended the author and the book to Locke, who had read it before arriving in London (Walmsley, 2008, n. 14). On 2 April 1668 Sydenham sent Boyle a letter concerning a second edition of the *Methodus* and noting the help of a new acquaintance: 'I perceive my friend, Mr. Locke, hath troubled you with an account of my practice, as he hath done himself in visiting with me very many of my variolous patients especially' (Dewhurst, 1966, p. 163). As well as attending visits to patients, Locke assisted in the preparation of the second edition, which contained a new chapter on the plague. Locke wrote a poem of fulsome praise for Sydenham's methodology:

SYDENHAM, at last, opposing both Fever and the Schools, both fever probed and treatment understood. Not for him, fires of occult corruption or those 'humours' that breed fevers ... Not for him those squabbles whose heat exceeds the fires (Sydenham, 1987, p. 227).

Locke also had a hand in the text's composition, providing a set of references to authors who supported Sydenham's regimen of venesection for the plague, which Sydenham duly noted in the new chapter (Meynell, 1993). In addition, Locke finally began to practise medicine, treating family, friends and even Sydenham's son, William. Locke carefully recorded the symptoms, treatment and progress of his patients – compiling just the clinical observations that Sydenham had recommended. Locke's medical skills were further tested in the successful delivery of Ashley's grandson, and in persuading Ashley to undertake a high-risk, life-saving operation (Meynell, 1988, p. 26).

As well as embracing the practice of medicine, Locke set about defending his new medical outlook in a pair of papers – 'Anatomia' and 'De Arte Medica' (Meynell, 1994). Locke fully embraced Sydenham's methodology and carefully articulated its underlying assumptions. We cannot arrive at an accurate understanding of disease because 'it is certainly some thing more subtile & fine then what our senses can take cognisance of that is the cause of the disease, they are the invisible & insensible spts that governe preserve & disorder the aeconomie of the body' (Dewhurst, 1966, p. 91). The physician must therefore rely upon clinical experience to compile natural histories of diseases: 'how regulate his dose, to mix his simples & to prescribe all in a due method, all this is only from history & the advantage of a diligent observation of these diseases, of their begining progresse & ways of cure' (op. cit., p. 86). More progress has not been made in this regard because doctors had spent time second-guessing nature, when perhaps only God himself can understand his creation, 'it being perhaps noe absurdity to thinke that this great & curious fabrique of the world the workemanship of the almighty cannot be perfectly comprehended by any understandg but his that made it' (op. cit., p. 82).

While in Oxford, Locke had worked hard to determine the nature and purpose of respiration. Such efforts he now dismissed as hopelessly misguided:

whether respiration serve to coole the bloud, or give vent to its vapours, or to adde a fermt to it, or to pound & mix its minute particles or whether any thing else is in dispute amongst the learned from whose controversys about it are like to arise rather more doubts then any cleare determination of the point (Dewhurst, 1966, p. 88).

Locke rejected all theories about natural phenomena, extending his prohibition to Galenic cooling, Helmontian ferments and the mechanists' pounding and mixing of particles.

By 1669 Locke was acting as Sydenham's amanuensis in the composition of a new work on smallpox, to be dedicated to Locke's patron, Ashley. The work never appeared, most likely because Sydenham was in the process of revising his views on disease, concluding that each year had a particular 'constitution' – a unique disease variant that required unique treatment. Over the next few years Sydenham assembled a comprehensive catalogue of these constitutions in a collection of essays entitled *Medical Observations*. These essays formed the core of Sydenham's 1676 *Observationes Medicae* – a landmark in therapeutics that was to secure his reputation. Locke drafted several of these essays at Sydenham's dictation, corrected both his own and Sydenham's work, and made fair copies of these notes for his own use – the last in the spring of 1671. The men were working in close partnership during this principal phase of the book's composition. Sydenham was later to praise Locke in the Dedication to the *Observationes* as a man who 'in the acuteness of his intellect, in the steadiness of his judgement, in the simplicity ... of his manners, has, amongst the present generation, few equals and no superiors' (Sydenham, 1848–50, vol. i, p. 6).

Thus it should occasion no surprise that when Locke began work on the *Essay* that spring of 1671, he should build upon the methodological principles his mentor had impressed upon him. In Draft A, Locke maintained that we have no knowledge of natural causes:

> because these alterations being made by particles soe small & minute that they come not within the observation of my senses I cannot get knowledg how they operate, but only am informd by my senses that the alterations are indeed made from whence by the by we may take a litle light how much in the information of our understandings we are beholding to our senses (Draft A, sect. 15, p. 31).

We should not trouble ourselves with theories about such unobservable processes, but instead settle for what we can know – our own experience: 'the clearest best & most certain knowledg that man kinde can possibly have of things existing without him is but Experience, which is noe thing but the Exercise & observation of his senses about particular objects' (Draft A, sect. 33, pp. 62–3). Such experience may not give us certainty or 'scientific KNOWLEDGE', but it will give us the 'highest degree of Probability':

> such are all the setled constitutions & propertys of natural things & the regular proceedings of causes & effects in the ordinary course of nature. v.g That the sun is sometimes to be seen in Spain. That fire turnd wood into ashes. That a bullet of lead sunke in water. &c. (Draft A, sect. 34, p. 63).

We can only create low-level empirical generalizations about observable processes.

As Locke continued to work on the *Essay* – and his career took him to France, back to England, and into exile in Holland – he kept in touch with the latest developments in

Sydenham's thought and consulted him on particularly difficult cases (Walmsley, 2008, *passim*). While Locke's thinking certainly evolved during the many years of the *Essay*'s development, he never wavered from the fundamental beliefs that Sydenham imparted to him:

> There is not so contemptible a Plant or Animal, that does not confound the most inlarged Understanding ... The Workmanship of the All-wise, and Powerful God, in the great Fabrick of the Universe, and every part thereof, further exceeds the Capacity and Comprehension of the most inquisitive and intelligent Man (*E*, III.vi.9, p. 444).

Since God's creation is too complex for us to understand we cannot discover the internal constitution of bodies or the REAL ESSENCE of species, and must be content with experience alone:

> In the Knowledge of Bodies, we must be content to glean, what we can, from particular Experiments: since we cannot from a Discovery of their real Essences, grasp at a time whole Sheaves; and in bundles, comprehend the Nature and Properties of whole Species together. Where our Enquiry is concerning Co-existence, or Repugnancy to co-exist, which by Contemplation of our *Ideas*, we cannot discover; there Experience, Observation, and NATURAL HISTORY, must give us by our Senses, and by retail, an insight into corporeal Substances (*E*, IV.xii.12, p. 647).

The processes by which nature works are unknown to us. We cannot know the REAL ESSENCES of substances. NATURAL HISTORY is the only means to understand the world. These are the fundamental limits to knowledge that Locke set down in the *Essay*. Such epistemic pessimism was far from the optimistic research of Hooke, Boyle, Willis and Lower – research which Locke had himself been actively pursuing before his acquaintance with Sydenham. Locke's attitude to our knowledge of nature in the *Essay* was, at bottom, Sydenham's medical methodology writ large. No other individual had such a clear and decisive impact on the development of Locke's philosophy.

BIBILIOGRAPHY
Primary Sources
Sydenham, Thomas, *The Works of Thomas Sydenham*, ed. R.G. Latham (London, 1848–50).
——, *Methodus Curandi Febres*, ed. G.G. Meynell (Folkestone, 1987).

Secondary Sources
Dewhurst, Kenneth, Dr. *Thomas Sydenham (1624–1689): His Life and Original Writings* (London, 1966).
Meynell, G.G., *Materials For A Biography Of Dr. Thomas Sydenham* (Folkestone, 1988).
——, 'Sydenham, Locke, and Sydenham's *De peste sive febre pestilentiali*', *Medical History*, vol. xxxvii (1993), pp. 330–2.
——, 'Locke as author of *Anatomia* and *De arte medica*', *The Locke Newsletter*, vol. xxv (1994), pp. 65–73.
Walmsley, Jonathan, 'Sydenham and the Development of Locke's Natural Philosophy', *British Journal for the History of Philosophy*, vol. xvi (2008), pp. 65–83.

Jonathan Walmsley

3

EARLY CRITICS

BERKELEY, George (1685–1753)

On 7 July 1688, William Molyneux addressed a letter to the publishers of the *Bibliothèque Universelle et Historique* (*Corr.*, vol. iii, pp. 482–3), containing 'A Problem Proposed to the Author of the "Essai Philosphique concernant L'Entendement"' regarding an 'Extrait' of this 'Essai' recently published in the journal (Locke, 1688). The author of this 'Extrait', John Locke, certainly received this letter, since it remains amongst his papers, but did not immediately deal with the problem it posed. It was only when Locke and Molyneux became acquainted in 1692, and the matter raised again in a letter of 2 March 1693 (*Corr.*, vol. iv, pp. 647–52), that Locke responded. In the first edition of the *Essay concerning Human Understanding*, Locke had supposed some ideas common to 'divers Senses'; 'we can receive and convey into our minds the ideas of the extension, figure, motion, and rest of bodies, both by seeing and feeling'. Molyneux questioned whether a blind man made to see, and given a globe and a cube, 'by his sight, before he touch'd them, he could now distinguish, and tell, which is the Globe, which the Cube?' The *Essay*'s second edition noted this problem, and agreed with Molyneux that the blind man would not immediately discern the difference by sight alone (*E*, II.ix.8, pp. 145–6).

If Molyneaux influenced the *Essay*'s content, he also played a role in its reception. Founder of the Dublin Philosophical Society, a writer on optics, and MP for the University of Dublin,

Molyneux reported to Locke that 'I was the First that recommended and lent to the Reverend Provost of Our University Dr Ashe, a most Learned and Ingenious Man, Your Essay, with which he was so wonderfully pleased and satisfyd, that he has Orderd it to be read by the Batchelors of the Colledge, and strictly examines them in their Progress therein' (*Corr.*, vol. iv, pp. 601–2). Thus, by the time a fifteen-year old George Berkeley matriculated at Trinity College Dublin in 1700, Locke was central to the CURRICULUM. After graduating BA in 1704, Berkeley devoted himself to mathematics, dedicating *Miscellanea mathematica*, part of his 1707 *Arithmetica Absque Algebra Aut Euclide Demonstrata*, to Molyneux's son, Samuel. Securing a Trinity fellowship that year, he undertook research in mathematics, motion, optics and the 'new philosophy'. A pair of notebooks used from 1707 to 1709, now referred to as the *Philosophical Commentaries*, provide a detailed record of the development of Berkeley's thinking. Locke had purposely avoided investigating the causal origins of ideas – 'I shall not at present meddle with the Physical Consideration of the Mind; or trouble my self to examine, wherein its Essence consists, or by what Motions of our Spirits, or Alterations of our Bodies, we come to have any Sensation by our Organs, or any *Ideas* in our Understandings' (*E*, I.i.2, p. 43). Berkeley, on the contrary, made a point of considering the mechanics of PERCEPTION in detail. Thus, while Locke inspired most of the notes in the *Commentaries*, Molyneux received the first direct reference, because the problem he posed struck at the heart of Locke's account of perception. Where Locke and Molyneux supposed the blind man would not know cube from sphere, Berkeley bluntly stated a more radical conclusion: 'Molyneux's Blind man would not know the sphere or cube to be bodies or extended at first sight' (Berkeley, 1944, item 32) – he would have no notion that the sensations of light and colours had any relation to his sensation of touch, and what he then understood 'bodies' to be. Locke was not just mistaken about ideas of 'divers Senses', his neglect of perception led to significant philosophical misconceptions. Such radical conclusions required substantial support.

Consequently, Berkeley's first major work, *An Essay Towards a New Theory of Vision* (Dublin, 1709), focused on the perceptual processes that Locke had sidestepped. Berkeley's aim was twofold – to 'shew the manner wherein we perceive by sight the distance, magnitude, and situation of objects. Also to consider the difference there is betwixt the ideas of sight and touch, and whether there be any idea common to both senses' (ibid., par. 1). These questions were exactly those raised by the MOLYNEUX PROBLEM. Berkeley argued that, while we correlate visible and tangible sensations through long association, they are in fact completely heterogeneous. Vision gives us ideas of light and colour alone – though changes in these are consistently related to tangible size and shape. Moreover, the spatial 'outness' we ascribe to visual sensations is a learned response to these associations, rather than direct visual perception of an external space. People confuse the association between visible and tangible with commonality. The confusion arises, Berkeley argues, because philosophers have supposed that we can 'abstract' some common 'extension' from ideas of both sight and touch. Using Locke's example of the abstract idea of a triangle, which 'must be neither Oblique, nor Rectangle, neither Equilateral, Equicrural, nor Scalenon; but all and none of these at once' (*E*, IV.vii.9, p. 596), Berkeley simply asserts that such an idea is an evident impossibility – 'abstraction' is a delusion (Berkeley, 1709, pars. 122–7). Thus, while we may use the same NAMES for ideas of sense and touch, they refer to very different things in the different senses. Berkeley concludes by noting that if Molyneux's blind man cannot tell the difference between the sphere and cube by looking, as both Molyneux and Locke concede, it must be because visible and tangible ideas are completely independent (ibid., pars. 132–5).

Berkeley refrained from drawing metaphysical conclusions in his perceptual theorizing – but the implications of this work were not long suppressed. Just after his twenty-fifth birthday, Berkeley published *A Treatise concerning the Principles of Human Knowledge* (Dublin, 1710). Locke's aim in writing the *Essay* was to 'enquire into the Original, Certainty, and Extent of humane Knowledge' (*E*, I.i.2, p. 43). Locke was pessimistic about the scope of our abilities, citing, as an end of his enquiry, a determination of the limits of our understanding; 'to be more cautious in meddling with things exceeding its Comprehension; to stop, when it is at the utmost Extent of its Tether; and sit down in a quiet Ignorance of those Things, which, upon Examination, are found to be beyond the reach of our Capacities' (*E*, I.i.4. pp. 44–5). Locke believed that there was much we were incurably ignorant of – the nature of SUBSTANCE in general, the ESSENCE of any particular substance, anything relating to the infinite. There was also much we could not prove, but must take for granted – for example, the existence of things outside us, or the connection between ideas of secondary qualities and their causes. Berkeley found this attitude deplorable, not least because of the scepticism it was apt to engender. It is not difficult to identify his target in the *Principles'* Introduction: 'It is said that the faculties we have are few, and those designed by nature for the support and comfort of life, and not to penetrate into the inward essence and constitution of things' (Berkeley, 1710, intro. par. 2). Berkeley's outlook was more hopeful: 'We should believe that God has dealt more bountifully with the sons of men, than to give them a strong desire for knowledge, which He has placed quite out of our reach ... I am inclined to think that the far greater part, if not all, of those difficulties which have hitherto amused philosophers, and blocked up the way to knowledge, are entirely owing to ourselves' (ibid., intro. par. 3). The Introduction continued with an attack on the notion of ABSTRACTION – elaborating on the points made in the *New Theory of Vision*, and again mentioning Locke as the notion's leading advocate. Berkeley promoted abstraction from an apparently harmless bad habit of language and thought, to a serious conceptual corruption – these 'abstract natures and notions' cause 'manifold inextricable labyrinths of error and dispute'. By grounding the reader in the primacy of raw ideas of sensation, Berkeley was carefully laying the groundwork for the more startling conclusions of his metaphysical project.

The first section of the *Principles* proper repeated Locke's views that the objects of the understanding are ideas of sensation or reflection which, when suitably concatenated, are accounted individual things – thus a certain shape, size, colour and taste combined together are deemed an 'apple'. The second section repeated Locke's view that these ideas are known, perceived and operated on by an active agent – which Berkeley terms '*mind, spirit, soul*, or *myself*' (ibid., par. 2). In the third section Berkeley surveys what we can thus far conclude exists – our minds, and our ideas – and nothing else. From these seemingly innocuous Lockean premises, Berkeley then draws the radical conclusion that nothing can possibly be known to exist outside of minds: 'For as to what is said of the absolute existence of unthinking things without any relation to their being perceived, that seems perfectly unintelligible' (ibid., par. 3). Section 4 drew attention to the 'opinion strangely prevailing amongst men, that houses, mountains, rivers, and in a word all sensible objects, have an existence, natural or real, distinct from their being perceived by the understanding' (ibid., par. 4). This view

Berkeley believes, contains a 'manifest contradiction. For, what are the fore-mentioned objects but the things we perceive by sense? and what do we perceive besides our own ideas or sensations? and is it not plainly repugnant that any one of these, or any combination of them, should exist unperceived?' (ibid.).

Section 5 then looks to the cause of this 'strangely prevailing' opinion: 'abstraction' – 'For can there be a nicer strain of abstraction than to distinguish the existence of sensible objects from their being perceived, so as to conceive them existing unperceived?' (ibid., par. 5). Once 'abstraction' is set aside, it is clear 'that all the choir of heaven and furniture of the earth, in a word all those bodies which compose the mighty frame of the world, have not any subsistence without a mind' (ibid., par. 6). Berkeley then thrusts home the consequence of his Lockean premises: 'From what has been said it follows there is not any other substance than spirit, or that which perceives.' In other words, there is no such thing as 'matter'. In seven short paragraphs, Berkeley has taken Locke's empiricist project of codifying common sense and recast it as a foundation for a revolutionary new metaphysics.

To demolish Locke's 'matter' more completely, and more clearly illustrate his new 'immaterialist' view, Berkeley next makes an extended attack on Locke's distinction between PRIMARY AND SECONDARY QUALITIES. Whether Berkeley was fair in his assessment of Locke's theory, which rests on the conceivability of corporeal causation, or whether this would have made any difference to his appreciation of Locke's views, since he thought ideas completely causally inert, is debatable. But he certainly highlighted Locke's rhetorical missteps, the peculiarity of any 'mechanist' metaphysics and the inherent implausibility of dualism. Surely, Berkeley argues, if ideas of the 'sensible qualities', like colour, taste and smell, exist in the mind alone, if they are inseparably mixed with ideas of the 'original qualities' of extension, shape and motion, and if they cannot be 'abstracted' from them, these original qualities must also exist in the mind – 'In short, extension, figure, and motion, abstracted from all other qualities, are inconceivable. Where therefore the other sensible qualities are, there must these be also, to wit, in the mind and nowhere else' (ibid., par. 10).

Berkeley also criticized Locke's definition of SUBSTANCE – 'If we inquire into what the most accurate philosophers declare themselves to mean by material substance, we shall find them acknowledge they have no other meaning annexed to those sounds but the idea of being in general, together with the relative notion of its supporting accidents' (ibid., par. 17). This was most objectionable: 'The general idea of Being appeareth to me the most abstract and incomprehensible of all others; and as for its supporting accidents, this … cannot be understood in the common sense of those words; it must therefore be taken in some other sense, but what that is they do not explain' (ibid.). Moreover, even were 'matter' to exist, 'how is it possible for us to know this?' (ibid., par. 18), since we cannot perceive anything other than ideas, or make reliable inferences to 'matter' since dreams show that ideas can occur without matter. Finally, even if 'matter' existed, no one can explain how this should cause ideas in us, 'since they own themselves unable to comprehend in what manner body can act upon spirit' (ibid., par. 19).

Even if Berkeley could dispatch Locke so quickly, he still had work to do in constructing and defending his own position. If objects amount to nothing more than collections of sensations, what happens when no one is there to perceive them? Equally, if there is no material cause of our ideas, how do these sensations of smell, colour, taste, size and shape always 'hang together' so as to produce the apple? Berkeley thought our sensations were so carefully ordered as to provide a 'language of nature' that allows us to learn, provide for ourselves and steer clear of harm. These advantages point to an author, and what could be responsible for the creation of ideas but another spirit – for where can ideas exist but in minds? God is responsible for these blessings. He creates the world for our benefit and stands on perpetual perceptual sentry duty for the world when no finite mind perceives it.

Berkeley's immaterialism failed to win immediate converts, but the cumulative impact of his writing was immense. Hume did to Berkeley what Berkeley did to Locke – destroying speculative metaphysics through the application of strict empiricism. The 'phenomenalism' that Berkeley pioneered endures to the present day. Locke often serves as the foil for Berkeley's criticisms, making it seem that Berkeley is relentlessly critical of Locke's errors. The impression is misleading. Berkeley concedes that Locke 'has so far distinguished himself from the generality of writers by the clearness and significancy of what he says' (Berkeley, 1709, par. 125). Moreover, Berkeley takes Locke's empiricism, vocabulary and methodology practically for granted. Locke thus provided both metaphysical target and empiricist ammunition for Berkeley's attack on the 'modern' philosophy. Berkeley nonetheless recognized the debt he owed Locke. Though his public praise appeared faint, Berkeley privately conceded the difficulty and value of Locke's pioneering achievements: 'Wonderful in Locke that he could … see at all thro a mist that had been so long a gathering & was consequently thick. This more to be admir'd than that he didn't see farther' (Berkeley, 1944, item 567).

BIBLIOGRAPHY
Primary Sources
Berkeley, George, *Arithmetica Absque Algebra Aut Euclide Demonstrata* (Dublin, 1709).
——, *An Essay Towards a New Theory of Vision* (Dublin, 1709).
——, *A Treatise concerning the Principles of Human Knowledge, Part I* (Dublin, 1710).
——, *Philosophical Commentaries generally called the Commonplace Book*, ed. A.A. Luce (London, 1944).
Locke, John, 'Extrait d'un Livre Anglois qui n'est pas encore publié, intitulé Essai

Philosophique concernant L'Entendement', *Bibliothèque Universelle et Historique*, vol. viii (January 1688), pp. 49–142.

Jonathan Walmsley

BURNET, Thomas (c. 1635–1715)

Thomas Burnet, author among other works of a *Telluris Theoria Sacra* (1681), in which he combines biblical exegesis and geological hypotheses on important matters from the Flood to the New Earth, Master of the Charterhouse, a follower of Ralph Cudworth and Henry More, and a friend of Archbishop Tillotson, criticizes Locke's *Essay* in his anonymous *Remarks upon an Essay concerning Human Understanding* (1697) and their continuation, the *Second Remarks* (1697) and *Third Remarks* (1699). Although the attack takes various angles – moral, psychological and metaphysical – the main line consists in an appeal to nature against convention.

Burnet claims that the distinction between moral good and evil is not only 'antecedent to all human laws', but also rests upon 'the intrinsic nature of the things themselves' (Burnet, 1989, p. 25). He is aware that Locke would agree about the first point, since the true standard of morality is the divine law, but not about the second, because the law is the effect of the will of God and, as such, is natural only in the sense that it is universal, not relative to particular societies. Burnet is a moral realist in the Platonic fashion. He objects to theological voluntarism (for the background of this discussion, see Ayers, 1991, vol. ii, pp. 131–4) by means of the old arsenal, that of Plato's *Euthyphro*: if moral distinctions are made by a lawmaker, either he follows a moral criterion, antecedent to the law, and in that case he does not make moral distinctions from scratch, or he makes them without drawing on a criterion, but then how

can we be sure that they are correct? Suppose that we are in a universe in which God has declared that rape is not bad. This seems incorrect. There are two ways to respond: one could say that (1) God is never wrong even when he decides that rape is not bad; or that (2) God would never do that because he is not only omnipotent, but also supremely good; therefore there are misdeeds that he would not do. The second answer would contradict the claim that moral distinctions are entirely made up by God and that God is omnipotent. The first answer entails that there is a gap between what morality is at the divine level and our common sense of morality.

The Cambridge Platonists strove to bridge that gap. From Benjamin Whichcote to Ralph Cudworth and Henry More, they constantly defended the univocity of the good: the meaning of 'good' for God cannot be utterly different from the meaning of 'good' for us. Our common notion of the good is a sure guide to understand what goodness is even at the divine level. There is a link between the argument against divine command accounts of morality and the recourse to preconceptions, what Burnet terms 'natural impressions' or 'obscure and indistinct notices' (Burnet, 1989, p. 63) – we recognize here the Stoic *prolepsis*, which Cudworth used to translate 'anticipation'. Human beings commonly understand the meaning of good. Thanks to this natural apparatus, they are able to recognize that a rule, whether divine or human, is just or not.

According to Burnet, there is an intrinsic connection between, on the one hand, our epistemic ability ('natural conscience' or 'sagacity') to grasp moral properties independently of external laws and, on the other hand, the reality of those properties, i.e. their foundation in nature (op. cit., p. 58). Putting stress on the immediacy of our 'inward sense' of good and evil (op. cit., p. 64), Burnet (as Tuveson pointed out) foreruns moral sense theories, whether rationalist or sentimentalist. The apprehension of values is not a matter of 'ratiocination', but is immediate as an emotion: "Tis not like a theorem which we come to know by the help of precedent demonstrations and postulatums, but it rises quick as any of our passions, or as laughter at the sight of a ridiculous accident or object' (op. cit., p. 24). Natural conscience is both 'a spring and motive of our actions' and 'a role or direction to our actions' (op. cit., p. 66). As with moral sense theories, Burnet's view is vulnerable to the charge of subjectivism. In the margin of Burnet's *Third Remarks* – Locke's autograph annotations (first published by Porter, 1887; edited by G. Watson in Burnet, 1989) on his copy of this volume, now held in the Beinecke Library at Yale, are abundant – Locke shrewdly notes 'it is not conscience that makes the distinction of good and evil – conscience only judging of an action by that which it takes to be the rule of good and evil' (op. cit., p. 59). Burnet's claim that natural conscience is a 'principle of distinguishing one thing from another in moral cases without ratiocination', seated in our soul (op. cit., p. 64), cannot be accepted, since we would then be judged in our own case. Or, as Locke puts it in the margin: 'He who confounds the judgement made with the rule or law upon which it is made, as the author doth here, may perhaps talk so' (op. cit., p. 65). Locke terms Burnet's scheme 'a foundation for ENTHUSIASM' (ibid.), because it exempts moral judgement from being grounded in an external standard. This sheds light on the chapter on enthusiasm that Locke added to the fourth edition of his *Essay*. Locke's argument against the claim to immediate evidence in matters of faith also debars moral judgement from being by itself the standard of value. Here we are very close to Jeremy Bentham's criticism of Shaftesburian and Hutchesonian moral sense theories as 'ipse-dixitism'. In this dispute Catharine Trotter (later Mrs COCKBURN), sided with Locke against Burnet and the moral-sensists (see Sheridan, 2007).

In an Appendix to his 1697 *Reply* to STILLINGFLEET's *Second Letter*, in which he responds scornfully to the *First Remarks*, Locke argues that Burnet's strictures against his moral theory are irrelevant (in a way that Burnet deemed 'snappish and peevish' (Burnet, 1989, p. 42)). Firstly, the *Essay* does not claim to demon-

strate morality, but only to show that it is '*capable* of demonstration as well as mathematics' (op. cit., p. 34). Therefore there is no ground for deploring the absence of such a demonstration in the *Essay*. Secondly, Burnet is wrong when he construes Locke's position as a simplistic empiricism that would derive moral notions from sensorial experience (op. cit., p. 35). In his *Second Remarks*, Burnet repeats this charge, since he ascribes to Locke the view that moral distinctions derive from sensation and reflection. It is clear that Burnet does not understand Locke's account of values as 'mixed MODES', i.e. notions that are relative to a rule. Since the true rule is the divine law, it is obvious that, for Locke, there is a ground for morality and that there is not an 'arbitrary difference of good and evil' (op. cit., p. 61).

BIBLIOGRAPHY
Primary Sources
Burnet, Thomas, *Remarks on John Locke* (with Locke's replies), ed. G. Watson (Doncaster, 1989).

Secondary Literature
Ayers, M., *Locke. Epistemology and Ontology*, 2 vols (London, 1991).
Grave, S.A., *Locke and Burnet* (Perth, 1981).
Pasini, M., *Thomas Burnet: una storia del mondo tra ragione, mito e rivelazione* (Florence, 1981).
Porter, N., 'Marginalia Locke-a-na', *New Englander and Yale Review*, vol. xlvii (1887), pp. 33–49.
Sheridan, P., 'Reflection, Nature and Moral Law: The Extent of Cockburn's Lockeanism in her Defence of Mr. Locke's Essay', *Hypatia*, vol. xxii, no. 3 (2007), pp. 133–51.
Tuveson, E., 'The Origins of the Moral Sense', *Huntington Library Quarterly*, vol. xi (1947–8), pp. 241–59.

Laurent Jaffro

EDWARDS, John (1637–1716)

John Edwards was the second son of Thomas Edwards, whose attacks on sectaries, heresies and malpractices in *Gangraena* (1646), created such a sensation that he fled to Holland before dying the following year. John Edwards was admitted BA (1657) at St John's College, Cambridge, and MA (1661), before ordination (1662) and serving several parishes. He returned to Cambridge for his BD (1668), but soon thereafter his theological opinions forced him from St John's to Trinity Hall. While maintaining occasional parish appointments, he proceeded to publish some forty books of sermons, biblical interpretation and theological controversy from 1665 until his death in 1716.

Little more than a month after its publication in August 1695, Locke's anonymous *Reasonableness of Christianity* came under fire from John Edwards in *Some Thoughts concerning the Several Causes and Occasions of Atheism*. Dedicated to Thomas Tenison, the Archbishop of Canterbury, the book launched a controversy that lasted several years, extended to others of Locke's works and engaged supporters on both sides. The exchanges, vitriolic and even malicious on both sides, reveal much about Locke and his times.

Edwards's book rehearsed nine relatively customary factors that contribute to atheism in its first half before turning his attention to what he saw as a recent and special threat of atheism from the rise of SOCINIANISM in England. In attacking various contributors to this movement, he cited and quoted with approval Locke writing on education as 'Another Ripewitted Naturalist' and later described Locke as 'that very Thoughtful and Ingenious Gentleman' (op.cit., pp. 93–4, 96). Thereafter, however, Edwards concluded his book with a twenty-page critique of the *Reasonableness*.

Edwards charged the author of the *Reasonableness* with having intentionally omitted mention of several biblical passages supporting the doctrines of the Trinity and the divinity of Christ. He also claimed the book neglected the Epistles because they required belief in a host of Christian doctrines that the book implicitly rejected. At the heart of Edwards's attack, however, was the charge that the *Reasonableness* required only one article of faith, that Jesus is the Messiah. This, he asserted, is the result of subjecting everything in Christianity to the test of reason, thus ridding it of all 'that is not plain, and exactly level to all mens Mother-wits' (op. cit., pp. 115–16). This rationalist method and its resulting single article of faith demonstrated to Edwards that the author sympathized with the Socinians and the English Unitarians, which in his view led directly to atheism.

Locke's authorship of the *Reasonableness* must have been quickly and widely rumoured. Even in this first attack Edwards feigns disbelief that the author could have been the person who 'writ of *Human Understanding* and *Education*'. While Edwards's style was sometimes crude and he intentionally misrepresented opponents, his specific charges against the *Reasonableness*, the association of the book with both foreign and domestic heresy, and its printed rumours of Locke's authorship posed a sufficient threat in Locke's mind to merit a spirited reply. By mid-November 1695 Locke had published *A Vindication of the Reasonableness of Christianity, &c. from Mr. Edwards's Reflections*. Therein he sought to refute each charge and ridicule Edwards's association of his book with Socinianism, Unitarianism and the rationalist approaches of others.

Edwards pressed his attack in two publications of 1696. *Socinianism Unmask'd* seems to have been written largely in late 1695, but was not published until April 1696. There Edwards undoubtedly grasped the distinctions upon which Locke's thesis rested, but he continued to misrepresent Locke's positions and extend his charges of heresy. The one article of faith required to make one a Christian Edwards presented as a flat denial of all other articles of faith. Locke's detailed rehearsal of Jesus' teachings was represented as rejection of the Epistles and all their doctrines. Silence about the Trinity and satisfaction for sins evidenced to Edwards opposition to those doctrines and association with Socinianism, Unitarianism, 'Mahometanism' and atheism.

The Socinian Creed, published late in 1696 but dated 1697, was dedicated to Edward STILLINGFLEET, the Bishop of Worcester, who was then engaged in a controversy with Locke over his *Essay concerning Human Understanding*. Edwards here named Locke as the author of the *Reasonableness* and sought to link Locke's *Essay* as well as the *Reasonableness* to Socinianism. Claiming that Socinus himself held the theory of a *tabula rasa*, Edwards asserted that the first book of Locke's *Essay* was merely an introduction to the heresies laid out in the *Reasonableness* (op. cit., p. 122). He even found a way to connect the *Reasonableness* to Locke's writings on money, charging him with presenting a '*Clipt* Christianity', 'a *False Coin*', and 'a *Counterfeit Stamp* in Religion (op. cit., p. 247). It was, he wrote, 'the worst book published in 1500 years' (op. cit., p. 264).

In the spring of 1697 Edwards extended the controversy in *A Brief Vindication of the Fundamental Articles of the Christian Faith*. His personal attacks on Locke and his character in this book were exacerbated by the fact that Edwards had obtained the imprimatur of four members of Cambridge University. Edwards reiterated all his previous charges against the *Reasonableness* in a point-by-point refutation of the book as well as Locke's *Vindication* and *Second Vindication*. He also repeated a charge first raised by Richard WILLIS in his anonymous *Occasional Paper* (1697) that Locke had borrowed the thesis of his book from Thomas HOBBES. In his inimitable fashion Edwards exclaimed, 'When that Writer was framing a *New Christianity*, he took *Hobbes's Leviathan* for the *New Testament*, and the *Philosopher of Malmsbury* for our *Saviour* and the *Apostles*' (op. cit., sig. A3ʳ).

Edwards repeated his charges against Locke in publications of 1699 and 1701. His frequent and forceful attacks were seconded by such contemporaries as William Payne, Stephen Lobb,

Richard West, Jonathan Edwards (Principal of Jesus College, Oxford) and Thomas Becconsall. Thus, by the time of Locke's death in 1704 he had faced a host of revilers of his *Reasonableness*. None, however, was more prolific or influential than John Edwards. Indeed, Edwards's attacks shaped the interpretation of the *Reasonableness* throughout the centuries. His charge that Locke had moulded Christianity to fit reason's bounds has been carried forward by historians who view Locke as a principal figure in the rise of English DEISM. Others have taken up Edwards's charge that Locke was secretly a Socinian and Unitarian. Finally, Edwards provided fodder for a group of scholars who built a case that Locke was a covert follower of Hobbes in religion as well as politics. Despite his excessive language, the multiplicity of irreconcilable charges, the utter lack of evidence in many instances and the intentional misrepresentation of facts in others, John Edwards shaped the interpretation of Locke's religious thought until the present day.

BIBLIOGRAPHY
Primary Sources
Dictionary of National Biography
Edwards, John, *Some Thought concerning the Several Causes and Occasions of Atheism* (London, 1695).
——, *Socinianism Unmask'd* (London, 1696).
——, *The Socinian Creed* (London, 1697).
——, *A Brief Vindication of the Fundamental Articles of the Christian Faith* (London, 1697).
[Locke, John,] *A Vindication of the Reasonableness of Christianity, &c. from Mr. Edwards's Reflections* (London, 1695).
[Locke, John], *A Second Vindication of the Reasonableness of Christianity, &c.* (London, 1697).
[Willis, Richard], *Occasional Paper*, I (London, 1697).

John C. Higgins-Biddle

LEIBNIZ, Gottfried Wilhelm (1646–1716)

Philosophers traditionally place Locke and Leibniz on opposite sides of a seemingly unbridgeable divide. Locke is viewed as the father of British empiricism, Leibniz as one of the great continental rationalists. No doubt the line ought not to be so sharply drawn. Locke no more outlaws human reason than Leibniz rejects empirical evidence. All the same, Locke's empirical account of human reason is contrasted with Leibniz's view that empirical evidence merely supports knowledge of truths provable, in principle, by a priori reasoning. This methodological divergence underpins differing goals. Locke's epistemological approach in his *Essay concerning Human Understanding* sets out to establish the origin, extent and limits of human understanding. Leibniz's goal is to develop a system of metaphysics that provides a true and complete account of reality. His speculative and sometimes dogmatic stance is in stark contrast to Locke's reserve and scepticism concerning the limits of human knowledge, particularly in respect of our knowledge of external material things.

Locke's quintessentially modern project sets out to clear the ground of inherited systems of thought so as to make clear the way for the experimental, mechanical philosophy being developed by the early-modern virtuosi. Leibniz's philosophy, on the other hand, bridges the ancient-modern divide, retaining aspects of ancient and medieval thought alongside the new science. Leibniz applauds the latter's capacity to explain particular natural events in terms of their efficient causes while also insisting that, metaphysically, the motion of matter must be underpinned by Aristotelian substantial forms present everywhere within matter. The laws of motion themselves must be accounted for through final causes that appeal to the considerations of goodness and perfection that guided God's decision to create the best possible world. In this way, mechanism rests ultimately on teleology.

These and other nuanced differences are discernible in the pages of Leibniz's *Nouveaux Essais sur l'entendement humain*. Locke would never read this work, but he did study a short set of remarks, *Quelques remarques sur le livre de Mons. Locke intitulé Essay of Understanding*, which Leibniz had prepared within six years of the publication of the first edition of Locke's *Essay*. The *Remarques* reveal that Leibniz studied Locke's work carefully and with understanding, despite its being in a language in which he was not particularly fluent. Attention is there focused on Books I and II, but the brevity of comments relating to Books III and IV does not necessarily indicate that Leibniz read these any less attentively. It may suggest only that he found less there with which he disagreed. Certainly, in the *Nouveaux Essais* themselves, comments on sections relating to the last two books tend to be affirmative, offering additional support or relatively minor modifications.

Locke read Leibniz's *Remarques* with equal care and attention. Leibniz had sent a copy of his *Remarques* to Thomas Burnett of Kemnay in March 1696 (Leibniz, 1875–90, vol. iii, p. 176). The following July, he granted Burnet permission to distribute the *Remarques* to whomever he saw fit, adding that if it fell into the hands of Locke or any of his friends, so much the better (Leibniz, 1875–90, vol. iii, p. 180). However, Burnett did not forward the remarks to Locke immediately. Instead, he sent copies to others, including Alexander Cunningham, a jurist who had met Leibniz in Florence in 1689 (Leibniz, 1962, p. xviii). Locke reports that he and Cunningham read this copy carefully 'paragraph by paragraph' in the summer of 1696 (*Corr.*, vol. vi, p. 86). On finally receiving the *Remarques* from Burnet (*Corr.*, vol. vi, pp. 60–1), Locke sent a copy to Molyneux. In the accompanying letter, Locke indicates that he can answer Leibniz's objections and notes, disparagingly, that 'Mr. Leibnitz's great name had raised in me an expectation which the sight of his paper did not answer' (*Corr.*, vol. vi, pp. 86–7).

Locke never answered Leibniz. Overwork, ill health and his lowered estimation of the

German philosopher are possible causes, as is annoyance on being informed, wrongly as it turns out, that Leibniz's *Remarques* were to be published in the French translation of Locke's *Essay* being prepared by Pierre Coste. Basnage de Beauval, the editor of the *Nouvelles de la République des Lettres*, had proposed the plan to Leibniz in January 1697 (Leibniz, 1875–90, vol. iii, p. 130). However, although Leibniz forwarded a copy of his *Remarques* to Basnage in his reply a month later, he refused permission to publish them in the French translation. Leibniz considered it unfair to print them with the *Essay* without Locke having scrutinised them and inappropriate because the *Remarques* had been written in order to give Locke the opportunity to clarify matters (Leibniz, 1875–90, vol. iii, p. 134). None of this was communicated by Basnage when he sent the *Remarques* to Le Clerc, who in April 1697 passed both a copy of the *Remarques* (*Corr.*, vol. vi, pp. 777ff.) and news of their intended publication to Locke (*Corr.*, vol. vi, p. 73).

The eventual publication in 1700 of Coste's French translation of the fourth edition of Locke's *Essay*, without Leibniz's *Remarques*, enabled Leibniz to read the *Essay* for the first time in a familiar language. A few years later, he began work on his *Nouveaux Essais*, a fictional debate in which Locke's views, often lifted directly from Coste's translation, are commented upon by the protagonist representing Leibniz. He probably started work on his *Nouveaux Essais* in 1703 and continued working on it until at least 1705. But Locke's death in 1704 meant that he was to conduct a merely imaginary debate with Locke and he abandoned plans to publish the *Nouveaux Essais*. They were published posthumously in 1765.

In the preface, Leibniz introduces the debate between himself and Locke in terms of the difference between the views of Aristotle and those of Plato (Leibniz, 1962 and 1982, pp. 47–8). The key point of contention is whether the mind contains innate principles and ideas. Like Locke, Aristotle regards the mind as a *tabula*

rasa (Leibniz, 1962 and 1982, p. 48). Plato, in contrast, allows that ideas and truths may be in the mind as 'inclinations, tendencies, or natural potentialities', which may be awakened or recollected through experience (Leibniz, 1962 and 1982, p. 52). Plato's doctrine of recollection, Leibniz describes as 'sheer myth', but it is, he says, 'entirely consistent with unadorned reason' (ibid.). In particular, it chimes well with Leibniz's own view that distinct perceptions are the result of the unfolding of what was implicitly in the soul and which the soul had previously perceived only confusedly.

The first book of Locke's *Essay* presents arguments against the prevalent doctrine of innate speculative and practical principles. The final chapter raises further objections against innate ideas in the mind, and thereby sets the scene for Locke's assertion early in Book II that all our ideas are acquired through experience. Leibniz's considered view is that 'all the thoughts and actions of our soul come from its own depths and could not be given to it by the senses', simply emerging as the individual's essence unfolds temporally. However, he declares himself willing, for the sake of discussion, to enter Locke's philosophical position so far as to accept the common distinction between ideas that are innate and ideas that we may be said to acquire through the interaction of our bodies' sense organs with the external world (Leibniz, 1962 and 1982, p. 74). Even conceding this much, Leibniz believes he can still defend some form of innatism: '... even within this framework, one should in my opinion say that there are ideas and principles which do not reach us through the senses, and which we find in ourselves without having formed them, though the senses bring them to our awareness' (ibid.).

Locke takes the innatist to be claiming that universal consent to certain speculative and practical principles is sufficient to prove them innate in all human beings. Accordingly, he bases his case against innatism on the denial of universal consent. Leibniz's position is more nuanced. He concedes Locke's point that there is no universal consent to any of the principles commonly regarded as innate. However, he insists that the lack of such consent does not disprove the doctrine of innatism, at least in the form in which he himself accepts it. The underlying issue here is Locke's thesis of the transparency of the mind. Locke restricts the contents of the mind to those and only those items of which the mind is aware. Leibniz, on the other hand, believes the mind contains much more. It contains an infinity of *petites perceptions* of which the mind is not conscious and it may be that the mind may use certain speculative principles, such as the Law of Contradiction, 'without paying distinct attention to it' (Leibniz, 1962 and 1982, p. 76). Due care and attention may make such principles explicit, but this is not to deny that they were implicitly and innately in the mind all along.

Petites perceptions play a larger role in Leibniz's discussion than their description might suggest. As qualities of substances, *petites perceptions* must not be excluded from accounts of SUBSTANCE and PERSONAL IDENTITY. Locke had claimed that although we can have ideas of the qualities of substances, we can have only a very obscure idea of substance in general as nothing more than a supposed '*Substratum*, wherein they do subsist, and from which they do result' (E, II.xxiii.1). We know that the substratum is '*something* besides the Extension, Figure, Solidity, Motion, Thinking, or other observable *Ideas*', but we do not actually know 'what it is' (E, II.xxiii.3). Leibniz observes that Locke has separated the attributes or qualities from substance itself, but in so doing, he has removed everything by which any substance could be identified. It is hardly surprising, then, that Locke has no clear idea of substance in itself. In Leibniz's opinion, however, attributes and qualities cannot be abstracted from the substances themselves. Consequently, for Leibniz, knowledge of substances is possible to the extent that we know their attributes and qualities. Inevitably, however, human knowledge of substances is limited. On this point, Locke and Leibniz agree,

but the reason for Leibniz's agreement rests on his claim that it is impossible for a finite being to know the infinity of qualities that make up an individual substance. '[I]ndividuality involves infinity,' he writes at III.iii.6 of the *Nouveaux Essais* (Leibniz, 1962 and 1982, p. 289). A finite being cannot, for instance, know the infinity of perceptions included in an individual's soul. Consequently, only God can have complete and true knowledge of the real identity of individual substances. Thus for Leibniz, *contra* Locke, while memory or consciousness provide evidence of personal identity, they cannot constitute it, since there is in them no awareness of the myriad *petites perceptions* that are also included in the individual being.

That the mind contains an infinity of insensible *petites perceptions* is also the reason why Leibniz agrees that finite minds can never have complete knowledge of external bodies. It is not possible that a finite being should distinctly perceive all the parts of an infinitely divided material body. Such parts, he insists are perceived by the soul only by confused *petites perceptions*. For the same reason, Leibniz disagrees with Locke over the simplicity of our ideas of PRIMARY AND SECONDARY QUALITIES. In Leibniz's view, such ideas only appear to be simple. In fact, they are infinitely complex. Our perception of the colour green, for instance, is made up of tiny perceptions of blue and yellow particles, from which Leibniz concludes that the idea of green would appear to be composed of the ideas of blue and yellow (Leibniz, 1962 and 1982, p. 120). Our sense perceptions of extended things are also complex. Extended objects are composed of infinitely many co-existing extended parts. Our perceptions of these parts are minute, insensible perceptions that do not allow us to distinguish the individual parts from each other. Our idea of extension is similarly complex, involving the component ideas of plurality, continuity and co-existence.

In contrast to Locke, Leibniz holds that bodies are neither substances nor entirely passive. For him, only indivisible unities qualify as substances. Bodies do not qualify because they are divisible, indeed actually divided, aggregates of living substances or monads, each of which possesses an organic body that is similarly an aggregate of living substances, *ad infinitum*. In this way, Leibnizian matter is imbued throughout with active beings, impregnated everywhere with living, perceiving substances. Whereas Locke's conception of the material world is inspired by the experimental work of the corpuscularian BOYLE, Leibniz's model draws upon the microscopic investigations of the early biologists Swammerdam, Malpighi and Leeuwenhoek. So it is that, in the *Nouveaux Essais*, Leibniz's fictional persona is Theophilus, the lover of God, activity and life, while Locke is represented as Philalethes, the promoter of lifeless, senseless matter whose implicit materialism threatens the immortality of the soul and undermines creaturely dependence on the divine.

Given Leibniz's keen interest in the REAL ESSENCES of substances, the nature of bodies and whether matter might think, it is unsurprising that he followed closely the controversy between Locke and Edward STILLINGFLEET, Bishop of Worcester. In this, he was assisted by Burnett, through whom he was to receive not only Stillingfleet's *Discourse in Vindication of the Doctrine of the Trinity* which sparked the exchange of letters between Locke and the Bishop, but also all the letters themselves, except for Locke's reply to Stillingfleet's first letter (Leibniz, 1875–90, vol. iii, pp. 268–9). Leibniz relayed his response to the early exchanges to Locke via Burnett in January 1699 (Leibniz, 1875–90, vol. iii, pp. 245–8) and a year later there followed his *Réflexions sur la seconde réplique de Locke* (Leibniz, 1962, 29–34), which were passed to Locke by Burnett (*Corr.*, vol. vii, pp. 57–8) in April 1700.

Burnett was not Leibniz's only contact with Locke in England. Towards the end of his life, Locke resided in the household of Francis and Damaris MASHAM. Leibniz corresponded with Lady Masham between 1703 and 1705 and, until Locke's death, he often urged her to consult Locke on the issues raised in their letters. But, to Leibniz's regret and to the detriment of philosophical endeavour generally, the pattern set by Burnett was continued with Lady Masham and Locke remained at one remove in his relations with Leibniz.

BIBLIOGRAPHY
Primary Sources
Leibniz, G.W., *Sämtliche Schriften und Briefe* (Darmstadt, 1923–; ser. VI, vol. vi, ed. André Robinet and Heinrich Schepers, Darmstadt, 1962).
——, *Die Philosophischen Schriften von G.W. Leibniz*, ed. C.I. Gerhardt, 7 vols (Berlin, 1875–90), vol. v (Berlin, 1882).

Translations
Leibniz, G.W., *New Essays on Human Understanding*, trans. and ed. Peter Remnant and Jonathan Bennett (Cambridge, 1981; repr. with corr., 1982).

Secondary Sources
Dewey, John, *Leibniz's 'New Essays concerning Human Understanding': A Critical Exposition* (Chicago, 1888).
Jolley, Nicholas, *Leibniz and Locke: a Study of the 'New Essays on Human Understanding'* (Oxford, 1984).
Duchesneau, François, and Jérémie Griard (eds), *Leibniz selon les Nouveaux Essais sur l'entendement humain* (Montreal and Vrin, 2006).

Pauline Phemister

MILNER, John (1628–1702)

Locke's religious thought attracted critical notices in his own day and has continued to do so. In this respect, there was nothing very remarkable about the anonymously published

An Account of Mr Lock's Religion in 1700. Like many other critiques and commentaries on Locke's religious thought at that time, it considered the charge that Locke's thought paralleled, if it did not reproduce, the heterodox doctrines of SOCINIANISM and concluded that such a charge was warranted. But in other respects, the *Account was* remarkable. It was the first comprehensive commentary on Locke's religious thought. It distinguished thirty-one theological topics about which Locke had expressed views at length or in passing and examined his thought holistically, taking up not only all his writings on religion up to 1700, but also his writings on philosophy and education. It was not (unlike Locke's major adversary John EDWARDS's critiques) a vituperative assault upon Locke's religious heterodoxy, but rather a sophisticated series of critical observations that put question marks against his orthodoxy through a scrupulous investigation of his consistency.

The anonymous writer was John Milner, who was, according to Humphrey Gower, the Master of St John's College, Cambridge, a man of 'great learning and piety' who 'deserve[d] a place amongst the best' ([Hunter], 1832, p. 18). Milner had had an established career as vicar of Leeds since 1677, but after the Glorious Revolution, unable to take the new oaths, he became a nonjuror. He was duly deprived of his preferments, but thanks to the hospitality of St John's College, enjoyed a satisfying retirement. Here, he had 'the more Leisure to revise, compose, and publish those learned Works for which his eminent Skill in … all manner of critical Learning, had admirably qualified him' (Thoresby, 1724, pp. 115–16). Amongst these works was the *Account*.

In prefacing the *Account* Milner informed his readers that as it had been '*the little Satisfaction and Consistency*' Locke had found in '*most of the Systems of Divinity*' which had apparently driven him to compose *The Reasonableness of Christianity*, so it was 'the little Satisfaction and Consistency' he had found in Locke's *Reasonableness* which was 'one Occasion' of

his composing the *Account* ([Milner], 1700, 'A Premonition to the *Reader*').

The structure of the *Account* was straightforward. For each theological topic identified, Milner first gave an account of Locke's views 'out of his own Writings, and in his own Words', so that 'neither [Locke] might have Cause to complain, nor the Reader to suspect that [Milner had] misrepresented him'. Furthermore, Milner made sure to include the 'good and justifiable' elements in Locke's account on each topic as well as those in which he 'depart[ed] from the Truth', lest he should be accused of failing to act in accordance with the Christian duty of impartiality. He then subjoined his own observations on Locke's account. In this way, Milner believed that he could fairly and effectively show how Locke had asserted the truth in one place but contradicted it in others (ibid.).

One such example was Locke's rejection of innate ideas. Milner noted that although Locke believed people could attain the knowledge of NATURAL LAW by their 'natural FACULTIES from natural Principles' (*E*, I.iii.13, 1–3 edn, p. 75), by denying innate ideas, he had deprived himself of the resources by which he could explain how people acquired these natural principles ([Milner], 1700, p. 60). Another example was Locke's insistence that there were whole nations of atheists. This was crucial evidence for his argument against innate ideas. But in urging this point, Milner argued, Locke had invalidated the argument for the existence of God from universal consent, and undermined in the process the plainness of the principles of natural religion, to the disadvantage of his stated belief both in God and natural religion (op. cit., pp. 2–9, 64–5).

Not only were Locke's arguments here self-defeating, they also came dangerously close to Socinus' arguments (particularly about natural religion (op. cit., p. 185)). Although Milner had become a nonjuror, he remained wedded intellectually to the Church of England, and the views he expressed in the *Account* reflected his desire to defend traditional Anglican positions against Socinian views. In the *Account* and the second of two appendices, 'A brief Enquiry whether *SOCINIANISM* be justly Charged upon Mr Lock', Milner reproached Locke for not being explicit about his thoughts on the doctrine of the satisfaction and the trinity, two doctrines that the Socinians notoriously denied (op. cit., chaps 8, 12, p. 180). He also criticized Locke for talking of the *only* article of faith required for justification – that is, 'Jesus is the Messiah' (op. cit., chaps 14, 22, 29). Milner argued that there was a 'distinction between fundamentals and non-fundamentals' (*ParN*, 'Introduction', pp. 34–5), a distinction, he thought, even Locke and the Socinians could accept. Therefore, if Locke was willing to admit more explicitly that his fundamental article was 'a brief Summary of all that we are requir'd to believe concerning Christ', i.e. 'as in the Creed', he could lessen public reproof ([Milner], 1700, pp. 184–5).

Furthermore, Milner questioned Locke on other typical Socinian issues such as original sin and the eternal punishment of the wicked. Again, noting that Locke was not forthcoming about these issues, Milner intimated that his silence smacked of closet Socinianism. Concerning original sin, Locke had failed to mention the 'Corruption of Human Nature in *Adam's* Posterity'. Concerning the sanctions in the afterlife, he had insisted that death could only mean 'ceasing to be', or annihilation, which suggested that he did not believe in *eternal* punishments (op. cit., chaps 15, 31, pp. 186–8). This suspicion could only increase when Locke left the possibility that spirits could be material, while maintaining that the immateriality of the soul proved its immortality (op. cit., chap. 25).

Locke made no formal response to Milner. There are at least three ways in which we can interpret Locke's reticence. First, Locke may have felt incapable of responding to Milner. According to George Hickes, Milner had so persuasively exposed Locke's inconsistencies, one must 'pity' him and 'almost despise his Works' (Carroll, 1709, p. [35]). Secondly,

Locke may have felt it pointless to respond. Many of the issues Milner addressed overlapped with those of his other controversies. Moreover, he had accounted for some of them already; for example, he had excised the expression 'natural Principles' (with which Milner had made great play) from the fourth edition of the *Essay concerning Human Understanding* (*E*, op. cit., 4–5 edn). A third possibility is that Locke *did* respond, but indirectly. Locke's later manuscripts and his final theological work, *A Paraphrase and Notes on the Epistles of St Paul* show some evidence that he had reflected on some of the issues raised by Milner (*ParN*, 'Introduction', pp. 34–5, 53).

Milner's profile in recent Locke scholarship has not been high, probably because Locke did not respond to him directly, as he had to others who questioned his theological respectability. But in his own time, Milner was highly esteemed: as Gower recalled, 'I had the happiness of much of his conversation, but still desired more' ([Hunter], 1832, p. 18). Although Milner did not draw Locke into a public controversy, contemporaries certainly took his *Account* of Locke's religion seriously; modern Locke scholars could do worse than follow their example.

BIBLIOGRAPHY
Primary Sources
Carroll, William, *Spinoza Reviv'd ... To which is added, A Preliminary Discourse ... by the Reverend Dr George Hicks* (1709).

[Hunter, Joseph] (ed.), *Letters of Eminent Men addressed to Ralph Thoresby* (London, 1832).

[Milner, John], *An Account of Mr Lock's Religion* (1700).

Thoresby, Ralph, *Vicaria Leodiensis* (1724).

J.K. Numao

NORRIS, John (1657–1712)

John Norris was born in Collingbourne-Kingston, Wiltshire and was educated at Winchester School and at Exeter College, Oxford. He was elected fellow of All Soul's College in 1680 and ordained an Anglican priest in 1684. He started his versatile career as a writer with translations from Latin and Greek classics, but was drawn to philosophy at an early stage and is first of all known as the most prominent British follower of the French Cartesian philosopher Nicolas MALEBRANCHE. Another important influence on Norris was Plato, and with his insistence that not even the Scriptures guarantee the existence of bodies, Norris advocated an immaterialism that went well beyond the philosophy of Malebranche.

In *Reason and Religion* (1689), Norris defended Malebranche's hypothesis of the vision of all things in God. According to Malebranche, since God has created all things, He has the ideas of all things; and when we see these things, we see them in God (Malebranche, *Recherche* vol. ii, 1962, III. II. vi). In 1690 Norris published the *Cursory reflections upon a book call'd, an Essay concerning human understanding. In a Letter to a Friend*, which was appended to his *Christian Blessedness*. The *Cursory Reflections* was the first published attack on John Locke's *Essay* after its appearance in December 1689. In the *Reflections* (Norris, 2001, p. 22), Norris complains about the absence of a clear definition of 'idea' in Locke's *Essay*. Norris argues that *Essay* II.viii.5 does not give a satisfactory explanation of the term. He desires to know the essence or nature of ideas. Are they real beings? Are they substances or modifications? And if they are substances, are they material or immaterial? A critical review of Norris's attack was published by Locke's friend Jean le Clerc in the *Bibliothèque Universelle et Historique* (1691), and an English translation of this review appeared in the third volume of the *Athenian Gazette* later that year. Norris replied to this English version in 1692 with *A Brief Consideration of the Remarques made upon the foregoing Reflections.*

Norris's relations with Locke were initially friendly, in spite of his criticism of the *Essay*, and Locke was instrumental in helping Norris to the rectorate of Bemerton in 1692 where he was to live for the rest of his life. On 22 October of that same year, however, Locke's landlord in London, Robert Pawling, wrote a letter to Locke in which he accused Norris of having opened and 'been peeping into' a letter entrusted by Lady MASHAM for delivery to Locke (*Corr.,* vol. iv, p. 548). The incident, although probably based on a trivial misunderstanding, incurred Locke's implacable wrath. It was only after this incident that Locke was motivated to draft three responses to both Norris and Malebranche himself. The manuscripts containing these reactions are currently deposited in the Bodleian Library but none was published during Locke's lifetime: (1) MS Locke c. 28, fols 107–12, 'JL to Mʳ Norris'/'JL Answer to Mʳ Norris Reflections 92', published in 1971 by Richard Acworth in 1971 (referred to hereafter as 'Answer to Norris'); (2) MS Locke d. 3, pp. 1–86, 'JL Of seeing all things in God 1693', published in 1706 by Peter King as 'An Examination of P. Malebranche's Opinion of Seeing All Things In God' (= 'Examination'); (3) MS Locke d. 3, pp. 89–109, 'Some other loose thoughts which I set down as they came in my way in a hasty perusal of some of Mʳ Norris's writeings', written in 1693 and published in 1720 by Pierre Des Maizeaux as 'Remarks upon Some of Mr. Norris's Books' (= 'Remarks'); (4) finally, there is an unpublished fourth text, 'Recherche'; MS Locke c. 28, fol. 159, probably written in 1693, devoted not to Norris but exclusively to the 'vision in God' and to related problems discussed in Malebranche's *Recherche de la verité* (III.II.i–iii, v).

Norris's role as catalyst for Locke's reactions has been underestimated, not in the least because Peter King in his edition of the 'Examination' had suppressed paragraphs 1, 3–5, and also a sarcastic allusion to 'A certain Gent' (par. 29), which all show that Norris

was very much at the centre of Locke's attention. Yet for all the importance of Norris in
occasioning Locke's replies, and in spite of
Norris being a philosopher in his own right,
who was not a slavish follower of
Malebranche, the fact remains that Norris
added little to the hypothesis of the 'vision in
God' that had not already been supplied by
Malebranche himself. Consequently it is not
surprising that the *substance* of Locke's arguments against the 'vision in God' is directed
against Malebranche, not against Norris. This
is not to say that all Norris's own critical observations went by unheeded. His remark in the
Cursory Reflections about the lack of a definition of 'idea' provoked an angry reaction by
Locke that formed the better part of the
'Answer to Norris'. Locke retorted that he had
given a definition of 'idea' in the introduction
(*E*, I.i.5, p. 45), where he had also explained
that he did not want to be drawn into speculations about 'the Physical consideration of the
Mind' (*E*, I.i.2, p. 43). He then supplied a characteristic example of his epistemological agnosticism: 'perhaps I was lazy and thought *the
plain historical method* I had proposed to my
selfe was enough for me ... nay possibly I found
that discovery beyond my reach' (MS Locke c.
28, fol. 109v), and he ends with a characterization of ideas as 'a sort of sullen things which
will only shew them selves but will not tell you
whence they come nor whether they goe nor
what they are made of' (MS Locke c. 28, fol.
110v, see also 'Remarks' par. 2, MS d. 3, p. 90).

Locke and Norris never reconciled. In 1697
word reached Locke that Norris was working
on another attack against the *Essay*. This
prompted William Molyneux to make the
remark that Norris was 'so overrun with Father
Malbranch and Plato, that its in vain to endeavour to sett him right. and I give him up as an
inconvincible Enemy' (Molyneux to Locke, 4
October 1697, *Corr.*, vol. vi, p. 220). The book
in question was Norris's *Essay towards the
Theory of the Ideal or Intelligible World*, published in 1701–4. Locke's young friend
Anthony Collins took the trouble of reading the

work and wrote an account that elicited
Locke's last comment on Norris in a letter of 21
March 1704, seven months before Locke's
death: 'Men of Mr Ns way seem to me to
decree rather than to argue' (Locke to Collins,
Corr., vol. viii, p. 254).

BIBLIOGRAPHY
Primary Sources
Locke, John, *Posthumous Works of Mr. John
Locke* ed. Peter King (1706).
——, 'Remarks upon Some of Mr. Norris's
Books', in *A Collection of Several Pieces of
Mr Locke, Never before printed, or not
exstant in his Works. Published by the
Author of the Life of the Ever Memorable
Mr John Hales*, [ed. Pierre Desmaizeaux]
(London, 1720).
Malebranche, Nicolas, *Recherche de la vérité*,
3 vols, ed. Geneviève Rodis-Lewis (Paris,
1962–4).
Norris, John, *Philosophical and Theological
Writings*, 8 vols, ed. Richard Acworth
(Bristol, 2001).
For Locke's writings against
Norris/Malebranche see also www.digital-
lockeproject.nl.

Secondary Literature
Acworth, Richard, 'Locke's First Reply to
Norris', *The Locke Newsletter*, vol. ii
(1971) pp. 8–11.
——, *The Philosophy of John Norris of
Bemerton (1652–1712)* (Hildesheim,
1979).
Johnston, Charlotte, 'Locke's *Examination of
Malebranche* and John Norris', *Journal of
the History of Ideas*, vol. xix (1958), pp.
551–8.
Milton, Philip, 'Pierre Des Maizeaux, A
Collection of Several Pieces of Mr. John
Locke, and the Formation of the Locke
Canon', *Eighteenth-Century Thought*, vol.
iii (2007), pp. 255–91.
Schuurman, Paul, 'Vision in God and
Thinking Matter. Locke's Epistemological
Agnosticism Used against Malebranche

and Stillingfleet', in Sarah Hutton and Paul Schuurman (eds), *Studies on Locke: Sources, Contemporaries and Legacy* (Dordrecht, 2008), pp. 177–93.

Paul Schuurman

PROAST, Jonas (c. 1642 –1710)

Son of a Calvinist minister of Dutch descent, Jonas Proast matriculated in 1659 at Queen's College, Oxford, gaining a BA in 1663 and then an MA from Gloucester Hall in 1666. After having studied for some years in Cambridge, he came back to Oxford in 1670, where he was appointed as a chaplain, first of Queen's College and then of All Souls College in 1677. A partisan of High Church ideas, Jonas Proast opposed both James II's policy of religious TOLERATION and his use of the power of dispensation to promote it in the Church and the university. In 1688 Proast defended the Anglican Church against popish influence in two unpublished tracts. In the first of them, he chastised the way James excluded several fellows from Magdalen College for having refused a Catholic warden ('A brief defence of the society of St Mary Magdalen College'). In the second, he vigorously criticized James's injunction to the clergy to read from the pulpit the declaration of indulgence ('The case of reading the declaration for liberty of conscience'). For Proast, toleration was first and foremost an absolutist policy by which James tried to bypass the existing legislation and to meddle unduly in ecclesiastical and academic affairs in order to promote his Catholic friends.

That same year – 1688 – Proast was expelled from his chaplaincy at All Souls College by the incumbent warden Leopold Finch. Finch, a Tory and a man of High Church leanings, had been proposed by James for this post, but the fellows were not disposed to elect him formally because of his rather dissolute personal behaviour. The college's visitor, Archbishop Sancroft, had already tried to block Finch's career in the preceding years and he was quite inimical towards his nomination for the All Souls Wardenship. Nevertheless, since the only credible alternative seemed to be the Catholic poet John Dryden, the fellows resolved to 'accept' Finch without 'electing' him.

Conflict between Finch and Proast crystallized in April 1688, when Finch stood for election to the Camden Chair of History in order to increase his income and pay off part of his debts. Proast refused to vote for Finch and actively campaigned for his rival, Henry Dodwell. His expulsion from All Souls was the result of his having managed to persuade three of the three hundred electors not to give their ballot to Finch, thus provoking the warden's defeat by a very thin margin.

After the Glorious Revolution of 1689, Proast could have expected to be reinstated in his chaplaincy since he could appear as one of the victims of the former regime. But High Church clerics such as Proast and Sancroft were in dispute with Low Church latitudinarians for the legacy of the revolution. William and Mary wanted to show that they dissociated themselves from High Church policy and that their victory would not mean any triumph for the kind of ecclesiastical ABSOLUTISM which Sancroft and Proast stood for. Proast's case was made all the more difficult since Archbishop Tillotson – a friend of Locke and a partisan of toleration and comprehension, whom Proast's High Church friends accused of being a heretic and a Socinian – was now the incumbent of Lambeth Palace. Tillotson dragged the whole thing out until 1692, when Proast finally got back his chaplaincy at All Souls. Proast died in 1710 in Oxford, where he is buried.

Proast's reputation as a writer and polemicist stems from his having been the only critic on the subject of religious toleration to whom John Locke responded in print. Proast published a first rejoinder to Locke's *Letter on Toleration* (*The Argument of the Letter concerning*

Toleration Briefly Consider'd and Answer'd, 1690); after Locke's answer (*Second Letter on Toleration*, 1690), he published a second tract (*A Third letter concerning Toleration in defence of the argument of the letter concerning toleration, briefly consider'd and answer'd*, 1691), but he waited twelve years after Locke's massive *Third letter* (1692) to publish a third tract confusingly entitled *A second Letter to the Author of the Three Letters for Toleration* (1704), which provoked Locke's unfinished *Fourth letter* (1704).

As Mark Goldie (Goldie, 1993) has shown, Proast's argument against toleration is not Erastian but theological. He readily admits that it is improper to use force instead of reason and argument in order to induce men to consent to a truth which is not self-evident, since everybody knows 'that the nature of the understanding is such that it cannot be compelled to the belief of anything by outward force' (Proast, 1690, p. 5). Notwithstanding this, force can be used, not to convince by its own proper efficacy, but to bring men to consider those reasons and arguments which are such as may convince them but which, without being forced, they would not consider. Usefulness is not enough, however, since force must also be shown to be necessary for its use to be lawful in order to procure the salvation of the souls. Such a necessity is not hard to demonstrate since, without force, men would stick to their own beliefs and prejudices, and never choose to consider any contrary proposition. So, asks Proast, 'who can deny but that, indirectly and at a distance, force does some service toward the bringing men to embrace that truth which otherwise, either through carelessness and negligence, they would never acquaint them with, or through prejudice they would reject and condemn unheard, under the notion of error?' (ibid.). Finally, if there is both use and necessity of outward force for the promoting of true religion, this is a good argument to prove that someone must have a right to use it for that end. And if there is such a right, who should have it, if not the civil magistrate in whom the power of compelling generally resides? Proast argues that Locke begs the question in saying that commonwealths are instituted only for the protection of our civil interests and that, on the contrary, they exist for the procurement of all the benefits they can yield. Thus, if it is jointly true that commonwealths are indirectly able to advance men's spiritual interests, that those interests are of paramount importance for men, and that they cannot be advanced otherwise than by the use of force, one must conclude that 'the procuring and advancing those interests must in all reason be reckoned among the ends of civil society, and so fall within the compass of the magistrate's jurisdiction' (Proast, 1690, p. 24).

BIBLIOGRAPHY
Primary Sources
Proast, J., *The Argument of the Letter concerning Toleration, briefly consider'd and answer'd* (Oxford, 1690).
——, *A Third Letter concerning Toleration: in defense of the argument of the Letter concerning Toleration briefly consider'd and answer'd* (Oxford, 1691).
——, *A second Letter to the author of the Three Letters for Toleration* (Oxford, 1704).
——, *The Case of Jonas Proast ... Chaplain of All Souls College* (n.p., 1690).

Secondary Literature
Goldie, M., 'John Locke, Jonas Proast and Religious Toleration 1688–1692', in J. Walsh, C. Haydon and S. Taylor (eds), *The Church of England c.1689–c.1833. From Toleration to Tractarianism* (Cambridge, 1993).
——, 'The Theory of Religious Intolerance in Restoration England', in O.P. Grell, J.I. Israel and N. Tyacke, *From Persecution to Toleration: The Glorious Revolution and Religion in England* (Oxford, 1991).
Vernon, R., *The Career of Toleration. John Locke, Jonas Proast and After* (Montreal, 1997).

Wolfson, A., 'Toleration and Relativism', *The Review of Politics*, vol. lix (1997), pp. 213–31.

Jean-Fabien Spitz

SERGEANT, John (1623–1707)

John Sergeant was an English Roman Catholic priest and a prolific author of theological and philosophical polemics. From the 1650s to the 1680s, Sergeant concentrated on theology, writing at length against noted Protestant divines including John Bramhall, John Tillotson and Locke's own adversary, Edward STILLINGFLEET. His principal theological theme was the absolute certainty of Christianity, with Church tradition rather than Scripture identified as its rule of faith. In the final years of the century, Sergeant turned his attention to philosophy, publishing two positive accounts of his own methodology and metaphysics (*The Method to Science*, 1696; *Transnatural Philosophy*, 1700), a detailed critique of Locke (*Solid Philosophy Asserted, Against the Fancies of the Ideists*, 1697), and a sequence of critical works against the Cartesians in general and Antoine Le Grand in particular (*Ideae Cartesianae*, 1698; *Non Ultra*, 1698; *Raillery Defeated by Calm Reason*, 1699). Sergeant's philosophical outlook was firmly Aristotelian. He viewed Aristotle's own works as containing the key to truth, and, although he felt that Aristotle's later scholastic interpreters had strayed from the path, he also had an especially high regard for the works of those other seventeenth-century English Catholic Aristotelians, his friends Sir Kenelm Digby and Thomas White.

In a letter to Locke of 10 May 1696, accompanying the gift of a copy of *The Method to Science*, Sergeant indicated that he had already written all but the Preface and Appendix to that work before a friend showed him a copy of Locke's *Essay* (*Corr.*, vol. v, pp. 635–7). A few comments on the *Essay* did make it into that Preface and Appendix, including some broadly supportive remarks on Locke's account of identity and diversity (Sergeant, 1696, pp. 427–8). But Sergeant became more critical in *Solid Philosophy Asserted*, wherein he followed the *Essay* chapter by chapter across more than 500 pages, in somewhat the same manner as Henry Lee's *Anti-Scepticism* or LEIBNIZ's *New Essays* afterwards. Sergeant unilaterally declared victory in the dispute, bragging 'that though this book sunke Mr. Locke's credit very much, yet he never reply'd one word.' (Sergeant, 1816, vol. iii, p. 123). Unbeknownst to Sergeant, however, the main importance of his book for us lies in the fact that, in contrast to those others, we do actually have the benefit of Locke's own responses to many of the points Sergeant raised. A copy of *Solid Philosophy Asserted*, with extensive marginal annotations in Locke's own hand, is in the library of St John's College, Cambridge, and has been published in facsimile.

Sergeant wholeheartedly agreed with Locke that none of the mind's contents were innate (Sergeant, 1696, pp. 17, 21–4; Sergeant, 1984, p. 119; Sergeant, 1700, pp. 85–7), but where they differed starkly was in their accounts of what the mind *did* contain. For the Aristotelian Sergeant, for the soul to acquire a 'notion' – his favoured term, in preference to Locke's 'idea' – meant for it to receive the form of the external object. But then, to the extent that the object's form constituted its essential nature, the soul would thereby come to contain the nature of the object. In Sergeant's opinion, this boiled down to saying that the soul contained the object *itself*, albeit in an intellectual way (Sergeant, 1696, pp. 2–3; Sergeant, 1984, pp. 25–7). One and the same thing, he insisted, could comfortably exist in different manners, both corporeally in the external world and intellectually in the soul, and the soul could thereby enter into a genuine intellectual union with the object of its thought (Sergeant, 1678, pp. 116–19; Sergeant, 1984, pp. 39–40). Given that a thought about an object is the sort of thing that can only exist within a mind, Sergeant argued, it must follow that each individual component of that thought will also need to exist therein, *including* its object (Sergeant, 1984, p. 29). Equally, Sergeant identified notions with linguistic meanings, but he insisted that what is meant by a word is the very thing itself. When we say that a stone is hard, for instance, we surely cannot mean that a mental image of a stone is hard – for it is not – but rather that a *stone* is hard. However, since Sergeant also insisted that meaning as such can only exist within a mind, it must again follow that the thing exists therein too (Sergeant, 1984, Preface, pp. b6v–b7r, and p. 33).

According to Locke's 'ideist' scheme, as Sergeant interpreted it, all that really existed in the mind were similitudes of objects, rather than the objects themselves. Consequently, when it came to knowledge, Sergeant felt that such a scheme could only ever offer us knowledge of these similitudes, and not of the things that they were supposed to be resembling (Sergeant, 1984, pp. 30, 50–1). Crucially, he argued that we would never be entitled to extrapolate from knowledge of our internal ideas to knowledge of the external objects they resembled, unless we were in a position to know *that* they resembled them. But this was something we could never do unless we were in a position to compare the ideas with the objects. And *that* was something we could never do unless both the ideas *and* the objects were in our minds (Sergeant, 1984, pp. 31–2; Sergeant, 1700, pp. 146–7).

In his marginal comments, Locke identified several points in Sergeant's theory that he found to be simply unintelligible, and he repeatedly dissociated himself from Sergeant's crude interpretation of his own position. In his very first comment, for instance, he asked 'where is it Mr Locke says Ideas are the similitudes of things? he expresly says most of them are not similitudes' (Locke in Sergeant, 1984, Epistle Dedicatory, p. A4v). It is very true that, for instance in the case of secondary qualities, Locke did indeed expressly deny that there was any resemblance between the ideas and the things themselves. But even if Sergeant had noticed this, he would probably just have replied that, if such ideas were neither going to be equated with the things, nor even allowed so much as to resemble them, then we – and our prospects for knowledge – would seem to be taken *even further* away from the things. At bottom, Sergeant's principal complaint was that, being so taken up in contemplation of his ideas, Locke had lost sight of the things that these were supposed to represent (Sergeant, 1984, p. 172). Anticipating such later critics as BERKELEY or Reid, Sergeant felt that the new way of ideas, by trapping us behind what has since become known as a 'veil of perception', led inexorably to scepticism.

BIBLIOGRAPHY
Primary Sources
S., J. [Sergeant, John], *Of Devotion* (n.p., 1678).
——, *The Method to Science* (1696).
——, *Transnatural Philosophy, or Metaphysiks* (1700).
Sergeant, John, 'The Literary Life of the Rev. John Serjeant, written by himself, and never before published', *Catholicon*, vol. ii (1816), pp. 132–6, 169–76, 217–24; vol. iii (1816), pp. 9–16, 55–64, 97–104, 121–7.
S., J. [Sergeant, John], *Solid Philosophy Asserted, Against the Fancies of the Ideists* (New York, 1984, repr. of Locke's annotated copy of 1697 edition).

Secondary Literature
Krook, Dorothea, *John Sergeant and his Circle: A Study of Three Seventeenth-Century English Aristotelians* (Leiden, 1993).
Yolton, John W., 'Locke's Unpublished Marginal Replies to John Sergeant', *Journal of the History of Ideas*, vol. xii (1951), pp. 528–59.

Jasper Reid

SHAFTESBURY, Third Earl of (1671–1713)

Anthony Ashley Cooper inherited the courtesy title of Lord Ashley on his grandfather's death in 1683, and became third Earl of Shaftesbury when his father died in 1699. According to his own account of his education, Locke supervised the upbringing of all his brothers and sisters, but he himself received special attention:

> I was his more peculiar Charge being as eldest Son, taken by my Grandfather & bred under his immediate Care: Mr Lock having the absolute Direction of my Education, and to whome next my immediate Parents as I must own the greatest Obligation, so I have ever preservd the highest Gratitude & Duty (Shaftesbury to Jean Le Clerc, 8 Feb. 1705, Barrell 1989, p. 87).

The closeness of Locke's involvement should not, however, be exaggerated: the boy's earliest education was placed in the hands of a governess, Elizabeth Birch, and in the early 1680s he attended a school in Clapham, where Locke periodically visited him to check his progress. After his grandfather's death, control over his education was resumed by his parents, with whom Locke's relations seem not to have been very good, and he was sent to Winchester School, an experience he did not enjoy.

Ashley's first surviving letters to Locke were written from Paris in November and December 1687, soon after he had visited Locke at Benjamin Furly's house in Rotterdam. Their tone is warm and gossipy, but there was no attempt to discuss matters of any intellectual significance. By the summer of 1689 Locke was back in London, and Ashley – who had recently been talking with him about these matters – wrote him a long letter (*Corr.*, vol. iii, pp. 666–71) on the immateriality or (as Ashley suspected) materiality of the soul. The style is turbulent and the expression of thought frequently opaque, but it was a serious – if muddled – attempt to grapple with questions of fundamental importance; there is no indication that Locke replied, and the subject is not mentioned in their subsequent correspondence.

In December 1691 Ashley visited Locke and the MASHAM family at Oates. On his return to London he sent Locke what is perhaps the strangest letter in the whole of Locke's correspondence. Locke was accused of having deprived Ashley of 'almost … one half of all the Pleasures of a Former Life':

> I know not indeed how to Define precisely what It is that You have done to Mee. But I am sure of this, that in the main It ought to be reckon'd a Diskindness to anybody to put 'em out of Conceit with what us'd to be most diverting and satisfactory to em in their Particular Life. and this I owe to You. Though to say truth you never seem'd all the while to have any malice or spleen against mee; but rather so much the contrary that It appears Strang how any such thing should have been brought about by You. But You appear least to be what you are, and can disguise so well … (Ashley to Locke, 31 December 1691, *Corr.*, vol. iv, p. 349.)

Passing then into French, Ashley described Locke as a wise and powerful enchanter, living in an enchanted castle, and in whose room the chambermaid had found frightful instruments and diabolical equipment. The last claim is certainly highly metaphorical – few men are less likely than Locke to have dabbled in black magic – but what was intended is extremely unclear. It is, however, quite apparent that Ashley was in a fragile state of mind, and it seems that at least intermittently he thought of Locke with some degree of resentment, and perhaps even aversion.

During the last years of Locke's life his correspondence with Ashley (from 1699 Earl of Shaftesbury) became increasingly infrequent, and the main subject was the annuity of £100 per annum that Locke had purchased from the first earl in 1674. Shaftesbury fully recognized that he was both morally and legally obliged to continue the payments, but it is clear that both he and other members of the family resented the drain on their resources, and payments were frequently in arrears. Locke did not need the money, but his correspondence with his tenants in Somerset shows that he was quite willing to pursue much less affluent men and women for much smaller debts.

A few months after Locke's death Shaftesbury began a long correspondence with Locke's translator, Pierre Coste, who had lived with Locke at Oates, and was now tutor to Edward Clarke's younger children. Shaftesbury kept a large number of Coste's letters – his own in reply are now mostly lost – and these reveal that both men were (in private) increasingly disrespectful of Locke's memory, though Shaftesbury restrained Coste from making his distaste public (Milton, 2008). Shaftesbury's estrangement from Locke's ideas and his caution in making this publicly known are also apparent in letters to other correspondents from around this time, notably those sent to General James Stanhope (Barrell, 1989, pp. 239–43) and to Michael Ainsworth, a young protégé of Shaftesbury who was being educated at Oxford. In a letter to Ainsworth of 3 June 1709, Locke was accused of subverting the foundations of morality:

> 'Twas Mr. LOCKE that struck at all Fundamentals, threw all *Order* and *Virtue* out of the World, and made the very *Ideas* of these (which are the same as those of God) *unnatural*, and without Foundation in our Minds. *Innate* is a Word he poorly plays upon: The right Word, tho' less used, is *connatural*. For what has *Birth* or *Progress* of the Foetus out of the Womb to do in this Case? The Question is not about the *Time* the Ideas enter'd, or the *Moment* that one Body came out of the other: But whether the Constitution of Man be such, that being adult and grown up, at such or such a Time, sooner or later (no matter when) the Idea and Sense of *Order*,

Administration, and a GOD will not infallibly, inevitably, and necessarily spring up in him (Shaftesbury, 1981, part II, vol. iv, pp. 402–3).

Shaftesbury had no patience with the ethnographical material that Locke had amassed in the first book of the *Essay*: 'Then comes credulous Mr. LOCKE, with his *Indian*, Barbarian Stories of wild Nations, that have no such Idea, (as Travellers, learned Authors! and Men of Truth! and great Philosophers! have inform'd him ...' (ibid.). In public, however, Shaftesbury kept quiet: there is indeed no mention of Locke by name in any of the works that he published during his own lifetime. When the letters to Ainsworth were printed in 1716, it was without the approval or authorization of his family.

Shaftesbury's increasing alienation from Locke's philosophy was partly a matter of doctrine, and partly one of outlook. He disliked many things of which Locke approved – empiricist accounts of the working of the human mind, mechanistic theories of the natural world, contract theories of government – but the two things that he loathed above all were voluntaristic theories of ethics in which good and evil were determined by the divine will, not fixed in the nature of things, and egoistic theories of human motivation. The former was to be found mainly in HOBBES, rather than in Locke, but there is no doubt that Locke put forward the latter in a form deeply offensive to Shaftesbury. Locke had praised the ethical doctrines of the Greek philosophers whom Shaftesbury so admired, but regarded them as ineffective in motivating good conduct:

> The Philosophers indeed shewed the beauty of Virtue: They set her off so as drew Mens Eyes and approbation to her: But leaving her unendowed, very few were willing to espouse her ... But now there being put into the Scales, on her side *An exceeding and immortal weight of Glory*, Interest is come about to her; And Virtue

now is visibly the most enriching purchase, and by much the best bargain (*RCh.*, p. 162).

Shaftesbury thought this both vulgar and morally debased. For him, as for Kant, motive was all-important: an action taken purely for reasons of self-interest was of no moral value: if someone does a right action merely out of self-interest and fear of punishment, 'There is no more of *Rectitude*, *Piety* or *Sanctity* in a Creature thus reform'd, than there is *Meekness* or *Gentleness* in a Tyger strongly chain'd, or *Innocence* and *Sobriety* in a Monkey under the Discipline of the Whip' (Shaftesbury, 1711, vol. ii, p. 55).

In politics Shaftesbury fully adhered to the Whig traditions of his family, though ill health prevented him from playing more than a minor role either in the House of Commons, where he was MP for Poole from 1695 to 1698, or in the House of Lords. In his support of religious TOL-ERATION and his deep dislike of the High Church party, he was fully in accordance with Locke's own sentiments, but his theoretical approach was entirely different. Government was a natural result of the sociability of humankind, not an artificial construction instituted by contract: as he remarked in one of his earliest published writings (*Sensus communis*, 1709), 'How the Wit of Man shou'd so puzzle this Cause, as to make Civil Government appear a kind of Invention, or Creature of Art, I know not.' (Shaftesbury, 1711, vol. i, p. 111.)

Shaftesbury's religious views also differed markedly from Locke's. He was certainly not irreligious in the way that many of his contemporaries among the deists were, but his piety was not fundamentally Christian – he had much more in common with Marcus Aurelius, or with the later Neoplatonists such as Proclus. In December 1704, when he thought that he might himself be dying, he sent an unidentified friend some derisive comments on Locke's posthumously delivered letter to Anthony Collins (23 August 1704, *Corr.*, vol. viii, pp. 417–9), saying that it put him in mind

of 'one of those dying Speeches which come out under the Title of a Christian Warning-Piece. I shou'd never have guess'd it to have been of a dying Philosopher' (Voitle, 1984, p. 229). There is evidence that Locke had detected Shaftesbury's inclinations towards infidelity, and had written to him to persuade him of the truth of Christianity, though the letters have not survived. In the second edition of the *Biographia Britannica*, the editor, Andrew Kippis, quoted a communication sent to him by a Mr Huntingford, probably George Isaac Huntingford, Warden of Winchester College:

> And hence it seems to have arisen, that the letters in which Mr. Locke recommended Christianity to his Lordship, were of no avail. It is to be lamented that these letters are not now to be found; though many years have not elapsed since they were read by two Gentlemen, who were so affected by the strong and pressing terms in which Mr. Locke expressed his sentiments, that they could not abstain from tears (*Biographia Britannica*, 1778–93, vol. iv, p. 286*).

Shaftesbury – it would seem – was less moved.

The greatest difference between Locke and Shaftesbury was in outlook. Shaftesbury's ideal of philosophy – and of good learning in general – was informal, playful, witty and above all *polite*. His writings are studded with remarks that Locke would never have made under any circumstances, for example that 'To *philosophize*, in a just Signification, is but To carry *Good-Breeding* a step higher' ('Miscellaneous Reflections', Shaftesbury, 1711, vol. iii, p. 161.) Locke was not shy of proclaiming his own status as a gentleman – the second and subsequent editions of the *Essay* have 'John Locke, Gent.' on their title-pages – but Shaftesbury's approach was far more aristocratic: his books were designed to appeal to an elegant, leisured audience that had little or no inclination to read formal treatises:

Wɪᴛ and Hᴜᴍᴏᴜʀ … will hardly bear to be examin'd in ponderous Sentences and pois'd Discourse. We might now perhaps do best, to lay aside the Gravity of strict Argument, and resume the way of *Chat*; which, thro Aversion to a contrary *formal manner*, is generally relish'd with more than ordinary Satisfaction (Shaftesbury, 1711, vol. iii, p. 97).

Locke – perhaps wisely – entirely eschewed the dialogue form in his writings, and clearly had no inclination to imitate the complex and subtle literary forms that Shaftesbury found increasingly congenial.

Shaftesbury's deepest interests were also very unlike Locke's. He was passionately concerned with beauty – in poetry, paintings, sculpture, buildings and gardens, though not (it seems) women. The pursuit of excellence in these matters was of supreme importance: as he once said, 'The great Business in this, (as in our Lives, or in the whole of Life) is "to correct our Taste"' ('Second Characters', Shaftesbury, 1981–, ser. 1, vol. v, p. 196). This was not at all how Locke thought: his own outlook was deeply prosaic, and his remarks on poetry in *Some Thoughts concerning Education* strikingly hostile: 'if he [a child] have a Poetick Vein, 'tis to me the strangest thing in the World, that the Father should desire, or suffer it to be cherished or improved. Methinks the Parents should labour to have it stifled, and suppressed, as much as may be …' (*STE*, sect. 174). Music and painting fared no better (*STE*, sects 197, 203). For Shaftesbury all these matters were an essential part of a gentleman's education:

'Tis not *Wit* merely, but a *Temper* that must form the Wᴇʟʟ-Bʀᴇᴅ Mᴀɴ. In the same manner, 'tis not a *Head* merely but a *Heart* and *Resolution* that must compleat the *real* Pʜɪʟᴏsᴏᴘʜᴇʀ. Both *Characters* aim at what is *excellent*, aspire to a *just Taste*, and carry in view the Model of what is *beautiful* and *becoming* (Shaftesbury, 1711, vol. iii, p. 161).

Although Shaftesbury was the only philosopher who could in any sense be described as a pupil of Locke, he was certainly not a disciple. As he remarked in an unpublished note made in the last year of his life:

Hence *Hobs Lock* &c. still the same Man, same Genius at the Bottom – '*Beauty* is nothing!' *Virtue* Nothing. – 'So Perspective Nothing Musick Nothing' – But these are the greatest Realitys of things, especially the Beauty & Order of Affections.

These Philosophers together with the *Anti-Virtuosi* may be calld by one common Name, viz, Barbarians ('Second Characters', Shaftesbury, 1981–, ser. 1, vol. v, pp. 233–4.)

BIBLIOGRAPHY
Unpublished Sources
Hampshire Record Office, Winchester, Malmesbury papers, 9M73/G255, letters of Pierre Coste to the third Earl of Shaftesbury.

Primary Sources
Anthony Ashley Cooper, Third Earl of Shaftesbury: Standard Edition, ed. Wolfram Benda *et al.*, (Stuttgart, 1981–).
Shaftesbury, *Characteristicks &c.* ([London], 1711).
Barrell, Rex A. (ed.), *Anthony Ashley Cooper Earl of Shaftesbury (1671–1713) and 'Le Refuge Français'-Correspondence* (Lewiston, New York, 1989).
Biographia Britannica, 2nd edn (London, 1778–93).

Secondary Literature
Klein, Lawrence E., *Shaftesbury and the Culture of Politeness* (Cambridge, 1994).
Milton, J.R., 'Pierre Coste, John Locke and the Third Earl of Shaftesbury', in Sarah Hutton and Paul Schuurman (eds), *Studies on Locke: Sources, Contemporaries, and Legacy* (Berlin, 2008).

Voitle, Robert, *The third Earl of Shaftesbury, 1671–1713* (Baton Rouge, 1984).

J.R. Milton

STILLINGFLEET, Edward (1635–99)

Edward Stillingfleet had arguably the best mind in the Church of England throughout the nearly forty-year history of his publications from *Irenicum* in 1659 to his controversy with Locke in the late 1690s, a debate which ended only with his death. He had one of the best private libraries in England, now the nucleus of Marsh's Library in Dublin. As Dean of St Paul's, London (1678–89) and Bishop of Worcester (1689–99), he was at the centre of the Anglican establishment. He was the only opponent to whom Locke paid serious attention in both the famous controversy over the Trinity in 1697–9 and in an earlier dispute over TOLERATION and nonconformity in 1680–1. It is likely that they had some contact in London, since Locke was SHAFTESBURY's patronage secretary in 1674 when Stillingfleet received the earl's favour in securing a living in Lincolnshire, but no evidence of any other contact survives, though they shared friendship with writers such as BOYLE, NEWTON and SYDENHAM.

Stillingfleet's writings present a mind both conservative and liberal. He retained some of the habits of SCHOLASTICISM and invoked the law of nature in the tradition of Grotius. He had a residual Platonism from his Cambridge undergraduate days as a student of Henry More and retained his belief in innate ideas to the end, marking a huge difference with Locke. In particular, his insistence that God 'hath imprinted an universal character of himself on the minds of men' (Stillingfleet, 1710, vol. ii, p. 242) would have made him alarmed by the first book of Locke's *Essay* which rejected innate ideas altogether. He retained the con-

viction of the Cambridge school that faith was a rational discursive act of the mind and the classic Anglican line that God asks us to believe things beyond our comprehension but never requires us to believe contradictions.

In many ways Stillingfleet was a progressive thinker, in spite of his castigation of the 'new Way of Ideas', in the narrow definition of it he made against Locke to contrast with his own 'Way of Reasoning'. He was familiar with the writings of DESCARTES, HOBBES, Spinoza and many European contemporaries with whom he corresponded. His belief in 'moral certainty' was an attempt to find a workable combination of faith and reason that would hold together a rational and progressive religion. His Latitudinarian sympathies, evident from the beginning in his efforts at an inclusive and comprehensive church in *Irenicum*, were a reasoned attempt to hold united a faith that kept tradition and innovation together. So he claimed, in the preface to the first edition of *Origines Sacrae*, that he wrote in response to a need for a fuller and more rational defence of religion than anything written hitherto. To accomplish this he was willing to vary his strategy, embracing Descartes's ontological argument for God's existence as well as arguments from design which Descartes would have spurned.

The conviction of the reconciliation of revelation and reason, of tradition and intellectual scepticism, took Stillingfleet through his entire writing career and enabled him to deal at a high level of critical scholarship with very varied topics. *Origines Britannicae* (1685), for example, was a careful examination of the evidence for the history of the early British church and was widely respected until the nineteenth century, though it had a polemical purpose in asserting that the early church had been independent of Rome. From the early 1660s to the early 1690s his time was taken up with his increasing church responsibilities – he narrowly missed becoming Archbishop of Canterbury after Tillotson's death in 1694 – and his publications concentrated sustained attacks on both left and right of the theological divide, targeting SOCINIANISM and Rome with persistent if repetitive effect.

It was during this period that Locke had his first clash with Stillingfleet; it was a controversy the latter knew nothing of as Locke's criticisms remained unpublished, as indeed they remain to this day as a manuscript (Oxford, Bodleian Library, MS Locke c.34), though an edition by John Marshall is promised. This 167-page manuscript, known as *Critical Notes*, was written in 1681 and is in three different hands. One is certainly Locke's, and there is a consistency of thought that has led John Marshall to argue for Locke's directing mind throughout the script; he was ill at the time and may have dictated the content. Locke was forty-nine years old and these notes represented, with early drafts of the *Essay*, some of his most substantial sustained thinking on paper to date. The context was a London sermon, *The Mischief of Separation*, preached by Stillingfleet on 1 May 1680, followed by a substantial tome, *The Unreasonableness of Separation*, published early in 1681. The political situation following the Popish Plot included the possibility of five bills before parliament for the relief of dissenters being passed. Stillingfleet argued for a national church united against Rome; dissenting objections were relatively minor and their effect schismatic. A general toleration he compared to a Trojan horse that would destroy the Church from within; the author of *Irenicum* had, it seemed to many, performed a *volte-face*. His two publications produced a flurry of nonconformist replies, but unknown to everyone was the most interesting response of all, that of Locke, who received both works in March 1681.

The *Critical Notes* show no interest in the dissenting replies and, more significantly, no interest in arguments from history and tradition; all religious traditions claim themselves to be 'sole deliverers of unmixed truth'. Religion is solely 'a transaction between me and God' (MS Locke, c.34, p. 19); churches are voluntary, self-governing bodies constituted to serve individual ends. Toleration has nothing to do

with the Church; the Church is concerned only for itself and 'meddles only with its owne body but neither gives nor denyes toleration' (op. cit., p. 7). It is a remarkably atomistic view of Church and society; society is only the effect of personal decisions by participating members. For one who twice affirms, 'I who am of the Church of England' (op. cit., pp. 5, 8), it is nevertheless a private faith that Locke relies on, 'I must chuse my own way to salvation' (op. cit., p. 52). A sustained anti-clericalism permeates the work; while Stillingfleet himself is commended for his efforts at accommodation of dissent – 'the first I have ever met with of the side in power that would ever hearken to the least abatement of what they had set up' (op. cit., p. 31) – he is rebuked for invoking mantra-like phrases like 'established communion … settled church' to shore up his conservatism, 'dextrously twisting in the civil power to inforce his ecclesiastical laws' (op. cit., p. 124). Locke dissolved all theological controversy by insisting that 'mutuall charity' and 'edification' were the guiding principles for Christians (op. cit., pp. 53, 86, 136). It was a very low view of the Church: nowhere is there a sense of the Church as a supernatural society constituted by God, nowhere is there a hint of Erastian support for the buttress of the state and nowhere is there any interest in tradition. Why did the work remain unpublished? It was, perhaps, because events overtook it; the dissolution of parliament just after Locke received the works, a tactic used frequently by Charles II when a difficult issue was threatening stability, ended the process of accommodating dissent and Locke himself was to go into exile in 1683. It is telling that after *An Essay concerning Toleration* (1667) Locke's next foray into the subject was *Epistola de Tolerantia* (1689): if matters had reached an impasse in England, a Latin publication would best suit the wider European stage.

Immersed in ecclesiastical matters and doctrinal disputes, by the early 1690s Stillingfleet was, nevertheless, becoming more aware of the dangers of philosophical atheism and the need for a contemporary philosophical case against them. He started to revise *Origines sacrae* for a second edition, of which only two chapters were written and published posthumously in 1702. The thrust of the new text is philosophical not historical: it was contemporary thinkers such as Descartes and Hobbes who attributed too much to the mechanical powers of matter and motion and who had to be met on their own philosophical terms. He used many ideas of Boyle and Newton, notably the corpuscular theories of the former and the theories of gravity of the latter, but insisted that they fitted in with the traditional theological principle of a provident creator or, quoting the 'Learned Physician' Sydenham, the 'Supreme Artificer' (Stillingfleet, 1710, vol. ii, p. 100). Locke worked closely with Sydenham and it is intriguing that Stillingfleet was familiar with the latter's works. Stillingfleet was appalled to conclude that Descartes's ideas had given legitimacy to Spinoza's attempt to prove the world to be God. The new *Origines sacrae* ends with a commendation of the discovery of gravitation which supposes a wise Creator, for as a principle it is 'not inherent and essential to Matter but ... a force given and directed by Divine Power and Wisdom' (op. cit., p. 116). He was heartened that 'in our Age a great improvement hath been made in Natural and Experimental Philosophy' and defended the way of experiments as tending more to the true knowledge of nature than mechanical and Aristotelian speculations about forms and qualities (op. cit., p. 99). In this opinion Locke would have wholly concurred. He finally shook off most of the Cartesian influences in his thought which had persisted through his life: Stillingfleet had agreed with Descartes on the nature of ideas but the Frenchman's rejection of final causes and the deficient sense of providence are seen in the end as decisive. Stillingfleet had in his library many travel books which provided the beginnings of knowledge of other faiths. Towards the end of the unfinished second edition he drew extensively on such works to argue for a universal sense of a prov-idential deity. Locke, by contrast, used travel accounts to argue there was no innate sense of God.

However, while Stillingfleet was thus engaged, Locke had already published *An Essay concerning Human Understanding* in 1690 and, though the bishop had a copy, he seems to have made little use of it early in the decade while engaged both on diocesan business and in devoting several attacks to an unexpected revival of Socinian thought. It was not until John Toland published *Christianity not Mysterious* in 1696 that Stillingfleet became suspicious of where these new expressions of old Unitarian heresies might be coming from. Toland had reduced Christianity to what could be grasped by reason and did not allow supra-rational mysteries; he had drawn out implications from Locke's *Essay* that gave him, alleged Stillingfleet, reason to reject all mysteries of faith based on Locke's grounds of certainty.

Indeed, Toland had clearly followed Locke in asserting that knowledge is nothing else but the PERCEPTION of the agreement or disagreement of ideas. Locke derived all the components of his ideas from sensation and reflection but to Stillingfleet that led to scepticism and did not provide for a faculty of reason that could interpret and correct the senses. A more fundamental principle was also at stake for Stillingfleet: there must be an underlying base to all general ideas of things, namely, SUBSTANCE. An individual's personhood derives from his own SUBSTANCE: a person is 'a compleat Intelligent Substance, with a peculiar manner of Subsistence' (Stillingfleet, 1710, vol. iii, p. 511). Locke would not allow any serious validity to the notion of substance while also saying that 'nature' and 'person' are merely abstract ideas. Stillingfleet saw this as a threat to the doctrine of the Trinity, since it displaced substance in favour of consciousness. Neither side, perhaps, really understood the other's concerns, or their strengths and weaknesses. Locke had little interest in doctrine or tradition and Stillingfleet's philosophical powers were limited. He could not see Locke's point that he never argued for clear and distinct ideas as the only basis for certainty; it was, rather, the perception of the agreement or disagreement of ideas that concerned Locke. Stillingfleet used rather old-fashioned language like 'General Principles of Reason', but such terms were suspect and ill-advised to Locke. He preferred intuited ideas derived from sensation and reflection, which were quite sufficient for an adequate sense of certainty; one can be certain of something even though the ideas about it may not be clear. Their Trinitarian debate was unsatisfactory because, while sharing some common philosophical language, the bishop was not as adept as Locke at handling the terms of idea, consciousness, personality and substance, and Locke was not willing to help the bishop, taking defence in quiet irony and conducting his argument largely in negatives. Neither man was at his best in the debate.

Nevertheless, Stillingfleet had put his finger on the undoubted lukewarmness of Locke's Trinitarian thought; Locke did not think the doctrine of the Trinity could be found in the Scriptures and he could find no strong evidence to support it, particularly through the notions of substance and person. Locke made witty play in confounding Stillingfleet, not least through an exploration of what substance a resurrected body could have. Suggesting that a person was a substance with MODES and attributes was to Locke a dubious speculation, even more so our knowledge of God as one substance in three persons. More fundamentally still, Locke split certitude of knowledge from faith in divine revelation; he argued that Stillingfleet's rational undergirding of revelation left no room for faith – 'this being to resolve all revelation perfectly and purely into natural reason' – and Stillingfleet is saddled with the conviction that a proposition divinely revealed, that cannot be proved by natural reason, is less credible than one that can. Besides being a clever debating ploy to thrust the implication of DEISM back in Stillingfleet's face, it also undermined the whole effort of Stillingfleet's rational theology. M.A. Stewart is right to claim that

there is altogether less room for philosophy in Locke's religion than in Stillingfleet's. As for doctrine, Locke was content to point out that the Apostles' Creed was the ground of baptism in the Church of England and that that creed had no Trinitarian formula. Though giving nothing away, Locke had nonetheless been rattled by the bishop's intuition that Locke was open to a Unitarian position.

BIBLIOGRAPHY
Unpublished Sources
Oxford, Bodleian Library, MS Locke c.34.

Primary Sources
Stillingfleet, Edward, *The Works of … Dr Edward Stillingfleet,* 6 vols (London, 1710).
Locke, John, *A Letter to the Right Reverend Edward, Ld Bishop of Worcester* (London, 1697).
——, *Mr Locke's Reply to the Right Reverend the Lord Bishop of Worcester's Answer to his Letter* (London, 1697).
——, *Mr Locke's Reply to the Right Reverend the Lord Bishop of Worcester's Answer to his Second Letter* (London, 1699).

Secondary Literature
Carroll, R.T., *The Commonsense Philosophy of Religion of Bishop Edward Stillingfleet* (The Hague, 1975).
Popkin, R.H., 'The Philosophy of Bishop Stillingfleet', *Journal of the History of Philosophy,* vol. ix (Jan 1971), pp. 303–19.
Marshall, J., *John Locke: Resistance, Religion and Responsibility* (Cambridge, 1994).
Stewart, M.A., 'Stillingfleet and the Way of Ideas', in M.A. Stewart (ed.), *English Philosophy in the Age of Locke* (Oxford, 2000).

Neil Fairlamb

WILLIS, Richard (1664–1734)

In the 'Preface' to *The Reasonableness of Christianity*, Locke wrote: '*If, upon a fair and unprejudiced Examination, thou findest I have mistaken the Sense and Tenor of the Gospel, I beseech thee, as a true Christian, in the Spirit of the Gospel, (which is that of Charity) and in the words of Sobriety, set me right in the Doctrine of Salvation*' (*RCh.*, p. 3). The corrections Locke requested were not slow in coming, most notably from John EDWARDS, an Anglican clergyman of intemperate disposition. In the second *Vindication* of the *Reasonableness*, however, Locke took note of 'another gentleman' who had responded to his *Reasonableness*, a gentleman 'of another sort of make, parts, and breeding' (*W*, vol. vii, p. 420). This was the anonymous author of *The Occasional Paper*, Richard Willis, later Bishop of Winchester.

Willis was a true philosopher and was committed to treating even 'the *worst* of Men' with 'a sort of Civility' ([Willis], 1697a, p. 3). In the first issue of the *Occasional Paper*, which included 'An Account of the Authors Design', Willis cautioned those who were concerned with the '*Truth*' to be '*doubly cautious*' as to how they 'indulge[d] their Passions', 'lest the reputation of their *Cause*, as well as their own, suffer by their warmth'; and 'the more *Divine* the *Cause* is, still the greater shou'd be the Caution' (ibid.). Willis's sincere method of enquiry initially gave Locke 'great hopes'. Yet Locke accused Willis of failing to live up to his own rules in his comments on the *Reasonableness*, noting that 'it is not so easy to be a fair and unprejudiced champion for truth as some, who profess it, think it to be' (*W*, vol. vii, p. 420).

Locke's discontent focused on two claims that Willis had made in the first *Occasional Paper*. First, Willis had claimed that Locke's proposition in the *Reasonableness* – that the only article necessary for salvation was 'Jesus is the Messiah' – was borrowed from Hobbes's *Leviathan* ([Willis], 1697a, p. 19). Locke first denied that Hobbes was his source, stating: 'I borrowed it only from the writers of the four Gospels and the

Acts' (*W*, vol. vii, p. 420). He then questioned whether in associating the *Reasonableness* with the *Leviathan*, Willis's intention was to 'increase or lessen' his 'credit', and also, asked whether this allegation would fairly represent his view as a whole (op. cit., pp. 420–1).

Willis's second claim which displeased Locke was that Locke's reflections on the priests – for example, that they 'excluded *Reason*' from religion 'to secure their Empire' (*RCh.*, p. 143; see also, pp. 144, 149) – were 'very bitter' ([Willis], 1697a, p. 30). Locke felt misrepresented as having 'a prejudice against the ministry of the Gospel, and their office' (*W*, vol. vii, p. 422). He responded by posing five questions to Willis: first, whether it was not clear that he was talking about the heathen and Jewish priests before Christ; secondly, whether his claims about them were not true; thirdly, whether his arguments against the pre-Christian priests could really be applied to the modern-day clergy; fourthly, whether Willis's claim that Locke's language by implication went beyond the pre-Christian priests and extended to the modern clergy was not merely a reflection of Willis's own concerns about the probity of the latter and his interest in protecting them from all criticism; and finally, if so, whether it was not Willis himself who was accusing the clergy while diverting the blame to Locke. Locke denied that his reflections were 'bitter', arguing that they were consonant with what Jesus pronounced against the Jewish leaders (op. cit., p. 423).

Willis was reluctant to become involved in a controversy over how he had treated Locke, but responded in the 'Postscript' to the fifth *Occasional Paper* out of good manners, since Locke was 'impatiently' expecting a response from him ([Willis], 1697b, p. 37). Willis started by replying to Locke's five questions in order. He defended himself by affirming that he had granted that Locke's criticisms were levelled at the heathen priests ([Willis], 1697a, p. 30), and that he could agree with what Locke had said about them if he had meant that there were 'ill Men' among them, and not that 'the Priests were all a *Pack* of Knaves and Rascals, who endeavour'd to obstruct all the Good which the honest Philosophers would have carry'd on' ([Willis], 1697b, pp. 38–9). Willis agreed that Locke's portrayal of the priests could reflect 'the Priesthood of the *present* Age', albeit 'obliquely' in his opinion; but he was aware that in the 'Mouth of every Libertine', the '*Priests of all Religions are the same*' (op. cit., p. 39). Willis argued that in his view, Locke's language *did* imply an application beyond the pre-Christian priests and that he wished that Locke had explicitly stated that 'he would not willingly have his Reflexions apply'd to the *Christian* Priest-hood, or at least not to that of the *Church* of *England*' (op. cit., p. 40). Finally, Willis reassured Locke that he was not suggesting that the clergy should be exempt from any censure. His worry was that by making the priesthood a target, religion would suffer: 'the *corruption* of Men will push on the Contempt of the *Ministers* of God, to the contempt of his *Worship* and his *Laws* too' (op. cit., p. 41).

Willis's next task was to respond to Locke's first complaint, that he was unjustly associating Locke with Hobbes. Willis replied that he would take Locke's word that the proposition in the *Reasonableness* was not borrowed from the *Leviathan*. But he objected that he could not see any lack of charity on his part for thinking so; the *Leviathan* being 'so noted a Book', it was hard to believe that someone of Locke's erudition would not take note of it (op. cit., p. 41). Willis reassured Locke that his intention in noting the similarity with Hobbes was neither to lessen his credibility nor to represent him unfairly. We may take Willis's word on this because, unusually for the time, he did not anathematize Hobbes ([Willis], 1697a, p. 21; *RCh.*, 'Introduction', p. lxxv). His intention, on the contrary, was simply to warn Locke's readers that although faith in the proposition 'Jesus is the Messiah' was sufficient to give one the title of a Christian, one would still be 'weak and imperfect', and 'there were *many* things to be learn'd and believ'd afterwards, to build them up in the *Religion* of *Jesus*' ([Willis], 1697b, p. 42). Willis noted that Locke agreed with him on this point, which was a 'rare thing in Controversies', but his criticism was that Locke was not 'explicit enough'.

The exchange between Locke and Willis was less acrimonious than most of Locke's other controversies (Nuovo, 2002, p. xv n2), not least because of Willis's philosophical method of enquiry. But precisely because of his apparent sincerity, it was problematical for Locke. Locke's philosophical and religious writings had already come under a strong suspicion of being relativistic and atheistic. Wherever Willis's true intentions lay, his comments associated Locke with the atheistical doctrine of Hobbes and alienated him from the established Church, seriously jeopardizing his reputation. The exchange between the two philosophers may have been temperate by the standards of the age, but it was not less discomfiting for that.

BIBLIOGRAPHY
Primary Sources
[Willis, Richard], *The Occasional Paper, Number I* (1697a).
The Occasional Paper, Number V: With a Post-script relating to the Author of The Reasonableness of Christianity (1697b).

Secondary Literature
Nuovo, Victor, 'Introduction', in *John Locke: Writings on Religion* (Cambridge, 2002).

J.K. Numao

4

CONCEPTS

ABSOLUTISM

In the *Two Treatises of Government* (1689), Locke's insistence that political authority derived from the collective consent of rational individuals was directed against rival theories of natural subjection and unlimited allegiance to absolute authority, particularly as advanced in Sir Robert FILMER's *Patriarcha* (1680). Defining absolute government as a condition in which a ruler held 'both Legislative and Executive Power in himself alone', Locke regarded such claims as both false and politically dangerous. First, he equated obedience to absolute authority with political slavery in submitting oneself 'to the inconstant, uncertain, unknown, Arbitrary Will of another Man' (*TTG* II.22). For this reason, 'Absolute Monarchy, which by some Men is counted the only Government in the World, is indeed inconsistent with Civil Society, and so can be no Form of Civil Government at all' (*TTG* II.90). Although undivided political sovereignty could, in theory, be vested in governments comprised of the one, the few or the many, Locke always assumed absolute authority to imply government of the one: monarchy. Secondly, Locke was alarmed by the theoretical fragility of Filmer's adherence to a 'strange kind of domineering Phantom, called the Fatherhood, which whoever could catch, presently got Empire, and unlimited absolute Power' (*TTG* I.6). Rejecting the parallels Filmer had drawn between paternal and political power, Locke sought to demonstrate that his opponent's patriarchal derivation of

absolute authority conferred neither legitimacy nor secure grounds for obedience. Although the main purpose of identifying the source of political authority was to differentiate between legitimate and illegitimate power, Locke claimed that Filmer's *Patriarcha* instead 'cuts up all Government by the Roots' (*TTG* I.126). Accordingly, 'a Book, which was to provide Chains for all Mankind', Locke perceived to be 'but a Rope of Sand' (*TTG* I.1).

Whilst Filmer's *Patriarcha* was first published in 1680, its author had died in 1653. In the preface to the *Two Treatises*, Locke acknowledged that he would usually have refrained from attacking a 'dead Adversary' and 'a Gentleman, long since past answering, had not the Pulpit of late Years, publicly owned his Doctrine, and made it the Current Divinity of the Times'. An equally forceful defence of unlimited political obedience to absolute authority had been advanced in Thomas HOBBES's *Leviathan* (1651), although Hobbes's absolutism had been predicated on theories of natural freedom, rather than subjection. The considerable controversy provoked by Hobbes's unorthodox philosophical and religious claims, however, restricted the influence of his political precepts on Restoration royalism. Likewise, the defence of absolute monarchy espoused in *Patriarcha* did not attract universal assent when Filmer had originally composed his manuscript tract in the late 1620s, as constitutional notions of mixed government and the sovereign authority of the 'King-in-Parliament' were being strenuously and vociferously asserted in Parliament. By contrast, however, as Locke observed, 'In this last age a generation of men has sprung up among us, who would flatter princes with an Opinion, that they have a Divine Right to absolute Power' (*TTG* I.3). By the 1680s Filmer's absolutist precepts epitomized the political beliefs of Charles II's Tory supporters who defended non-resistance to absolute monarchy against Whig opponents who unsuccessfully sought instead to assert the essentially mixed and limited character of monarchical authority. Filmer's defence of divine-right absolutism thus conformed to what Locke elsewhere identified as 'a certain number of opinions which are received and owned as the doctrines and tenets of that society' and which required the intervention of 'a serious and sober friend' to puncture their theoretical errors and pernicious potential ('On Study', in Locke, 1997, pp. 370–1).

In this capacity, Locke drew attention to the relative novelty of Filmerian absolutism in departing from 'the old way' of forming governments 'by contrivance, and the consent of Men' acting rationally (*TTG* I.6). To this end, Locke invoked the authority of 'the Judicious' Anglican theologian, Richard Hooker, whose *Laws of Ecclesiastical Polity* (1594–7) had acknowledged that government was founded 'on common consent ... without which consent there would be no reason that one man should take upon him to be lord or judge over another' (*TTG* II.15, 91). Filmer's insistence on natural subjection to monarchical authority thus diverged from claims of older absolutist theorists, whom Filmer himself acknowledged had 'admitted the Natural Liberty and Equality of Mankind' (*TTG* I.4) in envisaging an irrevocable surrender of authority by free individuals. Moreover, Filmer's assertions regarding unqualified obedience were also, as Locke showed, at variance with the ideas of even 'the great Champion of Absolute Monarchy', William Barclay, and another 'great stickler for the Power and Prerogative of Princes', Thomas Bilson, who had accorded subjects an

ultimate right of resistance in extraordinary circumstances. Identifying Charles I's Anglican clergy and civil war royalists 'who were Contemporaries with [Robert] Sibthorp and [Roger] Manwering' as responsible for promulgating contrary theories of absolute non-resistance to monarchy, Locke encouraged readers to recognize that Filmerian 'Civil Policy is so new, so dangerous, and so destructive to both Rulers and People' (*TTG* I.5 and II.239).

More broadly, Locke also held absolute and arbitrary power to be synonymous. Despite respectfully referring to James VI & I as 'that Learned King who well understood the Notions of things', he rejected James's distinctions between virtuous kingship and vicious tyranny as affording insufficient protection for subjects, particularly since other absolutists, like Filmer, elided the distinction when asserting, for example, that 'every power of making laws must be arbitrary' (Filmer, 1991, p. 132). Instead, Locke extended the right of resistance *in extremis*, upheld by previous absolutists such as Barclay, to normal circumstances, on the grounds that recognizing subjects' right to resist, as opposed to enforcing slavish subjection, supplied 'the best fence against Rebellion, and the probablest means to hinder it' (*TTG* II.226). Insisting that any ruler who sought to 'get another Man into his Absolute Power, does thereby put himself into a State of War with him', Locke deemed it irrational for men to fear 'what Mischiefs may be done them by Pole-Cats, or Foxes, but are content, nay think it Safety, to be devoured by Lions' (*TTG* II.17, 93).

Whilst Locke's precepts applied to all civil societies, contemporary resonance is discernible in his enumeration of the actions by which an absolute king degenerated into an unlawful tyrant. For example, a 'Prince [who] hinders the Legislative from assembling in due time, or from acting freely' (*TTG* II.215) echoed Whig criticisms of Charles II for his prolonged parliamentary prorogations and for perpetuating the same parliaments, rather than calling fresh elections. Attempts 'by the Arbitrary Power of the Prince' to alter 'the Electors, or ways of Election' (II.216) was reminiscent of the aggressive attempts of Charles II's ministers to remodel town charters and electoral franchises to secure Tory electoral success in the early 1680s. Locke's denunciation of rulers who engaged in 'a manifest perverting of Justice, and a barefaced wresting of the Laws', thereby promoting 'violence and injury, however colour'd with the Name, Pretences, or Forms of Law' (II.20), evoked the controversial series of 'show trials' staged to eliminate Charles's Whig enemies. Meanwhile, Locke's attack on a ruler who either delivers his people 'into the subjection of a foreign Power' or who 'neglects and abandons that charge' denounced, respectively, both the pro-French and Catholicizing policies of Charles II and the flight to France in 1688 of his successor, James II (II.217, 219).

Driving the 'vast Engine of Absolute Power and Tyranny' of patriarchal absolutism was Filmer's claim that God had vested Adam with a proprietary monopoly of the world and its inhabitants and all notions of political authority derived from that antecedent PROPERTY (*TTG* I.67). Whilst Locke shared John Selden's interpretation of Scripture that held God to have accorded an 'Original Community of all things amongst the Sons of Men' (*TTG* I.40), he also rejected the political implications that Filmer had drawn from Genesis. For Locke, 'the Person of a private Father, and a Title to Obedience, due to the Supreme Magistrate, are things inconsistent' (I.66). Since civil society was not a macrocosm of a private family, whatever authority fathers wielded within families had no determinative influence on the power of civil magistrates. For his part, Locke restricted private patriarchal duties to the procreation and raising of children. Once those obligations had been fulfilled, a husband's power was 'so far from that of an absolute Monarch ... that the Wife has, in many cases, a Liberty to separate from him' (II.82). At the same time, Locke satirically caricatured Filmer's version of patriarchal absolutism as entailing a requirement that sons should obtain their fathers' permission before enjoying conjugal rights with their spouses. Since this seemed only likely to frustrate God's intention that mankind should multiply, Locke wryly observed that Filmer evidently 'takes great care there should be Monarchs in this World, but very little that there should be People' (I.33).

Whilst much of Locke's posthumous political renown derives from his sustained attack on Filmerian patriarchalism in the *Two Treatises*, it is worth drawing attention to absolutist arguments that Locke himself advanced in the 'Two Tracts on Government' that he wrote, but did not publish, in the early 1660s. Having identified religious fanaticism and sectarian ambition as serious threats to civil society, Locke had held that 'the supreme magistrate of every nation what way soever created, must necessarily have an absolute and arbitrary power over all the indifferent actions of his people' (Locke, 1997, p. 9). Since the government's prime aim was to avert strife, Locke had endorsed the Erastian imposition of a state religion whereby men would 'mutually agree to give up the exercise of their native liberty' (ibid., p. 22) to ensure peace. Given most subjects' reluctance to compromise the perceived purity of their religious beliefs, however, Locke ultimately rejected this strategy for the political management of religion as unfeasible. Instead, he advocated TOLERATION of religious nonconformists in both an unpublished 'Essay on toleration', written in 1667, and in his *Letter concerning Toleration* (1689).

Finally, Locke's concern to demonstrate the dangerously new deformity of Filmerian absolutism conflicts, to some extent, with other passages in the *Two Treatises* that supply a conjectural history of political development. In these accounts, the history of civil society is seen as a progressive evolution from primitive monarchical absolutism to rational and civilized government by consent. As Locke observed, 'if we look back as far as History will direct us, towards the original of commonwealths, we shall generally find them under the Government and Administration of one Man'

(*TTG* II.105). Monarchy was instinctively 'simple, and most obvious to Men', with neither a knowledge of different forms of government nor adverse experience 'of the Encroachments of Prerogative, or the Inconveniences of Absolute Power' (II.107). For Locke, such an era remained, however, a 'Golden Age' before 'vain Ambition, and ... evil Concupiscence, had corrupted Mens minds' and prompted them 'to examine more carefully the Original and Rights of Government' (II.111). For his part, Locke concluded 'that as far as we have any light from History, we have reason to conclude, that all peaceful beginnings of Government have been laid in the Consent of the People' (I.112). History and human reason thus concurred in confirming the vision of government by consent and individual rights of resistance, outlined in Locke's *Two Treatises*, not the depiction of slavish subjection to absolutist tyranny, inculcated in Filmer's *Patriarcha*.

BIBLIOGRAPHY
Primary Sources
Filmer, Sir Robert, *Patriarcha and Other Writings*, ed. Johann P. Sommerville (Cambridge, 1991).
Locke, John, *Political Essays*, ed. Mark Goldie (Cambridge, 1997).

Clare Jackson

ABSTRACTION, UNIVERSALS AND SPECIES

Locke's account of universals has a chequered history. At Draft A's outset, universals were just NAMES: 'the minde or the man comeing to observe a certeine number of these simple Ideas to be found in several particular subjects ranks them togeather or else findes them ranked togeather by others under one general name, which we cal a species & if more comprehensive a genus' (Draft A, sect. 2, p. 8). For Locke, as for HOBBES, 'Species' were 'generall words (for I thinke I may say we have noe notion of generall things)' (Draft A, sect. 2, p. 9). However, Locke soon presented a different view: 'out of these [simple] Ideas we collect such a number as we have observd or doe thinke belong to one sort of things which presently becomes the Idea of a substantial species & the name we give to it the name of a species or a sort of being' (Draft A, sect. 5, p. 15). How this 'collection' formed the species idea was unclear. Locke later referred to the understanding's power to 'abstract' – a scholastic term describing the process of forming general ideas (Draft A, sect. 43, p. 75; sect. 27, p. 42).

In Draft B, where there were previously only 'generall words', Locke now believed there to be universal 'signes i e either Ideas or words' (Draft B, sect. 86, p. 193). Locke elucidated their role:

that Idea v.g of blew or bitter which exists in any ones understanding be but one single numericall thing, yet as it agrees to & represents all the qualitys of that kinde where soever existing it may be considerd as a Specific Idea & the word that stands for it a Specific word comprehending many particular things (Draft B, sect. 59, pp. 161–2).

The idea of 'one' suggested how general ideas may be formed: 'the notion of one (which is suggested by every individuall object of sense or action of the minde) is noe thing but the consideration of that thing alone precisely in its self without consideration of parts or reference to any thing else' (Draft B, sect. 50, p. 156). 'Precise' meant 'cut out' or 'separate from' – implying that this idea is created by a kind of mental 'separation'. Conversely, Locke also noted that the understanding 'can only come to have true notions by considering & collecting those simple Ideas it findes in particular things & by that means frame generall notions &

generall names' (Draft B, sect. 86, p. 193). Again, general ideas are formed from collecting ideas together. Draft B was clear that there were general ideas, but unclear how they were created.

Locke's first extended treatment of 'abstraction' occurs in 1676 Journal entries regarding the idea of space. Pure space has no parts, since parts require intervening bodies, and bodies render space impure. Thus, to measure distance in pure space, we consider space in a particular way:

> a man might have considerd as much of that distance from the star in Taurus as is answerable or commensurate to a yard without considering the rest which is abstraction but not soe much as mental division ... & I thinke noe body says that abstracting (i e considering light alone) light from heat in the sun is separateing light from heat, one is only a partial consideration of one only the other is a consideration of both & lookeing on them as existing separately (Locke, 1936, p. 79).

Partial consideration is simply looking upon the idea in a certain manner, not separating different parts of the idea from one another.

These sentiments were repeated in Draft C (Draft C, II.xvi.15). However, they now conflicted with Locke's explicit statements regarding universals:

> abstraction ... is nothing else but the Considering any Idea barely & precisely in it self stripd of all Externall Existence & circumstances. By this way of considering them Ideas taken from particular things become universal being reflected on as nakedly such appearances as in the minde without considering how or whence or with what others they came there (Draft C, II.xiii.6).

Here, abstraction is 'separation' – taking away parts of particulars to leave the general idea.

There is tension – abstraction is sometimes 'partial consideration', sometimes 'separation'.

The *Essay* removed this tension. In discussing Space, every reference to abstraction was removed (*E*, II.xiii.13, pp. 172–3). Locke's account of universals was emphatic: '*Ideas* become general, by separating from them the circumstances of Time, and Place, and any other *Ideas*, that may determine them to this or that particular Existence' (*E*, III.iii.6, p. 411). The abstract ideas produced are 'precise, naked Appearances in the Mind' (*E*, II.xi.9, p. 159). People do not put parts together to create universals: 'they make nothing new, but only leave out of the complex *Idea* they had of *Peter* and *James*, *Mary* and *Jane*, that which is peculiar to each, and retain only what is common to them all' (*E*, III.iii.7, p. 411). Abstraction proceeds by 'separation': 'That this is the *way, whereby Men first formed general* Ideas, *and general Names to them*, I think, is so evident, that there needs no other proof of it, but the considering of a Man's self (*E*, III.iii.9, p. 412). Locke then defined the 'nominal essence' by which we sort things: 'the *Essence* of each *Genus*, or Sort, comes to be nothing but that abstract *Idea* which the General ... Name stands for'. This was distinct from the 'real essence': 'the real internal, but generally in Substances, unknown Constitution of Things, whereon their discoverable Qualities depend' (*E*, III.iii.15, p. 417). Locke's treatment of abstraction thus neutralized the pernicious aspects of scholastic ontology. However, critics from BERKELEY onwards believed that 'ideas' cannot be broken down into their constituent parts – you cannot separate the colour from the square, which must always have some colour or other.

BIBLIOGRAPHY
Primary Sources
Locke, John, *An Early Draft of Locke's* Essay: *Together with Excerpts from His Journals*, ed. R.I. Aaron and Jocelyn Gibb (Oxford, 1936).

Jonathan Walmsley

ANCIENT CONSTITUTIONALISM

The term 'ancient constitutionalism' refers to a constellation of ideas, predominantly articulated by early-modern English common lawyers to supply a specific historical legitimation, or construal, of contemporary English laws and political institutions. Integral to opposition to James VI & I's proposals for closer Anglo-Scottish union in 1604, Parliamentarian resistance to Charles I during the 1640s and Whig disagreements with Charles II during the 'Exclusion Crisis' of the late 1670s and early 1680s, ancient constitutionalist claims were primarily invoked to portray unpopular royal initiatives as innovative and thereby unconstitutional. In time, however, defenders of the royal prerogative also appropriated the same political language.

Ancient constitutionalism comprised a number of interrelated theoretical components. In historical terms, the importance of 'Gothicism' was emphasized, from the mid-sixteenth century onwards, by antiquarians such as William Lambarde, Dudley Digges, Roger Owen and Nathaniel Bacon, who claimed that contemporary laws and institutions originally derived from those Germanic tribes that had succeeded the Roman Empire: in England's case, the Anglo-Saxons. Tacitus' *Germania* was invoked to identify the Saxon *witenagemot* as progenitor of the English Parliament (its Norman-French name notwithstanding), the Saxons as a 'free people' and Saxon kingship as elective, limited and capable of accommodating popular resistance in the event of monarchical misrule. Accompanying Gothicism was an attachment to immemorialism: the claim that certain political and legal principles and practices had obtained for as long as could be remembered or, alternatively, that no proof was available to indicate a time when such practices had not existed, with the date of Richard I's coronation (1189) taken as demarcating time before memory from time of memory. Immemoriality, in turn, encouraged a celebration of legal continuity. The repeated confirmations, by monarchs from the time of the

Magna Carta onwards, of the largely apocryphal laws and charters of earlier Saxon monarchs, especially Edward the Confessor (1042–66), underpinned denials that English common law had been affected by historical ruptures such as the Norman Conquest of 1066.

Accordingly, the doctrine of historical prescription became the means by which inherited rights, privileges and customs acquired legal status and force whilst, jurisprudentially, an emphasis on legal immemoriality, continuity and prescription elevated the authority of custom, or unwritten law (*ius non scripta*), over written law. Venerated as a unique body of customary rules, English common law was thereby held to embody the cumulative wisdom and tested reason of previous generations. Regarding law as a local embodiment of universal reason, the Chief Justice, Sir Edward Coke, confirmed in the *First Part of the Institutes* (1628), that 'the common law itself is nothing else but reason, which is to be understood of an artificial perfection of reason, gotten by long study, observation, and experience, and not of every mans natural reason'. Unsurprisingly, the common law's acclaimed perfections also encouraged an instinctive legal insularity. As the Irish Attorney-General, Sir John Davies, acknowledged in 1615, the common law was 'so framed and fitted to the nature and disposition' of the English people that it was 'connatural to the nation, so as it cannot possibly be ruled by any other law' (Wootton, 1986, p. 133).

The language of ancient constitutionalism fused arguments for Gothic freedoms, immemoriality, continuity, prescription, custom, rationality and unique adaptation to national circumstances; and it was invoked to claim an extensive range of contemporary rights and liberties as fundamental English birthrights. The framers of the Petition of Right (1628), for example, cited the binding authority of Edward the Confessor's laws to request the king to desist from, *inter alia*, imposing forced loans and other financial exactions without parliamentary consent, and declared arbitrary imprisonment, martial law in peace-time and the forced free quartering of troops on civilian populations as likewise unconstitutional. For his part, Charles I's *Answer to the Nineteen Propositions* (1642) undertook to maintain 'the ancient, equal, happy, well-poised, and never enough commended constitution of the government of this kingdom' (Wootton, 1986, p. 171). Further claims by Coke, published posthumously in the mid-1640s, that the House of Commons not only possessed an equal share in legislative sovereignty with monarch and Lords, but also that the English Commons enjoyed an immemorial and prescriptive right to parliamentary representation, inspired a subsequent generation of polemicists, including Bulstrode Whitelocke, William Petyt, Sir Robert Atkyns, Sir Roger Twysden, James Tyrrell and William Atwood, to uphold the immemorial perpetuity of parliaments as an article of faith.

At the same time, royalist counter-attacks started to focus on rejecting ancient constitutionalist claims. Sir Robert FILMER's *The Freeholders' Grand Inquest* (1648), for instance, denied any prescriptive right of the lower House to either parliamentary representation or legislative sovereignty by attributing all legislative authority to the monarch alone, whilst also insisting that the Commons had not enjoyed regular representation until 1265 (49 Hen.3), when the earliest extant writ of summons had been issued to knights of the shires. As Filmer elaborated in *Patriarcha*, posthumously published in 1680, 'Customs at first became lawful only by some superior power which did either command or consent unto their beginning' (Filmer, 1991, p. 45). For Filmer, if the Commons' existence could not be conclusively demonstrated to be immemorial, its existence derived from the grace of a pre-existing authority, which could, in future, legitimately withdraw those privileges and powers the Commons claimed as entrenched and unassailable.

Meanwhile, renewed interests in England's feudal history presented further challenges to

the immemorial dimension of ancient constitutionalism, as advanced in Sir Henry Spelman's posthumously published complete *Glossarium Archaeologus* (1664) and Robert Brady's *Introduction to the Old English History* (1684). Attacking ancient constitutionalist claims as inherently anachronistic, Brady emphasized the need for philological exactitude on the grounds that 'whoever reads our old historians and hath not a true understanding and apprehension' of medieval realities could never 'arrive at the knowledge our ancient government ... nor indeed what truly the liberties were they contended for' (quoted in Pocock, 1987, p. 209). According to Brady, England had formerly been a feudal lordship, wherein the monarch had granted landed estates (fiefs) to Norman vassals, meaning that the king's council had originally been a feudal *curia regis*, comprising those vassals in their capacity as tenants *in capite*, and hence neither the seventeenth-century Lords, nor Commons, could be deemed immemorial. Moreover, as J.G.A. Pocock observed in 1957, 'nor would any of the arguments in the armoury of the school of Coke suffice to prove that the common-law *feodum* was not the *feudum* of the feudal law, and without such a proof the whole theory of the ancient constitution lay open to devastating attack' (Pocock, 1987, p. 120).

Engagement with ancient constitutionalist argumentation is, on initial reading, conspicuous by its absence in Locke's works. Observing that the *Two Treatises* (1689) made 'no appeal to the prescriptive force of the ancient constitution', Quentin Skinner interpreted this 'extremely unusual lacuna for him to have left in his argument' as evidence that Locke was consciously 'rejecting and repudiating one of the most widespread and prestigious forms of political argument at the time' (Skinner, 1974, p. 286). By contrast, sustained discussions of English history appeared in the works of Locke's Whig colleagues, such as Henry Neville, Algernon Sidney and James Tyrrell. Yet when he discussed, in the *Two Treatises*, the type of polity best suited for late seventeenth-century England, Locke endorsed, tacitly, the type of mixed polities championed by ancient constitutionalists (*TTG* II.213). Likewise, when referring to the challenges facing members of the Convention debating the Revolution settlement in February 1689, Locke privately intimated that there 'was noe way so well don as by restoreing our ancient government, the best possibly that ever was if taken and put together all of a piece in its originall constitution' (Locke to Edward Clarke, 29 January–8 February 1689, *Corr.*, vol. iii, p. 538). Similar models had previously been championed in *The Fundamental Constitutions of Carolina* (first published c. 1670) as a means to 'avoid erecting a numerous democracy', whilst England's existing political institutions were deemed vulnerable to attack by arbitrary innovators aiming to 'have placed themselves, and their possessions, upon a surer bottom (as they think) than Magna Charta' in *A Letter from a Person of Quality* (1675) (Locke, 1997, p. 162 and 361).

More broadly, politics, for Locke, comprised two aspects that were 'very different the one from the other'. As he explained in 'Some Thoughts concerning Reading and Study for a Gentleman' (first published in 1720), the first, with which the *Two Treatises* was primarily concerned, related to 'the original or societies, and the rise and extent of political power', whilst the second addressed 'the art of governing men in society' and was 'best to be learned by experience and history, especially that of a man's own country'. In this context, Locke identified key contributions to the ancient constitutionalist canon as essential repositories of political knowledge, directing readers to 'the ancient lawyers ... such as are Bracton, Fleta, Henningham, *Mirror of Justice*, my Lord Coke on the second *Institutes* and *Modus Tenendi Parliamentum* and others of that kind', notwithstanding that the last text, which described the Saxon parliament, had already been exposed as a forgery by the legal antiquary, John Selden. Together with 'the late controversies between Mr Petyt, Mr Tyrrell, Mr Atwood, etc. with Dr.

Brady', Locke also recommended John Sadler's *Rights of the Kingdom, and Customs of Our Ancestors* (1649), wherein readers would 'find the ancient constitution of the government of England', as well, incidentally, as a constitutionalist defence of Charles I's regicide in 1649 (Locke, 1997, pp. 351–2).

Despite acknowledging the significance of history in political thinking, Locke rejected the conservative and obscurantist implications of prescriptive modes of argumentation. As he insisted in the *Two Treatises*, 'at best an Argument from what has been, to what should of right be, has no great force' (*TTG* II.103). His refusal to draw political deductions from historical claims was consistent with his philosophical treatment of innate ideas, which also derived from similar psychological propensities for humans to accord normative status to principles of whose origins they were unaware. In his discussion of 'Study' (composed in 1676), for example, Locke observed that whilst a man had 'opinions planted in him by education time out of mind; which by that means come to be as the municipal laws of the country, which must not be questioned', perhaps 'these so sacred opinions were but the oracles, or the traditional grave talk of those who pretend to inform our childhood, who receive them from hand to hand without ever examining them?' (Locke, 1997, p. 369) In the political sphere, there were particularly malevolent risks involved in accepting claims grounded primarily on historical precedent, irrespective of their inherent rectitude.

Aside from logical fallaciousness, Locke also distrusted the inescapable anachronism associated with ancient constitutionalism. Holding that it was 'with Commonwealths, as with particular persons, [that] they are commonly ignorant of their own births and infancies' (*TTG* II.101), Locke denied that the rationale of modern laws, institutions, customs and laws was to be located in the past. Ancient constitutionalist inclinations to venerate all ancient practices as inherently superior to later developments were thus misguided. Ironically echoing Robert Brady's attacks on the anachronistic limitations of ancient constitutionalist claims, Locke likewise regarded it as 'not at all strange' for primitive societies to have instituted simple forms of absolute monarchical government, but refused to accept that such precedents necessarily supplied ideal models for subsequent ages. Yet whilst Locke eschewed ancient constitutionalism as a legitimate mode of argumentation, he endorsed its constitutional realities. When revising the *Two Treatises* regarding the dissolution of political society, he amended the final sentence 'place it in a new form, or new hands' to read 'erect a new form, or under the old form place it in new hands', thereby conferring retrospective approval on the reassuring outcome of events in England in 1689.

BIBLIOGRAPHY
Primary Sources
Filmer, Sir Robert, *Patriarcha and Other Writings*, ed. Johann P. Sommerville (Cambridge, 1991).
Locke, John, *Political Essays*, ed. Mark Goldie (Cambridge, 1997).
Wootton, David (ed.), *Divine Right and Democracy. An Anthology of Political Writing in Stuart England* (Harmondsworth, 1986).

Secondary Literature
Pocock, J.G.A., *The Ancient Constitution and the Feudal Law. A Study of English Historical Thought in the Seventeenth Century. A Reissue with a Retrospect* (2nd edn, Cambridge, 1987 [first published 1957]).
Skinner, Quentin, 'Some Problems in the Analysis of Political Thought and Action', *Political Theory*, vol. ii (1974), pp. 277–303.

Clare Jackson

ASSOCIATION OF IDEAS

Locke is generally credited for coining the expression 'association of ideas'. It first appeared in the title of Chapter xxxiii of Book II of the *Essay*, which was added to the fourth edition in 1700. We first hear of his plan to write this chapter in a letter to William Molyneux in 1695, where he discusses additions he is intending to put into a Latin translation of the *Essay*. He tells Molyneux that this chapter will discuss 'the Connexion of Ideas, which has not, that I know, been hitherto consider'd and has, I guess, a greater influence upon our minds, than is usually taken notice of' (Locke to Molyneux, 26 April 1695, *Corr.*, vol. v, pp. 350–3). When Locke came to write the chapter, he was convinced that false associations of ideas are the source of 'the most dangerous' errors in the world – those which prevent people from investigating the truth, and from seeing it when it is presented to them (*E*, II.xxxiii.18, p. 400–1). He appeals to the principle of association of ideas to explain the 'Irreconcilable opposition' between factions in religion and politics.

He begins the chapter by pointing out that association accounts for what we recognize as 'Extravagant in the Opinions, Reasonings, and Actions of other Men' but fail to identify in ourselves (*E*, II.xxxiii,1, p. 394). He notes that such errors are usually ascribed to education, but he thinks this does not get to 'the root it springs from' (*E*, II.xxxiii.3, p. 395). It is a 'Disease', an 'opposition to Reason [which really] deserves that Name, and is really Madness' (*E*, II.xxxiii.4, p. 395). He refers back to an explanation of madness which he had previously given in Chapter xi of Book II where he had identified it as a defect of the faculty of imagination or fancy, and not of reason itself – a claim which is to be found as early as a Journal entry for 5 November 1677 (Dewhurst, 1963, p. 89). Madmen, Locke claimed, 'argue right from wrong Principles' (*E*, II.xi.13, p. 161). For example, there are inmates of Bedlam who wrongly imagine themselves to be kings, but correctly reason that they should have 'suitable Attendance, Respect and

Obedience'; others imagine themselves to be made out of glass, but rightly use 'the caution necessary to preserve such brittle Bodies'. Locke accounted for these wrong connections of ideas in the imagination by a 'sudden very strong impression', or by the 'long fixing [of one's] Fancy upon one sort of Thoughts'. Such trauma or obsession causes 'incoherent *Ideas*' to be 'cemented together so powerfully, as to remain united.' In this earlier chapter he had already noted that men who are otherwise sane may be as mad on one particular matter as these inmates of Bedlam.

In the new chapter on association of ideas Locke contrasts the connections between ideas discoverable by reason with those formed by association. The first are 'natural' and 'it is the Office ... of our Reason to trace these and hold them together' (*E*, II.xxxiii.5, p. 395). These natural relations are discovered by demonstration or experience. In contrast, associations of ideas arise though 'Chance or Custom'. These latter principles cause unrelated ideas to be joined in people's minds so that when the one appears in the mind so does the other, and it is 'very hard to separate them.'

Locke appealed to a Cartesian psycho-physiological explanation to account for the strength of the associations of ideas: He writes that 'Custom settles habits of Thinking in the Understanding, as well as of Determining in the Will, and of Motions in the Body; all which seems to be but Trains of Motion in the Animal Spirits, which once set a going continue on in the same steps they have been used to, which by often treading are worn into a smooth path, and the Motion in it becomes easy and as it were Natural' (*E*, II.xxxiii.6, p. 306). His source for this psycho-physiological account was probably Book 2, 'Of the imagination', of MALEBRANCHE's *Search after Truth*. In order to account for 'Intellectual Habits' such as the ability to play a musical instrument 'without any care or attention' to what one is doing, both writers appeal to the changes wrought in the brain by the animal spirits. Compare *Search after Truth* (Malebrunche, 1997, pp. 107–9).

Locke ascribes a variety of 'Sympathies and Antipathies' to the association of ideas (*E*, II.xxxiii.7, pp. 396–7). We cannot endure being in a room in which a friend has suffered and died (*E*, II. xxxiii.12, p. 398). We cannot help hating a person from whom we once received 'a sensible Injury' after we turn the incident over and over again in our minds (*E*, II.xxxiii.11, p. 398). The result is 'Quarrels propagated and continued in the World' – even when the original offence was unintentional and slight. Locke notes that when a person has once gained ascendancy over us in a social situation we often come afterwards 'to flag' in his presence, even though he is 'not otherwise superior' to us (*E*, II. xxxiii.15, p. 399). This too is the result of a false association of ideas.

In the *Essay*, as well as *The Conduct of the Understanding*, he stresses the ill effects of associations caused by teachers and other adults in a child's early life. He writes of foolish maids who tell children stories of '*Goblines* and *Sprights*' which come out in the dark; as a result, in later life the person always associates the appearance of darkness with those 'frightful *Ideas*' (*E*, II.xxxiii.10, pp. 397–8). The 'Pain ... endured at School' when children are corrected by insensitive teachers causes an aversion to reading and study. The children associate the ideas of pain and books, and so lose what could have been a 'great Pleasure of their Lives' (*E*, II.xxxiii.15, p. 309). In the *Conduct*, Locke remarks wryly that 'the great art and business of the teachers and guides in most sects [is] to suppress, as much as they can, [the] fundamental duty which every man owes himself' to investigate the grounds of their beliefs (*Conduct*, sect. 40, *W*, vol. iii, p. 276). What they should be teaching is the rule that they should 'never suffer any ideas to be joined in their understandings in any other or stronger combination than what their [i.e. the ideas'] own nature and correspondence give them' (ibid., p. 277).

In ascribing absurd opinions to the association of ideas, Locke acknowledges that many people do not 'impose wilfully' on themselves 'and knowingly refuse Truth offer'd by plain Reason'

(*E*, II.xxxiii.18, p. 400). These men 'pursue Truth sincerely; and therefore there must be something that blinds their Understandings, and makes them not see the falshood of what they embrace for real Truth'. A Roman Catholic for whom 'the *Idea* of Infallibility' has been 'inseparably join'd' to that of a certain person will believe on authority that 'one Body' can be 'in two Places at once' (*E*, II.xxxiii.17, p. 400), or 'that to be Flesh, which he sees to be Bread' (*E*, IV.xx.10, p. 713). Locke holds that Catholics really do believe in transubstantiation in spite of the contrary evidence of their reason and senses.

Locke's views on the association of ideas were developed by philosophers throughout the eighteenth century. Francis Hutcheson applied Locke's account of association of ideas in a systematic way to moral philosophy, arguing in his *Essay on the Nature and Conduct of the Passions* (1728) that association is the source of perverted values. He wrote that 'the common Effect of ... *Associations* of Ideas is ... that they raise the Passions into an extravagant Degree, beyond the proportion of real Good in the Object' (Hutcheson, 2004, p. 69). Even the best of passions may lead us into 'pernicious Actions' when led by '*confused Sensations*, and *fantastick Associations* of Ideas which attend them' (op. cit., p. 110–11). Like Locke, Hutcheson generally regarded the association of ideas as the source of error (op. cit., p. 21). However, this view of the association of ideas is self-consciously reversed in David Hume's philosophy. In his *Treatise of Human Nature* (1739–40) he developed Locke's claim (*E*, IV.xvi.6, p. 662) that our judgement of cause and effect is based on 'constant Experience', arguing that this experience determines this judgement through custom and the resulting association of ideas (Hume, 2007, 1.3.6.14–15 & 1.3.7.6). Thus for Hume, unlike Locke, the principle of association of ideas becomes the fundamental principle of human understanding.

BIBLIOGRAPHY
Primary Sources
Hume, David, *A Treatise of Human Nature: A Critical Edition*, ed. David Fate Norton and Mary J. Norton (Oxford, 2007).
Hutcheson, Francis, *An Essay on the Nature and Conduct of the Passions and Affections, with Illustrations on the Moral Sense*, ed. Aaron Garrett (Indianapolis, 2002).
Malebranche, Nicolas, *The Search After Truth*, trans. Thomas M. Lennon and Paul J. Olscamp (Cambridge, 1997).

Secondary Literature
Dewhurst, Kenneth, *John Locke (1632–1704), Physician and Philosopher: A Medical Biography* (London, 1963).
Gill, Michael B., 'Nature and Association in the Moral Theory of Francis Hutcheson', *History of Philosophy Quarterly*, vol. xii, no. 3 (July 1995), pp. 23–48.
Warren, Howard C., *A History of the Association Psychology* (New York, 1921).
Wright, John P., 'Association, Madness and the Measures of Probability in Locke and Hume', in Christopher Fox (ed.), *Psychology and Literature in the Eighteenth Century* (New York, 1987), pp. 103–27.
Yolton, John W., article on 'association of ideas' in *A Locke Dictionary* (Oxford, 1993), pp. 18–23.

John P. Wright

COINAGE

In the 1690s England's economy was plagued by severe trade imbalances and debts stemming from the Nine Years War (Appleby, 1978; Kelly, 1991; Morrison, 2008). These pressures led to a painful and disruptive contraction in the domestic money supply. Developed in this context, Locke's best-known writings dealing with matters of currency and coinage include *Some Considerations of the Consequences of the Lowering of Interest, and Raising the Value of Money* (1691; see *LoM*, pp. 209–342), *Short*

Observations on a Printed Paper (1695; see *LoM*, pp. 343–59), and *Further Considerations concerning Raising the Value of Money* (1695; see *LoM*, pp. 399–481).

Locke's writings on coinage were addressed to the dilemma of 'clipped' coins – most often stamped silver crown or shilling pieces whose smooth edges had been illegally trimmed and the surplus silver sold as bullion. Clipped coins circulated widely throughout England and were commonly accepted at par or face value in trade even if this exceeded the underlying value of their silver content. This led to widespread deterioration in the silver currency in circulation – and to corresponding hoarding of unclipped or full-weight milled coins. It was unclear what would remedy the situation. Policymakers could devalue or 'raise' the nominal rating of the coin to approximate the market value of the silver. Additionally, they could call in all the clipped coins and replace them with full-weight minted coins. Holders of clipped coins could either be compensated at par value or paid based on the current bullion weight of the coins. In the former case, there was the question of how to absorb the cost of the difference between the par value of these coins and the value of the degraded metal content.

Locke's interventions in the debates over recoinage revolve around two key issues. The first was the technical problem of how to deal with England's deteriorating stock of currency. Most acknowledged the need for some form of recoinage, even if there was widespread disagreement about how to proceed and who ought to bear the costs. The second and more complicated issue was whether to revalue the currency itself. Silver crown pieces denominated at sixty pence had become undervalued relative to the rising market price of the silver bullion they contained. This led not only to clipping but encouraged the melting of coins down into bullion which could be shipped abroad, further exacerbating England's trade deficit and depriving the nation of ready, circulating coinage for domestic trade. The crisis came to a head in early 1695: public confidence in England's

currency collapsed, trade was seriously interrupted and full-weight coins virtually disappeared from circulation. A special committee of parliament was formed and produced the so-called 'Fourteen Resolutions', which proposed both to recoin England's silver currency and to 'raise' the par value of silver coins (initially nine per cent, then later a hefty twenty per cent), bringing their denominative value in line with the rising price of silver bullion (Li, 1963; Appleby, 1978; Kelly, 1991). This was supposed to curtail the widespread practice of melting coinage.

The most famous proponent of this scheme of 'raising' the value of the coin and recoining degraded silver currency was William Lowndes, Secretary of the Treasury, who supported, in 1695, most of the Fourteen Resolutions. Locke countered Lowndes's case in his *Short Observations* and his *Further Considerations* in 1695. He argued that by raising the denominative value of silver money by twenty per cent 'the Landlord here and Creditor are each defrauded of 20 per Cent. of what they contracted for, and is their due' (*LoM*, p. 416). If the true value of money is ultimately determined by its underlying silver content, as Locke maintained, then they would have lent out more silver than they were to receive back in kind at the new denominative rate. This would be every bit as unjust as lowering the value of currency by twenty per cent and compelling debtors to pay back twenty per cent more in silver than they had borrowed (ibid.). Locke further rejected the notion that holders of clipped coins should be compensated from a fund to be established for these purposes by a public tax (*LoM*, pp. 476–7). People decided freely whether they would accept degraded coins, and redeeming coins at par value would only encourage speculation. Because currency represents a veritable social compact among members of society, changing the denominative value of currency was tantamount to voiding the terms of all private contracts (*LoM*, pp. 415–17).

Locke preferred a gradual process of recoinage, whereby clipped coins would be redeemed by weight at the mint and exchanged for newer milled coins of more exact measurement with serrated edges to discourage clipping (*LoM*, p. 431). Until then clipped coins should begin immediately to pass by weight to avoid the dangers of speculators, hoarding and the seizure of the whole monetary system. Locke's arguments against revaluing the standard for coinage ultimately proved persuasive, but the strategy of allowing clipped coins to continue to pass at par value – rather than by weight, as Locke had argued – until some indeterminate date in the future precipitated a severe currency crisis throughout 1696–7 (Li, 1963). Fearful of being caught with worthless currency, people refused to accept degraded silver currency at par value – or indeed at any value – and the law as implemented did nothing to draw out full-weight minted coins that had been hoarded. Although Locke is widely blamed for the debacle of the Great Recoinage, its implementation differed from the plan he favoured (Kelly, 1991, pp. 26–7 and 32–5).

At the heart of the celebrated exchanges between Locke and Lowndes were two enduring conceptual questions. First, did the value of England's currency stem from the underlying gold or silver *specie* it contained, as Locke contended, or was the value of money determined strictly by fiat, in which case metal content was largely irrelevant? While Locke insisted that currency's acceptance is ultimately a matter of 'common consent' – echoing his account of the origins of money in the *Two Treatises* – he was adamant that its 'intrinsic value' is almost solely a function of underlying bullion value (*LoM*, p. 410). Secondly, there was the broader question of whether England's exchange rate regime should, as Locke insisted, remain perpetually fixed. By contrast, Lowndes argued that the English system had always been periodically adjusted to reflect the changing price of commodities. Locke's position ultimately carried the day, yielding a major shift in British monetary policy towards fixed currency exchange rates that held sway until the rise of Keynesianism in the twentieth century (Morrison, 2008).

BIBLIOGRAPHY
Secondary Literature
Appleby, Joyce, *Economic Thought and Ideology in Seventeenth-Century England* (Princeton, 1978).
Kelly, Patrick Hyde, 'General Introduction: Locke on Money', in *LoM* (1991), vol. i, pp. 1–105.
Li, Ming-Hsun, *The Great Recoinage of 1696 to 1699* (London, 1963).
Morrison, James, 'An Unholy Trinity: The Influence of Locke, Smith, and Keynes on British Macroeconomic Stabilization Policy' (PhD Dissertation, Department of Political Science, Stanford University, 2008).

Richard Boyd

CONSENT AND SOCIAL CONTRACT

The social contract, much discussed by Anglophone thinkers in the early-modern period, was often derided in the century following the publication of Locke's *Two Treatises*. William Godwin was profoundly sceptical of the notion that government was founded on the consent of the people. 'What can be more absurd,' he wrote, 'than to present to me the laws of England in fifty volumes folio, and call upon me to give an honest and uninfluenced vote on its contents' (Godwin, 1946, vol. i, p. 186). For David Hume, too, the idea of original contracts that had established existing polities was historical nonsense. In spite of this condemnation, Locke's stress on consent and social contract continues to appeal to the political imagination today.

The *Two Treatises* presents two accounts of the formation of political society. In the first, human history is essentially divided into two periods, the STATE OF NATURE and civil society. The second story is a more anthropological and gradualist account of the way in which modern political institutions emerge from the family and the tribe (Waldron, 1989). Consent plays a crucial role in both stories as it establishes political obligations. This is due to the fact that God created men in such a way that no one can naturally claim authority over any other person or nation. Moreover, in the state of nature all mature individuals have the right to enforce NATURAL LAW. In these circumstances there are two possible ways in which a man may become obliged to another. The first is by becoming a slave as a punishment for a crime. The second is through consent, the basis of political community (*TTG* II.95).

Consent, for Locke, is always a voluntary action; it can never be the product of coercion. While consent is a necessary condition of legitimate government, it should not be regarded as a sufficient ground for political legitimacy. Indeed, governments that breach the laws of nature act illegitimately irrespective of popular consent. Although consent establishes political obligations, it does not generate any obligatory force. Rather, men are bound to keep their promises as part of their service to God. Moreover, there are some actions, such as suicide, that men can never be obliged to perform even if they are foolish enough to promise to do so. This is due to the fact that individuals can only legitimately consent to actions that they already have the right perform. A man has no right to take his own life, for his life belongs to God. In this light, consent is not merely a psychological state; properly understood, consent is a legal fact that describes the act of taking on political obligations (Dunn 1967, p. 156).

The social contract is the consensual event that takes men out of the state of nature by establishing a political community. Locke presents this as a two-stage process. First, men agree to leave their natural state and enter an artificial community in which their natural judicial and executive powers are ceded to the community (*TTG* II.87–8). Secondly, this new community, which can now be considered 'a

people', agrees upon a specific form of government (*TTG* II.96–8).

Political obligations may be incurred through express or tacit consent. In general terms, anyone who voluntarily enjoys the benefits of an existing political community can be assumed to consent to its authority. Locke makes this clear in the context of his discussion of property, arguing that 'every Man, that hath any Possession, or Enjoyment, of any part of the Dominions of any Government, doth thereby give his tacit Consent, and is as far forth obliged to Obedience to the Laws of that Government' (*TTG* II.119). Consequently, consent need not be expressed formally or even verbally.

Consent plays an important role within civil society, specifically in relation to taxation and marriage. Men have a right to own property, and, accordingly, subjects must give their consent if taxation is to be legitimate (*TTG* II.138). Locke accepts that the consent of the people may be given through their representatives, or the majority of their representatives in a legislative assembly. Yet he stresses that there is a danger to the property of subjects who are represented by an assembly that has developed a set of interests different from the people's interests. Turning to marriage, Locke states that 'Conjugal Society is made by a voluntary Compact between Man and Woman' for the purpose of producing and nurturing children (*TTG* II.78). Consequently, the broad terms of the relationship could be agreed between the contracting parties, so long as the relationship was still fit to perform its procreative function. Locke allows the husband some privileges in the relationship as he is 'the abler and the stronger' (*TTG* II.82). Even so, he goes so far as to say that once children have been nurtured, the relationship may be consensually terminated without injustice (*TTG* II.81).

Notably, consent had little part to play in Locke's understanding of the conquest of America. Amerindians, Locke claimed, are in the state of nature (*TTG* II.49). Consequently, they only have a right to the land that they are occupying and cultivating. European settlers could therefore take any territory in the New World that was not being cultivated without the consent of the indigenous people (*TTG* II.36). If Amerindians attempted to resist the conquest, European settlers were morally entitled to subdue them, without their consent, using their legitimate right of war in the face of aggression (*TTG* I.130–1; Tully, 1994). This approach towards the conquest of America is a stark reminder that, for all his stress on consent, Locke was no 'liberal' in our modern terms.

BIBLIOGRAPHY
Primary Sources
Godwin, William, *Enquiry concerning Political Justice*, 3 vols (Toronto, 1946).

Secondary Literature
Dunn, John, 'Consent in the Political Theory of John Locke', *The Historical Journal*, vol. x (1967), pp. 153–82.
Tully, James, 'Rediscovering America: The *Two Treatises* and Aboriginal Rights', in G.A.J. Rogers (ed.), *Locke's Philosophy: Content and Context* (Oxford, 1994), pp. 165–96.
Waldron, Jeremy, 'John Locke: Social Contract versus Political Anthropology', *Review of Politics*, vol. li (1989), pp. 2–28.

R.E.R. Bunce

CURRICULUM, THE

Locke devised the general plan of the curriculum in his correspondence with Edward Clarke (Mason, 1961, p. 271), and was to return to the subject in later short writings, but it is in *Some Thoughts concerning Education* that the continuities with his general doctrine of education are fully spelled out: here, the curriculum follows an order of learning in conformity with the development of human FACULTIES and rests on a conception about the natural connections among the disciplines (Yolton and Yolton, 1989, p. 33): advancement in learning is at once a training of the mental capacities and an exploration of the links among the parts of the map of knowledge.

Reading, writing and foreign languages constitute the first formative stages of the curriculum. Children will start to learn reading skills by playing with alphabet toys, and continue with some easy, pleasant reading, such as Aesop's *Fables*, possibly with accompanying pictures, together with the easier and morally instructive parts of Scripture. Writing will begin with the child's learning to handle specific instruments and postures and can be combined with some first lessons in drawing and shorthand, which may prove useful to a gentleman in his travels and studies (*STE*, sects 148–61).

As soon as the child can speak English, he is prepared to start his training in French and Latin as well. Greek is certainly useful for the scholar, but indifferent for the gentleman (*STE*, sect. 195). Languages are much better taught by reading, translation and conversation than by the usual grammar school methods (learning rules by rote, composing declamations). Reading, writing and learning languages reinforce each other, and are aided by the use of interlinear books (where each line of the original text is immediately followed by the English translation of that line). They also serve as an introduction to the rudiments of both manners and the sciences, through a judicious selection of materials for reading and discussion by the tutor (*STE*, sects 162–77).

The sciences are to be ordered in conformity with the faculties that develop first: instead of LOGIC or metaphysics, learning should begin with those disciplines that solicit 'the Eyes and Memory' (*STE*, sect. 178, p. 235). Geography is thus a good start, especially those parts of it that can train visual recognition and memory.

Arithmetic may be introduced next, as a first step to abstract reasoning, which will gradually make possible further advances in geography, with the comprehension of longitude and latitude and the ability to read maps. Terrestrial maps can soon be supplemented by celestial maps, and thus the first steps in astronomy may be taken, and a modicum of the Copernican system introduced. With a more advanced understanding of the 'globes', the passage to geometry can be made, with the aid of the first six books of Euclid (*STE*, sects 178–81).

Continuous with the steps taken in the study of geography are also the first rudiments of chronology, itself a preparation to the introduction of history, 'the great Mistress of Prudence and Civil Knowledge' (*STE*, sect. 182, p. 237). History is itself one important link in the curriculum; it will put to use the young man's knowledge of Latin in the reading of the Latin histories (gradually advancing to Cicero, Virgil and Horace), will corroborate his reading of Cicero (of *The Offices*) with his by now more advanced Bible reading in order to further his knowledge of virtue, and will ground his study of civil law (Pufendorf and Grotius on the natural rights and duties of men, and the origins of society), and English common law (*STE*, sects 182–7). In a parallel section of Locke's 'Draft Letter to the Countess of Peterborough', history and politics coalesce around 'morality', understood as that 'wherein a man may learn how to live', as opposed to the speculative ethics of the Schools (Locke, 1968, p. 395). Equally serving morality in this sense is the knowledge of men and customs obtained through well-planned travel (*STE*, sects 212–16), or from such writings on the passions of men as Aristotle's *Rhetoric* or la Bruyère's *Characters* (Locke, 1968, p. 403).

Underlying all these pursuits are what Locke prefers to call, instead of referring to the traditional disciplines of logic and rhetoric, the arts of right reasoning (which is 'to have right Notions, and a right Judgment of things … and to act accordingly') and of speaking well (i.e. 'clearly and perswasively') (*STE*, sect. 188, pp.

240–1), which are best imbibed by reading exemplary authors (e.g. Chillingworth and Cicero) and by repeated practice. Significantly, the same 'arts' are placed at the head of the curriculum in 'Some Thoughts concerning Reading and Study for a Gentleman' (Locke, 1968, pp. 398–9).

As for natural philosophy, Locke repeatedly revised and remained unsatisfied with the sections devoted to it (Mason, 1961, p. 286). Its main use seems to be to provide fit subjects for (serious) gentlemanly conversation. Ralph Cudworth's *Intellectual System* is a good review of the ancients, for instance, while DESCARTES, BOYLE and NEWTON are the worthiest to be studied among the moderns. At the same time, Locke recommends the study of 'spirits' (a portion of natural philosophy drawing from the Bible) in preparation for that of the bodies, as fit training for understanding the natural philosophical cum theological argument about the impossibility of matter generating 'the great Phaenomena of Nature' by itself (*STE*, sect. 192, p. 246).

Locke warned that 'learning' should be subservient to the other parts of education, 'virtue', 'wisdom' and 'breeding'; but the end of rightly pursued learning is the same as the end of the education into virtue and wisdom: they are facets of the same programme of building well-oriented mind habits, as well as a love and esteem for both knowledge and morality.

BIBLIOGRAPHY
Primary Sources
Locke, John, *The Educational Writings of John Locke*, ed. James L. Axtell (Cambridge, 1968).

Secondary Literature
Mason, M.G., 'How John Locke wrote *Some Thoughts concerning Education, 1693*', *Paedagogica Historica*, vol. i, no. 2 (1961), pp. 244–90.
Yolton, John W., and Jean S. Yolton, 'Introduction' to John Locke, *Some Thoughts concerning Education*, ed. John

W. Yolton and Jean S. Yolton (Oxford, 1989), pp. 1–75.

Sorana Corneanu

DEISM

Deism is the doctrine that states that there is only one God, who created the world and governs it providentially. It is a moral doctrine in so far as it asserts that God, who is the sum of all perfections, is the supreme legislator, the author and enforcer of a moral law of nature which is discoverable by reason, and that true religion consists of reverently acknowledging God and sincerely endeavouring to obey the divine law. In this respect, the term is synonymous with theism.

The term also has a special use applying to the advocacy of natural religion over its revealed counterparts. In this respect, deism signifies a religious movement with a variety of expressions that flourished from the mid-seventeenth century through the eighteenth century, wherever the Enlightenment took hold. According to this use, deists were theists who became sceptical of the truth claims of religious institutions purportedly founded on revelation and suspicious of their practices. They worried that such institutions tended to be hotbeds of superstition and instruments of social manipulation. Deists did not explicitly deny the possibility or the occurrence of divine revelation. Indeed, the forefather of modern deism, Lord Herbert of Cherbury (1583–1648), affirmed the reality of it as a special gift of divine grace. (Herbert, 1937, pp. 81, 308–13) And John Toland (1670–1722) allowed that God has 'revealed to us in *Scripture* several wonderful Matters of Fact, as *the Creation of the World, the last Judgment* ... which no Man left to himself could ever imagine', and likened these revelations to private thoughts. Toland

objected to the removal of any alleged revelation from public scrutiny and the special use of it to establish institutional religious power and authority, which impinged upon its civil counterparts and encroached upon individual religious liberty. The desired effect of public scrutiny, assisted by the employment of critical historical methods, was the recovery of the pure content of those revelations that Toland was satisfied were true, and their presentation to the world 'stript of all fabulous or superstitious disguises'. The result was a religion of simple piety and virtue. (Toland, 1696, p. 40; 1720) Before Toland, Charles Blount (1654–93) and his circle acclaimed the authority of natural religion over its revealed counterparts. They argued that because universality is an essential property of divine truth and because the doctrines of natural religion derive from right reason and are therefore properly universal, they are to be preferred to the doctrines of revealed religions, which are parochial and suspiciously political. The attribution of universality to a proposition did not, as they applied it, depend upon universal consent, but only upon its being everywhere and always true and discoverable. Moreover, because revealed religions teach contrary doctrines, reason must decide which among them is true; therefore it has authority over them (Blount, 1695, pp. 197–211). For Lord Herbert, Blount and Toland religion was a matter of individual conscience whose best judgements involved the use of impartial reason; accordingly, the proper place for religious discourse, practical and scholarly, was the public sphere, the republic of learning, where it would be free from the constraints of ecclesiastical authority. Deism, then, is a religion of the cultivated laity; books and pamphlets are its vehicles. Accordingly, deists were promoters of TOLERATION, of freedom of thought and expression.

Locke was familiar with writings of all three men and was often in agreement with them. In *An Essay concerning Human Understanding*, he affirmed Lord Herbert's five principles of natural religion, which had become a sort of deist creed: that there is one supreme God, that God ought to be worshipped, that virtue joined to piety is the best worship, that repentance is everyone's obligation, and that reward or punishment is meted out by God to all after this life. Whilst he denied that these principles were innate, he readily admitted that they were universal. (*E*, I.iii.15, p. 77) He appropriated them in *The Reasonableness of Christianity*, without acknowledging their source (*RCh*, pp. 139–40). In the same work he allied himself with deists on the question of original sin: charging that a doctrine that claims that moral guilt could be a natural inheritance dishonours God (*RCh*, p. 5). Like the deists, he assigned reason the task not only of authenticating every revelation, but also of interpreting it, which is to say, of representing its meaning within the frame of ordinary language (*E*, IV.xviii.8, p. 694). In the chapter on ENTHUSIASM, which first appeared in the fourth edition (1700) of the *Essay*, he asserted the continuity of reason and revelation: reason is natural revelation; revelation is natural reason enlarged (*E*, IV.xix.4, p. 698). Among his primary aims in *A Paraphrase and Notes to the Epistles of St Paul* was to show that St Paul was no enthusiast, and that although his mind was infused directly by the Holy Spirit with the whole gospel, he was always able to communicate it through reasoned argument and in MODES of discourse that accommodated its content to ordinary understanding. A methodological presupposition of *A Paraphrase and Notes* is that an author's meaning, indeed his very mind as an author, is recoverable through critical historical enquiry. The Holy Spirit may be at work, but always through the instrumentation of the natural cognitive FACULTIES. Locke also shared with deists a deep suspicion of clerical authority, viewing it as a means to self-aggrandizement and temporal power. He was a constant advocate of toleration, which he described as the principal virtue of a true church (*ETol*, pp. 58–9; *TTG*, p. 137). Because so much of Locke's theological programme is in accord with leading deists such as Lord Herbert,

Blount and Toland, it becomes necessary to explain why it seems proper to regard them as deists and not Locke also.

Any explanation surely must acknowledge these affinities with deism, for they represent integral aspects of Locke's religious thought. What seems to set him apart from deists is an unqualified commitment to the Christian revelation and the claim, noted above, that revelation expands the scope of reason beyond its natural and, in Locke's case, empirical limits. Thus, through revelation, the mind is able to contemplate the supersensible domains of spirit, of legions of angels and of God and Christ reigning over all; likewise the dispensations of history and spiritual conflicts from creation to the second coming of Christ, and the transfiguration of mortality into immortality, whereby through Christ the eternal bliss that Adam lost is restored to his progeny – such things as these, strange as it may seem, become the subject of philosophical reflection. By this means, in Locke's mind the Christian revelation becomes reasonable without being entirely reduced to concepts of mere reason, and philosophical reflection reaches beyond its mere temporal confinement.

In Locke's case, deism or natural religion operates as a foundation of revealed religion, and Locke's thought overall may be viewed as a synthesis of deism and Christian supernaturalism. By reason alone, Locke claims, we can be certain that God exists and is pure spirit (*E*, IV.x). By reason alone he concludes that we are as certain of the existence of spirits as we are of the existence of material bodies, although without knowing the essence of either (*E*, II.xxiii.16, p. 306). By reason alone, Locke claims to be able to conjecture with confidence that there are as many spiritual beings in domains beyond the physical universe as there are natural beings beneath us in the chain of being (*E*, IV.xi.11, p. 637). Concerning free agency and moral actions, he asserts that the proper focus of our reflection is not upon bodies but spirits (*E*, II.xxi.2, p. 234). These are central issues in the *Essay*. Concerning questions about the soul, whether it is mortal or immortal, or whether it is material or immaterial, Locke looks beyond natural reason to revelation for a decisive judgement ('Adversaria Theologica', Nuovo, 2002, pp. 28–30; 'Homos ante et post lapsum', ibid., p. 231; *RCh*, pp. 6–8). His theory of toleration and acceptance of a Christian establishment play an important role in his reflections on the establishment of civil society and commerce. In the Fundamental Constitutions of Carolina, which Locke helped to draft, the hope was expressed that in a tolerant society 'heathens, Jews, and other dissenters' would be persuaded that Christianity is 'true and reasonable' as well as peaceful and inoffensive in its ways (*ETol*, p. 301; Goldie, 1997, p. 178).

Deism or natural religion was not only a foundation for Christianity, Locke viewed it also as a fall-back. In the *Reasonableness of Christianity*, Locke appropriated Lord Herbert's principles and deist arguments against organized religion, using them to vindicate the Christian religion and its God. He used them to respond to a deist objection that a universal religious truth ought to be universally published abroad, yet this has not happened. His response is that God has done so by providing mankind with rational cognitive powers by which the principles of true religion are discoverable, and all who discover them and live by them will become the object of divine favour. The failure of the majority of mankind to achieve this he attributed to the corrosive influence of priestcraft and political ambition. In this frame, Locke represented the Christian revelation as not merely a supernatural supplement to natural religion, but its restorer (*RCh*, pp. 143–55).

Locke's synthesis of deism and Christian supernaturalism prevailed during the eighteenth century largely through the efforts of Edmund Law (1703–87) and William Paley (1743–1805), but among Locke's immediate successors, persons who in one way or another were close to him, John Toland, Anthony Collins (1676–1729) and the third Earl of SHAFTESBURY (1671–1713), it did not take hold.

BIBLIOGRAPHY
Primary Sources
Blount, Charles, *Miscellaneous Works* ed. Charles Gildon (London, 1695).
Herbert, Edward, Lord Herbert of Cherbury, *De Veritate*, trans. Meyrick H. Carré (Bristol, 1937).
Nuovo, Victor, *John Locke: Writings on Religion* (Oxford, 2002).
Toland, John, *Christianity not Mysterious* (1696).
——, *Tetrademus* (1720).

Secondary Literature
Goldie, Mark, *John Locke: Political Essays* (Cambridge, 1997).

Victor Nuovo

EDUCATION AND ITS METHODS

The general aim of Locke's programme of education is to seek the health of both body and mind. While the health of the body occupies a generous introductory portion of *Some Thoughts concerning Education*, where medical and moral considerations combine to support prescriptions towards the achievement of bodily temperance and strength, the bulk of the work, together with most of Locke's *Of the Conduct of the Understanding*, are devoted to the health, or else virtue, of the mind. Excellence of both character and intellect is a matter of 'set[ting] the *Mind* right, that on all Occasions it may be disposed to consent to nothing, but what may be suitable to the Dignity and Excellence of a rational Creature' (*STE*, sect. 31, p. 103). The process of education involves both desires and judgement and a cultivation of the human FACULTIES, which may bring 'the powers of the mind to perfection' (Locke, 2000, p. 158). The main methodological principle Locke postulates to that end is the gradual habituation of the mind to self-mastery and right reasoning by means of constant, initially tutored but gradually self-assumed, practice (Neill, 1989; Schuurman, 2001). Crucial to that habituation is a steady orientation of the mind, achieved by means of the development of a 'love' or 'relish' for truth and moral virtue.

The 'great secret' of education, Locke says, is to harmonize discipline and freedom, or the mastery over one's immediate appetites and the keeping of a 'Child's Spirit, easy, active and free' (STE, sect. 46, p. 112). Against two of the more frequent, yet terribly corrupting, parental methods of his time (beating and flattering), Locke proposes as the best means to that end the employment of '*Esteem* and *Disgrace*' as guides and incentives to a child's education into a love of virtue (STE, sect. 56, p. 116). The middle ground between discipline and freedom is expressed in the development of an 'inward Civility', which is a habit of mind built by means of 'Credit and Commendation' (STE, sect. 67, p. 125–6).

The main precept in conformity with this stress on encouragement by 'credit' is that teaching relies on play rather than on the imposition of tasks or prescription of rules. Equally, rather than textbook rules, much more effective are company and conversation, persuasion and reasoning, and learning by example. While the father plays an important role here in that he needs to be able to act first as a figure of authority and gradually transform himself into a friend and companion, an even more influential actor is the private tutor. Both father and tutor are figures for whom the education of children seems to be not only a task, but a test as well. The tutor needs to be himself an exemplary embodiment of virtue and wisdom, much more than merely a scholar, as well as a patient observer of the child's 'temper' (STE, sect. 100, p. 162). Locke insists on the particularity of each individual child's disposition, inclinations and capacities, and on the need that the educator discriminates them and adapts his methods accordingly. Play, encouragement,

example, conversation and attention to particular temper contribute to catalyse the main educational mechanism, that of bending potentially corrupting inclinations and building 'contrary Habits' (STE, sect. 105, p. 164), or else the virtues of both character and intellect.

A habituation to right reasoning is important, in Locke's view, to both character formation and the development of the understanding. One important part of the learning of morality is the discussion of particular 'Cases' in which the child should be heard and provoked to give his own reasons (STE, sect. 98, p. 161). Equally, a careful management of children's inquisitiveness is one of the main tasks of the tutor, who must always be ready to answer their questions in a precise and truthful manner, and explain matters in ways suited to their comprehension, as well as to provoke their enquiries. Locke's recommendations for the teaching of the languages and sciences also include the notion that the understanding faculties may be best habituated to right reasoning by following several rules of thumb: begin with what is simple, teach little at once, make sure notions are truly absorbed before you proceed, add simple idea to simple idea and advance by degrees (STE, sect. 180, p. 236).

The *Conduct* builds a similar case for the continued exercise of the understanding, well into one's mature age, as the right method of curing its 'weaknesses or defects' (Locke, 2000, p. 180) and enhancing its capacities. There, besides his oft-repeated attacks against scholastic disputation and encyclopedic learning (Yeo, 2006), Locke offers the mind-ordering exercise of mathematics, which trains the understanding into a 'habit of reasoning closely and in train' (Locke, 2000, p. 167), as well as the constant examination of principles, whetted by a steady 'love of truth' (ibid., p. 178), as ways to cure the mind of its inordinate tendencies. Chief among these is the passionate, hasty or else lazy, but always presumptuous and uncritical formation or absorption of opinions (see also *E*, IV.xx, p. 706–19). Moreover, the examination of principles is to be accompanied by frequent self-examination, and is best played out in the combination of reading, meditation and 'discourse with a friend' (Locke, 'Of Study', 1968, p. 422).

BIBLIOGRAPHY
Primary Sources
Locke, John, *The Educational Writings of John Locke*, ed. James L. Axtell (Cambridge, 1968).
———, *Of the Conduct of the Understanding*, ed. Paul Schuurman (Keele, 2000).

Secondary Literature
Neill, Alex, 'Locke on Habituation, Autonomy and Education', *Journal of the History of Philosophy*, vol. xxvii (1989), pp. 225–45.
Schuurman, Paul, 'Locke's Way of Ideas as Context for his Theory of Education in *Of The Conduct of the Understanding*', *History of European Ideas*, vol. xxvii (2001), pp. 45–59.
Yeo, Richard, 'John Locke and Polite Philosophy', in C. Condren, St. Gaukroger and I. Hunter (eds), *The Philosopher in Early Modern Europe: The Nature of a Contested Identity* (Cambridge, 2006), pp. 254–75.

Sorana Corneanu

EDUCATION AND ITS ROLE IN CIVIL SOCIETY

A quaint phrase that a present-day reader is likely to notice, and perhaps equally likely to pass over, became a watchword of Locke's philosophy: it is 'love of truth', which recurs throughout his writings but gains prominence from about 1689 onwards. Additions to the second edition of the *Essay*, published in 1694, are a signpost pointing the way Locke was going. He styled himself 'a Lover of Truth', and he also announced that it is 'Truth alone I seek' (*E*, epistle to the reader, p. 11; and II.xxi.72, p. 285). A close friend, Benjamin Furly, wrote to Locke in 1694 that he too was one of the 'impartiall men that seek Truth, for Truths sake' (Furly to Locke, 21 September/1 October 1694, *Corr.*, vol. v, p. 134). 'Love of Truth [is] necessary', Locke declared in the fourth edition of the *Essay*; it is necessary, he explained to Anthony Collins in 1703, because it 'is the principal part of humane perfection in this world and the seed plot of all other virtues' (*E*, IV.xix.1, p. 697; Locke to Collins, 29 October 1703, *Corr.*, vol. viii, p. 97).

Such claims about 'love of truth' did not strike an altogether new note, but they were of novel intensity and had, this author wishes to suggest, a decisive bearing on Locke's understanding of the purpose of education. In fact, they mark only the beginning of the road on which he set out. The crucial step he took was to commit himself to developing a method of education which would make the pupil care more about the claims of truth than about the claims of self-interest and of custom (cf. Tully, 1993, pp. 200–1). Furthermore, Locke's method was the direct expression of his vision of man and society, and of what life in society might be in an ideal situation. If the ideal society would, as he assumed, live by the love of truth, its antithesis was a society of pernicious self-love and blind submission to local custom. Presumably even in Locke's ideal society some would live (and most would intermittently live) as though human beings had no end other than their own wills, self-interest and individual taste. Still, insofar as the post-lapsarian condition of human beings permitted, the opposite extreme – loving truth – was the goal of human life and collective life in society.

Societies in Locke's Europe appeared to be in poor shape: they were dominated, not by the love of truth, but by self-love and the love of 'the common received Opinions' which men adopted without any examination (*E*, IV.xx.17–18, pp. 718–19). When Locke turned to consider why it was that 'there are very few lovers of Truth', he brought to bear a crucial assumption: men's minds had been 'corrupted by Education' (E, II.xxxiii.1, p. 394; IV.vii.11, p. 601; and IV.xix.1, p. 697). More precisely, he assumed that mental corruption resulted from the specific system of education prevalent in Europe, which was dominated by the rhetorical and linguistic disciplines of the *studia humanitatis* inherited from the Renaissance (see E, II.xxxiii.2–5, pp. 394–5). It followed that those who had entered a university and achieved a high standing in society were likely to have had their minds warped by their studies more than common people. As Locke put it in a stunning passage in the *Essay*, rhetorical education was likely 'to turn young Men's Minds from the sincere Search and Love of Truth ... and to make them doubt whether there is any such thing'. According to his book on *Education*, rhetorical exercises led pupils 'into a captious and fallacious use of doubtful Words, which ... least suits a Gentleman or a lover of Truth'. Hence, the fact that the English landed gentry did not possess 'the Qualities of Gentlemen' was not their own fault but the fault of the European educational system (E IV.vii.11, p.601; STE sects 188–9, pp. 240–3).

Yet it is also this understanding of the power of education that underlay the optimism of the plans for a new method. Although Locke was alarmed by how powerfully the youth were being moulded by existing processes of belief and character-formation, he could also draw encouragement from precisely the same phenomenon and live in the usual humanist hope that a new method of education could transform the way men see, think and behave. Men were to become 'lovers of truth', characterized by an effacement of self-concern (see STE, sects 38–9, pp. 107–9; sect. 94, p. 156; and sect. 147, pp. 207–8; cf. Dunn, 1969, p. 114, and Savonius, 2006). And as the rhetorical disciplines could not orientate youngsters to loving truth, Locke's alternative CURRICULUM was fundamentally anti-humanist: it centred, not on acquiring skills of persuasion and literary abilities which allowed the rhetorician to win the audience to his own point of view, but on inculcating the mental habit of rising above one's subjective perspective and always yielding to the objective truth (Savonius-Wroth, forthcoming in 2009; and, specifically on the discipline of LOGIC, see Schuurman, 2001 and 2004).

Above all, in Locke's educational philosophy there is the sense that the stakes are extremely high. After 1689 Locke saw more and more clearly that the moral rectitude of political life depends on education, and that failings in education could entail catastrophic consequences for the entire nation, neighbouring countries, perhaps even humankind at large in the context of religious warfare and military conquests, world trade and colonization. A dramatic example, given in the *Two Treatises*, of the excesses to which a human being may fall prey is the case of a king turned tyrant, surrounded by flatterers and sycophants. In general, absolute monarchies appeared to be structured around man's 'Love of himself' and 'his own Power, Profit, or Greatness' (TTG II.93; cf. E, IV.iii.20, p. 552). After the overthrow of absolutism – an illegitimate regime premised on self-love – there awaited the massive tasks of reconstruction and education. The success of a revolutionary needed to be followed by the success of a tutor. The stakes were very high on the individual level of belief-formation and moral psychology, from the start of each child's process of education.

BIBLIOGRAPHY
Secondary Literature
Dunn, John, *The Political Thought of John Locke: An Historical Account of the Argument of the* Two Treatises of Government (Cambridge, 1969).
Savonius, S.-J., 'The Role of Huguenot Tutors in John Locke's Programme of Social Reform', in Anne Dunan-Page (ed.), *The Religious Culture of the Huguenots from 1660 to 1789* (Aldershot, 2006), pp. 137–62.
Savonius-Wroth, S.-J., 'The Educational Revolution of John Locke and His Huguenot Allies', in Viviane Rosen-Prest and Geraldine Sheridan (eds), *Les Huguenots éducateurs*

(Paris, forthcoming in 2009).

Schuurman, Paul, 'Locke's Way of Ideas as Context for his Theory of Education in *Of the Conduct of Understanding*', *History of European Ideas*, vol. xxvii (2001), pp. 45–59.

Schuurman, Paul, *Ideas, Mental Faculties and Method: The Logic of Ideas of Descartes and Locke and Its Reception in the Dutch Republic, 1630–1750* (Leiden and Boston, 2004).

Tully, James, *An Approach to Political Philosophy: Locke in Contexts* (Cambridge, 1993).

S.-J. Savonius-Wroth

ENTHUSIASM

Enthusiasm is a state of conviction or certainty wrought by divine inspiration. By direct infusion, it was supposed, God had revealed his identity, will and purpose to chosen agents or prophets or whole communities, who were thereby endowed with special power and authority as bearers of divine truth. Enthusiasm became a controversial theme in England during the seventeenth century, especially following the Interregnum, when the disestablishment of the Church of England and TOLERATION occasioned the proliferation of sects whose claim of a higher authority for the doctrines they espoused threatened the dissolution of venerable institutions and, it was charged, were subversive of social order, morality and religion. After the Restoration, the terms 'Enthusiasm' and 'Enthusiast' were commonly employed as odious labels.

Locke's writings on enthusiasm, which range over nearly a quarter of a century (from c. 1681 until 1704), offer critical assessments of the phenomenon and its claimants that vary in scope and particularity, but overall they express a consistent outlook that is philosophically

interesting and that casts light on Locke's epistemological stance. The most comprehensive and definitive of these writings is a chapter added to the fourth edition of the *Essay* (IV. xix), which appeared in 1700. Locke began planning it five years before (Molyneux to Locke, 26 March 1695, *Corr.*, vol. v, pp. 316–7). Much of its content is anticipated in journal entries inscribed in 1681 and 1682 (Aaron and Gibb, 1936, pp. 114, 119, 123–5), and also in Locke's early correspondence with Damaris Cudworth (*Corr.*, 684, 687, 688, 696, 699, 784), which also dates from 1681, and in 'Immediate Inspiration' (1687), his critical notes on Robert Barclay's *Possibility and Necessity of the Inward Immediate Revelation of the Spirit of God* (Oxford, Bodleian Library, MS Locke c.27, fols 73–4; Nuovo, 2002, pp. 37–41). *A Paraphrase and Notes on the Epistles of St Paul* presents his last reflections on this theme. A primary aim of this work is to prove that St Paul was no mere enthusiast. Thus, whilst Locke accepted as true St Paul's claim to have received the whole Christian gospel directly from God, he was careful to show that the apostle communicated and defended the divine truth vouchsafed to him by using concepts and arguments that accommodated it to rational comprehension, and that he did so without compromising its supernatural origin and authority.

Two things are worth noting about these writings: first they display no change of view, but only greater clarity and detail; second, Locke's reflections on enthusiasm developed in the context of ongoing conversations with Damaris Cudworth, later Lady MASHAM.

Locke imagined enthusiasm, in contrast to authentic divine inspiration, to be a kind of madness, a fixation of the mind upon a religious belief motivated wholly by passion and hence not dependent upon reason. He identified it not only among sectarians, but also among contemporary Platonists. His earliest recorded reflections on the theme, recorded in an ongoing conversation with Damaris Cudworth, were about whether the contemplative state advocated by the Cambridge Platonist John Smith (1618–52) is an instance of enthusiasm. Smith described this state as one of self-transcendence: 'the true Metaphysical and Contemplative man ... who by *Universal Love and Holy Affection* abstracting himself from himself, endeavours the nearest Union with the Divine Essence ... knitting his own centre, if he have any, unto the centre of Divine Being' (Smith, 1673, p. 20). Cognition of this sort was not propositional, rather it was pure vision; it required no reasons or evidence, for it is evident in itself; in this state the contemplative man sees things as they are in themselves as God, or as a more modest Locke would say, angels see them. Locke did not deny the possibility of a purely contemplative cognitive state; indeed, it was the norm for unfettered spirits or transfigured resurrection bodies. But in the present state of humanity, which he described as one of mediocrity: that is, of being situated in the chain of being between incogitative bodies and pure spirits, it is unlikely and hence suspect. In this state, all knowledge, whose content derives from everyday perceptions, is propositional, and the only self-evident truths are self-evident propositions (Aaron and Gibb, 1936, pp. 123–5). All other knowledge and belief derives from the comparison of ideas, deduction or evidence of matters of fact. Those who presume to have been inspired by God are more than likely to have been deceived, for human cognitive power in its present state has no way of distinguishing between true and false inspiration. Some corroborating evidence is needed, such as miracles, which are also problematic, and which can be verified only by rational appraisal, and only in the context of their occurrence (*E*, IV.xix.15, p. 705; *A Discourse of Miracles* in Nuovo, 2002, pp. 44–50).

It is not clear why Locke decided to add a chapter on enthusiasm to the fourth edition of the *Essay* (IV.xix). Writing to William Molyneux in April 1695, he reports that he intended to treat it formally as a cognitive misadventure, as a 'false principle of reasoning often made use of' and would forgo a historical treatment of it. He does not seem to have been motivated by any recent instance of it (Locke to Molyneux, 26 April 1695, *Corr.*, vol. v, pp. 350–3). What is noteworthy is that at the same time that he was writing this chapter, he was engaged in reading MALEBRANCHE (on Molyneux's recommendation; Molyneux to Locke, 26 March 1695, *Corr.*, vol. v, pp. 316–17). This is contemporaneous with the period when Lady Masham was writing *A Discourse on the Love of God*. She characterized the Malebranchian stance of John NORRIS as enthusiasm. She noted that in a sermon on Matthew 22: 37 ('Thou shalt love the Lord thy God with all thy heart ...'), Norris insisted that God is the only proper object of human love and that Christians must forbear loving anything else, hence they must forbear all ordinary human affections (Norris, 1693, vol. iii, p. 12 and *passim*; Masham, 1696, pp. 7–9, and *passim*). He based this directive on the Malebranchian claim that we perceive all things in God, and that all our judgements, whether judgements of truth or of goodness pertain to God only; hence whatever delight we may take in things that please us should have God as its object, for God, in whom we perceive them, is the author and efficient cause of this delight.

Lady Masham responded that Norris, in his divine passion, had ignored the state of mediocrity and its empirical constraints. In this state we learn to love things in their particularity, and to love God only as we come to recognize him to be the author of them (Masham, 1696, pp. 51). There is an interesting analogy between Locke and Lady Masham's views regarding our being in a state of mediocrity: in our cognitive judgements we are required to measure our assent by the weight of evidence; and in our delight in things and in our desire of them, by their particular worth. Thus we love God above all, because he is the author of all good things, but we love these things also for the delight they bring. Moreover, we learn to love God only because of the delight we have in things, just as we learn about God through our knowledge of things (Masham, 1696, pp. 53, 86, 96, 101; *E*, IV.xix.1, p. 697). It would not be farfetched to suppose that Locke and Lady Masham were engaged in a common project in which enthusiasm was a foil, and that their common reflections found expression in these writings. *The Reasonableness of Christianity* could also be considered another expression of this common project; in her *Discourse*, Lady Masham represents Christianity as a reasonable religion well suited to persons living in a state of mediocrity (Masham, 1696, p. 126).

One of the main arguments that Locke makes against enthusiasm is the incapacity of human understanding in a state of mediocrity to distinguish between immediate divine inspiration and its counterfeits. This incapacity lies in the mind, but it relates directly to the reception and warrant of purported revelation. In *Essay* IV.xix.13 he relies on the powerful metaphor of light and darkness and its associations with knowledge and ignorance, and God and Satan. The latter is the 'Prince of Darkness' who is able to present himself as an angel of light.

Light, true Light in the Mind [in a state of mediocrity] is, or can be nothing else but the Evidence of the Truth of any Proposition ... To talk of any other light in the Understanding is to put ourselves in the dark, or in the power of the Prince of Darkness, and by our own consent, to give ourselves up to Delusion to believe a Lie. For if strength of Perswasion be the Light ... I ask how shall anyone distinguish between the delusions of Satan, and the inspirations of the Holy Ghost? (*E*, IV.xix.13, pp. 703-4).

There is a measure of irony in the fact that enthusiasm was rehabilitated by the THIRD EARL OF SHAFTESBURY, who grew up under Locke's tutelage and who was also a friend of Lady Masham and moved in her circle. Exploiting its polarities: good and bad angels, darkness and light, he transformed and transvalued Locke's purely grim notion into an aesthetic concept, namely, the sublime, which became a common notion of the Enlightenment.

For inspiration is a real feeling of the Divine Presence and enthusiasm a false one. But the passion they raise is much alike. For when the mind is taken up in vision and fixes its view either on any real object or mere spectre of divinity, when it sees, or thinks it sees, anything prodigious and more than human, its horror, delight, confusion, fear, admiration or whatever passion belongs to it or is uppermost on this occasion, will have something vast, 'immane' [monstrous, grotesque] and (as painters say) beyond life. And this is what gave occasion to the name of fanaticism, as it was used by the ancients in its original sense, for an apparition transporting the mind (Shaftesbury, 1999, p. 27).

BIBLIOGRAPHY
Manuscript Sources
Oxford, Bodleian Library, MS. Locke c.27.

Primary Sources
Cooper, Anthony Ashley, Third Earl of Shaftesbury, *Characteristics of Men, Manners, Opinions, Times*, ed. Lawrence E. Klein (Cambridge, 1999).
Masham, Damaris, *A Discourse concerning the Love of God* (1696).
Norris, John, *Practical Discourses on Divine Subjects*, 3 vols (1693).
Nuovo, Victor, *John Locke: Writings on Religion* (Oxford, 2002).
Smith, John, *Select Discourses* (2nd edn, Cambridge, 1673).

Victor Nuovo

ESSENCES, REAL AND NOMINAL

Locke introduced his distinction between real and nominal essences about halfway through the third chapter of the third book of the *Essay*. He had introduced the term 'essence' earlier in order to make two points: that general words signify sorts of thing by standing for abstract ideas and that abstract ideas are the 'workmanship of the understanding'. It is in order to clear up confusions about these two points that in III.iii.15 Locke distinguishes real from nominal essences. The real essence, also described by Locke as the original meaning of essence, is 'the very being of any thing, whereby it is what it is. And thus the real, internal, but generally in substances unknown constitution of things, whereon their discoverable Qualities depend, may be called their essence'. But this original use has been perverted, Locke says, and essences are now understood to be integral to sorting things into kinds or species. They tell us what is essential to being a member of a given species. Locke wants to call essences that sort 'nominal essences'. Since 'things are ranked under NAMES into sorts or *species*, only as they agree to certain abstract *Ideas*, to which we have annexed those Names, the *Essence* of each *Genus*, or Sort, comes to be nothing but that abstract idea, which the general, or *sortal* ... Name stands for.' Locke is warning against what might seem to be the confusions of the scholastic account, in which the substantial form constitutes both the essence of each species, that which makes each member the kind of thing it is, and also constitutes the abstract nature by means of which we identify sorts. Locke is telling us that the nominal essence, the abstract idea associated with the name of each species, is other than the real essence, the inner constitution of things on which their properties depend. The ontological essence is different from the ideational essence.

Things become more complicated when we realize that neither Locke's nominal essence nor his real essence can do the job essences had previously been held to perform. Nominal essences do not constitute fixed boundaries to species, standards to which we can appeal to decide whether an entity is or is not a human or a fish. Instead, as ABSTRACTIONS constructed by us from those ideas that have in our experience been found to go together, they depend heavily on our own history with humans or fish. Locke in fact describes the collections of simple ideas we each put together as 'uncertain

and various' and points out it is not only the case each person abstracts a different idea from the collections of ideas they have assembled, but that over time, each of our collections change, as we add some ideas and subtract others. Each such collection constitutes a species, and there are as many species or sorts as there are abstract ideas made by human minds.

The situation with respect to real essences is even more complex, if only because Locke's most frequent remark about them is that they are entirely unknown. It is always a mistake to think that our words stand for such unknown real essences. It is difficult to ascertain what job Locke thinks real essences perform. He thinks that each *particular* has a real essence, in the sense that each particular must have that whereby it is what it is. It is equally clear that Locke thinks, with respect to particulars, there are no properties a particular must have to be what it is. A PROPERTY can only be essential when it comes to sorts, which in turn are identified by means of abstract ideas. While it is possible Locke thinks those parts of the world picked out by nominal essences have something in common, like a molecular structure, it is unlikely that he would identify such a molecular structure with a real essence, as some have assumed, rather than an additional feature of the nominal essence. Real essences can only be that which necessitates the properties concerned, that on which they depend and from which they flow. Locke's discussion of real essences is not a proposal that, for example, corpuscularian science will uncover real essences or inner constitutions, but is instead intended to deflate our claims to be able to know or to use real essences in sorting the world in kinds.

If neither the nominal nor the real essence have explanatory jobs to do, then what is Locke's point in introducing them? He thinks there are two important roles for language: to communicate our ideas to others and to use our words to stand for things. He thinks there are two assumptions we make that can lead to miscommunication. We assume the ideas in our own minds are the same ideas in the minds of others, and we assume our words stand for what he calls 'the reality of things'. Locke's reconception of both real and nominal essences helps explain how we can overcome barriers to communication, by showing that in each case, the assumption is not something I can take for granted, but is instead a project I must work towards. If the abstract ideas to which we attach NAMES are of our own making, rather than something imposed on us by the world, then we should not simply assume we share ideas, but must work to make sure this is so. Similarly, when we use our words to refer to things, we will recognize that the ideas to which we attach names are not controlled by real essences, but rather represent a project on our part to construct ideas that reflect real essences by putting together ideas that have gone together. Locke's discussion of real and nominal essences is not a stray bit of metaphysics dropped into his account of language, but is central to the issues about language Locke wants to raise.

BIBLIOGRAPHY
Secondary Literature
Atherton, M.A., 'Locke on Essences and Classification', in Lex Newman (ed.), *The Cambridge Companion to Locke's* Essay (Cambridge, 2007) pp. 258–85.

Margaret Atherton

FACULTIES

In the introduction to his *Essay* Locke states the aim of finding out 'how far the Understanding can extend its view; how far it has Faculties to attain Certainty' (*E*, I.i.4, p. 45). Faculties are 'Powers of the Mind' (*E*, II.xxi.6, p. 236). The two main powers are those 'perceiving' and 'preferring'. The first belongs to the faculty of the understanding and the second to that of the will (*E*, II.xxi.5, p. 236). The faculty of the understanding, in turn, consists of several cognitive sub-faculties. The first faculty is that of PERCEPTION, which takes place when sensation or reflection has produced an idea in the mind (*E*, II.ix.3, p. 143). Next comes retention, which is when the mind is 'keeping' the simple Ideas that it has received from Sensation or Reflection. Retention is called 'contemplation' when the idea is a continued object of our attention after it has first been received, and called 'memory' when we revive an idea after it has been 'as it were laid aside out of sight' (*E*, II.x.2, p. 149). Another faculty of the mind is that of 'discerning and distinguishing between the several *Ideas* it has' (*E*, II.xi.1, p. 155). This is a vital faculty, because it is prerequisite for all knowledge. Whereas this faculty of discerning considers the (dis)similarities between ideas *absolutely*, the faculty of comparing considers ideas *under a certain respect,* for example, 'in respect of Extent, Degrees, Time, Place' (*E*, II.xi.4, p. 157). Finally, the faculty of composition puts several different simple ideas together into complex ideas; the faculty of enlarging joins several ideas of the same kind ('the Idea of a dozen'); and the faculty of ABSTRACTION makes particular ideas general, by robbing them of particularities (*E*, II. xi. 4, 6 and 9, pp. 157–9).

Locke's attention to the faculties of the mind was by no means original. Discussions of the faculties can already be found in Plato and Aristotle (especially in *De anima*). In the early-modern period, however, the topic gained new urgency because of several developments and trends. The new corpuscularian philosophy demanded a new theory of perception that could replace the scholastic theory of qualities and species. Moreover, the revival of scepticism elicited questions that were all connected with the faculties; how reliable are the different faculties? And should knowledge depend on sensory perception? Finally, the renewed interest in method was frequently phrased in terms of how we should use our cognitive apparatus.

Although Locke's interest in the mental faculties was not new, it is nevertheless possible to detect his own specific agenda on at least three different counts. Firstly, although Locke's opening statement in the *Essay*, and even its very title itself, seem unambiguously concerned with an interest in the faculty of the understanding, the *Essay* first concerns itself with a discussion of ideas. Of course there is a clear connection between faculties and ideas. In the introduction of the *Essay* Locke writes that he wants 'to consider the discerning Faculties of a Man, as they are emply'd about the Objects, which they have to do with' (*E*, I.i.2, pp. 43–4) and these objects are ideas. Locke's preoccupation with ideas was by no means inevitable. Many topics discussed in the *Essay* had already been covered by Nicolas MALEBRANCHE in the *Recherche de la vérité* (1674–5), but whereas Locke organized his book around ideas, Malebranche had structured his around the mental faculties.

Secondly, there is the relation between the understanding and the will. According to DESCARTES, the will has priority over the understanding, in the sense that every judgement depends on the active power of the will (*Principia* I. 34, Descartes, 1982, p. 18). It is clear that Locke disagreed with Descartes and denied this priority, but the precise nature of his own views on the subject is less certain. He discussed the problem in the chapter on 'Of Power' of the *Essay*. In this chapter he remarked that 'When we say the *Will* ... follows the Dictates of the *Understanding*', 'this way of speaking of *Faculties*, has misled many into a confused Notion of so many distinct Agents in us ... which has been no small occasion of wrangling, obscurity, and uncertainty in Questions relating to them' (*E*, II.xxi.6, p. 237). The chapter 'Of Power' caused Locke many problems and it was extensively revised, but the fragment given here was allowed to stand unchanged from the first edition onwards. Moreover, in 'Of the Conduct of the Understanding' (par. 1/sect. 1), Locke repeated the exact words of the phrase used in the *Essay*, but this time without any reservations at all: 'The will it self how absolute and uncontro;eable so ever it may be thought never fails in its obedience to the dictates of the

understanding'.

Thirdly and lastly, unlike Descartes and Malebranche, Locke's discussion of the faculties is tied up with a thoroughly empiricist outlook. Hence it is no coincidence that perception is given first in Locke's list of faculties: 'Perception is the first Operation of all our intellectual Faculties, and the inlet of all Knowledge into our Minds' (*E*, II.x.15, p. 149). Once it has received this empiricist footing, he can use the subsequent discussion of the other faculties against the existence of innate truths. For instance, he remarks that 'even very general Propositions, which have passed for innate Truths', 'in truth' depend *'upon this clear discerning Faculty* of the Mind, whereby it perceives two *Ideas* to be the same, or different' (*E*, II.xi.1, p. 156).

BIBLIOGRAPHY
Primary Sources
Locke, John, 'Of the Conduct of the Understanding', ed. Paul Schuurman (PhD thesis, University of Keele, 2000); see also www.digitallockeproject.nl.
Descartes, René, *Principia philosophiae. Oeuvres de Descartes*, ed. Charles Adam and Paul Tannery, vol. viii-i (Paris, 1982).

Secondary Literature
Buickerood, James G., 'The Natural History of the Understanding: Locke and the Rise of Facultative Logic in the Eighteenth Century', *History and Philosophy of Logic*, vol. vi (1985), pp. 157–90.
Schuurman, Paul, *Ideas, Mental Faculties and Method. The Logic of Ideas of Descartes and Locke and Its Reception in the Dutch Republic, 1630–1750* (Leiden, 2004).

Paul Schuurman

FAITH, REASON AND OPINION

Probability, for Locke, is the great guide to life (*E*, IV.xix.14, p. 704). Thus, two of the *Essay's* aims are to 'search out the *Bounds* between Opinion and Knowledge' and identify 'the Nature and Grounds of *Faith*, or *Opinion*' (*E*, I.i.3, p. 44). Opinion is to believe without a PERCEPTION of the agreement between ideas, to believe when their agreement is only '*presumed to be so*,' (*E*, IV.xiv.4, p. 653). Locke reserves the term 'judgement' for this presumption of an agreement between ideas. These presumptions are based on the PERCEPTION of the probability of an agreement between the two ideas and not on the perception of a probabilistic agreement relation between the ideas. For Locke, truth is never probabilistic, although there can be truths about probabilities.

Locke finds that probabilistic assent or judgement comes in a variety of degrees ranging from 'full *Assurance* and Confidence quite down to *Conjecture, Doubt,* and *Distrust,* (*E*, IV.xv.2, p. 655). There are, moreover, two sorts of judgements, those concerning observables, or 'matters of fact', and those concerning unobservables (*E*, IV.xvi.5, p. 661). Each has somewhat different grounds. Judgements concerning 'matters of fact' are grounded in their conformity with our observations and experiences and the testimony of others regarding their observations and experiences (*E*, IV.xv.4, p. 656 and IV.xvi.6–11, pp. 661–5). Judgements concerning unobservables, however, are grounded in their conformity with our knowledge and analogical reasoning (*E*, IV.xv.4, p. 656; IV.xvi.12, pp. 665–7; and *On the Conduct of the Understanding* (*W*, vol. iii, p. 275). These divisions between probable judgements regarding observables and those regarding unobservables, as well as the divisions of their grounds into personal experience and observation, testimony and ANALOGY are old, going back at least to the ancient medical empirics and sceptics.

Locke's primary concern in discussing assent is normative (*Conduct, W*, vol. iii, pp. 265–6).

He wants to identify how we do, and how we ought to, regulate judgement, hence the frequent scholarly emphasis on Locke's ethics of belief (Wolterstroff, 1996; Passmore, 1980). Locke's position is that for a judgement to be praiseworthy it must be regulated by Reason. The criteria that need to be satisfied are that, first and foremost, judgements must rest on a thorough examination of the grounds of their probabilities (*E*, IV.xv.5, p. 656). Ideally, such an examination would be complete, but Locke concedes that completeness is an ideal and that what actually suffices is 'as full and exact an enquiry as [one] can make,' (*E*, IV.xvi.1, p. 658 and *Conduct, W*, vol. iii, pp. 208–13 and 223). Secondly, the judgement must be proportional to the degree of assent warranted by its grounds, that is, proportional to how probable it actually appears that the ideas agree or disagree. Some sorts of experiences, observations and testimonies warrant greater credence than others (*E*, IV.xvi.6–11, pp. 661–5). Those that accord with the universal experience of all testifiers and with one's own experiences achieve the '*highest degree of Probability*', while those that 'contradict common Experience' or involve testimonies that 'clash with the ordinary course of Nature, or with one another' warrant mere '*Belief, Conjecture, Guess, Doubt, Wavering, Distrust,* [or] *Disbelief*' depending on 'the different Evidence and Probability of the thing'. Also, some analogies are more cogent, others less cogent, insofar 'as they more or less agree to Truths that are established in our Minds, and as they hold proportion to other parts of our Knowledge and Observation' (*E*, IV.xvi.12, p. 665). Thirdly, we must avoid the pitfalls of wrong assent: believing despite lacking proofs (*E*, IV.xx.2–4, pp. 706–9); believing despite an inability to use the available proofs (*E*, IV.xx.5, p. 709); believing despite refusing to use the available proofs (*E*, IV.xx.6, pp. 710–11); and believing based on the wrong measures of probability, which include accepting false principles of knowledge (*E*, IV.xx.8–10, pp. 711–13 and *Conduct, W*, vol. iii, pp. 216–18), accepting ungrounded hypotheses as principles of explanation (*E*, IV.xx.11, pp. 713–14), being seized by passions (*E*, IV.xx.12–14, pp. 714–16 and *Conduct, W*, vol. iii, p. 208), and blindly accepting authoritative pronouncements (*E*, IV.xx.17, pp. 718–19 and *Conduct, W*, vol. iii, p. 208). Essential to this is Reason, because Reason is that which creates the 'proofs' or the various grounds for and against an agreement between ideas.

Reason is a general capacity or power in the Understanding. It is the mental faculty for creating proofs or demonstrations. Unlike the Understanding's faculty of perception, Reason is both an active and passive faculty. It contains sagacity, the active power of discovering and perspicuously ordering intermediate ideas, and illation, the passive power of perceiving the connection in each of the proof's steps and perceiving the connection between the conclusion and proof as a whole, (*E*, IV.xvii.2–3, pp. 668–70). Reason is, moreover, that which distinguishes Man from beasts and is necessary for most knowledge and all judgements. This disparity between knowledge and judgement reflects the lack of anything like INTUITION in judgement. Regarding this lack, Owen has recently argued that in probabilistic proofs the connection between each intermediate idea is one of immediate belief (presumption) caused by either sensation or testimony (Owen, 2007, pp. 422–9).

Locke distinguishes propositions based on their relationship to Reason (*E*, IV.xvii.23, p. 687). Most propositions are in accordance with Reason, i.e. most are truths discoverable via natural deductions from the principles and ideas presented by sensation and reflection. Some are '*above Reason*,' i.e. truths that cannot be naturally deduced, even though true, and consequently have to be presented via revelation. Finally, some are '*contrary to Reason*,' i.e. 'inconsistent with, or irreconcilable to our clear and distinct *Ideas*'. Locke's examples of these three types of propositions are 'one God exists', 'the dead will be resurrected' and 'more than one God exists'.

Locke believed that religious faith was a species of assent and thus needed to be regulated by Reason. So Locke rejected the common dichotomy between Faith and Reason (*E*, IV.xvii.24, pp. 687–8). BERKELEY found Locke's position anathema (Berkeley, 1948, pp. 288–9), but for someone who had lived through the chaos of the Civil War and the Commonwealth such a sensitivity to the dangers of ENTHUSI-ASM and faith loosed from Reason's restraints were natural. Even so, Locke recognized that there was something to the dichotomy and identified a sense in which 'reason' might be opposed to religious 'faith'. The denotation of this special sense of 'reason' is not the mental faculty itself; rather, 'reason' in this sense is a success term denoting the establishment or justification of religious truths by the faculty of Reason: '*Reason*, therefore here, … [is] the discovery of the Certainty or Probability of such Propositions or Truths, which the Mind arrives at by Deductions made from such *Ideas*, which it has got by the use of its natural FACULTIES.' Faith, then, 'is the Assent to any Proposition, not thus made out by the Deduction of Reason; but upon the Credit of the Proposer, as coming from GOD, in some extraordinary way or Communication', i.e. by revelation (*E*, IV.xviii.2, p. 689). The only religious truth that satisfies Locke's special definition of 'reason' is God's existence. All others must be revealed.

Thus revelation plays the central role in Locke's conception of religious 'faith' (*E*, IV.xvi.14, pp. 667–8). Locke distinguished between *Original Revelation*, which is an impression on the mind made by God, and *Traditional Revelation*, which is the testimony of original revelation by prophets and sacred texts. Both types of revelation fall into the ambit of Locke's discussion. Like all kinds of assent, Reason is needed to regulate the presentations of revelation. Given the nature of God, we can know with certainty that 'if God reveals p, then p is true'. But in any purported case of revelation, the real issue is the satisfaction of the antecedent (*E*, IV.xix.14, p. 704). Let us distinguish between 'the revelation p'

and 'its being revealed that p'. 'The revelation p' refers simply to the propositional content of the revelation. 'Its being revealed that p' refers to the event during which the propositional content 'the revelation p' is revealed. Examinations of 'the revelation p' are important in that p's conformity with the dictates of Reason is a necessary condition for p's being revealed. The revelation might be above reason, but it may never be contrary to reason (E, IV.xviii.8, pp. 694–5). Moreover, such examinations might provide *sufficient* grounds for assenting to p – when it can be shown that p is a truth in accordance with Reason (E, IV.xviii.4, pp. 690–1) – but doing this obviates the justificatory role of revelation and even undermines the status of p as revealed since, as maintained in Locke's *Discourse of Miracles*, God would not reveal 'things indifferent, and of small moment, or that are knowable by the use of their natural faculties' because this 'would be to lessen the dignity of his majesty in favour of our sloth' (W, vol. ix, p. 262). The onus for Locke lies on Reason's establishing 'its being revealed that p.'

Locke is very suspicious when others claim a revelation and maintains that even in cases of original revelation, the assent with which we ought to accept p is relatively low and always needs to be judged against the evidence we have against its being a revelation. There is always, says Locke, the possibility that we deceive ourselves in ascribing p's presentation to God and that we misinterpret the meaning of p, which inherently lessens the revelation's epistemic status. Thus for a revelation to be accepted, Reason must determine with a relatively high degree of probability these two questions, 'how should p be interpreted' and 'what's the likelihood that p is actually revealed by God?' Locke has little to say about the former. Presumably, the coherence and conformity of p with all the dictates of Reason (known and judged) is the main criterion, but as Locke well knew such things are always underdetermined; hence the importance of miracles (E, IV.xvi.13, p. 667).

A miracle, according to Locke, is 'a sensible operation, which, being above the comprehension of the spectator, and in his opinion contrary to the established course of nature, is taken by him to be divine,' (W, vol. ix, p. 256). Miracles in Locke's eyes attach to the person rather than to the proposition and vouch for a prophet's status as prophet. They are God's ways of providing the prophet with general bona fides regarding his connection to the Divine (ibid., p. 259). Some seem to have been confused by this, asking something like which of a prophet's propositions are supported by the occurrence of a miracle? (Wolterstroff, 1994, p. 196). But for Locke all propositions alleged by a prophet to be revealed are supported by the prophet's miracle(s) by virtue of these miracles supporting his status as a true prophet. In other words, miracles support the prophet's testimony that propositions p_{1-n} are revelations rather than that these propositions are revealed. (Of course, in all cases, the revelations need to be properly interpreted.) Now, reason cannot just accept any perceived violation of the course of nature because 'bad angles have abilities and excellencies exceedingly beyond all our poor performances or narrow comprehensions' (W, vol. ix, p. 264), and one claiming revelation may be deluded by Satan. So, Locke adds that we ought to accept only those wonders which evince the 'greater and superior power' of God (ibid., pp. 259–60). As the case of Moses against the Pharaoh's magicians showed, the power of God is greater than any 'lying wonders'. This works only when two alleged prophets clash, of course. Where there is no clash of prophets, Locke advocates the 'number, variety, and greatness' of the prophet's miracles. Thus, Jesus ought to be accepted by even the most incredulous because the sheer number and variety of his miracles 'carry with them such strong marks of an extraordinary divine power' (ibid., p. 261).

BIBLIOGRAPHY
Primary Sources
Berkeley, George, *Alciphron or the Minute*

Philosopher, in A.A. Luce and T.E. Jessop (eds), *The Works of George Berkeley, Bishop of Cloyne*, vol. iii (London, 1948).

Secondary Literature

Owen, David, 'Locke on Judgment', in Lex Newman (ed.), *The Cambridge Companion to Locke's 'Essay concerning Human Understanding* (Cambridge, 2007), pp. 406–35.

Passmore, John, *Locke and the Ethics of Belief* (Oxford, 1980).

Wolterstroff, Nicholas, 'Locke's Philosophy of Religion', in Vere Chappell (ed.), *The Cambridge Companion to Locke* (Cambridge, 1994), pp. 172–98.

——, *John Locke and the Ethics of Belief* (Cambridge, 1996).

Benjamin Hill

FREE WILL AND VOLITION

Seventeenth-century writers about freedom and the will ordinarily associated themselves either with 'necessitarianism' or 'indifferentism'. Necessitarians hold that two people with the same circumstances, dispositions, mental states and history would necessarily choose and act in just the same way. Indifferentists, by contrast, hold that such people might choose and act in any of a variety of different ways. In his discussion of freedom and the will, which appears in 'Of Power' (*E*, II.xxi, pp. 233–87), the longest chapter of the *Essay*, Locke aligns himself with the necessitarians. But he makes two important and original contributions there. First, he offers a distinctive account of the nature of choice, or volition. Under his account, only persons are capable of choice and, as such, of guiding actions in the special way we do when acting voluntarily. Second, he offers a different version of the necessitarian position

from that offered by his predecessors. For Locke, that human choices and actions are necessitated is no obstacle to their being free in the senses that matter. If our actions are necessitated *by* our choices and our choices are necessitated *by* the good, then we are free in all the ways that it is worthwhile to be free.

Locke made careful changes to his account of volition between editions of the *Essay*. Here is his definition of volition in the first edition: '*Volition*, 'tis plain, is nothing but the actual choosing or preferring the forbearance to the doing, or doing to the forbearance, of any particular Action in our power, that we think on' (*E*, II.xxi.15, first edition, p. 241). Any thought in favour of an action – a desire, preference, wish – is a volition to perform that action. In the second and later editions, Locke cuts this remark and replaces it: '*Volition*, 'tis plain, is an Act of the Mind knowingly exerting that Dominion it takes itself to have over any part of the man, by imploying it in, or withholding it from, any particular Action' (*E*, II.xxi.15, p. 241). Locke's changes in this regard are systematic. Every first edition definition of volition under which any mental state favouring an action is a volition to perform it is replaced with a more restrictive definition. In his more restrictive account, Locke adds a self-conscious element to volition. A volition, in the later editions, is a mental state favouring an action that is conceived of by the agent as an exercise of power to produce the action. To bring about behaviour by choosing it is not *just* to bring that behaviour about, it is to bring it about through the recognition that one has the power to bring it about. If a person does not choose something, but merely wants it and moves towards it, then he thinks about that thing and moves towards it as a result of his thought about it, his desire for it. But if he *chooses* something and moves towards it, then, in addition to thinking about that thing, he also thinks about the fact that he is thinking about it. He then thinks about the fact that by thinking about it he is bringing it about. Finally, he moves towards it as a result of this complex thought. To act voluntarily is to exercise one's power to act by employing one's recognition of the fact that one has the power to act; it is to act as a result of 'knowingly exert[ing] one's dominion' over the action.

What is the significance of Locke's mature account of volition? In addition to this change in his account of volition, the chapter on PERSONAL IDENTITY was added to the second edition of the *Essay* (*E*, II.xxvii, pp. 328–48). There, Locke claims that the identity of a person is determined by 'consciousness'; an event is an event in a particular person's life just in case he is capable of a certain kind of awareness of it. Animal identity, including the human animal, by contrast, is not constituted by self-consciousness. Under Locke's revised account of volition, in choosing, we are self-consciously aware of the fact that we are endeavouring towards a particular action, and we are self-consciously aware of the causal push provided by our state of endeavouring. Thus, the very causal role of our thoughts about actions through which we bring those actions about is internal to the person. What follows, under Locke's account, is that there is a sense of ownership to be found in voluntary actions that is absent from the behaviour of any non-persons. In voluntary actions of persons, and not in the behaviour of any non-person, the causal role of one's guiding mental state is itself something internal to the agent of the act, and internal in a sense that is unique to persons.

One important question about Locke's view of freedom is what relationship it bears to HOBBES's position. Hobbesians hold that there is no more to freedom than freedom of action, where that is defined as dependency of conduct on choice. A person has freedom of action when he will act in a particular way if he chooses to act that way, and he will act in some other way if he chooses to act in that other way. Under this definition, the only things that take away from freedom are physical constraints, things that prevent our choices from causing the actions at which they aim. Nobody denies that freedom of action is necessary for

fully fledged freedom, but the Hobbesian makes the further claim that it is sufficient. Under Hobbesianism, the causes *of one's choices* are irrelevant to the freedom of the actions that follow those choices. After all, even if one could not have chosen otherwise than one did, it still might be the case that *had* one chosen otherwise, one would have done otherwise.

The question of whether Locke is a Hobbesian is important for assessing the philosophical interest of his position since Hobbesianism has several counter-intuitive implications. Under Hobbesianism, an agent who is coerced or indoctrinated to choose as he does is still free; an agent who chooses through mental illness, a child's ignorance, or addiction is still free. Those who think that these conditions do detract from freedom do not deny that freedom of action is part of fully fledged freedom, but they think there is more to fully fledged freedom than that. Let us define the term the 'Elusive Something' to refer to that, over and above freedom of action, with which the fully fledged free agent is invested. The Hobbesian denies that there is an Elusive Something. Most philosophers who, by contrast, accept that there is an Elusive Something – and thus deny that freedom of action is sufficient for fully fledged freedom – think that an agent who has it has a further form of freedom, usually labelled 'freedom *of will*'. According to such views, even if you have freedom of action, you are not free unless you *choose* freely. But there is space for another position under which there is an Elusive Something, but it is not, itself, a form of freedom. To take this position is to hold ground intermediate between the Hobbesians and those who assert that the Elusive Something is a form of freedom. It is this intermediate position that Locke holds.

Locke famously remarks that it is not the will that is free, but the man (cf. *E*, II.xxi.21, p. 244). Freedom of action is the power to act voluntarily or refrain, according to how one chooses, and the will is a power, the power to make choices. Since powers cannot have powers, it follows that the will cannot have freedom of action. Despite appearances, this does not amount to Hobbesianism. Locke's point in insisting that the will is not the sort of thing that can be free is to discourage philosophers from equating the Elusive Something with some form of freedom. His point is not to deny that there is an Elusive Something; he does not hold that freedom of action is sufficient for freedom (cf. *E*, II.xxi.47, p. 263). Instead, he is discouraging us from looking for what more there is to fully fledged freedom *by* looking for some kind of freedom over and above freedom of action. For Locke, and for the Hobbesian, physical constraints, which prevent a person from doing as he chooses, interfere with that person's abilities. The fully fledged free agent does not suffer from such interference; he can do as he chooses. But for Locke he must have other features also. In noting that it is not the will that is free, but the man, Locke is noting that these other features are not likely to be other abilities. The Elusive Something consists in something else. How, then, are the volitions of the fully fledged free agent caused, according to Locke?

Consider the following passage: '['T]is as much a *perfection, that the power of Preferring, should be determined by Good*, as that the power of Acting should be determined by the Will; and the certainer such determination is, the greater is, the perfection' (*E*, II.xxi.48, p. 264). Locke holds that fully fledged freedom should be equated with a pair of 'perfections'. An agent who has freedom of action enjoys perfection in the determination of action: it is good to act in a way that conforms with one's choices. An agent who has the Elusive Something enjoys perfection in the determination of volition. Locke tells us here what that perfection amounts to: determination by the good. There is something valuable about choosing in accordance with the good, or, at least, being able to. Further, Locke is a hedonist about value: he holds that something is good just in case it promises pleasure or a decrease in

pain (cf. *E*, II.xx.2, p. 229). So, in addition to having freedom of action, Locke is claiming that the fully fledged free agent's choices are determined, or necessitated, by what promises the most pleasure and the least pain (taking into considerations the pains and pleasures of the afterlife), or, if they are not, then such an agent could have done something that would have resulted in his choices being determined that way.

Locke expends some energy detailing the capacities a person needs to have in order to align his volitions with the good. The most important is the capacity to 'suspend' the effect of urges in order to 'contemplate' future pleasures and pains. This form of contemplation makes it possible to have *present* feelings, what Locke calls 'uneasinesses', that align with temporally *future* pleasures and pains (cf. *E*, II.xxi.52, pp. 266–7). By contemplating, we come to be affectively drawn towards actions that promise the most overall long-term pleasure, and affectively averse to actions that promise overall long-term pain. Locke's discussion of the sorts of capacities *required to have* the Elusive Something should not be mistaken with his account of the Elusive Something itself. Locke does not hold, for instance, that an agent has the Elusive Something when he has the capacity to suspend his uneasinesses and deliberate; if he can align his choices with the good without suspension and deliberation, he can still be a fully fledged free agent. Nor does Locke hold that an agent has the Elusive Something when her volitions accord with her (possibly mistaken) *judgements*, or beliefs, about what is best; you are not free if you get it wrong, and could not have got it right.

The insight of the Hobbesian view is that our conduct can realize something of value, and merit the name of freedom, even if it is necessitated: it can come from and depend upon our choices. The insight of Locke's alternative necessitarian position is twofold. First, our choices involve the exercise of the capacities that distinguish persons from animals, and make it possible to realize values that cannot be realized without them. Second, like our conduct, our choices, too, even if necessitated, can realize something of value and worthy of the name of freedom (even if not, literally, a form of freedom): they can align with what is of genuine value.

Gideon Yaffe

GOD

Like the majority of educated people in seventeenth-century England there is no reason to suppose that Locke ever seriously doubted the existence of God. He remained a practising member of the Church of England all his adult life. But his commitment to Christianity as his faith was philosophically of a different order from his belief in a personal God who had created the universe. Whilst commitment to both was for him grounded in reason, the existence of a Deity was for Locke a matter of certain demonstrable truth, whilst the acceptance of the Christian religion was built on an interpretation of the revelation contained in the Bible and especially in the New Testament. Locke explained the difference between these two kinds of religious belief like this. It is manifest, he said, to all who care to think about it that nobody can 'either doubt of the Being of a GOD, or of the Obedience due to Him ... the Precepts of Natural Religion are plain and very intelligible to all Mankind' (E, III. ix. 23, p. 490). However, the truths 'conveyed to us by Books and Languages, are liable to the common and natural obscurities and difficulties incident to Words'. We should therefore be 'less magisterial, positive and imperious, [in] our own sense and interpretation' of them, as the 'Volumes of Interpreters, and Commentators on the Old and New Testament are but too manifest proof' (E, III. ix. 23, p.

489). This distinction between the manifest and demonstrable truth of natural religion and the correct interpretation of sacred texts that are always to some extent problematic is central to his whole philosophy and to his religious beliefs. It is only the former of Locke's claims that this article considers.

Locke holds that there are three kinds and degrees of knowledge: intuitive, demonstrative and experiential. Intuitive truths are self-evident and demonstrative truths are composed of successive propositions of intuitive truths themselves intuitively obviously connected one to another. His proof of the existence of God assumes the correctness of this account of DEMONSTRATION.

Locke argues that the first existential claim of which we can be certain is that of our own existence. Remembering Locke's commitment to the empiricist principle it is no surprise to find him saying that 'Experience ... convinces us, that *we have an intuitive Knowledge of our own Existence*, and an internal infallible Perception that we are' (E, IV. ix. 2, pp. 618–19). The knowledge of our own existence is of the highest degree of certainty and it is this knowledge which, Locke holds, provides us with a route through to knowledge of the existence of God. Given the empirical principle, Locke cannot hold that we have an innate idea of God and therefore we have no innate knowledge of his existence. Granted that knowledge of the existence of God is not intuitive then, Locke holds, it must be knowledge that follows as the conclusion of an argument that itself follows from intuitively obvious, or other known, premises. Locke's argument is fully set out in Chapter X of Book IV of the *Essay*. The intuitively obvious premise from which Locke begins is our knowledge of our own existence. The second premise is also, Locke says, intuitively obvious: that 'bare *nothing can no more produce any real Being, than it can be equal to two right angles*' (E, IV. x. 3, p. 620). Although Locke's claim might be challenged – are these two truths as alike as he assumes? – let us pass on, though we should note that the appeal to a geometrical example will reappear again later. It follows from this that what has a beginning – ourselves – must have its beginning from some prior thing. Further, Locke claims, it is also intuitively obvious that whatever powers a being has, these must originate in the prior being that caused it. It follows from this that as I evidently have the powers of PERCEPTION and knowledge, my prior cause must also have had these powers, otherwise I could not myself have them. It is impossible to move from a state of there being nothing in the universe which has knowledge to a state where there is a being having knowledge, 'For it is as repugnant to the *Idea* of senseless Matter, that it should put into it self Sense, Perception, and Knowledge, as it is repugnant to the *Idea* of a Triangle, that it should put into it self greater Angles than two right ones' (*E*, IV. x. 5, pp. 620–1). Thus from a consideration of ourselves and our constitutions we are led to a knowledge of this 'certain and evident Truth, That *there is an eternal, most powerful, and most knowing Being*' (*E*, IV. x. 6, p. 621), i.e. God. We have, Locke says, a more certain knowledge of the existence of God than of anything else, except our own existence and of 'anything that our senses have not immediately discovered to us' (*E*, IV. x. 6, p. 621). We must remember that it is important in his philosophy that Locke establishes as certain knowledge that God exists, for it is this fact that grounds his moral philosophy and arguably his political theory, as well as his theology. It also defends his epistemology against the sceptic. Granted the existence of God it is, he holds, self-evident that we have a duty to carry out his command, which is to live according to the law of nature that God has prescribed: 'He ... that hath the *Idea* of an intelligent, but frail and weak Being, made by and depending on another, who is eternal, omnipotent, perfectly wise and good, will as certainly know that Man is to honour, fear and obey GOD, as that the Sun shines when he sees it' (*E*, IV. xiii. 3, p. 651). In its social dimensions this provides the political framework in which human beings should live their lives. And, granted that God has created us, he would not have done so and misled us about the way the world seems to us when we use our FACULTIES correctly. Knowledge of the existence of God, then, lies at the base of Locke's general philosophy. But the proof that he offers is constructed from entirely within his empiricist epistemology.

In the *Essay* Locke alludes to DESCARTES's famous proof of the existence of God generally known as the Ontological Argument. Descartes's argument claims that we can frame the idea of a most perfect being, which must necessarily include the idea of existence because a perfect being that did not exist would not be perfect at all. So, a perfect being must exist. Locke writes '*How far the* Idea *of a most perfect Being* which a Man may frame in his Mind, does, or does not prove the *Existence of a* GOD, I will not here examine (*E*, IV. x. 7, p. 621). The reason that Locke does not examine the proof, he says, is because it is contentious, some men finding it persuasive and others not. He almost certainly doubted that discussing it here when he had already provided what he considered a definitive proof was likely to be productive and would in any case be a hostage to fortune. But in his manuscripts there is a document which does consider it and which reaches a verdict. It is dated 1696, some six years after the first edition of the *Essay,* so he could have included it in later editions of his work but he never did. The paper – it is only about 1,000 words long – is headed 'DEUS. – Descartes's Proof of a God from the Idea of necessary Existence examined'. Locke begins by claiming that both the theist and the atheist agree that something has always existed, either a deity, which Locke characterizes as 'a knowing immaterial SUBSTANCE, that made and still keeps all the beings of the universe in that order in which they are preserved' (King, 1830, vol. ii, p. 134) or, for the atheist, 'senseless matter'. Locke points out that the notion of an 'eternal being, whether deity or matter, has in it the idea of existing, otherwise it would not be eternal, so that Descartes's argument is as useful (or useless) to the atheist as it is to the theist and so 'the question is begged on both sides' (King, 1830, vol. ii, p. 136). But the idea of necessarily existing matter or the idea of a necessarily existing deity in itself can never prove the existence of anything. And this is because

> our ideas make or alter nothing in the real existence of things, nor will it follow that anything really exists in nature answering it … But any idea, simple or complex, barely by being in our minds, is no evidence of the real existence of any thing out of our minds answering that idea. Real existence can be proved only by real existence; and therefore the real existence of God can only be proved by the real existence of other things (King, 1830, vol. ii, p. 138).

As a finale Locke alludes to the proof as we have it in the *Essay*. Our own existence, he continues, is given to us intuitively 'from whence therefore may be drawn, by a train of ideas, the surest and incontestable proof of the existence of a God' (King, 1830, vol. ii, p. 139).

It is of no surprise that the empiricist Locke should reject Descartes's ontological argument. But it is contrary to his stereotype to realize that he regarded his argument for the existence of God to be as conclusive as any other knowledge claim except that of his own existence. As we have stressed, which of the great religions best embodied other theological truths was for Locke quite another matter. But it is clear that he takes the possible candidates to be the monotheist ones as he knew them: the Jewish, Christian and Islamic faiths.

How then might we come to a proper knowledge of the nature of God? He is quite clear that our idea of God is not directly 'imprinted' on our minds in the ways in which our idea of an elephant might be. A true notion of God requires 'thought and meditation, and a right use of [our] Faculties' (*E*, I, iv. 15, p. 94). Locke stresses that a true idea of God is to be obtained only by considerable intellectual effort. But

this, he argues, is no criticism of the Deity for not providing us with such an idea at our creation. He has fitted us with faculties to obtain this knowledge. Just as we were not created already clothed but had to use our ingenuity to obtain clothes and other benefits, so we have to work hard intellectually to come to a proper understanding of God. Although simple people often suppose him to have a semi-human form – the white bearded figure of so many representations – our notion of God – he uses the word 'notion' about God more often than the word 'idea' – is not necessarily an image. For our limited intellects God must be understood as necessarily an 'incomprehensible and infinite Object' (*E*, I. iv. 17, p. 95). In one of his notebooks entitled 'Adversaria Theologica 94' he lists under 'Deus' the following properties: 'Unus [One], Trinus [Three], Omnipotens [Omnipotent], Omnisciens [Omniscient], Benignus [Good]' (Locke, 2002, p. 21). Although the notebook cannot be taken as a definitive source for Locke's idea of God, it is as full a source as we have and it is, with regard to natural theology, entirely consistent with his other beliefs. With the exception of the allusion to the doctrine of the Trinity, a matter of Christian doctrine about which Locke appears to have had serious reservations later in his life, the listed properties are all ones that Locke would see as being obtainable by the use of natural reason without reference to Scripture or any other form of revelation.

BIBLIOGRAPHY
Primary Sources
King, Peter, *The Life of John Locke, with Extracts from His Correspondence, Journals, and Common-Place Books. By Lord King* (new edn, 2 vols, 1830; repr., Bristol, 1991).
Locke, John, *Writings on Religion*, ed. Victor Nuovo (Oxford, 2002).

G.A.J. Rogers

HEDONISM

Hedonism is usually taken to be the doctrine that the pursuit of one's own pleasure is the only good in itself. Whilst there is a general scholarly consensus that Locke held to a form of hedonism, there is some disagreement as to the place that hedonism has within his ethics. In particular, the relationship between hedonism and NATURAL LAW within his ethical theory has been contested.

In the *Essay*, Locke maintained, 'Things then are Good or Evil, only in reference to Pleasure or Pain' (*E*, II.xx.2, p. 229). His empiricist doctrine entailed that the ideas we have of good and evil must come from reflection upon our sense experience, and he identified the source of these ideas in our experience of pleasure and pain. Although bodily pleasure and pain are part of this experience, Locke's main focus was on the mental pleasure and pain which accompany the entertaining of certain thoughts.

Locke certainly maintained a 'psychological' hedonism, in that he believed that pleasure and pain were what actually motivated human actions. His empiricism, moreover, and his denial of the existence of innate ideas, demanded that human experience of pleasure and pain (whether mental or sensory) was taken to be the only source of our ideas of good and evil. Enquiries by scholastic philosophers as to the nature of the greatest good, or '*Summum bonum*', were ridiculed by Locke as akin to disputes 'whether the best Relish were to be found in Apples, Plumbs, or Nuts' (*E*, II.xxi.55, p. 269), thus emphasizing the subjective and relativist nature of Locke's hedonism. It is evident, however, that hedonism was not the only element in his ethical theory. Locke also maintained that moral good and evil was 'only the conformity or disagreement of our voluntary actions to some law, whereby good or evil is drawn on us from the will and power of the law-maker'. As well as human laws, there was a 'divine law' given by God, to which he had annexed eternal rewards and punishments. Since it was possible, by reflection

on one's own existence and the world God had made, to know God's existence and his benevolence, it was also possible to know something of this 'divine law' which should govern men's actions through reason (*E*, II.xxviii.8, p. 352).

So whilst hedonism provided the philosophical basis for Locke's ethical theory, it was not straightforwardly utilitarian. Locke's hedonistic foundations for ethics appear to concur in some ways with those of HOBBES. Locke's more positive view of man's natural sociability, and his steady insistence that there is a valid standard, established by God, for judging men's behaviour objectively, repelled him from Hobbes's egoist conclusions. Apart from Hobbes, natural lawyers had typically maintained that actions are good or bad as they conform or fail to conform to the principles which govern the essential nature of man and the world. It was to Richard Hooker's version of natural law theory that Locke turned to argue, in the *Two Treatises*, that man, in the STATE OF NATURE, was at peace with his neighbour. It was this natural law tradition which Locke attempted to graft onto the stock of empiricist hedonism.

This tension within Locke's thought has been noted by modern commentators. Wilson has described Locke's 'two thought complexes'; as well as maintaining his empiricist perspective, Locke 'had strong realist intuitions' which 'push him toward a conception of absolute right and wrong independent of ideas and cultural practice' (Wilson, 2007, p. 383). Locke did not want radically to overturn received notions of morality, he wanted only to remove them from a basis in innate ideas, and place them instead on the foundation of empirical enquiry. Colman has attempted to show how Locke managed to hold both hedonism and 'ethical rationalism' together, although he has conceded that Locke's relativism 'can provide a rational foundation for only a minimal content of the law of nature' (Colman, 1983, p. 243)

Some commentators have, by contrast, attributed the apparent contradictions of the

Essay to the caution for which Locke is sometimes noted, thus seeking the 'real' Locke in the unpublished manuscripts. Vaughan, for example, commenting on some of Locke's unpublished philosophical writings, noted that they 'are all explicitly hedonistic' and 'confirm the guarded hedonism' of his published work (Vaughan, 1982, p. 84).

It is noteworthy that Locke appears to have modified his hedonistic doctrine after the first appearance of the *Essay*. The chapter 'On Power' was greatly expanded for the second edition. In doing so he promoted a 'negative' hedonism, in which the most pervasive motivation for action was the sense of unease. It was the fleeing of this pain, rather than the positive pursuit of pleasure, which took the place of the *summum bonum*, or dominant motivation for human action, in the later editions. 'Good and Evil, present and absent ... work upon the mind: But that which immediately determines the *Will*, from time to time, to every voluntary Action, is the *uneasiness* of *desire*, fixed on some absent good' (*E*, II.xxi.33, p. 252; see also Kraus, 1984, p. 51). It has even been maintained that the ambiguous nature of Locke's negative hedonism entailed that the good life was not incompatible with the coercive society: 'hedonism becomes utilitarianism or political hedonism' (Strauss, 1953, p. 251).

Whilst it is right to stress that Locke's ethics were neither Hobbesian materialism, nor mere utilitarianism, it is also right to recognize that the relativist and hedonistic elements in his thought might readily be used (as indeed they were) in ways that departed more radically from traditional Christian ethics and natural law theory than the cautious Locke himself would have countenanced.

BIBLIOGRAPHY
Secondary Literature
Coleman, John, *John Locke's Moral Philosophy* (Edinburgh, 1983).
Kraus, Pamela, 'Locke's Negative Hedonism', *The Locke Newsletter*, vol. xv (1984), pp. 43–63.
Strauss, Leo, *Natural Right and History* (Chicago, 1953).
Vaughan, Frederick, *The Tradition of Political Hedonism: from Hobbes to J.S. Mill* (New York, 1982).
Wilson, Catherine, 'The Moral Epistemology of Locke's *Essay*', in Lex Newman (ed.), *The Cambridge Companion to Locke's Essay concerning Human Understanding* (Cambridge, 2007), pp. 381–405.

Andrew Starkie

HYPOTHESIS AND ANALOGY

Locke took a dim view of hypotheses. Working with SYDENHAM in 1669, he wrote 'De Arte Medica', lamenting the poor state of contemporary medicine, and identifying its cause:

> Learned men of former ages imploid a great part of their time & thoughts in searching out the hidden causes of distempers, were curious in imagining the secret workemanship of nature & the severall unperceptible tooles wherwith she wrought, & puting all these phansies togeather fashioned to them selves systems & hypotheses (Dewhurst, 1966, p. 80).

Similar sentiments would be expressed in the *Essay*:

> He that shall consider, *how little general Maxims, precarious Principles, and Hypotheses laid down at Pleasure*, have promoted true Knowledge ... will think, we have Reason to thank those, who in this latter Age have taken another Course, and have trod out to us, though not an easier way to learned Ignorance, yet a surer way to profitable Knowledge (*E*, IV.xii.12, p. 647).

157

Consistent with Sydenham's medical methodology, Locke believed that 'getting, and *improving our Knowledge in Substances only by Experience* and History ... is all that the weakness of our FACULTIES in this State of *Mediocrity*, which we are in this world, can attain to' (*E*, IV.xii.10, p. 645).

Locke could countenance hypotheses in certain circumstances – they are 'great helps to the Memory, and often direct us to new discoveries'. But we should be circumspect in their adoption:

> we should *not take up any one too hastily* (which the Mind, that would always penetrate into the Causes of Things, and have Principles to rest on, is very apt to do,) till we have very well examined Particulars, and made several Experiments, in that thing which we would explain by our Hypotheses, and see whether it will agree to them all (*E*, IV.xii.13, p. 648).

Even then, we should still take care that hypotheses do not 'impose upon us, by making us receive that for an unquestionable Truth, which is really, at best, but a very doubtful conjecture, such as are most (I had almost said all) of the *Hypotheses* in natural Philosophy' (ibid.).

Locke nonetheless recognized that people made conjectures concerning unobservables, determining that '*In things which Sense cannot discover, Analogy is the great rule of Probability*' (*E*, IV.xvi.12, p. 665). Such conjectures 'appear more or less probable, only as they more or less agree to Truths that are established in our Minds, and as they hold proportion to other parts of our Knowledge and Observation' (ibid.). For example: 'observing that the bare rubbing of two Bodies violently one upon another, produces heat, and very often fire it self, we have reason to think, that what we call Heat and Fire, consists in a violent agitation of the imperceptible minute parts of the burning matter' (op. cit., pp. 665–6). Such analogy can, sometimes, afford us useful new truths: 'This sort of Probability, which is the best conduct of rational

Experiments, and the rise of Hypothesis, has also its Use and Influence; and a wary Reasoning from Analogy leads us often into the discovery of Truths, and useful Productions, which would otherwise lie concealed' (op. cit., pp. 666–7). Thus, if we are judicious, and fortunate, we can sometimes discover new truths, despite our ignorance of the ESSENCES of body: 'inquisitive and observing Men may, by strength of *Judgement*, penetrate farther, and on Probabilities taken from wary Observation, and Hints well laid together, often guess right at what Experience has not yet discovered to them' (*E*, IV.vi.13, p. 588). 'But,' Locke added, 'this is guessing still.' Thus, when composing a projected new chapter for the *Essay*, 'Of the Conduct of the Understanding', in spring 1697, Locke noted the limitations of even the most careful analogy:

> For example The acid oyle of Vitriol is found to be good in such a case therefor the Spirit of Nitre or Vinegar may be used in like case. If the good effect of it be oweing wholly to the acidity of it the trial may be justified, but if there be some thing else besides the acidity of the oyle of vitriol, which produces the good we desire in the case, we mistake that for analogie which is not, and suffer our understanding to be misguided by a wrong supposition of analogie where there is none (Locke, 2000, p. 228).

Since we do not know what is going on at the unobservable level, we may still misidentify nature's agency and be led astray.

Locke was thus content to adopt a wholly practical attitude to hypotheses. Explaining his medical methodology in a letter to Thomas Molyneux in 1693, Locke reiterated his belief, derived from his collaboration with Sydenham, that 'What we know of the works of Nature ... is only by the sensible effects, but not by any certainty we can have of the tools she uses, or the way she works by' (*Corr.*, vol. iv, p. 629). Consequently, we must do what works:

there is nothing left for a physician to do, but to observe well, and so by analogy argue to like cases, and thence make to himself rules of practice: and he that is this way most sagacious will, I imagine, make the best physician, tho' he should entertain distinct hypotheses concerning distinct species of diseases, subservient to this end, that were inconsistent one with another, they being made use of in those several sorts of diseases but as distinct arts of memory in those cases. And I the rather say this, that they might be rely'd on only as artificial helps to a physician, and not as philosophical truths to a naturalist (*Corr.*, vol. iv, pp. 629–30).

Efficacy trumps even consistency. Hypotheses are only as useful as the rules of thumb they précis, and the results they produce.

BIBLIOGRAPHY
Primary Sources
Dewhurst, Kenneth, *Dr. Thomas Sydenham (1624–1689): His Life and Original Writings*, (London, 1966).
Locke, John, *Of the Conduct of the Understanding*, ed. P. Schuurman, (PhD thesis, University of Keele, 2000).

Jonathan Walmsley

IDEAS

The aim of the *Essay* is to 'enquire into the Original, Certainty, and Extent of humane Knowledge' (*E*, I.i.2, p. 43). Central to this epistemological endeavour is the theory of ideas. Ideas are the 'materials', or 'instruments', of KNOWLEDGE. Ideas compose propositions, and knowledge of propositions consists in nothing more than perceiving the agreement or disagreement of their constituent ideas (*E*, IV.i.1,

p. 525). As such, ideas are the bedrock of Locke's epistemology. Perhaps because of this, they are also one of the most controversial aspects of his philosophy: his theory of ideas was the target of many of the earliest critics of the *Essay*, including NORRIS and STILLINGFLEET; their criticisms coalesced at the end of the early-modern period with Reid, and Locke's use of the term 'idea' continues to be controversial.

Locke was a proponent of what Stillingfleet famously described as the 'new way of ideas' (e.g. Stillingfleet, 1698, p. 120). Drawing on the Platonic and Neoplatonic traditions, the term 'idea' had been repopularized in the seventeenth century by DESCARTES. On the Continent, Descartes's use of the term gave rise to a celebrated dispute amongst Cartesians, centring around MALEBRANCHE and Arnauld. The terminology had advocates on the other side of the English Channel, too, including HOBBES, BOYLE and the Cambridge Platonists, More and Cudworth. To a greater or lesser extent, Locke was influenced by all these figures.

Apologizing for his frequent use of the term, Locke defines 'idea' in the Introduction of the *Essay* as 'whatsoever is the Object of the Understanding when a Man thinks', explaining that the term expresses 'whatever is meant by *Phantasm, Notion, Species*, or whatever it is, which the Mind can be employ'd about in thinking' (*E*, I.i.8, p. 47 and *E*, II.viii.8, p. 134). This definition is – presumably intentionally – consistent with most of the main theories of ideas abroad in the seventeenth century.

'Phantasm', 'notion' and 'species' were all originally Aristotelian terms, typically associated (respectively) with imagination, the intellect and sensation. But these terms were also used, often with related senses, by those hostile to the Aristotelian tradition: Descartes, for instance, often uses 'notion' to refer to ideas in the intellect, and Hobbes often uses 'phantasm' to refer to ideas in the imagination.

The claim that ideas are the 'Object of the Understanding' is equally undiscerning: the correct interpretation of this phrase was central to the dispute between Malebranche and Arnauld. Calling ideas 'objects' naturally suggests the view that ideas are themselves substances, or at least 'SUBSTANCE-like' entities. This was how Malebranche understood the phrase, arguing specifically that ideas are substance-like entities that exist 'in' the mind of God (Malebranche, 1997, sect. 3.2.1, 3.2.6, Elucidation 10). But Arnauld argued that this description is also consistent with the view that ideas are not themselves real beings, but intrinsically representational modifications of mind considered with respect to their intentional content, or the 'intentional objects' of these modifications of mind (Arnauld, 1990, chaps 5–6). This is a development of Descartes's famous claim in the *Meditations* that the term 'idea' is ambiguous, referring 'materially' to thoughts considered as modifications of mind, and 'objectively' to what those thoughts are thoughts *of*, e.g. the sun or a golden mountain (Descartes, 1985, vol. ii, pp. 7, 27–9).

Locke's critics have traditionally assumed that, like Malebranche, Locke thought of ideas as real beings (although unlike Malebranche, not 'in' God). This view is not obviously absurd; it continued to have proponents for centuries to come, particularly during the hey-day of sense-datum theories in the first half of the twentieth century. Nevertheless, Locke's critics argue that the interposition of 'shadowy' entities between perceiving subjects and material objects has disastrous epistemic consequences, leading either to external world scepticism, or at best – and dispensing with the mind-independent external world behind the 'veil of ideas' – Berkelian idealism (e.g. Reid, 1969).

Locke himself often lends support to this interpretation, frequently writing as though ideas are epistemic intermediaries between mind and world. Two notorious passages in particular contain the claims that material objects, unlike ideas, are not known 'immediately' (*E*, IV.iv.3, p. 563), are not 'present to the Understanding' (*E*, IV.xxi.4, p. 721), indeed are perhaps not perceived at all ('the Mind … perceives nothing but its own *Ideas*', *E*, IV.iv.3,

p. 563). These claims are strongly reminiscent of Malebranche's 'wandering soul' argument for the existence of ideas: that since the soul does not leave the body and 'stroll about the heavens' when it perceives objects external to itself, there must be something else distinct from these objects to which the soul is 'intimately joined' and that it thereby perceives directly (Malebranche, 1997, sect. 3.2.1).

But other passages cut against this interpretation, suggesting instead the more orthodox Cartesian view of Arnauld that ideas are nothing more than mental modifications considered with respect to their intentional objects (e.g. Yolton, 1984). Locke identifies ideas with acts of PERCEPTION on a number of occasions (e.g. *E*, I.iv.20, pp. 96–8 and II.x.2, pp. 149–50). Recalling Descartes's distinction between the material and objective reality of ideas, he talks at one point of ideas as being '*objectively in the Mind*' (*E*, p. 13). This interpretation also receives at least mitigated support from comments written by Locke on John Norris, the first published critic of the *Essay* and an English follower of Malebranche, and Malebranche himself. Indeed, in the discussion of Malebranche, Locke pre-empts what was to become a standard objection to indirect (often called 'Lockean') theories of perception, arguing that Malebranche's 'Vision in God' erects an impenetrable veil of ideas between perceiving subjects and material objects to disastrous epistemic effect: for 'how can I know that the picture of any thing is like that thing, when I never see that which it represents' (*W*, vol. ix, p. 250).

Nevertheless, simply 'de-ontologizing' ideas in this way is not an epistemological panacea. Even if ideas are merely intentional objects and not real beings, this does not by itself explain how ideas fulfil the function of guaranteeing our epistemic access to the world, given that in cases of illusion we can perceive objects to be other than they really are, and in cases of hallucination have perceptions as of objects that do not exist at all. Moreover, the overwhelmingly reticent tone of the posthumously published comments on Norris and Malebranche makes it difficult to attribute confidently to Locke any positive view about the nature of ideas. Consistent with his neutral definition of 'idea' in the *Essay*, it might be that Locke does not propose any positive theory of the metaphysics of ideas at all. As Locke himself says in response to Norris's complaint that he fails to give an account of the 'nature of ideas' – whether they are real beings or not, substances or modifications, material or immaterial – 'possibly I found that discovery beyond my reach & being one of those that doe not pretend to know all things am not ashamed to confesse my ignorance in this & a great many other' (Acworth, 1971, p. 10). That is, perhaps the metaphysical status of ideas is one of the things that the enquiry into the 'Original, Certainty, and Extent of humane Knowledge' ultimately shows lies beyond the 'compass of human understanding'.

Whatever their ontological status, Locke argues at length in Book 1 that no ideas are innate. Instead, all ideas derive ultimately from experience: either sensation, whereby objects produce ideas in us, or reflection, whereby we reflect on the operations of our own mind; 'These two are the Fountains of Knowledge, from whence all the *Ideas* we have, or can naturally have, do spring' (*E*, II.i.2, p. 104). But although experience is the ultimate origin of all our ideas, ideas differ depending on exactly how they derive from experience.

Simple ideas derive directly from experience, and in receiving them the mind is 'wholly passive' (*E*, II.xii.1, p. 163), although once received, these ideas can be actively discerned (*E*, II.xi.1, p. 155) and retained (*E*, II.x.1, p. 149). Simple ideas differ depending on their mode of entry into the mind: some simple ideas, like solidity and the secondary quality ideas of colour, sound, taste, smell, come only from one sense; some come from more than one sense, like the ideas of size, shape, motion; some come only from reflection, like the ideas of perception (or thinking) and VOLITION (or willing); and some, like pleasure, pain, power,

existence, unity, come from both sensation and reflection.

Complex ideas, in contrast, are produced out of simple ideas by various actions of the mind, including compounding, decompounding, repeating, comparing (e.g. *E*, II.xii.1, pp. 163–4). It is not entirely clear whether these actions of the mind are always voluntary. At times (*E*, II.xx.9, pp. 153–4) Locke seems to suggest that complex ideas derive directly from sensation; if so, the mind presumably binds together the simple ideas that 'enter by the Senses simple and unmixed' (*E*, II.ii.1, p. 119) (cf. Gibson, 1917, pp. 61–2; Chappell, 1994, p. 37). Elsewhere, however, Locke seems to distinguish complex ideas properly so called from mere 'Combinations of simple *Ideas*', of the sort a dog might 'take in' from his master (*E*, II.xi.7, p. 158). This would be consistent with the epistemological significance that Locke accords to the passivity of the mind in perception (cf. Bolton, 2007, pp. 86–7).

There are three types of complex idea (e.g. *E*, II.xii.3–8, pp. 164–6). First, there are ideas of particular substances, like a man or a sheep, which consist of particular qualities and the relative, obscure and confused, supposition of that in which these qualities inhere. Second, there are ideas of MODES of substances, of which there are in turn two types: simple modes, including space, number, power, and mixed modes, including obligation, drunkenness, lying. (Locke draws the distinction between simple and mixed modes in two not obviously equivalent ways, depending on whether the idea is a collection of distinct homogenous simple ideas (*E*, II.xii.5, p. 165) or modifications of the same simple idea (*E*, II.xiii.1, pp. 166–7).) Finally, and slightly more controversially, there are ideas of relations, like father, bigger and cause. These are slightly more controversial because changes to the fourth edition of the *Essay* are sometimes taken to suggest that Locke came to regard complex ideas and ideas of relations as mutually exclusive categories (*E*, II.xii.1, pp. 163–4; see e.g. Gibson, 1917, p. 65, but contrast Stewart, 1980).

Locke's distinction between simple and complex ideas raises a number of questions. Locke initially characterizes simple ideas in structural terms, as being in themselves 'uncompounded ... nothing but *one uniform Appearance*, or Conception in the mind' (*E*, II.ii.1, p. 132). On this view, simple ideas are like the atoms of the corpuscularian theory of matter (e.g. *E*, II.ii.2, pp. 119–20 and II.vii.10, pp. 131–2). This phenomenologically based structural distinction is in turn intended to ground the later semantic characterization of simple ideas, as ideas that have NAMES that are incapable of definition (*E*, III.iv.4, 7, pp. 421, 422). Yet the structural distinction between simple and complex ideas is not consistently adhered to: Locke admits elsewhere that the simple idea of extension is composed of parts, albeit other ideas of extension (*E*, II.xv.9, pp. 201–3); the simple idea of power 'includes' in it a relation to 'Action or Change'; and consequently paradigmatically uniform secondary quality ideas like colour involve relations, being as they are 'the *Powers* of different Bodies, in relation to our Perception, *etc.*' (*E*, II.xxi.3, p. 234). Even a purely genetic distinction between simple and complex ideas based on their relation to experience is problematic. We have already seen that it is unclear whether complex ideas can come directly from experience; the genetic story is still further complicated by Locke's claim that the mind by 'habitual custom' alters ideas received via the senses into ideas of three-dimensional figures (Bolton, 2007, pp. 81–3).

Crosscutting the distinction between simple and complex ideas are the coincident distinctions between particular and general, and concrete and abstract, ideas. Abstract ideas are the materials of general knowledge. They are formed by a different kind of mental activity, ABSTRACTION, which involves 'separating' ideas from 'the circumstances of Time, and Place, and any other *Ideas*, that may determine them to this or that particular Existence' (*E*, III.iii.6, p. 411).

Abstract ideas are the referents of general terms, like 'white', 'murder' and 'man'. Locke accepts the nominalistic principle that every-thing that exists is particular. Abstract ideas therefore play the role of universals, although they are not themselves universal: the universality of a general idea consists just in the fact that 'the particular *Ideas*, about which it is, are such, as more than one particular Thing can correspond with, and be represented by' (*E*, IV.xvii.8, p. 681). What is controversial is exactly how they fulfil this representative function.

Following BERKELEY (Berkeley, 1975, Introduction), it is traditionally assumed that Locke thinks of abstraction as a process for producing numerically distinct ideas, in which any features tying an idea to a particular spatio-temporal context are literally removed from it. On this view, abstraction is the converse of composition. This appears to be the view of abstraction proposed in the later Drafts of the *Essay* (Walmsley, 2000), and follows from a natural way of interpreting Locke's repeated claims in the *Essay* itself – especially in the second discussion of abstraction in Book III – that forming abstract ideas involves 'leaving out' those features that are peculiar to particular individuals (e.g. *E*, III.iii.7, 8, 9, pp. 411–12).

As Berkeley points out, such a view faces a number of problems. At the very least, it seems to require that abstract ideas have radically indeterminate contents: for instance, that the abstract idea of a man is an idea of a thing capable of voluntary motion, with sense and reason, joined to a body of a certain size, but such that this body is not any particular shape, size or colour. Worse, Locke even seems to suggest that the contents of abstract ideas are not just indeterminate, but internally inconsistent: for instance, that the abstract idea of a triangle 'must be neither Oblique, nor Rectangle, neither Equilateral, Equicural, nor Scalenon; but all and none of these at once' (*E*, IV.vii.9, p. 596).

With these problems in mind, a number of commentators have argued that Locke's considered theory of abstraction is actually the more innocuous view – effectively the view of abstraction that Berkeley himself proposes – that abstraction merely consists in 'partially considering' particular ideas, by selectively attending to some of their features whilst ignoring others (e.g. Ayers, 1991). This view is more strongly suggested by the earlier discussion of abstraction in Book II, where simple ideas of qualities are the main focus. As Locke remarks there, the mind is able to use ideas to represent ideas of a particular class by 'considering them as they are in the Mind such Appearances, separate from all other Existences, and the circumstances of real Existence, as Time, Place, or any other concomitant *Ideas*' (*E*, II.xi.9, p. 159). The mind frames the abstract idea of whiteness, for instance, when it 'considers that Appearance alone' which is common to chalk, snow and milk, without attending to any concomitant ideas, or taking into consideration anything that ties the simple idea of whiteness to its particular spatio-temporal context.

Locke's view of abstraction bears on a different question about the nature of ideas: are ideas images or concepts? There are different ways of understanding the contrast between images and concepts, but the view that all ideas are images (*imagism*) is typically associated with two related theses: first, that objects are presented in thought in the same general way as they are presented in sensation; and second, by way of explanation of this, that there is no rational intellectual faculty, distinct from the (sensory) imagination, of the kind that Descartes argues for by contrasting the mental activity of confusedly imagining a 1,000-sided chillagon with that of clearly conceiving of one (Descartes, 1985, vol. ii, pp. 50–1). The imagism debate bears on the debate about abstraction in the following way: because there can be no images with the kind of indeterminate content that the first model of abstraction (suggested by the Book III discussion) requires, an imagistic theory of ideas presupposes the view that abstract ideas are particular ideas partially considered.

As Ayers, who attributes an imagistic theory to Locke, notes, 'Hostility to Descartes's conception of intellect pervades the *Essay*' (Ayers, 1991, p. 48). Locke explicitly attempts to diffuse Descartes's argument for the existence of a distinct intellectual faculty, arguing that whilst we lack a clear conception of the *figure* of a chillagon, we are nevertheless able to think about it by virtue of having a clear conception of the *number* of its sides (*E*, II.xxix.13–4, pp. 368–9). Moreover, an imagistic theory of ideas is at least suggested by Locke's discussion of memory, with its abundant use of imagistic metaphor: memory is described, for example, as the faculty by virtue of which the mind is able to take previously experienced ideas and 'paint them anew on it self' (*E*, II.x.2, p. 150), even if '*The Pictures drawn in our Minds, are laid in fading Colours*' (*E*, II.x.5, p. 152).

Nevertheless, the evidence that Locke is a thorough-going imagist is equivocal. The first extant draft of the *Essay* opens with an explicit statement of imagism: 'simple Ideas or Images of things … are noe thing but the reviveing again in our mindes those imaginations which those objects when they affected our senses caused in us' (Draft A, sect. 1, p. 1). Yet Locke is less than forthright in the *Essay* itself: Locke's initial definition of idea is neutral between imagistic and non-imagistic theories (*E*, I.i.8, p. 47), and the term 'image' is used only sparingly elsewhere in the work. This might suggest that Locke subsequently became dissatisfied with the view, and perhaps with good reason. Although he is less epistemologically sanguine than Descartes, his scepticism is mitigated by knowledge claims that appear to require the existence of non-sensory intellectual concepts. Particularly problematic amongst the class of propositions that are putatively known are those which have as constituents ideas of our minds, God, powers, existence and morality. None of these ideas appear to be adequately represented imagistically (Soles, 1999).

Whether they are all images or not, Locke draws a number of further distinctions amongst the class of ideas depending on whether the ideas are clear or obscure, distinct or confused, real or fantastical, adequate or inadequate, and true or false.

IDEAS

The first pair of contrasts appropriate the famous Cartesian distinction. *Clear* ideas are those ideas of which the mind has 'a full and evident perception', whereas *distinct* ideas are those that the mind is able to distinguish from all other ideas (*E*, II.xxix.4, p. 364). Clarity and distinctness of ideas is necessary for propositions containing them to be known (e.g. *E*, II.xi.1, pp. 155–6).

The remaining pairs of contrasts relate to the representational features of ideas, or ideas 'in reference to things from whence they are taken, or which they may be supposed to represent' (*E*, II.xxx.1, p. 372). *Real* ideas 'agree to the reality of things' (*E*, II.xxx.1, p. 372). *Adequate* ideas agree to the reality of things completely: they 'perfectly represent those Archetypes, which the Mind supposes them taken from; which it intends them to stand for, and to which it refers them' (*E*, II.xxxi.1, p. 375). Finally, *true* ideas 'conform' to those things that the mind tacitly supposes them to refer to (*E*, II.xxxii.4, p. 385).

These further distinctions co-ordinate with the distinction between simple and complex ideas. Because the mind is wholly passive in the reception of simple ideas, simple ideas are all necessarily real, adequate and true. Simple ideas can represent in one of two ways: primary quality ideas represent by 'resemblance', being the 'Images, or Representations of what does exist' (*E*, II.xxx.2, p. 372), whereas secondary quality ideas represent by causal co-variation, being 'the Effects of Powers in Things without us, ordained by our Maker, to produce in us such Sensations' (*E*, II.xxx.2, p. 372). Either way, the 'steady correspondence' between these ideas and their causes guarantees that they represent them (*E*, II.xxx.2, p. 373), represent them completely (*E*, II.xxxi.2, pp. 375–6) and, as such, conform to them (*E*, II.xxxii.14, pp. 388–9).

This is epistemically important in two ways. First, because they are real, adequate and true, simple ideas are able to function as 'Marks of Distinction in Things' (*E*, II.xxxii.14, p. 388), thereby allowing for perceptually guided action:

simple ideas not only mark differences amongst particular substances by reliably corresponding to differences in these substances' powers to produce those ideas, but also mark the same substances over time so long as an object's powers to produce those ideas (in particular perceivers) remain constant. (The restriction to particular perceivers allows for the possibility of inter-subjective spectral inversion (*E*, II.xxxi.15, p. 389), an example perhaps inspired by Malebranche (Malebranche, 1997, sect. 1.13, p. 66).) Second, the steady correspondence between simple ideas and their causes is sufficient to secure the 'reality' of our knowledge of general propositions involving abstract simple ideas, thereby distinguishing our reasoning from the 'Visions of an Enthusiast' (*E*, IV.iv.1, p. 563).

It is unclear whether causal correspondence is both necessary *and* sufficient for simple ideas to fulfil their representative function. Locke sometimes seems to suggest that co-varying ideas only become representative of their causes when they are *taken* by the mind to be so: when they are 'tacitly referr'd' to their 'Archetypes' by the mind (*E*, II.xxx.1, p. 372 and II.xxxi.1, p. 375). But even if this is the case, Locke's thought seems to be that this 'taking' is an entirely 'natural' function of the mind: that simple ideas are therefore 'natural signs' of their causes, which somehow direct the mind to the mind-independent causes of those ideas (Ayers, 1991, pp. 60–6, Chappell, 1994, pp. 53–5). As such, this accords sensation an epistemologically foundational role.

Like simple ideas, complex ideas of modes and relations are also all real, adequate and true. But this is not because these ideas are passively caused by things distinct from ourselves – quite the opposite. Because these ideas are voluntarily determined by the mind, 'without reference to any real Archetypes, or standing Patterns, existing any where' (*E*, II.xxxi.3, p. 376), there is nothing for these ideas to fail to agree or conform to, hence their reality, adequacy and truth is, in a sense, trivial. This guarantees the possibility of knowledge in those

164

areas where knowledge consists in perceiving agreements or disagreements between ideas of modes, notably mathematics and, crucially for Locke, morality (see MORALITY AND ITS DEMONSTRATION).

Complex ideas of substances, in contrast, are all inadequate, and only sometimes real and true. They are real and true if our ideas are composed of simple ideas that are 'really united, and co-exist in Things without us' (*E*, II.xxx.5, p. 374), like the complex idea of a horse, but unlike the complex idea of a centaur. Yet whilst these complex ideas represent substances, they do not do so completely, and hence are inadequate: our complex ideas of substance neither represent the unknown REAL ESSENCES or inner constitutions of substances (*E*, II.xxxi.6–7, pp. 378–80), nor collect together all the observable properties of objects (*E*, II.xxxi.8–10, pp. 380–2), nor include the idea of substance in general (*E*, II.xxxi.13, p. 383). The inadequacy of our complex ideas of substances, which is due to the 'dull and weak' sensory FACULTIES (*E*, II.xxiii.12, p. 302) by which the mind is furnished with these ideas, is the source of one of the main limitations to the extent of human knowledge.

BIBLIOGRAPHY

Primary Sources
Arnauld, Antoine, *On True and False Ideas*, ed. Stephen Gaukroger (Manchester, 1990).
Berkeley, George, *The Principles of Human Knowledge*, in *Philosophical Works*, ed. Michael Ayers (London, 1975).
Descartes, René, *The Philosophical Writings of Descartes*, ed. John Cottingham, Robert Stoothoff and Dugald Murdoch, 3 vols (Cambridge, 1985; 1991).
Locke, John, 'JL Answer to Mr. Norris's Reflections', in Richard Acworth, 'Locke's First Reply to John Norris', *Locke Newsletter*, vol. ii (1971), pp. 8–11; text also available at www.digitallockeproject.nl.
Malebranche, Nicholas, *The Search After Truth*, ed. Thomas M. Lennon and Paul J. Olscamp (Cambridge, 1997).

Reid, Thomas, *Essays on the Intellectual Powers of Man*, ed. Baruch Brody (Cambridge, Massachusetts, 1969).
Stillingfleet, Edward, *The Bishop of Worcester's Answer to Mr. Locke's Second Letter* (London, 1698).

Secondary Literature
Ayers, Michael, *Locke* (London, 1991).
Bolton, Martha Brandt, 'The Taxonomy of Ideas in Locke's *Essay*', in Lex Newman (ed.), *The Cambridge Companion to 'Locke's Essay concerning Human Understanding'* (Cambridge, 2007).
Chappell, Vere, 'Locke's Theory of Ideas', in Vere Chappell (ed.), *The Cambridge Companion to Locke* (Cambridge 1994).
Gibson, James, *Locke's Theory of Knowledge and its Historical Relations* (Cambridge, 1917).
Soles, David, 'Is Locke an Imagist?', *The Locke Newsletter*, vol. xxx (1999), pp. 17–66.
Stewart, M.A., 'Locke's Mental Atomism and the Classification of Ideas: I and II', *Locke Newsletter*, vol. x (1979), pp. 53–82; vol. xi (1980), pp. 25–62.
Walmsley, Jonathan, 'The Development of Lockean Abstraction', *British Journal for the History of Philosophy*, vol. viii (2000), pp. 395–418.
Yolton, John, *Perceptual Acquaintance* (Oxford, 1984).

Keith Allen

INNATENESS

Locke devotes Book I of the *Essay* to the question of innateness. Against a widely held view (Yolton, 1956), he argues both that there are no innate 'speculative' or epistemological principles and no 'practical' or moral principles, including the idea of God. The purpose of his critique is to advance an alternative thesis that knowledge is acquired through experience and the assembling of ideas, to advocate reason as a (providentially) adequate faculty for knowledge, and to support experimental natural philosophy which does not rely on internal principles or 'maxims'. His position, especially on morals and the idea of God, generated enormous controversy.

In his discussion of speculative principles in Book I, chapter 2, Locke objects to the assumption that there are principles, characters or notions 'stamped upon the Mind of Man' and present in the soul from birth (*E*, I.ii.1, p. 48). While he refers to a literal or naïve view of innateness, he also addresses the dispositional account which asserts that these principles are assented to at a certain stage in human development (like the use of reason). Locke cites two examples of ostensibly innate maxims: *Whatsoever is, is*, and *That it is impossible for the same thing to be, and not be*. For Locke, these principles must receive universal assent from mankind to qualify as innate, but they fail to meet this condition. An imprinted truth must be perceived, according to Locke, but children and idiots do not assent to these statements, disproving their universality and the claim of innateness.

To those who modify the position by introducing the possession of reason as a dispositional requirement, Locke offers different answers depending on what is meant in this context: (1) if reason is necessary to discover innate truths, then everything discovered by reason must be described as innate. Locke rejects this as 'a very improper way of speaking' (*E*, I.ii.5, p. 50). (2) If by the use of reason is meant the moment at which assent is given, Locke does not detect circularity but rather suggests that the account is empirically false: in fact a long interval occurs between using reason and accepting or employing general propositions of this kind (as with children, illiterates or savages).

Locke maintains that innate truths must constitute a category clearly distinguishable from other truths or knowledge; by implication they should also be relatively limited or limitable in number. Accordingly, he concentrates on breaking down distinctions between ostensibly innate principles and other knowledge, and expanding their rank to such an extent that they are neither distinct nor economical. This strategy reappears in his reply to another proposed criterion of innateness – immediacy of assent. Locke indicates that on this basis the store of innate propositions would swell to include as many propositions as we have distinct ideas, together with every proposition of the form *x is not y* corresponding to all our stock of ideas – all of which receive immediate assent – but this would create 'Legions' of such propositions (*E*, I.ii17, p. 57).

Although compelling, Locke's arguments are not decisive. For example, he suggests that the proof from universal assent fails if any other way of accounting for such agreement can be found. This explains why in Book I he anticipates his impending, alternative theory, which he regards as offering a more satisfactory account of knowledge acquisition. Locke states that the 'Senses at first let in particular *Ideas*' (*E*, I.ii.15, p. 55), which are lodged in the memory and assigned NAMES; the mind subsequently abstracts them and learns to use more general names. These materials give employment to reason, but they all derive from acquired sources, not innate. Thus, when Locke stipulates that the constituent ideas of any innate principle must themselves be innate, he can argue that this would make 'all our *Ideas* of Colours, Sounds, Tastes, Figures, *etc.* innate', which contradicts 'Reason and Experience' (*E*, I.ii.18, p. 58).

Locke returns to these questions in his chapter 'Of Maxims' (*E*, IV.vii), which must be read in relation to his discussion of innate speculative principles (the chapters cross-reference one another). Locke makes it clear that he objects to innate principles being treated as foundational, while reiterating his alternative account of the foundations of knowledge. Locke also wants to show that they are not foundational logically; they do not provide the basis for deductions of other truths (*E*, IV.vii.10, p. 596). Finally, they do not advance the sciences or make new discoveries possible (*E*, IV.vii.11, pp. 599, 601–2). He takes the example of the vacuum to show the lack of value of general propositions. Cartesians would define the idea of body to mean nothing but extension. Using the maxim *What is, is* they would demonstrate that there is no space without body and thus deny a vacuum. Someone else, operating with a different definition of body, would defend the possibility of a vacuum, but each could use the maxim *What is, is* to support their argument. The real challenge is to prove the nature of bodies experimentally: 'for that we are left to our Senses, to discover … as far as they can' (*E*, IV.vii.14, p. 605).

In Book I, chapter 3, Locke examines the alleged innateness of *practical* or moral principles. Once again he argues that they require universal consent to be confirmed. In this context the absence of such agreement is 'much more visible' (*E*, I.iii.1, p. 65). By *modus tollens* the argument fails. In this context he also clarifies that universal consent is a necessary but not sufficient condition for demonstrating innate principles.

Locke introduces an important provision for his argument to work. Proponents of innate practical principles must not only show universal agreement but also what Locke calls 'Conformity of Action': actions, he says, are the 'best interpreters' of men's thoughts (*E*, I.iii.3, p. 67). He forestalls the response (which some critics still made) that consensus exists on moral principles but interpretations of them vary in different countries. Accordingly, Locke cites an array of diverse and incommensurable customs observed by travellers, ranging from practices of parricide, exposure of infants, or the abandonment of the ill, to cannibalism and immodest sexual customs. His anthropological references relate not only to primitive but also 'polite' societies, including the Greeks and Romans. Locke concludes with a rhetorical question: 'Where

then are those innate Principles, of Justice, Piety, Gratitude, Equity, Chastity? Or, where is that universal Consent, that assures us there are such inbred Rules?' (*E*, I.iii.9, p. 72). Locke concedes that breaking a rule does not mean that the rule is unknown, but he suggests that it is inconceivable that whole nations could flout what every one of its members knew to be a law. In answer to the counter-argument that custom and education are operative here, Locke replies that either innate principles must be incapable of eradication, in which case they should appear the same across mankind, or they can be altered, but then they should still remain apparent in children and illiterates who are closest to nature.

This discussion returns to a question Locke had addressed in his early *Essays on the Law of Nature* where he disputed the innateness of NATURAL LAW and common consent (*ELN*, pp. 136-45; 160-79). There too he made reference to diverse and incommensurable moral customs, drawing on a technique of argument well established in the sceptical tradition (Carey, 2006). But he is at pains to emphasize (both in his early work and in Book I of the *Essay*) that the lack of innate principles does not mean there are no moral truths. The law of nature remains knowable through the exercise of reason. In the *Essay* his larger point is that proponents of innateness fail to realize that moral principles are commands (e.g. *do unto others*), which explains how it is that we can ask 'why?' when they are stated, an absurd notion if they were innate (see Rickless, 2007, p. 55). If we reformulate these commands as propositions about duties, we will see that they 'cannot be understood without a Law' (*E*, I.iii.12, p. 74), which entails a lawmaker, and punishments and rewards (further developed in the *E*, II.xxviii). To count these propositions as innate, we must also show that the ideas of God, the afterlife, law, punishment, and obligation are innate.

This argument leads on to Locke's final chapter in Book I (chapter 4) in which he confirms that the idea of God is not innate (the absence of which tells against the plausibility of any other innate ideas since God would surely begin with himself if he intended to fit us with this kind of intellectual equipment). In addition to atheists recorded in antiquity and the suspicion of others existing at home, recent travel accounts confirmed that 'whole Nations' (*E*, I.iv.8, p. 87), both primitive and polite, exist without a notion of God or indeed any religion. Locke answers those who, like Grotius, intended to prove natural law or the deity on the basis of the consent of 'refined' peoples, a position Locke shared with Pufendorf. In reply to Bishop STILLINGFLEET, Locke later clarified his position by saying he had not dismantled the familiar proof of God's existence from consent (since he could trace unanimity to other sources). The number of atheists was small enough that the majority view could indeed be called 'the universal consent of mankind'. But an innate idea required universal confirmation 'in the strictest sense; one exception is a sufficient proof against it' (*W*, vol. iii, pp. 494–5).

This is disingenuous since Locke continued to mount up empirical evidence in succeeding editions of the *Essay*. In part Locke's argument depends on setting a condition similar to the requirement of 'Conformity of Action': everyone must share the same idea of God for the idea to qualify as universal. Thus polytheism provides evidence not of universal religious belief and therefore of innateness but merely demonstrates the absence of a 'true or tolerable Notion of a *Deity*' (*E*, I.iv.15, p. 93). Nor does Locke accept that universal agreement would be sufficient to defend innateness; on the contrary, he accounts for the widespread (if not universal) belief in God by saying that some people rightly use their FACULTIES to consider the creation and communicate the idea more widely; others simply follow words in use in their own countries, and the significance of the concept spreads itself. From Locke's perspective, God has provided reason to enable us to grasp his existence; to ask for Him to go further and imprint an idea of Himself would be like asking the one who gave us 'Reason, Hands, and Materials' to build bridges or houses for us at the same time (*E*, I.iv.12, p. 91). Locke's

impatience with this doctrine comes through in his peroration on the danger of enslaving our minds to others and refusing to examine received truths. Innateness forecloses discussion and inquiry.

Locke's position on practical principles and the idea of God met with opposition from many sources, including Stillingfleet, Henry Lee and SHAFTESBURY (Barnes, 1972; Carey, 2006; Colman, 1983; Yolton, 1956). Innateness provided a normative structure within nature, distinguishing between good and evil, and they replied by recirculating the dispositional, Stoic notion of *prolepsis* (Carey, 2006). Locke's acceptance of one innate principle – the desire for happiness and aversion to pain (*E*, I.iii.3, p. 67) – antagonized his critics since it was not normative.

Locke's position works only if his rather extreme requirements are accepted (conformity of action or a shared idea of God). Ultimately he succeeds in offering a coherent alternative theory, not a refutation of dispositional innateness. Locke's growing prestige made it difficult but certainly not impossible to defend innateness.

BIBLIOGRAPHY
Secondary Literature
Barnes, J., 'Mr. Locke's Darling Notion', *The Philosophical Quarterly*, vol. xxii (1972), pp. 193–214.
Carey, D., *Locke, Shaftesbury, and Hutcheson: Contesting Diversity in the Enlightenment and Beyond* (Cambridge, 2006).
Colman, J., *John Locke's Moral Philosophy* (Edinburgh, 1983).
Rickless, S.C., 'Locke's Polemic against Nativism', in Lex Newman (ed.), *The Cambridge Companion to Locke's 'Essay concerning Human Understanding'* (Cambridge, 2007), pp. 33–66.
Yolton, J., *John Locke and the Way of Ideas* (Oxford, 1956).

Daniel Carey

INTUITION AND DEMONSTRATION

Locke defined knowledge as the PERCEPTION of the agreement or disagreement between ideas (*E*, IV.i.2, p. 525). The perception of this agreement comes in three degrees, intuitive, demonstrative and sensitive. These degrees of knowledge involve different levels of directness in the perception of the agreement or disagreement: in intuitive knowledge, it is immediately apprehended; in demonstrative knowledge, it is apprehended mediately, via some middle term(s); and in sensory knowledge, it is apprehended via sensation. The significance of these differences lies in the degrees of clarity and certainty each brings.

Intuition is the immediate apprehension of an agreement obtaining between two ideas. It is the clearest perception we are capable of and carries with it the greatest certainty humans can hope to achieve (*E*, IV.ii.1, p. 531). Locke has little to say about intuition, probably because of its primitiveness. He gives an argument, however, for the claim that intuition possesses the highest degree of certainty: 'Man cannot conceive himself capable of a greater Certainty, than to know that any *Idea* in his Mind is such, as he perceives it to be; and that two *Ideas*, wherein he perceives a difference, are different, and not precisely the same' (ibid.). It looks as if the argument's linchpin is the principle that necessarily, nothing may be contained in the mind as an idea without our being conscious of it, which entails the corollary that if an idea is not perceived to have a quality or property, necessarily it does not have that quality or property. If that is the case, however, Locke generates serious problems for his account of the reality of intuitive knowledge, since it is not clear that ideas just as they are perceived will necessarily reflect the REAL ESSENCES of things, even in the cases of MODES and relations where the idea's nominal essence is its real essence. Often the understanding needs to investigate, to become conscious of, what 'necessarily connected' with the idea, i.e. what is contained but hidden in the idea. But,

if the above 'consciousness principle' is not the argument's linchpin, it is difficult to see how it could be valid. In any case, the relative clarity and certainty of intuitive knowledge is evident in the contrast with demonstration.

Demonstration is the apprehension of an agreement obtaining between two ideas mediated by a step-like series of intuitive apprehensions. Demonstration is less clear and certain than intuition, says Locke, although it is not obvious why it should be once a demonstration is apprehended. To be sure, not every good, graspable demonstration is apprehended (*E*, IV.ii.2, p. 531) since ''tis not without pains and attention: There must be more than one transient view to find it. A steddy application and pursuit is required ... and is not at first sight so knowable, especially to weak eyes' (*E*, IV.ii.4 and 6, pp. 532 and 533). But Locke maintains that demonstration 'is often with a great abatement of that evident luster and full assurance, that always accompany that which I call *intuitive*' knowledge, and he gives the metaphor of 'a Face reflected by several Mirrors one to another' which results 'in every successive reflection with a lessoning of that perfect Clearness and Distinctness' (*E*, IV.ii.6, p. 533). In my experience, the reflected image in such arrays of mirrors appears smaller and smaller, but I would not describe this as the image acquiring 'a great mixture of Dimness'. If, however, this diminution is not what Locke had in mind, it is difficult to see what he could have been thinking. But if this is what he did have in mind, it is difficult see how it applies to demonstration, since there is no diminution of ideas with each step in the demonstration. Perhaps Locke thought that memory was the cause of the diminishing – the awareness of the initial idea fades with each step in the demonstration since memory is such a faulty and fleeting faculty (*E*, II.x.4–5, pp. 150–2). To be sure, the role of memory in demonstration is a central one, and it is related in some way to its lower epistemic status, but that only seems to pertain to the grasping of the demonstration and its status as actual rather than habitual knowledge (*E*, IV.i.8–9, pp. 527–30). Once the entire demonstration is grasped, however, it is hard to see the memorial links as especially epistemically problematic. Another possibility, following the common idea that Locke believed sensitive knowledge to be less certain because it was susceptible to the hyperbolic dream doubt, would be to maintain that demonstration is less certain because it is susceptible to hyperbolic doubts regarding memory. One problem with this is that Locke does not seem to have been aware of hyperbolic memory scepticism, or at least sensitive to it in any way. Another is that it collapses the divide between intuitive and demonstrative knowledge on the one hand and sensitive knowledge on the other. Locke maintains that sensitive knowledge does not 'reach perfectly to either the foregoing degrees of certainty' (*E*, IV.ii.14, p. 537). This, it seems, is based on Locke's recognition that sensitive knowledge is susceptible to hyperbolic doubts in a way that intuitive and demonstrative knowledge are not. Yet in pushing the hyperbolic doubts past that line between sensitive knowledge and demonstrative and intuitive knowledge, it is a short and easy – and rational – step to seeing that intuition too is clearly susceptible to a hyperbolic doubt, the evil demon doubt. Consequently, there would seem to be little basis for maintaining an epistemic difference between any of the degrees of knowledge, unless one were to also maintain that being hyperbolic exhibits degrees, something for which there is no evidence in Locke and which is not clearly meaningful.

Another significant difference between intuition and demonstration is that demonstrative knowledge is prone to antecedent doubt. Because the agreement obtaining between the ideas is not self-evident, before working through the proof, one might easily have doubts about the agreement (*E*, IV.ii.5, pp. 532–3). Also, demonstrative knowledge, according to Locke, reaches far beyond mathematical and geometrical knowledge, encompassing natural philosophy (*E*, IV.ii.9–13, pp. 534–6) and even, famously, morality (*E*,

IV.iii.18, pp. 549–50). Finally, although it is not unusual to identify a Cartesian influence on Locke's account of intuition and demonstration, in reality the accounts of DESCARTES and Locke share a common root in Aristotle's *Prior* and *Posterior Analytics* (Aristotle, 1985), as filtered through Renaissance and late scholastic attempts to resolve the tensions between the allegedly empirical, inductive knowledge of first principles and the purely rational, demonstrative knowledge of scientific truth.

BIBLIOGRAPHY
Primary Sources
Aristotle, *Prior* and *Posterior Analytics*, in *The Complete Works of Aristotle*, ed. J. Barnes (Princeton, 1985), vol. i, pp. 39–166.

Benjamin Hill

KNOWLEDGE

Locke defines knowledge as '*the perception of the connexion and agreement, or disagreement and repugnancy of any of our Ideas*' (*E*, IV.i.2, p. 525). Here one can see the themes behind the justified true belief analysis of knowledge. Belief: knowledge requires an awareness or *perception* of the object of knowledge and its acceptance, in Locke's version assent to the agreement obtaining between the two ideas. Truth: Locke's focus on connection and agreement or disagreement and repugnancy hooks knowledge onto truth since what are true are, strictly speaking, mental propositions consisting of ideas that agree (affirmative propositions) or disagree (negative propositions), (*E*, IV.v, pp. 574–9). Justification: the knower's justification is the PERCEPTION of the agreement relation and, since the agreement relation *is* the truth-making relation, in Locke's account knowledge, when available (*E*, IV.iii, pp.

538–62), necessarily tracks truth. Nevertheless, Locke's formulation of the definition of knowledge raises a number of questions.

The phrase '*of any of our Ideas*' has long been identified as especially problematic. The most natural way to read that phrase is to equate it with 'between any two ideas'. Indeed, Locke's discussion in the *Essay* as well as the *Correspondence with Stillingfleet* seems to imply strongly that this is the only way to read that phrase. But reading it in that way throws up a number of philosophical problems. First, there is the problem of the veil-of-ideas, which leads right to radical, external world scepticism. If the agreements constituting truth and knowledge obtain only between ideas, how can truth and knowledge ever be about idea-independent reality? And if they are never about idea-independent reality, of what value are they? Very little, if any, it would seem. Second, without any connection to idea-independent reality, there is no rational basis for rejecting the internally consistent ravings of an enthusiast. Just so long as his perceptions are rooted in the agreements obtaining between his ideas, however ill-chosen, he has a claim to knowledge as equipotent and legitimate as ours. We may prefer our own ideas, or the ideas of our like-minded colleagues, but that would seem to be merely a matter of taste and not something rooted in reality itself. Third, insofar as sensitive knowledge (knowledge of the real existence of particulars via sense perception) is supposed to fit this characterization, it fails. In sensitive knowledge, it is not at all clear what the two agreeing ideas ought to be. The idea of existence seems the most likely candidate: thus, in knowing by sense '*x* exists', we perceive the idea of *x* and the idea of *existence* and the agreement obtaining between the two. But (1) just what perceiving such an agreement would consist in or be like is rather obscure, and (2) when we reflect on what knowing by sense involves, we can discern no such complex, triple perception. In sensitive knowledge, it seems as if Reid was right – we just see *x* and believe that it exists, (Reid, 2002, pp. 226–33).

As a result of these philosophical problems, many commentators deny that Locke meant it when he said that the perceived agreements are 'of our Ideas'. They posit that Lockean sensitive knowledge consists of the perception of an agreement between a sensed idea and idea-independent reality itself (Chappell, 1994, p. 168; Jolley, 1999, pp. 185–7; Lowe, 1995, pp. 174–5; Lowe, 2005, pp. 53–5; Woolzey, 1977, pp. 146–7; Yolton, 1970, pp. 110–12). However, the 'between ideas' reading cannot, and should not, be so easily dismissed. Locke was pressed hard by Edward STILLINGFLEET on this very issue (Stillingfleet, 1697, pp. 129–31 and 1698, pp. 6–15) and refused to renounce the problematic notion that it was an agreement *of* ideas. Indeed, Locke emphasized more than once that in sensitive knowledge two ideas are perceived to agree or disagree (W, vol. iv, p. 360). Thus, rather than dismiss Locke's requirement that the agreement obtain between ideas, we need to understand how such an ideational agreement can nevertheless be real and thus how Locke's definition of knowledge reconciles with real and sensitive knowledge.

A few scholars have taken Locke's commitment to agreements between ideas seriously and attempted a reconciliation (Hill, 2006; Mattern, 1998; Newman, 2004 and 2007; Soles, 1985 and 1988). Newman's reconciliation is interesting because he is attempting it while maintaining that Locke was committed to the representational theory of perception. Newman finds a distinction in Locke between 'strict *knowledge*' and '*sensitive* knowledge' or between '*knowledge* per se' and '*real* knowledge' (Newman, 2004, pp. 283–4 and 2007, pp. 346–9), which, he believes, effects the reconciliation. Sensitive knowledge is twofold, for Newman, involving a perceived agreement between the ideas of actual sensation and actual existence *and* a cognized agreement between the idea of *x* and reality. Unfortunately, in the end Newman's attempted reconciliation does not appear much better than the usual dismissals of ideational agreements in sensitive knowledge. For Newman, the cognized agreement, which is necessary to go beyond the trifling general claim that an actual sensation is of a real object, is merely a product of judgement and probability. This, however, does not amount to knowledge in Locke's sense any more than perceiving an agreement between ideas and reality. Moreover, given Locke's analysis of judgement and probability in terms of ideas, calling it a 'cognition' does nothing to get Locke outside the 'veil-of-ideas'. A more promising approach is suggested by Mattern and Soles, who propose that the propositional structure of knowledge is the key to understanding how knowledge can be real despite consisting of agreements between ideas. According to their approach, ideas possess, like words, inherently referential aspects which, in sensitive knowledge, are immediately perceived to be satisfied. This immediate perception is the perception of the agreement between the idea of x (as or when actually sensed) and the idea of actual existence (Hill, 2006). The view is that an idea of an object x, while being sensed, contains a non-phenomenal characteristic or aspect – *currently-being-sensed* – that is perceived and that is the first relatum of the agreement relation constituting sensitive knowledge.

Locke identifies four sorts of agreements constituting knowledge – (1) Identity or Diversity, (2) Relation, (3) Co-existence or Necessary Connection and (4) Real Existence (*E*, IV.i.3–7, pp. 525–7).

Identity or Diversity is connected with the mind's faculty of discerning (II.xi.1–3, pp. 155–7), but strictly speaking discerning and perceiving an agreement of identity or diversity are different mental activities. The difference is that perceiving an agreement is propositional, whereas discerning is not. In discerning two ideas, there is no mental act of endorsement or repudiation of the ideas' separation. The ideas are simply distinguished from one another. In the perception of an agreement of identity or diversity, the ideas are separated from one another *and* the mind mentally endorses or repudiates that separation. Consider a white square. According to Locke, we can discern the whiteness and the squareness. That is to say,

we can identify and distinguish the one quality from the other as they exist in the single idea of a white square, i.e. we can identify them as different aspects of the single idea obtaining before our minds. Now, because we can identify and distinguish each quality, we can abstract them from one another, which is to separate them mentally into free-standing ideas. Notice that here we still do not have a mental proposition nor a perception of an agreement of diversity. For that, we additionally need to copulate the ideas via a mental act of endorsement – we endorse the agreement that 'whiteness is not squareness' to generate that real, general truth and to have knowledge of their diversity. Without discernment, of course, we could never arrive at this knowledge of diversity. But that does not entail that discernment is sufficient for having such knowledge. For Locke the ability to construct propositions is just as necessary. It should also be noted that agreements of Identity and Diversity are self-evident and trifling (*E*, IV.viii.2–3, pp. 609–12).

Locke says little about Relational agreements. It is a large category, and what the agreement looks like must be reconstructed from the contrast with complex ideas of relations (*E*, II.xxv, pp. 319–24). A complex idea of relation is an abstract, general idea that necessarily connotes a co-relative idea. For example, the idea of husband necessarily connotes the co-relative idea of wife (and vice versa). Thus, wife is a part of the content of the idea of husband even though what 'appears' to the mind might simply be 'married man'. Because knowledge is propositional, to know that 'Cassius is husband (to Sempronia)', there must be agreements between the ideas of Cassius and husband and the ideas of Sempronia and wife, *and* these agreements must be perceived by the mind along with the connotative, co-relative relation between husband and wife.

Co-existence or Necessary Connection is central to Locke's views of scientific knowledge. Although potentially large, this category is in fact quite small, thinks Locke, because most such connections are *judged probable – presumed* rather than *perceived* to obtain. These connections generally obtain between qualities and properties. For instance, the whiteness and bitterness of manna are necessarily connected to some texture and, as a result, necessarily connected to one another. But because that texture is unknown, the necessary connections obtaining between manna's whiteness and its bitterness, as well as their necessary connections to the PRIMARY QUALITIES, cannot be perceived. In a triangle, however, having 180 degree interior angles and having an area equivalent to one-half its base times its height are properties necessarily connected one to another and to being a three-sided planar figure, and these necessary connections can be perceived via mathematical DEMONSTRATION.

Real Existence was mentioned above. It is the agreement obtaining between an idea (usually while being sensed) and the idea of existence. It is perceived intuitively in the first-person case, demonstratively in the case of God, and via sense in all other cases.

Perceptions of these four agreements may exist in the mind in one of three ways: actually, potentially in that one can remember the proposition but not its proof, or potentially in that one remembers the proof as well as the proposition known. The first is called Actual Knowledge, the present perception of an agreement between ideas. The other two are species of what Locke called Habitual Knowledge. Habitual Knowledge is not quite the same thing as what we call dispositional knowledge because Habitual Knowledge requires memory. One who stores in memory the perception of an agreement between ideas has Habitual Knowledge. The species depend on how this memory might be recalled. Call the first species 'Total Recall': in remembering the proposition one perceives anew the agreement between the ideas. Call the second species 'Credence Recall': in remembering the proposition one does not perceive the agreement but rather recalls having previously perceived such an agreement and feels anew the credence that perception provoked. Of course having Total Recall Habitual Knowledge is better than Credence Recall, but Locke's main point is that Credence Recall is nonetheless 'not short of perfect certainty, and is in effect true Knowledge' (*E*, IV.i.9, pp. 528–9).

BIBLIOGRAPHY
Primary Sources
Reid, Thomas, *Essays on the Intellectual Powers of Man*, ed. D.R. Brookes and K. Haakonssen (University Park, Pennsylvania, 2002).
Stillingfleet, Edward, *The Bishop of Worcester's Answer to Mr. Locke's Letter* (1697).
———, *The Bishop of Worcester's Answer to Mr. Locke's Second Letter* (1698).

Secondary Literature
Chappell, Vere, 'Locke's Theory of Knowledge', in Vere Chappell (ed.), *The Cambridge Companion to Locke* (Cambridge, 1994), pp. 146–71.
Hill, Benjamin, 'Reconciling Locke's Definition of Knowledge with Knowing Reality', *Southern Journal of Philosophy*, vol. xliv (2006), pp. 91–105.
Jolley, Nicholas, *Locke: His Philosophical Thought* (Oxford, 1999).
Lowe, E.J., *Locke on Human Understanding* (London, 1995).
———, *Locke* (New York, 2005).
Mattern, Ruth, 'Locke: "Our Knowledge, which All Consists in Propositions"', in Vere Chappell (ed.), *Locke* (Oxford, 1998), pp. 226–41.
Newman, Lex, 'Locke on Sensitive Knowledge and the Veil of Perception – Four Misconceptions', *Pacific Philosophical Quarterly*, vol. lxxxv (2004), pp. 273–300.
———, 'Locke on Knowledge', in Lex Newman (ed.), *The Cambridge Companion to Locke's 'Essay concerning Human Understanding* (Cambridge, 2007), pp. 313–51.

Soles, David, 'Locke on Knowledge and Propositions', *Philosophical Topics*, vol. xiii (1985), pp. 19–30.

——, 'Locke on Ideas, Words, and Knowledge', *Revue Internationale de Philosophie*, vol. xlii (1988), pp. 150–72.

Woolzey, A.D., 'Some Remarks on Locke's Account of Knowledge', in Ian Tipton (ed.), *Locke on Human Understanding: Selected Essays* (Oxford, 1977), pp. 141–8.

Yolton, John, *Locke and the Compass of Human Understanding* (Cambridge, 1970).

Benjamin Hill

LOGIC

At the beginning of the seventeenth century logic had lost the place of pre-eminence it had held in previous ages, but it remained in academic curricula, and its content and structure were still predominantly Aristotelian. Textbooks were mostly divided in three parts, containing a discussion of individual terms (words), propositions (composed of two terms), and syllogisms (composed of three propositions). Locke was well acquainted with this tradition; a small booklet (Bodleian Library MS Locke f.11, fols 7v–57) with accounts of money received from and disbursed for his pupils from 1661 to 1666, when he was tutor at Christ Church, lists various logical textbooks that were bought for the students under his supervision (by Philippe du Trieu, Samuel Smith and Robert Sanderson, all – near – contemporary authors). Locke's teaching experience did little to endear Aristotelian logic to him. Vituperations against this logic kept recurring in his work and his correspondence for the rest of his life. He attacked the merely verbal character of syllogisms (*E*, IV.xvii.4, pp. 670–8), which according to him were used for sterile disputations without making any real contribution to science; in the 'Of the Conduct of the Understanding', he pitted 'purely logical enquirys' against 'that admirable discovery of Mr NEWTON that all bodys gravitate to one an other' (par. 84, sect. 43).

Locke's *Essay* not only contains an attack on traditional Aristotelian logic, but it also provides an alternative logic, a 'logic of ideas'. Firstly, this new logic is not interested in words but in ideas, which are considered the true atoms of thinking. The structure of Locke's logic was not tripartite (terms – propositions – syllogisms) but bipartite: in the first stage we must take care that each of our individual ideas is clear and distinct, and in the second stage we reason by comparing two ideas with the help of one or more intermediate ideas. Secondly, instead of focusing on the formalization of reasoning, the new logic concentrates on a prior inspection of the mental FACULTIES. Thirdly, there is the topic of method. Different complex ideas demand different methods. In the case of MODES, e.g. the abstract ideas of mathematics (or ethics), the most suitable method is that of Euclid's geometrical demonstration (*E*, IV.xii.7, p. 643). In the case of ideas of substances, Locke advocates his 'Historical, plain method' (*E*, I.i.2, p. 44). This experience-based method accepts our very limited means of obtaining general knowledge of either spiritual or material substances and acquiesces in a step-by-step investigation of the phenomena, in much the same way as a physician examines the disease of a patient. These three elements are interconnected. Our mental faculties are 'about' our ideas, and the method by which we endeavour to obtain knowledge depends on the kind of ideas that are presented to our faculties. The result is a logic that is not so much interested in words as in epistemology and psychology.

Locke's critique of the old logic was not new. The privileged position of the syllogism had been under fierce attack ever since the Renaissance, and its most prominent critics before Locke had been Francis Bacon and René DESCARTES. Moreover, the trend towards a deeper interest in the epistemological and psychological aspects of human cognition had already announced itself in some of the textbooks that Locke himself had used when he served as Tutor at Christ Church, although the subject was to be treated much more radically by Descartes. In his *Regulae*, Descartes wrote about the importance of surveying our instruments of knowledge as an important step in the development of his method. According to him the main weakness of Aristotelian formal logic was its inability to reflect the natural powers of our mental faculties, which left to themselves are quite able to make a correct inference (*Regulae*, Regula III, Descartes, 1986, p. 368). This is thanks to a faculty that Descartes called our *lumen naturale* or *intuitus*. Locke expressed a similar confidence in what he termed our 'native rustick Reason' (*E*, IV.xvii.6, p. 679). But although Descartes discussed the basic notions of a new logic, he left it to his successors to develop these notions into a full system. Where Descartes's admirer Nicolas MALEBRANCHE used these elements to develop a rationalist system around the mental faculties, Locke took these elements to develop an empiricist system around his taxonomy of ideas.

Although Locke's *Essay* can be seen as an alternative for the conventional logic that Locke had taught in Oxford, and although 'immediately from its publication, [it] was read as an articulation of logical theory, despite any ambiguity in his intent' (Buickerood, 1985, p. 181), in 1693 he did not much like the idea of changing the *Essay* into the format of a textbook on logic himself (Locke to Molyneux, 20 January 1693, *Corr.*, vol. iv, p. 627). But he did not mind when two years later the Oxford professor John Wynne (1667–1743) set out to make an abridgement of the *Essay* with the express aim of using it as a textbook on logic, and he expressed delight when this text was indeed used in Oxford, 'in the place of an ordinary system of logick' (Locke to Molyneux, 26 April 1695, *Corr.*, vol. v, p. 351). And when he attacked 'the logick now in use' in the 'Conduct' (on which he started to work in

1697), he probably had come to see his own work as a new logic that formed an improvement on 'rules that have served the learned world these two or three thousand years' (par. 2, sect. 1).

BIBLIOGRAPHY
Primary Sources
Descartes, René, *Regulae ad directionem ingenii* in *Oeuvres de Descartes*, vol. x, ed. Charles Adam and Paul Tannery (Paris, 1986).
Locke, John, 'Of the Conduct of the Understanding', ed. Paul Schuurman (PhD thesis, University of Keele, 2000); see also http://www.digitallockeproject.nl/.

Secondary Literature
Buickerood, James G., 'The Natural History of the Understanding: Locke and the Rise of Facultative Logic in the Eighteenth Century', *History and Philosophy of Logic*, vol. vi (1985) pp. 157–90.
Schuurman, Paul, *Ideas, Mental Faculties and Method. The Logic of Ideas of Descartes and Locke and Its Reception in the Dutch Republic, 1630–1750* (Leiden, 2004).

Paul Schuurman

MEANING AND SIGNIFICATION

Locke is often cited as the *locus classicus* for the view that words signify ideas. He believes that language has two uses: first, to fix our ephemeral thoughts in our memories, and second, to communicate these otherwise hidden thoughts to others. Words can perform these functions because they are sensible, that is they are visible and audible, and can therefore act both as mnemonic signs to ourselves of the fleeting ideas they represent and as 'external' signs to others of the 'invisible' ideas they represent in ourselves (*E*, III.ii.1, p. 405). Locke is drawing here on both scholastic and Hellenistic theories of signification, according to which 'to signify' means, respectively, 'to make known' and 'to indicate' (just as sweat is a sign of pores). 'The use then of Words,' as Locke sums it up, 'is to be sensible Marks of *Ideas*; and the *Ideas* they stand for, are their proper and immediate Signification' (*E*, III.ii.1, p. 405). For Locke, 'signification' is synonymous with 'meaning', 'the meaning of words, being only the *Ideas* they are made to stand for by him that uses them' (*E*, III.iv.6, p. 422).

These are striking claims for modern readers. One way of making sense of the proposal that words 'mean' ideas is to recall what H.P. Grice called 'natural' meaning, whereby we say for example that 'those spots mean measles' (Grice, 1957). More generally however, one needs to recognize that for Locke and his contemporaries, meaning was a fundamentally extra-linguistic phenomenon. While we think of it as ineluctably linguistic and distinct from any subjective sensations we might associate with certain words, for Locke there were no peculiarly semantic entities. His was an unadulterated metaphysics, which postulated no distinction between the senses of words and associated ideas. The meaning of 'sun' was simply the speaker's (and hopefully the community's) idea of that object. A radical dualism between ideas and words therefore underpinned Locke's philosophy of language.

Locke's theory has been criticized from a number of angles. Not only is it urged that language is in certain ways prior to and constitutive of thought, but also that meaning, in addition to and in connection with being linguistic, must be public and normative. Following Wittgenstein, it is suggested that one mind is insufficient and incompetent to establish the correct use of words, that the rules of the game can get off the ground only in a community, and that consciousness cannot provide the criteria for semantic propriety. More broadly, and following Frege, it is proposed that since people communicate, meaning must be publicly accessible – a function, for example, of use or of external objects – and cannot therefore be constituted by private ideas. Related to this proposal is the claim that words refer not to ideas but to things, so that when we say that 'the sun rises', we do not mean that 'my idea of the sun rises' but the object itself.

For Locke, however, words could only be signs of ideas, since ideas, according to the most basic axiom of his epistemology, are all that we know. Moreover, his account of signification is not the naïve cartoon his critics assert but a complex, internally coherent argument that neither cuts words off from the world, nor ignores the obstacle of privacy and the role of the community in communication.

Locke explains that words signify ideas 'by a voluntary Imposition, whereby such a Word is made arbitrarily the Mark of such an *Idea*' (*E*, III.ii.1, p. 405). He suggests that language began with individuals such as Adam imposing certain sounds on certain ideas, creating connections which gradually filtered into 'common use' through a process of 'tacit Consent', the community deciding which words to keep and which to discard, and determining the contents of 'proper' speech (*E*, III.vi.45, p. 467; *E*, III.ii.8, p. 408).

The question remains how auditors gain access to the private ideas of the speaker. Locke's answer has four parts. First, we can know the ideas of others because we can have the same ideas as them; insofar as we are physiologically similar, Locke conjectures that we perceive both the world and the operations of our mind in a similar way and therefore have the same particular ideas of sensation and reflection (*E*, II.xxiii.12, p. 302). We come to share ideas of things of which we have no direct experience by abstracting from particular ideas. By focusing on the resemblances between, for example, mother, nurse and other figures who coo over our cot, we arrive at a universal idea of 'man' (*E*, III.iii.7, p. 411). Equipped now with shared, general ideas, we are able to agree which ideas should be affixed to which words by ostensive definition: we point to the thing

176

which causes a certain idea in us and name it 'man' (*E*, III.i.5, p. 403; cf. *E*, III.xi.18, p. 518; *E*, III.ix.9, p. 479). The final piece of the puzzle elucidates how we identify and name those ideas without public causes. Locke imagines that in the beginning people took the NAMES of sensible ideas and applied them to insensible ideas which resembled the sensible ones; '*Angel*', for example, originally signified 'Messenger' (*E*, III.i.5, p. 403). In explicating the accessibility of ideas of sensation and reflection, which are the building blocks for every conceivable idea, Locke can claim to have accounted for complete communication.

Contra Locke's critics, then, both common use and the external world play a part in the development of meaning. Indeed, when discussing the inverted spectrum, Locke somewhat inconsistently goes so far as to suggest that meaning is a function of public objects rather than private ideas (*E*, II.xxxii.15, p. 389). However, just as Locke has the resources to placate his critics, so might he have something to teach them: he intimates the possible depth of intersubjective experience through language, and evinces the way in which experience provides the indispensable raw materials out of which language is formed.

BIBLIOGRAPHY

Secondary Literature
Aarsleff, Hans, 'Leibniz on Locke on Language' in *From Locke to Saussure: Essays on the Study of Language and Intellectual History* (Minneapolis, 1982), pp. 42–83.
Ashworth, E.J., '"Do Words Signify Ideas or Things?" The Scholastic Sources of Locke's Theory of Language', *Journal of the History of Philosophy*, vol. xix (1981), pp. 299–326.
Dawson, Hannah, 'Locke on Private Language', *British Journal for the History of Philosophy*, vol. xi (2003), pp. 609–38.
———, *Locke, Language and Early-Modern Philosophy* (Cambridge, 2007).

Grice, H.P., 'Meaning', *Philosophical Review*, vol. lxvi (1957), pp. 377–88.
Kretzmann, Norman, 'The Main Thesis of Locke's Semantic Theory', *The Philosophical Review*, vol. lxxvii (1968), pp. 175–96.
Losonsky, Michael, 'Locke on Meaning and Signification' in G.A.J. Rogers (ed.), *Locke's Philosophy: Content and Context* (Oxford, 1994), pp. 123–41.

Hannah Dawson

MODES

Insofar as Locke's taxonomy of ideas is his reconstruction of the *Categories*, 'mode' constitutes a basic category. Traditionally, modes were conceived as properties standing in a dependence relation to their subjects, that of non-mutual separability (Suarez, 1965, vol. i, pp. 250–74). Unlike 'real' accidents, which could exist without their subjects and vice versa, modes could not exist without their subjects. DESCARTES, famously, invoked this notion in the *Meditationes*, while reconceiving extension in the light of his rejection of 'real' accidents. Thus during the course of the seventeenth century, 'mode' became more or less synonymous with 'accident' (e.g. Chauvin, 1713, s.v. *accidens praedicmentale*; Chambers, 1741, s.v. accident). Locke explicitly distanced himself from this tradition: 'if in this I use the word *Mode*, in somewhat a different sence from its ordinary signification, I beg pardon' (*E*, II.xii.4, p. 165). Locke's difference lay not in the dependence relation between modes and their subjects, which he explicitly retained. But precisely where that difference lies is a matter of analysis. One way of approaching such an analysis is to consider three aspects: (1) the elements compounded in an idea of mode; (2) the relations between the compounded elements; (3) the semantic characteristics of the ideas of modes.

Locke recognized two kinds of modes depending on the kinds of elements they contained. Simple modes are compoundings of the same species of element. Examples Locke discusses include the modes of space, duration, number (including infinity), the various modes of sensation, of thinking, and finally of pleasure or pain. The essential idea is that the simple modes exhibit complexity in terms of their various degrees. Saltiness, for example, is a simple mode of taste because it involves the same taste varying in intensity (E, II.xviii.5, p. 224) and '*Intention*' is a simple mode of contemplation because it involves the same attention as '*Remission*' only at a greater level of intensity (E, II.xix.3–4, pp. 227–8). The contrast is with mixed modes, which are compoundings of diverse species of elements. Examples Locke discusses include powers, various modes of sensation, of thinking and of pleasure or pain, moral properties like '*Lye*', and institutional activities like '*Triumphus*', among others. In mixed modes, there are layers of complexity in addition to variations in intensity. So the taste of salted licorice is a mixed mode because it involves the distinct flavours of salt, liquorice and anise alongside their various degrees of intensity, and nostalgia is a mixed mental mode because it involves remembrance bound to longing.

What is distinctive about both kinds of compoundings is that though truly predicated on their subjects, they do not inhere in their subjects. This is clearest in cases like '*Triumphus*' (the Roman victory ritual), which 'being Actions that require time to their performance, and so could never exist all together' (E, II.xxii.8, p. 291) and the modes of space, since space (expansion) is not a SUBSTANCE. But the same applies to modes that do exist all at once and are attributable to a substance, like beauty or being one metre long. In those cases the mode applies by virtue of the substance's qualities, but cannot be identified with those qualities.

Because of non-inherence, we have considerable freedom in constructing modes. '*The Mind*,' says Locke, 'often *exercises an active Power in the making these* several *Combinations*' and often 'without examining whether they exist so together in Nature' (E, II.xxii.2, p. 288). Locke's usual way of expressing this is to say that modes are made '*very arbitrarily*' (E, III.v.3–6 and 12–13, pp. 429–31 and 435–6). This is Locke's fundamental difference with modes in the traditional sense, which Suarez maintained were real because they flowed *ex natura re*. For Locke, qualities flow *ex natura re* but modes are imposed on to substances by the mind.

Another consequence of non-inherence is that they cannot be united by the substrata of their subjects of predication. For Locke it is the name that unifies the elements of the idea of mode *and* the different elements of the modal property (E, II.xxii.4 and 8, pp. 289–91; III.v.10–11, pp. 434–5; III.vi.44–5, pp. 466–8). By 'name', Locke means not a specific utterance but the codification of a name within a natural language or a linguistic community, since utterances or NAMES buried in an individual's mind and memory are just as fleeting and transient as the modes and their ideas themselves.

The two consequences of non-inherence raise a difficult problem – how can modes be *real*? If modes are arbitrarily constructed names imposed on the world, how could they not be 'fantastical' and all 'knowledge' involving them not be a mere 'castle in the air'? Were modes to involve only social or institutional knowledge, this would not seem such a problem, but for Locke arithmetical, geometrical and moral properties are modes. Indeed this is a pressing problem for Locke and the one that has most exercised scholars (Ayers, 1991, pp. 91–109; Jolley, 1999, pp. 155–61).

Locke maintained that what grounds the reality of modes is that their NOMINAL ESSENCES are identical to their REAL ESSENCES – the ideas of modes are themselves archetypes in other words (E, II.xxx.4, pp. 373–4; III.iii.18, pp. 418–19; III.v.14, pp. 436–7), which is supposed to follow from non-inherence and arbitrariness. (Logical consistency appears to some to be Locke's grounds for reality, but in fact logical consistency is a criterion for identifying real ideas of modes, but not their metaphysical grounds or basis; the reason why, for Locke, logical possibility is a mark of real ideas of modes is that they are themselves the archetypes for logical possibility.) Commentators have generally frowned on this, considering it, apparently, ad hoc. Certainly Locke ought to have said more, but the situation is not as dire as it is often presented. Given that modes were intended to delineate to the warp and woof of possibility (*E*, II.xxx.4, pp. 373–4; III.v.5, p. 430), Locke's account accords perfectly with his nominalism and appears to suffer from irreality no more than other nominalist accounts of possibility.

BIBLIOGRAPHY
Primary Sources
Chambers, Ephraim, *Cyclopaedia* (1741).
Chauvin, Stephen, *Lexicon philosophicum* (Leeuwarden, 1713).
Suarez, Francisco, *Disputationes metaphysicae* (Hildesheim, 1965, repr. of Paris, 1866).

Secondary Literature
Ayers, Michael, *Locke: Epistemology and Ontology*, 2 vols (New York, 1991).
Jolley, Nicholas, *Locke: His Philosophical Thought* (Oxford, 1999).

Benjamin Hill

MOLYNEUX PROBLEM, THE

On Saturday, 7 July 1688, the Irish scientist and politician William Molyneux (1656–98) sent a letter to Locke in which he put forward a problem that was inspired by Locke's French extract of his *Essay* (Locke, 1688). In this extract, Locke distinguished between ideas we acquire by means of one sense and those we acquire by means of more than one sense. He maintained that someone who lacks a sense will never be able to acquire the ideas pertaining to it. A blind man, for example, will never be able to have any idea of colour. Among the ideas we are able to acquire by means of a combination of senses, Locke reckoned those of space, rest, motion and figure. Molyneux's problem had to do with the last of these. He formulated his problem as follows:

A Problem Proposed to the Author of the Essai Philosophique concernant L'Entendement. A Man, being born blind, and having a Globe and a Cube, nigh of the same bigness, Committed into his Hands, and being taught or Told, which is Called the Globe, and which the Cube, so as easily to distinguish them by his Touch or Feeling; Then both being taken from Him, and Laid on a Table, Let us suppose his Sight Restored to Him; Whether he Could, by his sight, and before he touch them, know which is the Globe and which the Cube? Or Whether he Could know by his sight, before he stretched out his Hand, whether he Could not Reach them, though they were Removed 20 or 1000 feet from him? If the Learned and Ingenious Author of the Forementioned Treatise think this Problem Worth his Consideration and Answer, He may at any time Direct it to One that Much Esteems him, and is, His Humble servant William Molyneux (*Corr.*, vol. iii, pp. 482–3).

For reasons unknown, Locke never replied to this letter. However, a couple of years later, after the two philosophers had started an amicable correspondence, Molyneux returned to his problem, this time with success. The exchange of letters was a result of Molyneux's praise of Locke in his dedication of the *Dioptrica Nova* to the Royal Society:

But to none do we owe for a greater advancement in this part of philosophy [i.e., LOGIC], than to the incomparable Mr. Locke, who in his *Essay concerning Humane Understanding*, has rectified more received mistakes and delivered more profound truths, established on experience and observation, for the direction of man's mind in the prosecution of knowledge … than are to be met with in all the volumes of the ancients. He has clearly overthrown all those metaphysical whimsies, which infected men's brains with a spice of madness, whereby they *feigned a knowledge where they had none, by making a noise with sounds, without clear and distinct significations* (Molyneux, 1692, p. xl–xli).

Locke was sent a copy of the *Dioptrica Nova*, read Molyneux's flattering words and thanked the writer: '… if my trifle could possibly be an occasion of vanity to me; you have done most to make it so, since I could scarce forbear to applaud myself upon such a testimony from one, who so well understands DEMONSTRATION' (16 July 1692, *Corr.*, vol. iv, p. 480). He added: 'Sir, you have made great advances of friendship towards me, and you see they are not lost upon me' (*Corr.*, vol. iv, p. 480). There followed an exchange of letters mainly dealing with improvements to Locke's *Essay*. In one of these, dated 2 March 1692/3, Molyneux once again presented Locke with his problem of the person born blind, though in a somewhat altered form, asking Locke if he could perhaps find some place in his *Essay* to say something about it (*Corr.*, vol. iv, p. 651). This time Locke reacted with enthusiasm: 'Your ingenious problem will deserve to be published to the world' (28 March 1693, *Corr.*, vol. iv, p. 666). From the second edition of his Essay (1694), Locke included Molyneux's problem in his work and thereby made it accessible to a wider audience:

Suppose a Man born blind, and now adult, and taught by his touch to distinguish

between a Cube, and a Sphere of the same metal, and nighly of the same bigness, so as to tell, when he felt one and t'other; which is the Cube, which the Sphere. Suppose then the Cube and Sphere placed on a Table, and the Blind man to be made to see. Quaere, Whether by his sight, before he touch'd them, he could now distinguish, and tell, which is the Globe, which the Cube' (*E*, II.ix.8, p. 146).

The reader will have noticed that in this second version of his problem Molyneux omitted the question about distance. Perhaps he believed that the answer to the question regarding the distinguishing and naming of a sphere and a cube implied the answer to the distance question. It is also possible that he made the omission because in the *Dioptrica Nova* he had – clearly, he believed – demonstrated that distance cannot be seen and that the answer was therefore obvious.

The question that Molyneux put to Locke was actually a double question: if the man were to recover his power of sight would he be able to *distinguish* them by sight, without the help of the sense of touch, and would he be able to *name* them? Molyneux himself did not give separate answers to these two questions, for his answer was as follows:

Not. For though he has obtain'd the experience of, how a Globe, how a Cube affects his touch; yet he has not yet attained the Experience, that what affects his touch so or so, must affect his sight so or so; Or that a protuberant angle in the Cube, that pressed his hand unequally, shall appear to his eye, as it does in the Cube' (E, II.ix.8, p. 146; see also *Corr.*, vol. iv, p. 651).

Molyneux believed that the relationship between tactile and visual sensations of the shape of objects would not be immediately apparent but would have to be learnt.

In his *Essay*, Locke expressed agreement with Molyneux's statement, but he did not seem particularly interested in the link between the sense of touch and the faculty of sight: in the chapter dealing with PERCEPTION, he used Molyneux's problem to illustrate the thesis that we often have false beliefs about the way in which we perceive – without our taking notice of it. Locke stated that when, for instance, we look at a uniformly coloured sphere, the idea we get of it is that of a (flat) circle with a variety of shades and colours. But from experience we have learnt that this sort of idea is caused by a sphere and thus we interpret the idea of the unevenly coloured circle as the idea of a uniformly coloured sphere. This happens so quickly that we hardly notice it. In order to make this process clearer, Locke used a language metaphor that was to take on a persistent life of its own in discussions on Molyneux's problem. Whenever a person reads or listens to something with attention and understanding, stated Locke, he does not take note of the letters or the sounds but of the concepts that they call forth (*E*, II.ix.9, p. 147). Just as sounds are *signs* of concepts, so also is a circle a *sign* for a sphere. The passage in which Locke put his opinion regarding unconscious judgements reads as follows:

We are farther to consider concerning perception, that the *Ideas we receive by sensation, are* often in grown People *altered by the judgment*, without our taking notice of it. When we set before our Eyes a round Globe, of any uniform colour, *v.g.* Gold, Alabaster, or Jet, 'tis certain that the Idea thereby imprinted in our Mind, is of a flat Circle variously shadow'd, with several degrees of Light and Brightness coming to our Eyes. But we having by use been accustomed to perceive, what kind of appearance convex Bodies are wont to make in us; what alterations are made in the reflections of Light, by the difference of the sensible Figures of Bodies, the judgment presently, by an habitual custom, alters the Appearances into their Causes: So that from that, which truly is variety of shadow or

colour, collecting the Figure, it makes it pass for a mark of Figure, and frames to itself the perception of a convex Figure, and an uniform Colour; when the *Idea* we receive from thence, is only a Plain variously colour'd, as is evident in Painting' (*E*, II.ix.8, p. 145).

It is at this point that Locke introduced Molyneux's problem: 'To which purpose I shall here insert a Problem of that very Ingenious and Studious promoter of real Knowledge, the Learned and Worthy Mr. *Molineux*, which he was pleased to send me in a Letter some Months since' (*E*, II.ix.8, p. 145–6).

Locke apparently expected that his statement could be tested with the help of a person born blind who has recovered the power of sight. Such a person would not be prejudiced by habit as are all normally sighted adults. Locke responded to Molyneux's question saying that he believed that a person born blind would not be able to say immediately with any certainty which was the sphere and which the cube:

I agree with this thinking Gent. whom I am proud to call my Friend, in his answer to this his Problem; and am of the opinion, that the Blind Man, at first sight, would not be able with certainty to say, which was the Globe, which the Cube, whilst he only saw them: though he could unerringly name them by his touch, and certainly distinguish them by the difference of their Figures felt. This I have set down, and leave with my Reader, as an occasion for him to consider, how much he may be beholding to experience, improvement, and acquired notions, where he thinks, he has not the least use of, or help from them: And the rather, because this observing Gent. farther adds, that *having upon the occasion of my Book, proposed this to divers very ingenious Men, he hardly ever met with one, that at first gave the answer to it, which he thinks true, till by hearing his reasons they were convinced*' (*E*, II.ix.8, p. 146).

Molyneux thanked Locke with the following words: '... I can only Pour out my thanks to you for the Favourable Character under which you have transmitted me to posterity' (28 July 1694, *Corr.*, vol. v, p. 93).

What is noticeable here is that Locke did not deal with Molyneux's question regarding the ability of the newly sighted individual to distinguish between the sphere and the cube but only treated the question of *naming* the objects. A further point worth noting is that Locke believed that the man would be *unable to say with certainty* which was the sphere and which the cube.

After Molyneux and Locke had discussed Molyneux's problem, it was discussed by a large number of philosophers and other men of learning such as BERKELEY, LEIBNIZ, Voltaire, Diderot, La Mettrie, Helmholtz and William James. In the first instance, philosophers regarded Molyneux's problem as a thought-experiment, which could be dealt with only by reasoning. Empiricists such as Molyneux, Locke and Berkeley answered the question in the negative. More rationalist philosophers such as Synge, Lee and Leibniz gave an affirmative answer.

Discussion concerning Molyneux's problem took a new turn once the English surgeon and anatomist William Cheselden published an account of what a congenitally blind boy had seen after his cataracts had been removed (Cheselden, 1728). This publication led philosophers to regard Molyneux's problem no longer as a thought-experiment, but as a question that could be answered by experimentation. In his account, Cheselden noted that when the boy was first able to see, he did not know the shape of a thing and could not recognize one thing from another, regardless of how different in shape or magnitude they were. Some philosophers thought that Cheselden's observations were unequivocal and that they confirmed the HYPOTHESIS that a blind man restored to sight would not be able to distinguish objects and would have to learn to see. Most of these philosophers, we might mention

Voltaire, Camper and the elder Condillac as examples, were adherents of Berkeley's theory of vision, which had predicted a similar outcome. Others, however, such as La Mettrie and Diderot, regarded Cheselden's account as wholly ambiguous in its implications. They pointed out that it was possible that the boy had been unable to make valid perceptual judgements because his eyes had not been functioning properly. They suggested that this could have been due to the fact that his eyes had not been used for a long time, or to their not having had enough time to recover from the operation. They also pointed out that Cheselden had, perhaps, asked the boy leading questions. Some philosophers furthermore believed that the results of the inquiry depended on the intelligence of the patient. Those who criticized the significance of Cheselden's account in this way (such as the French *philosophes*) made proposals as to how to avoid the problems mentioned. They suggested that one should prepare the patient carefully for the operation and for the interrogation, that one should allow his eyes time to recover from the operation and that one should give him the opportunity to exercise his eyes in darkness. What is more, one should avoid asking leading questions. Some philosophers were even more radically critical of operations like that performed by Cheselden. Mérian, for example, noticed that Cheselden's observations, like all observations of blind people whose cataracts have been removed, present difficulties because cataracts do not cause complete blindness and complete blindness cannot be cured.

Discussions continued in the nineteenth and twentieth centuries, but describing them would take us too far afield (see Degenaar, 1996 for a comprehensive survey). It is worth pointing out, however, that it has recently been argued that modern developmental psychology and neurophysiology show that Locke and the empiricists were correct in their negative response to Molyneux's question (Gallagher, 2005, p. 153–72).

BIBLIOGRAPHY
Primary Sources
Cheselden, William, 'An Account of some Observations made by a young Gentleman, who was born blind, or lost his Sight so early, that he had no Remembrance of ever having seen, and was couched between 13 and 14 Years of Age', *Philosophical Transactions*, vol. ccccii (1728), pp. 447–50.
Locke, John, 'Extrait d'un Livre Anglois qui n'est pas encore publié, intitulé *Essai Philosophique concernant l'Entendement*, où l'on montre quelle est l'étendüe de nos connoissances certaines, et la manière dont nous y parvenons', *Bibliothèque Universelle et Historique*, vol. viii (1688), pp. 49–142.
Molyneux, William, *Dioptrica Nova* (1692).

Secondary Literature
Degenaar, M.J.L., *Molyneux's Problem: Three Centuries of Discussion on the Perception of Forms* (Dordrecht, 1996).
Gallagher, S., *How the Body Shapes the Mind* (Oxford, 2005).

Marjolein Degenaar and
Gert-Jan Lokhorst

MORALITY AND ITS DEMONSTRATION

In several places in the *Essay concerning Human Understanding* Locke states his belief that morality is capable of being made a demonstrative science. Such a demonstration would proceed according to Locke's 'way of ideas': 'shewing the Agreement, or Disagreement of two *Ideas*, by the intervention of one or more Proofs, which have a constant, immutable, and visible connexion one with another' (*E*, IV.xv.1, p. 654). Proofs are 'Those intervening *Ideas*, which serve to show the Agreement of any two others' (*E*, IV.ii.3, p. 532). Demonstration, then, is the tracing of conceptual connexions.

Moral demonstration is possible because 'the precise REAL ESSENCES of the Things moral Words stand for, may be perfectly known; and so the Congruity, or Incongruity of the Things themselves, be certainly discovered' (*E*, III.xi.16, p. 516; cf. *E*, IV.xii.8, p. 643). Like those of mathematics, ideas of morality are archetypes – not copies of things, but patterns to which things may conform. In their case, nominal and real essence exactly coincide, since the words standing for these complex ideas designate nothing other than the component simple ideas which the mind has put together. Moral ideas and words such as 'murder', 'revenge', 'temperance', provide the content of moral rules (see *E*, II.xxii.10, p. 293) and can be exactly defined: 'For they being Combinations of several *Ideas*, that the mind of Man has arbitrarily put together ... Men may ... exactly know the *Ideas*, that go to each Composition, and so both use these Words in a certain and undoubted Signification, and perfectly declare ... what they stand for' (*E*, III.xi.15, p. 516).

Locke raises the obvious objection to this account of morality: 'If *moral Knowledge* be placed in the Contemplation of our own *moral Ideas*, and those ... be of our own making, What strange Notions will there be of *Justice* and *Temperance*? What confusion of Vertues and Vices?' (*E*, IV.iv.9, p. 566). Moreover, the *Essay*'s hedonistic theory of motivation and of the Good also seems to run contrary to a rationalistic ethics. If happiness consists in pleasure and the absence of pain, if 'Good' refers to whatever promotes pleasure, and 'evil' to what promotes pain (*E*, II.xx.2, p. 229), the objects of desire are relative to the individual (*E*, II.xxi.55, p. 269).

Locke asserts that it is not up to the individual to construct moral ideas and assign NAMES to them. The proper meaning of terms in moral discourse is their usual signification in the public language of that discourse (ibid.). But is this only rejecting an individualistic moral relativism for a social moral relativism? At *Essay* II.xxviii.7f. pp. 352–7, Locke discusses three laws according to which actions are judged right or wrong: '1. The *Divine* Law. 2. The *Civil* Law. 3. The Law of *Opinion* or *Reputation*'. The first of these is 'that Law which God has set to the actions of Men, whether promulgated to them by the light of Nature or the voice of Revelation … This is the only touchstone of *moral Rectitude*'. However, in practice it is the third law which is applied in judgements of virtue and vice, right and wrong. Such judgements are made in accordance with the 'approbation or dislike, praise or blame, which by a secret and tacit consent establishes it self in the several Societies, Tribes, and Clubs of Men' (*E*, II.xxviii.10, p. 353). Locke does say that the Law of Opinion 'in a great measure every-where correspond[s] with the unchangeable Rule of Right and Wrong, which the Law of God hath established' (*E*, II.xxviii.11, p. 356). But how could such correspondence be known except by comparing the Law of Opinion with the Divine Law *as known by revelation*? Moral ideas which are solely constructions of the human mind can only belong to the Law of Opinion.

Of Locke's manuscripts pertaining to moral philosophy, that most relevant to demonstration is 'Morality' (Oxford, Bodleian Library, MS. Locke c.28, fols 139–40), an exposition of morality *more geometrico* which endeavours to establish the rules of morality on the basis of psychological HEDONISM. Locke asks why, if each of us is motivated by the desire for our own happiness, should people not break a compact when it is to their advantage to do so? If this were permissible for me it would be permissible for everyone and the purpose of compacts would be annulled. On this basis 'Justice' is established. But justice so construed provides only a minimalist morality. The altruistic virtues are conspicuously omitted. Locke mentions 'civility', 'charity' and 'liberality', 'which relate to society and soe border on Justice but yet are not comprised under direct articles of conduct'. The manuscript ends by defining civility as 'noething but outward expressing of goodwill and esteem or at least of noe contempt or hatred'. But civility as

a moral duty is not founded on respect for a person's PROPERTY created by compact, but rather respect for the person. Another manuscript, 'Ethica', dated 1692 (Oxford, Bodleian Library, MS. Locke c.42, p. 242), argues that the pleasure of altruistic action is longer lasting than that which is purely self-interested. But this hardly establishes duties of benevolence and altruism even when contrary to the agent's own happiness.

A science of morality as envisaged by Locke is undercut by the main reason he has for envisaging it: since in moral ideas real and NOMINAL ESSENCES coincide, morally significant actions can be precisely defined. A core of such ideas must exist across cultures if *moral* rules are to be distinguished from other rules of conduct such as etiquette or religious ritual. Granting that any morality will include some notion of justice and of morally wrong actions such as murder, there is still wide divergence as to what counts as justice or murder in concrete instances. Despite the urging of his friends, Locke never produced the demonstration he thought possible. It is telling that in *The Reasonableness of Christianity* he remarks that as the moral law has been *revealed* in the New Testament its demonstration is unnecessary (*RCh.*, pp. 149–54).

BIBLIOGRAPHY
Manuscript Sources
Oxford, Bodleian Library, MS. Locke c.28.
Oxford, Bodleian Library, MS. Locke c.42.

John Colman

NAMES

Book III of the *Essay* is entitled 'Of Words'. It focuses on 'names of *Ideas* in the Mind' (*E*, III.vii.1, p. 471). These include names of particular ideas, such as 'John', and – for the sake of communication and knowledge – names of general or abstract ideas such as 'man'. Locke divides these into three types: names of simple ideas, mixed MODES, and substances.

Names of simple ideas – abstract ideas of a single sensation or reflection, such as 'red', 'sweet' or 'doubting', and out of which every possible idea is composed – have three interesting features. The first, that they are indefinable, pushes home a fundamental principle of Locke's philosophy: language, like knowledge, depends on experience. The names of simple ideas cannot be understood through other words (which are ultimately just sounds) but only through personal acquaintance with the ideas themselves. At its base, language is meaningless except when it is conjoined with consciousness. 'He that thinks otherwise,' contends Locke, 'let him try if any Words can give him the taste of a Pineapple' (E, III.iv.11, p. 424). Locke's targets here are both scholastics and 'modern philosophers' who purport to define key words but, in the absence of the relevant simple ideas, only translate them into other words, creating a circle of empty signs. 'Light', for example, is defined in the schools as 'The Act of Perspicuous, as far forth as perspicuous', and by DESCARTES as 'a great number of little Globules, striking briskly on the bottom of the Eye' (E, III.iv.10, p. 423), all of which amounts to nothing more than insignificant noise in the ears of a blind man. While we might want to draw back from Locke's ideational characterization of meaning, and insist that a blind man can use the word 'scarlet' perfectly well, there is a sense in which he does not understand the word, nor know why a dress, or a woman, is scarlet.

The second noteworthy feature of names of simple ideas is that, while they immediately signify ideas, they 'intimate also some real Existence', confirming that for Locke ideas connect words to the world, rather than sever them from it (E, III.iv.2, p. 421). The third and related feature of this type of name is that insofar as the ideas they stand for are 'perfectly taken from the existence of things', they are not remotely 'arbitrary' (E, III.iv.17, p. 428), that is,

they have not been acted on by the will. Simple and unfabricated, they are therefore the same for all and, as such, ideal objects of communication.

Names of substances, such as 'Gold', tread a path between nature and the arbitrary. They signify collections of simple ideas that are regularly observed together, such as 'a Body yellow, of a certain weight, malleable, fusible, and fixed' (E, III.vi.2, p. 439). In forging these NOMINAL ESSENCES, as Locke calls them, speakers are obliged to 'follow Nature', and are under 'necessity' not to join, for example, the colour of lead with the weight of gold (E, III.vi.28, p. 455; E, III.vi.51, p. 471). However, while people ought to unite only ideas which are 'supposed to have a union in Nature', we have 'some latitude' not only in deciding which ideas to include (e.g. should 'Ductility' go in or not?), but also what is to count as a distinct SUBSTANCE and what not (e.g. why should 'water' be a distinct species from 'ice', or 'watch' from 'clock'?) (E, III.vi.28, p. 455; E, III.iv.17, p. 428; E, III.ix.13, p. 483; III.vi.39, p. 463). Locke's point, directed against scholastic 'substantial forms' and more generally against quotidian pretensions to essentialist realism, is that the essences of substances are 'made by the Mind, and not by Nature' (E, III.vi.26, p. 453). Names of substances cannot stand for REAL ESSENCES because (1) we have little experience of the real constitution of things, and (2) even if we did, we could not know how the PRIMARY QUALITIES relate to the secondary, and therefore which to incorporate and which to ignore. Moreover, Locke doubts the very existence of real essences; essences are just 'Sorts', or human constructs, there being nothing 'essential' to any 'individual parcel of Matter' (E, III.vi.4, p. 440; E, III.vi.6, p. 442). It is the nominal essences, those phenomenological confections which track our subjective encounters with the world and are demarcated by us, which are the absolute semantic limit to the names of substances.

Unlike the names of substances, the meanings of mixed modes – such as 'adultery', 'murder' and 'ambition' – 'are not only made by the

Mind, but made *very arbitrarily*, made without Patterns, or reference to any real Existence' (*E*, III.v.3, p. 429). They are entirely the products of will – diverse ideas, such as 'man, dies, wakes up', assembled together to forge the complex idea of 'resurrection'. Since these nominal essences are completely 'the Workmanship of the Mind', and are not signs of things beyond themselves in nature, they are also real essences (*E*, III.v.14, p. 436). They are therefore 'adequate' ideas, the things they stand for 'perfectly known', and the agreement or disagreement of 'the Things themselves' perfectly perceptible (*E*, IV.iv.7, p. 565; *E*, III.xi.16, p. 516). This is why, unlike in natural philosophy, where the nominal essences of substances fall short of the reality they are supposed to represent, Locke feels able to declare that morality is '*capable of Demonstration*' (*E*, III.xi.16, p. 516). Far from being reassured, however, his contemporaries saw his manmade characterization of moral ideas, coupled with his anti-innatism, as evidence of godless scepticism. While Locke's precise intentions remain controversial, his emphasis on the manufactured nature of moral essences is certainly a continuation of his anti-scholastic, and more generally anti-essentialist, polemic. In proving essences to be nothing more than 'an Artifice of the Understanding', Locke aims to denigrate all the mistaken talk about '*Genera*, and *Species*, and their *Essences*, as if they were Things regularly and constantly made by Nature' (*E*, III.v.9, p. 433). Instead, they are agglomerations of ideas so fleeting and naturally distinct that they require names to bring them into being and give them lasting life. The name is 'the Knot, that ties them fast together', on which 'the continuation and fixing of that Unity' depends (*E*, III.v.10, p. 434). Far from being universal concepts, they embody the 'customs and manner of life' of particular communities, instantiated in their own peculiar, often untranslatable, words (*E*, III.v.8, p. 432).

Locke's concentration on names has laid him open to two related criticisms. First, it is proposed that sentences rather than words are the basic units of meaning, and second, that language cannot be condensed into an unconnected series of words that signify ideas. While he would not have recognized the first point, he does draw a distinction between 'names' (words that signify ideas) and 'particles' (words that signify the actions the mind performs on its ideas, such as '*Is*, and *Is not*, … the general marks of the Mind, affirming or denying' (*E*, III.vii.1, p. 471)). Locke also indicates words that stand for mental actions which appraise these affirmations and denials, thereby accounting not only for propositional content, but propositional attitudes too (Ott, 2004, pp. 34–52).

BIBLIOGRAPHY

Ott, Walter, *Locke's Philosophy of Language* (Cambridge, 2004).

Hannah Dawson

NATURAL HISTORY

Bacon's project to revolutionize natural philosophy comprised two parts. First, a 'natural history' should be compiled. A large collection of facts should be gathered with an unprejudiced eye, and organized by 'heads' or 'titles'. Second, these natural histories should undergo a process of 'induction', where general axioms about the causes of these phenomena would be derived and improved over time.

Locke's notebooks record that his medical training in the 1660s comprised voracious reading of Galenist, Chymist and Mechanist alike. As his interest in chymistry grew, his research became more practical – attending Peter Stahl's chemistry course, and collaborating with Richard Lower and Robert BOYLE on research into respiration. The more practically minded he became, the more he was drawn to natural history. Following a suggestion from

Boyle in the *Philosophical Transactions*, Locke began a weather register in June 1666 – recording the atmospheric conditions every day for the next seventeen years. He also compiled a detailed agenda concerning the properties of the blood entitled 'Tryall about the bloud espetially humane'.

Locke undertook his own 'induction' on the basis of this research – proposing theories of disease and respiration, in both cases leaning towards the views of the chymists. Such theorizing did not survive Locke's acquaintance with Thomas SYDENHAM, first made in 1667. Sydenham believed that 'theory' had vitiated medical practice and should be dispensed with. Instead, the physician should compile natural histories of diseases and their susceptibility to cure. In short, Sydenham embraced Bacon's 'natural history', but rejected his 'induction'. Locke enthusiastically adopted this outlook – abandoning his previous theorizing, and embracing a practice of medicine founded solely on clinical experience and empirical effectiveness. He gave Sydenham's project extensive intellectual and practical support, accompanying him on visits to patients and working as his amanuensis on the manuscripts that were eventually to become Sydenham's landmark *Observationes Medicae* (1676). These papers comprised comprehensive natural histories of each year's 'epidemic constitution' – the particular diseases that dominated that year. For instance, Sydenham's essay on smallpox, which Locke copied for his own records, began: 'This is the naturall hystory of the Small-pox as comprehending the true & geniune Phaenomena belonging to them as they are in thier owne nature' (Sydenham, 1991, p. 74). Locke also wrote defences of Sydenham's method – 'Anatomia' and 'De Arte Medica' – bluntly stating his opposition to theorizing about nature's causes: 'Tis certaine therefor notwithstanding all our anatomicall scrutinys we are still ignorant & like to be soe of the true essentiall causes of diseases, their manner of production, formalities, & ways of ceaseing, & must be much more in the darke as to their cures upon such HYPOTHESIS' (Dewhurst, 1966,

p. 92). Natural history is the true path to knowledge: 'how regulate his dose, to mix his simples & to prescribe all in a due method, all this is only from history & the advantage of a diligent observation of these diseases, of their begining progresse & ways of cure' (op. cit., p. 86). The *Essay* shared this scepticism, which Locke now characterized as an inability to understand the REAL ESSENCES of substances. Consequently, natural history is the only path to knowledge:

> In the Knowledge of Bodies, we must be content to glean, what we can, from particular Experiments: since we cannot from a Discovery of their real Essences, grasp at a time whole Sheaves; and in bundles, comprehend the Nature and Properties of whole Species together ... Experience, Observation, and natural History, must give us by our Senses, and by retail, an insight into corporeal Substances (*E*, IV.xii.12, p. 647).

Locke believed that this method was applicable to all enquiries into the natures of things – not least, the Understanding. Locke began the *Essay* by stating that he would 'not at present meddle with the Physical Consideration of the Mind; or trouble my self to examine, wherein its Essence consists' (*E*, I.i.2, p. 43). Rather, he hoped that by an 'Historical, plain Method, I can give [an] Account of the Ways, whereby our Understandings come to attain those Notions of Things we have' (op. cit., p. 44). Indeed, after accounting for the origin of simple ideas, Locke concludes:

> And thus I have given a short, and, I think, true *History of the first beginnings of Humane Knowledge*; whence the Mind has its first Objects, and by what steps it makes its Progress to the laying in, and storing up those *Ideas*, out of which is to be framed all the Knowledge it is capable of (*E*, II.xi.15, p. 162).

In short, the *Essay*, begun in 1671, the time of Locke's closest collaboration with Sydenham, is a natural history of the Understanding – a careful catalogue of its contents, FACULTIES and properties, compiled without any theorizing concerning its underlying nature. Locke thus treated the Understanding as he would any other natural object of enquiry.

It is no surprise, therefore, that Locke continued to support the practice of natural history, 'soliciting' Boyle's 1684 *Memoirs for the Natural History of Human Blood*, and helping complete Boyle's *General History of the Air* in 1692 (which included Locke's diligently compiled weather register). Locke continued to eschew theories, dismissing them, when corresponding that year with Thomas Molyneux, as 'for the most part but a sort of waking dream'. In medicine, he averred, 'Dr. Sydenham has set them of a better way ... Nicely to observe the history of diseases in all their changes and circumstances' (*Corr.*, vol. iv, p. 629). After working with Sydenham, Locke never wavered in his belief that, given our ignorance of nature, natural history is all we can rely upon.

BIBLIOGRAPHY
Primary Sources
Dewhurst, Kenneth, Dr. *Thomas Sydenham (1624–1689): His Life and Original Writings*, (London, 1966).
Sydenham, Thomas, *Thomas Sydenham's 'Observationes medicae' and 'Medical Observations'*, ed. G.G. Meynell, (Folkestone, 1991).

Secondary Sources
Anstey, Peter, 'Locke, Bacon and Natural History', *Early Science and Medicine*, vol. vii (2002), pp. 65–92.
Walmsley, Jonathan, '*Morbus*: Locke's Early Essay on Disease', in *Early Science and Medicine*, vol. v (2000), pp. 366–93.
——, 'John Locke on Respiration', *Medical History*, vol. li (2007), pp. 453–76.

Jonathan Walmsley

NATURAL LAW

The idea of a universal moral law known by natural reason was a commonplace in seventeenth-century moral and political thought. Much of the reflection on natural law was still inspired by Thomas Aquinas and his later commentators. In the Thomist doctrine, natural law was seen as a part of the eternal law which was a rational principle guiding both God and human beings. Natural law consisted of the principles of practical reason, which directed human beings to maintain their existence and to achieve their natural perfection as rational beings capable of contemplating God. This rationalistic understanding of natural law had been challenged in the fourteenth century by Duns Scotus and William Ockham, who claimed that it questioned God's omnipotence. They did not deny its existence but insisted that it binds human beings as a law only because it is imposed on them by God's will (Schneewind, 1998, pp. 17–25).

The medieval discussion on natural law was transmitted to the seventeenth century by Spanish neo-scholastics, most famously by Francisco Suarez, whose works were appreciated also in Protestant school philosophy. The neo-scholastic model was, however, challenged by Hugo Grotius, Thomas HOBBES and Samuel Pufendorf, who aimed to formulate a natural law which would serve as a norm for all, irrespective of religious differences. In this purpose, they emphasized the independence of natural law from biblical revelation and theological concerns, and rejected the Aristotelian-Christian idea of human perfection as a criterion for the content of natural law. While their accounts of natural law differed in many respects significantly, they all associated its principal content with norms needed to maintain peaceful social life (Schneewind, 1998, pp. 58–140; Haakonssen, 2004).

Locke reflected on the character of natural law throughout his intellectual career, but he never published a systematic account on the topic. The question of how his diverse remarks on natural law fit together perplexed his contemporaries and also today scholars have different opinions on their coherence (Colman, 2003). In most of his discussions on moral philosophy Locke was interested in the epistemology and obligating power of natural law, not so much in defining its content. The exception is the *Two Treatises*, in which he offers an account of the politically relevant precepts of natural law as a normative foundation for an anti-absolutist constitutional theory.

Locke's earliest discussion on natural law consisted of lectures he gave in 1663–4 as Censor of Moral Philosophy at Christ Church, Oxford (later translated into English under the title *Essays on the Law of Nature*). In these lectures he addressed many themes, which he later explored in greater detail and sophistication in the *Essay concerning Human Understanding*. These included a primarily voluntaristic understanding of natural law, according to which its obligating character followed from the authority of God as the supremely wise creator of the human species (Schneewind, 1998, pp. 153–6; see MORAL OBLIGATION). Locke also rejected the widely shared assumption that knowledge of natural law is innate to human beings: according to the lectures, its precepts are discovered by applying reason to observations concerning the human condition (Marshall, 1994, pp. 28–32).

In the *Essay*, the rejection of inborn moral knowledge became part of a general attack upon the existence of innate ideas and was connected to a descriptive account of human morality. Locke pointed out that moral knowledge was even more evidently not innate than speculative knowledge. Speculative principles – such as 'the whole is bigger than a part' – were at least self-evident and therefore universally accepted, whereas moral rules lacked such immediate certainty and were a subject of considerable disagreement among human beings. As a proof, Locke referred to what contemporary travel literature told about the vile practices among many non-European nations. He admitted that most nations seemed to follow the precepts of natural law most indispensable for the maintenance of social life. This, however, was no proof of the innate character of such principles, as many nations obeyed these rules only amongst themselves and not in their dealings with strangers. Moreover, as human beings were capable of observing the connection between their well-being and orderly social life, they followed the central precepts of natural law as rules of convenience, but lacked a proper understanding of their morally obligating character as God's commands (*E*, I.iii.1–13, pp. 65–75; Colman, 1983, pp. 51–75).

In Locke's view, moral opinions were considered innate because they were taught to children and were later confirmed by prevailing customs. Men had no recollection of how they had first adopted these precepts and were, therefore, inclined to think that they are innate and natural. Since the great majority were busy with the 'daily Labours of their Callings', few questioned the moral views held in their community (*E*, I.iii.22–6, pp. 81–4). Accordingly, the norm by which people usually judged the rectitude or depravity of their actions was neither the law imposed on them by God nor the civil law, but 'the Law of Opinion or Reputation'. This consisted of prevailing views concerning virtue and vice and was sanctioned by other people's approbation and condemnation (*E*, II.xxviii.10, pp. 353–4).

Many contemporaries, including some of Locke's friends, held that the above descriptive account of human morality indicated the rejection of all objective moral distinctions. Locke himself, however, insisted that while the great majority took their moral views from 'the Law of Opinion', human reason was capable of recognizing the true moral law God had imposed on the human species and even presenting its content and obligating power with demonstrative certainty. Yet most readers have felt that in the *Essay* Locke failed to explain how such moral knowledge is to be achieved, leaving especially unclear how human reason is able to discover God's benevolence and the existence of afterlife rewards and punishments. What made the latter omission problematic was Locke's hedonistic theory of motivation, which made it difficult to conceive how human beings could be inclined to obey God's commands without the idea of pleasure or pain awaiting them in the hereafter. On the other hand, how could they be disinclined to obey God's commands when they did have the idea of afterlife enjoyments and hardships? (Schneewind, 1994, pp. 200–8; Colman, 1983, pp. 206–34; see HEDONISM). Such difficulties notwithstanding, in his subsequent theological works Locke restated the view that human reason is capable of recognizing and perhaps even demonstrating the moral law – although in the *Reasonableness of Christianity* he emphasized that achieving a full understanding of natural law had been extremely difficult before Jesus had clarified this law and its sanctions (Haakonssen, 1996, pp. 56–8).

Such epistemological concerns are absent from the *Two Treatises*. In this work Locke was interested in the content of natural law insofar as it was relevant for understanding the proper character of political society. His method of using natural law may have been inspired by Pufendorf's *De Jure Naturae et Gentium* (1672), which he described, in *Some Thoughts concerning Education*, as a book in which a young gentleman 'will be instructed in the natural Rights of Men, and the Original and Foundations of Society, and the Duties resulting from thence' (*STE*, p. 239). Locke endorsed Pufendorf's idea of a pre-political STATE OF NATURE as the generic starting point of political theory, but rejected HOBBES's infamous claim that in such a condition natural law is silent. While people were free and equal in the state of nature, they were all obliged to obey natural law. This law was 'plain and intelligible' for those who studied it, though many people failed to do so, which was one of the motives for establishing civil society (*TTG* II.12 and 124).

Locke did not, however, adopt Pufendorf's idea of the cultivation of sociality as the fundamental principle of natural law. Instead, he declared that as God wants humankind to increase and multiply, the fundamental law of nature is to preserve it (*TTG* I.41 and II.16). This gave his account of natural law a voluntaristic flavour, though some scholars have argued that we can also find a proto-Kantian secular element in the *Two Treatises* (e.g. Simmons, 1992, pp. 36–46). The duty to preserve humankind indicated a duty to preserve one's own life and a duty to preserve others when one's own preservation was not in danger. The latter duty, in its turn, included both a negative duty to abstain from harming others, and a positive duty of charity to help others to survive in cases of extreme need (*TTG* II.6).

The duty to preserve one's own life gave individuals living in the state of nature a subjective right of preservation. This included, first of all, the right to take 'Meat and Drink, and such other things Nature affords for their subsistence' from the earth God had given to all human beings in common (*TTG* II.25). As a reply to Robert FILMER's critique of the contractual theory of PROPERTY Locke pointed out that in the state of nature property was not founded on consent, but on the fact that by making the survival of human beings dependent on the work of their hands, God had commanded them to labour. As a result, labour had the moral capacity to transform fruits of the earth as well as the earth itself into private property (*TTG* II.27–32). After the introduction of money, it became possible to own more land than one needed for oneself, and there emerged significant differences in material wealth (*TTG* II.46–9). The introduction of money did not, however, remove the duty of charity which 'gives every Man a Title to so much out of another's Plenty, as will keep him from extream want, where he has no means to subsist otherwise' (*TTG* I.42).

The duty to preserve oneself and others also gave rise to the rights of protecting one's 'Life, Liberty and Estates' (*TTG* II.87) and punishing those who violated natural law (*TTG* II.7–9).

Here Locke departed not only from those contemporaries who held that rulers receive their power to punish directly from God but also from Pufendorf, according to whom the right to punish came into being through the contract by which civil society was established. A natural right to punish had been supported by some previous theorists, such as Grotius, but Locke gave this doctrine a new orientation by connecting it with the right to resist a tyrant. He emphasized that while people entering a civil society gave up their right to punish the violations of natural law, the principles of natural law applied also within the civil society, standing as 'an Eternal Rule to all Men, Legislators as well as others' (*TTG* II.135). Therefore, a ruler who failed to follow or enforce natural law not only lost his authority but also declared a war against his subjects. In such a situation people regained their right to punish, and gained the right of armed RESISTANCE AND REVOLUTION (Marshall, 1994, pp. 205–91).

BIBLIOGRAPHY
Secondary Literature
Colman, John, *John Locke's Moral Philosophy* (Edinburgh, 1983).
——, 'Locke's Empiricist Theory of Natural Law', in Peter R. Anstey (ed.), *The Philosophy of John Locke: New Perspectives* (London and New York, 2003), pp. 106–26.
Haakonssen, Knud, *Natural Law and Moral Philosophy: From Grotius to the Scottish Enlightenment* (Cambridge, 1996).
——, 'Protestant Natural Law Theory: A General Interpretation', in Natalie Brender and Larry Krasnoff (eds), *New Essays on the History of Autonomy: A Collection Honoring J.B. Schneewind* (Cambridge, 2004), pp. 92–109.
Marshall, John, *John Locke: Resistance, Religion and Responsibility* (Cambridge, 1994).
Schneewind, J.B., 'Locke's Moral Philosophy', in Vere Chappell (ed.), *The Cambridge Companion to Locke* (Cambridge, 1994), pp. 199–225.
——, *The Invention of Autonomy* (Cambridge, 1998).
Simmons. A. John, *The Lockean Theory of Rights* (Princeton, 1992).

Kari Saastamoinen

NUMBER AND INFINITY

Ideas of numbers are treated by Locke as ideas of simple MODES, the basic unit of which is an idea of unity. The idea of unity is one of the ideas that 'convey themselves into the Mind, by all the ways of Sensation and Reflection' (*E*, II.vii.1, p. XXX), and it is 'suggested to the Understanding, by every Object without, and every *Idea* within' (*E*, II.vii.7, p. 131). According to Locke, 'whatever we can consider as one thing, whether a real Being, or *Idea*, suggests to the Understanding, the *Idea* of Unity' (ibid.). Thus, the idea of unity is given to the understanding through the mental act of *considering* various items *as* one thing.

Once the mind acquires the idea of unity, it frames ideas of various numbers by 'repeating this *Idea* in our Minds, and adding the Repetitions together' (*E*, II.xvi.2, p. 205). These various numbers, however close they are to each other, are 'distinct' from each other (*E*, II.xvi.3, p. 205). Because their unit (the idea of unity) is definite and immutable, they are different from each other at least by one unit. Therefore, according to Locke, though it is difficult for the mind to recognize the slightest difference between two different degrees of white colour or the slightest difference between two different sizes of extension, 'The simple modes of Number are of all other the most distinct' (ibid.).

Ideas of numbers framed in this way are retained in the memory. However, since they are framed by repetition of the same idea of unity, they are 'so many Combinations of Unities, which have no variety, nor are capable of any other difference, but more or less' (*E*, II.xvi.5, pp. 206–207). Therefore, to count numbers as distinct items, one needs 'distinct NAMES' (ibid.); 'without such Names or Marks, we can hardly well make use of Numbers in reckoning' (ibid.). For this reason, the ability to manage numbers depends on the richness of their names.

According to Locke, ideas of modes are generally framed by the mind without any archetypes. Ideas of numbers are one of these ideas. Therefore, mathematics that treats simple modes (like morality that treats ideas of mixed modes) assumes a character different from that of empirical sciences. Regarding 'physical Things' Locke says, 'I am apt to doubt that, how far so ever humane Industry may advance useful and *experimental* Philosophy *in physical Things*, *scientifical* will still be out of our reach' (*E*, IV.iii.26, p. 556). In contrast, 'In some of our *Ideas* there are certain Relations, Habitudes, and Connexions, so visibly included in the Nature of the *Ideas* themselves, [and] in these only, we are capable of certain and universal Knowledge' (*E*, IV.iii.29, p. 559); at least concerning 'the *Ideas* of *Number*, *Extension*, and *Figure*' (*E*, IV.ii.9, p. 535), there is a possibility to attain such knowledge. Locke's view of this matter is based on his basic view that, whereas complex ideas of substances generally express only 'NOMINAL ESSENCES' of things, complex ideas of modes are generally their own archetypes and express their 'REAL ESSENCES'.

As for infinity, we think of it not only concerning space, duration and number, but also concerning God. However, we think of God's infinity 'primarily in respect of his Duration and Ubiquity' (*E*, II.xvii.1, p. 210), and 'more figuratively [in respect of] his Power, Wisdom, and Goodness, and other Attributes' (ibid.); in the latter cases we can just try to 'multiply [these Attributes] in our Thoughts, as far as we can, with all the infinity of endless number' (ibid.). Moreover, when we consider the infinity

of space and duration, we also take note of a kind of numerical processing in our minds. Thus, 'of all other *Ideas*, it is *Number* ... which, I think, *furnishes us with the clearest and most distinct* Idea *of Infinity*' (*E*, II.xvii.9, p. 215).

The idea of number is, as stated above, framed by repeated addition of the idea of unity, and for Locke the essential content of the idea of infinity consists in the fact that we can continue this procedure endlessly. We can say the same thing concerning the infinity of space or duration. According to Locke, 'when [the Mind] has added together as many millions, *etc.* as it pleases, of known lengths of Space or Duration, the clearest *Idea*, it can get of Infinity is the confused incomprehensible remainder of endless addible Numbers, which affords no prospect of Stop or Boundary' (ibid.).

For this reason, the idea of infinity is not 'positive' (*E*, II.xvii.13, pp. 216–17), it is merely a negative one. If the idea of infinity is positive and it is an idea of a determined number or a certain determined size of space or duration, we can still multiply it; in this sense, it has a contradiction within it. Therefore, the ideas of *infinite* number, *infinite* space, and *infinite* duration are contradictory, and are different from the ideas of *infinity of* number, *infinity of* space, and *infinity of* duration.

According to Locke,

even *the most abstruse* Ideas, how remote so ever they may seem from Sense, or from any operation of our own Minds, are yet only such, as the Understanding frames to it self, by repeating and joining together *Ideas*, that it had either from Objects of Sense, or from its own operations about them (*E*, II.xii.8, p. 166).

For him, 'even the *Idea* we have of *Infinity*, how remote so ever it may seem to be from any Object of Sense, or Operation of our Mind, has nevertheless, as all our other *Ideas*, its Original [in *Sensation* and *Reflection*]' (*E*, II.xvii.22, p. 223). After his discussions about simple ideas, Locke takes up space, duration, number and infinity before any other complex ideas. This procedure is obviously based on his intention to clarify the above point.

Yasuhiko Tomida

OBLIGATION, MORAL

Locke's thoughts on moral obligation are written in the idiom of NATURAL LAW. By 1690 the phrase 'natural law' had at least two distinct meanings. First, it was used in the work of thinkers such as Isaac NEWTON to describe the regularities of the natural world. Secondly, it was also used to describe a moral law that was independent of civil law or human custom. This second usage had a far more extensive genealogy than the first, stretching back to classical antiquity. Locke's discussion of the law of nature owes much to this second tradition. His ambition was nothing less than to create a science of morality. However, despite several valiant attempts, a scientific account of morality eluded him.

Locke's first extended treatment of the subject is contained in a series of Latin manuscripts completed between 1660 and 1664, which were posthumously published as *Essays on the Law of Nature*. His decision not to publish these manuscripts may well indicate that he was not satisfied with their argument. Nonetheless, the essays discuss some aspects of natural law in much greater detail than any of his published works and are therefore worthy of attention. The essays take the view that there is a fundamental moral law which all men are obliged to obey. Locke argues that this law binds in two senses: 'effectively' and 'terminativly' (*ELN*, p. 185). First, men are bound to observe this moral law due to the fact that it is God's will. God is, after all, humanity's creator and sustainer, and has therefore the right to require humanity to act as he sees fit. The 'will of a superior' then is the prime or 'effective' cause of the human obligation.

Secondly, men are also bound 'terminativly', that is to say, they are obliged to follow natural law because God has made it known. Rational investigation of nature teaches that there is a God who created and sustains mankind and who has an active will which ought to be obeyed. If God's law were hidden, Locke claims, it could not be considered compelling. However, as God's will for humanity, the law of nature, is declared through human nature, it is sufficiently accessible that men are bound to obey it.

The *Two Treatises* does not contain a coherent or detailed account of natural law; indeed the text explicitly omits a discussion of its precepts. Nonetheless, it echoes the optimism of the earlier essays concerning the ease with which natural law can be discovered by human reason (*TTG* II.12). According to the *Two Treatises*, humanity is, first of all, bound by natural law in the STATE OF NATURE (*TTG* II.6). Men, including rulers, are also bound by the law of nature in civil society. For this reason, the rights of government are limited by natural law as civil laws are only valid insofar as they conform to the law of nature. The source of moral obligation in the *Two Treatises* is obscure. Nonetheless, Locke does describe natural law as 'the Law of Reason' (e.g., *TTG* I. 101), and seems to argue that the law of nature can be discerned from human nature – an argument that is clearly familiar from the early essays. Evidence that Locke retained this essential understanding of the obligatory force of the law of nature into the late 1670s and early 1680s can be found in his journal entries for 15 July 1678, entitled '*Lex naturae*', and for 26 June 1681, where he comments on Richard Hooker's view of natural law (Von Leyden, 1956, p. 35; and Von Leyden, 1954, p. 67). Still, the *Two Treatises* has no explicit discussion concerning the obligatory force of the law of nature.

The *Essay concerning Human Understanding* marks a clear departure as it introduces the notion that morality is related to pleasure and pain. This conception, which is absent from the 1671 drafts of the *Essay*, first appeared in Locke's manuscript 'Of ethick in general' (c. 1686–7). It may well reflect the influence of Pierre Gassendi's disciples, whom Locke met during his stay in France. Clearly, knowledge of natural law is not innate; but Locke does accept that there are 'natural tendencies imprinted on the Minds of Men' (*E*, I.iii.3, p. 67) or 'lodged in Men's Appetites' (*E*, I.iii.13, p. 75) which spur men to action. The desire for happiness and the aversion to misery are Locke's prime examples of such principles.

Yet these tendencies are not moral principles. Experience of pleasure and pain can lead to ideas of good and evil. Actions that tend to produce pleasure are called good; those that produce pain are termed evil. However, these 'natural' definitions fall short of true moral knowledge, for morality must be based on law. Indeed, reason and sensation teach that duty presupposes law; and law in turn presupposes a lawmaker who, of necessity, has the power to punish and reward. According to Locke, God is such a lawmaker: consequently, rational men will act morally in order to reach the pleasures of heaven and avoid the misery of hell. In this way, the *Essay* links human HEDONISM and human motivation with God's will and moral obligation.

What does Locke mean by authority? Why does God, according to Locke, have the right to punish or reward? What are all the precepts of natural law? The problems in Locke's account have led some modern commentators to doubt the sincerity of his claims regarding the existence of God and moral law. Leo Strauss, for example, essentially accused Locke of Hobbism (Strauss, 1958; see Yolton, 1958, and Schneewind, 1994). It seems to be more plausible to argue that Locke was simply never able to produce an entirely coherent account of moral obligation.

BIBLIOGRAPHY
Secondary Literature
Schneewind, J.B., 'Locke's Moral Philosophy', in Vere Chappell (ed.), *The Cambridge Companion to Locke* (Cambridge, 1994), pp. 199–225.
Strauss, Leo, 'Locke's Doctrine of Natural Law', *American Political Science Review*, vol. lii (1958), pp. 490–501.
Von Leyden, W., 'Introduction', in John Locke, *Essays on the Law of Nature*, ed. W. von Leyden (Oxford, 1954), pp. 1–91.
——, 'John Locke and Natural Law', *Philosophy*, vol. xxxi (1956), pp. 23–35.
Yolton, John W., 'Locke on the Law of Nature', *Philosophical Review*, vol. lxvii (1958), pp. 23–35.

R.E.R. Bunce

PERCEPTION

Locke often uses the term 'perception' broadly, as a synonym to 'thought' (e.g. *E*, II.vi.2, p. 128). In the 'propriety of the *English* Tongue' (*E*, II.ix.1, p. 143), however, 'perception' refers to the passive operation of the mind that Locke more usually calls 'sensation'.

Along with reflection, sensation furnishes the mind with IDEAS, the 'materials' of KNOWLEDGE. Much knowledge is knowledge of general truths. But perception is also a way of acquiring 'sensitive knowledge': knowledge of the existence of particular finite substances and their observable qualities (*E*, IV.ii.14–15, pp. 536–8 and IV.xi, pp. 630–9).

It is controversial whether sensitive knowledge is consistent with Locke's official definition of knowledge (in which 'perception' is used in the general sense), as '*the perception of the connexion and agreement, or disagreement and repugnancy of any of our Ideas* (*E*, IV.i.2, p. 525). In particular, knowledge of the existence of 'things without the mind' appears to depend not on agreement between ideas, but on the agreement of ideas with the world.

Locke's thought seems to be that sensation carries with it an awareness that it is the 'the actual receiving of *Ideas* from without' (*E*, IV.xi.2, p. 630), in the same way that memory is supposed to consist in reviving ideas with the 'additional Perception annexed to them, that it has had them before' (*E*, II.x.2, p. 150). There is some suggestion that this additional awareness is grounded in differences in the ideas involved: that the awareness of an external cause is tied to the greater force and vivacity of ideas of sensation, and the feeling of familiarity of recalled ideas to their comparative lack of force and vivacity (these ideas are '*laid in fading colours*', *E*, II.x.5, p. 152). Hence Locke asks the sceptic: is there not 'a very manifest difference between dreaming of being in the Fire, and actually being in it'? (*E*, IV.ii.14, p. 537).

This response to scepticism is not unproblematic. The distinction between sensation on the one hand and memory and dreaming on the other is not obviously co-extensive with the distinction between more and less forceful and vivacious ideas: there can be dull sensations and forceful memories and dreams. Worse, this response threatens to beg the sceptic's question, who wants a reason for thinking that greater force and vivacity is in fact a mark of an external cause.

For his part, Locke suggests extreme sceptical doubt is self-undermining, because it calls into question the reliability of the FACULTIES necessary to ask the sceptical question in the first place: 'For we cannot act any thing, but by our Faculties; nor talk of Knowledge it self, but by the help of those Faculties, which are fitted to apprehend even what Knowledge is' (*E*, IV.xi.3, p. 631). But although Locke offers a number of additional 'concurrent Reasons' for rejecting the sceptical hypothesis (*E*, IV.xi.4–7, pp. 632–4), he is ultimately not overly concerned by the sceptical challenge: the attendance of ideas of sensation, unlike memory and dreaming, with pleasure and pain is at least sufficient for our purposes as moral subjects (*E*, IV.ii.14, pp. 536–8 and IV.xi.8, pp. 634–5).

The passivity of the mind in perception is central to Locke's account of sensitive knowledge, as it guarantees that ideas of sensation are caused by things distinct from ourselves. This epistemologically central claim is therefore somewhat compromised by Locke's claim that the ideas received in sensation are often altered by 'judgement' or 'habitual custom', as when the idea of 'a flat Circle variously shadow'd, with several degrees of Light and Brightness' is transformed into 'the perception of a convex Figure, and an uniform Colour' (*E*, II.ix.8, p. 145). This claim prefaces the discussion of the 'MOLYNEUX PROBLEM', added to the second edition of the *Essay*. Molyneux asked Locke (Molyneux to Locke, 2 March 1693, *Corr.*, vol. iv, p. 651) whether a man born blind and made to see would be able to distinguish by sight a globe from a cube, correctly anticipating that Locke would answer the question negatively. Locke explains that the blind man '*has not yet attained the Experience, that what affects his touch so or so, must affect his sight so or so*' (*E*, II.ix.8, p. 146).

Following BERKELEY (1975, sect. 133), it is often assumed that the issue turns on the 'heterogeneity' of ideas received via different senses: that the ideas of extension received by sight and touch differ fundamentally in kind, and can only be associated as a result of experience of their conjunction. But this does not sit well with Locke's claims that the idea of extension is a simple idea that we perceive via more than one sense (e.g. *E*, II.v, p. 127 and II.xiii.5, 24, pp. 168 and 178–9), and moreover a simple idea that resembles qualities of objects, and so presumably other simple ideas of extension. If so, why *could* a man born blind not be able to distinguish a cube from a globe on being made to see?

It is therefore more likely that Locke's negative answer to the Molyneux Problem depends instead upon the view that light and colours are the 'direct' objects of sight (Bolton, 1994). The blind man would be unable to distinguish the cube from the globe because he would lack the experience necessary for judgement to transform patterns of light and colour ('from that, which truly is a variety of shadow and colour, collecting the Figure') into two-dimensional plane figures, and these two-dimensional plane figures into three-dimensional solid figures (see also *W*, vol. iii, p. 325).

Even so, problems remain. Locke's claim

that the transformation occurs 'without our taking notice of it' appears to conflict with the claim, central to his polemic against innate ideas, that it is 'hardly intelligible' that there should be ideas in our minds of which we are unaware (*E*, I.ii.5, pp. 49–51). Likewise, the claim that judgement 'alters the appearances into their causes' stands in tension with Locke's epistemologically fundamental claim that all simple ideas represent properties of objects perfectly – are 'real' and 'adequate' – because in receiving them the mind is purely passive, and so they cannot but correspond to their causes.

BIBLIOGRAPHY
Primary Sources
Berkeley, George, *An Essay Towards A New Theory of Vision*, in Michael Ayers (ed.), *Philosophical Works* (London, 1975).

Secondary Literature
Bolton, Martha Brandt, 'The Real Molyneux Question', in G.A.J. Rogers (ed.), *Locke's Philosophy. Content and Context* (Oxford, 1994).

Keith Allen

PERSONAL IDENTITY

Locke's account of personal identity, appearing in II.xxvii ('Of Identity and Diversity') in the second edition of his *Essay,* is one of his most innovative and influential contributions to philosophical debate. Locke composed the chapter in mid-1693 at the suggestion of William Molyneux, however his first journal note dealing explicitly with personal identity dates from 1683 (Dewhurst, 1963, pp. 222–3), and there are even some thoughts relevant to his later theory in a note on immortality of 1682 (Locke, 1936, pp. 121–3).

Locke makes several remarks touching on personal identity in the first edition of the *Essay* when discussing both the resurrection and the Cartesian doctrine that the soul always thinks (*E*, I.iv.4–5, p. 86; II.i.11–2, p. 110). In one of them, Locke indicates that for him personal identity has to do with the 'Consciousness of our Actions and Sensations, especially of Pleasure and Pain, and the concernment that accompanies it' (*E*, II.i.1, p. 110). The two central notions in this comment, *consciousness* and self-*concern*, are crucial also to his theory as developed in the second edition chapter. Indeed, it was these remarks that inspired Molyneux to suggest a chapter on the topic.

Locke's account in terms of a self-relating consciousness challenges traditional views about personality and identity. He clearly refers to earlier accounts of the issue when he notes the 'great deal of that Confusion, which often occurs about this Matter' (*E*, II.xxvii.7, p. 332; cf II.xxvii.28, pp. 347–8). Locke does not indicate which texts he has in mind, but it is plain that one of the debates to which he is referring is the heated controversy between William Sherlock and Robert South about the Trinity – a debate which took place just before the writing and publication of Locke's chapter and created widespread interest (Thiel, 1983, pp. 61–4, 105–18; Thiel, 2000). This controversy, dealing with the identity of human persons and self-consciousness as well as with the theological issue, hints at the complex historical context from which Locke's new theory emerged. Some of the relevant background can be gleaned from references in Locke's text: background such as the debates about the scholastic search for a principle of individuation and related debates about diachronic identity in general, discussions about the immortality of the soul and the resurrection of the body, related views about the nature of the human soul and the human body, especially in Cartesian and anti-Cartesian early-modern thought, and traditional notions of responsibility, the law, just rewards and punishments in this life and the afterlife. Other relevant background is not obvious from Locke's published text: for example traditional ideas of consciousness and related notions such as conscience, memory and debates about the very concept of a person from Boethius onwards. Regarding the notion of consciousness, Locke's journal note from 1682 reflects his reading of the Cambridge Platonist Ralph Cudworth, who introduced the term 'consciousness' into the English philosophical terminology, using it as a translation of Plotinus' 'synaisthesis' (Thiel, 1991, p. 89). Locke's note of 1683 echoes passages in Lucretius that relate to the importance of memory to identity (Martin and Barresi, 2000, pp. 3–5).

For Locke, identity in general is an issue that pertains to our concepts of those things whose identity is in question – a view that occurred before Locke in some form or other in thinkers as diverse as Clauberg, Geulincx, HOBBES and BOYLE. In Locke, this view is connected to his rejection of substantial forms and his denial that we can have knowledge of the real essences of substances. On this basis Locke holds that the answer to the question of how much a thing may change without losing its identity must be in terms of our abstract ideas of those beings whose identity is under consideration. That is why Locke believes it is crucial to stick to that abstract idea of any being whose identity we consider: 'whatever makes the specifick *Idea*, to which the name is applied, if that *Idea* be steadily kept to, the distinction of any thing into the same, and divers will easily be conceived, and there can arise no doubt about it' (*E*, II.xxvii.28, p. 348).

In accordance with this general theory of identity, Locke argues that 'to find wherein *personal Identity* consists, we must consider what *Person* stands for' (*E*, II.xxvii.9, p. 335). And to be clear about the concept of a person, we have to distinguish it carefully from those of a thinking SUBSTANCE or soul or spirit, and of a man or human being. (*E*, II.xxvii.7, 15; pp. 332, 340). As Locke argues that we cannot know the real essence of the soul, he holds that speculations about the soul's materiality or immateriality are irrelevant to an understanding of the subject as a person and to personal identity. Accordingly, Locke does not ultimately choose between a Cartesian dualist account of man and the view of man as an 'organiz'd living Body' (*E*, II.xxvii.8, p. 333). He favours the latter, but only in so far as our ordinary idea of man is concerned. And whichever account of the soul, as substance, or man we may choose, we would still have to distinguish both from the notion of person.

Locke argues that 'it is the consciousness ... which makes the same *Person* and constitutes this inseparable *self*' (*E*, II.xxvii.17, p. 341). Consciousness constitutes the person and its identity by functioning as a unifier of thoughts and actions (*E*, II.xxvii.16, p. 340). It relates to the present as well as to the immediately preceding moments, connecting present and past experiences and thereby making them part of one identical person. Clearly then, contrary to what many writers on the topic have for a long time assumed, consciousness in Locke's account is not to be identified with memory alone. However, for Locke memory is a form of consciousness and it, too, plays a role in constituting personal identity (*E*, II.xxvii.23, pp. 344–5): to establish personal identity across time, it is not sufficient to point to a chain of direct, overlapping consciousness-links; it must also be possible that the past thoughts and actions be recalled, that is 'be brought home to the mind, and made present' (*E*, II.xxi.37, p. 254).

For Locke, 'person' or 'personality' is not just a cognitive unity of thoughts and actions. It is also that aspect or quality of a human subject with respect to which it is morally and legally responsible; it is a 'Forensick Term' (*E*, II.xxvii.26, p. 346). And here the notion of self-concern plays an important role (Thiel, 1983, pp. 128–51; Thiel, 1998, pp. 894–7). Its main function is to relate the present human subject, as person, to its own future, for the consciousness of thoughts and sensations includes the consciousness of pleasure and pain, and 'that which is conscious of Pleasure and Pain' desires 'that that *self*, that is conscious, should be happy'. Therefore Locke says that a 'concern for Happiness' is 'the unavoidable concomitant of consciousness' (*E*, II.xxvii.26, p. 346). And it is through its link with self-concern that consciousness relates to the future person: we are now motivated to act in such a way as to avoid future pain and to attain happiness. This includes the desire that I will not have to ascribe actions to myself that will result in punishment, i.e. misery.

Locke argues that 'person' can be applied only to free, rational beings, 'capable of a Law, and Happiness and Misery' (*E*, II.xxvii.26, p. 346), but that morally and legally relevant action attribution requires consciousness (and memory) in addition to freedom and rationality. However, Locke's idea that 'punishment ... [is] annexed to personality, and personality to consciousness' (*E*, II.xxvii.22, p. 344), creates a problem for his account. This is revealed in his discussion of the issue of drunkenness (*E*, II.xxvii.22, pp. 343–4) which he discusses also in his correspondence with Molyneux (e.g. Locke to Molyneux, 19 Jan 1694, *Corr.* vol. iv, p. 785). Human courts, Locke seems to concede in this context, cannot always distinguish between genuine and pretended lack of consciousness. And this makes Locke's claim that *personal* identity is the foundation of 'all the Right and Justice of Reward and Punishment' (*E*, II.xxvii.18, p. 341) problematic.

Yet, for Locke, when pursued rationally, the 'concern for happiness' relates to happiness in the afterlife (*E*, II.xxi.38, 60, 70; pp. 255, 273–4, 281–2). And since our happiness or misery in the future life depends on God's judgement of our actions in this life, we are concerned to be able to ascribe actions to ourselves which conform to the divine moral law, a law available to us through reason and revelation. Moreover, with respect to the Last Judgement the problem of the genuineness of self-ascription of actions through consciousness does not arise, for 'the Secrets of all Hearts shall be laid open' and 'no one shall be made to answer for what he knows nothing of' (*E*, II.xxvii.22, p. 344).

Locke's theory aroused vehement controversy almost immediately after its first publication, and it dominated the disputes over personal identity in the eighteenth century. Some of the early criticisms that relate to the logic of Locke's argument are still being discussed today. This includes the charge of circularity, urging that consciousness presupposes personal identity and therefore cannot constitute personal identity. However, this objection presupposes the very thing Locke challenged, namely that the person is an object to which consciousness relates as to an already individuated being. Another standard criticism maintains that Locke's theory is inconsistent with the undeniable transitivity of identity, i.e. with the principle that if *a* is identical with *b* and *b* identical with *c*, then *a* is identical with *c*. It is argued that, while identity is transitive, consciousness is not. This objection is more difficult to combat than the charge of circularity, although it has been argued that it can be met if consciousness is not equated with memory. Such defences are problematic, however, when they assume that the ability to recollect past individual actions is not at all essential to Locke's account (e.g. Garrett, 2003, p. 110).

Matters of interpretation continue to be debated as well. For a long time, many commentators focused almost exclusively on the cognitive side of Locke's account and the notion of consciousness (e.g. Flew, 1968). At the other end, some more recent writers have emphasized the practical aspect of Locke's theory to such an extent that they ascribe to self-concern even a certain priority over consciousness in the constitution of personal identity (e.g. Brandt, 2006, p. 41). Both extremes are problematic; neither is compatible with Locke's text. For Locke, both consciousness and self-concern are central, but consciousness has priority. As Locke notes: 'it is impossible to make personal identity to consist in any thing but consciousness' (*E*, II.xxvii.21, p. 343). Self-concern is merely an 'unavoidable concomitant of consciousness', and it reaches only 'as far as ... consciousness extends' (*E*, II.xxvii.17, p. 341).

BIBLIOGRAPHY
Primary Sources
Locke, John, *An Early Draft of Locke's Essay. Together with Excerpts from his Journals*, ed. R.I. Aaron and J. Gibb (Oxford, 1936).

Secondary Sources
Brandt, Reinhard, 'John Lockes Konzept der persönlichen Identität. Ein Resümee', *Aufklärung*, vol. xviii (2006), pp. 37–54.
Dewhurst, Kenneth, *John Locke: Physician and Philosopher* (London, 1963).
Flew, Antony, 'Locke and the Problem of Personal Identity', in C.B. Martin and D.M. Armstrong (eds), *Locke and Berkeley. A Collection of Critical Essays* (London, 1968), pp. 155–78.
Garrett, Don, 'Locke on Personal Identity', *Philosophical Topics*, vol. xxxi (2003), pp. 95–125.
Martin, Raymond, and John Barresi, *Naturalization of the Soul. Self and Personal Identity in the Eighteenth Century* (London and New York, 2000).
Thiel, Udo, *Lockes Theorie der Personalen Identität* (Bonn, 1983).
——, 'Cudworth and Seventeenth-Century Theories of Consciousness', in S. Gaukroger (ed.), *The Uses of Antiquity* (Dordrecht, 1991), pp. 79–99.
——, 'Personal Identity', in D. Garber and M. Ayers (eds), *The Cambridge History of Seventeenth-Century Philosophy* (Cambridge, 1998), pp. 868–912.
——, 'The Trinity and Human Personal Identity', in M.A. Stewart (ed.), *English Philosophy in the Age of Locke* (Oxford, 2000), pp. 217–43.

Udo Thiel

PRIMARY AND SECONDARY QUALITIES

Locke's distinction between the primary and secondary qualities of body was anticipated by Galileo, DESCARTES, BOYLE and HOBBES, as well as the ancient atomists. But his version stands out from its predecessors and has become the classic statement of the distinction. This is partly, no doubt, because it standardized the terminology, but it is also because of the subtlety with which Locke interprets the relations between quality, power and idea, and because of the range of considerations he offers the reader in favour of the distinction.

Primary qualities, for Locke, have two fundamental characteristics. Firstly, they belong to a body categorically, or 'as it is in it self' (*E*, II.viii.23, p. 140). Secondly they are inseparable from body 'in what estate soever it be', and thus are determinables of *each and every* body (*E*, II.viii.9, p. 134). Such qualities include solidity, extension, shape, size, motion and rest, and number.

While primary qualities bring with them powers, secondary qualities, on the other hand, are defined as being *only* powers – powers to produce certain perceptual ideas in us, including those of colour, taste, smell, heat and cold, and sound. Thus when we smell a violet, or see the reddish colour of porphyry, there is in fact nothing in the objects that resembles the perceived scent or colour; but when we see or feel the shape or size of these things, our PERCEPTION resembles the objects themselves.

Sometimes, following BERKELEY, Locke has been interpreted as saying that secondary qualities are in the mind. Such an interpretation is not entirely without textual warrant, but it is now usually thought to misrepresent Locke's considered position. This holds that only *ideas* of secondary qualities are in the mind, and that the *qualities* themselves involve a dispositional relation between bodies and mind. In fact, we may even say that secondary qualities belong to bodies, if we understand their mode of belonging as one of power, not intrinsic property. Locke writes that secondary qualities are 'nothing in the Objects themselves, but [i.e. except] Powers to produce various Sensations by their *primary Qualities* ... of their insensible parts' (*E*, II.viii.10, p. 135).

Secondary qualities are thus powers founded on the primary qualities of imperceptible particles – the scent of a perfume, for example, would be caused by the size, shape and motion of the minute corpuscles that make up an emission. Primary qualities are then, in addition to being the only categorical properties of bodies, also the ground of the causal powers of body, amongst which secondary qualities are numbered.

Locke also talks of 'a third sort' of qualities (*E*, II.viii.10, p. 135), which are generally termed 'tertiary qualities' by commentators. These, like secondary qualities, are the powers of objects rather than their intrinsic properties. More particularly, they are powers that objects have to change the qualities (primary and secondary) of other objects. For example, fire has the power to change the colour or consistency of wax or clay (*E*, II.viii.10, p. 135). Tertiary qualities differ from secondary qualities in that, while both are powers, only secondary qualities are generally assumed actually to qualify the objects themselves, and thus only they are a common source of philosophical perplexity.

Locke's basis for making the distinction between primary and secondary qualities was traditionally thought to be a reflection on everyday perceptual experience. Some of Locke's arguments are indeed of this kind. For example, he points out that perceptions of secondary qualities change as the states of the perceiver change. Thus if our hands are different temperatures, 'the same Water, at the same time, may produce the Idea of Cold by one Hand, and of Heat by the other' (*E*, II.viii.21, p. 139). Equally, while at one distance fire produces a sensation of warmth, at a nearer approach it produces a painful, burning sensation. If the pain is thought not to reside in the fire, why should we suppose that the warmth resides there? Locke concludes that fire has, 'by its primary Qualities', the power to produce in us sensations of both warmth and burning (*E*, II.viii.16, p. 137).

More recent interpretations have been directed to the scientific background of the distinction. Commentators since Maurice Mandelbaum (Mandelbaum, 1964) and Peter Alexander (Alexander, 1985) have tended to see Locke as systematizing and expounding the ontology of the corpuscularian HYPOTHESIS, in which only primary qualities are intrinsic to the particles that make up nature. This scientific interpretation has significant textual backing and many of the arguments that Locke advances for distinguishing between primary and secondary qualities clearly point to the explanatory power of corpuscularianism (the discussion of the purgative manna, at *E*, II.viii.18, p. 138, is one example). Locke even apologizes to the reader for his 'Excursion into Natural Philosophy' (*E*, II.viii 22, p. 140).

Locke's preference for corpuscularian explanations should not, however, be taken to be merely the expression of a deference to natural science. He thought corpuscularianism exploited a fundamental fact about our ability to understand physical causation, which we might call his 'impulse principle'. Impulse 'is the only way which we can conceive Bodies operate in' (*E*, II.viii.11, p. 136), Locke states, as a prelude to his presentation of the many cases of perception on which commentators have tended to concentrate their analysis. The impulse principle means that only mechanical contact-action – which relies exclusively on the primary qualities of the bodies concerned – is perspicuous to us. It is because corpuscularian science respects this principle, excluding other forms of causal power, that it recommends itself as uniquely intelligible and is therefore philosophically acceptable.

BIBLIOGRAPHY
Secondary Literature
Alexander, Peter, *Ideas, Qualities and Corpuscles: Locke and Boyle on the External World* (Cambridge, 1985).
Hill, James, 'The Impulse Principle and Locke's Distinction between Primary and Secondary Qualities', *The British Journal*

for the History of Philosophy, vol. xvii, no.
1 (2009), pp. 85–98.

Mandelbaum, Maurice, 'Locke's Realism' in
Maurice Mandelbaum, Philosophy, Science
and Sense Perception: Historical and
Critical Studies (Baltimore, 1964), pp.
1–60.

McCann, Edwin, 'Locke's Philosophy of
Body', in Vere Chappell (ed.), The
Cambridge Companion to John Locke
(Cambridge, 1994), pp. 56–88.

James Hill

PROPERTY

Locke's notion of natural, labour-based
property rights in chapter five, 'Of Property', of
the 'Second Treatise' is among the most hotly
debated topics in the history of political
thought. Famously, Locke himself wrote to
Richard King on 25 August 1703 that
'Propriety, I have no where found more clearly
explain'd than in a Book intituled, Two
Treatises of Government' (see Laslett, 1988, p.
3). Nonetheless the reception history of Locke's
ideas on property shows a confusing variety of
often contradictory accounts of their genesis,
meaning and status within his political and
moral philosophical thought. In the last
decades, the progress of research on Locke's
politics has entailed a drastic reduction in the
space for interpreting his views on property.

Since the nineteenth century Locke's conception of property has flown many different
flags. Socialist appraisals of his notion of
property culminated in C.B. Macpherson's
(1962) exposition of Locke as a possessive individualist; these were, in turn, pruned back by
John Dunn's (1969) landmark study of the
Two Treatises. J.G.A. Pocock subsequently
influenced the discussion of Locke's legacy on
modernity by acclaiming the destruction of the

proto-liberal 'myth' and denying Locke a place
in the presentation of his paradigm of the
'Atlantic republican tradition' (Pocock, 1975
and 1980). More recently scholars have discussed the image of Locke as a liberal supporter of English colonialism, in order to recon-
stitute his relation to the development of
America as well as to re-evaluate the transmission of Lockean ideas to the American continent in the eighteenth century (Armitage, 2000
and 2004; Arneil, 1994 and 1996; Kramnick,
1990; Tully, 1980 and 1993; Tuck, 1999; see
also the earlier work by Appleby, 1976 and
1978).

A major difficulty in establishing the meaning
of Locke's chapter five lies in disagreements
among Locke scholars about its relation to the
rest of the 'Second Treatise' and, in general,
about the composition and dating of the Two
Treatises. Often the chapter 'Of Property' has
been studied in isolation from the other
chapters of the 'Second Treatise', and one
possible reason for this arises from the ongoing
discussion about its dating and context.
According to Peter Laslett, chapter five was
written together with the main part of the
'Second Treatise' before 1680 and incorporated into a new structure to refute FILMER's
Patriarcha (Laslett, 1988, pp. 59–66; TTG
II.25 note). By contrast, new research has made
a strong case for pushing forward the composition of the 'Second Treatise' to 1681–2. It
has been argued that the specific aim of chapter
five was not to refute Filmer, but either to assail
Pufendorf's theory of natural sociability and,
thereby, William Penn's outlook on the rights
of the native inhabitants of America (Tuck,
1999, pp. 167–78), or to develop the theory
behind Locke's Fundamental Constitutions of
Carolina, which he was revising in 1682
(Armitage, 2004). Furthermore, in looking elsewhere, beyond Filmer, to explain why Locke set
up his comprehensive argument about the
origins of property rights and the socio-
economic development of properly constructed
civil societies, these accounts also are consistent
with and strengthen the interpretation that

Locke sketched mankind in the state of nature as a 'negative community', instead of one in which each man had a property right in the earth (cf. Tully, 1980, pp. 60–1 and 111–16).

While the context in which Locke wrote and the question of his fundamental analytical principles have recently attracted attention, it is also important to notice that the chapter on property was included in a natural jurisprudence treatise, whose direct aim was to refute Filmer's argument that the authority of rulers over subjects and territory came directly from God. Likewise, the chapter of property was a profound rebuttal of Filmer's idea that God-given property rights belonged to rulers instead of to 'Mankind in common' (*TTG* II.25). Against Filmer, Locke defended but redeveloped Grotius's theory, which next to a notion of negative community included the idea that consent lay at the basis of individual property rights. Locke's primary focus was on construing a theoretical transition from the conditions of the state of nature (of 'plenty of natural provisions' and land) via the emergence of money to the state. A ramification of this way of anchoring civil society in labour-based property – which has often been overlooked in political philosophers' discussions about Locke's ideas of justice and inequality – is that the overarching logic of this theory perhaps cannot be described in terms of unchanging individual rights, but can be grasped only through Locke's 'workmanship' perspective (Tully, 1980; Sreenivasan, 1995; cf. Kramer, 1997). Through this natural jurisprudence perspective, Locke developed in chapter five a conjectural history of the natural socio-economic development of a well-constituted political order, which functioned as a normative basis for assessing the validity of property distributions in civil societies. This can be recognized by looking more precisely at Locke's argument about America.

As pointed out by Stephen Buckle, Locke did not describe America as being either in the state of nature – without the institution of money, without political authority – or as a place that colonial settlers could consider to

be in the state of nature (Buckle, 2001, pp. 258–62). Instead, it was in 'want of People and [the widespread use of] Money'(*TTG* II.108). When Locke argued that 'in the beginning all the World was *America*' (*TTG* II.49), he suggested that America's socio-economic structures had not evolved *despite* the existence of money, government and property. There was a sharp discrepancy between Locke's model of the material perfection of humankind and the reality that America presented, which was the basis for his view that settlers could rightfully occupy lands in America. Yet the main contrast lay not in the cultivation of land, but more generally in the growth of population and markets, such as had taken place in England, where there were 'Plenty of People under Government who have Money and Commerce' (*TTG* II.35; see also Buckle, 2001, pp. 268–72). God had given the earth to the 'Industrious and Rational' to promote 'Comfort' rather than need satisfaction, and money drove the process by which man increased his 'conveniencies of Life' (*TTG* II.34 and II.44). The combination of Locke's recognition of money as the essential instrument for the continuing perfection of humankind (Hont and Ignatieff, 1983, pp. 35–42; cf. Tully, 1980, pp. 150–3) and his awareness of the barriers that may block natural progress, offers an insight into the reasons for his later works on money and activities on the Board of Trade as efforts to accommodate the natural laws of property with suitable legislation.

Based on the above, Buckle's suggestion (2001, pp. 273–5) that America itself was of marginal concern in Locke's argument on property makes some sense. Chapter five contained a Protestant theory of *imperium* that neatly circumscribed limited justifications for territorial empire (Armitage, 2000), but that theory itself was part of a wider model for the natural order of human improvement. Ultimately, a more analytically precise reading of the argument on property in chapter five will not only be useful for reconsidering Locke's role on the Board of Trade or his vision of the development of Carolina, but sustains a rein-sertion of Locke into the history of political thought in the Atlantic tradition with regard to the issues of commercial society, state debts, financial competition, international trade, empire and the reform of the interstate system. Perhaps Locke's political legacy should not be seen primarily in terms of the transmission across the Atlantic in the late seventeenth and eighteenth centuries of liberal or republican political ideas, which carries the risk of ending up with the same old retrospective ideological impositions in a new form. When, instead, Locke's views on the relation between consent, money, property and political authority are seen as a form of early political economy, it becomes possible to see his intellectual and political enterprise in the same way as did his eighteenth-century Italian translators (Pagnini and Tavanti, 1751) and as was acknowledged by a contemporary review (*Novelle letterarie*, 1751), where Locke was described as having provided an enduringly relevant vision for the dominant eighteenth-century problem of rec-onciling international peace and trade.

BIBLIOGRAPHY
Primary Sources
Pagnini, Giovanni Francesco, and Angelo Tavanti (eds), *Ragionamenti sopra la moneta l'interesse del danaro le finanze e il commer-cio scritti e pubblicati in diverse occasioni dal signor Giovanni Locke*, 2 vols (Florence, 1751).
Novelle letterarie, vol. xxii, no. 42 (1751), pp. 657–62.

Secondary Literature
Appleby, Joyce, 'Locke, Liberalism and the Natural Law of Money', *Past and Present*, vol. lxxi (1976), pp. 43–69.
Appleby, Joyce, *Economic Thought and Ideology in Seventeenth-Century England* (Princeton, 1978).
Armitage, David, *The Ideological Origins of the British Empire* (Cambridge, 2000).
——, 'John Locke, Carolina, and the *Two Treatises of Government*', *Political Theory*, vol. xxxii (2004), pp. 602–27.
Arneil, Barbara, 'Trade, Plantations, and Property: John Locke and the Economic Defense of Colonialism', *Journal of the History of Ideas*, vol. lv (1994), pp. 591–609.
——, *John Locke and America: the Defence of English Colonialism* (Oxford, 1996).
Buckle, Stephen, *Natural Law and the Theory of Property: Grotius to Hume* (Oxford, 1991).
——, 'Tully, Locke and America', *British Journal for the History of Philosophy*, vol. ix (2001), pp. 245–81.
Dunn, John, *The Political Thought of John Locke: An Historical Account of the Argument of the* Two Treatises of Government (Cambridge, 1969).
Hont, Istvan, and Michael Ignatieff, 'Needs and Justice in the *Wealth of Nations*: An Introductory Essay', in Istvan Hont and Michael Ignatieff (eds), *Wealth and Virtue: The Shaping of Political Economy in the Scottish Enlightenment* (Cambridge, 1983), pp. 1–44.
Kramer, Matthew H., *John Locke and the Origins of Private Property: Philosophical Explorations of Individualism, Community, and Equality* (Cambridge, 1997).
Kramnick, Isaac, *Republicanism and Bourgeois Radicalism* (Ithaca, New York, 1990).
Laslett, Peter, 'Introduction', in *TTG* (1988), pp. 3–133.
Macpherson, C.B., *The Political Theory of Possessive Individualism: From Hobbes to Locke* (Oxford, 1962).
Pocock, J.G.A., *The Machiavellian Moment: Florentine Political Thought and the Atlantic Republican Tradition* (Princeton, 1975).
——, 'The Myth of John Locke and the Obsession with Liberalism', in *John Locke: Papers Read at a Clark Library Seminar by J.G.A. Pocock and Richard Ashcraft* (Los Angeles, 1980), pp. 1–24.
Sreenivasan, Gopal, *The Limits of Lockean Rights in Property* (Oxford, 1995).
Tuck, Richard, *The Rights of War and Peace:*

Political Thought and the International Order from Grotius to Kant (Oxford, 1999).
Tully, James, *A Discourse on Property: John Locke and His Adversaries* (Cambridge, 1980).
——, *An Approach to Political Philosophy: Locke in Contexts* (Cambridge, 1993).

Koen Stapelbroek

RATE OF INTEREST

Locke's participation in economic debates over the proper rate of interest date back to an early memorandum of 1668, entitled 'Some of the Consequences that are like to Follow upon lessening of interest to 4 per Cent', possibly drafted at the behest of the first Earl of SHAFTESBURY, who was then Chancellor of the Exchequer (Kelly, 1991, pp. 3–12; and *LoM*, pp. 167–202 (the memorandum of 1668)). In addition to addressing proposals floated in the House of Commons in the spring of 1668 to lower interest rates from six per cent to four per cent, Locke's paper responded to claims advanced in Josiah Child's influential pamphlet, the *Brief Observations* of 1668, many of which were reiterated that same year by Thomas Culpeper.

After putting these writings aside for more than two decades, Locke returned to the topic in the 1690s when proposals were made to lower interest rates in response to a profound crisis in the English economy stemming from the Nine Years War. A sharp decrease in the money supply was slowing trade, and one likely culprit was England's rate of interest. Inspired by the example of the Dutch case, where commercial prosperity accompanied low interest rates, many claimed that lowering interest rates would encourage commerce, stimulate the English economy and raise falling rents. At the prompting of John Somers, Edward Clarke and John Freke, Locke revised and considerably expanded the original 1668 memorandum for publication. This more comprehensive work, entitled *Some Considerations of the Consequences of the Lowering of Interest, and Raising the Value of Money*, was published in 1691 in the midst of renewed attempts to lower the legal rate of interest from six per cent to four per cent per annum (see *LoM*, pp. 203–342).

Substantively, Locke's writings on interest revolve around the following main arguments. First, the rate of interest charged on money is no different from any other commodity: it depends on available supply and demand. Like any other commodity, money has a 'Naturall' or 'intrinsick' price that depends both on its availability and the number and necessity of those who require it (*LoM*, pp. 170–3 and 243–9). By speaking of a 'natural' price Locke did not mean to endorse the scholastic or Aristotelian position that money has an inherent or essential value and that to charge more for its use is a moral crime. Rather, terms like 'natural' or 'intrinsic' are posed in contradistinction to 'artificial' or 'external' efforts by governments to control by law the equilibrium rate of interest.

After outlining the true determinants of the price of money, Locke's *Some Considerations* deals with potentially negative consequences of suppressing interest rates artificially. If legal rates of interest are lowered by the government below the 'natural' rate, several things will follow. Most importantly, rather than letting money out at an artificially depressed rate, would-be lenders will simply keep the money themselves or give their funds to bankers, thereby stifling the money supply necessary for trade. One of Locke's key assumptions is that the circulation of money serves as the main facilitator of wealth and trade, the veritable life-blood of a nation's economy (*LoM*, p. 172, 221, and 235–7). What was needed in England above all else was an acceleration of that flow; the key to commercial prosperity was the volume and rapidity of money's circulation.

Locke appreciated that the interest rate, or

price of money, has a necessary relationship to the price of other goods in which one might choose to invest, particularly the price of land and land rents. Responding to the claims of Child and others, he argued that artificial suppression of interest rates was unlikely to raise the price of land or other commodities (*LoM*, pp. 178–96 and 243–84).

Locke also appreciated that, in an international economy, England's decision to lower rates of interest unilaterally could either provoke an outflow of capital to other nations or, alternatively, discourage foreign lenders from hazarding loans overseas (*LoM*, pp. 168–70). The best way to increase the circulation of money and restore the commerce of England was to restore a more favourable balance of payments with other nations. Only by selling more and buying less abroad could England halt the flow of specie to other nations and increase the domestic circulation of money (*LoM*, pp. 231–2).

Locke's argument was baldly prudential and realistic. Laws dictating an artificially lowered interest rate were likely to be widely ignored or circumvented, contributing to a broader disregard for the laws themselves and, hence, causing 'great Perjury in the Nation' (*LoM*, p. 212). It was just as improbable that the government could successfully regulate the price of money as it could 'set a rate on Victualls in a time of famine' (*LoM*, p. 170).

Many commentators have been tempted to find the origins of a modern 'science' of economics in Locke's writings on trade and banking (Letwin, 1963; Vaughn, 1980; Harpham, 1985). Were his writings, then, a step in the direction of liberating a nascent science of economics from its classical and Christian antecedents? He does lay great emphasis on the ways in which interest, or the price of money, is governed by economic laws no different from those governing the price of any other commodity. Moreover, Aristotelian or Christian aversions to usury are certainly anathema to Locke's position. Nonetheless, his formal economic theory cannot be divorced

from prevailing classical or Christian precepts about the moral underpinnings of the market economy (Boyd, 2002). For example, Locke delved into the distributional effects of artificially lowering interest rates, in particular the consequences for widows, orphans and pensioners, whose support depended on interest on their savings (*LoM*, p. 212 and 219–20). Depressing interest rates was alleged to harm those living on a fixed income, to discourage important social virtues such as industry and frugality, and to punish creditors for taking risks.

Locke's concerns about the distributional effects of interest rate policy – both within England but also between England and other nations – demonstrate that the ultimate justification for letting the free market set the rate of interest is not any sacrosanct notion of equilibrium price or economic efficiency but a general solicitude for the 'public interest'. Notwithstanding his prescient insights into the spontaneous formation of prices and his aversion to state regulation, Locke's writings are more exemplary of a classical political economy with its superintending concern for the commonweal. Arguments for letting the free market determine interest rates are inseparable from mercantilist assumptions that governed his economic thinking more generally. What was at stake was the policy, in the context of international economic competition, most conducive to England's affluence and wellbeing (*LoM*, pp. 221–32). 'A Kingdom,' Locke emphasizes, 'grows Rich, or Poor, just as a Farmer doth, and no otherwise', namely by producing rather than spending abroad (*LoM*, p. 230). Without free circulation of money throughout the economy, the trade that constituted England's chief advantage would have been squandered.

BIBLIOGRAPHY
Secondary Literature
Boyd, Richard, 'The Calvinist Origins of Lockean Political Economy', *History of Political Thought*, vol. xxiii (2002), pp.

30–60.

Harpham, Edward J., 'Class, Commerce, and the State: Economic Discourse and Lockean Liberalism in the Seventeenth Century', *Western Political Quarterly*, vol. xxxviii (1985), pp. 565–82.

Kelly, Patrick Hyde, 'General Introduction: Locke on Money', in *LoM* (1991), vol. i, pp. 1–105.

Letwin, William, *The Origins of Scientific Economics* (London, 1963).

Vaughn, Karen, *John Locke: Economist and Social Scientist* (Chicago, 1980).

Richard Boyd

REPUBLICANISM

Classical republicanism refers in early-modern Britain to political ideals that were based on those of ancient Greek and Roman republican models. Although similar traditions of thought can be found in many other European countries, the term has a specifically British resonance. This is no doubt mainly due to the fact that the term, classical republicanism, was coined by Zera S. Fink in his *Classical Republicans: An Essay in the Recovery of a Pattern of Thought in Seventeenth Century England* (1945). Another path-breaking study, especially for the latter part of the seventeenth and the eighteenth century, is Caroline Robbins's *The Eighteenth-century Commonwealthman* (1959).

Fink defined his central concept in the following way: 'By a "classical republican" I mean a person who advocated or admired a republic, and who took his ideas for such a government in whole or in part from the ancient masterpieces of political organization, their supposed modern counterparts, or their ancient and modern expositors' (Fink, 1945, p. x). Fink was aware of the difficulty of defining the term

'republic'; in order to avoid confusion, he took his 'criteria from those of the classical republicans themselves'. 'When they spoke of a republic,' he wrote, 'they had in mind primarily a state which was not headed by a king and in which the hereditary principle did not prevail in whole or in part in determining the headship' (Fink, 1945, p. x). Although he acknowledged that early-modern Englishmen learned numerous things from their classical heroes, Fink mainly focused his attention on the concept of mixed government, and how 'the one, the few, and the many would act as effective checks on one another' (Fink, 1945, p. 2).

Classical republicanism is most closely linked with the republican thinkers of the Civil War and Interregnum period (1640–60), as well as of the late seventeenth century. There were very few, if any, authors in pre-Civil War England who advocated a republican form of government. Yet it is widely agreed that classical republican modes of thought were well known from the beginning of the sixteenth century, when such central early-Tudor humanists as Thomas More and Thomas Starkey expounded them. Walter Haddon, a mid-Tudor humanist, noted in 1552 that in the *De officiis* Cicero had fitted Plato's laws into 'a new republican form' (Haddon, 1567, p. 75; Harris, 2007). These ideas were never lost between that period and the mid seventeenth century. Indeed, Thomas HOBBES argued that it was above all the crucial impact of classical republicanism that had caused the Civil War and Revolution. In *Leviathan* (1651) he wrote: 'And as to Rebellion in particular against Monarchy; one of the most frequent causes of it, is the Reading of the books of Policy, and Histories of the antient Greeks, and Romans ... From the reading, I say, of such books, men have undertaken to kill their Kings' (Hobbes, 1991, pp. 225–6).

There were two chief ways in which classical republican concepts entered the mainstream of English political thinking in the sixteenth century and the early seventeenth century. First, in the course of the latter part of the sixteenth century and the early years of the seventeenth century, all the key classical sources associated most closely with classical republicanism were translated into English. Practically the whole canon of classical republican thought was available in English by the early seventeenth century. The second and even more important way was through grammar schools, where the values of classical citizenship were inculcated in generations of schoolboys. As one schoolmaster put it in 1579, 'in matters concerning the common wealth, hee is never taken for a good Citizen, which is touched with no love of the common wealth, which beareth no friendly, loving, nor favourable goodwill to his fellowe Citizens, and their affayres, which in all thinges seeketh himselfe, without aniue regarde of others' (Stockwood, 1579, fols 27ᵛ–28ʳ).

Every schoolboy was expected to have an intimate knowledge of Cicero's *De officiis*, and was also exposed on a daily basis to republican politics in his training in rhetoric, which had an absolutely central place in grammar school curricula. In the context of Hobbes's remark in *Leviathan*, it is highly interesting to note that in a popular school textbook a speech against tyranny was one of the model speeches. It emphasized the usefulness and facility of tyrannicide, arguing that 'no followers are needed to attack tyranny' and that 'judges' vote will be sufficient to destroy all the power of tyranny' (Aphthonius [c. 1520], sig. b.iiiʳ). The most popular edition of this work provided a list of classical sources that eulogized tyrannicide (Aphthonius, 1575, fols 97ᵛ–98ʳ). Similarly, a collection of Cicero's letters, edited by a master of Manchester grammar school in 1602 for grammar school use, contained many of Cicero's most openly republican letters. The editor provided summaries of the letters in which he briefly explained their republican context. For instance, from a letter to Cassius in May 44 BC – where Cicero persuaded Cassius, Decius and Brutus to continue their work for the republic, but without actually mentioning that this meant the killing of Antony – schoolboys were advised to read out

the following: 'When Caesar's murderers escape from the city, and Antonius, who already directs to imperial disposition, performs everything by his own lust, Cicero, by writing to the fugitives ... teaching that all the hope of liberty is in Decius and Marcus Brutus and Cassius, kindles them to the killing of Antonius' (Cicero, 1602, p. 98).

In the course of the 1640s republican ideals and values, if not the actual republican constitutional arrangements, were examined by John Milton and by Marchamont Nedham, who by the latter part of the 1640s was beginning to explore Machiavellian themes in his Leveller pamphlets. After the execution of Charles I in January 1649, a republic was finally established in England. A week after the execution it was announced that 'the office of a king in this nation ... is unnecessary, burdensome, and dangerous to the liberty, safety and public interests of the people'. In late March a declaration changed 'the *Government* of this *Nation* from the former *Monarchy* ... into a *Republique*' (Scott, 2004, p. 252 and 255). In the early 1650s the new regime was defended by republican principles in its own newspaper, *Mercurius Politicus*. Nedham, its editor, also defended the republic in *The Case of the Commonwealth* (1650) and again in *A True State of the Case of the Commonwealth* (1654).

One of the most common features of seventeenth-century classical republicanism was the fact that it was often developed not only as an answer to some urgent political questions but more often than not also as a critical reaction to existing political circumstances. Thus in 1656 Nedham published a revised version of his editorial from *Mercurius Politicus* in *The Excellencie of a Free-state* as an attack against Oliver Cromwell, whom Nedham exhorted not to undermine republican values. At the same time, John Streater, Henry Vane and James Harrington also used these values to criticize the current regime. Cromwell's death in September 1658 triggered a process in which first the Protectorate fell in the winter of 1658–9 and then the restored republic collapsed in the course of the following winter. During this intense period such authors as Harrington, Milton and Henry Stubbe remained steadfast to their republican cause and made their last intellectual efforts to devise a lasting republic.

Although the restored monarchy hunted down and either assassinated, executed or imprisoned many republicans, classical republicanism did not vanish from the English intellectual landscape. The most important republican author of the Restoration was Algernon Sidney, who had been active already during the Interregnum. In his *Court Maxims* (written in 1664–5 but unpublished until 1996), he offered an analysis of tyranny, but in his *Discourses concerning Government* (written in 1681–3 and published posthumously in 1698), Sidney explored republican themes more widely. In the 1690s a group of republicans, including Robert Molesworth, John Toland and Walter Moyle, not only produced their own republican contributions but also brought earlier republican texts into print, thus bequeathing a republican canon to the eighteenth century. These included Sidney's *Discourses*, Milton's prose works in 1698, Henry Neville's *Plato Redivivus* (1698) and James Harrington's works (1700).

At the centre of classical republicanism was the concept of liberty. As Nedham put it in 1656, liberty was 'the most precious Jewel under the sun ... of more worth than your Estates, or your lives' (quoted in Scott, 2004, p. 156). Classical republicans advocated a theory of liberty that was mainly derived from classical Roman moralists, historians and legal sources. According to this theory, someone was free when he was not dependent on the will of someone else. Liberty was not simply an absence of coercion but even of its possibility. Freedom was thus contrasted with slavery. In the case of a civil association this meant that it possessed freedom when it was a self-governing community and its laws were made by the whole community. It followed that a republic could lose its liberty if it was 'coercively deprived of its ability to act at will in pursuit of its chosen ends' (Skinner, 1998, p. 48; Skinner, 2008).

Another central value in classical republicanism was virtue, which for some scholars is its defining characteristic (Worden, 1994, pp. 46–7). Virtues included the classical cardinal virtues of prudence, courage, temperance and justice, but for many republicans also a Machiavellian *virtù*, where ethical considerations gave way to the centrality of the common good. Both liberty and virtue as highest political values were prerequisites for republican citizenship. Classical republicanism included a very strong commitment to politically active citizenship, although its precise social limits could vary.

Perhaps the most distinctive aspect of seventeenth-century English classical republican thought was its heavy indebtedness to Machiavelli's *Discorsi*. This was most evident in the eager embrace of the Machiavellian notion of *grandezza*. Following the Florentine, many English republicans drew a distinction between aristocratic republics, such as Sparta and Venice, which aimed at longevity and safety on the one hand, and more democratic ones, such as Rome, which aimed at expansion, glory and *grandezza* on the other.

Liberty, based on virtuous citizenship and the rule of law, was the central political value of classical republicanism. When Fink launched the concept 'classical republicans', he argued that mixed government was the defining character of this concept, but more recent scholarship has challenged this view. It has been pointed out that for many early-modern republicans the precise constitutional arrangement was much less important than the more general values of liberty and virtue. And even those republicans who were interested in constitutional questions placed much less emphasis on the mixed constitution than Fink assumed. Locke's relationship with classical republican discourse is a case in point. He was no constitutional republican and does not satisfy any criterion of doctrinaire republicanism, as he never argued for the superiority of a republican form of government. Yet recent scholars have largely abandoned the earlier view that the republican tradition is irrelevant for gaining an understanding of Locke's political philosophy. They have emphasized that the republican concept of liberty is of crucial importance to his *Two Treatises* and that the issue of a life of virtue surfaces in his work on *Education*.

BIBLIOGRAPHY
Primary Sources
Aphthonius, *Aphthonii sophistae praeexercitamenta interprete viro doctissimo*, trans. and ed. Gentian Hervet ([c. 1520]).
———, *Aphthonii sophistae progymnasmata, partim a Rodolpho Agricola, partim a Ioanne Maria Cataneo Latinitate donata: cum luculentis & utilibus in eadem scholijs Reinhardi Lorichij Hadamatij* (1575).
Cicero, M.T., *Epistolarum familiarium M.T. Ciceronis epitome secundum tria genera libro secundo epistola tertia proposita: nuntiatorium, iocosum, & graue ... Thoma Coganno medico, quondam Ludimagistro Mancuniensi collectore. Ad usum scholarum* (Cambridge, 1602).
Haddon, Walter, *G. Haddoni legum doctoris, S. Reginae Elisabethae à supplicum libellis, lucubrationes passim collectae, & editae* (1567).
Hobbes, Thomas, *Leviathan*, ed. Richard Tuck (Cambridge, 1991).
Stockwood, John, *A Very Fruiteful Sermon Preched at Paules Crosse the Tenth of May Last ... in Which Are Conteined Very Necessary and Profitable Lessons and Instructions for This Time* (1579).

Secondary Literature
Fink, Zera S., *The Classical Republicans: An Essay in the Recovery of a Pattern of Thought in Seventeenth Century England* (Evanston, Illinois, 1945).
Harris, Cathie R., 'Cicero's *De officiis* and Moral Education in the Res Publica of Elizabethan and Early Stuart England'

(MPhil thesis, University of Cambridge), 2007.
Robbins, Caroline, *The Eighteenth-century Commonwealthman* (Cambridge, 1959).
Scott, Jonathan, *The Commonwealth Principles. Republican Writing of the English Revolution* (Cambridge, 2004).
Skinner, Quentin, *Liberty before Liberalism* (Cambridge, 1998).
———, *Hobbes and Republican Liberty* (Cambridge, 2008).
Worden, Blair, 'Marchamont Nedham and the Beginnings of English Republicanism, 1649–1656', in David Wootton (ed.), *Republicanism, Liberty and Commercial Society 1649–1776* (Stanford, 1994), pp. 45–81.

Markku Peltonen

RESISTANCE AND REVOLUTION

In the early 1680s revolution was anticipated and feared, but in practice it did not occur in England. It was a great achievement for Charles II's regime to escape from the Exclusion Crisis without yielding to the Whigs' demands, and then to carry out a successful campaign of repression against all dissent, securing peace and strengthening the powers of the crown. To Locke, who was associated with the vanquished Whigs, Charles II's peace meant 'Violence and Rapine', a peace 'maintain'd only for the benefit of Robbers and Oppressors' (paraphrased from *TTG* II.228). The king's actions constituted, Locke intimated in the *Two Treatises*, a betrayal of trust that entitled his subjects to overthrow him by means of revolution (or aided by foreign conquest) and to set up a new government and new governors as they saw fit. Locke's position lay on the radical flank of Whiggery; the majority recoiled from such justifications of armed resistance, fearing a repetition of the civil wars of the 1640s.

In the 'Second Treatise', Locke made a bold move by defending a right of resistance which is, in its moral foundation, an individual right to 'appeal to heaven'. The basic principle is that, 'where the Body of the People, or any single Man, is deprived of their Right, or is under the Exercise of a power without right, and have no Appeal on Earth, there they have a liberty to appeal to Heaven' (*TTG* II.168, II.207, and II.241–2). The germ of Locke's argument may be found in the classical Roman accounts of the citizen's appellate power. Under the Roman Republic, the *provocatio ad populum*, subsequently known as *appellatio*, denoted an individual citizen's appeal from the magistrate's verdict to the people – or even to gods in heaven. It was considered a citadel of civil liberty. Locke, an inheritor of the resistance theories of the Reformation, transposed the classical notion of *provocatio* to the early-modern idiom of natural rights. However, while the monarchomachs' earlier theories had relied on corporations of some judiciary status to oppose a tyrant, Locke's right to appeal went one step further, assuming individuals reasonable enough to hold the power to compel a prince (Savonius, 2006; Skinner, 1978, vol. ii, esp. pp. 338–9).

Absolutists denounced such resistance theories as recipes for civil war and anarchy. The core problem – for Robert FILMER, Thomas HOBBES, and, in the 1660s, for Locke himself – was human subjectivity, the partiality and fickleness of each man's personal judgement. Since any government might in principle appear tyrannical to an individual subject, it seemed that an individual right to 'appeal to heaven' entails a perpetual danger of rebellion. In the 1680s his own political experience forced Locke, however, to consider the problem of subjectivity from another angle: reason appeared to have lost its restraint, not upon individual malcontents who might rebel, but upon the rulers of Stuart England and Bourbon France (Dunn, 1969).

In 1689, after the Stuart regime had col-lapsed, Locke was able to publish his *Two Treatises* in order to 'establish the Throne of our Great Restorer, Our present King William' (*TTG*, preface). Yet it seems that he did not compose his work in order to justify the Revolution of 1688–9. On the basis of cir-cumstantial evidence, Peter Laslett argued that it had been written in 1679–83 to call for a rev-olution yet to come (Laslett, 1988, pp. 46–7). Subsequently, Richard Ashcraft stressed that the revolution to come never came true: that Locke demanded a more democratic and radical revolution than the one actually con-summated in 1688–9 (Ashcraft, 1986, pp. 3–9, and chaps 6 and 11; see also Goldie, 1980).

There is evidence which casts doubt on Ashcraft's account of how Locke perceived England's political situation and future prospects (Goldie, 1992; Marshall, 1994). In 1689 the English were offered, Lady Mordaunt wrote to Locke, 'an occasion not of amending the government: but of melting itt downe and make all new'. It is unclear whether Locke's remark that the English should restore 'our ancient government ... in its originall constitu-tion' implied constitutional reforms and a lib-eration from the past – a 'radical' use of ANCIENT CONSTITUTIONALISM – or simply a 'restorationist' re-establishment of a mixed monarchy with a different head (Carey Mordaunt, Viscountess Mordaunt, to Locke, 21/31 January [1689]; and Locke to Edward Clarke, 29 January/8 February 1689, *Corr.*, vol. iii, p. 538 and 545).

It is clear, however, that the 'revolution' – or 'restoration' – Locke defended in 1689 was merely the first stage in the plan for cleansing Europe of oppressors. He wished to see com-pleted 'the designes which his Majestie has soe gloriously began for the redeeming England and with it all Europe' (Locke to Charles Mordaunt, Viscount Mordaunt, 21 February 1689, *Corr.*, vol. iii, pp. 575–6). The French translation of Locke's 'Second Treatise', pub-lished in 1691 when there was hope for a military victory over France, justified the title to rulership of a conqueror who had delivered a nation from oppression (Locke, 1691, section XVI.1). Locke's works launched the ideology of revolutionary action and military intervention, articulated in an idiom of individual rights, more persuasive today than at the time.

BIBLIOGRAPHY
Primary Sources
Locke, John, *Du Gouvernement Civil* [trans. David Mazel] (Amsterdam, 1691).

Secondary Literature
Ashcraft, Richard, *Revolutionary Politics & Locke's* Two Treatises of Government (Princeton, New Jersey, 1986).
Dunn, John, *The Political Thought of John Locke: An Historical Account of the Argument of the* Two Treatises of Government (Cambridge, 1969).
Goldie, Mark, 'The Roots of True Whiggism, 1688–1694', *History of Political Thought*, vol. i (1980), pp. 195–236.
Goldie, Mark, 'John Locke's Circle and James II', *Historical Journal*, vol. xxxv (1992), pp. 557–86.
Laslett, Peter, 'Introduction', in *TTG* (1988), pp. 3–133.
Marshall, John, *John Locke: Resistance, Religion and Responsibility* (Cambridge, 1994).
Savonius, S.-J., 'The Lockean Rightholders', in Petter Korkman and Virpi Mäkinen (eds), *Transformations in Medieval and Early-Modern Rights Discourse* (Dordrecht, 2006), pp. 285–306.
Skinner, Quentin, *The Foundations of Modern Political Thought*, 2 vols (Cambridge, 1978).

S.-J. Savonius-Wroth

SCHOLASTICISM

Locke's comments on the scholastics are consistently critical and sometimes satirical or openly dismissive. Like other practitioners of the new science, he contrasted an openness to experiment and new discovery with what he saw as the hidebound, barely intelligible Aristotelianism of the schools. Locke's opposition to scholasticism is, however, not just a negative affair: it helped motivate him in his theoretical inquiry into language and meaning. In addition, his philosophy showed more continuity with scholasticism than he was prepared to admit.

There are two main strands to Locke's treatment of scholasticism: firstly his reaction to the practice and style of philosophy in the schools and secondly his view of actual scholastic doctrines. In relation to practice, Locke was particularly critical of the art of disputation. He had first-hand experience of formal disputations and in one letter wrote that he 'feared there would be noe other way to decide the controversy betweene them but by cuffs' (Locke to [John Strachey?], [early January 1666?], *Corr.*, vol. i, p. 182). 'Wrangling' – as he liked to refer to it – is not, in Locke's view, conducive to the seeking of truth. Instead, it encourages a variety of intellectual vices: disputants tend to pretend to more knowledge than they in fact have, to alter the meaning of terms to suit the given polemical context, and to use obscure terminology (*E*, III.x.6–8, pp. 493–5).

The practice of disputation is thus linked by Locke to what is his principal criticism of the style of scholastic philosophy, its lack of intelligibility. Intelligibility was a central concern to Locke, and he charged the schoolmen with weaving 'a curious and unexplicable Web of perplexed Words' and of spinning a 'learned Gibberish' (*E*, III.x.8–9, pp. 494–5). We may suppose that he had scholastic language principally in mind when he famously described himself as an 'Under-Labourer' to the great scientists of his time, 'removing some of the

Rubbish, that lies in the way of Knowledge', including 'the learned but frivolous use of uncouth, affected, or unintelligible Terms' (*E*, 'The Epistle to the Reader', p. 10).

DESCARTES had, of course, held similar reservations about the usefulness and intelligibility of much of scholastic terminology. His strategy tended to be the diplomatic one of remaining silent about the scholastic concepts he rejected, concentrating instead on the development of his new system that did without them. Locke, on the other hand, provided a direct critique of scholastic language. The third book of the *Essay*, devoted to the question of the 'signification of words', culminates in an examination of the abuse of words by the scholastics, as well as others (*E*, III.x, pp. 490–508). In linking the question of a philosophical account of meaning with a critique of scholastic jargon, Locke was (whether consciously or not) continuing the approach of HOBBES's seminal work on language in *Leviathan* ('Of Speech', pt I, chap. 4).

In relation to doctrine, Locke took particular exception to the kinds of explanation offered by the scholastics. Drawing on his experience in medicine, he satirizes the appeal to FACULTIES such as a 'digestive faculty', an 'expulsive faculty' and a 'motive faculty' to explain digestion, excretion and movement. There was a danger, he thought, that the same kind of pseudo-explanation was at work in appeals to the intellect and the will to explain mental behaviour. In particular, to say the will 'wills' or 'commands' is as empty as saying the digestive faculty (or the ability to digest) digests (*E*, II.xxi.20, pp. 243–4).

Locke opposed the use of general maxims that in scholasticism were often treated as the foundation of a deductive, syllogistic science or *scientia*. The special status given to such maxims as 'the whole is equal to all its parts' obscures the role of the particular empirical truths that precede our knowledge of these generalizations. The use of maxims also leads to a kind of armchair science which eschews experimentation and practical investigation, something Locke argues as early as 'De Arte Medica' of 1669, where he unfavourably compares scholastic knowledge of nature with that of gardeners, tanners, ploughmen and bakers (f. 54r).

Locke's opposition to scholastic doctrine also involved a rejection of the Aristotelian doctrine of four causes. Locke was only interested in efficient causation: formal, material and final causes are dismissed early in Draft A of the *Essay* because 'I doe not at present soe well understand their efficacy or causality' (Draft A, sect. 15, p. 31). In the *Essay* itself he has also clearly done away with scholastic animal and vegetative souls and, in so far as Locke tends towards granting a soul to humans, he seems to have in mind a Cartesian SUBSTANCE, not the substantial form of the scholastics.

Despite Locke's negative appraisal of scholastic doctrine, there remain notable continuities between his philosophy in the *Essay* and that of the schools. Most importantly his empiricism is in agreement with the official Thomist tenet that the mind, at its beginning, is a blank slate. Locke actually uses the scholastic term *tabula rasa* in this connection in the first drafts (Draft A, sect. 2, p. 8; Draft B, sect. 17, p. 128), although in the *Essay* he prefers 'white Paper, void of all Characters' (*E*, II.i.2, p. 104). Locke also clearly went along with the related Thomist principle that 'nothing is in the intellect that has not been already in sense' (*nihil est in intellectu quod non prius fuerit in sensu*). Locke explained the acquisition of geometrical, mathematical and other concepts by the faculty of ABSTRACTION – an approach generally favoured by the scholastics. In addition, scholastic ontological concepts, such as substance, essence and quality, remained central to Locke's thought. Indeed, his adoption and reinterpretation of these terms gave rise to some of the most original and influential chapters of the *Essay*.

BIBLIOGRAPHY
Primary Sources
Hobbes, Thomas, *Leviathan* (1651).
Locke, John, 'De Arte Medica', National Archives, London (MSS PRO 30/24/47/2), ff. 47–56.

Secondary Literature
Jolley, Nicholas, *Locke: His Philosophical Thought* (Oxford, 1999).
Milton, J.R., 'The Scholastic Background to Locke's Thought', *Locke Newsletter*, vol. xv (1984), pp. 25–34.
Woolhouse, R.S., *Locke* (Minnesota, 1984).

James Hill

SOCINIANISM

Locke was often accused of inclining towards Socinianism, not least by John EDWARDS, who declared in 1695 that Locke's thought was 'all over Socinianiz'd', and by John MILNER, who paralleled Locke's arguments with Socinian arguments in his 1700 *An Account of Mr Lock's Religion*. In the 1690s Bishop STILLINGFLEET pressed Locke to deny that he held Socinian sympathies and suggested that Locke's 'new way of ideas' in the *Essay concerning Human Understanding* compromised Trinitarianism. In 1709 LEIBNIZ suggested that, by countenancing the possibility of matter thinking in the *Essay*, Locke had countenanced the mortality of the soul, in common with Socinians (Jolley, 1984; Marshall, 2000).

In the seventeenth century, the accusation of 'Socinianism' was levelled frequently against what seemed to accusers to be an undue emphasis on reason in matters of faith or an undue limitation of Christian faith to a few non-Trinitarian doctrines, and often attacked many whose beliefs could be called Unitarian rather than specifically Socinian, as they held an essentially Arian Christology in believing that Christ was pre-existent but not eternal; for Socinians, Christ was a divinely inspired prophet who had been given rulership over the world at his resurrection. Both Arians and Socinians disbelieved in the Trinitarian orthodoxy of three co-eternal, co-equal, consub-stantial persons in the Godhead. For Socinians, Christ had not paid an equivalent for all humanity's sins – the interpretation of the atonement stressed by sixteenth and seventeenth-century Calvinists. Socinianism was a non-dogmatic religious movement that issued no official creedal statement, emphasizing instead the individual search of Scripture, and was frequently amalgamated with other strands of thought by the later seventeenth century, including combinations of Socinianism, Arianism and Arminianism. Unitarians in the later seventeenth century sometimes combined an Arminian understanding of the atonement as involving a voluntary payment for sin, but not the payment of an equivalent for sin, with an Arian or Socinian understanding of Christ's nature, and refused the label 'Socinian', designating themselves followers of non-Trinitarian primitive Christianity and of the words of Scripture itself (McLachlan, 1951; Mulsow, 2005; Snobelen, 2001; Wilbur 1946–52).

The accusation of Socinianism against Locke involved several major areas of his thought and their cumulative combination in his works as they together designated his considerable distance from contemporary Protestant orthodoxy. First was Locke's thought about the Trinity and the related doctrines of Christ's priesthood and the satisfaction for sin. Edwards identified Locke as giving 'proof of his being Socinianiz'd by his utter silence about Christ's satisfying for us, and purchasing salvation by virtue of his death'. Next were Locke's position on original sin and his arguments about the set of doctrines associated with the afterlife: the doctrine of the immortality of the soul, the eternity of punishment in hell, and the resurrection of the body. Finally, and more broadly, Locke was labelled Socinian for his emphasis upon reason in the examination of Christian doctrine and rejection of innate ideas; and for his arguments for religious TOLERATION and for creedal minimalism (Snobelen, 2001; Wootton, 1989).

In his *Reasonableness of Christianity*, its defences and his later *Paraphrase on the*

Epistles of St Paul, Locke did not support the Trinity of co-eternal, co-equal and consubstantial persons in the Godhead. Like many Socinians, Locke explicated 'Son Of God' as meaning 'the Messiah' and paralleled Christ's sonship with that of Adam. When pressed to testify to Trinitarian belief, Locke refused, declaring in his *Reply to the Bishop of Worcester's Answer* and *Reply to the Bishop of Worcester's Answer to His Second Letter* that he had never read in his Bible 'in these precise words' that 'there are three persons in one nature, or, there are two natures and one person'. Like Socinians, in the *Reasonableness*, Locke did not support Christ's priestly role and departed significantly from most contemporary accounts of the satisfaction for sin. In his *Paraphrase on the Epistles of St Paul* he emphasized God's forgiveness of sin as being of his 'free bounty'. Like Socinians, Locke simultaneously denied the then orthodox doctrine of original sin, writing in the *Reasonableness* that 'none are truly punished but for their own deeds' and denying a 'corruption' in the 'nature' of Adam's posterity. Like Socinians, Locke privately supported the annihilation of the wicked after their punishment, denying the eternity of punishment in Hell, and in revisions to the *Essay* he argued for the resurrection of the dead but not of their bodies. Like Socinians, Locke supported toleration and emphasized creedal minimalism and individual interpretation of Scripture. Locke held that belief in Jesus as the Messiah was sufficient to make one a Christian, and that beyond that belief individuals were to search Scripture for themselves for its meaning. Like many Socinians, Locke stressed reason and denied innatism (Marshall, 1994 and 2000; Snobelen, 2001).

Locke was probably significantly influenced by Socinian works. He owned eighty-three anti-Trinitarian works, including many by Faustus Socinus and his most important followers, Johann Crell and Johann Volkel, and many Arian works. His manuscripts and interleaved Bibles show that he had taken notes from Socinian works, despite professing publicly never to have read a page of various Socinian works. In addition, he engaged in private biblical criticism with anti-Trinitarian Arians such as Isaac NEWTON, and tried to secure publication for Newton's manuscript attack on Trinitarian corruptions of Scripture. Locke provided patronage for other anti-Trinitarians, some of whom consulted him about the interpretation of Scripture. His manuscript collection includes a lengthy, unpublished Socinian argument by Jacques Souverain. On the Trinity, by the end of his life Locke seems to have believed, like most Arians, in a pre-existent Christ, but emphasized, like Socinians, Christ's prophetic role and post-resurrectional rulership. Locke certainly never became a sectarian Socinian: he was an eclectic deeply hostile to any systematic theology (Mulsow, 2005; Marshall, 1994, 2000 and 2006; Snobelen, 2001).

BIBLIOGRAPHY
Secondary Literature
Jolley, Nicholas, *Leibniz and Locke: A Study of the New Essays on Human Understanding* (Oxford, 1984).
Marshall, John, *John Locke: Resistance, Religion and Responsibility* (Cambridge, 1994).
——, 'Locke, Socinianism, "Socinianism" and Unitarianism', in M.A. Stewart (ed.), *English Philosophy in the Age of Locke* (Oxford, 2000), pp. 111–82.
——, *John Locke, Toleration and Early Enlightenment Culture: Religious Intolerance and Arguments for Religious Toleration in Early Modern and 'Early Enlightenment' Europe* (Cambridge, 2006).
McLachlan, H.J., *Socinianism in Seventeenth-Century England* (London, 1951).
Mulsow, Martin, 'The "New Socinians"', in Martin Mulsow and Jan Rohls (eds), *Socinianism and Arminianism: Antitrinitarians, Calvinists and Cultural Exchange in Seventeenth-Century Europe* (Leiden, 2005), pp. 49–78.

Snobelen, Stephen D., 'Socinianism, Heresy and John Locke's *Reasonableness of Christianity*', *Enlightenment and Dissent*, vol. xx (2001), pp. 88–125.

Wilbur, Earl Morse, *A History of Unitarianism*, 2 vols (Cambridge, Massachusetts, 1946–52).

Wootton, David, 'John Locke: Socinian or Natural Law Theorist?', in James E. Crimmins (ed.), *Religion, Secularization and Political Thought: Thomas Hobbes to J.S. Mill* (London, 1989), pp. 39–67.

John Marshall

SPACE AND TIME

The thorniest questions about space concern its ontological status – is it a something or a nothing, corporeal or incorporeal, SUBSTANCE or accident? (Sorabji, 1988, pp. 124–215; Grant, 1981). Locke refused to be drawn into such debates (*E*, II.xiii.17–20, pp. 174–5). But whatever its nature, Locke believed that we possess a real idea of space that allows us to identify a number of its properties. And this idea is broadly Epicurean, and anti-Aristotelian and anti-Cartesian (Lennon, 1983; idem, 1993, pp. 276–88).

Locke distinguishes *Extension*, the 'continuity of solid, separable, and moveable parts' (*E*, II.iv.5, p. 126), from *Expansion*, the 'continuity of unsolid, inseparable, and immoveable' parts (ibid.) or the quantity of 'Space in general, with or without solid Matter possessing it' (*E*, II.xiii.26, p. 180; II.xv.1, p. 196). Both are acquired by sight and touch (*E*, II.v p. 127; II.xiii.2, p. 167). Regardless of which we are addressing, two questions arise: (1) in what way is the simple idea of space simple? and (2) what kind of simple idea is it?

Locke's admission that the simple idea of space consists of parts makes the former more pressing (*E*, II.xv.9, pp. 201–3). Two possibilities appear, *minima sensibilia* and simplicity as the terminus of conceptual analysis. *Minima sensibilia* appear to be embraced: 'I may be allowed to call [this least portion of space] a *sensible* Point, meaning thereby the least Particle of Matter or Space we can discern' (*E*, II.xv.9, pp. 202–3). But this position threatens Locke's more considered views regarding simplicity. M. Barbeyrac brought this home to Locke. Locke responded in a footnote appended to the fifth edition, by maintaining that simplicity excludes the composition of different species of ideas rather than numerically distinct ideas of the same species (*Essay*, footnote to II.xv.9, pp. 201–2). Yet this undermines the distinction between simple ideas and the complex ideas of simple MODES. Thus one might think that Locke should have adopted analytic simplicity as his model. The drawback with analytic simplicity, however, is the implication of a merely relative simplicity – because *partes extra partes* entails infinite divisibility, no idea designated *the* simple idea of space could ever be absolutely simple.

The second question, 'what kind of simple idea is the simple idea of space', is rarely asked but deserves consideration. The simple idea of space clearly cannot be qualitative. The obvious place for it is as a simple *modal* idea. If the 'simple' idea of space turns out to be really a complex idea of a simple mode, this would be straightforward. But if Locke took the idea's simplicity serious, how can it be classified as modal? As of yet, there is no answer to this puzzle.

Locke does not talk explicitly about the interstitial void, but he accepts the possibilities of intracosmic and extracosmic voids. He provides traditional arguments for both. In *Essay* II.xiii.21[bis], we find the annihilation argument – God can annihilate matter while preventing anything else from moving into the annihilated matter's place. Locke also provides a naturalized relative of the annihilation argument: since the motion of any bit of matter is independent of the motion of any other, we can conceive of one bit moving without conceiving of another moving into the former's place (*E*, II.iv.3, p. 124). But the argument that Locke privileges is the Epicurean argument that motion entails a void – motion exists; for movement to begin, there must be some empty space for the moving object to occupy first; therefore, a void must exist (*E*, II.xiii.22, pp. 177–8).

Locke's argument for the possibility of the extracosmic void goes back to Archytas (Archytas, 1987, frag. 7, p. 182; Lucretius, 2001, 1:969–84, p. 29): Body, or the realm of body, cannot be infinite; Thus there must be an edge to the realm of body; supposing that you were placed at this edge of the realm of body, could you extend your hand beyond this edge? If no, what prevents it? If yes, then there is void space beyond the edge of the cosmos (*E*, II.xiii.21, pp. 175–6).

Archytas' argument leads to another for the infinity of space. Because this thought-experiment may be endlessly repeated, the infinity of space is implied as strongly as the extracosmic void is. According to Locke, we can possess this sort of notion of the infinity of space, although we can never possess the idea of an infinite space (*E*, II.xvii.7–8, pp. 213–15). In essence, then, for Locke empty space is simply the prerequisite for the possibilities of motion and place in usual Epicurean fashion (*E*, II.xiii.26, p. 179).

According to Locke, the ideas of space and time have different geneses. Space is a sensitive idea, whereas time is a reflective idea acquired by the mind's taking notice of the change of its ideas, which suggests the idea of succession, the simplest temporal idea. The complex temporal idea of duration follows in that it consists of the idea of the length of a series of successions. But other than that, they are very similar ideas (*E*, II.xv, pp. 196–204). The ontological issues surrounding them are more or less the same as are the properties we can attribute to them. Their only difference is that time is '*as it were the length of one straight Line*'. What Locke means is that we can move around in the infinity of space, but not in the

infinity of time – when it exists, a time 'equally comprehends' all parts of Being and has none of its parts existing together, but space, where it exists, 'comprehends' only a part of Being and has all its parts necessarily existing together, inseparably (*E*, II.xv.11–12, pp. 203–4).

BIBLIOGRAPHY
Primary Sources
Archytas of Tarentum, *The Fragments of Archytas*, in Kenneth Sylvan Guthrie and David Fideler (eds), *The Pythagorean Sourcebook and Library* (Grand Rapids, Michigan, 1987), pp. 177–201.
Lucretius, *On the Nature of Things*, trans. Martin Ferguson Smith (Indianapolis, 2001).

Secondary Literature
Grant, Edward, *Much Ado about Nothing* (Cambridge, 1981).
Lennon, Thomas, *The Battle of the Gods and Giants* (Princeton, New Jersey, 1993).
——— , 'Sources et signification de la théorie lockienne de l'espace', *Dialogue*, vol. xxii (1983), pp. 3–14.
Sorabji, Richard, *Matter, Space, and Motion* (London, 1988).

Benjamin Hill

STATE OF NATURE, THE

The notion of the state of nature plays a key role in the political theory Locke puts forward in the *Two Treatises*. It encapsulates his main arguments against Robert FILMER's political theory and also offers a normative foundation for his theories of political authority and resistance. The notion itself was not Locke's own invention. It had been used most notably by Thomas HOBBES, in whose theory it typically referred to a hypothetical social condition in which human beings live without effective government and other forms of organized social life. Locke, however, spoke about the state of nature in two different yet interrelated ways. Firstly, according to Locke's deployment of the term, it denotes a moral condition God has imposed on adult human beings through the features he has given them. Secondly, it refers to a historical social condition in which political government does not exist. A number of scholars have argued that Locke's remarks concerning the state of nature as a social condition should not be taken at face value or should at least be seen as irrelevant for his political theory (Dunn, 1969; Ashcraft, 1968; Simmons, 1989). Others, however, are of the opinion that these remarks should be taken seriously, especially since they enable Locke to present European civil societies as the *telos* of human development, which some other civilizations have not reached (Hindess, 2007).

The state of nature in the first mentioned sense is described by Locke as a condition of 'perfect Freedom', in which human beings are entitled 'to order their actions and dispose of their possessions and persons, as they think fit, within the bounds of the Law of Nature, without depending upon the will of any other man'. It is also a 'State of Equality' in the sense that no one has a right to impose legislation on others and everyone is entitled to punish those who violate NATURAL LAW (*TTG* II.4 and II.7–9). Locke's argument for such independence and equality relies on the observation that human beings are 'Creatures of the same species and rank promiscuously born to the same advantages of Nature, and the use of the same FACULTIES'. He concludes that unless God has by some 'manifest Declaration of his Will' established power relations among human beings, they should be regarded as 'equal one amongst another without Subordination or Subjection' (*TTG* II.4). In the 'First Treatise', Locke argues, *pace* Filmer, that no such announcement can be found in the Bible. Thus human beings must be seen as free and equal by nature (see Waldron, 2002, pp. 44–82).

In his theory, Hobbes had infamously argued that the commands of the law of nature are silent in the state of nature, and people are entitled to do whatever they see as necessary for their own survival. By contrast, Locke maintained that the state of nature has 'the Law of Nature to govern it, which obliges every one' (*TTG* II.6). The fundamental law of nature is to preserve humankind, which includes both a duty to preserve one's own life and a duty to preserve others when one's own preservation is not in danger. These duties give rise to the natural right to protect one's 'Life, Liberty and Estates' and the right to punish those who violate natural law (*TTG* II.7–9 and II.87).

Locke also rejected Hobbes's claim that the state of nature is a state of war, making a conceptual distinction between these two conditions. In the state of nature human beings are obliged to obey the law of nature, which directs them towards 'Peace, Good Will, Mutual Assistance and Preservation'. However, while the state of nature is never a Hobbesian war of every man against every other, it is still a condition 'full of fears and continual dangers' because there is no authoritative judge to settle disputes between an aggressor and his victims (*TTG* II.123–4). If someone threatens other people's lives or attempts to subject them under his absolute power (which is the same thing), he steps outside human moral community and introduces a state of war. As a result, other people are entitled to treat the aggressor 'as beast of Prey' and to kill him for the same reasons one kills wolves and lions (*TTG* II.16–19).

The state of nature is a moral condition in which 'all Men are naturally in' and 'remain so, till by their own Consent they make themselves Members of some Politick Society' (*TTG* II.15). This does not mean that human beings would be born in the state of nature, as children are by nature obliged to obey their parents (*TTG* II.55). However, *pace* Filmer, paternal power is not absolute and it terminates when children reach maturity. As adults, they may adopt new duties towards others through contracts, and consent to political authority, but they will always remain in the state of nature with regard to those who are not members of their own political society (see CONSENT AND SOCIAL CONTRACT).

In addition to presenting his account of the God-imposed moral condition, Locke also addressed Filmer's historical claim that in reality political societies have never been established by free and equal people. He admitted that since literacy has hardly ever preceded civil society, history 'gives us but a very little account of Men, that lived together in the State of Nature'. It is, however, an 'evident matter of fact' that Rome and Venice were founded by 'several Men free and independent one of another'. Moreover, before the arrival of Europeans, many people in America lived in groups with no proper political authority. This Locke saw as 'a Pattern of the first Ages in Asia and Europe', concluding that 'in the beginning all the World was *America*' (*TTG* II.49, II.101–2, and II.108).

BIBLIOGRAPHY
Secondary Literature
Ashcraft, Richard, 'Locke's State of Nature: Historical Fact of Moral Fiction', *American Political Science Review*, vol. lxii (1968), pp. 898–915.
Dunn, John, *The Political Thought of John Locke: An Historical Account of the Argument of the* Two Treatises of Government (Cambridge, 1969).
Hindess, Barry, 'Locke's State of Nature', *History of the Human Sciences*, vol. xx (2007), pp. 1–20.
Simmons, A. John, 'Locke's State of Nature', *Political Theory*, vol. xvii (1989), pp. 449–70.
Waldron, Jeremy, *God, Locke and Equality: Christian Foundations in Locke's Political Thought* (Cambridge, 2002).

Kari Saastamoinen

SUBSTANCE

Locke's argument about the role of the idea of substance in our thought is often misunderstood, partly because it is continuously and allusively polemical, partly because its centrality to his philosophy often goes unrecognized. The argument was directed, in general, against any pretension to have achieved, or to possess the method to achieve, certain theoretical knowledge of nature. It responded, in particular, to Aristotelian SCHOLASTICISM and Cartesian philosophy, both of which built on Platonic themes. But Locke also turned a critical eye on the kind of 'corpuscularian' mechanism that he himself had come to favour as at any rate the best available model for the physical world.

For Aristotelians, the category of substance is primary in two related ways. First, substances (*things*) are the ultimate subjects of predication. Entities falling into other categories comprise ways substances are, their extent, ways they act or are acted upon, and other relations to other things. Substances are in this way logically and ontologically independent as qualities, quantities, actions and relations are not. Substances are what are most real – 'real', by origin, simply meant 'thingish'. Universal predicates in this first category, primitive 'substantives' such as 'dog', have as their subjects the individual substances themselves, the primary existents. Such specific predicates simply name their subject – they say 'what it is'. They do so in a very strong sense, since the individual dog precisely is the (or, in another view, *an*) embodied 'specific form' of *dog*.

Accordingly, substances constitute the ultimate subject matter of natural science. They are the things and stuffs that must be identified and classified, and whose specific natures must be known, if the ultimate demonstrative natural science is to be achieved. Such a science would be founded on 'real' (as opposed to merely 'nominal') definitions of substances by genus and difference – definitions that are 'simple' in that they would unpack the unitary ESSENCES from which the peculiar 'properties' of (i.e.

attributes proper to) each species of thing, with its genera, could be deduced and explained teleologically, by reference to the function or perfection of that kind of thing.

Aristotle proposed a four-stage process by which essential definitions may be achieved. First comes sense PERCEPTION and secondly 'experience', when recurrent associations are noted. Then a universal conception is formed – that is, perceived individuals are assigned to a kind. Then, after close observation, the peculiar functional 'difference' is identified from which flow other properties of the kind (whether species or genus) (cf., for example, *Posterior Analytics* B19, Aristotle, 1985, pp. 165–6). A worked-out natural science would present the species of substances as linked hierarchically by division of ever-wider genera, ultimately of the category of substance itself – the so-called Tree of Porphyry. To adopt this conception of natural science is to accept that biological individuals and species are scientifically basic, as they are logically basic in natural language. But it also implies that the many attributes of, and changes in, particular things that are not deducible from essence, so-called 'accidents', are not susceptible to scientific explanation, at least at this level. Indeed Aristotle affirms that there is no science of accidents. Scholastic accounts that, explicitly or implicitly, accord 'reality' to accidents – to sensible qualities and powers in particular – as things mysteriously inherent in substances, became a favourite target of opponents of Aristotelianism (cf., e.g., *E*, II.xiii.19, p. 175).

Seventeenth-century corpuscularians, rejecting the assumption that biology and chemistry (or alchemy) are basic sciences, followed the ancient atomists in postulating one universal physical substance, matter or 'body'. Aristotelian 'matter' is in itself featureless, the mere bearer of form and an ABSTRACTION from the embodied substantial form that is the concrete individual. Corpuscularians, in contrast, held matter to have a geometrical or mechanical essence and properties in its own right, and biological and chemical kinds to be differentiated only by mechanical structure and motion of parts. Substantial forms and teleology made way for more 'intelligible' mechanical explanation.

DESCARTES proposed that the chief attribute of matter, the foundation of its properties, is extension itself, from which mobility and impenetrability follow. Conflating the extension of space with the extension of matter, he denied the possibility of a vacuum. The laws of motion are the rules by which an immutable God orders created matter. But others, most notably Gassendi, favoured the ancient doctrine that placed material atoms in empty space. HOBBES, too, while believing that there is in fact no vacuum in nature, criticized Descartes's denial of any real distinction between space and matter, and purported to deduce the laws of mechanics from the nature of matter alone, without recourse to the arbitrary will of a creator. In name or in effect the 'new philosophers' admitted a class of 'accidents', namely the 'MODES' or 'modifications' of matter such as roundness or determinate motion. But these are simply the quantitative determinations of determinable properties of matter, as such by no means excluded from mechanics. Other qualities and powers ordinarily ascribed to things were explained in terms of the effects of the things' material structure on other things and on perceiving minds. This neat way of presenting the substance-accident relation as intelligible in the case of material substance was an undoubted attraction of the corpuscularian model, although the same plausible tidiness did not extend to mind or spirit.

Some corpuscularians argued that mechanical processes, like the necessary truths of geometry, appear intelligible to us because of the availability of an innate idea of matter that the intellect brings to the interpretation of sensory input. In *Meditations*, Descartes suggested that we can make this innate idea explicit by considering what is left in our conception of, for example, a piece of wax in abstraction from all the accidental changes that it can be perceived to undergo (*The Philosophical Writings of Descartes*, vol. ii, pp. 20–2). In his Objections to the *Meditations*, a copy of which Locke owned, Gassendi argued that, whereas everyone agrees that the concept of the substance of the wax can be abstracted from the concepts of its accidents, that does not mean that 'the substance or nature of the wax is itself distinctly conceived' (*The Philosophical Writings of Descartes*, vol. ii, p. 189). We conceive of 'something which is the subject of the accidents and changes we observe; but what this subject is, or what its nature is, we do not know.' (For more on theories of substance before Locke's *Essay* see Ayers, 1991, vol. ii, pt 1, pp. 18–30, 32–6 and *passim*.)

In his earliest extant discussions of substance, in the 1671 manuscripts known as Drafts A and B of the *Essay*, Locke laid out a response to dogmatic theories much like Gassendi's. It was refined and developed in the published work, partly, at least, as a result of his further reading, but it remained fundamentally unchanged. Draft A begins significantly. A very brief version of Locke's trademark claim that all our simple ideas are acquired by sense and reflection flows smoothly into an account of how we come to form 'our Ideas of Substantiall or materiall objects' (Draft A, sect. 1, p. 2, cf. Draft B, sects 60–1, 63). Ideas of sensible qualities, 'the first objects of our understandings' (or the sensible qualities themselves, confusingly here, as often in the *Essay* itself, also called 'simple ideas' – cf. Draft B, sect. 61, p. 164) are found by experience of 'certain objects' to 'goe constantly togeather'. It soon appears that 'simple ideas', and even 'qualities', include powers (cf. Draft A, sect. 14, p. 29). We take such a recurring cluster of qualities and powers to 'belong to one thing' and call them 'soe united in one subject' by one name. By 'one thing' Locke evidently had in mind one kind of thing, his exemplary 'NAMES' being 'man', 'horse', 'sun', 'water' and 'iron'. Finally, 'by inadvertency', we mistake our idea of the one thing to be 'one simple idea', when it is in fact a complex of the simple ideas of the qualities by which we identify the kind of thing in question. Knowledge of what it is that binds

the defining qualities together in all observed instances, the 'fit and common subject' responsible for their regular concurrence, is beyond us. We suppose that there is such a 'subject' or 'substance' because it is not intelligible that the qualities and powers should 'subsist alone', i.e. have no unifying foundation in nature (Draft A, sect. 1, p. 1). This account follows the Aristotelian account closely, except that, all-importantly, the fourth and final stage of arriving at a grasp of the unitary nature of the substance is replaced by a mere illusion of possessing such a simple conception.

It is next argued that our definitions depend on our experience to date. Hence different people employ different definitions and ideas under the same name, leading to confusion and merely verbal disputes. Further experience and observation can lead to improvements in our classificatory ideas, but only by increasing our grasp of which sensible qualities and powers may be expected to go together. The distinction of species and genus exists only because one complex idea may comprise just some of the simple ideas included in another, widening its 'comprehension' (Draft A, sects 1–2; Draft B, sects 67–78, 90–3j). Locke concludes that universal propositions about substances, if certain, are merely verbal – true by definition. If they are 'instructive', then they are uncertain, at best probable (Draft A, sects 13, 27, 29, 31). The same applies to the underlying 'substance or mater' (as Locke once calls it, in Draft A, sect. 1, p. 2) taken in general. If we accept Descartes's definition of matter as extension, his proof of the impossibility of a vacuum is valid; but the conclusion, although certain, is merely verbal, a consequence of an arbitrary decision to use 'those 3 names Extension Body Space ... for one & the same Idea' (Draft A, sect. 27, p. 45). No other definition we can come up with, as by adding 'resistability' to extension, advances our knowledge of what matter ultimately is. Nevertheless, we distinguish body from spirit, since we do not understand 'how body can produce' the 'operations of our own minds' available to reflection.

Another argument, however, suggests that the generality of the 'name *Substance*' arises from its being 'applicable to anything wherein we find any of our simple Ideas', rather than the postulation of a general stuff, matter. Our supposition that observable qualities need the support of an enduring cause of their union creates the illusion that we have an idea of the substance distinct from our ideas of the qualities, 'though in reality we have no such Idea' beyond that relative one (Draft B, sect. 92, p. 199). Locke further urges, in effect, that nothing is gained by insisting on the ontological status of a substance as a fundamental entity. The general idea of existence or being, abstracted from the determinate ideas of sense and reflection that can give it content, adds nothing to the thought that 'something' has certain sensible qualities and effects on other things. Nothing of all that philosophers say about 'entyty or Being' is any help 'to the least discovery nor ... any notion of the Substance or Substratum of either extended or thinking beings' (Draft A, sect. 8, p. 20; cf. Draft B, sect. 93, p. 200).

The 1671 Drafts set out the main shape and themes (and often the very words) of Locke's treatment of substance in the *Essay* in a form that clarifies its absolute centrality to his philosophical position. The topics of the idea of substance, our ideas of the species and genera of substances (and their names), and the limitations on our knowledge of substances by comparison with knowledge about modes, topics dealt with more or less continuously in Draft A, are to an extent driven apart by the order of exposition of the *Essay*. Moreover the traditional emphasis on Books I and II of the *Essay* has tended to represent the first extended discussion of the idea of substance, in II.xxiii, as a lame effort to deal with a late-considered counter-example to the thesis that all our ideas come from experience. It is, on the contrary, a crucial, basic step on the way to Locke's fully explained argument that, whereas non-vacuous universal knowledge of mathematical and moral truths is open to us, as not going beyond

clear ideas we have, the limitations of our faculties cuts us off from 'instructive' universal knowledge of nature. Our ideas of the kinds of substances always fall short of being ideas of their essences, and the hierarchy of species and genus is not natural, but constructed by the mind 'for the conveniency of marshalling its owne Ideas, recording its owne thoughts and signifying them to others' (Draft B, sect. 91, p. 198). If we think of the 'fit and common subject' of qualities simply as matter, even the most stripped-down idea of matter, in this like our idea of spirit, is restricted to what is experienced – extension and the cohesion of parts. To try to 'peirce farther into the nature of things' is to fall into 'darkenesse and obscurity' (Draft B, sect. 94, p. 212).

Essay II.xxiii, 'Of our Complex Ideas of Substances', starts by repeating the deflationary commentary on the Aristotelian route to essential definitions and simple conceptions of substances. Next, Locke turns to the content of the ordinary person's '*Notion of pure Substance in general*', which is simply the idea of 'he knows not what support of [observable] Qualities' (*E*, II.xxiii.2, p. 295). These qualities may be said to inhere in 'the solid extended parts' (a corpuscularian answer), but then the question arises as to what 'that Solidity and Extension inhere in'. The only answer available is that it is 'something' which we 'have no distinct idea of at all, and so are perfectly in the dark' (*E*, II.xxiii.2, pp. 295–6).

Several things have conspired to mislead readers of this passage. One is that corpuscularian theory plays a much greater role in the *Essay* than in the Drafts. There are passages, such as II.viii, on PRIMARY AND SECONDARY QUALITIES, or passages in III.vi that contemplate what it would be to know the 'real essence' of a species, in which Locke can seem to have come to believe that the essence of matter consists in the PRIMARY QUALITIES, in particular extension and solidity, and that specific 'real essences' consist simply in the determinate ways this matter is modified. Given such a view of essence, what could it mean to say that, if the question is raised of what the solidity and extension of material particles inhere in, the only possible answer is that it is something, we know not what? Does this not imply that something further underlies even essence, as essence underlies observable qualities? It may seem that the unknown subject or substance must be some more mysterious metaphysical entity than essence, a 'bare subject', Locke's (perhaps half-hearted) belief in which has been somehow generated by the logical structure of language.

Locke's rhetoric has served to reinforce this interpretation. The famous comparison in this section with the 'Indian philosopher' who supposed the world to rest on an elephant that rests on a tortoise that rests on 'something, he knew not what', or with children who, when asked 'what such a thing is', reply 'something', may suggest that Locke is making fun of the notion of substance itself, almost to the extent of treating it as a functionless excrescence in our thought, a merely logical entity – or non-entity (cf. the polemic at *E*, II.xiii.17–20, pp. 306–7). STILLINGFLEET accused Locke of almost excluding substance from the world (*W*, vol. iv, p. 16f), and BERKELEY took a similar line in item 89 of his *Philosophical Commentaries* (Berkeley, 1944, p. 23). Locke's attitude towards corpuscularian theory, however, is more nuanced than wholesale acceptance. Briefly, it was for him the best available inadequate theory, and was employed in argument as such. Sometimes its virtues, sometimes its shortcomings are emphasized. The legendary Indian is here specifically compared to a corpuscularian who first offers a positive account of matter before having to admit that he is ignorant of the ultimate nature of solid extended substance – a message driven home at length later in the chapter. Moreover, the imagined child is presented with an unquestionably substantial object. His reply 'Something' is in response to the Aristotelian question, 'What is it?' The child is guilty of a pretence to knowledge of the kind and nature of the thing, which is the accusation Locke is bringing against both Aristotelian and corpuscularian accounts of substance.

Nevertheless, there is something both odd and interesting in the way Locke attempts to bring logical or linguistic points to bear in his attack on claims to know essence. In *Essay*, II.xxiii.3, he moves on from the 'obscure and relative *Idea* of Substance in general' to '*Ideas of particular Sorts of Substances*'. These comprise simple ideas of qualities observed to exist together, and (since these are taken to flow from 'the particular internal Constitution, or unknown Essence of that substance') 'have always the confused *Idea* of *something* to which [the qualities] belong, and in which they subsist'. To mark this mystery ingredient, we always define the substance as 'a *thing* having such or such Qualities', and distinguish the substance from the accidents that exist 'in' it: 'as Body is a *thing* that is extended, figured and capable of motion, ... and ... Hardness, Friability, and Power to draw Iron, we say, are Qualities to be found in a Loadstone.' Such 'fashions of speaking intimate that the Substance is supposed always *something* besides' the observable qualities, 'though we know not what it is' (*E*, II.xxiii.3, pp. 296–7). It is easy to see how this passage has fed the mistaken idea that 'substance' is for Locke a bare subject, and LEIBNIZ, discussing *Essay*, II.xxiii.2, in effect accused him of being committed to that conclusion: 'if you distinguish [attributes or predicates from their common subject] it is no wonder that you cannot conceive anything special in the subject' (Leibniz, 1996, p. 218). It may seem undeniable that, even if we knew the essence of matter, its definition would still take the grammatical form 'Matter is a substance that is such and such'. Locke, however, thought otherwise, and (like Leibniz, on the other side) was contributing to an ongoing debate precisely related to such 'fashions of speaking', and to the significance of the distinction between primitive noun-predicates – names of 'things' such as 'dog' or 'matter' – and adjectival predicates and their nominalizations.

For Descartes matter *is* extension, in accordance with the Aristotelian principle that substance and essence are one and the same. The merely conceptual distinction between them is the result of abstracting a formal concept of substance, also applicable to spirit, from concrete content (cf. *The Principles of Philosophy* I.63; *The Philosophical Writings of Descartes*, vol. i, p. 213). Following Descartes, MALEBRANCHE in *The Search for Truth*, asserts that extension is a substance, as if the noun 'matter' was, if not inappropriate, at any rate redundant. To suppose that something underlies extension is to base ontology on 'a general idea from LOGIC'. If logic leads us to postulate a subject underlying extension with another nature or 'principle', 'a new *subject* and a new *principle* of this subject of extension could be imagined, and so on to infinity' (Malebranche, 1980, pp. 243–4).

The Port Royal *Logic*, also broadly Cartesian, takes a partly different view. It accepts the logical propriety of primitive noun-predicates such as 'spirit' or 'matter' to name or 'directly signify' substances, while nominalized predicates (such as 'roundness') directly signify modes. But most noun-predicates (e.g. 'dog' or 'gold') are logically composite, naming 'modified things', since we commonly name things according to their sensible modes. Hence the defining 'essence' of (say) gold can be legitimately abstracted from the substance, its (Cartesian) matter. Philosophers are liable to carry on the process, illegitimately thinking of man as having *humanitas*, body as having *corporeitas*. Significantly, *ratio* is added to the list of misconceived terms, and *extensio* might well have joined it. Where Malebranche rates the nominalized predicate above the primitive noun-predicate, the *Logic* argues the reverse, but for both the logico-ontological sin is to treat a substance's true essence as if it were distinct from the substance.

Locke believed that, in the case of substances, we never commit this sin, since we have no knowledge of essences, and only ever know things through their accidents. Locke studied both the *Logic* and *Search* carefully in the decade following 1671. He evidently chose to up-end their arguments that language encourages an illegitimate distinction between matter and extension, man (or mind) and reason. For Locke, if we knew the essence of something, it would indeed be wrong to distinguish it from the substance, but ordinary talk simply and rightly reflects an acknowledgement of our ignorance. He appeals to ordinary language against 'those who find it necessary to confound [the] Signification' of 'body' and 'extension': (*E*, III.x.6, p. 493). We speak as we do because 'The *Essence* of anything, in respect of us, is the whole complex *Idea*, … and in Substances, besides the several distinct simple *Ideas* that make them up, the confused [idea] of Substance, or of an unknown Support and Cause of their Union, is always a part; and therefore the Essence of Body is not bare Extension, but an extended solid thing' (*E*, III.vi.21, p. 450). Likewise, 'No one will say, That Rationality is capable of Conversation, because it makes not the whole Essence, to which we give the Name Man'. The argument implies that, if we knew its true essence, rather than just an essence 'in respect of us', then our idea of matter would not include the general idea of substance, and its name would legitimately take the form of a nominalized predicate or 'abstract' noun. This conclusion is made explicit with the claim that the proper function of abstract nouns is to name real essences, where they are known (*E*, III.viii.2, pp. 474–5). The artificiality of such terms as '*animalitas*' or '*humanitas*', in contrast to such ordinary terms as 'whiteness', 'justice' and 'equality', bespeaks 'the confession of all Mankind, that they have no *Ideas* of the real Essences of Substances'. Only 'the Doctrine of *substantial Forms*, and the confidence of mistaken Pretenders to Knowledge' gave rise to such terms. If we had the Creator's knowledge of matter, however, 'Grammar it self' would be different (*E*, IV.x.18, p. 629). (For more on the context and content of Locke's argument from language see Ayers, 1991, vol. ii, pp. 51–64.)

The latter, larger part of II.xxiii is taken up with what may appear conflicting themes.

Locke first asserts that, having no more notion of 'the *Substance* of Matter' than of 'the *Substance* of Spirit', we have no more reason to deny the existence of the latter than that of the former. But then, in turning to the species of material substances, he focuses on a contrast between the known sensible qualities by which we distinguish them and the unknown primary qualities of the 'minute parts', 'on which their real Constitutions and Differences depend'. Very soon, however, Locke proposes strict limits on what mechanistic explanation can achieve. The extension of a body itself consists in the cohesion of its parts, and corpuscularian explanations of that leave us with the mystery of the internal coherence of the particles themselves (*E*, II.xxiii.23–7, pp. 308–11). The communication of motion by impulse and the paradoxes of infinite divisibility are other enigmas (*E*, II.xxiii.28, 31, pp. 311–13), and elsewhere Locke cites the law of attraction as further evidence of our ignorance of the nature or substance of matter (*W*, vol. iv, p. 467f; cf. *W*, vol. iii, p. 304f).

Locke's account of our idea of substance impinges on virtually every area of his epistemology and metaphysics, meshing closely with argument on other topics – the possibility of thinking matter, moral theory, the existence of God, natural classification and method, language, PERSONAL IDENTITY and many more. The interpretation of that account is still controversial. What is certain is that, if we want to understand Locke's general philosophy, we had better understand his theory of substance.

BIBLIOGRAPHY
Primary Sources
Aristotle, *The Complete Works of Aristotle: The Revised Oxford Translation*, ed. Jonathan Barnes (Oxford, 1985).
Arnauld, A. and Nicole, P., *La Logique ou l'Art de Penser*, ed. P. Clair and F. Girbal (Paris, 1965).
Berkeley, George, *Philosophical Commentaries generally called the Commonplace Book*, ed. A.A. Luce (London, 1944).
Harrison, John and Laslett, Peter, *The Library of John Locke* (Oxford, 1965).
Leibniz, G.W., *New Essays on Human Understanding*, trans. P. Remnant and J. Bennett (Cambridge, 1981).
Malebranche, N., *The Search after Truth*, trans. T.M. Lennon and P.J. Olscamp (Columbus, 1980).

Secondary Sources
Ayers, M., *Locke: Epistemology and Ontology*, 2 vols (London, 1991).

Michael Ayers

TOLERATION

All societies are tolerant (as John Coffey has noted); they just tolerate different things. Locke's particular view of what should and should not be tolerated has, for some, almost come to define toleration. Other commentators have in turn reacted to the 'Locke obsession' which, they object, has unreasonably attributed the advent of toleration to 'the intellectual achievements of a great and lonely thinker' (Coffey, 2000, p. 5).

Locke was not, of course, a lonely thinker, but a player in the political and religious conflicts of Restoration England, and indeed late seventeenth-century Europe. Locke's advocacy of religious toleration was intrinsically linked to his theory of religious knowledge and his doctrine of the Church, as well as his theory of government.

His early 'tracts' on government, written between 1660 and 1662 whilst a don at Christ Church, Oxford, unpublished until 1967, appear to be standard conformist defences of an enforced 'Anglican' settlement, and opposed to religious toleration. The civil magistrate had a right to impose 'things indifferent'. However, the 'heterodoxies' in Locke's early tracts were telling, and suggested the future development of his thought: coercion should be used only for outward conformity; religious *adiaphora* – that is, matters indifferent to salvation, typically points of ritual or church organization – were not to be distinguished from civil *adiaphora*; and the clergy had no distinctive role to play in society. The debt to parts three and four of HOBBES's *Leviathan* (though judiciously unacknowledged) is evident (Rose, 2005, p. 619 and 621).

The patronage of the Earl of SHAFTESBURY put Locke close to the heart of a court circle around Charles II, which promoted religious toleration through royal indulgence. His manuscript essay concerning toleration, written in 1667, maintained many of the themes of the 'tracts', most notably the right of the civil magistrate to enforce things indifferent. However, Locke now considered the scope of the civil power more limited. Laws should only be made 'for the security of the government & protection of the people in their lives, estates and Libertys' (*ETol*, p. 31). This thus precluded any punishment of religious dissent that did not affect the public good in this secular sense. Locke may have been influenced in his thinking by his experience of visiting the city of Cleves in 1665–6 and seeing religious toleration in practice. He wrote of the citizens that they 'quietly permit one another to choose their way to heaven' (Locke to Boyle, 12/22 December 1665, *Corr.*, vol. i, p. 228).

When, in the mid-1680s, Locke returned to the subject of religious toleration, he was again in continental Europe. Charles II had turned against Shaftesbury and sought support from an emerging 'High Church' and 'Tory' group. Plotting and allegations of plotting had made life difficult for those close to Shaftesbury's party. Locke's *Epistola de Tolerantia* was composed, in 1685, for the Remonstrant theologian Philip van LIMBORCH. It was 'undoubtedly written with the European fate of Protestantism … at the forefront of Locke's mind' (Marshall, 1994, p. 358). The persecu-

tion of Huguenots, culminating in the Revocation of the Edict of Nantes, together with the crisis over the succession of James II, a Roman Catholic, to the English throne, provide the political context for Locke's *Epistola*. As well as being more removed from merely English concerns, the *Epistola* departed from the early essay on toleration in countenancing resistance by individuals to persecuting governments (*EdT*, p. 146).

The *Epistola* and its English translation, *A Letter concerning Toleration*, were published after the Revolution of 1688–9. James II's downfall was due not least to his perceived misuse of the royal prerogative to promote tolerationist policies. The Williamite regime which ousted James did not bring the religious toleration for which Locke had argued. Locke himself would have preferred a comprehensive English Church that demanded less from its adherents, whilst allowing Protestant dissenters freedom to worship and civil liberties. In the event, the 'Toleration Act' allowed freedom of worship to all Trinitarian Protestants, but did not give full civil liberties to dissenters, whilst the Convocation of the Church of England refused to change its liturgy or laws to accommodate its dissenting critics.

The *Letter* was attacked by JONAS PROAST. Locke, in his turn, replied to Proast in a *Second* (1690) and *Third Letter on Toleration* (1692), and in an unfinished *Fourth* (1704). These later letters emphasize morality as the proper concern of the civil magistrate, thus marking a departure from the *laissez-faire* toleration of the essay of 1667 (Marshall, 1994, pp. 376ff).

Locke's views still have the popular reputation as the basis of modern, secular pluralism. Locke even proposed the toleration of non-Christian religions. In practice, however, there were severe limits to the toleration he advocated. In the *Epistola* Locke exempted from toleration those who 'arrogate to themselves, and to those of their own sect, some peculiar prerogative, contrary to civil right' (*EdT*, p. 130). Thus, those who claim that princes who are excommunicated forfeit their crowns, or that 'dominion is founded in grace', cannot be tolerated. Neither can those who 'refuse to teach that dissenters from their own religion should be tolerated', nor those whose church is 'so constituted that all who enter it *ipso facto* pass into the allegiance and service of another prince' (*EdT*, p. 132), thus, in Locke's view precluding toleration for Roman Catholics, insofar as the pope was a foreign prince. Nor were atheists to be tolerated, because their oaths could not be trusted (*EdT*, p. 134).

Locke's view of the Church entailed that it was a voluntary society made up of men who were already compacted together in the state. Thus, it had to be subject to the state in all its dealings. Whilst the state had no right to interfere with men's purely religious concerns, should a church claim a right to an allegiance before or above that of the state, it represented a political threat to the public peace and could not then be tolerated.

The practical problem for Locke's view of religious toleration was that almost all churches of his era, whatever otherwise divided them, did claim some sort of divine authority which was both older than and superior to that of the state, for their doctrine and ministry. The exceptions to toleration outlined in the *Epistola* 'would perhaps have excluded from its benefits almost all the churches of Locke's day except the Quakers' (Tarcov, 1999, pp. 179–80). His reflections 'undercut not only the Anglican case but also that of the Dissenters' (Stanton, 2006, p. 90). It is, therefore, important to recognize that Locke was not an advocate for absolute, unlimited toleration, despite the claim for such a toleration in the Introduction to the English edition of the *Epistola*. Locke's theory of toleration was, as John Dunn has noted, concerned exclusively with worship and theoretical religious beliefs, since their goal was the attainment of eternal life, and they could not 'damage the rights of fellow citizens' (Dunn, 1991, p. 185). He was in favour of what has been called 'the paradoxical establishment of a sort of civil religion of toleration – an established religion albeit one potentially shared by

many otherwise diverse churches' (Tarcov, 1999, p. 180). Whilst appearing to promote toleration *per se*, Locke's *Epistola* was in fact advocating a fundamental shift in what a society should tolerate – and doing so on a basis that was in part theological.

At the root of Locke's version of toleration lay a scepticism concerning religious knowledge and a denial of the Church as a divinely instituted visible earthly entity, allied with an optimism concerning human nature. Yet Christian tradition also motivated Locke's view of toleration, as he maintained that each believer would be held accountable for his beliefs at the last judgement and therefore must be free to believe sincerely.

Locke did not think that belief in a truth could be compelled by force. It is clear, however, that neither did his opponents; this was almost universally agreed. Advocates of civil penalties in religious matters, such as Proast, held only that force may remove the 'negligence' and 'prejudice' which prevented people from attending to the truth. (The same sort of justification is at work in present-day secular democracies when, for example, the state compels motorists who are caught speeding to attend classes where they are shown the horrific consequences of car crashes and given statistics of fatalities at various speeds – or else face fines and other penalties. The use of coercion to assist right belief is still present, though attached to a different understanding of right belief.)

Locke himself tacitly conceded that the will does have an indirect influence on belief, when he claimed that 'civility and good usage prepared man for considering arguments' (Marshall, 1994, p. 361). One can choose what to consider, and this is a crucial factor in determining belief. The belief that I adopt after having been forced to consider certain propositions is not, because of the coercion, less genuine. Should I be compelled to look at snow at the point of a bayonet, my belief that snow is white is not likely to function any differently from that of someone who did not need to be so coerced (Waldron, 1991, p. 118).

The crucial claim in Locke's defence against Proast is, therefore, not that coercion does not work, but that the civil magistrate is not in a privileged position to know which religion is the true one. It is this scepticism concerning religious knowledge, rather than a commitment to toleration *per se* that underlies Locke's avowal of religious toleration.

Whilst the Toleration Act of 1689 was not the settlement that Locke advocated, Locke's understanding of toleration did find expression in the writings of some prominent Latitudinarian churchmen of the late seventeenth and early eighteenth centuries, notably Gilbert Burnet and Benjamin Hoadly. Locke had Burnet's *Pastoral Care* at his side as he wrote his *Third Letter* against Proast (Goldie, 1993, p. 165). Lockean justifications underpinned the campaign by Hoadly, when Bishop of Bangor, to repeal the Occasional Conformity and Schism Acts – Tory legislation of Queen Anne's reign, which disadvantaged Protestant Dissenters. The start of this campaign, the publication of Hoadly's sermon, *The Nature of the Kingdom, or Church, of Christ* (1717), sparked the 'Bangorian controversy'. Opposition to repeal of these Acts, even from moderate Whigs, was due in no small part to the perception that this was the thin end of a wedge, which would have seen the effective establishment of a civil religion with little dogmatic content. Hoadly, like Locke, saw comprehension of Protestants within the national Church as preferable to the widespread adherence to over-scrupulous Dissent.

Like many other political thinkers of his era, Locke was seeking to come to terms with the demise of Christendom, which followed the Reformation. His doctrine of toleration challenged the received wisdom concerning public religion in seventeenth-century England, not because it was inherently more tolerant, but because it marked a significant shift in belief about the grounds for toleration and, consequently, about what the state ought to tolerate.

BIBLIOGRAPHY
Secondary Literature
Coffey, John, *Persecution and Toleration in Protestant England 1558–1689* (Harlow, 2000).
Dunn, John, 'The Claim to Freedom of Conscience: Freedom of Speech, Freedom of Thought, Freedom of Worship?', in Ole Peter Grell, Jonathan Israel, and Nicholas Tyacke (eds), *From Persecution to Toleration* (Oxford, 1991), pp. 171–93.
Goldie, Mark, 'John Locke, Jonas Proast and Religious Toleration 1688–1692', in John Walsh, Colin Haydon and Stephen Taylor (eds), *The Church of England c.1689–c.1833: From Toleration to Tractarianism* (Cambridge, 1993), pp. 143–71.
Marshall, John, *John Locke: Resistance, Religion and Responsibility* (Cambridge, 1994).
Rose, Jacqueline, 'John Locke, "Matters indifferent" and the Restoration of the Church of England', *Historical Journal*, vol. xlviii (2005), pp. 601–21.
Stanton, Timothy, 'Locke and the Politics and Theology of Toleration', *Political Studies*, vol. liv (2006), pp. 84–102.
Tarcov, Nathan, 'John Locke and the Foundations of Toleration', in Alan Levine (ed.), *Early Modern Skepticism and the Origins of Toleration* (Lanham, Maryland, 1999), pp. 179–95.
Waldron, Jeremy, 'Locke: Toleration and the Rationality of Persecution', in John Horton and Susan Mendus (eds), *John Locke: A Letter concerning Toleration in Focus* (London, 1991), pp. 98–124.

Andrew Starkie

TRUTH AND FALSITY

Locke mentions 'moral' and 'metaphysical' truth (*E*, IV.v.11, pp. 578–9), which correspond to moral certainty (DESCARTES, 1984, vol. i, pp. 289–91; Shapiro, 1983, *passim*) and material truth and falsity (Descartes, 1984, vol. ii, pp. 29–30), but his focus is clearly on truth in the received philosophical sense. Locke recognizes that some speak as if ideas were true or false, but that is, he believes, mistaken. 'For our *Ideas*,' Locke argues, 'being nothing but bare Appearances or Perceptions in our Minds, cannot properly and simply in themselves be said to be *true* or *false*, no more than a single Name of any thing, can be said to be *true* or *false*' (*E*, II.xxxii.1, p. 384). Locke defines truth as '*the joining or separating of Signs, as the Things signified by them, do agree or disagree one with another*' (*E*, IV.v.2, p. 574). Falsity is the contrary, the joining or separating of signs otherwise than as the things signified by them agree or disagree one with another (*E*, IV.v.9, p. 578).

Locke adopted the traditional, scholastic, psychologistic account of truth. Truth requires a proposition as its bearer, and propositions exist only if uttered or thought. There are two types of propositions corresponding to the two types of signs (*E*, IV.v.2, p. 574 and IV.xxi.4, pp. 720–1), mental propositions consisting of ideas joined or separated by a mental act and verbal propositions consisting of words joined or separated by a verbal copula. This division between mental and verbal propositions is not about whether the propositions are 'in the head'. Rather, it concerns what the constitutive terms of the proposition are. For example, the proposition '*S* is *P*' existing 'in the head' will be mental if and only if the terms *S* and *P* appear as ideas joined by a mental act of separation or union; if either *S* or *P* appears as words, or if their connection appears as the verbal copula 'is', the proposition is verbal even though it is contained entirely 'in the head'. Of course, written and uttered propositions are always verbal according to Locke.

The joining or separating of signs concerns the copulation of the signs involved. In the mental case, this is performed by the adoption of a certain kind of attitude towards the possible union of the two ideas, either an attitude of endorsement or repudiation. No union of ideas is actually effected by the copulation of the mental signs – it is not the construction of a complex idea in accordance with the mental operations of compounding, comparing or abstracting (*E*, II.xii.12, pp. 163–4). In a mental proposition, the copulated ideas remain individual ideas. Mental copulation is nothing more than the mental act of endorsement or repudiation that connects ideas in a single judgement. In the verbal case, this copulation is performed (ideally) by the syncategormatic terms 'is' or 'is not' (Hill, 2006, pp. 93–5).

Although Locke does not appear aware of it, his psychologistic account of truth is susceptible to all the well-known objections to which such an account is prone – that there is no truth before the existence of humans and their formulations of propositions, that truth extends only so far as humans have happened to formulate propositions, that Divine Truth is discontinuous with human truth, etc. Nevertheless, Locke develops a rather baroque theory of truth.

Locke's taxonomy of truth is as follows: (1) real mental truth, (2) real verbal truth, (3) nominal mental truth, and (4) nominal verbal truth. One of the benefits of such a taxonomy is that it easily allows us to make sense of the INTUITION that fictional 'truths' are different from other falsehoods without obliging one to maintain their real truth. 'Sherlock Holmes is a detective' is not materially equivalent to 'Sherlock Holmes is Brazilian' because the former is *nominally true* and *really false* whereas the latter is *nominally false* as well as *really false*. The core of the taxonomy concerns the ways in which the signs involved in the proposition signify. There are two types of signifying that apply to both types of propositions. Locke calls the two types of truths generated by these different ways of signifying as '*Real*' truth and '*purely Verbal*' or '*barely nominal*' truth (*E*,

IV.v.6, p. 576 and IV.v.8, pp. 577–8). To avoid confusion, let us use 'Real' and 'Nominal' to characterize the distinction. A real (and instructive) truth is one in which the agreement between the signs is rooted in or founded on the agreement obtaining between the real objects ultimately signified by the signs, and a nominal (and trifling) truth is one in which the agreement is rooted in or founded on the agreement obtaining between the nominal definitions of the signs. This distinction corresponds to the traditional distinction between *de re* and *de dicto* KNOWLEDGE: nominal truths involve agreements between the descriptive content of the signs, or how the sign represents its significate, whereas real truths involve agreements between the significata themselves, between the objects represented by the signs or their meanings themselves.

Because words and ideas relate to real things differently, mediately versus immediately (*E*, III.ii.2, pp. 405–6), the relations establishing verbal truths differ slightly from those establishing mental truths. The question is whether the idea, that is the immediate signification of the word, is treated by the mind as a sign or as an object. In nominal truth, the idea is not treated as a sign but as an object, whereas in real truth, it is treated as a sign. Technical scholastic terminology (which Locke did not make use of) makes Locke's point much more clearly: in nominal truth, the idea that is signified by (verbal propositions) or constitutes (mental propositions) the subject term has only *material supposition*. Thus it refers only to its own descriptive content. In real truth, however, that idea has *personal supposition*. Thus it refers to its archetype, that real object which the idea immediately signifies. Whereas the verbal-mental division concerns the types of signs constituting the proposition (words versus ideas) and so is a purely psychological distinction, the nominal-real division is a semantic distinction that arises from how the signs (whatever their psychological manifestations) codify truth conditions (materially, as in 'cat' is a three-letter word,' or personally, as in 'cat is an animal').

Consider the following examples: The verbal proposition 'a chimera is an animal' is nominally true because the idea of chimera contains the idea of animality. But it is not really true because the idea of chimera is a fantastical idea (*E*, II.xxx.5, p. 374). The mental proposition 'a chimera is an animal' is nominally true too, because the idea of chimera contains the idea of animality. It also fails to be really true because, again, the idea of a chimera is a fantastical idea. But on the other hand, the verbal proposition 'gold is malleable' is really true (putting aside Locke's doubts about the adequacy of our SUBSTANCE ideas) because the idea of gold signifies a substance with a real essence (a corpuscular constitution) such that malleableness necessarily flows from it. The same applies for the mental proposition 'gold is mallable:' the idea of gold signifies a substance with a real essence such that the objects signified really agree.

What is the conceptual relationship between real and nominal truth? It might initially seem as if every real truth will also be nominally true, but not every nominal truth will be really true. Sometimes, however, both relationships will obtain. In cases involving simple, modal and relational ideas as subject terms, this will certainly happen because their NOMINAL ESSENCES are their REAL ESSENCES. Thus in those cases, whatever is really true is nominally true *and* whatever is nominally true is really true. With substance ideas, the tables are turned, however. Sometimes, as in the chimera case, a proposition will be nominally true but not really true. *And* sometimes a proposition involving substance terms will be really true but not nominally true, which happens when on the basis of experiments the predicate is perceived to agree with the subject but that quality has not (yet) been established as part of the subject term's nominal essence. Given the right linguistic community, the above example of gold's malleableness would illustrate this.

'It will be objected, That if Truth be nothing but the joining or separating of Words in Propositions, as the *Ideas* they stand for agree or disagree in Men's Minds, the Knowledge of

Truth is not so valuable a Thing,' Locke realized, since 'it amounts to no more than the conformity of Words, to the *Chimaeras* of Men's Brains' (*E*, IV.v.7, p. 577). This 'problem of correspondence', a problem with the possibility of real truth, is analogous to the problem with the possibility of real knowledge (*E*, IV.iv, pp. 562–73), and Locke directs us there for the details of his solution (*E*, IV.v.8, pp. 577–8). It is the reality of the ideas involved in the proposition that dictate whether there is the possibility of real truth – agreements perceived to obtain between two ideas are real agreements if and only if the ideas between which they are perceived to obtain are real. And ideas are real in different ways depending on their type (*E*, II.xxx.2–5, pp. 372–4); all simple, modal and relational ideas are real, the former by virtue of a nomological connection and the latter two by logical consistency. But only some particular ideas of substance are real, namely those (excepting God and the self) that have been sensed. Locke's theory of truth, then, is a correspondence theory, despite initially looking as if it would be a coherence theory.

BIBLIOGRAPHY
Primary Sources
Descartes, René, *The Philosophical Writings of Descartes*, trans. John Cottingham, Robert Stoothoff, et al., 3 vols (Cambridge, 1984).

Secondary Sources
Hill, Benjamin, 'Reconciling Locke's Definition of Knowledge with Knowing Reality', *Southern Journal of Philosophy*, vol. xliv (2006), pp. 91–105.
Shapiro, Barbara, *Probability and Certainty in Seventeenth-century England* (Princeton, New Jersey, 1983).

Benjamin Hill

VALUE AND WEALTH

Locke's writings on money are mainly famous within the history of economic thought for containing an early clear expression of the quantity theory of value. According to this theory, price levels follow the amount of available money in a particular country at a given moment (Leigh, 1974; Eltis, 1995; Vaughn, 1980). Despite the fact that Locke, in contrast to classical economists, developed the quantity theorem in a static form only, parts of his monetary theory are frequently judged to surpass the views of many eighteenth-century writers (Kelly, 1991, pp. 75–86 and 91). Most of the modern scholarly debate over Locke's theory of value has focused on the adequacy, in terms of economic theory, of the passages where Locke, arguing under *ceteris paribus* conditions, sets out to refute the main logic of his opponents on the effects of lowering interest rates and a devaluationary recoinage on the price of lands, investments, consumption levels and economic competitiveness. From the perspective of economic theory, his ideas about value tend to be qualified as generally representative of the antiquated principles of 'mercantilism' (see Kelly, 1991, pp. 67–71). There can be no doubt that refuting his opponents' economic logic was Locke's primary aim. Still, a more sustained focus on the *political significance* of his ideas about value paves the way for a more authentic understanding of these ideas in conjunction with his main political theory.

In his monetary works, Locke distinguished between, but also related, three ideas of the 'intrinsick value' of money: (1) the physical qualities of durability, scarcity and divisibility of gold and silver, (2) the use value that resulted when gold and silver were turned into money, and (3) the value of money as a sort of commodity, 'perfectly in the same Condition with other Commodities', in the exchange of goods between people (*LoM*, pp. 233–4 and 410–11; cf. pp. 82–3 and 86–9). Perhaps surprisingly, Locke added only at the last minute an elaborate discussion of the basic economic laws to the manuscript of *Some Considerations of the Consequences of the Lowering of Interest, and Raising the Value of Money* (published in 1691; cf. Kelly, 1991, p. 82). This discussion provides us with a more abstract perspective on Locke's political views on money.

In the 1690s Locke strenuously maintained that debts had to be satisfied according to the legal standard (*LoM*, pp. 417–19): '[m]en in their bargains contract not for denominations or sounds, but for the intrinsique value, which is the quantity of silver by public authority ascertained'. The nominal value of money that had been 'setled by publique authority' and 'grown into common use,' according to Locke, 'should not be alterd but on absolute necessity if any such there can be' (*LoM*, p. 375). Contracts should be protected, instead of being violated. Locke compared devaluation to clipping coins by the government (*LoM*, p. 307, 322, and 402–4). As public debts had risen during the war, the issue of the satisfaction of debt obligations became very significant. Devaluation might alienate the state's creditors from the state. Locke judged that devaluation was utterly unjust, as those who 'assisted our present necessities, upon Acts of Parliament, in the Million Lottery, Bank Act, and other Loans, shall be defrauded of 20 per Cent. in all their Debts and setled Revenues' (*LoM*, p. 419).

The satisfaction of contractual obligation was not only an important requirement for political stability, but also for stable economic growth. Locke held that economic growth was best served by a slowly but steadily rising level of money within the country (*LoM*, p. 266; cf. p. 79, 85 and 90–1). Building upon his theory of the value of money in international trade, Locke sketched a model of how a country with no money but an impressive wool production (England) would outcompete a state (Spain) that abounded in gold and silver mines (*LoM*, pp. 228–9). Enhanced competitiveness created new income distributions, investment opportunities and higher prices and labour costs.

Through the international comparability of the price of money, the relative development of a national economy could be gauged. Here, Locke followed the political reasoning of Benjamin Worsley, who saw trade and power as directly related (*LoM*, pp. 70–1, 79, 220, 222 and 280–1).

Locke's vision was underlined by the idea – increasingly prominent in his monetary works – that gold and silver were 'the means of Plenty and Power' (*LoM*, p. 71). Reasoning from an entirely different perspective, Nicholas Barbon objected to this idea. Barbon denied that money had a use value. He asserted that silver and gold had an intrinsic value as metals *and* had been given an extrinsic value by public authority. It was only because '[s]ome Men have so great an Esteem for Gold and Silver, that they believe they have an intrinsick Value in themselves, and cast up the value of every thing by them' (Barbon, 1690; 1696). When Henry Layton criticized Locke for pretending that 'the Government had no more power in Politicks than in Naturals' (Layton, 1697, p. 15), he came closer to grasping the logic of Locke's thinking. For Locke, the use value of money emerged 'out of the bounds of Societie' by 'common consent' (*LoM*, pp. 233–4 and pp. 410–11) or 'tacit Agreement' (*TTG* II.36), i.e. by a concurrence in the development of human affairs. It was on this theoretical construct, couched in terms of the discourse of natural jurisprudence, that much of Locke's vision of the importance of monetary politics rested: a monetary politics carrying forward, simultaneously, the progress of humankind and English commercial empire.

BIBLIOGRAPHY
Primary Sources
Barbon, Nicholas, *A Discourse of Trade* (1690).
——, *A Discourse concerning Coining the New Money Lighter* (1696).
Layton, Henry, *Observations concerning Money and Coin* (1697).

Secondary Literature

Eltis, Walter, 'John Locke, the Quantity Theory of Money, and the Establishment of a Sound Currency', in Mark Blaug (ed.), *The Quantity Theory of Money: From Locke to Keynes and Friedman* (Aldershot, 1995), pp. 4–26.

Kelly, Patrick Hyde, 'General Introduction: Locke on Money', in *LoM* (1991), vol. i, pp. 1–105.

Leigh, Arthur H., 'John Locke and the Quantity Theory of Money', *History of Political Economy*, vol. vi (1974), pp. 200–19.

Vaughn, Karen I., *John Locke, Economist and Social Scientist* (Chicago, 1980).

Koen Stapelbroek

WORDS, THEIR IMPERFECTIONS AND ABUSES

The polemical purpose of Locke's examination of language was not to insist that words signify concepts; this was a commonplace of which his contemporaries needed no persuading. Instead, the thrust of his analysis was to expose the difficulties inherent in the linguistic theory to which they all subscribed. While his forebears had long complained about the abuses of words, Locke was concerned about not only malign manipulations of speech, but also the imperfections of words themselves that cause people to talk poorly. His concerns bear witness to his awareness of the impediments which the private, ideational nature of meaning put in the way of both communication and reference, and which his critics have accused him of overlooking. His concerns might be grouped into three.

The first involves the obscurity, vacuity and pretence of our talk about the world. Words signify ideas, and while these might be caused by qualities in things, they do not grasp the REAL ESSENCES of those things. SUBSTANCE terms therefore 'convey so little Knowledge or Certainty in our Discourses' (*E*, III.x.18, p. 500). This imperfection is exacerbated by the reality of the terms themselves, which, irrespective of their light ideational load, *seem* to reach further and 'stand for … The real constitution of Things' (*E*, III.ix.12, p. 482). The imperfection shades into an abuse when people set words '*in the place of Things, which they do or can by no means signify*' (*E*, III.x.17, p. 500). Eager to make up for the deficit in our understanding, we 'tacit[ly]', 'secret[ly]' refer words such as 'gold' to real essences, so that they come 'to have no signification at all' (*E*, III.x.19, p. 501).

Locke's second concern is with semantic instability, whereby sounds are not fixed to meanings and misunderstanding follows. This is in part precipitated by speakers wilfully wrenching words from their proper significations, obstructing 'Truth and Knowledge' and bringing 'Confusion, Disorder and Uncertainty into the Affairs of Mankind' (*E*, III.x.34, p. 508; *E*, III.x.12, p. 496). Locke lists a series of these abuses of common use, including equivocation (when, for example, 'dog' is applied now to an animal, now to a star) and all the tropes of rhetoric (when, for example, I call that 'frugality' which others call 'covetousness') (*E*, III.x.5, p. 492; *E*, III.x.34, p. 508; *E*, III.x.33, p. 507). In addition to these 'cheats', Locke diagnoses more innocent causes of semantic instability. As with his first concern, his diagnosis follows from pushing to its logical conclusions, and in the context of his innovative epistemology, the contemporary axiom that words signify ideas. Locke points out that if this is so, words can only signify the ideas that individual speakers happen to have, and if these differ, they do not communicate. Since complex ideas are made by us, they might be – and often are – made differently, with the result that people speak 'a distinct Language, though the same Words' (*E*, III.ix.22, p. 489). The complex ideas signified by substance terms vary between people not only because they decide which ideas to include, but also because people have varying levels of experience of the same substance (a boy, for example, might know only 'the bright shining yellow colour' in 'gold', a 'Chymist' 'Solubility in *Aqua Regia*') (*E*, III.ix.13, p. 483; *E*, III.ii.3, p. 406). The problem is even graver in the case of the NAMES of mixed MODES, the meanings of which have no natural standards to keep them even in the same ballpark. As entirely 'arbitrary' ideas, 'put together at the pleasure of the Mind', they can diverge unrestrictedly, so that, as Locke glumly conjectures, 'moral words' (the most important subsection of mixed modes) 'have seldom, in two different Men, the same precise signification; since one Man's complex *Idea* seldom agrees with anothers, and often differs from his own, from that which he had yesterday' (*E*, III.ix.6, p. 478; *E*, III.ix.7, p. 478). 'The Rule of Propriety', which ought to settle the meanings of words, is of little help, it being an unpromulgated and barely legislated law, 'no body having an Authority to establish the precise signification of Words' (*E*, III.ix.8, p. 479). Indeed, under the glare of Locke's verdict of endemic semantic instability, *common* use – the means by which public meaning is established – reduces to an overlapping assortment of individual uses. Rather than simply presenting linguistic contracts which speakers dishonestly break, Locke casts doubt on the very existence of these contracts, and therefore on the possibility of communication.

The third concern is about the practical priority and destructive power of words. While words are supposed to be subservient to, and merely sensible incarnations of ideas, in practice they dominate not only in communication, where all we have are the words, but in thought as well, where sensible words stick much more easily in our sensuous minds than their abstruse and ephemeral cargo. They thereby conceal both the vacuity and the instability described above, and promote the nonsense and miscommunication that result. Again, Locke departs from his contemporaries in stressing that the deceptive force of words is not simply a function of the corrupt desire to mislead, but is the inexorable consequence of language and human psychol-

ogy. He catalogues a number of ways in which words are used – more or less innocently – to betray their contents. Uncomfortable with the possibility that we do not understand each other, we automatically suppose that we signify the same ideas by our words (*E*, III.x.22, p. 503; *E*, III.ii.4, p. 406). Disconcerted by the short reach of our knowledge, and keen to 'palliate' our ignorance, we take words for things, constructing elaborate stories about the world that we have no right to tell (*E*, III.ii.5, p. 407; *E*, III.x.14, p. 497). Having from our cradles learnt easy words before difficult ideas, and then being too lazy, obtuse and obsequious to authority and fashion to investigate and question what these sounds mean, they lodge in our minds either entirely insignificantly, or else riddled with error and perplexity (*E*, III.ix.9, p. 479; *E*, III.x.4, p. 491). It is because words do not slavishly express the ideas they represent, but usurp them, sowing gibberish and confusion, that Locke takes the unusual step of inserting an entire book about words into an essay about the mind. In justifying the insertion, Locke explains that words 'interpose themselves so much between our Understandings, and the Truth, which it would contemplate and apprehend, that like the *Medium* through which visible Objects pass, their Obscurity and Disorder does not seldom cast a mist before our Eyes, and impose upon our Understandings' (*E*, III.ix.21, p. 488).

BIBLIOGRAPHY

Dawson, Hannah, 'Locke on Language in (Civil) Society', *History of Political Thought*, vol. xxvi (2005), pp. 398–425.

——, 'A Ridiculous Plan: Locke and the Universal Language Movement', *Locke Studies* (2007), pp. 137–58.

——, 'The Rebellion of Language against Reason in Early-Modern Philosophy', *Intellectual History Review*, vol. xvii (2007), pp. 277–90.

Hannah Dawson

5

SYNOPSES OF KEY WRITINGS

AN ESSAY CONCERNING HUMAN UNDERSTANDING

Locke described the *Essay*'s origin in its 'Epistle to the Reader':

Were it fit to trouble thee with the History of this Essay, I should tell thee that five or six Friends meeting at my Chamber, and discoursing on a Subject very remote from this, found themselves quickly at a stand, by the Difficulties that rose on every side. After we had a while puzzled our selves, without coming any nearer a Resolution of those Doubts which perplexed us, it came into my Thoughts, that we took a wrong course; and that, before we set our selves upon Enquiries of that Nature, it was necessary to examine our own Abilities, and see, what Objects our Understandings were, or were not fitted to deal with. This I proposed to the Company, who all readily assented; and thereupon it was agreed, that this should be our first Enquiry. Some hasty and undigested Thoughts, on a Subject I had never before considered, which I set down against our next Meeting, gave the first entrance into this Discourse, which having been begun by Chance, was continued by Intreaty; written by incoherent parcels; and after long intervals of neglect, resum'd again, as my Humour or Occasion permitted; and at last, in a retirement, where an Attendance on my Health gave me

leisure, it was brought into that order thou now seest it (*Essay*, p. 7).

Locke thought he would quickly wrap up his enquiries: 'I thought all I should have to say on this Matter, would have been contained in one sheet of Paper; but the farther I went, the larger Prospect I had' (*Essay*, pp. 7–8). James Tyrrell, a friend of Locke's from Oxford, in his copy of the *Essay* (British Library, shelfmark C.122.f.14), wrote in the margin next to the 'Epistle': 'I remember being myself one of those that then met there when the discourse began about the principles of morality and reveal'd religion'. Locke confirms that 'our Conduct' was 'that which gave the first *Rise* to this Essay concerning the Understanding (*E*, I.i.6–7, pp. 46–7). Damaris MASHAM, in her 'Character of Mr Locke', corroborated Tyrrell's claim: 'In the year 1670 or 71, as I am inform'd, Mr Locke began to lay the first foundations of his *Essay concerning humane Understanding* at the desire of Mr Tyrel Doctor Thomas and other of his Friends' (Woolhouse, 2003, p. 178).

Locke decided to provide a NATURAL HISTORY of the understanding, just as SYDENHAM provided natural histories in medicine:

in this Historical, plain Method, I can give [an] Account of the Ways, whereby our Understandings come to attain those Notions of Things we have, and can set down any Measures of the Certainty of our Knowledge, or the Grounds of those

Perswasions, which are to be found amongst Men (*E*, I.i.2, p. 44).

Locke then outlined his plan:

First, I shall inquire into the *Original* of those *Ideas*, Notions, or whatever else you please to call them, which a Man observes, and is conscious to himself he has in his Mind; and the ways whereby the Understanding comes to be furnished with them.

Secondly, I shall endeavour to shew, what *Knowledge* the Understanding hath by those *Ideas*; and the Certainty, Evidence, and Extent of it.

Thirdly, I shall make some Enquiry into the Nature and Grounds of *Faith*, or *Opinion*: whereby I mean that Assent, which we give to any Proposition as true, of whose Truth yet we have no certain Knowledge: And here we shall have Occasion to examine the Reasons and Degrees of Assent (*E*, I.i.3, p. 44).

The earliest example of what was to become the *Essay*, now referred to as Draft A, is entitled 'Intellectus humanus cum cognitionis certitudine, et assensûs firmitate' – 'Human understanding with certainty of knowledge and firmness of assent' – and dated 1671. Taking up thirty-five pages of a large commonplace book, the Draft is not the 'one sheet of Paper' that Locke first set down. It is, however, 'hasty and undigested', full of digressions, corrections, deletions, insertions and addenda. The first two sections in particular are long and discursive – Locke hastily jots down related thoughts before they escape him. Later sections include large additions that distort a more orderly discussion. Yet Draft A has an intelligible structure roughly consistent with Locke's plan.

Locke's beginning is robustly empiricist:

I imagin that all knowledg is founded on and ultimately derives its self from sense, or something analogous to it & may be cald sensation, which is donne by our senses conversant about particular objects which give us the simple Ideas or Images of things & thus we come to have Ideas of heat & light, hard & soft (Draft A, sect. 1, p. 1).

These sensations form our conceptions of objects:

The senses by frequent conversation with certain objects finde that a certeine number of those simple Ideas goe constantly togeather which therefor the understanding takes to belong to one thing & therefor words following our apprehensions are called soe united in one subject by one name ... & soe are all Ideas of substances such as man, horse sun water Iron (ibid.).

Yet there is something more to objects than mere concatenation of sensation. A man collects together the ideas

which because he cannot apprehend how they should subsist alone he supposes they rest & are united in some fit & common subject which being as it were the support of those sensible qualitys he cals substance or mater, though it be certain that he hath noe other idea of that matter but what he hath barely of those sensible qualitys supposd to be inhærent in it (Draft A, sect. 1, pp. 1–2).

The understanding supposes a substance, then imposes it upon a set of ideas, because we 'cannot apprehend how they should subsist alone'. Applying similar reasoning to our ideas from internal sensation, Locke noted the obscurity of both these concepts. We may 'take notice that the idea of matter is as remote from our understandings & apprehensions as that of spirit & therefor from our not haveing any notion of the essence of the one we can noe more conclude its non existence then we can of the other' (Draft A, sect. 1, p. 2). Opposing the doctrinaire positions of HOBBES and DESCARTES, Locke believed that matter and spirit were equally mysterious and that we know the essence of neither.

Locke then went back to add something that had apparently just occurred to him:

Imperfect & wrong definition of words cause endless doubt confusions & errors in mens owne mindes by them selves as wel as in their discourses with others, which is a thing of great moment in our present enquiry & well to be considerd if we would make any discovery what knowledg our understandings are capable of (Draft A, sect. 1, p. 4, n. 9).

A consideration of words, and not just ideas, will be critical to Locke's project. Indeed, this first section ends discussing the definition of simple ideas.

Section two turns to: 'The other fountaine of all our knowledge though it be not sense, yet is some thing very like it & may properly enough be called sensation & is noething but the experience of the operations of our owne mindes within' (Draft A, sect. 2, p. 7). Reaffirming that we have as little idea of the essence of spirit as body, Locke then summarized his view about the foundations of knowledge:

These two (I say) viz the objects of our senses & the operations of our owne minds are the two only principles or originals from which we receive any simple Ideas whatsoever & that all the knowledge we have beyond this is noe thing else but the compareing uniting compounding enlarging & otherwise diversifying these simple Ideas one with another (Draft A, sect. 2, pp. 7–8)

Consequences cascade quickly from these premises. Concerning particular substances, he 'who knows the most of the sensible qualitys that are in it, or the powers of it' knows it best (Draft A, sect. 2, p. 8). People not only make ideas of individual substances, they 'observe a certeine number of these simple Ideas to be found in several particular subjects ranks them togeather or else findes them ranked togeather by others under one general name, which we cal a species' (ibid.). Genus and species are collections of ideas united under a name, occasioning another discussion of words. If ideas of external bodies are compounded of sensation's simple ideas, so ideas of spiritual creatures must be compositions of ideas of reflection:

& even the best notions or Idea we can have of god is but attributeing the same simple Ideas of thinkeing knowing willing existence without beginning & all those powers & operations we finde in ourselves … to him in an higher & unlimited degree (Draft A, sect. 2, p. 10).

The section concludes with a discussion of artificial species, noting that their NAMES are well defined, being determined by us, rather than nature.

Section 3 introduces relations, Section 4 noting their most important type, 'which is the rectitude of actions which is noething but the relation or conformity of the actions of men to some rule & this is that which we call moral goodnesse and badnesse' (Draft A, sect. 4, p. 12). The discussion quickly turns to moral words, noting how the schoolmen have distorted common meanings.

Sections 5 and 6 summarize the findings to date and, in Section 7, Locke discusses what we may know of these ideas. Simple ideas are perfectly known, since we can never mistake one for another. But of 'compounded Ideas' (not yet 'complex') there may be degrees of knowledge, depending on how accurately we collect ideas from their models in nature. Locke notes, in Section 8, that ideas themselves cannot be true or false, but only in so far as they are (mis)applied to names, drawing the conclusion, in Section 9, that TRUTH AND FALSITY are not dependent on ideas themselves, but rather upon the action of the understanding on them: 'The next thing it doth is to joyne two of these Ideas considerd as destinct togeather or separate them one from an other by way of affirmation or negation, which when it comes to be expressed in words is cald proposition & in this lies all truth & falshood' (Draft A, sect. 9, p. 20).

Locke then considered the different types of proposition, first noting the most important – those asserting the existence of those things we have ideas of. Here Locke makes his first direct reference to Descartes, acknowledging that for anyone 'according to Des Cartes ... [it is] ... past doubt that whilst he writes, or thinkes that he writes, he that thinkes, doth exist' (Draft A, sect. 10, p. 21). Locke nonetheless dismissed the extreme scepticism that drove Descartes's thinking: 'This certainty I say of a things existing when we have the testimony of our senses for it is not only as great as our frame can attaine too but as our condition needs' (ibid.). Locke's practical outlook left little room for abstruse sceptical considerations.

Locke next discussed relations of number, but then changed tack to consider how and when we include ideas in particular substances. This led, in Sections 14–16, to a treatment of the powers of substances. Though we see relations of cause and effect, we are ignorant of how such relations are brought about – 'a comprehensive knowledg of causes and effects as I have last mentioned is I thinke out of the reach of humane understanding' (Draft A, sect. 15, p. 30). Locke further classified different types of relation, again dwelling upon 'actions relateing to a rule ... [which are] cald morall, & this sort of relation is of all the most considerable espetially in reference to our present designe' (Draft A, sect. 19, p. 35). Knowledge of moral relations should be straightforward: 'The notions to which they apply severall words being wholly in mens owne making & depending not at all upon things without ... Therefor of these moral Ideas we may have a certain knowledge (Draft A, sect. 26, pp. 40–1). This implied that morality could be certain, but that anyone can create moral rules. There is, however, 'Another sort of Moral Ideas or rules', which are

not of our owne making but depending on something without us & soe are not made by us, but for us & these are the rules set to our actions by the declard will or laws of another who hath power to punish our aberrations. These are properly & truly the rules of good & evill because conformity or disagreement of our actions with these bring upon us good or evill (Draft A, sect. 26, p. 41).

Locke's conception of the divine lawgiver was both traditional and orthodox, but he did not now deal with the subject that had occasioned his enquiry: 'I must only at present suppose this rule till a fit place to speake of those god the Law of nature & revalation' (ibid.).

Locke then considered the knowledge we might lay claim to. We know that we exist, and that when things affect our senses, they exist. We can compare certain ideas in proportion and likeness, and see evidence of cause and effect. That is all. Consequently, 'all that a man can certainly know of things existing without him is only particular propositions, for which he hath demonstration by his senses' (Draft A, sect. 27, p. 43). Regarding general propositions, Locke believed 'a man may have a certaine infallible knowledg of universal affirmative identicall propositions' and 'have a certain infallible knowledg of universall negative propositions where one of his simple Ideas is denied of another' (Draft A, sect. 31, p. 58). But beyond that, 'a man can have noe certain knowledg of the 1 existence 2 Union. 3 Eficacy 4 Concomitancy of any of these simple Ideas without him but only by the testimony of his owne senses conversant about those particulars' (Draft A, sect. 31, p. 60).

The boundaries of knowledge drawn up, Locke next considered the 'several degrees & grounds of Probability & Assent or Faith' (Draft A, sect. 32, p. 62). Their grounds are twofold: 'Agreeableness of our owne experience: And Testimony of witnesses vouching their Experience' (Draft A, sect. 33, p. 62). Locke then outlined the different degrees of probability, and its estimation in realms beyond our senses. Finally, he noted why people sometimes judge probabilities incorrectly – they lack proofs, are lazy or prejudiced, or simply refuse to assent to the most probable for reasons of religion or personal investment.

Having examined our ideas, knowledge and probability as planned, Locke ended his work. Nevertheless, the Draft contains additional sections dealing with 'the objections that I have hitherto met with against what is before said' (Draft A, sect. 43, p. 74), doubtless based on the reaction of the friends it was written for. The first was that 'we had certain innate Ideas or principles of whose truth we are certain though our senses could never come to any observation of them' (ibid.). While Section 27 had mentioned these in passing, Locke now firmly asserted that 'I never said the truth of all propositions was to be made out to us by our senses for this was to leave noe room for reason at all' (Draft A, sect. 43, p. 75). Reason allows us to determine truths that the senses alone could not discover, but that does not make these truths innate. It is perhaps unsurprising that Locke's friends found fault in this respect; Locke's remarks regarding demonstration and reason most often appeared in repeated criticisms of the scholastics' obsession with disputation, 'wrangleing' and 'learned gibberish'.

The second objection concerned the idea of the infinite, and whether this could possibly have been derived from ideas furnished by the senses (Draft A, sect. 44–5, pp. 78–82). Locke questioned whether his adversaries 'consider whether the notion they have of Infinite how positive so ever they thinke it be any new Idea but only the Ideas of Number or Extension inlargd or considerd without limits which was a power I always acknowledgd to be in our mindes' (Draft A, sect. 45, pp. 81–2). Although he was writing what was effectively an appendix, Locke promised to discuss the idea of power 'hereafter' (Draft A, sect. 44, p. 79).

A 'Memorandum' at the end of the Draft further signalled Locke's intent to continue work on his subject. He distinguished ideas and qualities:

> soe that Idea when it is spoken of as being in our understanding is the very perception or thought we have there, when it is spoken of as existing without is the cause of that perception. & is supposed to be resembled by it. & this also I call quality (Draft A, sect. 45, p. 82).

Despite constant criticism of the scholastics, Locke often relied on the scholastic intellectual framework. He assumed that knowledge required certainty, since scholastic 'science' required it. He adopted categories such as substance, quality, essence and species, seeking to redefine these on his empiricist premises. Scholastic 'qualities' could reside both in objects and in the mind. Locke's firm separation of qualities in bodies from ideas in the mind showed progress away from SCHOLASTICISM.

Scholastic influence is also evident in Locke's descriptions of the powers of bodies as active and passive, actual and potential (Draft A, sect. 2, p. 8, sect. 14, p. 29, sect. 45, p. 83) – a typical scholastic taxonomy. Corpuscularianism played a small role in Draft A. There are corpuscularian examples (Draft A, sect. 17, p. 32, sect. 15, p. 31), but there are also examples from rival theories. For instance, discussing events beyond our senses, Locke cites 'Natural spirits in animals. The forme soule or Effluviums of a load stone whereby it draws iron' (Draft A, sect. 38, p. 66), countenancing at least Aristotelean, and possibly Helmontian, explanations. Locke held that we have no definitive knowledge of natural agency: 'because these alterations being made by particles soe small & minute that they come not within the observation of my senses I cannot get knowledg how they operate' (Draft A, sect. 15, p. 31).

Locke was unsatisfied with Draft A – not only with what he wrote, but also how he wrote it. A bound volume was not suited to the writing and revision of a large treatise; smaller insertions were crammed into the margin, and longer insertions had to be made several pages away. Recommencing his work, Locke adopted the method of composition he had used for the 1667 *Essay concerning Toleration* (*ETol.*, pp. 162–72). He took sheets of paper, folded and cut them to create gatherings of eight leaves. Locke wrote on the right-hand pages, leaving the left-hand page free for corrections and additions. Where these exceeded the space available, Locke would insert a folded quarter sheet into the gathering, creating additional space. He could now place additions wherever he liked, and extend his work indefinitely.

Though also dated 1671, the next extant Draft, 'An Essay concerning The Understanding, Knowledge, Opinion and Assent' (Draft B, sect. 1, pp. 100–1), commonly known as Draft B, was much more coherent than its predecessor. Sections were generally much shorter and dealt with only one topic at a time (though the new writing method allowed Locke to insert extensive additions, occasionally distorting his more focused approach). Whereas innate ideas were an afterthought in Draft A, Draft B began with a sixteen-section refutation of innatism. This completely restructured Locke's work, and anticipated Book I of the *Essay*. After a general introduction (sects 1–3), the critique of innatism covered first practical, then speculative principles (sects 4–15), and concluded by noting that innate principles required innate ideas, which few would suppose children, for example, have (sects 16). Significant portions of this material were derived from Locke's earlier *Essays on the Law of Nature* (*ELN*, pp. 63–6).

Draft B more clearly distinguished simple and complex ideas. With one exception, simple ideas were discussed in Sections 17 to 59, complex ideas in Sections 60 to 162. In the sections on simple ideas Locke first elucidated their origin in sensation and reflection, but then, as in Draft A, deviated from the simple/complex split, and immediately concluded that we have no ideas of the essence of material or spiritual substance (sects 18–19). This point made, Locke returned to his consideration of simple ideas, elaborating on the capacities of the understanding, such as discerning, comparing, retaining, etc. (sects 21–9). Again following Draft A, Locke next outlined the knowledge we have from simple ideas (sects 32–40), following this with discussions of extension and number (sects 41–52), then recapitulating his conclusions to date (sects 53–9).

Turning to complex ideas, Locke discussed the ideas of substances (sects 60–3), including collective substances, for example, an army. This occasioned an extended treatment of the importance of words, with Locke discussing the different types of words, their difficulties and imperfections (sects 64–93f). Though inelegantly located within Draft B, it provided a place for a topic that had repeatedly appeared in Draft A, and which Locke clearly thought one of the most important innovations of his project. It also served as a prelude to Book III of the *Essay*. Locke next sought to determine what knowledge we have of substances (sects 93g–95).

Considering relations (sects 96–128), Locke gave a detailed treatment of time and duration, topics hardly mentioned in Draft A. Locke extensively revised his treatment during correction of the Draft, adding two new gatherings to accommodate this discussion (sects 101–28, cf. Walmsley, 2006, pp. 332–3).

Locke initially paused here, the remaining sections being written at a later date (Walmsley, 2006, *passim*). Resuming his work, Locke added two more sections on duration (sects 129–30), a treatment of cause and effect (sects 131–41), and relations of place (sects 141–4). The final sections of the Draft concerned 'relations principally belonging to men' (Draft B, contents, p. 97, cf. sects 145–62, pp. 260–70), and concluded with a discussion of moral relations, largely derived from Draft A, and entailing the same complications. Regarding universal moral rules, Locke once more deferred discussion 'till a fit place to speake of these viz God & the Law of Nature' (Draft B, sect. 160, p. 269). The Draft ends abruptly only two sections later, half-way through a sentence.

If Locke made little progress on morality, his thinking elsewhere expanded greatly. Where scholastic 'essence' and 'species' were discussed only in passing in Draft A, Draft B presented a rigorous analysis: 'that only is properly essential to any species expressed by any name, which is one of those simple Ideas that always goes to makeing up that complex Idea which either common usage or a definition hath applyd that specific name to' (Draft B, sect. 73, p. 179). 'Species' were merely stipulated similarities amongst objects without ontological significance. Aristotelian 'forms' were dismissed as 'unintelligible' (Draft B, sect. 72, pp. 176–7).

This criticism of scholasticism was coupled with more aggressive support for corpuscular theory. Locke asserted that 'The efficacy of causes can be imagind to be noething but motion' (Draft B, contents, p. 97, cf. sect. 138, p. 256). Thus, when considering how ideas are produced in us, we can only conceive this to happen mechanically, allowing us to infer that

> sensible qualitys in bodies as heate cold colours smels tasts & all the objects of sense & the Ideas thereof produced in us are probably in the bodys wherein we imagin they reside noe thing but different bulke & figure & in us those appeareances or sensations of them are noe thing but the effects of various impulses made upon our organs by particles or little masses of bodys of different sise figure & motion (Draft B, sect. 94, p. 209).

This allowed Locke to identify the 'primary qualitys or propertys of body viz. Extension & cohæsion of parts' (Draft B, sect. 94, p. 210), a precursor to the *Essay*'s primary and secondary quality distinction.

There was no systematic treatment of MODES in the early Drafts, but they were mentioned in Draft B, often as insertions. An interesting example occurs in a sheet inserted into sect. 98, where Locke listed the types of ideas he had dealt with 'v.g. simple Ideas. Substances. Modes

& even Relations' (Draft B, sect. 98, p. 219). Locke apparently conceived the taxonomy of complex ideas that would become standard in the *Essay*, but at a late stage of Draft B's composition – too late to affect the Draft's structure, but not too late for minor modifications to be made to the manuscript as Locke reviewed his work. For example, in sect. 97, Locke inserted 'modes' into the text some five times (Draft B, sect. 97, p. 217). Locke appears to have gone back to Draft A, and inserted modes there also (Draft A, sect. 6, p. 16, sect. 27, p. 49).

Locke also revised his opinion of 'demonstration'. In Draft A, he had derided this practice, but in Draft B, in the context of mathematics, 'when we would arive at that great certainty which we call Demonstration. we usualy appeale to our eyes'. He continued with 'what we come to know this way is not by proofe but INTUITION', which, he held was 'noe thing else but shewing men how they shall see right' (Draft B, sect. 44, p. 153). Locke believed that demonstration was nothing more than extended intuition, anticipating the position later expressed in the *Essay*.

While improving on Draft A, Draft B had its own structural problems. There was no consistent treatment of time, space and number, each regarded as both simple idea and relation. Locke provided separate accounts of the knowledge consequent to both simple and complex ideas. Since there was no unified discussion of knowledge, Draft B had no natural place for a treatment of faith, probability and opinion, and this discussion was omitted from the draft.

In April 1672 Ashley was created Earl of SHAFTESBURY and in November appointed Lord Chancellor. Locke's workload increased commensurately, and his health worsened. To remedy this, from 1675 to 1679 Locke travelled in France, recording occasional notes on his 'Essay' in his journals. Thus, for example, having covered time in Draft B, Locke wrote several entries on space, extension and body in the first half of 1676. The most extensive of these, written on 20 June, was later to comprise the bulk of *Essay*, II.xiii (Locke, 1936, pp. 77–80). While space was still presented as a relation, it was firmly differentiated from body, distancing Locke from Descartes, where the earlier Drafts had been ambivalent about the Cartesian position (Draft A, sect. 27, pp. 45–6; Draft B, sect. 29, p. 139).

On 13 July Locke noted four basic types of simple ideas of reflection – perception, willing, pleasure and pain – these latter two, he believed 'joyn themselves upon occasion and are produced by allmost all the Ideas both of body and minde' (Locke, 1936, pp. 80–1). An entry written three days later gave a detailed exposition of these new ideas, noting that 'To know our passions, then, and to have right ideas of them, we ought to consider pleasure and pain and the things that produce them in us, and how they operate and move us' (*ELN*, p. 265). Pleasure and pain are the sole motivations; desire 'is nothing but a pain the mind suffers in the absence of some good' (*ELN*, p. 270), leading to a discussion of the idea of power. These reflections were to form the basis of *Essay*, II.xx–xxi.

Philosophical entries were fewer in 1677, often concerning more general matters – the nature of the understanding, what it was suited to, and how it weighed arguments (Locke, 1936, pp. 84–90, 90–1, 97–8). In late 1677 and early 1678 Locke returned to the question of space in several entries (op. cit., pp. 94–6, 99–103, 105). That some version of the 'Essay' accompanied Locke while in France is evidenced by the fact that, on 2 July 1678, when leaving Paris for a trip, he 'Put into a black trunck to be left at Madame Herinx's' … 'Essay de Intellctu fol.' (Lough, 1953, p. 202).

Returning to England in 1679, Locke found himself in the midst of the Exclusion Crisis, in which Shaftesbury was playing an active role. These distractions seem to have kept Locke from his 'Essay' – there are fewer notes in his journals from this period. Nonetheless, those that do appear are often significant. On 26 June 1681 Locke proposed that there were 'two sorts of knowledg in the world generall and

particular founded upon two different principles i.e. true Ideas and matter of fact or history' (Locke, 1936, p. 116). Concerning mathematics, for example, 'he that hath the true Idea of a triangle or circle is capeable of knowing any demonstration concerning these figures' (ibid.) – building on his views of demonstration in Draft B. But, Locke went on, any 'true Ideas' can found demonstration, 'which the minde being capeable of haveing of morall things as well as figure I cannot but think morality as well as mathematiques capeable of demonstration' (op. cit., p. 117). Moral reasoning could provide certainty; the questions of 'morality and reveal'd religion' Locke had set out to investigate might be definitively resolved.

Notes from 1682 concerned religious 'ENTHUSIASM' (op. cit., pp. 119–21, 123–5) – religious convictions 'if there be noe proofs of them they can passe for noething but mear imaginations of the phansy' (op. cit., p. 119), again setting clear bounds for the *Essay*'s initial subject. Finally, on 5 June 1683 Locke made a brief but consequential note:

> The identity of persons lies not in having the same numericall body made up of the same particles, nor if the minde consists of corporeal spirits in their being the same, but in the memory and knowledg of ones part self and actions continued on under consciousnesse of being the same person whereby every man ownes himself (Dewhurst, 1963, pp. 222–3).

Locke had identified, and plausibly resolved, a new philosophical issue – that of PERSONAL IDENTITY.

News of the Rye House plot became public a week later. Given the resulting political climate, and his former association with Shaftesbury, Locke thought it prudent to withdraw to the Netherlands. There, he found time to set his thoughts on human understanding into a coherent order. Writing to the Earl of Pembroke in November 1684, Locke defended himself against accusations that he had written libellous pamphlets explaining that 'upon that my old theme de Intellectu humano (on which your Lordship knows I have been a good while a hammering), has my head been beating' (*Corr.*, vol. ii, p. 665). Locke offered 'to present to your Lordships view by the first opportunity a part of what I have been doeing here' (op. cit., p. 666). To that end, Locke sent an 'Epitome' of his 'Essay' to Pembroke in May 1685 (Walmsley, 2004, *passim*), a copy of which still survives.

Comprising highly compressed abbreviations of Locke's work to date, the 'Epitome' has the same basic structure and content as the published *Essay*. Book I dealt with innate ideas, but since this was only a propaedeutic to the larger project, it was referenced only to note its omission. Book II dealt with ideas. This began with a consideration of the origin of simple ideas through sensation, from one sense or many, ideas of reflection and ideas from both. Locke then warned us that though we may think these simple ideas are 'resemblances of something in the objects that produce them in us ... for the most part, they are not' (King, 1830, pp. 235–6). Developing his thinking on mechanism from Draft B, Locke explained that there are different kinds of qualities of bodies. Solidity, extension, figure, number, motion or rest were the 'original qualities' of body, since 'whatsoever state body is put ... [they are] ... always inseperable from it' (op. cit., p. 237). Locke next considered 'how bodies operate one upon another; and the only way intelligible to me is by impulse' (ibid.). Thus, when something produces an idea in us of these original qualities, for example, by sight, 'the impulse made on the organ must be by some insensible particles coming from the object to the eyes, and by a continuation of that motion to the brain, those ideas are produced in us' (ibid.). Equally, Locke continued, 'by the same way we may also conceive how the ideas of the colour and smell of a violet may as well be produced in us as of its figure, viz. by a certain impulse on our eyes or noses' (ibid.). Consequently, we can distinguish these original

or PRIMARY QUALITIES from the secondary, and infer that 'the ideas of the primary qualities of bodies are resemblances of them, and their archetypes do really exist in the bodies themselves; but the ideas produced in us by these secondary qualities have no resemblance of them at all' (op. cit., p. 238).

Expanding upon his work in Draft B, Locke next considered the ideas of space, time, NUMBER AND INFINITY. He then turned to ideas of pleasure and pain, and their fundamental role in morality: 'whatsoever, has an aptness to cause, increase, or continue pleasure in us, or to lessen or shorten any pain, we call good, and the contrary we call evil' (op. cit., p. 245). As in his journal notes, this led to a consideration of power. Just 171 words long, this ended with the thought that 'The power we find in ourselves to act, or not to act, conformable to such preference of our minds, gives us the idea we call liberty' (op. cit., p. 247). This hardly presages the fact that the chapter on this subject was eventually to become the *Essay*'s longest.

Locke turned next to complex ideas, dividing them into substances, modes and relations. Concerning substances, Locke, unusually, presented an argument that appeared in no other version of the *Essay*. Concerning body, Locke asked:

> what other idea a man has of body, but of solidity, extension, and mobility, joined together, which are all simple ideas received from sense. Perhaps some one here will be ready to say, that to have a complete idea of body, the idea of substance must be added to solidity and extension. But of him that makes that objection, I shall demand what his idea of substance is? (op. cit., p. 248)

He concluded that:

> substance in both is but a supposed but unknown substratum of those qualities, something, we know not what, that supports their existence; so that all the

ideas we have of the substance of anything is an obscure idea of what it does, and not any idea of what it is (op. cit., p. 249).

This account notably fails to convey Locke's view that the understanding of necessity infers the idea of substance to explain the coherence of our ideas of objects. As he had previously, he noted the difficulties in the ideas of both matter and spirit, now adding a critique of Bernoulli's pressure explanation for the coherence of matter. Our idea of God, as in Draft B, was just that of our own understanding and power multiplied, so all other ideas of substances are just combinations of our simple ideas. Locke next distinguished modes, simple or mixed, combining the same or different ideas, respectively. And finally, at the end of Book II, the 'Epitome' provides a summary of relations (though it does not touch on any specific topic in detail).

From the first sections of Draft A, and to his own apparent surprise, Locke had noted the importance of words to his project. The 'Epitome' now devoted Book III to their consideration, further altering the structure he had planned for his work. He began by noting that it 'was impossible to discourse of knowledge with the clearness that one should, without first saying something first of words and language' (op. cit., p. 255). His thinking had advanced markedly from Draft B, and was remarkably close to the published *Essay*. Locke dealt with the signification of words, general terms, NAMES of simple ideas, modes, relations and substances, the imperfection and abuses of words, and the remedies that might be applied to these. He ended with a brief reference to differences between abstract and concrete terms. Locke's paraphrasing is also arguably more effective than it had been in Book II – the sections are longer, the points clearer, the import more evident.

Since our ideas are invisible to one another, Locke believed, in order to communicate, we create signs for them. The most convenient of these signs, articulate sounds, we call words. Words, in short, 'are signs of ideas' (op. cit., p.

256). To facilitate communication, people make two additional suppositions – 'that they are signs of ideas in the mind of him with whom we communicate' and 'that words stand not only for ideas, but for the things themselves' (op. cit., p. 257). Regarding general terms, Locke believed they stood for general ideas: 'ideas become general only by being abstracted from time and place and other particularities, that make them the representatives only of individuals, by which separation of some ideas which annexed to them make them particular, they are made capable of agreeing to several particulars' (op. cit., p. 258). This separation theory of ABSTRACTION, somewhat redolent of scholastic accounts, had not appeared in either earlier Draft. Having reduced scholastic genus and species to complex ideas in Draft B, Locke could now state that they were nothing but these abstract ideas.

This then allowed Locke to redefine the scholastic concept of 'essence'. He stated that 'every particular thing has a real constitution by which it is what it is', but that the scholastics, in considering genus and species, 'commonly look on ESSENCES to belong to the sorts of things' – abstract ideas. Locke now distinguished these two types of 'essence': 'The first of these may be called the real, the second the nominal essence, which sometimes are the same, sometimes quite different one from another' (op. cit., p. 259). For example, in simple ideas and modes, they are identical, but 'The names of substances signify only their nominal essence, and not their real essence' (op. cit., p. 262):

> sensible qualities, make up the complex idea men have in their minds, to which they give the name gold; but the texture of the insensible parts, or whatever else it be, on which these sensible qualities depend, which is its real constitution or essence, is quite a different thing ... but since we have no idea of that constitution, and can signify nothing by our words but the ideas we have, our name gold cannot signify that real essence (op. cit., pp. 262–3).

The remainder of Book III outlined how words can obscure knowledge, why people might undertake such obfuscation, and what might be done to remedy this. Here Locke expanded upon the many criticisms of scholasticism from the early Drafts. He also considered how people might avoid obscurity in their use of words, exemplifying a reformist tendency evident throughout the writing of the *Essay*.

The Epitome's summary of Book IV is also close to the published *Essay*. Locke considered knowledge in general, then dealt with its degrees, extent and reality. Holding that 'knowledge is nothing but the perception of the agreement or disagreement of any two ideas', he noted its four classes: identity, coexistence, real existence and relation (op. cit., p. 275). The immediate perception of agreement or disagreement of ideas he termed 'intuition' and reintroduced the scholastic term 'demonstration' as '[w]hen the agreement or disagreement of any two ideas cannot be immediately perceived, … the mind makes use of the intervention of other ideas to show it', as hinted in his Draft B remarks (op. cit., p. 277). Our ideas set the boundaries to our knowledge, and within these boundaries, not all ideas can be connected or compared. Moreover, knowledge of things outside us, confined to 'the actual presence of particular things to our senses, is much narrower than either of the former' (op. cit., pp. 278–9). Human knowledge is thus severely limited in scope. Knowledge derived through ideas is real in so far as our ideas are conformable to the reality of things. Since simple ideas cannot be made by the mind, they must conform to the powers that produce them, so knowledge of them is real (op. cit., p. 281). Modes and relations are created by the understanding and cannot but conform to themselves (op. cit., pp. 281–2). Knowledge of substances is again different, however – since we cannot know the internal constitution of things, our knowledge of substances is generally very limited.

Having built this account of knowledge, Locke developed his account of truth.

Expanding upon his work in Draft A, he believed truth was 'the joining or separating of signs according as thing themselves agree or disagree' (op. cit., pp. 282–3). These signs 'being of two sorts, viz. ideas and words', there are both verbal and mental truths (op. cit., p. 283). As in Sections 27–9 of Draft A, Locke then outlined the different types of universal truths, the content and relative unimportance of scholastic maxims, and the trifling propositions they are apt to engender.

Turning to existence, Locke stated that 'The knowledge of existence goes no further than particulars of our own existences' (op. cit., p. 287). Regarding God, Locke believed that 'there is demonstration, for which we need go no farther than ourselves for a proof' (ibid.), but broke off without providing this, implying that it was not yet drafted to his satisfaction. Regarding the existence of everything else, Locke believed 'our knowledge reaches … as far as our senses, and no further' (ibid.), again strictly limiting our knowledge.

Given these restrictions, Locke next considered how we might improve our knowledge – in substances through 'experiment and observation in particulars', in modes and relations through 'clear and steady ideas' (op. cit., p. 288). His discussion of knowledge complete, Locke provided an account of judgement, probability, assent (and where it can go awry), reason, faith and revelation, drawing heavily on his initial thinking on these matters from Draft A. Book IV concluded with a threefold division of the sciences – 'Φυσική' – 'the knowledge of things', 'Πρακτική' – 'the rule of operation … which concern our conduct', and 'Σημιωτική' – 'the knowledge of signs, i.e. ideas and words' (op. cit., p. 293).

It is perhaps unremarkable that Locke's thinking was so far advanced at this point in the *Essay*'s composition – he had, after all, been working on the subject for thirteen years. What might occasion more surprise is that Locke had not made more progress towards his original goal – a discussion of our conduct. While he touched on good and evil in his consideration of pleasure and pain, indicated his belief in a proof of the existence of God, noted once again that 'that Ethics might be improved to a much greater degree of certainty, if men, affixing moral names to clear and settled ideas, could with freedom and indifferency pursue them' (op. cit., pp. 288–9), carefully distinguished faith and reason, and included our conduct as one of the three key fields of human knowledge, there is no consistent ethical theory in his work. Locke certainly set the bounds of human knowledge, but this apparently did not help him resolve the problems he set out to examine.

Locke continued to refine his thinking over the next several months, producing new versions of Books I and II in the early part of 1686, a copy of which, known as Draft C, is still extant (Walmsley, 2004, p. 222). Book I expanded upon the first sixteen sections of Draft B, but reordered the text so that speculative principles were dealt with before practical. Book II differed from the Epitome in several instances, most notably in several additions to the text. Where the Epitome had touched on the FACULTIES of the understanding in passing, Draft C provided a chapter for each of perception, retention, discerning, comparing, composing and denomination and abstraction. Where, in the Epitome, consideration of complex ideas and modes began after the idea of power, in Draft C this was brought forward immediately to follow discussion of the capacities – most likely because space, time and infinity, whilst grounded in simple ideas, were much more than that. Before considering other modes, Locke inserted a new chapter on Solidity – an important part of his distinction between space and body, presumably, therefore, requiring additional elucidation. Following Section 61 of Draft B, Locke added a chapter on the collective ideas of substances.

In the 'Epitome', Book II ended with a consideration of relations. Consistent with this in Draft C, at the end of Book II, Chapter 31, 'Of other Relations', Locke appended 'Sic cogitavit JL', indicating the end of the work. However, taking advantage of the flexibility of his writing method, he added two new gatherings to accommodate the new chapters 'Of Clear & Destinct Obscure & confused Ideas' and 'Of Real & Phantasticall Adequate & inadequate Ideas', providing additional guidance for the reformation of our ideas. He also introduced a new method of textual correction: inserting and binding small strips of paper into gatherings to replace deleted text – for example, in Draft C, II.xviii.13.

Locke produced new versions of Book III in August 1686, and Book IV in December (Walmsley, 2004, p. 222). He also considered new additions. Two of these survive amongst his manuscripts; an extended treatment of the division of the sciences, and a chapter entitled 'Of Ethick in General', intended to be the twentieth and twenty-first chapters of Book IV, and thus the conclusion of the *Essay* (Oxford, Bodleian Library, MS Locke c.28, fols 155–6, 145–52 cf. *ELN*, p. 69). Perhaps Locke felt that, having set the limits of human understanding, he should, finally, consider the subject that had prompted the writing of the *Essay*.

Locke asserted that good and evil were a consequence of pleasure and pain, but also supposed a NATURAL LAW we must all obey. Section 8 initially combined these two principles, revealing their inherent tension:

This moral rectitude which when considered is conformity to the naturall law of god, would signifie noething and moral goodnesse be noe reason to direct my action were there not really pleasure that would follow from the doeing of it and pain avoided greater than is to be found in the action it self (op. cit., fol. 149v).

Not all moral actions are pleasurable, nor immoral painful. Locke deleted this passage. In Sections 10 and 11, he returned to the final sections of Draft B, taking the text almost word for word, and supposing an ultimate moral law 'till a fit place to Speak of these viz God and the Law of nature' (op. cit., fol. 151r cf. Draft B, sect. 160, p. 269). In Draft B, he had not kept this promise. In the next section of this projected chapter, he laid out his plan to do so:

To establish morality therefor upon its proper basis and such foundations as may carry an obligation with them we must first prove a law which always supposes a law maker ... The next thing then to shew is that there are certain rules certain dictates which it is his will all men should conforme their actions to, and that this will of his is sufficiently promulgated and made known to all mankinde (op. cit., fol. 152r).

The discussion abruptly ends here – much as it had in Draft B. Though Locke had already written extensively on the Law of Nature during his time at Oxford, and had much material he could have reused to substantiate his arguments, he did not do so. Perhaps he felt he was straying too far from the *Essay*'s project, perhaps that it would lengthen an already lengthy work. But the suspicion remains that he could not reconcile his ethical theory with traditional Christianity, and could not firmly ground knowledge of a universal law, once he had dismissed innatism. The chapter was scrapped; Locke never provided a detailed treatment of ethics (*ELN*, pp. 9–10, 75).

Having confirmed Pembroke's support for his work, Locke set about publishing the 'Epitome', and then the *Essay* proper. The former found a home in the *Bibliothèque Universelle et Historique*, a journal edited by Locke's friend Jean Le Clerc. Translated into French by Le Clerc, Locke's work appeared in spring 1688 under the title 'Extrait d'un Livre Anglois qui n'est pas encore publié, intitulé ESSAI PHILOSOPHIQUE concernant L'EN-TENDEMENT' (Locke, 1688). Though closely corresponding to the Epitome, there were a number of changes, reflecting the developments in the *Essay*'s structure. As indicated by Draft C, these were mostly additions to Book II. The Extrait included summary chapters on perception and reten-

tion. It also included a summary of the operations of mind on its ideas – '1. Les discerner ou les distinguer: 2. Les comparer: 3. Les composer & les étendre: 4. & en former des abstractions' (op. cit., p. 59) – compressing several chapters from Draft C into one. As in Draft C, Locke included a chapter on solidity after that on Infinity, and followed it with chapters on other simple modes, and modes of thinking. As he had in Draft C, Locke drew forward the discussion of mixed modes that had appeared at the end of the Epitome's summary chapter on substance, and added it to the chapter on complex ideas which, in the Extrait, still preceded that on substance. Locke also added summaries of the chapters on clear and distinct, and real and fantastical ideas. He then split adequate and inadequate ideas into their own chapters, and added a new section on true and false ideas, further extending Book II. The sole addition to Books III and IV was the proof of God's existence that had been indicated, but not included, in the 'Epitome'. This comprised a translation of what would, with a few minor changes, become the first six sections of the corresponding chapter in the *Essay* (Hill and Milton, 2003, p. 7).

Locke had copies of his abridgement printed separately and, appending a dedication to Pembroke, sent them to friends and colleagues for their opinion. Not every response was positive – BOYLE thought 'the author either knew not or concealed the menstruum for the greate work' (David Thomas to Locke, 10 May 1688, *Corr.*, vol. iii, p. 453). The Glorious Revolution had changed England's political climate and in February 1689 Locke felt safe enough to return home. Back in London, he signed a contract to publish the *Essay* with Thomas Basset on 24 May (*Essay*, p. xv). He had made further changes since the publication of the Extrait, again, for the most part, in Book II. The chapter on Solidity, which had succeeded that on Infinity, now succeeded that on 'Ideas of One Sense'. In addition, he reworked his thinking on Complex ideas into a single chapter preceding his discussions of space, time and infinity. Combining content from Draft C and the Epitome, this more clearly distinguished simple and complex ideas, categorized the different types of complex ideas, and furnished brief introductions to modes, substances and relations. Locke added a chapter 'Of Particles' to Book III and made 'Of Wrong Assent, or Error' the penultimate chapter of Book IV. As Locke himself conceded, his method of composition made the published *Essay* somewhat digressive, rambling and repetitive (*Essay*, p. 8).

Locke received his own bound copies in early December (*Essay*, p. xv), and in a letter on the 19th, Tyrrell reported that the *Essay* 'came downe to oxford last weeke and many copyes are sold of it, and I hear it is well approved of by those who have begun the readeing of it (*Corr.*, vol. iii, p. 763). Yet questions soon emerged, and, on 30 June 1690 Tyrrell reported that 'discourseing with some thinke-ing men at Oxford ... I found them dissatisfied with what you have sayed concerning the Law of nature, (or reason,) whereby we distinguish moral good, from evil and vertue, from vice' (*Corr.*, vol. iv, p. 101), providing a detailed review of their critiques. Locke's reply does not survive, but was apparently intemperate –Tyrrell ended his next letter 'if you doe not like that I should tell you what objections the world make against what you write, I shall for the future be more reserved' (*Corr.*, vol. iv, p. 109). But he also provided suggestions as to how Locke might meet these objections:

I know you have made long since a Treatise or Lectures upon the Law of nature which I could wish you would revise, and make publick, since I know none more able, then your self to doe it. and which would likewise make a second part to the former worke (ibid.).

Tyrrell was apparently unaware that Locke had already tried and failed to complete the *Essay* in exactly this manner.

Locke's work had its defenders, not least because it provided a philosophical foundation for the new science. One such supporter, William Molyneux, dedicated his 1692 treatise on optics, *Dioptrica Nova*, to Locke. The two began a lengthy correspondence of significant consequence for the evolution of the *Essay*. Though Locke did not agree to Moyneux's request, in a letter of 27 August 1692, to create a '*Treatise of Morals*', drawn up according to the Hints you frequently give in Your Essay, Of their Being Demonstrable according to the Mathematical Method (*Corr.*, vol. iv, p. 508), he did seek Molyneux's advice on the next edition of the *Essay*. In a letter of 20 September 1692, Locke wondered 'whether it would not be better now to pare off, in a second edition, a great part of that which cannot but appear superfluous to an intelligent and attentive reader' (*Corr.*, vol. iv, p. 523). Molyneux saw no reason for concision: 'I never quarrelled with a book for being too prolix, especially where the prolixity is pleasant, and tends to the illustration of the matter in hand' (op. cit., p. 600). Molyneux did, however, suggest updates to Locke's work. Regarding power, Locke responded to Molyneux's questions by noting that VOLITION had a self-consciousness element. This emphasis on 'consciousness' found further expression in a new chapter that Molyneux had solicited: 'Of Identity and Diversity', con-cerning personal identity, expanding upon Locke's 1683 journal notes. The second edition's chapter on Perception also included 'the MOLYNEUX PROBLEM' – whether a man born blind and made to see could distinguish a sphere from a cube. Locke thought not. At Molyneux's request, Locke further added marginal summaries of each section, and an analytical index. He also made several changes of wording throughout to refine his views, express himself more clearly, or fix errata (*Essay*, pp. xix–xxv).

The new edition went to press in early 1694. Mindful of the owners of the first edition, Locke made a special request of the printer:

For as to the larger additions and alterations, I have obliged him, and he has promised me to print them by themselves, so that the former Edition may not be wholly lost to those who have it, but by the inserting in their proper places the passages that will be imprinted alone, to that purpose, the former Book may be made as little defective as possible (*Essay*, p. 12, n. 19).

Locke treated the printed book in the same way he had his manuscript – allowing for the insertion and binding of new gatherings and small fragments into the text to correct and expand upon his previous opinions. Publication was only one stage in the *Essay*'s evolution.

The book continued to sell well, and a third edition was produced in 1695 which, while it amended minor errors from the second, did not add any significant new content. But even as this edition was going to press, in a letter of 8 March, Locke mentioned possible new additions to Molyneux, suggesting something on 'Enthusiasm' and 'P. MALEBRANCHE's opinion concerning seeing all things in god' (*Corr.*, vol. v, p. 287), and then deciding, in a letter of 26 April, for the former and against the latter, preferring a new chapter on the 'Connexion of Ideas', since it 'has not, that I know, been hitherto consider'd and has, I guess, a greater influence upon our minds, than is usually taken notice of' (op. cit., pp. 352–3).

Locke's work had begun to provoke significant controversy, much along the lines Tyrrell had earlier outlined. The *Essay*'s denial of innate principles, the cursory discussion of natural law and the adoption of HEDONISM appeared to undercut Christian morality. Locke's focus on ideas seemed to engender scepticism. His account of substance appeared to eviscerate a fundamental ontological concept, if not dismiss it altogether – casting doubt on the Trinity. Locke's casual aside that, given our limited understanding, God might, for all we know, give matter the power to think (*E*, IV.iii.6), seemingly opened the door to materialism. Since Locke had not provided a coherent ethical or religious outlook in the *Essay*, a succession of critics – NORRIS, SERGEANT and BURNET – did it for him, implying that the *Essay* was at best misguided, at worst, a poorly disguised exhortation to atheism. These suspicions appeared vindicated by Toland's *Christianity not Mysterious* (London, 1696), which used Locke's epistemology to ground a critique of the Trinity and transubstantiation. This provoked a strong response from Edward STILLINGFLEET, Bishop of Worcester, in *A Discourse in Vindication of the Doctrine of the Trinity* (London, 1697). While Locke was much more responsive to compliments than criticism, Stillingfleet's rank necessitated some reply. The book began a series of open letters between the two about the *Essay* and its implications, ending only with Stillingfleet's death in 1699.

Locke's work on religious enthusiasm and the ASSOCIATION OF IDEAS, and their respective deleterious effects, set Locke thinking on how the understanding should conduct itself. Beginning in 1697, he set down a long series of reflections in a number of manuscripts. Projected to succeed his chapter on Enthusiasm in Book IV, 'Of the Conduct of the Understanding' would have been the *Essay*'s longest chapter, outlining the two basic errors to which the understanding was prey – a lack of determined ideas, and careless reasoning. However, the controversy with Stillingfleet distracted Locke from pursuing this planned addition. Thus, when the fourth edition was published in 1700, the last in Locke's lifetime, it only contained the new chapters II.xxxiii 'Of the Association of Ideas' and IV.xix 'Of Enthusiasm', as well as numerous other minor changes, which Locke again arranged to be printed separately so that they could be bound into copies of previous editions (*Essay*, pp. xxviii–xxxi). Locke's final years were devoted to theological matters, but he still managed to make some small updates to his *Essay*, most notably in the chapter on Power. These were included in the fifth edition, published two years after his death (*Essay*, pp. xxxi–xxxiii).

The *Essay* remained unfinished. As his work progressed, Locke became more interested in the nature of the understanding than in the questions of 'morality and reveal'd religion' he had originally set out to investigate. He became as interested in fixing the problems of the understanding as cataloguing them, opening large new areas of enquiry that he could never really hope to compass. Perhaps this was only to be expected in a work whose method of composition encouraged endless expansion, and whose pursuit was more profitable than its intended conclusion.

BIBLIOGRAPHY
Primary Sources
Locke, John, 'Extrait d'un Livre Anglois qui n'est pas encore publié, intitulé ESSAI PHILOSOPHIQUE concernant L'ENTENDEMENT', *Bibliothèque Universelle et Historique*, vol. viii (1688), pp. 49–142.
———, *An Early Draft of Locke's* Essay: *Together with Excerpts from His Journals*, ed. R.I. Aaron and Jocelyn Gibb (Oxford, 1936).
———, *Abstract of the* Essay, in P. King, *The Life of John Locke* (London, 1830), vol. ii, pp. 231–93.

Secondary Sources
Dewhurst, K., *John Locke: Physician and Philosopher* (London, 1963).
Hill, J., and J.R. Milton, 'The Epitome (Abrégé) of Locke's *Essay*', in Peter R. Anstey (ed.), *The Philosophy of John Locke: New Perspectives* (London, 2003), pp. 3–25.
Lough, John, *Locke's Travels in France, 1675–1679* (Cambridge, 1953).
Walmsley, J., 'Dating the 'Epitome' of the *Essay*', *Locke Studies*, vol. iv (2004), pp. 205–22.
———, 'Locke, Mechanism and Draft B, a Correction', *The British Journal for the History of Philosophy*, vol. xiv (2006), pp. 331–5.
Woolhouse, R.S., 'Lady Masham's Account of Locke', *Locke Studies*, vol. iii (2003), pp. 167–93.

Jonathan Walmsley

TWO TREATISES OF GOVERNMENT

I

Locke's main work on political theory contains two separate treatises, which are generally seen as unequal in importance and ambition. The first, which 'detects and overthrows' 'the false principles and foundation of Sir Robert FILMER, and his followers' (*TTG*, title page), is now often considered the lesser treatise in quality. It does not have the virtue of being complete either; its last paragraph, number 169, breaks off in the middle of a sentence, and the rest is missing. The lost portion of Locke's manuscript was, he noted in the preface to his work, longer than the extant parts he had published in 1689. Present-day commentators have habitually allotted a greater significance to the 'Second Treatise'. Entitled 'An essay concerning the true original, extent, and end of civil government', it runs to 243 paragraphs. After a detailed and thorough demolition, in the 'First Treatise', of Filmer's theory of patriarchal and absolutist kingship, in the 'Second' Locke turned to discuss such issues as civil liberty, political obligation, authority and property in more general and abstract terms, and also to defend the right of armed resistance against tyrants.

Today the 'Second Treatise' has the status of being considered the humus from which political liberalism grew subsequently; it has the status of one of the canonical works defining the horizon of liberal culture in the West. During the Cold War it was alleged that just as the Eastern bloc referred to Karl Marx's works in order to justify its practices of government, so the West could rely on Lockean ideas. Hence, purportedly, there took place an intellectual war between Marxism and Lockean principles (cf., for instance, Lloyd Thomas, 1995, pp. 11–12). Historians and political commentators have argued with force that Marx's authentic aims, however flawed, should not be linked to the reality of communist totalitarianism in Eastern Europe and Asia. But fewer have undertaken the equally relevant task of highlighting the distance between Locke's original aspirations and ours in our representative democracies and capitalist societies (on this distance, see Dunn, 1969 and 1990; on the reception of Locke's politics, see Goldie, 1999 and 2004). Typically, both the critics and the defenders of modern liberalism have instead endorsed the view that our contemporary language of individualist politics is grounded in a tradition which stretches back to Locke's vision of man and society (see, e.g., Colletti, 1972, esp. pp. 150–1; Macpherson, 1973, pp. 224–37; Simmons, 1992, e.g. p. 14; Waldron, 1993, p. 1).

It is, then, commonplace to assume that there is something distinctly 'modern' about the 'Second Treatise'. What are Locke's credentials as a man of modernity? When seen from our contemporary vantage point, there are six key assertions in the 'Second Treatise'. The first is that the human condition without (and before) the establishment of political society and government is a *state of nature*. Human beings are, by nature, in this state 'of perfect Equality' and 'of perfect Freedom' (*TTG* II.4–7), in which there are no political institutions. In the STATE OF NATURE individuals possess *natural rights*; in practice, however, it may be impossible for them to uphold their rights as they cannot, when disputes over their rights arise, appeal to any judge or authority in order to resolve the dispute. For instance, although an individual has a particular natural right, 'yet the Enjoyment of it is very uncertain, and constantly exposed to the Invasion of others'. The state of nature is a condition, 'which however free, is full of fears and continual dangers' (*TTG* II.123). There is, then, always a risk of the state of nature collapsing

into a state of war. The instability and precariousness of their condition makes individuals willing to establish a political society – or what Locke also termed 'civil society' – 'for the mutual Preservation of their Lives, Liberties and Estates, which I call by the general Name, Property' (*TTG* II.123). The 'Second Treatise' is famous for the emphasis on individuals as rightholders who enter into society to protect their natural rights – their 'property'. The way in which early-modern theorists of natural jurisprudence – and perhaps especially Locke – inflected the language of natural rights is usually held to have laid the groundwork for our present-day notions of *human rights*.

The second key assertion is that the foundational moral legitimacy of a political society depends on the consent of all its full members. Locke insisted that individuals must not be coerced into leaving the state of nature and its freedom: 'Men being ... by Nature, all free, equal and independent, no one can be put out of this Estate, and subjected to the Political Power of another, without his own Consent' (*TTG* II.95). The Lockean theme of government by consent reverberates powerfully through our current discussions about representative government, but in fact we have largely abandoned Locke's original stance on the issue. According to the 'Second Treatise', no one is a full member of a political society without having consented to it. In Locke's England a son, for example, was *de facto* born under the English monarchy, but *de jure* 'a Child is born a Subject of no Country or Government ... there is no Tye upon him by his Father being a Subject of this Kingdom'. When he comes of age, 'he is a Free-man, at liberty' to 'unite himself to' any existing country or to help establish a new society (*TTG* II.118).

This understanding of consent as the source of legitimacy entails the third key point: all legitimate political societies arise from voluntary agreement between individuals who quit the state of nature, form a community and submit themselves to the 'determination of the majority' in the community, and subsequently decide what constitutional form of government to create. Modern scholars refer habitually to this foundational agreement as the 'social contract'. In the 'Second Treatise' it is typically called a 'compact', the 'original Compact' (*TTG* II.97; see CONSENT AND SOCIAL CONTRACT). It is the equal individuals who make, first, the compact with each other and, then, the collective majority decision to delegate their power to specific trustees, that is, legislators. There is no social contract between people and government; government is only a trust. In passing, it is worth noting that Locke applied a similar approach to marriage: 'Conjugal Society is made by a voluntary Compact between Man and Woman' (*TTG* II.78).

The fourth key assertion is that, when individuals deliberate on which constitutional form of government to create, they cannot agree to be ruled by an absolute monarch. Hypothetically, if they were to transfer all power to a single individual, they would in effect renounce their own humanity. They would turn themselves into slaves, mere instruments of their master, who could use them and their property without any regard to their rights; a master-slave relationship would supersede rational citizenship. This 'Slavish Condition' would defeat the purpose of coming out of the state of nature and entering into civil society: it would compromise 'the great and chief end … of Mens uniting into Commonwealths, and putting themselves under Government', namely, 'the Preservation of their Property' (*TTG* II.124 and 149). Hence, while they 'might set up what form of Government they thought fit', they cannot choose absolute monarchy, which is 'inconsistent with Civil Society, and so can be no Form of Civil Government at all' (*TTG* II.90, 106, 220, and 243). What does this proviso have to do with modern liberalism? It is important because it may be taken to limit the ruler's power and, hence, to limit what government is entitled to do to any citizen and the citizen's property. When Locke's political philosophy is viewed in this perspective, it is a philosophy of limited government.

There remain two more key arguments, which may also be seen as corollaries of the previous arguments. The fifth concerns the problem of political sovereignty – that is, the problem of who ought to have the highest power in a society. According to the 'Second Treatise', whatever the chosen form of government, there obtains a separation of powers. Here it is important to guard against the present-day tendency to assimilate or confuse the doctrines of Locke and Montesquieu. The doctrine of the separation of powers, in its more familiar form, purportedly derived from Montesquieu's politics, has the objective of promoting civil liberty by vesting the state's power in the legislative, executive and judiciary institutions, which balance one another. In the 'Second Treatise', the trio of governmental powers is legislative, executive and federative power (*TTG* II.88 and 143–8). The judiciary, separate in Montesquieu's system, is subsumed under the legislative power; the separate federative power, which pertains to international relations, Montesquieu would subsume under the executive power. Strikingly, according to Locke, although 'the Executive and Federative Power of every Community be really distinct in themselves', they are usually wielded by the same persons or person, who may, moreover, also have 'a share in the Legislative' (*TTG* II.148, 151 and 159). All three powers may be vested in a single person because the aim is not to achieve a constitutional balance by placing the distinct functions of government on a comparatively equal footing. Rather, the aim is to establish that there is 'one Supream Power, which is the Legislative, to which all the rest are and must be subordinate'. The key point is that the executive and federative powers are to be controlled by the legislative power, which, in its turn, is controlled by the extra-constitutional power of the community that has entrusted the legislators with power. Hence, 'the Community may be said in this respect to be always the Supream Power' (*TTG* II.149).

This assertion eliminates the possibility of absolute monarchy and the passive subjection characteristic of ABSOLUTISM, and it implies a continual and vigorous exercise of individual rights against abuses of power. So long as the individuals who form the community are fully human – so long as they are not slaves, dehumanized automata – their community retains the supreme political power. On the other hand, should their legitimate ruler betray the trust and try to bring them into 'a Slavish Condition, they will always have a right ... to rid themselves of' the ruler (*TTG* II.149). This is the final key assertion in the 'Second Treatise': individuals are always entitled to take up arms against even a legitimate ruler if the ruler, in their judgement, has turned tyrant. They have a right to take human life. When they cannot appeal to the positive laws of their society, they can 'appeal to Heaven' and uphold their rights by killing the ruler who attempts to curtail their rights. After a successful revolution – to quote the last words of the book – 'the People have a Right to act as Supreme, and continue the Legislative in themselves, or erect a new Form, or under the old form place it in new hands, as they think good' (*TTG* II.168 and 243; see RESISTANCE AND REVOLUTION).

II

When we come to the 'First Treatise', we encounter a different atmosphere and literary form. At first glance, the 'Second Treatise', an exposition of Locke's own system, is the more accessible book today. Just what is the 'First Treatise'? Its original purpose was to free the English from the illusion, created by the seventeenth-century champions of absolutism, that 'they are Slaves, and ought to be so'. It offered a therapy for moral and political corruption, taking the form of a relentless criticism of FILMER's *Patriarcha*, 'a Book, which was to provide Chains for all Mankind' (*TTG* I.1). At the outset, Locke managed to summarize the contents of the *Patriarcha* and Filmer's other political writings in two sentences:

Filmer's system was 'no more but this, *That all Government is absolute Monarchy.* And the Ground he builds on, is this, *that no Man is Born free*' (*TTG* I.2).

In the seventeenth century such prominent absolutists as Grotius, HOBBES and Pufendorf started from the assumption that human beings, born free, alienate their natural freedom to the ruler. Filmer, by contrast, defended a theory of natural subjection which was patriarchal: the political relations in a monarchy were to mirror the relations characteristic of a patriarchal family and household where the father exercised natural and unlimited power over his wife, children, servants, labourers and property. In Filmer's patriarchalism, there was an essential analogy between family and state, between paternal and regal authority. In chapter 2 of the 'First Treatise', Locke glossed this position by insisting that, according to Filmer, 'a Father or a Prince' has such power 'over the Lives, Liberties, and Estates of his Children and Subjects ... that he may take or alienate their Estates, sell, castrate, or use their Persons as he pleases, they being all his Slaves, and he Lord or Proprietor of every Thing, and his unbounded Will their Law' (*TTG* I.9). It is of crucial importance that when Locke began writing the *Two Treatises*, he set out to refute Filmer's defence of natural subjection – rather than, say, Hobbes's absolutist theory of natural freedom – because the challenge presented by Filmer shaped Locke's own theory.

Filmer's patriarchalism was connected to his interpretation of Mosaic history. The great claim Filmer made was that God had given the world and everything in it to the first man, Adam, whose proprietary monopoly and absolute rulership stood as a paradigm for all his male heirs, including the king of Filmer's England (cf. *TTG* I.67). Locke's 'First Treatise' was primarily an effort to contest Filmer's deployment of Scripture proofs from Genesis; it was not an attempt to undermine the discourse of politics rooted in biblical exegesis so much as an attempt to justify a rival reading of Scripture.

Both Filmer and Locke aimed to resolve problems posed by religious warfare and civil conflict in a confessionally fragmented Europe. In general, when early-modern thinkers tackled the core problem of how to pacify Europe, the central questions for them included the following: Who is supreme in constitution? Who determines succession to the throne? How should the royal prerogative be used? Can it be right to resist a regime that is seen as tyrannical? Much of the seventeenth-century controversy over these questions could be condensed into 'the Great Question which in all Ages has disturbed Mankind, and brought on them the greatest part of those Mischiefs which have ruin'd Cities, depopulated Countries'. According to the 'First Treatise', the great question was, 'Not whether there be Power in the World, nor whence it came, but who should have it' (*TTG* I.106). The answers given in the *Patriarcha* and the *Two Treatises* revealed diametrically opposite political imaginations. Filmer claimed that political power resides naturally in one individual, the king, who has inherited Adam's status, and others are simply to obey him. According to Locke, by contrast, each individual capable of reason has and ought to have power, and the individual's political obligations are to equals in a horizontal fashion, not to a superior in a vertical, hierarchical fashion (see Dunn, 1985, p. 65). Both answers were innovative, sweeping aside the historicizing traditions of ancient and mixed constitutionalism (cf. *TTG* II.103, and Tully, 1995, esp. pp. 70–8 and 150–1), but Locke's was perhaps the more radical and implausible in the reality of political life.

The case Locke wished to put in the *Two Treatises* was that individuals can and should act politically for themselves. In the 'First Treatise', his claim that people are able to govern themselves conditioned his interpretation of the Genesis story about the building of the city of Babel. He stressed that its building was 'not by the Command of one Monarch, but by the Consultation of many, a Free People … They built it for themselves as Free-men, not as Slaves for their Lord'. The builders were 'at liberty to part asunder, but desired to keep in one Body'. Babel's political cohesion did not depend on the Filmerian notion of men's being 'tyed together under the Government of one Monarch': it depended, in the absence of a monarchical hierarchy which would have put external pressure on the subject's will, on the free men's will to co-operate and on their common rationality (*TTG* I.146).

In the 'Second Treatise', Locke transposed his argument into the Grotian and Pufendorfian idiom of 'modern' natural jurisprudence (see NATURAL LAW; on the scholarly debate over the emergence of a 'modern' theory of natural law, see Haakonssen, 1996; Schneewind, 1998, pp. 58–140; Swanson, 1997; Tierney, 1997; Tuck, 1993; and Zagorin, 2000). In natural jurisprudence, the leitmotiv was the idea that natural law is universally binding upon all human beings and that it is obligatory independently of what other forms of law prescribe. In the 'Second Treatise', it supersedes all written, positive laws and can be used to judge their soundness: 'the Municipal Laws of Countries … are only so far right, as they are founded on the Law of Nature, by which they are to be regulated and interpreted' (*TTG* II.12). Who, then, has the power to judge whether the law of nature has been violated and to punish those who have transgressed it? In the state of nature – which is, importantly, 'not a State of Licence', but a state of freedom 'within the bounds of the Law of Nature' (*TTG* II.4, 6 and 7) – 'every Man hath a Right to punish the Offender, and be Executioner of the Law of Nature' (*TTG* II.8). This 'natural' practice of direct individual self-government is a defective system, partly because of human partiality (*TTG* II.124–5). Hence, according to Locke, individuals agree to form a self-governing community, which entrusts the 'executive power of the law of nature' (the power to enforce that which is objectively right) to legislators, who are trustees and representatives. As noted above, if legislators betray their trust, people can take back their original political power.

III

In order to recover the authentic spirit of Locke's political theory, it is essential to keep clearly in focus the historical circumstance that the *Two Treatises* did not result from academic research work into political philosophy. Neither Locke and his allies nor their opponents were professional philosophers. To free our historical imagination, it may also be beneficial to abstract, for the moment, from the assumptions that Locke was right against his adversaries and that Filmer's doctrine of patriarchal kingship must have turned into a quaint relic of the past as soon as Locke's refutation had appeared.

In Restoration England, FILMER *was* a man of the past: he had died in 1653; his longest work on politics, the *Patriarcha*, had been composed before the Civil War broke out, perhaps as early as in 1628–31, in defence of Charles I's regime (Sommerville, 1991). Nevertheless, when the first edition, dated 1680, of the *Patriarcha* appeared, Filmer's doctrine seemed to be a herald of what might be expected in Charles II's England. The *Patriarcha* was conscripted into the service of the 'Tory' ideology at the time of the so-called Exclusion Crisis. This crisis had its roots in the contention between 'Cavalier' royalists, who became Tories, and the 'Country' opposition, which modulated into the Whig movement, championed by the Earl of SHAFTESBURY, Locke's patron. The Whigs challenged the king by attempting to exclude James, the openly Roman Catholic heir to the throne, from the order of succession: their First Exclusion Bill was introduced into the Commons in 1679, followed by the Second in 1680 and the Third in 1681; each was defeated, either by the Lords' votes or the king's countermeasure, the dissolution of parliament.

After the Third Exclusion parliament had been dissolved in Oxford in March 1681, it appeared that Charles II had no intention of calling another parliament. England might, it was feared, head towards another civil war; however, it seemed more likely that the king would campaign vigorously and successfully against all dissent, exact his revenge on Whigs, ally himself with Louis XIV, and pave the way for a Roman Catholic dynasty. In 1682–3, the Whigs' efforts in parliament having failed, their radical flank may have been driven to plot to assassinate the king (Ashcraft, 1986; Marshall, 1994, esp. pp. 91–3, 212–20 and 241–3).

In the middle of 1681 James Tyrrell, who was at the time Locke's closest intellectual associate, published his attack on Filmer's doctrine, *Patriarcha non Monarcha*. In 1681–3 Algernon Sidney appears to have been drafting his refutation of Filmer, the *Discourses concerning Government*: a copy of the unfinished manuscript was discovered in Sidney's house when he was arrested on a charge of treason in June 1683, and was used as evidence of treasonable intent when he was sentenced to death. Locke's response to the challenge of Filmer falls into company with Tyrrell's and Sidney's, despite the fact that it was *published* in 1689 to justify the overthrow of James II's regime and to 'establish the Throne of our Great Restorer, Our present King William' (*TTG*, preface).

Whilst modern historians have made remarkable advances in the dating of the *Two Treatises*, the precise circumstances in which it was written still elude us and are likely to remain unclear, at least unless new manuscript evidence comes to light. Still, it now seems reasonably clear that the 'First Treatise' was sketched around 1680 and that the 'Second' was drafted sometime after the dissolution of the Oxford Parliament in 1681, when Sidney and others whom Locke knew may have canvassed tyrannicide as the solution to England's troubles. If so, Locke was drafting a violently seditious work during a time of precariousness and considerable danger. As there survives no manuscript version of the *Two Treatises*, historians are unable to ascertain which portions of the work he composed before leaving for the safety of the Dutch Republic in 1683 (Laslett, 1970, pp. 45–66; 1988, p. 35, pp. 46–7 and 50–1; Marshall, 1994, p. xvi, pp. 220–1 and 241–3; and cf. Wootton, 1993, p. 14, 21, pp. 72–3 and 77–89).

When he published the *Two Treatises* after his return to England in 1689, Locke did not contribute to debates akin to those conducted by today's academics so much as entered an arena of political contention that was inhabited predominantly by the clergy and the gentry. The first edition of Filmer's *Patriarcha* had been published at Archbishop Sancroft's instigation, and in 1685 Sancroft had aided Edmund Bohun to publish an improved edition. In the preface to his work Locke remarked that he 'should not have Writ against Sir Robert', 'a dead Adversary', had it not been for 'Men amongst us … crying up his Books, and espousing his Doctrine'. These men were clerics in the Church of England: 'the Pulpit' had 'publickly owned his Doctrine, and made it the Currant Divinity of the Times'; 'taking on them to be Teachers', the clergy had 'dangerously misled others' in their sermons (on preaching in England at the time, see Green, 2006).

For Locke, the deepest problem was the restoration of political life in a corrupt monarchy. If England was to be cleansed of royal and clerical hubris, the solution could not be narrowly constitutional. The primary solution, for Locke and his allies in the 1690s, was to re-educate people: to have a long revolution, or even a permanent revolution, in the form of an educational process. One stage of this process was to refute Filmer's *Patriarcha*, used 'by such, whose Skill and Business it is to raise a Dust, and [who] would blind the People, the better to mislead them' (adapted from *TTG* I.1). During the Allegiance Controversy, which followed the Revolution of 1688–9, Whigs sympathetic towards Locke's politics considered the diffusion of his *Two Treatises*, Mark Goldie has recently observed, a part of 'a deliberate programme of political education' (Goldie, 1999b, p. xxxiii; on the other stages of the process of re-education, see Savonius, 2006). The few Whig writers who paraphrased the *Two Treatises* or alluded to it in the 1690s wanted to eliminate the 'ridiculous and false' notions typical of the Stuart era (Goldie, 1999a,

vol. i, p. 6). In 1690 William Atwood recommended that the *Two Treatises* be read 'every morning' as a 'Catholicon' against Tory absolutism (Goldie, 1999a, vol. i, p. 38; and Goldie, 1999b, p. xxxiii).

IV

In the 'Second Treatise', Locke portrayed the champions of absolute monarchy as innovators whose 'Civil Policy is so new, so dangerous, and so destructive' that 'former Ages never could bear the broaching of it' (*TTG* II.239). The age of Filmer was degraded: pretensions to absolute power went hand in hand with selfishness and ambition, flattery and fawning. It was clear to Locke that the primitive condition, 'the Golden Age', had had 'more Virtue, and consequently better Governors, as well as less vicious Subjects' than his own age. 'In the beginning of things', as Locke saw it, the 'way of living … afforded little matter for Covetousness or Ambition'; material life was simple in small-scale communities defined by an honest economy of real needs (*TTG* II.107–8).

This was Locke's vision of how things had stood in the earliest societies of Asia and Europe, but it was equally important to his politics that human societies were no longer, and could no longer be, like that (except in, say, America, 'which is still a Pattern of the first Ages in Asia and Europe' (*TTG* II.108)). The primitive harmony of interests had been destabilized and succeeded by new forms of collective life which carried with them a propensity to set men's principal interests against one another. There had emerged a new constant, conflict of interest, which was associated with a competitive monetary economy and which had, as its moral and psychological groundwork, 'vain Ambition, and *amor sceleratus habendi* [the accursed love of possessing], evil Concupiscence' (*TTG* II.111.1–5; see Property).

Locke's *Two Treatises* was not an invitation to his contemporaries to restore the virtuous equality, unspoilt trust and simple life of the lost golden age. Rather, it was an exhortation to pass through the absolutist age of corruption to a time when collective life would once again exhibit a relative integrity and moral health. If we ask why it was that Locke expected the future to be open to such a decisive improvement upon its past, the key to the answer lies in his belief in the power of education. After the clergy had been 'Propagating wrong Notions concerning Government', the Revolution of 1688–9 gave him reason to hope that the future ages 'will abhor the Memory of such servile Flatterers, who whilst it seem'd to serve their turn, resolv'd all Government into absolute Tyranny' (*TTG* preface and II.239).

BIBLIOGRAPHY

Secondary Literature

Ashcraft, Richard, *Revolutionary Politics & Locke's* Two Treatises of Government (Princeton, New Jersey, 1986).

Colletti, Lucio, *From Rousseau to Lenin: Studies in Ideology and Society* (New York and London, 1972).

Dunn, John, *The Political Thought of John Locke: An Historical Account of the Argument of the* Two Treatises of Government (Cambridge, 1969).

——, 'From Applied Theology to Social Analysis: The Break between John Locke and the Scottish Enlightenment', in John Dunn, *Rethinking Modern Political Theory:* Essays 1979–83 (Cambridge, 1985), pp. 55–67.

——, 'What Is Living and What Is Dead in the Political Theory of John Locke?', in John Dunn, *Interpreting Political Responsibility:* Essays 1981–1989 (Cambridge, 1990), pp. 9–25.

Goldie, Mark (ed.), *The Reception of Locke's Politics*, 6 vols (London, 1999a).

——, 'Introduction', in Mark Goldie (ed.), *The Reception of Locke's Politics*, 6 vols (London, 1999b), vol. i, pp. xvii–lxxi.

——, 'John Locke: Icon of Liberty', *History Today*, vol. liv (2004), pp. 31–6.

Green, Ian, 'Orality, Script and Print: The Case of the English Sermon *c.* 1530–1700',

in Heinz Schilling and István György Tóth (eds), *Cultural Exchange in Early Modern Europe: Volume 1: Religion and Cultural Exchange in Europe, 1400–1700* (Cambridge, 2006), pp. 236–55.

Haakonssen, Knud, *Natural Law and Moral Philosophy: From Grotius to the Scottish Enlightenment* (Cambridge, 1996).

Laslett, Peter, 'Introduction', in John Locke, *Two Treatises of Government*, ed. Peter Laslett (2nd edn, Cambridge, 1970).

——, 'Introduction', in *TTG* (1988), pp. 3–133.

Lloyd Thomas, D.A., *Locke on Government* (London and New York, 1995).

Macpherson, C.B., *Democratic Theory: Essays in Retrieval* (Oxford, 1973).

Marshall, John, *John Locke: Resistance, Religion and Responsibility* (Cambridge, 1994).

Savonius, S.-J., 'The Lockean Rightholders', in Petter Korkman and Virpi Mäkinen (eds), *Transformations in Medieval and Early-Modern Rights Discourse* (Dordrecht, 2006), pp. 285–306.

Schneewind, J.B., *The Invention of Autonomy: A History of Modern Moral Philosophy* (Cambridge, 1998).

Simmons, A. John, *The Lockean Theory of Rights* (Princeton, New Jersey, 1992).

Swanson, Scott G., 'The Medieval Foundations of John Locke's Theory of Natural Rights: Rights of Subsistence and the Principle of Extreme Necessity', *History of Political Thought*, vol. xviii (1997), pp. 399–459.

Sommerville, Johann P., 'Introduction' and editorial apparatus, in Sir Robert Filmer, *Patriarcha and Other Writings*, ed. Johann P. Sommerville (Cambridge, 1991), pp. ix–xlvi.

Tierney, Brian, *The Idea of Natural Rights. Studies on Natural Rights, Natural Law and Church Law, 1150–1625* (Atlanta, Georgia, 1997).

Tuck, Richard, *Philosophy and Government, 1572–1651* (Cambridge, 1993).

Tully, James, *Strange Multiplicity: Constitutionalism in an Age of Diversity* (Cambridge, 1995).

Waldron, Jeremy, *Liberal Rights: Collected Papers 1981–1991* (Cambridge, 1993).

Wootton, David, 'Introduction', in John Locke, *Political Writings* (Harmondsworth, 1993), pp. 7–122.

Zagorin, Perez, 'Hobbes without Grotius', *History of Political Thought*, vol. xxi (2000), pp. 16–40.

S.-J. Savonius-Wroth

LETTERS CONCERNING TOLERATION

John Locke was the author of three letters on TOLERATION published during his lifetime and began a fourth, which remained unfinished at his death. The first letter is a touchstone of liberal thinking and a political classic. The lasting link that posterity has made between Locke's name and the idea of toleration rests squarely upon it; the later letters by comparison are little known and little read today, even by Locke scholars and students of his writings. Many scholars have judged these letters 'dull, repetitious and prolix' (Nicholson, 1991, p. 184n). If this judgement is understandable, the later letters have, for all that, received less attention than they deserve – for they develop arguments against an objection to toleration as he conceived it that Locke's first letter had not addressed explicitly, and in ways that shed much light on his own position.

Locke's first letter on toleration was written, in Latin, in Amsterdam, between early November and the middle of December 1685 (Locke, 1963, p. xv). At that time the prospects for toleration in England and on the Continent looked as bleak as Locke's personal circumstances were precarious (see Woolhouse, 2007, p. 219). Toleration was under attack on two fronts. In October 1685 Louis XIV of France had formally revoked the Edict of Nantes, which had granted toleration to generations of French Protestants, and turned the full force of the law and the army against those who refused to convert to Catholicism. In November of the same year in England James II moved against the Test Act, which excluded Catholics from public office – a development that gave grounds for fearing the use of French methods against English Protestants. If this situation was scarcely of his making, the arguments about toleration that Locke elaborated in its shadow were very much his own.

Locke's arguments were first published in April 1689, anonymously, under the title *Epistola de toleratia* at Gouda in the Netherlands. The publication was supervised by Locke's friend, the Remonstrant theologian Philippus van LIMBORCH, to whom the *Epistola* was dedicated in the mysterious series of initials on its title-page which, if deciphered, simultaneously identified Locke as its author (see Woolhouse, 2007, p. 270). Less than six months later an English translation appeared in London, again anonymously, with a new preface and minus the potentially incriminating initials, as *A Letter concerning Toleration*. The translation and the preface were the work of William Popple, a Unitarian merchant with whom Locke was also friendly. It was Locke who supplied Popple with a copy of the Latin original to work from but it seems that he did not at the same time confide his authorship: in his will Locke was to write, with characteristic circumspection, that the *Epistola* had been translated into English 'without my privity', that is, without his express consent as author, though not without his knowledge (*Corr.*, vol. viii, p. 426; see Locke, 1963, pp. xxxi–xl). In any event, Locke's later letters defended the English version when its arguments were challenged publicly. But we must turn to the style and the detail of its arguments in order to grasp the nature of that challenge.

Locke's style was to argue without rhetorical excess or the constant invocation of authorities, on the basis of distinctions established more comprehensively elsewhere in his writings. The fundamental distinction on which he relied was that between the ends and authority of states and those of churches. Locke had worked on the assumption that states and churches were categorically different bodies since 1667, when his *Essay concerning Toleration* had premised that religious worship as such lay outside the magistrate's control (*ETol.*, p. 270). The second of his *Two Treatises of Government* had validated that premise by providing an explanation of political authority and its extent in which religious concerns did not figure (*TTG* II.87–9 and II.134–42). This explanation suggested that the authority of the state extended only to people's civil interests and that it did not – and, more pointedly, could not – legitimately encompass matters of salvation. *A Letter concerning Toleration* reiterated this conclusion and supplemented it with an account of the ends and authority of churches and their standing relative to the state and to each other. So much is apparent from the structure of the *Letter*, which first insists on the necessity of distinguishing between political and religious institutions and practices, and adduces three considerations in favour of maintaining this distinction, before turning to consider the nature of churches and the practical conclusions about toleration and related matters that follow from its conceptions of church and state.

The first of Locke's three considerations was that God had not committed, nor could the consent of people commit, the care of souls to the magistrate (Locke, 1689b, p. 7). If these two claims were obviously different, they were connected by the supposition that the authority of the magistrate came from God via the free actions of people acting in conformity with his wishes. Thus, since he had nowhere indicated that he wished any one human being to have authority over another in matters of religion, it followed that people themselves could not rightly give that authority to the magistrate. This consideration tended to a second, for it implied that all human beings were responsible

for taking care of their own salvation and that only what they themselves judged pleasing to God would be valuable in that connection. They could not therefore disavow their own judgements and take up the dictates of the magistrate at will because they would be hazarding their own salvation by doing so – but also because it was a fortiori impossible for them to do so, since their judgements could not be changed at will.

The second consideration was that the magistrate's power consisted only in outward force, whereas true and saving religion involved the inward persuasion of the mind (Locke, 1689b, p. 7). Since force was incapable of altering the contents of the mind, it was incapable of bringing people to true and saving religion. Locke's third consideration was that, even supposing that force *was* capable of changing the contents of the mind into conformity with the dictates of the magistrate, this would not help with the salvation of souls because, while there was only one true religion and so one way to salvation, the magistrates of the world differed violently over which religion was true and could not all be right (Locke, 1689b, pp. 8–9). The odds against finding oneself in a country whose magistrate happened to hold the true religion were very high indeed – as high as 500:1, Locke later estimated (*W*, vol. vi, p. 566). Besides this, it was hard to reconcile what was effectively salvation by lottery with the notion of a Deity who held people responsible for taking care of their own salvation – for people were hardly responsible for the place of their nativity. If these considerations were not exhaustive, taken together they were, Locke thought, sufficient to show that religion was and could be none of the magistrate's business. Religion was rather the business of churches, to which his attention duly turned.

Churches he defined as 'voluntary Societ[ies] of Men, joining themselves together of their own accord, in order to the publick worshipping of God, in such a manner as they judge acceptable to him, and effectual to the Salvation of their Souls' (Locke, 1689b, p. 9). As such, they were constituted by nothing other than a coalition of human wills on the basis of judgements held in common about which professions and modes of worship God would find most pleasing. That churches were simply productions of human intellect and will implied a view of both capacities: that these capacities were naturally adequate to recognizing and discharging the responsibilities to God, themselves and others under which people laboured. The same view underwrote the claim that all men 'know and acknowledge that God ought to be publickly worshipped' (Locke, 1689b, p. 27). Locke used this view to undermine rival understandings of churches. More exactly, he used it to bypass the notion that one true church exclusively had been constituted directly by God with authority over all believers, which provided means of salvation unavailable to those who remained outside it. Locke's strategy was to encourage the abandonment of this notion by questioning the paradigm on which it was based.

This strategy had two aspects, one positive and the other negative. The positive aspect highlighted the requirements of true religion. The true religion was revealed in the Holy Scriptures, which declared in express words all that was necessary to salvation. The negative aspect cut against the idea of one true Church. Locke asked whether it would not be better for churches to understand themselves solely in reference to the Scriptures as opposed to some special divine warrant. Concomitantly he suggested that the apostolic succession was unnecessary to identify a church as true and observed that the dissensions among those who claimed to bear it both necessitated and allowed individual believers to choose to which churches they would adhere (Locke, 1689b, p. 11). The effect was to place all churches on the same footing with respect to truth, since each one believed itself to be the true and there was no common judge on earth to determine which, if any, was right (Locke, 1689b, p. 16). In short, it was left to every individual to join with the body in which he or she believed the true

religion could be found. It was emphatically not for a church to nominate itself as the true to the exclusion of every other and to demand the adherence of every individual on that basis or to attempt to compel it by force. Force was an instrument that belonged to the magistrate not to churches.

Locke inferred that by a like token the magistrate could have no role in upholding a particular church or assaulting others in the name of religious truth. For the magistrate was no better placed than any other individual to judge where the truth lay in matters of religion. His superiority in power over his subjects did not translate into superiority in knowledge (Locke, 1689b, p. 23). Neither did he enjoy special access to truth about religion (or anything else) in virtue of belonging to a particular church and with it the right to require the obedience of his subjects in religious matters (Locke, 1689b, p. 24). Not only was such a claim question-begging, it was incompatible with the strict distinction upon which Locke insisted between civil matters, which fell under the magistrate's jurisdiction, and religious matters, which did not. If the paradigm that Locke was questioning presupposed that church and state were complicit in a distinctively Christian enterprise – the promotion of salvation – which required the combined resources and efforts of both (see Goldie, 1984, Harris, 2002 and Stanton, 2006 for discussion), the alternative he was proposing indicated that church and state were separate and independent bodies that could not be jumbled together without bringing unqualified misery and disaster to both (Locke, 1689b, p. 18).

Locke's alternative implied the existence of a plurality of churches within a state. How would these churches relate to each other and the magistrate to them? Locke's answer to the first question was that churches stood in the same relation as private persons one to another: none had any rights or jurisdiction over another (Locke, 1689b, p. 15). Where differences arose between them, they should emulate the example of Christ, whose message of holiness, benignity, decency and meekness called Christians to deal with one another with charity and love. Hence Locke's striking assertion that toleration was the 'chief Characteristical Mark of the True Church' – for a true church was just a church organized around the requirements of the true religion, and the true religion required tolerance of its followers (Locke, 1689b, p. 1). Mutual toleration was in this sense a Christian duty, something owed by one church to another no less than by one Christian to another (Locke, 1689b, p. 15). This did not mean that individual Christians could not persuade or admonish their brethren, or that individual churches could not expel members who were finally unwilling to live by their rules, but neither admonition nor excommunication could be allied to, or triggered, civil penalties (Locke, 1689b, pp. 13–14). Individuals' civil rights and enjoyments belonged to them as members of the state, not as members of particular churches or religions.

What of the magistrate's relation to particular churches? In Locke's view, the magistrate had the same rights as any private person to persuade and admonish in religion but no additional rights over religion accrued to him in virtue of his civil office. Thus Locke argued that 'the Magistrate has no Power to enforce by Law, either in his Church, or much less in another, the use of any Rites or Ceremonies whatsoever in the Worship of God' (Locke, 1689b, p. 28). Nor had he 'any Power to forbid the use of such Rites and Ceremonies as are already received, approved, and practised by any Church' since this would amount to the power to dissolve churches, which their individual members alone could do (Locke, 1689b, p. 32). Even in cases where it appeared otherwise, as when the magistrate forbade the killing of livestock for sacrifice in times of famine, he enjoyed and exercised no power over religious matters *per se*. In the case in point, he banned the slaughter of animals, not their sacrifice – a civil, not a religious activity. To Locke's mind, it seemed that either the magistrate could alter nothing in religion, or *anything*; Locke insisted

upon the former (Locke, 1689b, pp. 33–4). Congruently, he denied that the magistrate should punish idolatry or otherwise annex civil punishments to perceived deviations from Christian truth, for there was 'absolutely no such thing, under the Gospel, as a Christian Commonwealth' (Locke, 1689b, pp. 36–7). Christianity, therefore, was not the magistrate's business: his business was the protection of civil interests only.

To this end, certain exclusions from the scope of toleration were necessary, for some beliefs could be of interest to the magistrate if they endangered civil interests. The danger was twofold, from beliefs that threatened civil peace and from beliefs that threatened the very fabric of civil society. These beliefs would be practical rather than purely speculative, since by Locke's own definitions speculative beliefs terminated in the understanding and did not affect civil society (Locke, 1689b, p. 39; cf. *ETol.*, p. 271). First Locke identified the beliefs that membership of a particular church brought with it special civil privileges or licensed interference in the affairs of other churches. The magistrate should not, he thought, tolerate those who exempted themselves from the duty to tolerate others. To these were added those whose church membership went hand-in-hand with allegiance to a foreign power. In the minds of many, this meant Roman Catholics, though Locke did not distinguish this group by name, preferring the example of Muslims, whose political loyalty belonged to the Mufti of Constantinople (Locke, 1689b, p. 47). His point was that any group standing in this relation to a foreign power was suspect, and on the same grounds: they were intolerable because politically subversive.

Another group – atheists – was intolerable on rather different grounds. Atheism not only subverted government but all that it existed to protect. The purpose of civil government was to uphold civil society. It followed that 'No Opinions contrary to human Society, or to those moral Rules, which are necessary to the preservation of Civil Society, are to be tolerated by the Magistrate'. Atheism endangered civil society because 'Promises, Covenants, and Oaths, which are the Bonds of Humane Society, can have no hold upon an Atheist' (Locke, 1689b, p. 45). This was so because God assured the authenticity of these undertakings. To swear an oath before him was to offer a guarantee of one's veracity, because he would punish bad dealing in the afterlife. The atheist's promises offered no such guarantee, and so could not be trusted. Neither could atheists display justice in their actions. Locke was sure that the practice of justice was the 'bond of every society' (*ELN*, p. 214). Justice involved tailoring one's actions to the requirements of NATURAL LAW; without this, civil life was impossible. Atheists did not recognize these requirements, and since (as Locke supposed) actions flowed from the understanding, their cognitive blindness rendered them incapable of just action. In other words, atheism was not a purely speculative attitude to religion; it had practical implications that made it a legitimate object of the magistrate's attentions. Locke presented those implications very starkly indeed: 'The taking away of God, tho but even in thought, dissolves all' (Locke, 1689b, p. 48). Atheists were intolerable and the magistrate should root them out (see Dunn, 1984, pp. 58–9).

Of course Locke held that belief in a deity was rational, which was why he could count those who failed to acknowledge him among 'the most dangerous sorts of wild beasts' (*ETol.*, p. 308). But the *Letter* nowhere specified that the deity must be a peculiarly Christian one, only that he should command an afterlife to provide effective sanction to oaths. If atheists were intolerable because they acknowledged no deity, then Jews, Muslims and even theistic pagans satisfied Locke's criterion, and so were not to be excluded from the civil rights of the commonwealth. That is to say, because Locke supposed that civil society depended upon the adherence to *a* God, the limits of toleration, other things being equal, were set by the bounds of theism. This is obvious enough once

we recollect that with Locke the public worship of God was a duty under natural law (*ELN.*, p. 156). Only those who recognized natural law could therefore claim the concomitant right to worship as they chose. That this right lay along a juridical axis that did not at any point intersect with the juridical axis of politics implies at least two noteworthy considerations.

One consideration is that the rights that found their home along one axis could not be passed along the other (Locke, 1689b, p. 15). A second, and potentially more alarming, consideration is that when the attempted exercise of rights secured along one axis clashed with the exercise of rights secured along the other axis, there was no judge on earth capable of mediating the claims of each (Locke, 1689b, p. 45). Again, this juridical arrangement suggested that if there were reciprocal duties between religious believers and rights held one against another in the same capacity, religious believers possessed no *civil* right to toleration at the magistrate's hands. Neither did the magistrate *qua* magistrate have the duty to tolerate *them*. So while it is certainly true that Locke's position accommodates toleration – though not for those who espoused no religion – and liberty of conscience – the liberty to join or leave the Church of one's own choosing – it does so in terms quite unlike those in which Locke's closest contemporaries typically dealt and very far from those in which it is usually presented today.

Something of the suspicion which Locke's positions aroused among his contemporaries is discernable in one of the earliest attacks upon the *Letter*, the anonymous *The Argument of the Letter concerning Toleration, Briefly Consider'd and Answer'd* (1690). The author of this short pamphlet was the Anglican clergyman Jonas PROAST. Proast was a convinced adherent of the paradigm Locke wished to supplant, and a wily defender of its merits. Rather than merely juxtaposing his own opinions to Locke's he engaged with Locke's, and raised a possibility that Locke had not obviously considered. Proast agreed with Locke that the use of outward force could not push the mind into compliance with the dictates of another – a point which modern commentary forgets when asserting that Locke argued for toleration only in terms of the ineffectiveness of force in changing belief – but suggested that it might 'bring men to consider those Reasons and Arguments which are proper and sufficient to convince them, but which, without being forced, they would not consider'. Proast's position was that force could work 'indirectly and at a distance' to persuade people to embrace voluntarily the true religion which alone could secure their salvation (Proast, 1690, p. 5; cf. Waldron, 1988). We might conveniently label it 'persecution without tears'.

Proast buttressed his position with the claim that Locke had begged the question when insisting that the magistrate had no business besides the civil interests of his subjects. This presupposed that only civil interests could be defended or furthered by the magistrate. But if it were the case that 'the Spiritual and Eternal Interests of men may any way be procured or advanced by Political Government', these too would fall under his jurisdiction (Proast, 1690, pp. 18–19). If force, sensitively applied, could direct people to the truth, the magistrate might have a place in the economy of salvation after all. Proast went on to dispute each of Locke's three considerations against this possibility in turn, arguing that the magistrate had been committed to care for the souls of his subjects to some degree, that the power at his disposal was effective to this end, and that it belonged to him in order to bring men not to his own, but only to the true religion. Persecution without tears meant that even if the magistrate mistook a false religion for the true, the mildness of his penalties ensured that people would suffer only 'some tolerable Inconveniences' when, after due consideration of his alternative, they followed their own reason and consciences newly reassured of the truth of their convictions (Proast, 1690, pp. 21–7).

If Proast's challenge was succinct and temperate, Locke's response was neither. A Second Letter concerning Toleration (1690) was cast as the work of an admirer of the first letter now entering the fray under the pseudonym 'Philanthropus' (lover of mankind) – not that anyone was long deceived (see Proast, 1704). Locke picked apart the implications of Proast's position and testily impugned his scholarly abilities. He suggested that Proast had misunderstood the style of his argument when supposing that it relied on a single fundamental premise or argument – this was as foolish as supposing 'only one Beam of a House had any strength in it, when there are several others that would support the Building' (Locke, 1690, p. 5). Proast's own arguments, in contradistinction, depended entirely upon one

lurking Supposition, that the National Religion now in England, back'd by the Publick Authority of the Law, is the only True Religion, and therefore no other is to be tolerated. Which being a Supposition equally unavoidable, and equally just, in other Countries (unless we can imagine that every where but in England Men believe what at the same time they think to be a Lie) will in other Places exclude Toleration, and thereby hinder Truth from the means of propagating it self (Locke, 1690, p. 4).

If this supposition, once stripped of its rhetorical veneer of moderation, was indeed central to the paradigm which Proast accepted, it was not one that Locke was disposed to accept.

Locke chipped away at its veneer by enquiring who would be penalized, and for what, under Proast's scheme. He suggested that most magistrates were interested only in external compliance, not the convictions of their subjects, and surmised that those in the firing line would turn out to be not those members of the national church who had not once reflected upon what they believed, and lived very dissolutely, but rather the usual suspects – the dissenters – who had already received ample inducements to reflect upon their convictions. In other words, Proast's scheme would authorize in practice what it formally repudiated, the use of compulsion to bring people into the church the magistrate preferred, and so his valorization of 'true' religion was mere trifling (Proast, 1690, p. 21; Locke, 1690, p. 27).

Locke did not directly deny Proast's claim that indirect force might produce positive results – by *Accident* as he derisively put it (Locke, 1690, p. 7). His silence has puzzled many commentators (cf. Waldron, 1988; Vernon, 1997; Tuckness, 2002), but a flat denial would have been superfluous. Locke's position was that even if compulsion *did* work, it was unnecessary and illegitimate. The first *Letter* proclaimed that religion should not be propagated by force of arms (Locke, 1689b, p. 18). The *Second Letter* offered a more expansive explanation of why it should not. Locke argued that there was no authorization in Scripture for the use of force to promote true religion and so that it was not a means that Christians could properly employ (Locke, 1690, p. 22). Neither could a warrant for force, absent in Scripture, be derived from popular consent.

In Locke's view, people agreed to enter civil society to obtain benefits they could not secure or advance without it. This rationale did not apply to salvation, which they could obtain without 'the Force of Civil Society'. Indeed, salvation was something for which they were individually responsible, a responsibility they could not evade or sensibly be thought to trade off or entrust to another (Locke, 1690, pp. 53–4). People could not, therefore, appoint their spiritual welfare as one of the ends of civil society, which, since they had made it themselves for other secular purposes, was confined to those purposes alone. Proast's view, Locke argued, implied that any organization could legitimately expand its remit to include ends its members had not originally foreseen if those ends could in 'any way be procured or advanced' by it. Thus the Church of Rome was perfectly within its rights to pursue secular advantages and interests, a position for which Locke had not expected to find support from a Protestant writer – 'But there is a time for all

things' (Locke, 1690, p. 53). This provocation did not go unanswered. Proast returned to print (again anonymously) to defend himself in *A Third Letter concerning Toleration* (1691).

Proast's *Third Letter* echoed Locke's *Second Letter* in its style and temper. For the most part it simply exposed the distance between its author's views and Locke's. Where Locke was confident that the true religion did not require the assistance of human authority to prevail, Proast believed that 'the Corruption and Pravity of Humane Nature' necessitated its support at the hands of a godly magistrate (Locke, 1690, p. 3; Proast, 1691, p. 7). But it raised at least one interesting question when it asked why, if the magistrate could not be trusted with people's spiritual welfare, he could be trusted to look after their civil interests. *A Second Letter* had suggested that God, recognizing that magistrates were no less liable to prejudice and error than anyone else, had excluded force as a means of promoting true religion (Locke, 1690, p. 21). Proast countered that the same liabilities ought to disqualify him from promoting anything else impartially. To his mind, the magistrate's authority over civil affairs and over spiritual affairs stood and fell together. Locke thought very differently. The gargantuan reply he composed to Proast's *Third Letter* developed many of the points in his earlier letters, even as its sustained discussions of true religion looked forward to the concerns of *The Reasonableness of Christianity*; but it also tackled Proast's question head-on.

Locke's *A Third Letter for Toleration* (1692) played up the magistrate's responsibility to restrain the vices and immorality that damaged civil society which his first letter, and other writings before that, had mentioned in passing (Locke, 1692, p. 282; Locke, 1689b, p. 3; *ETol.*, p. 281). It reiterated the claims that Proast's distinction between the magistrate's religion and the true religion dissolved in practice, that true religion was unforced and that this excluded 'all the *Humane Means* of Force from being *necessary*, or so much as lawful to be used' in religion (Locke, 1692, p. 200, p. 318, see Stanton, 2006, p. 94). But it argued that force was both necessary and legitimate in politics. For the ends of civil society were served by placing force in the hands of men, whereas those of religion were not. Civil society was brought into existence to protect and preserve people's civil interests. In order to serve these ends, when it came to making laws, magistrates, be they 'as humoursom, passionate, and prejudiced as they will', were 'by their own Interest obliged to make best use of their best Skill, and with their most unprejudiced and sedatest Thoughts take care of the Government and endeavour to preserve the Common-wealth'. Thus, 'notwithstanding their *Humours and Passions*, their liableness to *Error and Prejudice*, they do provide pretty well for the Support of Society', because the causal impetuses for joining civil society in the first place (their particular needs, interests and situational difficulties) pushed them in the direction of impartiality in civil legislation (Locke, 1692, p. 313–14; see Tuckness, 2002).

Whether cowed by the brilliance of Locke's arguments or exhausted by their length, Proast did not respond immediately. When he did respond, twelve years later, it was as much to show that he was not cowed as it was to deplore the invocation of Locke's arguments in recent writings by dissenters. Proast's *A Second Letter to the Author of the Three Letters for Toleration* (1704) redug old ground, adding little beyond a clumsy attempt to make the distinction between true religion and the rest stick, by insisting that '*Full Assurance*' came with the former and authorized persecution without tears in its name (Proast, 1704, p. 6). Dutifully, Locke began a reply, which made short shrift of Proast's efforts, but he was by this time a sick man and he would not live to complete *A Fourth Letter for Toleration*, which was published imperfectly in his posthumous works (*W*, vol. vi, pp. 549–73).

Reputation is not a reliable guide to worth, as Locke knew only too well. For every place in which his later letters on toleration reflect the law of diminishing returns, there is another in which Locke develops views which every serious scholar and student of his thought would do well to consider. This essay has commented on only a small number of these; it is for readers to investigate further.

BIBLIOGRAPHY
Primary Works
Locke, John, *Epistola de tolerantia* (Gouda, 1689a).
——, *A Letter concerning Toleration* (London, 1689b).
——, *A Second Letter concerning Toleration* (London, 1690).
——, *A Third Letter for Toleration* (London, 1692).
——, *A Letter concerning Toleration* ed. Mario Montuori (The Hague, 1963).
Proast, Jonas, *The Argument of the Letter concerning Toleration, Briefly Consider'd and Answer'd* (Oxford, 1690).
——, *A Third Letter concerning Toleration* (Oxford, 1691).
——, *A Second Letter to the Author of the Three Letters for Toleration* (Oxford, 1704).

Secondary Literature
Dunn, John, *Locke* (Oxford, 1984).
Goldie, Mark, 'The Theory of Religious Intolerance in Restoration England', in W. Sheils (ed.), *Persecution and Toleration* (Oxford, 1984), pp. 331–68.
Harris, Ian, 'Tolérance, Église et État chez Locke', in Y.C. Zarka, F. Lessay and G.A.J. Rogers (eds), *Les fondements philosophiques sur la tolerance*, 3 vols (Paris, 2002), vol. i, pp. 175–218.
Nicholson, Peter, 'John Locke's Later Letters on Toleration', in J. Horton and S. Mendus (eds), *John Locke: A Letter concerning Toleration in Focus* (London, 1991), pp. 163–87.
Stanton, Timothy, 'Locke and the Politics and Theology of Toleration', *Political Studies*, vol. liv (2006), pp. 84–102.
Tuckness, Alex, *Locke and the Legislative*

Point of View (Princeton, 2002).

Vernon, Richard, *The Career of Toleration: John Locke, Jonas Proast, and After* (Montreal, 1997).

Waldron, Jeremy, 'Locke: Toleration and the Rationality of Persecution', in S. Mendus (ed.), *Justifying Toleration* (Cambridge, 1988).

Wolfson, Adam, *Persecution or Toleration: An Explication of the Locke-Proast Quarrel, 1689–1704* (Lanham, 2010).

Timothy Stanton

SOME THOUGHTS CONCERNING EDUCATION

Some Thoughts concerning Education originated in 1684, when Mr Edward Clarke, a
friend of Locke's, asked for advice in bringing up
his son. Locke began a series of letters to the
Clarkes on the subject while in Holland, and
went on for two more years after his return to
England in 1689. In 1693 *Some Thoughts* was
published after some amount of revision and
expansion of the material of those letters,
followed by new modified editions in 1695,
1699 and 1705. In the dedicatory preface ('To
Edward Clarke of Chipley, Esq.') Locke warned
that this was not a complete treatise on education, but that the subject was of great importance, and that he himself was not without some
successful experience in the field. Indeed, Locke
was an Oxford tutor, as well as a private adviser
of several noble and gentlemanly families'
children, among whom the third Earl of
SHAFTESBURY is the most famous (Yolton and
Yolton, 1989, pp. 5–8; Axtell, 1968, pp. 38–48).

The shaping power of education is a credo
which Locke openly declares from the very
beginning, in a famous formulation: 'I think I
may say, that of all the Men we meet with, Nine
Parts of Ten are what they are, Good or Evil,
useful or not, by their Education' (*STE*, sect. 1,
p. 83). The credo had many advocates in early-
modern educational thought, and it was often
expressed by means of metaphors such as the
moulding of wax or clay, the channelling of
waters, the dying of wool, or the tilling of land.
Locke was of a mind here with Erasmus,
Montaigne, Roger Ascham, Henry Peacham,
Richard Allestree, Jean Gailhard or Obadiah
Walker. Contrary to what is sometimes believed,
however, these metaphors never imply that education works with a featureless, infinitely malleable lump; on the contrary, they are always
accompanied by discussions of the child's (often
the individual child's) capacities, inclinations
and dispositions, which need to be carefully
observed if education is to work at all. This is
also important to Locke (Neill, 1989 *contra*
Passmore, 1965), who also shares a number of
other notions with these works, for example,
that the transformative work of education is
expressed in the formation of habits of both
virtue and judgement, or that education proceeds
by careful guidance, play, conversation, example,
by the management of shame and praise, and by
the cultivation of a love for knowledge and
virtue. Locke may be said thus to have absorbed
a rich Christian humanist tradition of educational thought, while at the same time formulating a new idiom, in which the psychological
and practical details acquire a richness they had
not known before, and where education starts to
become a visible companion of theories of
knowledge and of political government.

The Juvenalian *mens sana in corpore sano* is
the educational aim Locke places at the head of
his work. In looking at the health of the body in
sections 2 to 30 of *Some Thoughts*, Locke formulates several principles which actually apply
generally to the training of both mind and body:
'health' aptly translates as both 'strength' and
'temperance', or a mastery over self-indulging
inclinations; it can be achieved by a gradual
habituation in self-denial which begins early and
proceeds by degrees through a confrontation
with hardships; the art of education is to devise
the exercises meant to develop virtuous habits.

As far as the body is concerned, Locke goes
through a series of recommendations on how
to habituate the body to the cold (by swimming

in cold water, spending time in the open air, as well as, rather shockingly for today's sensibilities, having children wear leaky shoes to let water in), on sartorial habits (clothes should never encumber the body's free motions or be too warm), on a plain and simple diet (plenty of dry bread and little meat, little salt and sugar and no spices, only light beer and never wine or strong drinks, very moderate fruit consumption, generally temperate and never strictly scheduled meals), on sleeping habits (children should sleep alone, use hard beds, vary sleeping postures and rise early), and on how to avoid constipation (accustoming the body to regular bowel movements, rather than administering medicine). Faithful to his experimental approach, Locke always interweaves his advice with instances of personal, often medical, observation, as well as with examples provided by his wide readings in travel literature or ancient authors.

Sections 31 to 42 introduce the general principles governing the health of the mind. Early beginnings are again emphasized, as is the core educational mechanism of building habits by practice and exercise. The parallel with the body also serves to formulate the definition of the health, or virtue, of the mind, which is formed by enduring hardships, and whose great principle is 'That a Man is able to *deny himself* his own Desires, cross his own Inclinations, and purely follow what Reason directs as best, tho' the appetite lean the other way' (*STE*, sect. 33, p. 103). Much more emphasis than in the sections devoted to the body, however, is placed here on the figures surrounding the young child: echoing again a frequent complaint in other educational works, Locke condemns the corrupting influence of foolish parents, tutors and servants and makes a repeated point of the need 'That none but discreet People should be about them [children]' (*STE*, sect. 39, p. 108). Fathers and tutors in particular bear the responsibility of setting up worthy examples for the child, of carefully and affectionately steering his course in learning the good habits, and thus, crucially, of impersonating for him the standard

of reason by which he needs to measure his mind before he becomes capable of using his own reason to the full (*STE*, sects 36, 42).

The ensuing large portion of the work (sects 43 to 132) aims to spell out the educational discipline in more detail. In keeping with his definition of virtue, Locke describes the aim, or 'the great Art', of education as the reconciliation of two seemingly contrary desiderata: mastery over appetites, inclinations and will, and the freedom of an active and supple mind (*STE*, sect. 46). The means to that end can never be such as encourage either looseness or slavishness of mind, and Locke spends a lot of ink condemning both the brutality of beating and the flattery of easy rewards. Instead he proposes 'esteem' and 'disgrace', or 'credit' and 'shame', as the form that the powerful guides of rewards and punishments should take. Indeed, Locke proposes, 'reputation' seen as the recognition of virtuous action by other rational men (perhaps especially by the 'discreet') is closest to 'the true Principle and Measure of Vertue', which consists in 'the Knowledge of a Man's Duty, and the Satisfaction it is to obey his Maker, in following the Dictates of that Light God has given him, with the Hopes of Acceptation and Reward' (*STE*, sect. 61, p. 119). Credit and shame are the two great tools in the hands of the educator by which he may motivate and guide his pupil towards developing moral and intellectual habits. The main function of credit and shame, Locke suggests, is to enable the development of a 'love' or 'relish' for virtue and knowledge which in turn makes possible the practice conducive to virtuous habits (*STE*, sects 58, 70, 98).

The strategies Locke proposes in this sense are given more in the manner of general educational guidelines than of a strict, rule-bound methodology. All teaching, he insists, should be done as play, rather than by rules, and should never appear as a task or burden (*STE*, sects 63, 73, 75, 130). This is the best route to giving children a 'Liking and Inclination to what you propose to them to be learn'd' (*STE*, sect. 72, p. 134). Encouragement can never be used enough, and rebuke had rather take the form of meaningful looks, displeased wonder and gentle persuasion, than of beating, passionate chiding or untimely prohibitions (*STE*, sects 77, 80, 83, 85). Example is another powerful educator for Locke, who comes back repeatedly to the shaping force of the live examples the child's immediate company offers (*STE*, sects 67–71, 89, 93, 146). It is not only by passive imitation that example works, however; it also has a more active role in that one important task of the educator is to draw the child's attention to instances around him and provoke his reasoning powers by inviting him to consider and judge them (*STE*, sect. 82). Thus, conversation – one suited to the reasoning powers of the child at various stages, and based on a discussion of cases rather than on theoretical principles – is another important educational method (*STE*, sects 81–2, 98). But fundamentally, all strategies need to start from a consideration of the child's dispositional baggage, or what Locke variously calls 'tempers', 'capacities', 'dispositions', 'the peculiar *Physiognomy of the Mind*' (*STE*, sect. 101, p. 163), or his '*native Propensities*' (*STE*, sect. 102, p. 163).

A patient and concerned observation of the child's temper, capacities and inclinations is one important task of the private tutor, who should be a 'discreet' observer and prudent guide of them, as well as a companion in conversation. At several moments in this part, Locke leaves the main thread of his 'method' in order to elaborate on the tutor's virtues and paint the portrait of a figure endowed with patience, skill, gentleness and prudence (*STE*, sect. 76), care, attention and observation (*STE*, sect. 78), sobriety, temperance, tenderness, diligence and discretion (*STE*, sect. 90), virtue, civility (*STE*, sect. 93) and wisdom (*STE*, sect. 94). It is by his wise management of esteem and disgrace, his encouragement, persuasion and conversation, by his prudent direction of the child's observation and reflection, and by an attentive study of the child's temper and capacities, that the tutor is capable of devising the best method for his individual pupil, and of

guiding the major work of education, that is, the bending of potentially corrupting inclinations and their turning into 'contrary habits'.

An exemplification of the latter occupies sections 103 to 132, where Locke draws a list of moral virtues seen as so many reoriented bad tendencies: children's 'love of dominion' (combined with 'covetousness' and 'self-love') is to be countered by learning the mastery of desires, civility, liberality, justice and honesty (*STE*, sects 103–7, 109–10), their domineering attitude and pride, by learning submission and patience (*STE*, sect. 112), their softness and effeminacy of spirit, by learning 'insensibility' of mind (*STE*, sects 113–14), their fear and cowardice, by learning courage (*STE*, sect. 115), their cruelty, by learning benignity, compassion and humanity (*STE*, sects 116–17), and their lying, by a cultivation of ingenuity (*STE*, sects 131–2). The natural inquisitiveness of children is a good inclination which the tutor should carefully cultivate by exercising their reasoning faculty and acting as an open and sincere companion of discussion (*STE*, sects 108, 118–22); but if the child is listless and shows a 'sauntering' humour, the same methods employed in the building of contrary habits can be tried (persuasion, encouragement, shame), unless it is due to their natural constitution, in which case all manner of incentives to activity should be sought (*STE*, sects 123–7) (see also Tarcov, 1984).

The sections on the 'contrary habits' and on the tutor's virtues are in direct correspondence with the next large portion of the work (*STE*, sects 134–16), dedicated to what Locke calls the main parts of education: virtue, wisdom, breeding and learning, with the latter the least imperative of the list. Virtue grows out of a double foundation: a true notion of God, as well as love and reverence for him, and the honesty of speaking the truth and of being good-natured to others (*STE*, sects 135–9). Wisdom (or prudence) rests on a combination of good natural temper, application of mind and experience, which a child can only begin to acquire in his tender years, by becoming accustomed to seeking 'true Notions of things' and to avoiding 'Falshood, and Cunning' (*STE*, sect. 140, p. 199). Good breeding (or civility, or decency) is foremost among the 'social virtues'. It is the outward expression of a disposition of the mind (what Locke had earlier called 'inward Civility', *STE*, sect. 67, p. 126) and is defined as the esteem and good will we have for both others and ourselves (*STE*, sects 141–5).

Last on Locke's list of the parts of education is 'learning', or the CURRICULUM of languages, sciences and other 'accomplishments'. The subordinate role of learning compared to virtue, wisdom/prudence and breeding/civility is a theme Locke emphasizes repeatedly throughout this part. A scholar's learning devoid of them actually enhances 'foolishness', but learning added to a 'well-disposed mind' and pursued in such a way as to further build a sound mind is indeed a good asset (*STE*, sects 147, 155, 177, 200). Locke itemizes the parts of the curriculum, while emphasizing their interconnections and the right order of pursuing them: reading, writing, Latin, French; geography, arithmetic, astronomy, geometry, chronology, history, ethics, civil law, English common law, the arts of right reasoning (LOGIC) and of speaking well (rhetoric), natural philosophy; dancing, riding, fencing, wrestling; the manual arts and accounting; travel (or the study of men and customs) (*STE*, sects 147–216).

The main business of the teaching of languages and sciences, again one of the tutor's chief tasks, is to accustom the pupil gradually to right judgement, by building up from simple to complex, making clear connections of ideas, making sure that notions are assimilated before further steps are taken, and always paying attention to the capacities and inclinations of the child at every stage (*STE*, sect. 180). The futility of rules, importance of credit, play and conversation, and the major mechanism of habit-building are emphasized again, as is the centrality of a 'right disposition' of the mind as the purpose of the pursuit of studies: the tutor's business is 'not so much to teach him all that is knowable, as to raise in him a love and esteem of Knowledge; and to put him in the right way of knowing, and improving himself, when he has a Mind to it' (*STE*, sect. 195, p. 249).

Towards the middle of the text, Locke formulates one core theme of his educational doctrine, which is actually a persistent undercurrent of most of his philosophical thought: the greatest care a man should have is to cleanse and improve his understanding, seek knowledge that is fit for his FACULTIES and useful for the conduct of his life, and thus fulfil a duty towards himself and towards his Creator (cf. *E*, I.i.5, 6, pp. 45–6). With Seneca, Locke deplores the kind of knowledge pursuit that fails in that task: 'we learn not to Live, but to Dispute; and our Education fits us rather for the University, than the World' (*STE*, sect. 94, p. 157).

BIBLIOGRAPHY
Secondary Literature

Axtell, James L., 'Introduction', John Locke, *The Educational Writings of John Locke*, ed. James L. Axtell (Cambridge, 1968), pp. 3–97.

Neill, Alex, 'Locke on Habituation, Autonomy and Education', *Journal of the History of Philosophy*, vol. xxvii (1989), pp. 225–45.

Passmore, John A., 'The Malleability of Man in Eighteenth-Century Thought', in Earl R. Wasserman (ed.), *Aspects of the Eighteenth Century* (Baltimore and London, 1965), pp. 27–46.

Tarcov, Nathan, *Locke's Education for Liberty* (Chicago, 1984).

Yolton, John W., and Jean S. Yolton, 'Introduction', John Locke, *Some Thoughts concerning Education*, ed. John W. Yolton and Jean S. Yolton (Oxford, 1989), pp. 1–75.

Sorana Corneanu

THE REASONABLENESS OF CHRISTIANITY AND ITS VINDICATIONS

Locke's principal subjects – religious TOLERA-TION, epistemology, political theory, education and economics – were not in his age the separate subjects and disciplines they have become in the intervening centuries. Religious thinking was then an integral aspect of virtually all these subjects. To understand the full dimensions of Locke's writings, it is necessary to consider his major works on religion, including *The Reasonableness of Christianity* and its two vindications.

From his earliest extant writings on NATURAL LAW and infallibility, Locke was never far from the popular religious debates of his day. As he entered his seventh decade of turbulent times, his attention was drawn to a debate among Dissenters from the Church of England over the nature of Christian faith that led to justification – making a sinner righteous before God, thereby achieving salvation. He later recalled it was this controversy that led him to consider over the winter of 1694–5 the nature of faith and to publish anonymously in August *The Reasonableness of Christianity*. In contrast to the Calvinist tradition in which he was raised and to the Dissenters' debates, Locke did not inquire into faith as a free gift of divine grace, rather than a human action deserving of some credit. Nor did he trouble much over the implications grace had on human freedom or the responsibility to perform good works. Rather, he asked, what faith brought justification? What must one believe to attain salvation (Locke, 1697, sig. A7^{r-v})?

Although posing his question in terms of assent to propositions set Locke off from the Dissenters, the method by which he sought to answer his question kept him firmly within the Protestant camp. Locke turned to what he considered to be the infallible authority of the Bible. He compiled large lists of biblical quotations and citations (see *RCh.*, Appendices, pp. 172–226), seeking to determine what Jesus

had required his followers to believe as recorded in the Gospels and the book of *Acts*. So detailed and thorough was he that the largest portion of the *Reasonableness* came to be an attempt to record in chronological order the life and teachings of Jesus. This method of depending on Jesus' teachings had roots in Protestant attempts to refute Roman Catholic appeals to oral traditions, claimed to be derived from teachings by the resurrected Christ. However, Locke's attempt to reconstruct the earliest teachings of Christianity led him beyond most Protestant predecessors to write a virtual 'life of Jesus'. He even attempted to deal with Jesus' thoughts and intentions, including the apparent attempt to hide his true identity – what would later be called the 'messianic secret'. This concern to return to the earliest teachings of Jesus and his disciples led Locke to focus on what he thought were the more historical portions of the New Testament over the more doctrinal epistles of the New Testament.

Locke concluded from his analysis of the Gospels and *Acts* that all Jesus and his disciples required followers to believe was the one fundamental article that Jesus was the Messiah (*RCh.*, pp. 22–3). However, he also pointed out that, since Jesus had preached to the Jews, it was assumed that his followers must also believe in God. Moreover, although Locke asserted that the meaning of 'Messiah' was easy to understand, it included believing in his miracles, resurrection, ascension and appointment as the ruler and future judge of the world. Such beliefs he said were 'concomitant' articles of faith (*RCh.*, pp. 22, 25–6, 31, 106, 164). While believing these articles of faith were sufficient to *make* one a Christian, Locke was quick to add that Christians were also required to believe everything in divine revelation once they come to know it (*RCh.*, pp. 167–9) and to repent and obey all God's laws (*RCh.*, pp. 111–12). Christianity, Locke concluded, was simple and easy for anyone to understand, resting upon belief of a few propositions. All the systems of theology that had divided Christians over the centuries and in his day were far from the heart of this simple faith.

Locke's book was immediately subjected to virulent attacks by people defending those systems of theology. A Cambridge divine, John EDWARDS, mentioned the *Reasonableness* in a sermon within a month of its publication and then published its first critique (Edwards, 1695). To his dire warnings about multiple causes of atheism, especially the rise of SOCINIANISM and Unitarianism, Edwards appended a twenty-page attack on the *Reasonableness*. Accusing its author of neglecting the doctrines of the Trinity, the divinity of Christ, satisfaction for sins, and the New Testament's epistles, he focused attention on the claim (as he misstated it) that only one article of faith was required of Christians. This conclusion, he asserted, was the result of subjecting everything in Christianity to a test of reason, which proved the author was secretly a Socinian and his book would ultimately lead to atheism.

Locke responded quickly and publicly to Edwards's attack. In November 1695 he published, again anonymously, *A Vindication of the Reasonableness of Christianity, &c. from Mr. Edwards's Reflections*. He met Edwards's ridicule in kind and sought to quote some phrases from *The Reasonableness* to counter charges of his sins of omission. He also indicated that he had, as the title showed, written to 'those who were not yet thoroughly or firmly Christians', those who 'either wholly disbelieved or doubted of the truth of the Christian Religion' (Locke, 1695, pp. 6–7). Thus, he asserted, he had focused on those doctrines upon which Christians were agreed.

In April 1696 Edwards published *Socinianism Unmask'd* and followed it with *The Socinian Creed* at the end of that year. In these attacks he continued his misrepresentation of and charges against the *Reasonableness*, and he first hinted, then openly stated, Locke's authorship. He dedicated the latter book to Edward STILLINGFLEET, Bishop of Worcester, who was at the time engaged in a published debate with Locke. Stillingfleet had suggested (Stillingfleet, 1697) that Locke's *Essay* contributed to the Socinian and Unitarian cause and provided a foundation for John Toland's anonymous *Christianity Not Mysterious*, a classic exposition of DEISM published in 1696. About the same time Richard WILLIS (*Occasional Paper*, 1697) and Richard West (*Animadversions*, 1697) charged that the *Reasonableness* had borrowed its thesis from Thomas HOBBES, a claim later repeated by Edwards.

Amid what Locke termed 'the buz, and flutter, and noise' (Locke, 1695, p. 10) surrounding the publication of the *Reasonableness*, he did find some support; much of it likely unwanted. John Toland anonymously published a brief defence, more of himself than Locke, against Edwards's attack (*Miscellaneous Letters*, 1695). Another anonymous writer also assailed Edwards, but did so to refute the doctrine of the Trinity (*The Exceptions of Mr. Edwards*, 1695). In 1696 two more supporters ([Stephens], 1696; anon., *A Letter to the Deists*, 1696) only further connected the *Reasonableness* to the deist cause. It was not until Samuel Bold, of Jesus College, Oxford and the parish of Steeple in Dorset, came to his defence late in 1696 that Locke found a supporter to value. Bold issued a tract, together with a sermon (Bold, 1697), that defended Locke and attacked Edwards and other detractors of the *Reasonableness*. Although his defence depended heavily on an understanding of faith that Locke may not have shared, Bold repeated his support in additional publications over the following years. Nevertheless, within just over a year after its publication, Locke's book had been associated with deism, Socinianism or Unitarianism, and Hobbism, three of the most widely decried traditions by those within the Church of England.

Locke vehemently defended himself against all these charges. He claimed in *A Second Vindication* (Locke, 1697, sig. a2^r) to have written his book *against* the deists 'who thought either that there was no need of Revelation at all, or that the Revelation of our

Saviour required the Belief of such Articles for Salvation, which the settled Notions and their way of reasoning in some, and want of Understanding in others, made impossible to them'. While evidence supporting Locke's real intentions in writing is meagre, he had recorded in a commonplace book in 1695 a note reading 'Uriel Acosta the father and patriarch of the Deists' (Oxford, Bodleian Library, MS Locke d. 10, p. 33). Locke may well have encountered Acosta's claims of the sufficiency of natural religion and denial of the need for revelation from a book by his friend Philippus van LIMBORCH (van Limborch, 1687). He might also have known Toland's work even though it was not published until the year after the *Reasonableness* appeared. He knew Toland well enough to have lent him money and while he was writing his book, Locke received 'Mr. T's Papers', possibly a manuscript portion of *Christianity Not Mysterious* (John Freke and Edward Clarke to Locke, 9 April 1695, *Corr.*, vol. v, pp. 326–7). Although Toland had borrowed extensively from the *Essay*, he departed from Locke in crucial ways. Locke had maintained that faith must accept any proposition delivered in a clear or evident revelation if it was not contradicted by certain knowledge, which led him to accept a wide range of revealed propositions (*E*, IV.xviii.8–10, pp. 694–6). Toland, however, held that one should not accept anything that cannot be confirmed by reason, leading to his rejection of whatever he found to be mysteries. The *Reasonableness* sought to refute those, like Acosta, who found no need for revelation and those, like Toland, who claimed reason could know or confirm any truth (*RCh.*, pp. 141–64). Locke's thesis of a simple, reasonable Christianity was suited, he asserted, to all people – both those who cannot determine the truth on their own or those who find some truths to be above reason.

In countering the charges that he was a Socinian and a Hobbist, Locke claimed never to have read the writings of the Socinians (Locke, 1695, pp. 22–3; Locke, 1697, pp. 223–4, 350)

as he also claimed not to be well read in Hobbes (Locke, 1699, p. 422). His assertions, however, appear to be contradicted by his ownership of their books and by evidence of notes he had taken on them. While such prevarication may be grounds for suspecting Locke's veracity, little evidence exists of Locke's religious thinking being directly influenced by the Socinians, the English Unitarians, or even Hobbes.

Making a case for his substantial agreement with the Socinians and Unitarians is complicated by determining the distinguishing marks of these groups and by the limited records of Locke's opinions on many fine points of theology. In the case of Hobbes, however, the two agreed almost precisely on what was required to become a Christian. However, there is also strong evidence that Locke owned, read and approved the books of many authors besides Hobbes, Socinians or Unitarians who proposed a few, simple articles of faith as a means of unifying Christianity.

Having lived through civil wars and constant turmoil over religion, Locke had concluded while at Christ Church that no one possessed infallible knowledge in religion (Biddle, 1977). Soon thereafter he decided that Christians should tolerate one another's differences, finding unity in matters on which they could agree (*ETol.*) and later published anonymously *Epistola de tolerantia* (*EdT*). So when Locke sought in the *Reasonableness* to find what Jesus required his followers to believe, he approached the issue with an expectation that God had made clear a means for all to agree and unite on what was required to be believed to become a Christian, no matter how they might divide themselves on non-essential matters. In this effort he drew upon a long tradition within Christianity – the way of fundamentals.

Irenic theologians of Catholic and Protestant persuasions throughout the sixteenth and seventeenth centuries had drawn upon an ancient Christian tradition emphasizing fundamental articles of faith over matters of lesser importance, sometimes termed *adiaphora* or things indifferent, on which a variety of opinions or practice could be legitimately held. Using this way of fundamentals, reformers such as Erasmus, Castellio and Acontius sought to bridge the gulfs created by the divisions of the Reformation. Their followers in mid seventeenth-century England, including William Chillingworth, applied this approach to bring unity amid splits within the Church of England. Jeremy Taylor, Richard Baxter, Benjamin Whichcote, John Smith, Simon Patrick and others who came to be called Latitudinarians, used the way of fundamentals to seek unity without uniformity. Locke's case in the *Reasonableness* followed this tradition and he explicitly appealed to it (*RCh.*, p. 8; Locke, 1695, pp. 37–8; Locke, 1697, pp. 126, 216, 228). Indeed, he went beyond his predecessors in two respects. He sought to provide a list of the fundamental articles of faith derived from the Bible alone and he maintained that they were so simple and clear therein that everyone, regardless of intellectual capacities, could discover and understand them. In this way he thought his book would contribute to 'Peace and Union amongst Christians' (Locke, 1697, sig. a3ʳ).

Locke's policy of religious TOLERATION provided a context for the few, simple fundamental articles of faith in the Bible. Thus, although he wrote almost exactly what Hobbes had written, Locke's statement was in diametric opposition to Hobbes and any political or religious coercion based upon claims to infallible knowledge. He rejected innate principles and propounded a way of ideas in the *Essay* in part to provide a basis in knowledge and faith for everyone to establish beliefs and opinions free from the dictates of magistrates or systems of theology. In arguing for toleration, Locke cited 'mutual toleration among Christians' as the distinguishing mark of a 'true church'. He urged that Church membership requirements include only what Scripture declared to be necessary (*EdT*, pp. 58–9, 74–5). The *Reasonableness* set forth what Locke considered to be that fundamental faith, grounded in the Bible itself and available for all to understand, leaving Christians free to tolerate each others' differences on matters indifferent.

BIBLIOGRAPHY

Primary Sources

[Anon.], *A Letter to the Deists* (London, 1696).

——, *Exceptions of Mr. Edwards, The,* in *A Third Collection of Tracts* ([London], 1695).

——, *Miscellaneous Letters,* vol. xix ([London], September 1695), pp. 465–7.

Biddle, John C., 'John Locke's Essay on Infallibility: Introduction, Text and Translation', *Journal of Church and State,* vol. xix (1977), pp. 301–27.

Bold, Samuel, *Some Passages in the Reasonableness of Christianity, &c. and its Vindication; with Some Animadversions on Mr. Edward's Reflections on the Reasonableness of Christianity, and on his Book, Entitled Socinism Unmask'd* (London, 1697).

Edwards, John, *Some Thoughts concerning the Several Causes and Occasions of Atheism* (London, 1695).

——, *Socinianism Unmask'd* (London, 1696).

——, *The Socinian Creed* (London, 1697).

[Locke, John,] *A Vindication of the Reasonableness of Christianity, &c. from Mr. Edwards's Reflections* (London, 1695).

——, *A Second Vindication of the Reasonableness of Christianity, &c.* (London, 1697).

Locke, John, *Mr. Locke's Reply to the Right Reverend the Lord Bishop of Worcester's Answer to his Second Letter* (London, 1699).

[Stephens, William], *An Account of the Growth of Deism in England* (London, 1696).

Stillingfleet, Edward, *A Discourse in Vindication of the Doctrine of the Trinity* (London, 1697).

Toland, John, *Christianity Not Mysterious* (London, 1696).

Van Limborch, Philippus, *De veritate religionis Christianae* (Gouda, 1687).

[West, Richard], *Animadversions on a Late Book Entituled The Reasonableness of Christianity* (Oxford, 1697).

[Richard Willis], *Occasional Paper*, vol. i (London, 1697).

John C. Higgins-Biddle

PAPERS ON MONEY

In 1988 Patrick Kelly commented that Locke's works on interest and money that were 'a major source for the interpretation of the *Two Treatises* [lay] still virtually unexploited amongst the author's own papers'. To some extent the potential to develop a firmer understanding of Locke's politics through these works remains unfulfilled, even after Kelly's having provided a seminal contribution to bringing that objective within reach with his two-volume edition of *Locke on Money*. Thanks to Kelly's rich annotations and carefully crafted introduction (*LoM*, pp. 1–162), we know a great deal about the direct contexts, gestation and dating of different pieces as well as the interrelations among Locke's economic writings. In addition, Kelly discussed such longstanding issues as the position of Locke in the history of economic thought, and the quantity theorem in particular, and the role Locke actually played in the debates leading up to the Great Recoinage of 1696.

Roughly speaking, Locke's works on money belong to two different periods. His first writing on money, which consists of three parts and remained unpublished during his lifetime, stems from the context of the years 1668 and 1674. As a member of the household of the later Earl of SHAFTESBURY, which he joined in 1667,

Locke drew up 'Some of the Consequences that are like to follow upon Lessening of Interest to 4 per Cent' (*LoM*, pp. 167–202). In order to resolve the capital problems of the East India Company and the English national debt crisis that was reinforced by lagging tax revenues in the aftermath of the Second Anglo-Dutch War, Josiah Child had argued that the key to increasing international commercial competitiveness lay in a reduction of the legal interest rate to four percent (Child, 1668; Keirn and Melton, 1990). Child's proposal sparked a small debate in which he was accused of promoting partisan interests. That Locke, who – like Shaftesbury – busied himself with colonial trade and politics, responded to Child's monetary proposal becomes less of a surprise once the wider perspective of his early text on money is considered. Locke's writing was not so much a direct refutation of Child as a more programmatically inspired analysis of the real effects of legal alterations of the value of money. As Kelly suggests, Locke's venture into the field of monetary politics must be seen in connection with the striking vision of aggressive commercial empire developed by Benjamin Worsley, which Locke appears to have shared (*LoM*, pp. 6–7 and 10). Guided by the perspective of his earlier studies in NATURAL LAW, the way in which Locke understood the function of money and his idea of there being a 'natural RATE OF INTEREST' resulted in a thorough critique of Child's entire outlook on money that, moreover, accorded neatly with Worsley's and Shaftesbury's views of commercial policy.

Locke's more famous – and influential – writings on money were written in the 1690s. Upon his return from Holland in 1689 and the publication of his main works he was solicited by the later Lord Chancellor John Somers to give his views on two proposals, for an interest reduction and a devaluation, that had already failed to pass before the Commons. This request would by a chance of events lead to the publication by Locke of three pamphlets between 1691 and 1696 that are part of a wider debate associated with the Great Recoinage of

1696 (Li, 1963; Horsefield, 1960). The initial occasion resembled the earlier context in which Locke dedicated himself to monetary politics. Backed by the publication of Child's *A Discourse about Trade*, some prominent members of the East India Company argued for the necessity to lower the interest rate in order to safeguard the English economy and sustain its military efforts in the Nine Years War (Child, 1690). In order to resolve problems arising from a deteriorating currency, others proposed devaluation. Based on his earlier views, as he acknowledged himself (*LoM*, p. 210) in his first anonymous pamphlet *Some Considerations of the Consequences of the Lowering of Interest, and Raising the Value of Money* (1691), Locke engaged with the very LOGIC that was behind their economic arguments, and he concluded that since the measures proposed were grounded on faulty presuppositions, they could never have their desired effects (*LoM*, pp. 209–342). If the tone of this pamphlet appears more detached from particular circumstances, its sequel, *Short Observations on a Printed Paper*, was more directly bound up with its political purpose (*LoM*, pp. 346–59). Written in 1693, at the moment Charles Montague first came out advocating a devaluation policy, the *Short Observations* was published in 1695 as an immediate response to the 'Fourteen Resolutions' put forward by a committee established by Montague who, supported by the officials of the Tower Mint, pleaded for a nine per cent devaluation of the coin. Locke's *Further Considerations concerning Raising the Value of Money* (1695) contained, as its subtitle indicated, more detailed arguments on the same topic to refute the *Report* published by William Lowndes, the Treasury Secretary, in support of a recoinage combined with a devaluation (*LoM*, pp. 403–81, cf. pp. 363–97). This last pamphlet, which included the gist of his policy memoranda requested by the government in 1695, extended and deepened Locke's involvement, somewhat against his will, in the same protracted controversy. The debate came to an end in 1696 with the decision for a non-devalua-tionary recoinage with which Locke's name has ever since been associated (Fay, 1933; Kleer, 2004). It is to Patrick Kelly's credit (*LoM*, pp. 106–9) that Montague's role in the political process was revealed and that the myth of Locke's influence on the government's eventual decision was exposed – the myth which had become a commonplace in the eighteenth century (Galiani, 1751, pp. 163–4; Pagnini and Tavanti, 1751, vol. i, p. xxiii).

As Kelly has emphasized (1988, pp. 273–4; *LoM*, p. 3), further study on Locke's writings of money is due to shed new light on the later sections of chapter five of the 'Second Treatise' (*TTG* II.45–50): this is where Locke sketches his vision of the progress of civilization by reference to the emergence of money. Yet, when situated in the context of an English debate on commercial empire, Locke's idea of money in chapter 5 of the 'Second Treatise' can be seen as a theoretical support for his fundamental objections to financial politics as an appropriate field for interstate competition. Analysis of Locke's pamphlets in closer conjunction with ideas about foreign trade that prevailed in circles in which Locke moved (Clarke, Freke, James and John Houblon, Shaftesbury, Worsley, Cary), and in contrast to the vision laid out by Child and others, will produce a sharper outlook on the rival visions of commercial empire in late seventeenth-century English politics (cf. Harpham, 1985; Davison and Keirn, 1988; Appleby, 1976 and 1978). Such a perspective may be useful for a long overdue reconsideration of Locke's membership of the Board of Trade (Laslett, 1969). Finally, dissociating Locke's works on money from the narrow context of the Great Recoinage may pave the way for explaining their enduring attraction to eighteenth-century political thinkers in all corners of Europe. If his views on 'the relationship between money and trade' gave a distinctive impulse to the course of political economic thought, as Kelly suggested (Kelly, 1988, p. 276), Locke's works on money still merit to be studied in closer relation to their political contexts.

BIBLIOGRAPHY
Primary Sources
Child, Josiah, *Brief Observations concerning Trade, and Interest of Money* (1668).
——, *A New Discourse of Trade* (1690).
Galiani, Ferdinando, *Della moneta* (Naples, 1751).
Pagnini, Giovanni Francesco, and Angelo Tavanti (eds), *Ragionamenti sopra la moneta l'interesse del danaro le finanze e il commercio scritti e pubblicati in diverse occasioni dal signor Giovanni Locke*, 2 vols (Florence, 1751).

Secondary Literature
Appleby, Joyce, 'Locke, Liberalism and the Natural Law of Money', *Past and Present*, vol. lxxi (1976), pp. 43–69.
——, *Economic Thought and Ideology in Seventeenth-Century England* (Princeton, 1978).
Davison, Lee, and Tim Keirn, 'John Locke, Edward Clarke, and the 1696 Guineas Legislation', *Parliamentary History*, vol. vii (1988), pp. 228–40.
Fay, C.R., 'Locke versus Lowndes', *Historical Journal*, vol. iv (1933), pp. 143–55.
Harpham, Edward J., 'Class, Commerce, and the State: Economic Discourse and Lockean Liberalism in the Seventeenth Century', *Western Political Quarterly*, vol. xxxviii (1985), pp. 565–82.
Horsefield, J. Keith, *British Monetary Experiments 1650–1710* (Cambridge, Massachusetts, 1960).
Keirn, Tim, and Frank T. Melton, 'Thomas Manley and the Rate-of-Interest Debate, 1668–1673', *The Journal of British Studies*, vol. xxix (1990), pp. 147–73.
Kelly, Patrick, '"All things richly to enjoy": Economics and Politics in Locke's *Two Treatises of Government*', *Political Studies*, vol. xxxvi (1988), pp. 273–93.
——, 'General Introduction: Locke on Money', in *LoM* (1991), vol. i, pp. 1–105.
Kleer, Richard A., '"The ruine of their Diana": Lowndes, Locke, and the Bankers', *History of Political Economy*, vol. xxxvi (2004), pp. 533–56.
Laslett, Peter, 'John Locke, the Great Recoinage, and the Origins of the Board of Trade: 1695–1698', in John W. Yolton (ed.), *John Locke, Problems and Perspectives: A Collection of New Essays* (Cambridge, 1969), pp. 137–64.
Li, Ming-Hsun, *The Great Recoinage of 1696 to 1699* (London, 1963).

Koen Stapelbroek

OF THE CONDUCT OF THE UNDERSTANDING

In 1697 Locke started work on a chapter that he intended to include in the fourth edition of the *Essay concerning Human Understanding*. The name of the chapter was 'Of the Conduct of the Understanding'. The 'Conduct' was never finished and in 1706, two years after Locke's death, his kinsman Peter King included the work in a volume of *Posthumous Works*. The 'Conduct' is a jumble of topics and themes. King made a start with ordering the text, but it is not surprising that he was defeated at an early stage. His edition in the *Posthumous Works* basically follows the order of the original manuscripts (Bodleian Library, MS Locke e.1 and MS Locke c.28, fols 121–38).

In the introductory paragraphs to the 'Conduct', Locke stresses the importance of the understanding, its liability to errors of all kinds and the possibility of curing these errors. Although its catalogue of errors is rather bewildering in its lack of order, the 'Conduct' has a clear function in the broader context formed by Locke's main work, the *Essay*. This exceptionally rich work can be seen, amongst other things, as an alternative LOGIC that revolved not around 'empty' words, like traditional Aristotelian logic, but around ideas as the signs for 'things themselves'. In the same way as Aristotle had written a separate treatise on the errors that are relevant for his syllogistic logic *(De sophisticis elenchis)*, the 'Conduct' can be seen as an analysis of error in the context of Locke's new logic of ideas. This logic consists of two stages. In the first stage we should take care to start with ideas that are clear and distinct. The second stage consists of reasoning that is based on these clear and distinct ideas. Locke's analysis of error in the 'Conduct' runs parallel to the two stages in his logic of ideas. An error of the first kind is to accept ideas that are obscure or confused as the basis of subsequent reasoning; an error of the second kind is a defect in reasoning itself.

Reference to the 'Conduct' is to the paragraph numbers established by Paul Schuurman, followed by the traditional section numbers used by King and subsequent editions. Quotations are taken not from King but from the original manuscripts.

In par. 98 (sect. 3) of the 'Conduct', Locke characterizes the two main kinds of error as '[1] the want of determined Ideas and of Sagacity and [2] exercise in finding out and laying in order intermediate Ideas'. An important example of an error of the first kind is the 'custom of takeing up with principles that are not self evident and very often not soe much as true' (par. 10/sect. 5). When discussing this error, Locke gives special attention to Aristotelian schoolmen who waste the time of their pupils with 'purely logical enquirys' (par. 84/sect. 43) and to the 'zealous bigots' (par. 67/sect. 34) of the various religions; both fail to analyse the principles they build on. Another error of the first kind is not so much that of having wrong principles, but that of starting with one-sided principles, i.e. erecting our opinions 'upon a single view' (par. 24/sect. 7).

Once we have taken the first hurdle of a prior examination of our principles, we should take care in the subsequent process of reasoning to observe 'the connection of Ideas and following them in train' (par. 17/sect. 6). Things go wrong at this stage when we reason either erroneously or not at all. On the whole, Locke seems to be more afraid of errors of the first kind than of errors in reasoning itself. Once we have managed to get before us the basic material, clear and distinct ideas, we are not likely to make mistakes in any subsequent reasoning (see par. 98/sect. 3).

Locke discusses two general causes of error. Some errors arise because factors from outside impede the proper functioning of our understanding. Other errors are caused by defects in the understanding itself. In the *Essay*, Locke had explained that the main extraneous cause of our errors is formed by an *'uneasiness* of desire', which usually takes the form of a passion, such as fear, anger, envy or shame (*E*, II.xxi.39, pp. 256–7). Passions often determine our will, and when this happens, we are prone to error. Our 'natural tempers and passions' influence our judgement (par. 40/sect. 14); men 'espouse opinions that best comport with their power, profit or credit' (par. 41/sect. 15); and their partiality prompts them to 'a phantastical and wilde attributeing all knowledg to the Ancients alone or to the Modernes' (par. 49/sect. 24).

Defects in our understanding form another source of error. Here the great problem is habit or custom. It is custom that causes a 'takeing up with principles that are not self evident and very often not soe much as true' (par. 11/sect. 6). The most interesting instance of the nefarious influence of 'the empire of habit' is that of the gradual but wrong association of different ideas, a process by which 'unnatural connections become by custom as natural to the mind, as sun and light' (par. 77/sect. 41). According to Locke, knowledge is based on our ability to see the agreement and disagreement between individual ideas. The danger of association is that it vitiates this very ability by contaminating the individual ideas under consideration with other ideas. Moreover, a man is prone to wrong association in every state of mind, not only when he is 'under the power of an unruly Passion', but also in perfectly calm circumstances; and since it is 'a very hard thing to convince any one that things are not soe, and naturaly soe as they constantly appear to him' (par. 76/sect. 41), it is an error that is difficult to eradicate.

Locke notes, however, that there are 'a great many natural defects in the understanding capable of amendment' (par. 5/sect. 2). His favourite remedy for error is mental exercise or practice. The relation between errors caused by habit or custom, and remedies consisting of practice, is one of *similia similibus curantur*. In the *Essay*, he had explained that wrong habits or customs are caused by the frequent repetition of 'Trains of Motion in the Animal Spirits' (*E*, II. xxxiii.6, p. 396) and in the 'Conduct', he stresses that wrong repetitions must be prevented or cured by right repetitions provided by practice; 'practise must setle the habit' (par. 8/sect. 4). The mind is like the body; both can be raised to a higher pitch only by repeated actions (par. 7/sect. 4). Since 'we are of the ruminating kinde' (par. 45/sect. 20), repetition corresponds well with our nature. Exercise helps us to look into our own individual principles and helps us 'in finding out and laying in order intermediate Ideas' (par. 77/sect. 41).

In this way the analysis of the nature and causes of error and its remedies in the 'Conduct' forms a practical and didactic complement to the *Essay concerning Human Understanding*.

BIBLIOGRAPHY
Primary Sources
Locke, John, *Posthumous Works of Mr. John Locke: viz. I. Of the Conduct of the Understanding* ..., ed. Peter King (London, 1706).
——, 'Of the Conduct of the Understanding', ed. Paul Schuurman (PhD thesis, University of Keele, 2000), accessible at www.digitallockeproject.nl.

Paul Schuurman

A PARAPHRASE AND NOTES ON THE EPISTLES OF ST PAUL

A Paraphrase and Notes on the Epistles of St Paul is John Locke's last major work. It was incomplete at his death and was published posthumously (1705–7). The published work treats only five of the apostle's letters: Galatians, 1st and 2nd Corinthians, Romans and Ephesians. Locke had intended to comment on all the canonical Pauline epistles, as well as Hebrews, which was traditionally attributed to St Paul, but whose authorship was even then in dispute. Locke's acceptance of the authenticity of all these letters should not be dismissed as naïvety. His judgement of authorship seems to have been based on sound historical critical principles, among them literary genre, historical context, authorial intention, the author's cast of mind, his style and his virtuosity as a publicist for the Christian religion. These principles are set forth in Locke's masterful 'Essay for the Understanding of St Paul's Epistles by understanding St Paul himself', which was printed as a preface to the whole work (*ParN*, pp. 103–16). In preparing his commentary, Locke employed a polyglot New Testament (in French, Latin and Greek), which he had interleaved and rebound in five volumes (Harrison and Laslett, 1971, no. 2864, Oxford, Bodleian Library, Shelf mark: Locke. 9.103–7). His notes on interleaved pages of these volumes and on additional inserts inform us of his sources and methods, and they record his progress on unfinished letters.

The reasons that led Locke late in life to undertake so large a task remain unclear (*ParN*, p. 2). There appears to have been no serious external challenge that led him to it. More likely, the study of St Paul's writings came as a proper climax of a life devoted to biblical study, which Locke pursued not out of mere curiosity or scholarly disinterest, but from a duty that he admonished all Christians to follow, to 'betake ourselves in earnest to the Study of the way of Salvation, in those holy Writings wherein God has reveal'd it from Heaven, and propos'd it to the World, seeking our Religion where we are sure it is in Truth to be found' (*ParN*, p. 116). By this process, Locke was sure that he would not only discover divine truth, but also enlarge his rational understanding of his place in the world (*E*, IV.xix.4, p. 698).

Pauline themes were not new to Locke. The argument of *The Reasonableness of Christianity* is framed by St Paul's idea of the two Adams: the first Adam brought mortality to the human race, the latter restored it to immortality (1 Cor. 15: 22); and the Pauline themes of justification and the opposition of law and faith figure prominently in it (*RCh*, pp. 11, 19–21). Now Locke sought something more comprehensive than an understanding of these basic themes. He believed that by divine infusion St Paul had come to possess the entire Christian revelation, that he had 'thoroughly digested it', that all the parts of it 'were formed together in his Mind, into one well-contracted harmonious Body' (*ParN*, p. 113). Locke studied St Paul with the expectation that by comprehending his mind, he might bring his own understanding of the Christian religion to as perfect a consummation as might be expected in this life.

The preface to *A Paraphrase and Notes* provides the reader with insight into Locke's hermeneutics and his theory of the art of reading. He acknowledged that St Paul's letters, or any other part of the Bible, presented readers with obstacles much like those they encountered when approaching any antiquarian text. Readers removed in time and place and unfamiliar with the language and circumstance of a text will fail to understand its meaning until they have discovered its historical context, its occasion and the author's purpose in writing it. In this respect, Locke holds to an objective theory of meaning. 'The Genuine Sense of the Author' is attainable through reading: an author's thoughts, once let loose and followed in writing, are retrieved by readers (*E*, Epistle to the Reader, p. 6), although only by diligent effort and discernment, and with an attentiveness to the style and temperament and circum-

stances of the author (*ParN*, p. 105). Attentive reading requires that readers of the New Testament be aware that it was 'written in a Language peculiar to itself', a vulgar form of Greek employed by writers whose idiom was Hebrew and Aramaic; they should also take note of genre, in this instance letters directed to particular audiences of varying temperaments, culture and circumstance. They must be especially attentive to the mind of the author, expressed in the design and purpose of his particular writings, his chosen themes and arguments. The whole tenor of the author's expression, reconstructed in the imagination of the reader, is the objective rule that shows or declares itself to the diligent reader. By this means, the careful reader interprets St Paul's letters by consulting St Paul himself (*ParN*, pp. 109–10, 113). Locke is insistent that there is no other rule. St Paul's meaning replaces every rule of faith: creeds, confessions and suchlike.

To this end the careful reader is advised to shun familiar and authoritative guides, among them the printed text of the Bible. The division of chapter and verse superimposed on biblical texts give the particular verses an aphoristic quality never intended by the author; texts are fragmented and the pieces employed as proof texts for various systems of divinity. The eye deceives the mind, when it is 'constantly disturb'd with loose Sentences, that … appear as so many distinct Fragments' (*ParN*, p. 105).

Contrary to this, Locke contends correctly that St Paul's letters were written as continuous discourses, and so are best read straight through. The meaning of any sentence must be decided by its context, by what comes before and after it in the text; all of this translates in the mind of the reader into a train of thought. Similar misdirection follows from dividing the text into lections for liturgical use. These pericopes are more easily established in the memory than any extended rational discourse; and we have been schooled in them from early childhood. The careful reader must disable the effect of these practices.

It should not be supposed from all this that Locke was proposing to replace traditional piety with a secular historical critical attitude. Rather, by this method of reading Scripture he hoped to gain access to divine truth, which is a saving truth. What sets this apprehension of divine truth apart from conventional piety is its recognition of no other authority but the truth itself, expressed in the meaning of what the apostle has written. Locke credits divine providence with ordaining 'that St. Paul has writ a great Number of Epistles' that, notwithstanding differences of occasion and circumstance, all pertain to his apostolic mission and to related themes (*ParN*, p. 113). *À propos* to this is the important biblical rule that Scripture is to be interpreted by Scripture, spiritual things by spiritual things, and, accordingly, St Paul by St Paul. But Locke cautions that this comparing is not to be done randomly or with premeditated dogmatic philosophical design but by comparing texts that are thematically the same, while accounting for contextual differences (*ParN*, pp. 112–13).

By this method of critical comparison, Locke supposed that the diligent reader would begin to espy the entire Christian revelation, which is the ultimate rule of faith that once resided in the mind of the apostle. Locke could have said of this truth that it is a whole in the form of a system; that it is not a sum of doctrine, but a mode of subjectivity: the mind of the apostle comprehended by the Christian scholar. This may seem an austere form of religion, and it is, but it is quite in keeping with Puritan and Reformed models of piety.

Locke's paraphrases and notes are intended to provide proof of his theory of interpretation; each division of his text is a trial of his method. The mind of St Paul is also on trial. Overall, his method is experimental. Locke intended to show that, notwithstanding his ebullient cast of mind and the effect on it of having received visions and revelations directly from God (2 Cor. 12: 1; *ParN*, p. 307), St Paul was no enthusiast. His style is difficult because his mind is so rich in content that, although it 'lay all

clear and in order open to his view', when it came forth, it 'flow'd like a Torrent' (*ParN*, p. 113). Yet Locke claimed to perceive in his letters a conceptual clarity and a consistency in argument. His commentary was intended to provide proof of this. It was also meant to provide proof that St Paul was fit to carry out his divine commission, that he was a proper instrument of the divine purpose. In a similar vein, Locke's lengthy exposition of messianic secrecy in *The Reasonableness of Christianity*, is offered as proof of the harmony of divine providence in Jesus' actions as Messiah and therefore proof of his messianic calling (*RCh*, pp. 40–108).

Among the themes treated in Locke's commentary, foremost among them is St Paul's 'political theology' (Taubes, 2004). As apostle to the Gentiles, St Paul was engaged in transforming traditional biblical religion into a universal faith. But this religion, in its older or newer varieties, was connected with a nation, Israel, whose ruler was the Messiah, who ruled unseen even before he became incarnate and whose coming into the world was prophesied (*ParN*, pp. 616, 806). St Paul's apostolic mission involved the reconstitution of the nation of Israel as a universal society that in the end of times would replace all political dominion, and the establishment within it of a new law, a law of faith, in contrast to the Mosaic law. This theme is recurrent in the Corinthian letters and Galatians, but is most systematically developed in Romans 9–11 (*ParN*, pp. 560–81). Locke's exposition of these chapters provides the reader with a comprehensive account of his vision of history. The political history of the world is taken to be an expression of divine sovereignty over all nations and civil societies. The rise and fall of nations, their adventures and misadventures, their fortunes and misfortunes, are all governed by an absolute power that builds them up or breaks them down as it pleases the divine will. These events are not altogether arbitrary, however. They reflect the religious and moral practices of nations and are expressions of divine approval and disapproval; although in every respect, there is divine contrivance, God hardening the hearts of those whom he would punish, as he did Pharaoh, and in the destruction of the Jewish nation as punishment for their failure to acknowledge Jesus as their Messiah and King. God was believed to have contrived this also! Yet, according to St Paul, Locke also approving, the purpose of all this apparent injustice is to bring to fruition a divine plan of universal redemption that would conclude with a conversion of the whole nation of Israel. Locke departs from St Paul, however, by placing a limit on this display of divine contrivance of the vicissitudes of history: divine arbitrariness affects only the temporal fortunes of a nation, not the eternal destiny of the people individually, which is altogether a matter of their faith and obedience. In doing so, however,

he limits the scope of the universal salvation envisioned by St Paul. In sum, Locke's commentary reflects a curious combination of ahistorical moral religion, which is essentially individualistic and private, and a particular historical mythology claiming universality. This curious combination is an enduring aspect of his thought.

BIBLIOGRAPHY
Secondary Sources
Harrison, John, and Peter Laslett, *The Library of John Locke* (2nd edn, Oxford, 1971).
Taubes, Jacob, *The Political Theology of Paul* (Stanford, 2004).

Victor Nuovo

6

INFLUENCE

THE INFLUENCE OF LOCKE'S PHILOSOPHY IN THE EIGHTEENTH CENTURY: EPISTEMOLOGY AND POLITICS

The impact of Locke's writings in the eighteenth century is difficult to overstate. It is doubtful if any other thinker at any time in modern European history has had more of an impact in so many different directions, as he did throughout the century. Locke does not rival Aristotle in the longevity of that impact or the inspirational quality of Plato's thought over more than two millennia, but his empiricist epistemology, as embodied primarily in the *Essay concerning Human Understanding*, provided the foundation for much of the thinking of the century, not only in philosophy but also in protestant theology and for much of the enquiry in the natural sciences. Nor was this true only in the English-speaking world: his epistemology was also widely absorbed in Europe. As Hegel, writing in the 1820s, expressed it:

The philosophy of Locke is much esteemed; it is still, for the most part, the philosophy of the English and the French, and likewise in a certain sense of the Germans. To put it in a few words, it asserts on the one hand that truth and knowledge rest upon experience and observation; and on the other the analysis of ABSTRACTION from general determinations is prescribed as the method of knowledge; it is, so to speak, a metaphysical

empiricism, and this is the ordinary method adopted in the sciences (Hegel, 1892, vol. iii, p. 298).

It was not only Locke's epistemology that had this major impact. It was also his political philosophy as expounded particularly in the second *Treatise of Government*, and also in his *Letter on Toleration*. The argument of the former was adopted widely by American radicals in their justification for rejecting British rule and by those framing the constitution of the new country. For those seeking intellectual justification for the revolution in France it supplied argument for the removal of despotic monarchy and the establishment of a republic.

With hindsight it is possible to see Locke's influence passing through various phases in the course of the eighteenth century. In England, by those already well disposed towards the 'new philosophy' associated with Bacon and the Royal Society, his philosophy was warmly received, but it was strongly challenged by others who saw it as a threat to standard theology, morality and traditional scholastic philosophy. From its inception and through the earlier decades of the century there was powerful opposition from many within the Anglican Church. But by the 1730s the hostility became less overt and the number of books published either supporting Locke or drawing on his arguments to support similar positions increased. By this stage, too, Locke's epistemology was closely linked to the natural philosophy of NEWTON as providing a comprehensive account of the mental and physical world (cf. Feingold, 1988, Rogers, 1979, 1982). Its impact in France strengthened through the century and emerged powerfully in the works of *les philosophes* associated with the project of the *Encyclopédie*. But by the end of the century Locke's place in the landscape was diminishing, both from the impact of poets and thinkers associated with the Romantic movement and the rise of a new philosophical vision powerfully articulated in the achievement of Immanuel Kant.

To justify these claims, we must begin with the early reception of Locke's works, and to do so we must remind ourselves of some of the key features of the intellectual context in which they were to appear. But first a general point: novel philosophical positions are rarely, perhaps never, universally welcomed. New philosophy must necessarily challenge accepted positions, and those with a vested interest in the status quo often jealously guard it. It usually takes a while for new ideas to find an audience and followers. This was widely true in the seventeenth century, a time of novel philosophy on a scale not seen since the fourth century BC. Among the first of the new thinkers, Francis Bacon, himself following in the steps of several Renaissance Italian philosophers of the sixteenth century, argued the need for a new LOGIC to achieve knowledge of the natural world, a new method of enquiry, based upon co-operation between experimentalists who force nature to reveal its secrets for the benefit of humanity. On the Continent, however, two of the most important thinkers, Galileo and DESCARTES, recognized Bacon's originality even if he had not given a large enough place in his method to mathematics. It was mathematics, and especially geometry, that provided the paradigm of knowledge that featured powerfully in philosophy and natural philosophy through much of the century. The twin forces of Baconian induction and Euclidean geometry cut through the old teaching to reveal the new men of genius. Locke himself was indebted to Descartes and the Baconian-inspired members of the early

Royal Society, of which he himself was a member. When the *Essay* was published, it was dedicated to the then President of the Royal Society, the Earl of Pembroke. Pembroke was not only a man of learning and friend of Locke, he was politically one of the most powerful men in the country. The association of the *Essay* with the Royal Society and with the new political order in England following the Revolution of 1688 was indicative of the place the work was to acquire in English life in the early decades of the eighteenth century. Many of those who praised its argument at its first publication were often Locke's personal friends, fellow members of the Royal Society, who were well placed as opinion-formers in the coffee houses of London. In the universities and amongst the clergy more widely there was less warmth and often open hostility. All were well aware that Locke had been expelled from Christ Church on the express order of Charles II in 1684 and that he was strongly associated with the Whig cause. Oxford had been for some time prior to 1688 a Tory stronghold and was to remain so for decades to come. Philosophically, the college fellows were generally committed to the doctrine of innate ideas to account for religious and moral knowledge and were therefore immediately opposed to Locke's rejection of innate ideas and suspicious of his whole argument (cf. Tyrrell to Locke, *Corr.*, vol. iv, p. 11). Although Descartes had been making some impact on the teaching for some while, many of the universities were still closely wedded to the scholastic syllabus in both their teaching and their beliefs. In Cambridge, similar resistance to Locke's philosophy was present from its appearance, partly because there remained a strong intellectual inheritance from the Cambridge Platonists, especially Henry More and Ralph Cudworth.

That resistance, however, was to be weakened early in the course of the century, witnessed by the advice given to students about reading and the many reprintings of Locke's works. By 1730 Daniel Waterland, in his *Advice to a Young Student, with a method of study of the first four years*, aimed at under-graduates, recommended Locke's *Conduct of the Understanding* and otherwise commended him. The *Conduct* itself went through eight editions in the century, as well as translations into Dutch, German and Italian. The *Essay* went through fifty-six English editions (or print-ings) by 1800, with numerous editions of Pierre Coste's French translation as well those into German, Latin and Polish. Almost as popular was John Wynne's Abridgement of the *Essay*, a work of which Locke approved, which was published in about fifteen editions (or printings) with translations into French, Italian, German and Greek, and an extract in Russian in 1782. The only other philosophical work of compa-rable reach in the eighteenth century was Pierre Bayle's *Dictionaire historique et critique* (1st edn, 1697), which had enormous sales through-out the eighteenth century but which, whilst sharing many intellectual roots, is such a dif-ferent work from that of Locke that compar-isons are pointless.

Descartes, in his *Principia Philosophiæ* (1644), had offered an account of knowledge and the world that was the most comprehensive system of philosophy to have emerged since Aristotle. Locke's philosophy as we have it in the *Essay*, and produced in the shadow of Descartes, did not attempt to rival it in scope. It deliberately stayed clear of any attempt to offer a natural philosophy, and modestly dis-guised a major tome under the label 'Essay' even though it ran to 360 pages folio, at the time possibly the largest work of epistemology ever written. But as epistemological questions lie at the base of all human inquiry, it was not altogether surprising that it was to provide such a foundation for many intellectual disciplines in the course of the century.

An example of Locke's direct influence is to be found in the logic textbook of Richard Bentham, *An Introduction to Logick, Scholastick and Rational* (a contrast itself indicative), which was widely used in Oxford after its publication in 1773. Locke himself was strongly opposed to the teaching of

scholastic logic, as he made very clear in the *Essay*, but it was to be taught as standard until well into the twentieth century. Bentham's book, in its Section I, 'Of the Soul, its Power and Operations', offers an epistemology entirely Lockean in vocabulary and direction. It begins with a brief account of the senses and the ways in which they provide the *under-standing* with *ideas*. Section II, 'Of Words and their several Kinds', introduces simple and complex ideas and draws on a Lockean account of language. At the close of the book, Bentham sets down a list of questions that can-didates were likely to be asked in examinations and the answers he recommends. These include the rejection of innate ideas, the division of ideas into simple and complex, and a host of questions that are drawn directly from a reading of the *Essay*. By the middle of the century Locke's influence in the CURRICULUM was everywhere to be found (cf. Yolton, 1986). Another author of a logic, the dissenting minister Isaac Watts, also drew enormously on Locke's *Essay* in his widely used *Logick: or the right use of reason in the enquiry after truth* (1725), even though he did not altogether follow Locke in his rejection of innate ideas. That a dissenter was so strongly influenced by Locke's work is indicative of Locke's wider influence outside the established Church and universities. But perhaps this is not so surpris-ing when we remember that Locke is the author of the *Letter on Toleration*. It was not difficult for dissenting ministers and their congregation to see that Locke's account of TOLERATION pointed towards a more just and secure future for their religious practice than had until then existed.

To appreciate Locke's influence on the understanding of logic in the eighteenth century we need to look further at the impact of the Cartesian emphasis on ideas on the under-standing of logic as a discipline. As Paul Schuurman (Schuurman, 2004) has empha-sized, whereas it has been normal practice for historians of philosophy to contrast the ratio-nalist Descartes with the empiricist Locke, with regard to logic both stood on the same side against the scholastic logic teaching of the schools. The 'New Way of Ideas', though not without problems of its own, came to dominate philosophy in the eighteenth century, in both its rationalist and empiricist MODES, even though the latter came to be the more widely accepted version. This dominance was to last until the philosophy of Kant appeared on the scene at the end of the century.

Locke's rejection of classical logic was of course contentious, as was his rejection of virtually the whole of scholastic philosophy, and it is no surprise to find that with the publication of the *Essay* he was very soon attacked by the English Catholic, John SERGEANT, in his *Solid Philosophy asserted against the Fancies of the Ideists* (1697). The 'Ideists' were in particular Descartes and Locke, who Sergeant read as claiming that ideas intervene between us and the world and thereby completely destroy the possibility of 'solid' knowledge of physical reality. Sergeant was one of the few major critics who did not attack Locke for his rejection of innate ideas. And he was one of the first philosophers to see that Descartes and Locke were in important ways on the same side. Sergeant was hardly a typical Catholic – he was dismissed by fellow Catholics as being heretical – but in many ways his response to the *Essay* represented many within the universities and the churches who were still wedded to scholastic philosophy.

William Molyneux, a Protestant citizen of Dublin, had in 1692 recommended Locke's *Essay* to the Provost of Trinity College, who was so impressed with it that he ordered it to be read and examined in the college. So Trinity College, Dublin became the first university to put Locke's work on the curriculum. The effect was significant not only for that reason but because the decision guaranteed that, when George BERKELEY became a student at Trinity in 1700, he was soon introduced to Locke's work, an experience that was probably to have a more profound impact on his philosophical thinking than any other.

This emerges very clearly in Berkeley's early notebooks, known as his *Philosophical Commentaries*, where Locke is by far the most cited philosopher. Berkeley takes over much of Locke's philosophical vocabulary, including the language of ideas as the objects of human understanding, the distinction between PRIMARY AND SECONDARY QUALITIES, which Berkeley was later vigorously to attack, and many other features of the 'Way of Ideas', as the new philosophy was characterized. The *Philosophical Commentaries* were written for Berkeley's personal benefit and not intended to be made public, but it clearly emerges that Berkeley was already seeing Locke as the philosopher whom it is his ambition to confront and refute. Locke is the giant and Berkeley is the pigmy confronting him (Berkeley, 1944, p. 239). Something of Berkeley's regard for Locke as a philosopher can be seen in the paper he almost certainly gave to the Dublin Philosophical Society in 1707 entitled 'Of Infinites', in which Berkeley refers to Locke's *Essay* as 'the incomparable Mr Locke's treatise of *Human Understanding*' (Berkeley, 1951, vol. iv, p. 235). Part 1 of his most famous work of philosophy, *Of the Principles of Human Knowledge*, begins with words that appear to express an entirely Lockean epistemology:

It is evident to anyone who takes a survey of the objects of human knowledge, that they are either ideas actually imprinted on the senses, or else such as are perceived by attending to the passions and operations of the mind, or lastly ideas formed by help of memory and imagination, either compounding, dividing, or barely representing those originally perceived in the aforesaid way (Berkeley, 1951, vol. ii, p. 41).

He then goes on to argue that all those philosophers, such as Locke, who claim that there exist material substances lying behind our ideas as their cause subscribe to a position that is incoherent and unintelligible. That Berkeley delivers a sustained and substantial attack on Locke's philosophy cannot disguise the fact that it is delivered from within an intellectual framework that Berkeley drew from Locke's own philosophical position. Berkeley's assault begins with his rejection of what he takes to be Locke's account of the origin of our 'abstract general ideas'. Berkeley's argument is heavily dependent on reading Locke as taking ideas to be visible images of the things for which they stand. But this reading is open to serious challenge. If Berkeley is correct, then much of his argument against the coherence of the notion of material SUBSTANCE goes through and his ontology of minds and ideas is, at best, very difficult to refute. But the fact remains that, whilst his readers found his argument clever and powerful, it persuaded almost nobody. Locke's philosophy needed adjustment, not rejection, and for the most part the Lockean inheritance was substantially unruffled by Berkeley's intervention.

Famously, Locke, in the Epistle to the Reader prefacing the *Essay*, had announced that he saw his task as an under-labourer clearing the ground for the master-builders, such as BOYLE and Newton. His task was not to offer a comprehensive philosophy, which would have to include a natural philosophy, a physics and cosmology to account for the natural world in the way in which Aristotle and Descartes had provided that much wider picture. Berkeley followed Locke in this narrower conception of the philosopher's task, substantially offering an epistemology and metaphysics without a fully developed physics to go with it, even though he had plenty to say about central physical concepts such as space, time and force, which were highly critical of the version expounded by Newton. But, despite the merit in Berkeley's objections, and rather as in the case of Locke's philosophy, Newton's conceptions prevailed and the Newtonian picture dominated natural philosophy well into the next century.

Meanwhile, Locke's reception in England in the early decades of the century was substan-

tially a battleground, not only in respect of the *Essay* but also with regard to Locke's writings on toleration and religion. We shall return to these later, but we look first at the response to the *Essay*. The first published attack to appear was that of John NORRIS, whose pamphlet 'Cursory Reflections upon a Book Call'd, *An Essay concerning Human Understanding*' was published within a year of the *Essay* itself and reprinted two years later. Like many later critics and the ones that we have seen Tyrrell signal in Oxford, Norris's target was Locke's rejection of innate ideas. A similar but longer assault followed from James Lowde in 1694, *A Discourse concerning the Nature of Man, Both in his Natural and Political Capacity*. In 1697 appeared (anonymously) Thomas BURNET's short *Remarks upon an Essay concerning Human Understanding: in a Letter address'd to the Author*, to be followed shortly by two further *Remarks*. Although Locke defended himself in print against Burnet, he was also strongly supported in 1702 by Catherine COCKBURN in her *A Defence of the 'Essay of Human Understanding'*. Cockburn also wrote another defence of Locke, not published until after her death in 1749. It was aimed at Winch Holdsworth's sermon, significantly delivered in Oxford, charging Locke with SOCINIANISM on the basis of Locke's account of PERSONAL IDENTITY given in the *Essay*. Holdsworth's attack is a good example of the way in which philosophical issues in the *Essay* could rapidly spill out into a major theological dispute. Cockburn argued with some force that, contrary to Locke's detractors, there was no conflict between his empiricism and orthodox Anglican theology and moral theory (cf. Cockburn, 1751). Henry Lee, in 1702, published *Anti-Scepticsm*, which was a critical commentary on each chapter of the *Essay* and which, like Sergeant, identified Locke as amongst the sceptics. Locke's claim that, for all we know, God could add to matter a power of thought, produced a sustained response in John Broughton's *Psychologia; or, An Account of the Nature of the Rational Soul* (1703), anticipating a major issue in Locke commentary for the remainder of the century. Broughton himself came under criticism from Samuel Bold, who defended Locke both for the *Essay* and his *Reasonableness of Christianity* in a series of works from 1697 to 1706, of which the most comprehensive was his *A Collection of Tracts Publish'd in Vindication of Mr Locke's 'Reasonableness of Christianity... and of his 'Essay concerning Humane Understanding'* (1706).

Virtually all the writers we have mentioned who defended or attacked Locke, with the obvious exceptions of Cockburn and Sergeant, were members of the Anglican clergy, nicely reflecting the fact that Locke's philosophy both raised issues central to Anglican theology and the divide between those of a Platonic sympathy, such as John Norris, and those whose inclination was towards the spirit of Baconianism that characterized the 'New Philosophy'. It is no surprise to learn that, at the beginning of his early notebooks, Berkeley, on 7 December 1706, set out some rules for a society which includes the words 'That the business of our meeting be to discourse on some part of the new Philosophy' (Berkeley, 1944, p. 3). What the new philosophy was would have been clear to all the participants, it was embodied in the thought of Locke and the science of Newton.

If Berkeley was the first great philosopher to be strongly influenced by Locke, then the second must be David Hume. By the time that Hume went to Edinburgh University in 1723 the philosophy of Locke and Newton was well established in the curriculum and it appears that Hume absorbed Locke's empiricism into his intellectual map of the world at an early age (he was only thirteen when he went to Edinburgh). In his first major work, *A Treatise of Human Nature* (1739), although Hume is rarely inclined to indicate his debts to earlier thinkers, he acknowledges Bacon and Locke as primary movers in putting the 'science of man on a new footing' (Hume, 1739, p. xxi). And he immediately goes on to identify his position

on the possibility of knowledge as one identical with that of Locke: 'to me it seems evident, that the essence of mind being equally unknown to us with that of eternal bodies, it must be equally impossible to form any notion of its powers and qualities otherwise than from careful and exact experiments' (ibid). Like Locke, too, Hume begins from 'the perceptions of the human mind', which he calls impressions and ideas, and which, again following Locke, he divides into simple and complex. He then goes on to draw on the Lockean notion of the ASSOCIATION OF IDEAS as central to his account of our mental life. These early debts to Locke must not hide the great differences between them, including in their understanding of ideas and impressions. And they do not, of course, detract from Hume's achievements as a philosopher, which emerge in his celebrated analysis of causation, induction, motivation and moral theory, but it does illustrate the way in which Hume's philosophy was largely built on foundations supplied by Locke.

Hume's influence, no more than that of Berkeley, was not to supplant that of Locke in the eighteenth century. But it is generally reckoned to have become very important late in the century through its impact on Kant. In his own testimony, Kant was awoken from his 'dogmatic slumbers' by reading him. If indeed Hume was the catalyst that generated Kant's philosophy, there is a sense in which Hume was crucial to supplanting Locke's philosophy as transcendental idealism came to displace British empiricism as the dominant philosophy in European thought. But there were many things to happen in the world of philosophy and Locke's place in it before that was to happen.

The first published account of Locke's *Essay concerning Human Understanding* appeared not in English but in French. In 1688, in the *Bibliothèque universelle et historique*, edited by Jean Le Clerc and published in Amsterdam, appeared Locke's Abstract of the *Essay*, translated by Jean Le Clerc. It was to the Francophone world, then, that Locke's work was first announced. When the *Essay* was published at the end of the following year, it is no surprise that there was soon a demand for a French edition and Locke was himself keen for that to be realized, but it was to be another ten years before one appeared. It was the work of Pierre Coste, a young Huguenot who through Le Clerc and Locke came to act as a tutor of the MASHAM son, Francis, at Oates where Locke lived for the last fifteen years of his life. Coste was therefore able to discuss the translation with Locke himself. In the course of the century there were at least fifteen French editions of Coste's translation, testifying to its popularity throughout the century.

When we turn to its actual influence in France, the obvious place to begin is with Voltaire. His enthusiasm for Locke's account of knowledge and for Locke's whole intellectual approach was famously expressed in his *Lettres sur les Anglais* (1734). After attacking Descartes and MALEBRANCHE, he turns to Locke: 'After so many random reasoners had been thus forming what might have been called the Romance of the Soul, a sage appears who has modestly presented us with the history of it. Mr Locke has developed human reason to man, just as a skilful anatomist explains the springs and structure of the human body' (Voltaire, 1950, p. 177). Voltaire saw Locke and Newton as the twin founders of a new understanding of the mental and physical world. It was not a message altogether welcomed in France, any more than it had been in England, where Descartes had found wider favour after early opposition. However, a recognition of the merits of both thinkers gradually emerged in the following decades and it was not long before important works began to appear that espoused an essentially Lockean epistemology and a Newtonian physics. This was an image of the two thinkers that was also strongly fostered in England and elsewhere, where popular accounts of Newton's science were often, perhaps always, prefaced with a Lockean epistemology (cf. Pemberton, 1728; Maclaurin, 1748).

Voltaire had drawn attention to the passage in which Locke had conjectured that God might superadd to matter a power of thought. He noted that this speculation had immediately brought down wrath on Locke in England as it was also to do in France. But he also noted that Locke was not thereby committing himself to any kind of materialism. Not only did Locke believe in the possibility of the immortality of the soul, but he had never asserted that matter actually does think, but only that he could see no contradiction in supposing that it may if it is the will of God that it should do so. Voltaire reported that every day his ears were dinned with the exclamations 'Locke denies the immortality of the soul; Locke destroys morality' (Voltaire, 1950, p. 179).

As Voltaire reports it, Locke was notoriously regarded as a free thinker. But, although the charge was unjustified, as Voltaire knew, it nevertheless encouraged radical thinkers to read him. It was not long before French philosophers were producing works that reflected Locke's thought and in some cases advanced beyond it. Important in this regard was Etienne Bonnot de Condillac, whose most important work *Essai sur l'origine des connaissances humaines* (1746), was translated as *An Essay on the Origin of Human Knowledge being a Supplement to Mr Locke's Essay on the Human Understanding* (1756). There can be no doubt at all of Condillac's debts to Locke. He writes in the Introduction to his *Essay* of two kinds of metaphysics, the one that has the ambition of 'solving all mysteries' and 'turns all nature into a kind of enchantment'. With it errors are multiplied endlessly and the mind is satisfied with 'words without meaning'. Most philosophy and philosophers fall into this first class. The other kind of metaphysics 'is more modest and adjusts its inquiries to the weakness of the human mind'. Locke is the only philosopher who has followed this path, whom Condillac contrasts favourably with Descartes. Like Voltaire, Condillac sees Locke as having limited 'himself to the study of the human mind and has completed his task with success'

287

(Condillac, 2001, pp. 3–4). Crucial to Condillac's philosophy is his empiricism. He tells us that the peripatetics were the first to adopt the principle that all knowledge comes from the senses, but it was a truth they did not really understand or explain and it was Locke who had 'the distinction of being the first to demonstrate it' (Condillac, 2001, p. 7).

Condillac concedes that Locke's *Essay* has many faults. It is repetitive and badly organized. His refutation of innate ideas is overdone and he begins his account of words only in Book III, rather than Book II where it should have been. He was, nevertheless, the first to have written on this as 'a true philosopher' (Condillac, 2001, p. 8). It was Condillac's achievement to appreciate the importance of language to knowledge in a way in which it had never before been recognized. It is a paradigmatic example of how Locke's influence was to lead to a philosophical advance that was to be fundamental to the late eighteenth century and beyond.

Condillac was scarcely the last of *les philosophes* to owe much to Locke. Another major figure much in his debt was Marie-Jean-Antoine-Nicolas Critat, Marquis de Condorcet. His *Sketch for a Historical Picture of the Progress of the Human Mind* (1795), a title which in itself tells much about Enlightenment optimism, was apparently completed by Condorcet in hiding soon before his incarceration in a prison cell as a dangerous aristocrat and where he died, perhaps through suicide, in 1794.

In his *Sketch*, Condorcet divided human history into ten stages, of which the last was looking to the future. The ninth was entitled 'From Descartes to the foundation of the French Republic'. He saw the establishment of political economy on mathematical and rational grounds as central to progress, which itself had to be founded in general philosophy and metaphysics. Descartes had brought 'philosophy back to reason' and at last

Locke grasped the thread by which philosophy should be guided; he showed that an exact and precise analysis of ideas, which reduces them step by step to other ideas of more immediate origin or of simpler composition, is the only way to avoid being lost in that chaos of incomplete, incoherent and indeterminate notions which chance presents to us at hazard and we unthinkingly accept (Condorcet, 2001, pp. 132–3).

Locke had established an empiricist philosophy that generated precision. He had been, furthermore, 'the first man who dared set a limit to the human understanding' and its capacities (Condorcet, 2001, p. 133). Locke's method, he went on to claim, 'was soon adopted by all philosophers and … [applied] to politics and to social economy': 'this metaphysical method became virtually a universal instrument … applied to various undertakings of the human understanding' (Condorcet, 2001, p. 134). Locke's philosophy, as Condorcet saw it, lay at the heart of all the achievements of the Enlightenment.

Another thinker as much influenced by Locke as Condillac and Condorcet was Jean d'Alembert, who, with his co-editor Denis Diderot, was largely responsible for the great project of the *Encyclopédie*. It is not so much that Locke's philosophy is argued for in that work but presupposed. Both main authors and most of the contributors (perhaps all) accepted Locke's epistemological premises and proceeded on that basis. It also flirted with the materialist implications in his philosophy, as some readers of Locke found in his refusal to exclude the possibility of thinking matter. This was an issue in Locke's philosophy that had haunted his standing since it had been raised by Bishop STILLINGFLEET soon after the publication of the *Essay*. As Yolton showed, it was to reverberate throughout the French Enlightenment (Yolton, 1991).

If Locke's impact on French thought in the eighteenth century was as substantial as has been suggested, it must also be remembered that French had generally replaced Latin as the language of intellectual exchange throughout

Europe. Coste's translation of the *Essay* was read from Amsterdam to Prague and from Warsaw to Florence. But translations into other languages also became popular as the century advanced. Burridge's Latin translation appeared in 1701 in London, and in Leipzig in 1709, 1741 and 1758, indicating a fairly brisk German market. Burridge's translation was also published in Naples in five volumes 1788–91. There was a Polish translation published in Cracow in 1784 and a three-volume German translation published in Leipzig, 1795–7.

Locke's direct influence on German philosophy in the eighteenth century was never of the same order as his impact in France. LEIBNIZ, the greatest German philosopher before Kant, had attempted to make direct contact with Locke in 1699 but without much success. His letter about the *Essay* was treated with disdain by Locke, who knew of Leibniz primarily as a mathematician, not as a philosopher, a misapprehension in part excused when it is remembered that most of Leibniz's philosophical works were still to appear. Leibniz's assessment of the *Essay*, the *New Essays on the Understanding*, was not published until 1765. In it Leibniz is full of praise for Locke, but shows his own philosophical position was very different, even though he had had hopes of a possible synthesis. In 1765 Leibniz was still a powerful philosophical influence, but it is unclear if his work generated any interest in Locke's thought in Germany. Before this, however, Christian Thomasius, one of Leibniz's teachers, had expressed an empiricist epistemology at virtually the same time as Locke. It was not widely accepted, however, as it was the rationalism of Leibniz, Spinoza and Christian Wolff that was the more influential in German thought until French Enlightenment thinking, and via it Locke's thought, made its full impact towards the end of the century. By the time that we reach Kant it is worth remembering that many other British empiricist philosophers, of whom Berkeley and Hume were only two of several, had published works that began from

Lockean premises and which were also being read and were beginning to be influential.

In the Netherlands, it is not clear how much impact Locke's epistemology made. It is easier to see his influence as part of a wider acceptance of 'the logic of ideas' and Newton's mathematical physics more generally than to find disciples of Locke (on this see especially Schuurman, 2004) and it is not surprising that Descartes and Spinoza remained powerful influences there throughout the century. It is of note that, though all had the *Essay* on their shelves, only a few Dutch thinkers became fully committed to empiricism as a philosophy, or to any other particular school of thought, and remained for the most part eclectic in their outlook.

The story was different in the English New England colonies. Throughout the seventeenth century they were strongly Calvinist and in the eighteenth there was a strong commitment to the view that the individual was responsible for his own salvation. The first important thinker to articulate this was Jonathan Edwards (1703–1758), regarded as the most able philosopher of the century in North America. He was educated at Yale College, where, like at Harvard, Locke's *Essay* was central to the syllabus. Its impact on Edwards was crucial – it was 'the formative document in Edwards's development' (Kuklick, 2001, p. 8).

It was not, of course, only Locke's *Essay* that was widely read throughout Europe in the eighteenth century. Almost as important were his *Two Treatises of Government* (1690), especially the second. The English edition was republished about ten times in the century as well as in the many editions of the *Works*. Significantly there was an edition published in Boston in 1773. There was a French translation in 1691 of the Second Treatise only, and a further ten printings to 1795. There was a German translation in 1718, a Dutch in 1728, Swedish in 1726 and Italian in 1773. The number of French printings in the period leading up to the Revolution is striking and it is possible that the French version actually reflected Locke's own wish (Laslett in *TTG*, p.13). All the translations were only of the second Treatise and also omitted the first bridging chapter of that. The effect is to make the work appear to be advocating an account of society which is at least in spirit republican rather than of a limited monarchy.

In the North American colonies in the eighteenth century leading up to the war of independence, the place of Locke's *Two Treatises* was once regarded as central and obvious, but in the mid and late twentieth century this reading was challenged by several highly regarded scholars. However, the work of more recent historians has once again claimed 'the great Mr Locke' as the leading philosophical source for a justification for the right to revolution and also as setting the framework for the constitution that actually was adopted for the new republic (cf. Dworetz, 1990, *passim*). Not only was Locke's political theory widely read and cited, but his epistemology and theology, implicitly or explicitly, lay behind the sermons of the New England clergy. As Carl Becker expressed it, in the eighteenth century 'most Americans had absorbed Locke's works as a kind of political gospel' (Becker, 1958, p. 27).

Locke's *A Letter concerning Toleration* was also extensively read throughout the eighteenth century. It appeared in Latin, English and Dutch in 1689 and there were many later editions, together with the *Second and Third Letters*. In 1710 was published *Oeuvres Diverses de Monsieur John Locke*, which contained a translation of the *Letter*, and there was an edition of the *Traité sur la Tolerance* in 1764. Editions were published in Boston in 1743 and Wilmington in 1764. Equally widely available in many editions and translations were *The Reasonableness of Christianity* and *Some Thoughts concerning Education*.

Gilbert Ryle drew attention to Locke's influence by claiming, with only slight exaggeration, that it is possible just by reading a sermon of the period to detect whether or not it had been given before or after the publication of the *Essay* (Ryle, 1990, p. 147). Not only did

Locke's epistemology set the agenda for philosophy but his philosophy and his religious writings were central to much, probably most, protestant religious writing in the English-speaking world throughout the century. Of course only a minority of theologians would have been prepared to describe themselves as Lockeans, but there were none who were not familiar with his epistemology and *The Reasonableness of Christianity*. The list of those whose own writings were directly influenced by Locke's thought is long indeed (cf. Sell, 1997, *passim*). Perhaps, as Sell claims, Locke's most important contribution to theology was to encourage 'many divines to set out from the starting point of epistemology and to seek a reason for their faith' (Sell, 1997, p. 270) rather than to rely on traditional authority for religious certainties. It was always Locke's strong message in epistemological, religious and moral issues to turn to the power of the individual intellect to provide answers, or to come to recognize its limits, and not succumb to claims of authority that when examined usually were found to be based on unsubstantiated foundations.

We have already noted some of the large number of editions of Locke's works and indicated some of the very many responses both positive and negative that they generated in the century, but one initial work should be noted. It is that of Thomas Morell. In 1794 he published *Notes and Annotations on Locke on the Human Understanding. Written by Order of the Queen*. Queen Charlotte was a lady with serious intellectual interests and she had clearly decided that she should know about the thought of England's most famous philosopher. By the end of the century Locke was regarded as the country's official philosopher, confirmed by copies of his collected works in all the grand libraries of lords and gentlemen throughout the land – even if they did not always show much sign of having been read. His expulsion from Christ Church in 1684 by order of the king was a very distant memory.

BIBLIOGRAPHY
Primary Sources
Bayle, Pierre, *Dictionaire historique et critique* (Amsterdam, 1697; 2nd edn, 1702).

Bentham, Richard, *An Introduction to Logick, Scholastick and Rational* (Oxford, 1773).

Berkeley, George, *Philosophical Commentaries*, ed. A.A. Luce (1944).

——, *The Works of George Berkeley*, 9 vols, ed. A.A. Luce (1951).

Bold, Samuel, *A Collection of Tracts Publish'd in Vindication of Mr Locke's 'Reasonableness of Christianity' … and of his 'Essay concerning Humane Understanding'* (1706).

Broughton, John, *Psychologia; or An Account of the Rational Soul* (1703).

[Burnet, Thomas], *Remarks upon an Essay concerning Human Understanding: in a Letter address'd to the Author* (1697).

Cockburn, Catherine, *A Defence of the 'Essay of Human Understanding'* (1702).

——, *A Vindication of Mr Locke's Christian Principles, from the injurious Imputations of Dr Holdsworth, Parts I and II*, in *The Works of Mrs Catherine Cockburn*, 2 vols (1751), vol. i, pp. 157–377.

Condillac, Etienne Bonnot, *Essay on the Origin of Human Knowledge*, ed. Hans Aarsleff (Cambridge, 2001).

Condorcet, Nicolas de, *Sketch for a Historical Picture of the Progress of the Human Mind*, trans. June Barraclough, with an Introduction by Stuart Hampshire (1955).

Hegel, G.W.F., *Lectures on the History of Philosophy*, 3 vols, trans. E.S. Haldane and F.H. Simson (1892).

Hume, David, *A Treatise of Human Nature* (1739), ed. L.A. Selby-Bigge (Oxford, 1888).

Lee, Henry, *Anti-Scepticsm* (1702).

Leibniz, G.W., *New Essays on Human Understanding*, trans. and ed. P. Remnant and J. Bennett (Cambridge, 1981).

Locke, John, *An Abridgement of Mr Locke's Essay concerning Human Understanding* [by John Wynne] (1696).

[Lowde, James], *A Discourse concerning the Nature of Man, Both in his Natural and Political Capacity* (1694).

Maclaurin, Colin, *An Account of Sir Isaac Newton's Philosophical Discoveries* (1748).

Morell, Thomas, *Notes and Annotations on Locke on the Human Understanding. Written by Order of the Queen* (1794).

Norris, John, *Cursory Reflections upon a Book Call'd*, An Essay concerning Human Understanding (1692).

Pemberton, Henry, *A View of Sir Isaac Newton's Philosophy* (1728).

Sergeant, John, *Solid Philosophy asserted against the Fancies of the Ideists* (1697).

Voltaire, *Letters concerning the English*, ed. Desmond Flower (1950).

Waterland, Daniel (1950), *Advice to a Young Student, with a method of study of the first four years* (Cambridge and Oxford, 1755).

Watts, Isaac, *Logick: or the right use of reason in the enquiry after truth* (1725).

Secondary Literature
Becker, Carl, *The Declaration of Independence* (New York, 1958).

Dworetz, Steven M., *The Unvarnished Doctrine. Locke, Liberalism and the American Revolution* (Durham, North Carolina, 1990).

Feingold, Mordechai, 'Partnership in Glory: Newton and Locke through the Enlightenment and Beyond', *Newton's Scientific and Philosophical Legacy* (Dordrecht, 1988) pp. 291–308.

Kuklick, Bruce, *A History of Philosophy in America, 1720–2000* (Oxford, 2001).

Rogers, G.A.J., 'Locke's *Essay* and Newton's *Principia, Journal of the History of Ideas*, vol. xxxix (1978), pp. 217–32.

——, 'The System of Locke and Newton', *Contemporary Newtonian Research*, ed. Zev Bechler (Dordrecht, 1982), pp. 215–38.

Ryle, Gilbert, 'John Locke', in *Collected Papers*, 2 vols (1971; repr. Bristol, 1990), vol. i, pp. 147–57.

Schuurman, Paul, *Ideas, Mental Faculties and Method. The Logic of Ideas of Descartes and Locke and Its Reception in the Dutch Republic, 1630–1750* (Leiden, 2004).

Sell, Alan P.F., *John Locke and the Eighteenth-Century Divines* (Cardiff, 1997).

Yolton, J., 'Schoolmen, Logic and Philosophy', *The History of Oxford University, Volume 5, The Eighteenth Century*, ed. L.S. Sutherland and L.G. Mitchell (Oxford, 1986), pp. 565–91.

Yolton, John W., *Locke and French Materialism* (Oxford, 1991).

G.A.J. Rogers

THE RECEPTION OF LOCKE IN ENGLAND IN THE EARLY EIGHTEENTH CENTURY: METAPHYSICS, RELIGION AND THE STATE

Henry Longueville Mansel once observed that in the first half of the eighteenth century in England, 'both the assailants and the defenders of Christianity borrowed their weapons from the armoury of Locke' (Mansel, 1873, p. 296). Mansel's observation brings out well the heterogeneous character of some of Locke's readers' responses to his writings during this period. It also suggests something of the sheer intellectual power to which they were responding in Locke. For it is a mark of intellectual power that it evokes further thought in many directions – as much by repulsion as by attraction – and often along lines that could not have been predicted. Consequently, it becomes difficult to identify confidently when a response has been evoked, and more difficult still to

capture the overall shape of these responses in a single picture that makes sense of them collectively. When intellectual power is exercised over a wide range of topics, as it was by Locke, then the difficulties increase exponentially. As there is no way round these difficulties, this essay must tiptoe its way through them along a very narrow path.

To consider the reception of Locke is in effect to pose two questions about him: what difference did he make to posterity, and why did he make the difference that he did? These questions may be posed with different purposes in mind, and answers to them may be pursued in many different ways. Sometimes the purpose is iconoclastic – to dispel 'a myth of Locke, which presents his thinking as ubiquitous, and sometimes of exclusive importance, in eighteenth-century thought and culture' (Pocock, 1991, p. 45) or to show that the difference Locke made to a particular constituency of opinion has been wildly overstated (Dunn, 1969). Sometimes the purpose is revisionary – to reassert Locke's catalytic role in subsequent thought by identifying, selecting and collecting together some of the vast array of texts which in one way or another reacted to his cues (Goldie, 1999), to trace the contours of his posthumous reputation (Goldie, 2007), or to argue for his active influence in the formation of a particular brand of ideology (Ashcraft and Goldsmith, 1983) or politics (Moore, 1991). Often the question about the difference Locke made subsumes the question about just why he made such a difference, and the answer to the second question has to be distilled from the answer to the first. This essay is unusual in taking a different approach to these questions.

That approach is to consider the second question before the first – to endeavour to explain what it was that Locke did to make the difference he did and thereafter to trace the ramifications of what he did through the types of intellectual response he evoked in the early eighteenth century. In other words, the essay attempts to say something about why Locke's readers might have responded to him as they did. Mansel's was one such attempt; others since have made further attempts (compare Mansel, 1873; Pocock, 1991; Dunn, 2003; Harris, 2007). Each one illuminates Locke's thinking and the elements of his thought that commanded the attention of his successors in a striking and original way. If this essay has more modest aspirations, it follows their example in drawing together a range of superficially disparate considerations into a single explanatory account – in this case, of Locke's impact on conceptions of the relationship between religion and civil society in the first few decades of the eighteenth century. To be specific: it argues that Locke's readers were responding to a shift of mind that his writings embodied (see Harris, 2007, p. 144). This shift had metaphysical origins, but its implications were very far-reaching indeed, because it implied that the terms in which some central themes, notions and institutions in theology, religion and politics had been discussed in the past did not make much sense. In what did this shift of mind consist?

Broadly speaking, it consisted in a shift away from Aristotelian assumptions in metaphysics. Now Locke was by no means the first thinker to doubt the adequacy or the sufficiency of those assumptions, and it would be a long task indeed to expound in its entirety the story of those before and beside him, including DESCARTES, Galileo, Gassendi, HOBBES and Kepler, who had expressed similar doubts. But there is another side to this story, and that is the resilience and persistence of Aristotelian assumptions in many areas of thought and discussion in the seventeenth century (see at length Garber and Ayers, 2003). For it happened that these were the assumptions on the basis of which most orthodox discussions in theology, religion and politics were still conducted. To understand what these assumptions were, and to get some sense of how pervasively they patterned a wide variety of explanations in Locke's day, it will be helpful to survey briefly the ways in which they underwrote and were manifested in the theological, religious and political posi-

tions of a suitably upright and representative figure, the Anglican divine Edward STILLINGFLEET.

Stillingfleet's positions were based on a conception of human nature as radically weakened in the Fall of Man and requiring the gracious support of God. This support was thought to be delivered through the true Church, the embodiment and vehicle of God's grace, which enlisted the civil government in its task of salvation, whilst civil society was taken to be necessary to buttress the true Church. These positions turned on his view of human nature, and this view was made possible by certain metaphysical assumptions. More precisely, it assumed a realism about species of a broadly Aristotelian stripe. Stillingfleet suggested that every individual of the same kind had the same SUBSTANCE or real essence,

for that alone is it which makes it to be what it is. Peter and James and John are all true and real men; but what makes them so? Is it the attributing a General name to them? No certainly, but that the true and Real Essence of a Man is in every one of them ... They take there Denomination of being Men from that common Nature, or Essence which is in them (Stillingfleet, 1697, p. 258).

It was this common nature which Adam's sin was supposed to have depraved, a depravation subsequently propagated and imputed to each individual who shared that nature (Stillingfleet, 1735, pp. 346–56).

Stillingfleet relied on the same assumptions when discussing the doctrine of the Trinity, and did so again when explaining the mechanism by which Christ, being at once human and divine, was able to atone for the sin of Adam and thereby release mankind from the captivity of sin. The divinity of Christ turned on his being of one substance (*homoousios*) with God. As Stillingfleet put it, 'the three Persons of Father, Son and Holy Ghost' each had 'distinct Subsistences, and incommunicable Properties, and one and the same divine Essence' (Stillingfleet, 1697, p. 111 and 119). In the Incarnation, meanwhile, the 'divine Person' of Christ had 'come down from Heaven and take[n] our Nature upon Him', by way of a hypostatical union of the sort that 'we all grant to be so between Soul and Body' (Stillingfleet, 1710, vol. iii, pp. 355–6; see Stanton, 2006a, p. 96). If assumptions about substance were thus fundamental to the theological explanations Stillingfleet propounded, they were not less important to the political and ecclesiastical explanations that went along with them. For Stillingfleet assumed that Church and state could be understood on the same model as persons, that the typology of the one applied to the other. Accordingly, he discussed the Church and the state as if they were two different modes of subsistence of the same substance. To account for the differences between the two, Stillingfleet once more turned to Aristotle.

Stillingfleet's account employed a variation on the traditional Aristotelian treatment of causal power. Nowadays we typically think of causality on the Humean model, as a brute connection in which B is the result of A, as when an artist makes a figure out of clay. Aristotle took a broader view, incorporating the purpose or end for which the artist acted (embodied in the final cause), the agency by which the artist brought the figure into existence (the efficient cause), the matter – the clay – which was acted upon (the material cause), and the pattern to which the artist's activity contributed or conformed (the formal cause). Stillingfleet applied these categories to the single body that he supposed civil and ecclesiastical society to comprise, using the categories of formal and efficient cause to distinguish the functions of the governors of Church and state without separating their persons – and thereby ruling out the possibility of two powers competing for dominance over the same body (Stillingfleet, 1662, pp. 41–6). If he did not dwell upon final or material causes, it was only because he assumed that Church and state were complicit in the one purpose – the mutual pro-

motion of salvation and defence of Christian truth – and co-extensive.

Perhaps inevitably, these assumptions generated their own set of resistances in ecclesiastical politics. They did so because they implied that allowing people to leave the national Church *eo ipso* involved the destruction of a substantial unity. On such assumptions as these it is hardly surprising that Stillingfleet should have persistently opposed TOLERATION, advocating a comprehensive but unitary church. In his view, the proper order was laid down according to a divine pattern and entrusted to the care of a godly magistrate (Stillingfleet, 1662, p. 39); it was not and could not be constructed by individuals using their own capacities and initiative. What is more, every individual could have certain knowledge of the authoritative nature of that pattern and of the institutions – into which they were born and to which they owed their adherence – that reflected it. With Stillingfleet, a combination of innatism and Scripture, illuminated by the grace of the Holy Spirit mediated through the Church of England, delivered this certain knowledge. Those who sought alternative political and ecclesiastical arrangements were therefore supposed by him to be acting irrationally – as those in want of grace were bound to act (Stillingfleet, 1672, p. 493). If these wider views did not make direct use of Aristotelian postulates, they fell into a common pattern with them. If, however, a different set of postulates were substituted in the place of Aristotle's, then those views, along with the pattern of explanation to which they conformed, could quite easily begin to look very odd and unprepossessing. Certainly they did not entice Locke.

Locke developed an alternative pattern of explanation, which befitted his different metaphysical postulates. His explanations referred to substance hardly at all, and made no use of it as a typological model. These explanations presupposed his view of the human understanding, in which considerable doubt was expressed about the possibility of knowing substances or REAL ESSENCES with the perspicacity and precision that Stillingfleet imagined (*E*, II.xxiii.2, pp. 295–6). Locke's doubts about the explanatory viability of substance were supplemented by a suspicion of the Aristotelian view of causality. He preferred to think of causality only in terms of efficient causes, 'for as for the other 3 sorts of causes soe cald I doe not at present soe well understand their efficacy or causality' (Draft A, sect. 16, p. 31; see Harris, 2007, p. 146). In short, neither Locke's view of causality nor his metaphysical postulates matched Stillingfleet's. Accordingly the pattern of explanation that followed from them differed from his, too.

Locke's explanations, by contrast to Stillingfleet's, were patterned on the model of relations, that is to say, connections and comparisons between different IDEAS, institutions and persons, made by people themselves. This alternative pattern was evident first of all in Locke's accounts of civil and ecclesiastical society and of the distinction between the two. How did he account for these items? As Locke had it, the conceptual identity of civil society depended on its difference from ecclesiastical society, and in order to establish this difference he compared the two together. Comparison disclosed that the two societies, so far from being complicit and co-extensive, were independent contraries which people brought into existence for wholly different ends. The 'End of Civill Society', Locke noted in a manuscript of 1674, 'is the preservation of the Society and every Member theereof [*sic*] in a free and peaceable enjoyment of all the good things of this life that belong to each of them'. This end was understood in parallel with religious society, which aimed at 'the attaining happinesse after this life in another world'. It followed, therefore, that civil society 'beyond the concernments of this life… hath noething to doe at all' (*ETol.*, p. 327). Civil society, that is to say, answered to secular purposes only.

Secular did not denote in this case an absence of theological reference. In fact Locke explained civil society in terms of divine intentions, but intentions that concerned only life on earth.

This allowed him to explain the authority of civil government while excluding from its terms of reference any spiritual matters. Thus Stillingfleet's belief that a proper order would reflect God's intentions reappeared in Locke in a new guise.

With Locke God was an efficient cause of this order, and in two senses: he produced the characteristics, needs and situational difficulties which drove people into civil society and he produced the FACULTIES and norms (promulgated in the law of nature) from which flowed the rights which authorized civil government (*TTG* I.56, II.58 and 77; Harris, 2007, p. 150). That is to say, God set people about certain purposes and made them fit and responsible for fulfilling those purposes. On this basis Locke argued that humankind's natural faculties were adequate to the creation and maintenance of civil society: it was something that they themselves made and sustained in conformity with divine guidelines, using their own capacities and initiative. If, as Locke indicated, civil society did not require the direct intervention of the deity in its construction or support, it was easier to suppose that spiritual purposes did not figure within its terms. It could be seen as a human construction answering to terrestrial interests, needs and purposes. Locke, however, understood civil society in relation to ecclesiastical society. What did his characterization of civil society imply here?

It implied an analogous treatment. Locke suggested that humankind's natural faculties were also adequate for the construction of ecclesiastical society. Neither human coercion nor the assistance of divine grace was necessary to people's joining or constituting a church. Locke suggested that no one was born a member of a particular church, that people became members of churches voluntarily by exercising their faculties to enter into new relations with others of the same mind as they were 'for the public worship of God in such manner as they believe will be acceptable to the Deity for the salvation of their souls' (*EdT*, p. 71). Understanding the Church as a natural body for the purpose of its relations with the state allowed Locke to recast those relations in a novel way: he could disregard as irrelevant in terms of these relations the claims of particular churches to embody supernatural truth (which civil society could be called upon to underwrite). Thus he was able to treat civil and ecclesiastical society as distinct and independent, rather than complicit, each one made by people (through their own rationality and efficient causality) as a device to secure the ends God intended for them. This treatment had another aspect to it, namely its potentiality. It enabled Locke to discuss dissensions from particular churches without speaking in terms of separation or error. Where Stillingfleet's view of substance encouraged him to see plurality as destruction, Locke's view of relation encouraged him to see unity in charitable dealings among a plurality of churches within a state, each emerging spontaneously from the free choices and wills of its members. He called this arrangement 'toleration' (*EdT*, p. 81).

Locke's discussions of civil and ecclesiastical society also advanced positions on some central theological topics, if only by implication. In particular, they suggested that the consequences of original sin, whatever they were, had not affected human beings so radically that they were no longer capable of doing what God required of them unbidden – their ability freely to make and sustain institutions which fell in with his wishes told another story. When Locke considered the question of original sin and related items of revealed theology more directly, he continued the pattern of explanation that ran through his political discussions. He indicated that the ubiquity of human misconduct was attributable to 'fashen & example', not to any substantial corruption of human nature (Oxford, Bodleian Library, MS Locke f.3, fols 112–13). Congruently, his conception of personhood omitted any positive role for substance, which made it hard to explain how every *person* could have been damaged in the Fall of Man.

The same conception told against the presence of a generic sin in mankind for which Christ could be supposed to satisfy or atone. Thus his role would have to be explained in other terms. Locke argued in 1695 that Christ had interposed with a new order of things, the 'law of faith', by which, where people were unable to fulfil the obligations of NATURAL LAW, 'Faith is allowed to supply the defect of full Obedience; and so the Believers are admitted to Life and Immortality as if they were Righteous' (*RCh.*, p. 19). The law of faith, therefore, completed rather than replaced the law of nature, compensating for people's defective performance of that law through faith. And the faith which God counted as righteousness was the faith that Jesus was the Messiah sent by him (*RCh.*, pp. 22–36). Now, to believe that Jesus is the Messiah does not require one to take a decided view of his divinity or humanity, or to explain how he could be human and divine at one and the same time. Neither does this belief obviously demand that Christ has sacrificed himself in propitiation for our sins, which alleviates in its turn the need to explain his divinity (Stanton, 2006a, p. 98). In Locke's theological explanations, no less than in his political explanations, the language of substance is scarcely detectable.

Of course, these explanations assumed that revelation was a source of authentic information about God's wants. But they did not adduce it as a source of knowledge that overrode the claims of reason – rather, as an object of faith and reflection that might produce certainty in its way (see Stewart, 2006, p. 687). Neither, for that matter, did Locke's philosophical writings suggest that there was much to be said for innatism as a shortcut to knowledge (*E*, I.ii.1–28, pp. 48–65). They suggested, on the contrary, that all ideas derived from sensation and reflection, however abstracted or compounded, and that knowledge lay paradigmatically in the PERCEPTION of the relation of those ideas. If Locke was ready to concede that this did not leave much content for ideas of substance or much knowledge of it, those of

Stillingfleet's mind were less relaxed about such suggestions. As Stillingfleet himself pointed out, in Locke's way of thinking it was impossible to have clear ideas of things or persons as substances in which certain attributes and properties inhered. Consequently there could be no knowledge of God as a divine nature or essence in which the three persons of Father, Son and Holy Spirit inhered (Stillingfleet, 1697, pp. 245–62). This effectively put most of the fundamental articles of the Christian religion, not least those of the Trinity and the Incarnation, beyond human understanding (see Moore, 1991, p. 64). Locke protested that he had not mentioned the Trinity in *An Essay concerning Human Understanding*, still less had he objected to it (W, vol. iv, p. 3). Quite so: he had done something more sweeping and more disconcerting.

Locke had established in his writings a pattern of explanation that was almost limitless in its potential and he had licensed assumptions upon which far bolder structures than he cared for might be made to stand. This was why he made such a difference; we are now in a position to consider the difference he made.

The potentialities of the Lockean style of explanation were not disclosed all at once. But its potency was quickly recognized by many. Among the first to recognize the constructive possibilities in Locke's arguments and to capitalize upon them were the dissenters. Earlier generations of dissent had been hobbled by the disjunction between their practical needs and their explanatory resources. They needed toleration but both doctrinally and temperamentally they were opposed to it. It did not help their efforts to find a way out of this bind that their assumptions were essentially those of Stillingfleet. The extreme discomfort that this disjunction produced is evident in thinkers as diverse as Richard Baxter and John Owen, John Humfrey and Thomas Wall, John Barrett and Vincent Alsop (for discussion, see Stanton, 2006b, pp. 164–70). If the Toleration Act of 1689, which countenanced separation in practice, did not prompt deep reflection about

these assumptions among dissenters, the move made early in the next century by the supporters of the established Church to ban occasional conformity (by which dissenters evaded the sting of the Test Act) demanded a response on the plane of explanation. The dissenters were challenged to justify their attitudes and practices. How could they do so? Locke provided an explanatory means to their practical ends.

These means were employed to arresting effect in two pioneering works. Edmund Calamy's tripartite *Defence of Moderate Non-Conformity* first cited Locke's *Letter concerning Toleration* and then his first, second and third letters corporately to buttress its positions (Calamy, 1704, p. 29, and 1705, p. 85). John Shute Barrington's *The Rights of Protestant Dissenters* was more briskly self-assertive (Shute, 1704). In these works, dissenters for the first time abandoned the implicit aspiration to substitute their own for the established Church and embraced pluralism on a Lockean model, along with the conception of churches as voluntary societies that made it possible (Goldie, 1999, vol. i, p. xlii).

If Lockean arguments were used to justify the practical postures of one party, they were also used to assault those of another: the doctrines and practices of the established Church began to be assailed with Lockean weapons. At the vanguard of the assault was Matthew Tindal. Tindal's *The Rights of the Christian Church Asserted* (1706) suggested that the Church of England's claim to pronounce on doctrinal matters to the nation, and to occupy a privileged position in its political life, was bogus. All Christians had the right to judge for themselves what should and should not be believed, and the Anglican body – like any other church – was simply a coalition of like-minded believers who had chosen to associate together on the basis of what they shared. Its priests and ministers did not imbue it with a higher authority or monopolize the means of grace (whatever they were) and on that basis warrant for it the special support of the state. If Tindal referenced Locke by name only once, and then in passing (Tindal, 1706, p. 302), it was because he had swallowed down and absorbed Locke's assumptions very much earlier in his intellectual career, when he had used Lockean ideas to support sneak attacks on the doctrine of the Trinity (Tindal, 1694; see Moore, 1991, p. 71). When pushed to defend his view of the Church, Tindal ventriloquized Locke, insisting that all were equally capable of deciding for themselves, by their own judgement and agreement, how God ought to be worshipped (Tindal, 1708, p. 28). But in his final work he went beyond Locke in suggesting that from this natural equality of capacity it could be inferred that revelation was redundant, and probably inauthentic (Tindal, 1730, p. 370).

Tindal's suggestion showed how Lockean assumptions could be used to support deist conclusions. Tindal burst through a door at which Locke had gestured and which John Toland had pushed ajar. The alarm had been triggered by Toland, who had used a coarsened version of Locke's epistemology to put question marks against the very notion of mysteries in religion (Toland, 1696) – it was via Toland's provocations, of course, that Stillingfleet had been alerted to the Lockean menace. Toland's lead was followed by Anthony Collins, a friend and protégé of Locke. In his *An Essay concerning the Use of Reason* (1707), Collins agreed with Locke in making knowledge consist in the perception of the agreement or disagreement of ideas. But he differed from Locke – though not from Toland – in making such perception the sole condition of all assent, in matters of faith as much as in everything else (Collins, 1707). In Collins's view, nothing could be above reason – or at least nothing worth bothering about (compare *E*, IV.xviii.9–11, pp. 695–6). Whatever was truly of interest to man could be known by reason, and so known by all; to suppose otherwise was incompatible with God's goodness and impartiality. Thus religion could have no mystery in it and would need no interpreter beyond everyone's own reason: Christ himself had merely reiterated what reason could discover. He had not completed the law of nature, because it was already complete. Again following in Toland's footsteps, Collins referred belief in religious mysteries to the mischief and chicanery of priests, a refrain to which he never tired of returning (see Collins, 1709; 1713).

Locke's assumptions were used to raise difficulties for priests on another score. Recall that Stillingfleet, reflecting the assumptions of his day, had relied upon an Aristotelian view of causality to establish the distinction between the spiritual power of the clergy and the temporal power of the magistrate. This provided him with a means of deflecting accusations that the clergy were pursuing temporal ambitions in fulfilling their priestly and ministerial offices, because these offices were of a different order altogether from the office of the magistrate. However, if Stillingfleet's assumptions were exchanged for Locke's, but the institutional complicity of Church and state remained unchanged, it might look as if 'the Distinction between Temporal and Spiritual Power, as now made, is a Distinction without Difference', and that priests were reserving to themselves lucrative temporal offices under the cover of a unique spiritual mission (anon., 1735, p. 10). In other words, it could seem that the clergy were not only knavish but greedy with it – as Toland and Collins, too, had claimed. Thus Locke's ideas and explanations could be received as invitations to push for the disestablishment of the Church of England. But they could be received in other ways too.

Locke's ideas and explanations could also be placed in the service of the Church of England, as they were by Benjamin Hoadly, successively bishop of Bangor, Hereford, Salisbury and Winchester. Hoadly's was perhaps the most sustained early attempt to work through the implications for the Anglican Church of the shift of mind that Locke had elaborated and to use Locke's style of explanation positively, to reformulate the grounds on which the Church stood and issued its pronouncements. This attempt had at least three aspects: to show that a proper appreciation of

St Paul's *Epistles* supported the distinction between civil and ecclesiastical society which Locke's political explanations took for granted, to deny that Locke's politics were theologically disreputable, and to do the same courtesy to his account of churches and toleration. Hoadly developed each of these aspects in turn, with great lucidity if not great concision. *The Measures of Submission to the Civil Magistrate Consider'd* (1706) echoed Locke's claim that the magistrate had authority only to preserve and extend the happiness and good of human society. Hoadly agreed with Locke, too, when he suggested that people could take measures to redress their grievances if these purposes were crossed, rather than served, by the powers that be, for they had been ordained to these ends, and only these ends – as St Paul himself had indicated (Hoadly, 1706, p. 10; compare *W*, vol. vii, pp. 405–6). In *The Original and Institution of Civil Government Discuss'd* (1710), Hoadly's debts to Locke were even more pronounced.

There, Hoadly argued, on Lockean grounds, for the absence of any scriptural warrant for divine right monarchy and paternal rule. He went on to explain civil government in the terms that Locke had explained it, though he used the language of Richard Hooker when doing so in order to underline the point that what had been respectable in Hooker, 'the Darling of the Old Church of England … and as great a Lover of Government and Order as could be', could not be objectionable in Locke, either theologically or politically (Hoadly, 1710, p. 130). Hoadly repeated Locke's view that God did not institute government directly but was its 'Fountain and Author' in the sense that he had authorized people to make it for themselves and provided them with the means of doing so (Hoadly, 1710, p. 198). The extra ingredient Hoadly added to this Lockean mix was a strong emphasis on God's providence and the special importance of Christ in evidencing it before the world (Hoadly, 1710, pp. 73–4). The role of Christ was expanded further in *The Nature of the Kingdom, or Church, of*

Christ (1717) in which Hoadly argued that Christ's kingdom was not of this world, that he was not the founder of a priesthood, and that he had left behind no vice-gerents or successors whom he had authorized to cajole or punish in his name: in sum, that Christ was an advocate of Lockean toleration *avant la lettre*. He alone legislated for Christians, who were all equal subjects in his kingdom and all equally responsible for interpreting his wishes and doing them in the manner they judged best (Hoadly, 1717, pp. 11–24). It should be remembered at this point that Hoadly was a bishop.

At the same time, it should be remembered that his positions also gave a central role to Scripture in the economy of salvation and that he used terminology friendly to the doctrines of the Incarnation and the Trinity while developing his positions. In this respect, Hoadly's formulations made Locke's arguments 'available not just to Anglicans but to other trinitarian churches as well' (Moore, 1991, p. 76). No doubt he intended to be reassuring, to show that it was possible to follow in Locke's footsteps without overturning the established Church and the Christian religion in the process. But many were not reassured, as the controversy which *The Nature of the Kingdom, or Church, of Christ* provoked – the so-called Bangorian controversy – showed only too clearly (see Kenyon, 1977; Starkie, 2007). For many remained wedded to Stillingfleet's way of thinking and his style of explanation in religion, theology and politics. Locke's way of thinking seemed to them a deep, dark cave of Polyphemus, from which there was no return – all the footsteps pointed one way. Among this number the most hostile, and certainly the most penetrating critic, was the non-juror Charles Leslie. He received Locke with dismay, and saw in his arguments the preface to disaster.

Leslie thought that Locke's views would be fatal to the established Church and to the monarchical government of England, that they constituted a pernicious corruption of moral and political life. In defence of both Church and monarchy, Leslie presented a revivified version of divine right patriarchalism – the version in which it was attacked by Hoadly (see Leslie, 1703, 1705b, 1707, and compare Hoadly, 1709). His response to Hoadly's attack on his own views showed just how far the danger posed by Lockean explanations extended in his eyes. 'The Sum of the Matter betwixt Mr. Hoadly and Me,' Leslie wrote, 'is this, I think it most Natural that Authority shou'd Descend, that is, be Derived from a Superiour to an Inferiour, from God to Fathers and Kings; and from Kings and Fathers to Sons and Servants: But Mr. Hoadly wou'd have it, Ascend, from Sons to Fathers, and from Subjects to Sovereigns; nay to God Himself, whose Kingship the Men of the Rights [i.e. Tindal] say, is derived to Him from the People! And the Argument does Naturally Carry it all that Way. For if Authority does Ascend, it must Ascend to the Height' (Leslie, 1711, p. 87; see Dunn, 1969, p. 64). Thus, as Leslie saw it, the Lockean style of explanation eviscerated all that it touched, for it suggested that everything should not only be understood in terms of relation, but as being constituted *by* relation, and so constituted by people themselves, even unto God himself. All that was solid melted into air.

If Stillingfleet had worried that this tendency was present within Locke's thinking (Stillingfleet, 1697, p. 246), Leslie took it for the signature of Locke's thinking and pursued its implications with tenacity, to all parts. He purposed to show that Locke's assumptions and the explanations that followed upon them were a self-deconstructing individualist nightmare – and a blasphemous one at that. Locke and his successors had 'Disolv'd all Government in Heaven, or on Earth' and so were 'Guilty of the Very Sin of Lucifer', of rebelling against what God had laid down (Leslie, 1705a). He discussed with incredulity a household run along Lockean lines, in which the ties which bound children to their fathers, wives to their husbands and servants to their masters were the products of agreement or contract, and was no less incredulous when

this pattern of explanation was repeated to account for the relations between subjects and rulers in Church and state. The idea that these institutions depended on the consent of every constituent member, and had no authority otherwise, was so preposterous that Leslie found it difficult to believe that Locke could really have meant what he wrote (Dunn, 1969, p. 65). For if he meant what he wrote, it would be man, not God, who was the true creator of the world in which people lived and moved and had their being.

Leslie's views illustrate one way in which Locke was received, as 'an incubus in need of exorcism', just as the views of Tindal, Toland, Calamy and the rest show him becoming 'an instrument in political causes', if not yet 'a totem to whom obeisance must be done' (Goldie, 1999, vol. i, p. xviii). Readers who require further illustrations of the selective and sometimes sharply opposed character of some other responses over a longer run, and an authoritative treatment of the ways in which modern historiography has registered the reception of Locke on the whole, should turn to the work by Mark Goldie listed in the bibliography below (and compare Stewart, 2006). This essay has offered a tentative explanation of why Locke's successors in the early eighteenth century may have responded to him and cared about him as they did. Put summarily, the explanation runs as follows.

Locke's assumptions and his style of explanation were diametrically opposed to the Aristotelian assumptions and explanations current in his day. These assumptions were fundamental to a whole series of explanations across a wide range of topics, in politics, religion, theology and philosophy. Consequently, when the assumptions that supported those explanations were put into question, so too were the explanations which eventuated upon them. Locke provided materials from which alternative explanations could be developed. How his readers received these materials, and what they did with them, was always a matter for them. But it was very hard for them to carry on in the same way as before, as if nothing had happened.

If it is difficult for us, as readers of Locke today, to appreciate adequately the force of the shake he gave to speculation right across the board, it is because most of us have become so accustomed to thinking on Lockean assumptions and pursuing Lockean styles of explanation that we rarely pause to consider alternatives: this is another mark of the intellectual power that distinguishes Locke (see Dunn, 2003; and Harris, 2007). We have – most of us at least – found it rather easier than did Leslie to believe that Locke meant what he wrote. Whether we have thought long or hard enough about the more unsettling potentialities in what Locke wrote that Leslie's reading identified is another matter again, but one upon which we would be well advised to reflect and to ruminate.

BIBLIOGRAPHY
Manuscript Sources
Oxford, Bodleian Library, MS Locke f.3.

Printed Primary Sources
[Anon.], *The Powers Claim'd by the Church-Hierarchy, Examined* (1735).
Calamy, Edmund, *A Defence of Moderate Non-Conformity*, Part II (1704).
——, *A Defence of Moderate Non-Conformity*, Part III (1705).
Collins, Anthony, *An Essay concerning the Use of Reason* (1707).
——, *Priestcraft in Perfection* (1709).
——, *A Discourse of Freethinking* (1713).
Hoadly, Benjamin, *The Measures of Submission to the Civil Magistrate Consider'd* (1706).
——, *An Humble Reply to the Right Reverend the Lord Bishop of Exeter's Answer* (1709).
——, *The Original and Institution of Civil Government Discuss'd* (1710).
——, *The Nature of the Kingdom, or Church, of Christ* (1717).
[Leslie, Charles], *The New Association*, Part II, appendix (1703).

——, *The Rehearsal*, no. 58 (1705a).
——, *The Rehearsal*, no. 59 (1705b).
——, *A Second Part of the Wolf Stript* (1707).
——, *The Finishing Stroke* (1711).
[Shute, John, Viscount Barrington], *The Rights of Protestant Dissenters* (1704).
Stillingfleet, Edward, *Irenicum, A Weapon-Salve for the Churches Wounds* (2nd edn, 1662).
——, *A Discourse concerning the Idolatry practised in the Church of Rome* (1672).
——, *A Discourse in Vindication of the Doctrine of the Trinity* (1697).
——, *The Works of Dr. Edward Stillingfleet* 6 vols (1710).
——, *Miscellaneous Discourses on Several Occasions* (1735).
[Tindal, Matthew], *A Letter to the Reverend the Clergy of Both Universities, concerning the Trinity and the Athanasian Creed* (1694).
——, *The Rights of the Christian Church Asserted* (1706).
——, *A Second Defence of the Rights of the Christian Church* (1708).
——, *Christianity as Old as the Creation*, vol. i [no more published] (1730).
[Toland, John], *Christianity not Mysterious* (1696).

Secondary Literature
Ashcraft, Richard, and M.M. Goldsmith, 'Locke, Revolution Principles and the Formation of Whig Ideology', *Historical Journal*, vol. xxvi (1983), pp. 773–800.
Dunn, John, 'The Politics of Locke in England and America in the Eighteenth Century', in John W. Yolton (ed.), *John Locke: Problems and Perspectives* (Cambridge, 1969), pp. 45–80.
Dunn, John, 'Measuring Locke's Shadow', in Ian Shapiro (ed.), *John Locke, Two Treatises of Government and A Letter concerning Toleration* (New Haven, 2003), pp. 257–85.
Garber, Daniel, and Michael Ayers (eds), *The*

Cambridge History of Seventeenth-Century Philosophy, 2 vols (Cambridge, 2003).

Goldie, Mark (ed.), *The Reception of Locke's Politics*, 6 vols (London, 1999).

Goldie, Mark, 'The Early Lives of Locke', *Eighteenth-Century Thought*, vol. iii (2007), pp. 57–87.

Harris, Ian, 'The Legacy of *Two Treatises of Government*', *Eighteenth-Century Thought*, vol. iii (2007), pp. 143–67.

Kenyon, John, *Revolution Principles: The Politics of Party 1689–1720* (Cambridge, 1977).

Mansel, Henry Longueville, 'Freethinking – Its History and Tendencies', in Henry W. Chandler (ed.), *Letters, Lectures, and Reviews* (London, 1873), pp. 293–336.

Moore, James, 'Theological Politics: A Study of the Reception of Locke's *Two Treatises of Government* in England and Scotland in the Early Eighteenth Century', in Martyn P. Thompson (ed.), *John Locke und Immanuel Kant: Historische Rezeption und Gegenwärtige Relevanz* (Berlin, 1991), pp. 62–86.

Pocock, J.G.A., 'Negative and Positive Aspects of Locke's Place in Eighteenth-Century Discourse', in Martyn P. Thompson (ed.), *John Locke und Immanuel Kant: Historische Rezeption und Gegenwärtige Relevanz* (Berlin, 1991), pp. 45–61.

Stanton, Timothy, 'Locke and the Politics and Theology of Toleration', *Political Studies*, vol. liv (2006a), pp. 84–102.

——, 'The Name and Nature of Locke's "Defence of Nonconformity"', *Locke Studies*, vol. vi (2006b), pp. 143–72.

Starkie, Andrew, *The Church of England and the Bangorian Controversy, 1716–1721* (Woodbridge, 2007).

Stewart, M.A., 'Revealed Religion, the British Debate', in Knud Haakonssen (ed.), *The Cambridge History of Eighteenth-Century Philosophy* (Cambridge, 2006) pp. 683–709.

Timothy Stanton

LOCKE'S CIVIL PHILOSOPHY IN THE EARLY EIGHTEENTH-CENTURY *RÉPUBLIQUE DES LETTRES*: AN IMPORTANT FOOTNOTE

Scholarship today increasingly recognizes that Locke's writings aimed not only at an English, but at a broader European audience. Locke can thus be seen as consciously carving out a role for himself in the European *République des lettres*, publishing in French and having his works translated in order to speak to the broader international audience of his day. Nevertheless, much of the making of the 'Jean Locke' – his Francophone literary name – whom the Continent learnt to know was the job of others. It was, more specifically, the affair of a fairly small and specific group of people who shared some of Locke's key concerns, but who were also happy to turn his thought to uses that were less fully in line with original authorial intentions. To a not inconsiderable degree, Locke's fame in the eighteenth century was based on 'Lockean' views that he had not himself in fact championed. This is at its clearest in French debates on materialism in the 1750s, a debate that has been discussed in some detail by John Yolton (1996). References to Locke were thus no certain sign of any influence of his writings, and in the heat of debate there really was no need actually to read Locke – in fact, that would in many cases have been of no help at all – to know precisely what one was accused of (or praised for) when being called a 'Lockean'.

This contribution provides some outlines of the constellations in which Locke's name and (often but not always) his ideas were held up as torches, brandished as weapons, twisted and bent, or trodden into the ground in Francophone debates. It focuses on the early period of the dissemination of his ideas, a time period stretching roughly from his death in 1704 to the early 1740s, when the materialism debate began to overshadow the earlier focus in the continental reception. The celebratory remarks on Locke in Diderot's *Encyclopédie*, in

Voltaire's writings, or the use made of Locke in Montesquieu, are perhaps more widely known, but without the earlier Francophone mediation of his ideas, it is unlikely any of these would have occurred. Such remarks have long given support to a conviction that Locke was a crucial influence on the Continent, or even that he provided the French Enlightenment with much of its key intellectual content (Jonathan Israel cites a number of scholars holding such views in Israel, 2006, pp. 370–1). This entry charts the early stages of the makings of the story of Locke the Enlightenment hero.

Jealousy is a strong motive force. For centuries, the majority of historians – or at least writers of general historical overviews – were content with granting the French pride of place as the ones who inaugurated the era of Enlightenment in Europe: it was the French *philosophes* who undertook what amounts to a revolution of prevailing cultural, intellectual and political modes of existence. The critical and questioning provocations of Diderot, d'Alembert, Montesquieu, Voltaire and other French luminaries led, as the majority of school children in the West still learn today, to replacing religious authority as a source of certainty with the individual's own rational faculty, and to replacing the received religious worldview with secularist rationalism and the new natural science – it led to what a broad, liberally minded consensus agrees with the *philosophes* in viewing as a progress from medieval or *ancien régime* darkness towards the electric lights of modernity. That picture of the Enlightenment has, in scholarly literature at least, been challenged and in many respects thoroughly revised, and yet the old understanding has, with a stubbornness characteristic of foundational myths, remained the popular understanding of matters (for a rapid walkthrough of Enlightenment conceptions in scholarship see Robertson, 2005, pp. 2–28).

In political terms, the schoolbook Enlightenment, if such a term may be used, appears as the source of political liberalism and democracy. Through its emphasis on TOLERA-

TION and on individual self-governance in matters of belief especially, the *philosophes* paved the way for the future, for the liberal, democratic West as we know it. The Enlightenment as a movement was, furthermore, easy to locate in geographical and chronological terms. This 'Age of Enlightenment', as Norman Torrey characteristically argued in 1960, 'is a term applied to a definite Revolution in the history of thought which took place in France in the eighteenth century. The leaders of the movement were called *philosophes*' (Torrey, 1960, p. 10). This is where one might become envious, unless one is French of course. The traditional Anglo-Saxon cure to that envy has, quite literally, been John Locke. For generations of schoolchildren in the Anglophone world, the revolution of the French *philosophes* has stood out as in the end a British achievement. Locke has (together with NEWTON) been hailed as the real source of the new secular scientific and empiricist worldview allegedly propagated by the *philosophes*, as 'the father of the Enlightenment' (Cushman, 1911, p. 145), making Britain the source of a 'light from the North' that would challenge what Paul Hazard characterized as the intellectual hegemony in Europe of 'the Latin races' (Hazard, 1953, p. 55). The lasting impression imprinted in Anglophone minds is one of Locke as the father of the French Revolution, of modern liberal politics, and of the Enlightenment empirical scientific ethos that would replace religious discourse as the framework for a more or less shared Western worldview.

Histories have histories, and while the present article does not claim to cover a very large portion of the history of Locke receptions, yet even the early continental reception sheds quite a bit of light on how Locke came to acquire his special position in the history of ideas. For the early European reception of his ideas, the Huguenots constituted a particularly important group. After Louis XIV annulled the Edict of Nantes in 1685, French Calvinists (also known as 'Huguenots') fled from France in great numbers (in most accounts over 100,000 individuals and wilder approximations suggest much larger numbers). The Huguenots henceforth constituted a small but influential segment of the population in many Protestant European countries, not least in the Netherlands, the Swiss republics, and Brandenburg-Prussia. Their French-language journals provided Protestant perspectives on the world of learning in a language that was rapidly replacing Latin as the common tongue for learned debate.

The Huguenots thus constituted a key element of the *République des lettres* of their time, and incidentally, without Pierre Bayle's hugely influential journal *Nouvelles de la République des Lettres*, the concept itself would quite possibly not be in use today. Through the *Nouvelles*, later edited by Jacques Bernard, and through Jean Le Clerc's influential journals *Bibliothèque Universelle et Historique* (Amsterdam, 1686–93), *Bibliothèque Choisie* (Amsterdam, 1703–13), and *Bibliothèque Ancienne et Moderne* (Amsterdam, 1714–26), the learned and indeed an increasingly wide circle of readers would get a brief reader's digest of most books written in English, Latin, German, Italian and sometimes other less well-known European languages. Frequently, the journals were written by internationally oriented thinkers who favoured an intellectualist and rationalist approach to religion, where the heroes of Protestantism were not so much Luther or Calvin but rather Erasmus and Grotius, and soon also Le Clerc, Locke and others favouring an approach to religion that demanded scholarly rigour in biblical exegesis, reasonable ethics as the foundation for interpreting the moral message of Christianity, and tolerance at least between Protestant denominations: such thinkers can be bracketed together as 'liberal Protestants'. The liberal Protestant journals, together with their Catholic competitors published in France – most famously the Paris-based *Journal des Savans* (1665–1792) and the Jesuit *Journal de Trévoux* (1701–67) – constituted the 'institutional core' of the Francophone *République des lettres*.

Originally, the journals were explicitly made up of personal letters between learned persons reporting on books being published in their different locales. This tells us two important things about the Republic of Letters: first, that it was concretely a republic based on (personal) letters and, secondly, that this is from its inception a network to help those interested in staying updated about recent publications.

The Protestant Francophone journals often used a language and imagery that fits well with what has later come to be viewed as Enlightenment thought. Thus in the opening 'Avertissement' of the first number of the *Bibliothèque Raisonnée des Savans de l'Europe* (Amsterdam, 1728–52), the journal explains as its mission to provide the kind of free and unbiased coverage of all good books published in Europe that is possible only in one other country in addition to the Dutch provinces. The journalists are also to remain anonymous, the 'Avertissement' explains, otherwise their independence would be impaired: the reviewers would hold back their true opinions because of the dangers involved in openly criticizing views cherished and articulated by various religious orthodoxies, and would be likely to refrain from commending a book containing views that influential religious groups deem heretical (ibid., 1728, pp. xii–xiii). The *Bibliothèque Raisonnée* journalists saw themselves as working for a more open society; thus one of them confirmed that, should a full freedom of judgement be granted to all, the despotic and intolerant defenders of inquisition would lose all credibility. 'Matters being as they now are,' the same author continues, 'all one can do is to conserve, strengthen, clarify [*éclaircir*] and renew from time to time the ideas of a honest Liberty in those places where it is permitted to say what one thinks.' The other country of freedom alluded to in the 'Avertissement' is, furthermore, Great Britain.

This anonymous author could well have been Jean Barbeyrac, one of the key journalists of the journal, and a thinker singled out by Ross Hutchison as the only Francophone thinker before Voltaire to make substantial use of Locke (Hutchison 1991, p. 227; but see Savonius, 2004, p. 52). Barbeyrac was, as a highly visible translator and commentator of political theory for the French readership, a key mediator of Locke's political thought. One reason why Barbeyrac stands out as a particularly early author to make substantial use of Locke's ideas is that he, unusually for his time, generally provided exact references even when discussing ideas put forth by contemporary authors. Traditionally, exact references were given only to figures of authority, mainly to ancient thinkers and biblical passages. Le Clerc notes that many readers were shocked by Barbeyrac's habit (Le Clerc, 1706, pp. 391–2). Barbeyrac was not as alone in making use of Locke as Hutchison suggests. He was simply one of the most widely read and most avid users of Lockean ideas and language in a group of liberal Protestant intellectuals who, in the *République des lettres* of the first half of the eighteenth century, articulated a commitment to what we might today designate as Enlightenment ideals: religious TOLERATION, freedom of thought and expression, anti-authoritarianism and critique of despotic power. For such thinkers, Le Clerc and Barbeyrac among them, Locke was a crucial point of reference (see Savonius, 2004). It was even in order to understand Locke's thought better that Barbeyrac – who spent important portions of his life in Berlin without learning a word of German and who spent over half of his active career in Groningen without apparently learning any Dutch – decided to learn English, which he soon mastered well enough to translate the sermons of another important British religious thinker, Archbishop Tillotson. Through Barbeyrac's summaries of Lockean viewpoints, key passages and statements in Locke were disseminated very effectively. This is the company in which Locke entered the European scene, and this entrée was to mark also the continuation of the Lockean presence there.

If the early reception of Locke's ideas was marked by Huguenot (and, as we shall soon see, Remonstrant) sensibilities, and if, as has

been plausibly suggested, the later French reception was strongly encouraged by Jansenists, another group of religious thinkers subject to intolerant attitudes in France, then this provides an excellent occasion to raise a classic question about the relationship between religion and the Enlightenment. For some, both in the scholarly debates and in more popular forums, the genuine Enlightenment champions were those who opposed a worldview based on religious convictions and strove to replace it with secular thought. In this reading, the Enlightenment is a project to replace religion with science, and the power of priests and Church with a modern secular state and democratic rule. Neither Locke nor his Huguenot mediators fit that description well, deeply entrenched as their thought was in discussions of theological and religious issues. Indeed, reading the Enlightenment as a combat between Christian and secularist intellectual forces is quite awkward. Verbal attacks on the power of the clergy, on superstition, slavish conformism or on the pointlessness and groundlessness of metaphysical theological speculation were all familiar themes in apologetic context, and formed a natural part of a debate on what religion should be like. It is only gradually that the project of reforming Christianity into something more rational was transformed into a project for replacing it with something other than religion, and in fact that project did not flower properly until the twentieth century. The tenacity of the story of the Enlightenment, and thus also of Locke as one of its key thinkers, as a project for replacing religion with (empiricist) science clearly owes much to the reverberations of twentieth-century positivism.

At the other extreme, some see the Enlightenment as something happening within Christian thought specifically, even to a point where egalitarian Enlightenment ideals or ideas about religious toleration are presented as natural outgrowths of Christian thought, as 'inspired by religious values' and as 'fundamentally religious in character' (Zagorin, 2003, p. 289). The question about religion and

Enlightenment is one of those where history is particularly intimately part of a political or ideological debate. If equality and toleration are a secular ideology opposed to religion and Christian traditions, then promoting an Enlightened, democratic way of life may well go hand in hand with promoting secularism, whereas if the real source of tolerance and equality are thought to be found within Christianity specifically, a conservative conclusion may be that Christian values should be promoted in order to defend the so-called open society. Locke and his influence in the *République des lettres* is an interesting case to study in regard to this question. Thus while some scholars emphasize his immersion in the religious debates of his time, others would either see Locke as a secularist philosopher or suggest that the religious character of his contribution to political debates was precisely why he is not a central Enlightenment figure in any real sense of the word (see, for example, Hunter, 2007, pp. 162–6).

For his Huguenot readers, Locke was not a philosopher attacking religion from the outside, but a member of a specific group of Protestant thinkers articulating what we can learn and how from Scripture as well from reasoning about human nature and divine intentions (Savonius, 2004 and 2006, esp. pp. 142–8). The prominence of secular-rational arguments in the discussion was for Locke, Le Clerc, Barbeyrac, Tillotson and others a significant aspect about what they thought religion should be like, not a sign of their being concerned with secular issues as opposed to religion. For many of his first continental readers and disseminators, Locke's oeuvre was essentially an amalgamation of superficially separate discussions unified by one overreaching goal. This goal was to provide an updated and reasonable view of what Christianity could and should be in the new century. Thus when Locke's by far the most important salesman on the Continent, the Remonstrant theologian whose academic journals we have already mentioned, Jean Le Clerc, summarizes the significance of Locke's

life's work, he emphasizes how important it is 'for all who are seriously committed to searching for the Truth [*la recherche de la Vérité*] and to the study of Christianity' (Le Clerc, 1710, p. xxii). Locke's productions constitute 'an example to close the mouths of all those who imagine that Piety is incompatible with finesse in reasoning and with the study of philosophy, as if religion were made only for those who reason not!' (Le Clerc, 1710, p. ii).

Locke was on close terms with several central Remonstrant thinkers. In private letters, the Arminian theologian Philippus van LIMBORCH repeatedly suggested that Locke's moral theological thought was very close to that of the Remonstrant leader Episcopius, and Locke did indeed read theological works by both Episcopius and van Limborch himself. In his 'Eloge', which was of central importance for the early Enlightenment understanding of Locke's thought, Le Clerc emphasizes how impressed Locke was with Remonstrant theology, and suggests that his publications constitute an application of the same (ibid., p. xlix). Le Clerc portrayed Locke as a champion for a philosophy built around a core of Remonstrant theological views (on Locke's connection with Arminianism, see Marshall, 1996, esp. pp. 331–6).

Locke's efforts towards establishing a minimalist credo took the idea, much in vogue amongst Remonstrants, of a limited set of core beliefs that suffice for a man to be called a Christian. His version of the 'fundamental dogma' discussion famously narrows down the number of beliefs necessary for a person to be termed a Christian to one: the belief that Jesus is the Messiah (*RCh.*, p. 352) – this, too, was an idea he could have picked up from a number of Remonstrant sources. Le Clerc was not slow to exploit this situation, and he soon became actively engaged in an effort to convince the European *République des lettres* that Anglicans on the whole were liberal-minded thinkers with rationalist leanings like Locke and Tillotson, and that this reasonable Christian approach did not only happen to be in tune with the ideas of the Remonstrants – who continually had to face challenges from the Calvinist majority in the Netherlands – but that the Anglicans basically had learned their moral theology from the Remonstrants. When the *Bibliothèque Raisonnée des Savans de l'Europe* adds (in its 'Avertissement', 1728, p. x) that the British hardly publish anything into which they would not have mixed theology, the picture emerging is increasingly one where British intellectuals are seen as doing little else but elaborate on Remonstrant theology.

This situation contributed substantially to the spread of Anglophile sentiments in the republic of European letters. The idea that Anglicans and Remonstrants were of a mind in defending an inclusive and tolerant Protestant Church that would not demand adherence to complicated formulae of religious dogma but only to very few fundamentals shared by all Christians was very useful for supporting optimism about the future of 'liberal Protestantism'. For Le Clerc and Barbeyrac, the dream is clearly of a Europe and a world where both Catholicism and authoritarian Protestantism have lost their role and an inclusive liberal Protestant Church has stepped into their place. A quite imaginary England with Locke as key figure stood for a hope that was later to be readapted and used as such, apart from the role of Protestantism, by Voltaire and the *philosophes*. It was in the interest of the rather marginal continental defenders of 'reasonable Christianity' to refer readers to the equally pretty marginal British defenders of the same, while exaggerating their role in British intellectual life, and the imaginary England they created continued to be loved by Voltaire, just as it has been cherished and kept alive in Anglophone accounts in the schoolbook Enlightenment genre. This, I suggest, is the narrative context for the rather strong language used to praise 'l'illustre Mr. Locke', and it is a factor not to forget in understanding how Locke's reputation as an influence on continental thought was made. French *philosophes* from Voltaire onwards may well have remained

Catholics, but they were certainly ready to sympathize with the demand to rethink religion in more rational terms, making them sensible to the main selling points in Le Clerc's Arminian campaign for 'Jean Locke the reasonable Christian'. Thus Voltaire, who is sometimes thought of as the author who introduced Locke on the Continent, characteristically celebrates Locke and Le Clerc together as being among the greatest philosophers and ablest pens, in his openly Anglophile *English Letters*.

Locke's career as a publishing philosopher entered a new phase in 1688 with the publication of the 'Extrait d'un livre anglois qui n'est pas encore publié', that is, the French-language summary of the *Essay concerning Human Understanding*. This digest of the *Essay*, translated by Le Clerc, was in essence Locke's first substantial philosophical publication, and became a hit at once, and the *Essay* itself, published in Coste's French translation in 1700, was published six more times within the fifty years after that – not very much, given how small editions generally were in the period, but also not much less than the ten English editions published in the same interval. It is much more than the *Two Treatises*, which was available in a partial translation as *Du Gouvernement Civil* (from 1691, translation attributed to David Mazel) containing the second book but without its first chapter, and which was republished only twice before 1750, or the *Epistola de Tolerantia*, which was translated by Le Clerc and published in the *Oeuvres Diverses de Mr. Jean Locke* in 1710 (republished once, in 1732, but the work also sold in Europe in the Latin original). In comparison, the *Reasonableness of Christianity* sold in six French editions, and the *Education des Enfants* (the French translation of *Some Thoughts concerning Education*) sold in at least sixteen editions within this same time period (with several more editions appearing in print in the second half of the century).

Locke was quite desirous of becoming part of the Protestant university CURRICULUM of ethics and politics. That curriculum was, at least for those interested in modern alternatives rather than a rehash of Aristotle, dominated by the NATURAL LAW theories of Grotius and Pufendorf. In Sweden and in many German states, Pufendorf and Grotius were among the five most quoted authors in doctoral dissertations, and Pufendorf's shorter main work, *De Officio Hominis et Civis*, remained a popular university textbook for over a century. Natural law theory was taught either in philosophy departments or at law faculties, where a number of chairs in *jus naturale et gentium* was created. While natural law in Catholic universities often remained more linked to Aristotelian models, the works of Pufendorf and Grotius were circulated and discussed, in spite of being banned, and were in fact translated into both Italian and eventually (although only in the nineteenth century) into Spanish.

Locke was thus, as current scholarship indeed suggests, actively seeking to establish himself as a curriculum philosopher in natural law; in some respects, however, his project failed (Savonius, 2002, p. 70). The *Du Gouvernement* did not sell well, nor did, on the whole, the *Epistola de Tolerantia*, both considered key works today. This does not mean that Locke the political philosopher failed to penetrate to the Continent. As a visible translator and commentator, Barbeyrac introduced his readers to many of the key passages in both works, making Locke an important footnote and more often than not corrective to Pufendorf. In this sense, Locke did become part of the natural law curriculum after all, albeit more as important footnote material than as an author in his own right. All over Europe, Barbeyrac's annotated editions of Pufendorf's main works were eagerly used, and provided the mainstay of most lecture series on the topic. Of the forty-five editions that 'the big Pufendorf', that is, *De Jure Naturae et Gentium* (1672), underwent before the eighteenth century was at its end, over half were based on Barbeyrac's French translation (*Le Droit de la Nature et des Gens*, first published in 1706) – thus, even in the English translation, the reader is introduced to the Huguenot Anglophile's Jean Locke, the hero of liberal Protestantism.

When Barbeyrac discusses the science of natural law in general terms in his preface to, and in the first chapter of, *Le Droit de la Nature et des Gens*, he draws on Locke's support for the idea that there can be a demonstrative science of morality. Pufendorf based the science of natural law – or of morality, politics and jurisprudence, as Barbeyrac sums up the area covered by natural law – on observations about how human beings need rule-based co-operation in order to survive. Barbeyrac brings in Locke to suggest further that laws and other 'moral entities' are logically intertwined in ways that make a demonstrative moral science possible. Locke's well-known passage, from the *Essay*, on how the concept of injury presupposes that of PROPERTY follows. Barbeyrac summarizes Locke's argument about demonstrable moral science by quoting a combination of passages, several pages long, from the *Essay*: together these are aimed to explain further in what sense natural law has a certain foundation as a secular-rational science about divine intentions (Barbeyrac 1740, pp. xvii–xx). Locke is thus introduced to a significant segment of his continental readership as an author who helps establish the status of Pufendorfian natural law as a science.

In a similar fashion, Locke's discussion of innate ideas comes to serve as an elucidation on Pufendorf's epistemological claims. Pufendorf discussed and rejected the idea that moral knowledge or principles pre-exist in men's minds from birth. Human beings learn to think of various actions as morally evil or good much like they learn their mother tongue. That the laws of nature are written in the heart of men must therefore not be taken to imply that humans would have some inborn knowledge of good and evil, or of natural law, Pufendorf explains. The matter was important because it concerned both the status and the very possibility of a secular science of morality. Many conservative Protestant divines thought that rejecting innate ideas entailed relativism and atheism (discussion in Barbeyrac, 1740, pp. xxxiii–xxxiv; see also Pufendorf, 1740, pp. 231–2). It is of course true that this approach leaves more room for doubt about received truths than does the assumption of eternal verities branded once and for all on the heart, and that is arguably part of the point. By arguing that norms are in reality learned through socialization and experience (written on the heart in a very figurative sense indeed), Pufendorf and Locke provide place for a secular-rational science of moral and legal norms. This also makes room for reasoning and doubt concerning received religious verities.

Locke's prominent place in Barbeyrac's discussion of natural law as a science also relates to how the British philosopher used secular-rational arguments in his discussions of Scripture and religion. The idea that there is a secular universal science of morality, which nevertheless presents morality as divinely imposed, was an important defining feature of the sort of liberal Protestant thought that the Remonstrants and Huguenots who transmitted Locke's thought to continental audiences favoured. In his *Traité du Jeu*, Barbeyrac insists that all the moral duties found in Scripture are in fact based on reason, and that this is the true meaning of St Paul's dictum that divine commandments are written on the heart. God gave men reason and this came with the capacity to acquire, through experience, observation and reasoning, a solid understanding of ethics and even a science of morality. Barbeyrac goes on to quote Locke to the effect that revelation was needed mainly in order to remind human beings of their rationally knowable but oft-forgotten moral duties, and to lend to these norms more explicitly the authority of God: the underlying assumption is, as Barbeyrac also makes clear a few pages earlier, that most (though not all) moral principles taught by Jesus are basically the same as those of natural morality, or 'the duties that reason can teach to all men' (Barbeyrac, 1709, t. 1, pp. 33–6). This makes natural law as a secular-rational science of duties and rights, the most certain and universally available source of insights concerning divine intentions. While Barbeyrac here uses Locke as part of a project of rethinking Christianity and religion from within rather than attack it from the outside, the impli-

cations are no less radical and in some ways perhaps more so. From the perspective of the *Traité du Jeu*, Locke is, together with Le Clerc, and Barbeyrac himself, part of a crew of new lay theologians whose work provides a truer continuation of the reformation than Luther, Calvin or their conservative descendants.

In political terms, the Huguenots and Arminians shared an understandable concern regarding the position of religious minorities. The Huguenot case – the Revocation of the Edict of Nantes and the ensuing *Refuge* – further strengthened the worry about political regimes that might strive to assume a right to force religious dissenters to submit to majority views on religion. While Protestant conservatives were bad enough, the threat of French dominance in Europe constituted an even more sinister cloud on the horizon. Thus it is not surprising to find that continental readers, as Locke had intended, read the *Du Gouvernment*, as 'an anti-absolutist critique of the French regime' (Savonius, 2004, p. 51). While the implied and often explicit attack on Catholics and on France was likely to draw in some of the Protestant conservatives, the other edge of the sword was sharpened to cut back at authoritarian approaches within Protestantism, branding all who do not accept a full right to freedom of religion to Arminians and rationalist dissenters as suffering from remnants of 'papism'. The *Epistola de Tolerantia* was similarly, for European readers, more a pamphlet in a war against French and Catholic influence (and a battle cry against conservative authoritarian strands within Protestantism) than a call for peace between denominations. It demanded, in a tone familiar from Le Clerc's journals, that all reasonable Protestants should be tolerated, but that Catholics and intolerant Protestants must not be tolerated because their intolerance constitutes a breach of secular-rational natural law, and thus is against the divine will as we know it.

While natural law theory as presented by Pufendorf did provide elements for a secular-rational political theory, the case for religious toleration was not a central theme within it.

The coexistence of several religious denominations was for Pufendorf a 'disorderly' situation: he felt that the Dutch practice of accepting several denominations was 'messy'. Barbeyrac, who, like Le Clerc, was very unhappy about Pufendorf's lack of support for the tolerationism that they themselves favoured, made both the *Du Gouvernement* and the *Epistola* into central resources for rethinking Pufendorfian natural law, making more room within it for inalienable rights and toleration than Pufendorf had. It is this somewhat Lockeified Pufendorf that continental audiences came to enjoy, and it was to become a central source for the language of 'natural and inalienable rights' that the American and French declarations of human rights later in the century were to solidify.

Locke thus became a corrective to Pufendorfian natural law theory, especially for the point that the state has a duty to tolerate religious minorities – minorities that serve God peacefully in accordance with the demands of their consciences (Barbeyrac, 1740, t.1, p. 58 and 158–9). Furthermore, according to Barbeyrac, Pufendorf should have stayed with the Grotian notion that injuries against natural law can be punished in the state of nature by those injured or third parties – a view that Locke had thankfully revived (ibid., pp. 319–20) – and he should not have adopted the view that property is always based on consent or contract, and again Locke is the author whose solution should be preferred (ibid., t. 2, p. 247). These seemingly disparate points are interrelated parts of an effort at reformulating Pufendorf's firmly duty-based or law-based understanding of *jus naturale* with a more rights-based approach. Barbeyrac understood property in Locke to refer quite generally to rights (Tully, 1982, p. 7). What his criticisms entail is a picture where individuals have rights in a proper sense prior to contracts, and where the social contract is – as Barbeyrac states explicitly – created at least partly for the purpose of defending those rights. These rights constitute their liberty, Barbeyrac explains,

which one must and can never entirely give up – the reference is to Locke's *Epistola* and 'Second Treatise' (Barbeyrac, 1740, t. 3, pp. 148–9 and 231–2). If a sovereign injures a citizen's inalienable rights, he thereby dispels the contract and by the same token makes himself subject to punishment by both the injured individual or group and third parties – in effect, by the rest of the (now former) citizens (the reference is to *TTG* II.203). In Pufendorf's view, a citizen directly and unjustly attacked by a superior can at most defend his own life but can never gain a right to punish the sovereign (Pufendorf, 1998, t. 2, p. 730).

Barbeyrac understands ABSOLUTISM as a failure of the state to respect the right to self-governance of peaceful religious minorities. While his exact positions are not identical to Locke's, he found in the *Du Gouvernement* and the *Epistola* a combination of arguments which gave his reworking of duty-based natural law into a theory of rights a distinctly Lockean flavour. His rights theory builds up to a theory of resistance against oppression that bears clear Lockean marks. Barbeyrac quotes the parallel with a shipmaster steering for Algiers, an interesting example adduced by Locke, referring to the slave market in Algiers where many Huguenot refugees ended up, instead of reaching the British shores they were often aiming for (Savonius 2002, p. 102). The civil state, Barbeyrac explains, is entered in order to procure a safety that the state of nature does not offer – but absolutism is in this regard, as Locke had argued, even worse. This is why a sovereign striving to usurp absolute power over the citizens (as Louis XIV did in revoking the Edict of Nantes, if not before) must be thought to wage war on his citizens, just as the shipmaster in the above example. In such situations, Barbeyrac argues, passive and active resistance is justified, as Locke had shown.

Pufendorf, Barbeyrac complains, failed to draw the substantial tolerationist consequences from the premise that he had laid down. For Pufendorf, state and Church are distinct institutions, and governing the religious life of citizens does not belong to the tasks of civil government as such. For Barbeyrac, as for Locke, Pufendorf's secularist premise entails that minority churches are autonomous and that their right to freedom of religion – within the limits set by security – must be respected by the government. Barbeyrac thus provides a précis of Locke's argument in the *Epistola*, arguing that these conclusions by 'l'illustre Monsieur Locke' follow directly from Pufendorf's principles (Barbeyrac, 1740, t. 3, pp. 148–9). As a response to the atrocities committed by Louis XIV, Pufendorf's statism, on its own, was not much of a reply. The Edict of Fontainebleau that annulled the Edict of Nantes was not phrased in terms of converting and saving souls: it was worded as articulating measures 'thought necessary for maintaining the tranquillity' of France. What the Huguenots (and minorities within Protestantism) needed was a theory about a right to serve God in accordance with their own conscience. Locke's theory provided several layers of argument with which to refine Pufendorf's theory. If Locke remained a footnote in the curriculum of natural law that dominated political theory in the eighteenth century, then at least he was quite an important footnote.

The French translation of Locke's *Reasonableness of Christianity* was published with a dissertation setting out to explain 'how on the principles of Reasonable Christianity, it would not be difficult to reunite all Christians in spite of their differences of opinion' (Locke, 1731, p. vii). The tract of reunification is a good example of where the dreams of 'reasonable Christians' for the future of Europe and Christianity pointed. The dream is of one inclusive Church in which all Christians could find place for worship, and the basic premise is that once disagreement on dogma is no longer viewed as a sufficient ground for exclusion, all Christians could commune within a single Church. Yet, in Locke's time (as in ours), those with a favourable attitude to dogmatic flexibility were a specific sort of Christians. When Le Clerc, Barbeyrac and other liberal Protestants used Locke to buttress the claims of a rationalist approach to religion where the secular science of natural law provides the foundations of Christian life while the role of dogma is minimized, their work is framed not by a desire to see authoritarian Calvinists and Lutherans live side by side with Arminians. They work towards a historical horizon where Europe and the world have been conquered by a reasonable sort of Christianity, where all share the conviction that dogma really matters very little. Thus, after quoting Locke's *unum necessarium*, the author concludes that every Christian 'has a duty to obey the laws and doctrines of Jesus Christ in scripture with all the application of which he is capable', while retaining the understanding that interpretations may differ: all are equally authorized in holding their own opinion of what Scripture says if they study it with due care (ibid., pp. 365–6). The author rejects almost in passing the possibility that Catholics could be part of the new universal Church but is more interested in establishing that no genuine Protestant could (as of course did many influential Protestant divines including central Francophone Calvinists such as Pierre Jurieu) condemn as a heretic a person who holds unusual religious views but believes in Jesus Christ and who instructs himself. Interestingly, then, the future of Christianity dreamt up in the work is based on one inclusive Church without either Catholics or intolerant Protestants: in that Church, the dominant eighteenth-century understandings of Christianity would have no place.

The reunification tract is significant in revealing a framework within which various parts of Locke's publications hang together for readers in the early eighteenth-century *République des lettres*. Locke's attack on absolutism was read as an attack on the Louis XIV regime and as an argument against the state's right to intervene against reasonable and tolerant (Protestant) groups, such as Arminians, Socinians and others whom religious conservatives often considered heterodox. At the same time, the plea for toleration suggested that intolerant conservatives should be kept in check by secular powers, and even that intolerant authoritarianism (Catholicism being the convenient example, but authoritarian Protestant orthodoxies often constituting the more pressing threat) is a crime against secular morality. As efforts to secure the foundations of a secular moral science within a project for reasonable Christianity, Locke's discussions of innate ideas and empirical science became part of an early Enlightenment project with a distinct religious profile.

The early reception of Locke's thought on the Continent was thus to a significant degree the work of thinkers who, like Le Clerc and Barbeyrac, strove to secure freedom of thought and toleration for unorthodox rationalist Protestants, and who wanted to rework Christianity from within. They inserted Locke's thought as a refinement of the secularist moral science known as natural law theory, and emphasized in particular his emphasis on toleration, and his critique of absolutism. Doing so in terms that were designed to target the French crown in particular, layered with criticism against authoritarian clergies in general, the Jean Locke of liberal Protestants also appealed to Voltaire and others who, in the latter half of the century especially, radicalized the effort to rethink Christian assumptions, bringing it to bear also on key metaphysical themes such as the existence of an immaterial soul. In general Voltaire shared the ideal of a tolerant religion focusing more on rational ethics and making very limited claims regarding dogma.

This is the outline, then, of Francophone Anglophilia in the early eighteenth century, and it is not, against this background, surprising to find that thinkers such as Locke became emblematic for what the British thought. On the Continent, Locke in fact came to stand as one of the main figures of 'liberal Protestantism', both for its proponents and its critics. Thus when Père Ceillier in his voluminous *Apologie de la Morale des Peres de*

l'Eglise (1718, see esp. pp. 257–78) attacks liberal Protestants, accusing them of emptying religion of all its contents, it is Locke in particular that he singles out for his bombardment. Locke's name thus came to stand out as one to praise and condemn not only for faults or strengths internal to his arguments, but also for the dream with which his name became associated, largely thanks to his early mediators – a dream of a more reasonable Christianity rethought on a secular-rational basis, and formulated in sufficiently general terms that its Protestant sensibilities would not alienate, say, Voltaire from it. And in fact, if the dream is said to build on 'religious motivations', then we must ask ourselves what 'religious' should be taken to mean in this context. Let us therefore return to the question posed at the beginning of this contribution. In what sense was the Enlightenment project a religious or anti-religious one?

The Lockean religious project as Barbeyrac understood and mediated it is one for overcoming the 'illusions of the heart' stemming from prejudice, passion, corrupt traditions and bad education. Self-serving ecclesiastic authorities have through the ages actively hindered rational ethical reflection in order to retain their power over the population, Barbeyrac explains. The continuing rivalry between denominations has led some to cram their tenets down other people's throats, taking away all freedom to examine matters rationally, he continues, quoting Locke's *Essay*. The subjected part of humanity should, the quote continues, 'with Egyptian bondage, expect Egyptian darkness', were it not for the 'sacred light' (*lumiére sacrée*) put by God in each human, that no human power can entirely extinguish (Barbeyrac, 1740, p. xxxix; *E*, IV.iii.20, p. 552). Although God did send Jesus to teach natural law, corruption soon had its say again until providence eventually raised up Grotius to make people use their rational FACULTIES again. This is the revolution of which Locke was now a central symbol and hero, together with Le Clerc and Barbeyrac himself.

Locke's ideas were formulated, mediated and used in a time when religious issues were both at the heart of political debate, because of the denominational quarrels, and a natural part of everyman's worldview. Rethinking religion or rethinking Christianity was not, in that context, something separate from rethinking the future of Europe and the world. In this sense, formulating a secularist rationalism as a universal foundation for both political thought and a more reasonable religion was not either a religious or anti-religious project, but both. Locke's position within this project is that of an important footnote, but he was also appointed a further role as part of a rhetorical construction of the Anglophile's England. In this sense, overstating Locke's importance as a source of the European Enlightenment has deep historical roots.

BIBLIOGRAPHY

Primary Sources
[Anon.], 'Avertissement', in *Bibliothèque Raisonnée des Savans de l'Europe*, vol. i, (Amsterdam, 1728).
Barbeyrac, Jean, *Traité de la Morale des Péres de l'Eglise* (Amsterdam, 1728).
——, *Traité du Jeu* (Amsterdam, 1709).
Ceillier, Dom Remy, *Apologie de la Morale des Peres de l'Eglise* (Paris, 1718).
Le Clerc, Jean, *Bibliothèque Choisie*, vol. ix (Amsterdam, 1706).
——, 'Éloge historique', in John Locke, *Œuvres diverses de Monsieur Jean Locke* (Rotterdam, 1710).
Locke, John, *Le Christianisme Raisonnable* (Amsterdam, 1731).
Pufendorf, Samuel von, *De Jure Naturae et Gentium Libri Octo* (Berlin, 1998).
——, *Le Droit de la Nature et des Gens*, ed. and trans. Jean Barbeyrac (1740).

Secondary Literature
Cushman, Herbert Ernest, *A Beginner's History of Philosophy* (Michigan, 1911).
Hazard, Paul, *The European Mind, 1680–1715* (London, 1953).
Hunter, Ian, *The Secularisation of the Confessional State: The Political Thought of Christian Thomasius* (Cambridge, 2007).
Hutchison, Ross, *Locke in France, 1688–1734* (Oxford, 1991).
Israel, Jonathan, *Enlightenment Contested: Philosophy, Modernity, and the Emancipation of Man 1670–1751* (Oxford, 2006).
Marshall, John, *John Locke: Resistance, Religion and Responsibility* (Cambridge, 1996).
Othmer, Sieglinde, *Berlin und die Verbreitung des Naturrechts in Europa* (Berlin, 1970).
Robertson, John, *The Case for the Enlightenment: Scotland and Naples, 1680–1760* (Cambridge, 2005).
Savonius, Sami-Juhani, 'John Locke and the Civil Philosophy of the *Bibliothécaires, circa* 1688–*circa* 1702' (PhD thesis, Cambridge, 2002).
——, 'Locke in French: The *Du Gouvernement Civil* of 1691 and Its Readers', *Historical Journal*, vol. xlvii (2004), pp. 47–79.
——, 'The Role of Huguenot Tutors in John Locke's Programme of Social Reform', in Anne Dunan-Page (ed.), *The Religious Culture of the Huguenots from 1660 to 1789* (Aldershot, 2006), pp. 137–62.
Torrey, Norman, *Les Philosophes: the Philosophers of the Enlightenment and Modern Democracy* (New York, 1960).
Tully, James, *A Discourse on Property: John Locke and His Adversaries* (Cambridge, 1980).
Yolton, John, *Locke and the Way of Ideas* (Bristol, 1996, repr. of Oxford, 1956).
Zagorin, Perez, *How the Idea of Religious Toleration Came to the West* (Princeton, 2003).

Petter Korkman

CONTEMPORARY LOCKE SCHOLARSHIP

Since World War II Locke studies have burgeoned. Bibliographies show a steady increase from twelve entries in 1946, through seventy-five in 1976, to ninety-nine in 2006 (Hall and Woolhouse, 1983; Hall, 1971–2000 and 2001–). Partly, this reflects the general increase in academic publication, but there are particular reasons too.

In 1975 the Clarendon Press, Oxford, undertook to publish (in an expected thirty or so volumes) a new collected edition of Locke's writings (Nidditch et al., 1975–). Much of the material for this was to come from the Lovelace Collection of Locke's manuscripts purchased soon after the war by the Bodleian Library, Oxford, on the advice of von Leyden (1954, pp. 1–7), who had examined the collection closely. The accessibility of these manuscripts stimulated new work on Locke, including of course the editing and gradual publication of the manuscripts themselves in the Clarendon edition and elsewhere (see, for example, Axtell, 1968; De Beer, 1976–; Dewhurst, 1963; Higgins-Biddle, 1999; Kelly, 1991; Lough, 1953; Milton and Milton, 2006; Nidditch, 1975; Nuovo, 2002; 2012; Romanell, 1984; Von Leyden, 1954; Yolton and Yolton, 1999; for others see Attig, 2004, *passim*).

Pervading the study of Locke (and other figures) in recent years have been questions regarding the purpose and method of studying the history of philosophy. Should Locke be studied contextually, against his own historical background, or should he be approached textually, and as dealing with perennial problems with which we ourselves are still concerned (Ayers, 1991, pp. 1–10; Bennett, 2001, vol. i, pp. 1–9; Wilson, 1992)? An early and influential exponent of the first approach was Yolton (1956). A powerful exponent of the second (an approach which has been described by the opposition as tomb-robbing by contrast with serious archeology) has been Bennett (1971, 2001; also Mackie, 1976).

Naturally, a large proportion of Locke studies has been devoted to the ontology and epistemology of his *Essay concerning Human Understanding* (of which Nidditch, 1975 is the definitive edition). Stimulated by Mandelbaum (1964) there has been a tendency to read the *Essay* as addressing questions which arose in the context of the natural philosophy of the time, in particular that of BOYLE, NEWTON and the virtuosi of the Royal Society (see Anstey, 2011). This is frequently exhibited in the work on various popular areas of concern. Does Locke, as was and still is conventionally thought, hold a representational theory of PERCEPTION – and would he be right or wrong if he did? – or is he a direct realist? (Bolton, 1978; Lowe, 1995, pp. 38–47; Mackie, 1976, pp. 37–71; Matthews, 1971; Yolton, 1970, pp. 131–3.) What exactly is his doctrine of PRIMARY AND SECONDARY QUALITIES, and how does it relate to his theory of perception? Is it simply taken over from Boyle? (Alexander, 1974; 1985, pt. 2; Bennett, 1965; 1971, pp. 89–123; Curley, 1972; Lowe, 1995, pp. 47–53; Mackie, 1976, pp. 7–36.) How should we understand the distinction between the two kinds of complex idea, substances and MODES, and the associated notions of real and nominal essence? (Atherton, 1984; 1991; Ayers, 1981; 1991, vol. ii, pt. 1; Bolton, 1976; Lowe, 1995, pp. 78–83; Mattern, 1986.) What exactly does Locke think about 'substratum', and is it defensible? Does he reject it as some of his contemporaries thought, and what is its relation to real essence? Is it a logico-linguistic notion, unconnected with the idea of an unknown physical micro-structure, as Bennett has argued, or, as Ayers has maintained, is it to be associated with that idea? (Ayers, 1975; 1991, vol. ii, pt. 1; Bennett, 1971, ch. 3; 2001, ch. 27; Lowe, 1995, pp. 72–8; Mackie, 1976, ch. 3.) Is Locke a thoroughgoing mechanist: do *all* the qualities and powers of a body 'flow from' its real essence, or are some voluntarily 'superadded' by God? (Ayers, 1991, vol. ii, chs. 11–13; McCann, 1985; Wilson, 1979).

There have been other frequently addressed topics in the *Essay*, unrelated to Locke's interest in contemporary natural philosophy. What he says about PERSONAL IDENTITY has received much attention, even though, or perhaps because, its interpretation and defensibility is open to discussion. (Allison, 1966; Ayers, 1991, vol. ii, pp. 254–92; Flew, 1951; Hughes, 1975; Lolordo, 2012; Lowe 1991; 1995, pp. 102–14; Mackie, 1976, ch. 6; Strawson, 2011; Thiel, 2011, chs. 3–6). The account of FREE WILL and voluntary action has been the subject of even more disagreement, both as to its meaning and its adequacy. Is Locke a libertarian, or a compatibilist? (Bricke, 1985; Chappell, 1994; 1998; Jolley, 1999, ch. 7; Lowe, 1986; 1995, ch. 6; 2004; Yaffe, 2000.) His philosophy of language, too, has constantly come under review – though in some markedly different ways. From the perspective of fashionable modern interests, it has been asked whether he falls foul of Wittgensteinian strictures against private language (Brykman, 1992; Hacker, 1972, pp. 224–31), and whether his semantics of natural kind terms anticipates that of Kripke or of Putnam (Galperin, 1995; Mackie, 1976, pp. 93–100). From a more historical perspective, his relation to various linguistic ideas current in his day in the Royal Society (Howell, 1971, pp. 264–98, 448–502; Land, 1974, ch. 1), and his possible debts to earlier scholastic thinking have been in focus (Ashworth, 1980; Dawson, 2007; Ott, 2004).

Locke's political thought has been much discussed. In the 1950s Strauss unmasked Locke as a secret follower of HOBBES whose avowed concern with God and NATURAL LAW was a front behind which he wished to advance a radically atheistic doctrine of natural right. Strauss's claims were extended by Cox and have been redacted many times since (Strauss, 1953; Cox, 1960; Myers, 1998; Zuckert, 1994; 2002).

Strauss was not alone in suspecting Locke's professions about God and natural law. MacPherson (1962) identified Locke's hidden agendum as the unlimited acquisition of PROPERTY by the capitalist class and his remarks about God and religion as ideological instruments designed to secure the compliance of a sub-rational labouring class. MacPherson agreed that Locke's was a theory of natural right, the right in question being to his mind the right to acquire beyond one's needs in a commercial society. Succeeding liberal interpreters disagreed with Strauss and MacPherson but continued their emphasis on natural right (Seliger, 1968; and cf. Simmons, 1992).

Historians in this period avoided overarching claims about conceptual content. Cranston's biography (1957) showed that Locke was obsessively secretive but revealed little about his thinking. However, Laslett's celebrated edition (1960) of the *Two Treatises of Government* put Locke's thought in a new light. Laslett argued that Locke wrote the bulk of the *Two Treatises* between 1679 and 1683 and so could not have written it to justify the Glorious Revolution of 1688 as generations of interpreters had supposed. If Laslett's dating remains problematical (see Milton, 1995), Locke scholars have accepted his basic argument and elaborated its implications.

Ashcraft (1986) depicted Locke as an ideologist of dissent, committed in word and deed to armed resistance and insurrection against the Stuarts. Dunn (1969a) combined the historical and the conceptual in establishing the centrality of theological conceptions to Locke's political arguments. Dunn considered Locke's thinking as an integrated whole; his method was contextual insofar as it understood Locke to belong to a culturally distant and in many respects alien world in which God suffused everything (and so to have little to say to the present). After Dunn, the question for most Locke scholars was not whether Locke's professions about God and natural law were genuine, but how exactly they related to his political thinking. The same question prompted renewed interest in Locke's religious views.

Tully (1980) first used Dunn's methodology to criticize MacPherson's claims about Locke on property and later (1993) to identify a colonial context for the arguments of the *Two Treatises*, which provided the cue for further accounts of the matter (Armitage, 2004). The role of those arguments in shaping the American Revolution remained a controversial question, and one in which the claims of Strauss and MacPherson continued to ramify (Dunn, 1969b; Dworetz, 1990; Pangle, 1988). The role of Locke's arguments in establishing a public/private distinction used to relegate the status of women in subsequent liberal thought was also scrutinized (Elshtain, 1981; Pateman, 1988).

Marshall (1994; 2006) examined the whole of Locke's political and religious thinking through a series of highly specific contexts. His conclusion was that, if it made sense to regard Locke's thinking as an integrated whole at all, over time it had been developed in very inconsistent ways. By contrast Harris (1994a) considered Locke's political theory as part of a continuous sequence of thought which connected the argument of the *Two Treatises* to his claims about TOLERATION.

Most modern interpreters followed Waldron (1988) in assuming that toleration for Locke followed directly from the premise that belief could not be coerced and for that reason found Locke's view inadequate. Wootton (1993) and Stanton (2006) found it more adequate. Milton and Milton (2006) edited and contextualized Locke's early writings on toleration; Goldie (1991; 1993) juxtaposed Locke's arguments to contemporaneous Anglican arguments for intolerance. Tuckness (2002) discovered in Locke's *Third Letter for Toleration* a distinctive argument for toleration from a 'legislative point of view'. Dunn (1991) exposed the distance between Locke's position and modern assumptions about freedom of conscience.

Although Harris (1994b) registered the political implications of Locke's understanding of Christianity, whether and how far Locke's positions about politics and toleration *depended* upon distinctively Christian commitments remained hard questions (see Waldron, 2002). So too the specific content of those commitments: some interpreters (Reventlow, 1980, pp. 401–69; Spellman, 1988) confidently aligned Locke's religious views with Latitudinarianism, others more cautiously

(Ashcraft, 1992; Marshall, 1992). Marshall (2000) decided that by the 1690s Locke had abandoned Latitudinarianism for SOCINIANISM. Nuovo (2002) and Higgins-Biddle (1999, pp. xlii–lxxiv) disagreed.

Work on Locke's abiding interest in medicine has focused on the relation between his general empiricist epistemology as expounded in the *Essay* and the mature medical methodology that he learnt from his association with SYDENHAM (Aspelin, 1949; Duchesneau, 1970; Romanell, 1984; Milton, 2001).

Regular editions of his *Thoughts on Education* (e.g. Axtell, 1968; Yolton and Yolton, 1999) and chapter length expositions of it (e.g. Curtis and Boultwood, 1953, ch. 10; Price, 1962, ch. 6) testify to a continuing interest in Locke's educational ideas. There has not been a huge amount of detailed critical work in this area, but it is certainly not absent (e.g. Benne, 1965; Leites, 1979; Neill, 1989; Tarkov, 1984; Yolton, 1998).

Locke's economic thought and his involvement in the recoinage have been duly recognized in general histories of economics (Horsefield, 1960, pp. 57–60; Li, 1963, ch. 6; Letwin, 1963, ch. 6). There have been some more extensive and specialized studies, both philosophical (Vaughn, 1980; Eltis, 1995; Leigh, 1974) and historical (Kelly, 1991; Laslett, 1957). Most recently, work has been done on the relation between Locke's interests in medicine and in economics (Caffentzis, 2003; Coleman, 2000).

All this work embodies methodological differences – about whether Locke's views should be explicated with reference to schools of thought that allegedly exerted an influence upon his thinking or in their own terms and, if so, how – which are unlikely to disappear. Happily, contemporary Locke scholarship seems much the richer for these differences.

BIBLIOGRAPHY
Alexander, Peter, 'Boyle and Locke on Primary and Secondary Qualities', *Ratio*, vol. xvi (1974), pp. 51–67.

——, *Ideas, Qualities and Corpuscles: Locke and Boyle on the External World* (Cambridge, 1985).

Allison, H.E., 'Locke's Theory of Personal Identity: A Re-examination', *Journal of the History of Ideas*, vol. xxvii (1966), pp. 41–58.

Anstey, Peter, *John Locke and Natural Philosophy* (Oxford, 2011).

Armitage, David, 'John Locke, Carolina and the *Two Treatises of Government*', *Political Theory*, vol. xxxii (2004), pp. 602–26.

Ashcraft, Richard, *Revolutionary Politics & Locke's Two Treatises of Government* (Princeton, 1986).

——, 'Latitudinarianism and Toleration: Historical Myth versus Political History', in R. Kroll et al. (eds), *Philosophy, Science and Religion in England, 1640–1700* (Cambridge, 1992), pp. 151–77.

Ashworth, E.J., 'The Scholastic Background to Locke's Theory of Language', in Konrad Koerner (ed.), *Progress in Linguistic Historiography* (Amsterdam, 1980), pp. 59–68.

Aspelin, G., 'Locke and Sydenham', *Theoria*, vol. xv (1949), pp. 29–37.

Atherton, Margaret, 'Knowledge of Substance and Knowledge of Essence in Locke's *Essay*', *History of Philosophy Quarterly*, vol. i (1984), pp. 413–28.

——, 'Corpuscles, Mechanism, and Essentialism in Berkeley and Locke', *Journal of the History of Philosophy*, vol. xxix (1991), pp. 47–67.

Attig, John C., 'John Locke Manuscripts' (2004–), http://www.libraries.psu.edu/tas/locke/.

Ayers, Michael, 'Substance, Reality, and the Great, Dead Philosophers', *American Philosophical Quarterly*, vol. vii (1970), pp. 38–49.

——, 'The Ideas of Power and Substance in Locke's Philosophy', *Philosophical Quarterly*, vol. xxv (1975), pp. 1–27.

——, 'Locke versus Aristotle on Natural Kinds', *Journal of Philosophy*, vol. lxxviii (1981), pp. 247–71.

——, *Locke*, 2 vols (London, 1991).

Axtell, J.L., *The Educational Writings of John Locke* (Cambridge, 1968).

Benne, K.D., 'The Gentleman: Locke', in P. Nash et al. (eds), *The Educated Man* (New York, 1965), pp. 190–223.

Bennett, Jonathan, 'Substance, Reality, and Primary Qualities', *American Philosophical Quarterly*, vol. ii (1965), pp. 1–17.

——, *Locke, Berkeley, Hume* (Oxford, 1971).

——, *Learning from Six Philosophers: Descartes, Spinoza, Leibniz, Locke, Berkeley, Hume*, 2 vols (Oxford, 2001).

Bolton, M.B., 'Substances, Substrata, and Names of Substances in Locke's *Essay*, *Philosophical Review*, vol. lxxxv (1976), pp. 305–16.

——, 'A Defense of Locke and the Representative Theory of Perception', *Canadian Journal of Philosophy*, supp. vol. iv (1978), pp. 101–20.

Bricke, John, 'Locke, Hume and the Nature of Volitions', *Hume Studies*, supp. (1985), pp. 15–51.

Brykman, G., 'Locke on Private Language', in P.D. Cummins and G. Zoeller, *Minds, Ideas, Objects* (Atascadero, California, 1992).

Caffentzis, C.G., 'Medical Metaphors and Monetary Strategies in the Political Economy of Locke and Berkeley', *History of Political Economy*, vol. xxxv: annual supp. (2003), pp. 204–33.

Chappell, Vere, 'Locke on the Freedom of the Will', in G.A.J. Rogers (ed.), *Locke's Philosophy: Content and Context* (Oxford, 1994), pp. 101–21.

——, 'Locke on the Suspension of Desire', *The Locke Newsletter*, vol. xxix (1998), pp. 23–38.

Coleman, W.O., 'The Significance of John Locke's Medical Studies for his Economic Thought', *History of Political Economy*, vol. xxxii (2000), pp. 711–31.

Cox, Richard H., *Locke on War and Peace* (Oxford, 1960).

Cranston, Maurice, *John Locke: A Biography* (London, 1957).

Curley, E.M., 'Locke, Boyle, and the Distinction between Primary and Secondary Qualities', *Philosophical Review*, vol. lxxxi (1972), pp. 438–64.

Curtis, S.J., and Boultwood, M.E.A., *A Short History of Educational Ideas* (London, 1953).

Dawson, Hannah, *Locke, Language and Early Modern Philosophy* (Cambridge, 2007).

De Beer, E.S. (ed.), *The Correspondence of John Locke*, 9 vols (Oxford, 1976–).

Dewhurst, Kenneth, *John Locke (1632–1704): A Medical Biography* (London, 1963).

Duchesneau, F., 'La Philosophie médicale de Sydenham', *Dialogue*, vol. ix (1970), pp. 54–68.

Dunn, John, *The Political Thought of John Locke* (Cambridge, 1969a).

——, 'The Politics of Locke in England and America in the Eighteenth Century', in J. Yolton (ed.), *John Locke: Problems and Perspectives* (Cambridge, 1969b), pp. 45–80.

——, 'The Claim to Freedom of Conscience: Freedom of Speech, Freedom of Thought, Freedom of Worship', in O.P. Grell et al. (eds), *From Persecution to Toleration: The Glorious Revolution and Religion in England* (Oxford, 1991), pp. 171–93.

Dworetz, Stephen M., *The Unvarnished Doctrine: Locke, Liberalism and the American Revolution* (London, 1990).

Elshtain, Jean Bethke, *Public Man, Private Woman: Women in Social and Political Thought* (Princeton, New Jersey, 1981).

Eltis, W., 'John Locke, the Quantity Theory of Money and the Establishment of a Sound Economy', in Mark Blaug et al. (eds), *The Quantity Theory of Money from Locke to Keynes and Friedman* (Brookfield, Vermont, 1995), pp. 4–26.

Flew, Antony, 'Locke and the Problem of Personal Identity', *Philosophy*, vol. xxvi (1951), pp. 155–78.

Galperin, D., 'Locke as Anticipator of Putnam rather than Kripke on Natural Kinds', *History of Philosophy Quarterly*, vol. xii (1995), pp. 367–85.

Goldie, Mark, 'The Theory of Religious Intolerance in Restoration England', in O.P. Grell et al. (eds), *From Persecution to Toleration: The Glorious Revolution and Religion in England* (Oxford, 1991), pp. 331–68.

——, 'John Locke, Jonas Proast and Religious Toleration 1688–1692', in J. Walsh et al. (eds), *The Church of England, c.1689-c.1833: from Toleration to Tractarianism* (Cambridge, 1993).

Grell, O.P., et al. (eds), *From Persecution to Toleration: The Glorious Revolution and Religion in England* (Oxford, 1991).

Hacker, P.M.S., *Insight and Illusion* (Oxford, 1972).

Hall, Roland, 'Recent Publications on Locke', *The Locke Newsletter*, vols 1–31 (1971–2000), *passim*.

——, 'Recent Publications on Locke', *Locke Studies*, vols 1– (2001–).

——, and Roger Woolhouse, *Eighty Years of Locke Scholarship* (Edinburgh, 1983).

Harris, Ian, *The Mind of John Locke* (Cambridge, 1994a).

——, 'The Politics of Christianity' [1994b], in G.A.J. Rogers (ed.), *Locke's Philosophy: Content and Context* (Oxford, 1994), pp. 197–215.

Higgins-Biddle, John C. (ed.), *The Reasonableness of Christianity* (Oxford, 1999).

Horsefield, J.K., *British Monetary Experiments, 1650–1710* (London, 1960).

Howell, W.S., *Eighteenth-Century British Logic and Rhetoric* (Princeton, New Jersey, 1971).

Hughes, M.W., 'Personal Identity: A Defence of Locke', *Philosophy*, vol. l (1975), pp. 169–87.

Kelly, Patrick Hyde (ed.), *Locke on Money*, 2 vols (Oxford, 1991).

Land, S.K., 'The Semantics of Locke and the Royal Society', *From Signs to Propositions* (London, 1974).

Laslett, Peter, 'John Locke, the Great Recoinage, and the Origins of the Board of Trade: 1695–1698', *William and Mary Quarterly*, vol. xiv (1957), pp. 370–92.

——, (ed.) *John Locke: Two Treatises of Government* (Cambridge, 1960).

Leigh, A.H., 'John Locke and the Quantity Theory of Money', *History of Political Economy*, vol. vi (1974), pp. 200–19.

Leites, E., 'Locke's Liberal Theory of Parenthood', in O. O'Neill et al. (eds), *Having Children* (New York, 1979), pp. 306–18.

Letwin, W., *The Origins of Scientific Economics: English Economic Thought 1660–1776* (Westport, Connecticut, 1963).

Li, Ming-Hsun, *The Great Recoinage of 1696–1699* (London, 1963).

Lolordo, Antonia, *Locke's Moral Man* (Oxford, 2012).

Lough, John (ed.), *Locke's Travels in France, 1675–1679* (Cambridge, 1953).

Lowe, E.J., 'Necessity and Will in Locke's Theory of Action', *History of Philosophy Quarterly*, vol. iii (1986), pp. 149–63.

——, 'Substance and Selfhood', *Philosophy*, vol. lxvi (1991), pp. 81–99.

——, *Locke* (London, 1995).

——, 'Locke, Compatibilist Event-Causalist or Libertarian Substance Causalist?', *Philosophy and Phenomenological Research*, vol. lxviii (2004), pp. 688–701.

Mackie, John, *Problems from Locke* (Oxford, 1976).

Macpherson, C.B., *The Political Theory of Possessive Individualism* (Oxford, 1963).

Mandelbaum, Maurice, 'Locke's Realism', *Philosophy, Science, and Sense Perception* (Baltimore, 1964), pp. 1–60.

Marshall, John, 'John Locke and Latitudinarianism', in Richard Kroll et al. (eds), *Philosophy, Science, and Religion in England 1640–1700* (Cambridge, 1992), pp. 253–82.

——, *John Locke: Resistance, Religion and Responsibility* (Cambridge, 1994).

——, 'Locke, Socinianism, 'Socinianism,' and Unitarianism' in M.A. Stewart (ed.), *English Philosophy in the Age of Locke* (Oxford, 2000), pp. 111–82.

——, *John Locke, Toleration and Early Enlightenment Culture* (Cambridge, 2006).

Mattern, Ruth, 'Locke on Natural Kinds as the "Workmanship of the Understanding"', *The Locke Newsletter*, vol. xvii (1986), pp. 45–92.

Matthews, H.E., 'Locke, Malebranche and the Representative Theory of Perception', *The Locke Newsletter*, vol. ii (1971), pp. 12–21.

McCann, Edwin, 'Lockean Mechanism', in A.J. Holland (ed.), *Philosophy, its History and Historiography* (Dordrecht, 1985).

Milton, J.R., 'Dating Locke's *Second Treatise*', *History of Political Thought*, vol. xvi (1995), pp. 356–90.

——, 'Locke, Medicine and the Mechanical Philosophy', *British Journal for the History of Philosophy*, vol. ix (2001), pp. 221–43.

——, and Philip Milton, *John Locke: An Essay concerning Toleration, and Other Writings on Law and Politics, 1667–1683* (Oxford, 2006).

Myers, Peter C., *Our Only Star and Compass: Locke and the Struggle for Political Rationality* (Lanham, Maryland, 1998).

Neill, A., 'Locke on Habituation, Autonomy, and Education', *Journal of the History of Philosophy*, vol. xxvii (1989), pp. 225–45.

Nidditch, P.H., et al. (general ed.), *The Clarendon Edition of the Works of John Locke* (Oxford, 1975–).

——, (ed.), *John Locke, An Essay concerning Human Understanding* (Oxford, 1975).

Nuovo, Victor, *John Locke: Writings on Religion* (Oxford, 2002).

——, (ed.), *John Locke, Vindications of the Reasonableness of Christianity* (Oxford, 2012).

Ott, Walter, *Locke's Philosophy of Language* (Cambridge, 2004).

Pangle, Thomas, *The Spirit of Modern Republicanism* (Chicago, 1988).

Pateman, Carole, *The Sexual Contract* (Stanford, 1988).

Price, K., *Education and Philosophical Thought* (Boston, 1962).

Reventlow, Henning Graf, *Bibelautorität und Geist der Moderne* (Göttingen, 1980).

Rogers, G.A.J. (ed.), *Locke's Philosophy: Content and Context* (Oxford, 1994).

Romanell, Patrick, *John Locke and Medicine* (New York, 1984).

Seliger, Martin, *The Liberal Politics of John Locke* (London, 1968).

Simmons, A. John, *The Lockean Theory of Rights* (Princeton, 1992).

Spellman, William M. *John Locke and the Problem of Depravity* (Oxford, 1988).

Stanton, Timothy, 'Locke and the Politics and Theology of Toleration', *Political Studies*, vol. liv (2006), pp. 84–102.

Strauss, Leo, *Natural Right and History* (Chicago, 1953).

Strawson, Galen, *Locke on Personal Identity: Consciousness and Concernment* (Princeton, 2011).

Tarkov, Nathan, *Locke's Education for Liberty* (Chicago, 1984).

Thiel, Udo, *The Early Modern Subject: Consciousness and Personal Identity from Descartes to Hume* (Oxford, 2011).

Tuckness, Alex, *Locke and the Legislative Point of View* (Princeton, New Jersey, 2002).

Tully, James, *A Discourse of Property: John Locke and his Adversaries* (Cambridge, 1980).

——, 'Rediscovering America: The Two Treatises and Aboriginal Rights', *An Approach to Political Philosophy: Locke in Contexts* (Cambridge, 1993), pp. 137–76.

Vaughn, K.I., *John Locke: Economist and Social Scientist* (London, 1980).

Von Leyden, W. (ed.) *John Locke: Essays on the Law of Nature* (Oxford, 1954).

Waldron, Jeremy, 'Locke, Toleration and the Rationality of Persecution', in S. Mendus (ed.), *Justifying Toleration* (Cambridge, 1988).

——, *God, Locke and Equality: Christian Foundations in Locke's Political Thought* (Cambridge, 2002).

Wilson, Margaret D., 'Superadded Properties: The Limits of Mechanism in Locke', *American Philosophical Quarterly*, vol. xvi (1979), pp. 143–50.

——, 'History of Philosophy in Philosophy Today; and the Case of the Sensible Qualities', *The Philosophical Review*, vol. ci (1992), pp. 191–243.

Wootton, David, *John Locke: Political Writings* (Harmondsworth, 1993).

Yaffe, Gideon, *Liberty worth the Name: Locke on Free Agency* (Princeton, New Jersey, 2000).

Yolton, John, *Locke and the Way of Ideas* (Oxford, 1956).

——, *Locke and the Compass of Human Understanding* (Cambridge, 1970).

——, 'Locke – Education for Virtue', in A.O. Rorty (ed.), *Philosophers on Education* (London, 1998), pp. 173–89.

——, and Jean Yolton (eds), *John Locke: Some Thoughts concerning Education* (Oxford, 1999).

Zuckert, Michael, *Natural Rights and the New Republicanism* (Princeton, New Jersey, 1994).

——, *Launching Liberalism: on Lockean Political Philosophy* (Kansas, 2002).

Roger Woolhouse and Timothy Stanton

INDEX OF LOCKE'S WORKS

A Discourse on Miracles 41, 142, 149

A Paraphrase and Notes on the Epistles of St Paul xi, 45, 102, 213, 214, **277–80**

An Essay concerning Human Understanding ix, xi, 3, 8, 13, 15, 20, 21, 25, 26, 27, 29, 37, 39, 40, 41, 42, 47, 49, 50, 51, 54, 55, 61, 63, 64, 67, 68, 71, 74, 78, 82, 87, 89, 93, 94, 96, 97, 98, 102, 104, 110, 113, 114, 115, 127, 128, 135, 136, 139, 140, 141, 142, 143, 146, 147, 150, 151, 153, 155, 156, 157, 158, 159, 160, 161, 162, 163, 167, 168, 179, 180, 183, 184, 188, 189, 193, 195, 196, 212, 213, 215, 220, 221, 222, **234–49**, 271, 275, 276, 277, 281, 282, 283, 284, 285, 286, 288, 289, 297, 307, 308, 312, 314, 316

An Essay concerning Toleration and Other Writings on Law and Politics x, 37, 45, 46, 82, 114, 239, 258

Clarendon Edition of the Works of John Locke ix, xii, 42, 43, 44, 45, 314

Epistola de Tolerantia 3, 21, 39, 42, 66, 67, 114, 225, 226, 257, 271, 307, 308, 309, 311

Essay on the Poor Law 30, 40, 45

Essays on the Law of Nature ix, 6, 13, 27, 45, 63, 85, 167, 189, 193, 239

Fundamental Constitutions of Carolina 12, 13, 37, 126, 201

Further Considerations concerning Raising the Value of Money 41, 43, 45, 130, 274

Letters concerning Toleration 12, 17, 23, 25, 32, 33, 39, 40, 42, 43, 44, 105, 106, 121, 225, 245, **257–65**, 258, 261, 262, 263, 281, 283, 290, 297, 316

Of the Conduct of the Understanding xi, 27, 40, 128, 137, 138, 147, 148, 158, **275–7**, 283

Papers on Money x, **273–5**

Posthumous Works of Mr John Locke 41, 44, 45, 275

Short Observations on a Printed Paper 43, 130, 274

Some Considerations of the Consequences of the Lowering of the Interest 12, 25, 40, 43, 129, 204, 231, 274

Some Thoughts concerning Education x, xi, 10, 15, 20, 21, 25, 28, 40, 43, 74, 112, 137, 140, 190, 209, **265–8**, 290, 307, 316

The Reasonableness of Christianity x, xi, 20, 25, 27, 28, 40, 43, 45, 64, 95, 96, 101, 117, 137, 143, 184, 190, 213, 214, 263, **269–73**, 278, 279, 286, 290, 311

Two Treatises of Government ix, xi, 2, 7, 9, 13, 17, 20, 21, 22, 23, 24, 25, 28, 30, 32, 33, 38, 39, 40, 41, 42, 45, 57, 59, 60, 61, 63, 82, 83, 119, 121, 122, 125, 126, 131, 140, 156, 189, 190, 193, 201, 209, 216, **249–57**, 258, 273, 289, 290, 307, 315

INDEX OF NAMES

Aikenhead, Thomas 27, 40
Ainsworth, Michael 110
Alembert, Jean le Rond d' 288, 303
Allestree, Richard 265
Alsop, Vincent 297
Aquinas, Thomas 188
Anne, Queen 41, 227
Archytas 216
Aristotle 1, 34, 57, 98, 107, 134, 145, 170,
   219, 276, 281, 283, 285, 294, 308
Arminius, Jacob 20, 66
Arnauld, Antoine 37, 69, 70, 71, 159, 160
Ascham, Roger 265
Astell, Mary 29, 33, 40, 73
Atwood, William 24, 125, 126, 255
Aubrey, John 9, 61
Augustine, St 21

Bacon, Francis 48, 49, 174, 186, 187, 281,
   282, 286
Bagshaw, Edward 5, 62
Barbeyrac, Jean 41, 215, 304, 305, 306, 307,
   308, 309, 310, 311, 312
Barbon, Nicholas 231
Barclay, Robert 141
Barclay, William 120
Barrett, John 297
Barrington, John Shute, first Viscount 33,
   297
Basset, Thomas 246
Baxter, Richard 272, 297
Bayle, Pierre 21, 39, 40, 69, 74, 283, 304
Becconsall, Thomas 96
Bentham, Jeremy 94
Bentham, Richard 283

Berkeley, Elizabeth 27
Berkeley, George 41, **89–93**, 108, 123, 148,
   162, 182, 195, 199, 222, 184, 285, 286,
   289
Bernard, Jacques 21, 304
Bernoulli, Jacob 243
Bilson, Thomas 120
Birch, Thomas 51, 52
Bodin, Jean 58
Bold, Samuel 26, 34, 270, 286
Boyle, Robert 6, 21, 26, 37, 40, **47–51**, 53,
   62, 76, 77, 78, 84, 85, 87, 100,
   113,115,134, 159, 186, 187, 188, 197,
   199, 246, 285, 314
Brady, Robert 125, 126, 127
Bramhall, John 107
Broughton, John 285, 286
Brounower, Sylvester 32
Burnet, Gilbert 227
Burnet, Thomas 33, 44, 51, 52, **93–6**, 248,
   285
Burnett, Thomas 97, 100
Burridge, Ezekiel 26, 41, 42, 289

Calamy, Edmund 33, 297, 300
Calvin, John 58, 304, 309
Cato 10
Charles I 2, 4, 17, 37, 58, 80, 81, 120, 124,
   125, 207, 254
Charles II 3, 7, 9, 10, 11, 13, 16, 18, 19, 34,
   37, 38, 39, 59, 114, 120, 121, 124, 209,
   225, 254, 282
Charleton, Walter 77
Charlotte, Queen 290
Cheselden, William 182

Chillingworth, William 134, 272
Churchill, Awnsham 29, 34
Clarke, Edward 18, 21, 23, 29, 31, 32, 38,
    39, 43, 110, 126, 133, 204, 210, 265,
    271, 274
Clarke, Samuel 41, 51, 52
Cockburn, Catherine 51–3, 74, 94, 285, 286
Cole, William 4
Collins, Anthony 20, 34, 41, 104, 111, 137,
    139, 298
Condillac, Étienne Bonnot de 287, 288
Condorcet, Nicolas, Marquis de 288
Cooper, Anthony Ashley see Shaftesbury
Cordemoy, Gérauld de 53, 69
Coste, Pierre 20, 26, 40, 41, 43, 45, 71, 73,
    82, 98, 110, 112, 283, 287, 289, 307
Courcelles, Étienne de 65, 66
Cromwell, Oliver 2, 4, 37, 80, 207
Cudworth, Ralph 28, 38, 62, 72, 74, 76, 77,
    93, 154, 159, 197, 282
Culpeper, Thomas 204
Cumberland, Richard 63
Cunningham, Alexander 97

Danby, Thomas Osbourne, Earl of 81
Defoe, Daniel 32
Des Maizeaux, Pierre 13, 14, 45, 82, 103
Descartes, René 4, 28, 37, 53–7, 69, 77, 84,
    113, 115, 134, 146, 154, 155, 159, 160,
    163, 170, 174, 175, 177, 185, 199, 212,
    219, 220, 222, 223, 228, 236, 237, 241,
    282, 283, 284, 285, 287, 288, 289, 293
Diderot, Denis 182, 288, 302, 303
Digby, Kenelm 77, 107
Dodwell, Henry 105
Dryden, John 3, 105
Duns Scotus 188

Edwards, John 25, 29, 40, 43, 44, 95–6, 101,
    107, 182, 213, 222
Edwards, Jonathan 289
Edwards, Thomas 95, 96
Episcopius, Simon 65, 66, 306
Erasmus 265, 272, 304
Essex, Arthur Capell, first Earl of 18, 24, 39
Evance, Stephen 31
Eyre, Lady 32

Fell, John 5, 18
Fénelon, François 40
Ferguson, Robert 8, 18, 25, 38
Filmer, Robert 17, 24, 33, 38, 57–61, 119,
    120, 121, 125, 190, 201, 202, 210, 216,
    217, 218, 249, 252, 253, 254, 255
Finch, Leopold 105
Forge, Louis de la 53, 69
Frege, Gottlob 176
Freke, John 204, 271, 274
Furly, Benjamin 20, 24, 28, 39, 67, 109, 139

Gailhard, Jean 265
Galileo 77, 199, 282, 293
Gassendi, Pierre 48, 77, 193, 219, 220, 293
Glanvill, Joseph 77
Godwin, William 131
Grotius, Hugo 113, 134, 168, 188, 191, 202,
    252, 304, 308, 312

Haddon, Walter 206
Halley, Edmund 15, 76
Harrington, James 37, 207, 208
Helmont, Jean-Baptiste van 29
Herbert, Thomas 19, 42
Hoadly, Benjamin 227, 298, 299, 300
Hobbes, Thomas 3, 9, 26, 37, 59, 61–5, 70,
    77, 96, 110, 113, 115, 117, 118, 119,
    122, 151, 152, 156, 159, 188, 190, 197,
    199, 206, 207, 210, 212, 216, 217, 219,
    225, 236, 252, 270, 271, 271, 293, 315
Holdsworth, Winch 52, 285
Holloway, Richard 18
Hooke, Robert 3, 38, 85, 87
Hooker, Richard 120, 156, 193, 299
Horace 4, 34, 134
Hume, David 92, 129, 131, 286
Humfrey, John 297
Hunton, Philip 58
Hutcheson, Francis 52, 129
Huyghens (Huygens), Christiaan 47, 77
Hyde, Edward, Earl of Clarendon 41, 62, 81

James I 58, 120, 124
James VI see James I
James, William 182

Kant, Immanuel 111, 282, 284, 286, 289
Kepler, Johannes 293
King, Peter 34, 40, 70, 103, 275, 276
Kneller, Godfrey 29

Law, Edmund 137
Lawson, George 62
Layton, Henry 231
Le Clerc, Jean 19, 20, 21, 26, 39, 44, 53, 65, 72, 76, 78, 82, 98, 103, 246, 286, 287, 304, 305, 306, 307, 309, 310, 311, 312
Le Grand, Antoine 107
Lee, Henry 107, 168, 182, 285
Leibniz, Gottfried Wilhelm 29, 41, 73, 74, 97–100, 107, 182, 213, 222, 289
Leslie, Charles 32, 41, 299, 300, 301
Limborch, Philippus van 17, 20, 21, 29, 39, 42, 44, 65–8, 74, 225, 257, 271, 306
Lobb, Stephen 96
Louis XIV 10, 14, 15, 20, 22, 32, 39, 81, 254, 257, 303, 310, 311
Lovelace, Earls of ix, 34
Lowde, James 285
Lowndes, William 29, 43, 130, 131, 274
Lucretius 48, 197, 216
Luther, Martin 304, 309

Machiavelli 208
Malebranche, Nicolas 15, 27, 38, 40, 44, 68–72, 73, 103, 104, 128, 142, 146, 159, 160, 161, 164, 175, 223, 248, 287
Mansel, Henry Longueville 292, 293
Marvell, Andrew 17, 38
Mary II 22, 23, 24, 39, 105
Masham, Damaris 4, 28, 29, 30, 34, 38, 40, 41, 53, 65, 72–6, 78, 100, 103, 109, 141, 142, 143, 234, 287
Masham, Francis 28, 34, 39, 72, 73, 100, 287
Mazel, David 20, 42, 307
Milner, John 100–2, 213
Milton, John 59, 207, 208
Molesworth, Robert 208
Molyneux, William 26, 28, 30, 40, 44, 54, 68, 89, 90, 97, 104, 127, 142, 158, 179, 180, 181, 182, 188, 195, 196, 198, 247, 248, 284
Monmouth, James Scott, first Duke of 19, 39

Montaigne, Michel de 15, 265
Montesquieu, Charles de 251, 303
Mordaunt, Carey, Viscountess 8, 22, 23, 210
Mordaunt, Charles, Second Viscount 9, 22, 23, 24, 39, 210
More, Henry 76, 77, 93, 113, 159, 282
Morel, Thomas 290
Moreri, Louis 72
Moyle, Walter 208

Nedham, Marchamont 207, 208
Neville, Henry 125, 208
Newton, Isaac 1, 20, 26, 29, 33, 39, 41, 47, 61, 64, 76–80, 113, 115, 134, 174, 193, 214, 281, 285, 286, 287, 289, 303, 314
Nicole, Pierre 15, 37, 38, 45, 69
Norris, John 27, 29, 40, 45, 69, 73, 74, 103–5, 142, 159, 160, 161 248, 285, 286

Ockham, William 188
Ovid 4
Owen, John 4, 297

Paley, William 137
Parker, Henry 58
Parker, Samuel 37, 78
Parry, Elinor 5
Patrick, Simon 272
Pawling, Robert 18, 28, 32, 103
Payne, William 96
Peacham, Henry 265
Penn, William 19, 21, 201
Petty, William 38
Plato 5, 76, 93, 98, 103, 104, 145, 206, 281
Plotinus 197
Pococke, Edward 4, 45
Popham, Alexander 3, 37
Popple, William 21, 27, 28, 32, 40, 257
Prideaux, Humphrey 18
Proast, Jonas 25, 33, 39, 42, 43, 67, 105–7, 225, 226, 227, 261, 262, 263, 264
Pufendorf, Samuel 14, 37, 38, 62, 134, 168, 188, 190, 191, 201, 252, 308, 309, 310, 311

Régis, Pierre Sylvain 53
Rohault, Jacques 5

Russell, William 18, 38

Sadler, John 14, 126
Sanderson, Robert 174
Selden, John 121, 126
Seneca 268
Sergeant, John 107–8, 248, 284, 285, 286
Shaftesbury, Anthony Ashley Cooper, first
    Earl of 6, 8, 9, 10, 11, 12, 14, 16, 17,
    18, 22, 34, 37, 38, 44, 52, 80–4, 113,
    168, 204, 225, 240, 241, 254, 273, 274
Shaftesbury, Anthony Ashley Cooper, third
    Earl of 14, 18, 26, 39, 41, 82, 109–13,
    137, 143, 265, 273
Sherlock, William 24, 26, 196
Sidney, Algernon 18, 38, 40, 59, 125, 208,
    254
Sloane, Hans 40
Smith, John 28, 73, 131, 162, 272
Smith, Samuel 174
Smith, Thomas 14
Socinus, Faustus 27, 96, 101, 214
Somers, John 9, 31, 32, 39, 43, 104, 273
South, Robert 196
Souverain, Jacques 214
Spinoza, Benedict de (Baruch) 21, 37, 70,
    113, 115, 289
Stahl, Peter 6, 186
Stanhope, James 110
Starkey, Thomas 206
Stillingfleet, Edward ix, 17, 25, 26, 36, 38,
    40, 42, 44, 45, 63, 94, 96, 100, 107,
    113–16, 159, 168, 171, 213, 222, 248,
    270, 288, 293, 294, 295, 296, 297, 298,
    299, 300
Streater, John 207
Stubbe, Henry 62, 63, 208
Suarez, Francisco 178, 188
Swift, Jonathan 32
Sydenham, Thomas 6, 15, 21, 47, 49, 77,
    84–8, 113, 115, 157, 158, 187, 188, 234,
    316

Tacitus 4, 124
Taylor, Jeremy 272
Templer, John 62, 63
Tenison, Thomas 62, 63, 95
Tindal, Matthew 297, 298, 300
Toinard, Nicolas 15, 33, 38
Toland, John 20, 27, 40, 115, 135, 136, 137,
    208, 248, 270, 271, 298, 300
Trieu, Philippe du 174
Tyrrell, James 13, 14, 17, 18, 19, 26, 28, 38,
    59, 64, 82, 125, 126, 234, 247, 248,
    254, 285

Vane, Henry 207
Virgil 4, 134
Voltaire 182, 287, 303, 305, 307, 312

Walker, Obadiah 265
Wall, Thomas 297
Wallis, John 62
Ward, Seth 62
Waterland, Daniel 282
Watts, Isaac 283
West, Richard 96, 270
West, Robert 18
Whichcote, Benjamin 93, 272
William III 17, 21, 22, 23, 24, 31, 38, 39, 41,
    84, 105, 210, 254
William of Orange see William III
Willis, Richard 96, 117–18, 270
Willis, Thomas 6, 85
Wittgenstein, Ludwig 176
Wolff, Christian 289
Wood, Anthony 4, 19
Worsley, Benjamin 231, 273, 274
Wren, Christopher 4, 134, 207
Wynne, John 26, 42, 175, 283

Yonge, Walter 31
York, James, Duke of 16, 37, 59, 81, 83

INDEX OF TOPICS

Absolutism 31, 58, 63, 105, **119–22**, 252, 310, 311, 312

abstraction 90, 91, **122–3**, 144, 145, 162, 163, 165, 212, 219, 243, 245, 246, 281

agnosticism 54, 70

America xii, 11, 30, 132, 133, 201, 202, 218, 255, 289

Amsterdam 18, 19, 20, 39, 42, 43, 65, 71, 83, 257, 286, 289

analogy 47, 50, 142, **157–9**

Anglican Church 3, 105, 281, 298

Anglicanism/Anglicans 5, 21, 19, 37, 199, 306, 307

anti-popery 17

Aristotelianism 211, 219

Arminianism/Arminians 2, 65, 66, 213, 306, 309, 311

Association Oath 24, 29

astronomy 15, 134, 268

atheism/atheists 26, 95, 96, 101, 114, 168, 226, 248, 260, 261, 270, 308

Bangorian controversy 227, 299

Bank of England 31, 34, 40

Bibliothèque Ancienne et Moderne 304

Bibliothèque Choisie 44, 304

Bibliothèque Universelle et Historique 20, 39, 89, 246, 304

biology 57, 60, 219

Board of Trade 11, 25, 30, 31, 32, 40, 45, 202, 274

Boyle's Law 47

Calvinism/Calvinists 2, 7, 10, 21, 213, 303, 311

Cambridge 24, 25, 29, 72, 76, 77, 78, 95, 105, 113

Cambridge Platonists 20, 54, 72, 76, 93, 159, 282

Cambridge University 29, 76, 96, 101, 107

Cartesianism 69, 73

Catholicism/Catholics 7, 10, 11, 16, 17, 19, 21, 23, 38, 39, 81, 83, 129, 226, 257, 260, 284, 307, 309, 311, 312

Cavalier party 14

chemistry/chymistry 6, 47, 84, 85, 186, 219

Christ Church (Oxford) 4, 5, 18, 19, 24, 34, 37, 39, 62, 174, 175, 189, 224, 271, 281, 290

Christianity/Christians 20, 21, 66, 95, 96, 111, 114, 142, 143, 153, 213, 246, 260, 263, 269, 270, 271, 272, 277, 297, 299, 304, 305, 306, 307, 309, 311, 312, 313, 316

chronology 15, **37–41**, 134, 268

Church of England 2, 3, 4, 101, 113, 114, 116, 141, 225, 255, 269, 270, 272, 297, 298, 299

Civil War(s) 1, 2, 14, 16, 17, 22, 37, 58, 80, 84, 148, 206, 254

Cleves 7, 8, 19, 37, 66, 225

coinage 29, **129–31**

consciousness 26, 115, 116, 151, 169, 176, 185, 196, 197, 198, 247

consent 17, 31, 60, 70, 98, 99, 101, 119, 120, 121, 122, 131, **131–3**, 135, 143, 167, 168, 176, 184, 190, 202, 203, 217, 218, 231, 250, 263, 310

constitutionalism, ancient **124–7**, 210

Convention 22, 23, 32, 39, 126

corpuscularianism 48, 50, 200, 238
Country party 13, 14, 31, 32
currency 25, 29, 61, 129, 130, 131, 274
curriculum 89, **133–4**, 283, 284, 286, 307

deism 27, 96, **135–7**, 270
democracy 12, 14, 126, 303
demonstration 33, 72, 94, 153, **169–70**, 173, 180, 240, 241, 244
devaluation 29, 231, 273, 274
dissenters 3, 16, 19, 23, 29, 33, 38, 39, 63, 66, 81, 114, 137, 225, 226, 227, 264, 269, 297, 309
Dordrecht, Synod of 65, 66
Dover, Treaty of 10
dualism 77, 91, 176
Dutch Republic 10, 54, 65, 254
Dutch Wars 7, 10

East India Company 15, 34, 273, 274
economics xi, 12, 25, 205, 269, 316
Edict of Nantes 20, 39, 225, 257, 303, 309, 310, 311
empiricism 13, 52, 56, 76, 85, 92, 94, 156, 212, 281, 285, 286, 288, 289
Enlightenment xi, 1, 20, 21, 27, 34, 135, 143, 288, 289, 303, 304, 305, 306, 307, 312, 313
enthusiasm 2, 25, 42, 68, 94, 136, **141–3**, 241, 248
epistemology xi, 6, 13, 54, 55, 61, 79, 154, 159, 174, 232, 269, 281, 283, 284, 285, 287, 289, 290, 298, 314, 316
equality 58, 60, 61, 120, 217, 223, 250, 255, 298, 306
essences
  nominal 49, **143–5**, 185, 186
  real 49, 87, 100, **143–5**, 186, 187, 221, 223, 232
ethics xi, 13, 72, 73, 74, 110, 134, 147, 156, 157, 174, 183, 245, 246, 268, 304, 307, 309, 312

faculties 55, 56, 136, 137, **145–6**, 148, 149, 158, 165, 174, 175, 195, 212, 217, 295
France xii, 10, 14, 15, 19, 20, 21, 22, 23, 32, 37, 38, 39, 40, 41, 53, 54, 80, 81, 83, 87, 121, 194, 210, 240, 241, 257, 281, 282, 287, 289, 303, 304, 305, 309, 311
free will **150–3**

geography 133, 134, 268
geometry 50, 72, 77, 134, 219, 268, 282
Germany 29, 289

Habeas Corpus Act 38
hedonism **156–7**, 184, 190, 248
history, natural 87, **186–8**, 234
Hobbism 61, 63, 64, 194, 270
Holland ix, 8, 10, 18, 19, 20, 21, 22, 23, 29, 38, 39, 69, 72, 76, 77, 78, 82, 87, 95, 265, 273
Huguenots 20, 21, 39, 225, 303, 304, 309, 311
hypothesis 48, 49, 50, 74, 79, 103, 104, **157–9**, 182, 187, 195, 200

idealism 160, 286
ideas, association of 25, 42, **127–9**, 248, 276, 286
identity, personal 99, **196–9**, 241, 247
immaterialism 92, 103
Indulgence, Declaration of 10, 39, 81
innateness **165–8**
innatism 26, 28, 52, 54, 98, 99, 186, 214, 239, 246, 294, 296
Inquisition 17, 67
interest rate 12, 204, 205, 273, 274
Interregnum 141, 206, 208
intuition **169–70**, 240, 241, 244
Ireland xii, 22, 30, 32, 39, 40

Jacobites 22, 24, 39
Jews 137, 261, 269
Journal des sçavans 304

Latitudinarians 66, 105, 272
law, natural 63, 64, 156, 157, 168, **188–91**, 193, 194, 217, 253, 261, 269, 308, 309, 310, 311, 312, 315
liberalism 2, 249, 250, 251, 303
liberty 1, 6, 13, 17, 23, 27, 30, 33, 60, 61, 62, 67, 82, 105, 121, 135, 207, 208, 209, 210, 242, 249, 251, 261, 310

Licensing Act 27
logic 51, 54, 69, 140, **174–5**, 180, 223, 268, 276, 282, 284
London 3, 6, 8, 11, 16, 17, 21, 28, 29, 32, 37, 38, 41, 42, 48, 51, 61, 76, 77, 78, 80, 82, 83, 84, 85, 103, 109, 246, 257, 282, 289
  Great Fire of 37
  Tower of 16, 18, 38, 81, 83
Lovelace Collection ix, 314
Lutherans 7, 311

Magna Carta 22, 124, 126
Marxism 250
mathematics 50, 76, 77, 89, 138, 165, 174, 183, 192, 282
metaphysics 4, 59, 70, 71, 91, 92, 97, 107, 133, 145, 176, 224, 285, 287, 288, **292–302**
modes 72, 94, 161, 164, 165, 169, 174, **177–9**, 185, 191, 192, 215, 219, 221, 223, 233, 240, 242, 243, 244, 245, 246, 247, 284, 314
Molyneux Problem 26, **179–83**, 195
morality 13, 26, 27, 52, 64, 70, 72, 73, 74, 78, 93, 94, 110, 134, 138, 141, 156, 163, 165, 170, **183–4**, 186, 189, 192, 193, 194, 225, 234, 237, 240, 241, 141, 148, 249, 281, 287, 308, 309, 312
Muslims 260, 261

nature, state of 63, 132, 190, 193, 202, **216–18**, 250, 251, 253, 310
Netherlands, the xii, 19, 20, 54, 65, 83, 241, 257, 289, 304, 307
Nine Years War 22, 39, 129, 204, 274

Oates 28, 29, 32, 34, 40, 41, 72, 78, 109, 110, 287
occasionalism 69, 70, 73, 74
optics 77, 89, 247
Oxford 4, 5, 7, 8, 9, 16, 17, 18, 25, 26, 28, 37, 38, 40, 41, 48, 49, 53, 62, 64, 81, 82, 85, 86, 96, 103, 105, 110, 175, 189, 234, 246, 247, 254, 265, 270, 282, 283, 285, 314
Oxford Parliament 16, 17, 38, 83, 254

Oxford University **4–6**, 34, 38

Paris 9, 15, 38, 54, 68, 109, 241, 304
Parliamentarians 2, 5, 13, 14
Pensford 1
perception 49, 54, 55, 70, 90, **145–6**, 148, 153, 154, 160, 161, 162, 164, 169, 171, 172, 173, 181, **194–6**, 199, 200, 238, 241, 244, 246, 298, 314
philosophy
  mechanical 6, 48, 97
  moral 5, 6, 13, 15, 26, 37, 73, 129, 184
  natural 4, 6, 47, 48, 50, 53, 54, 59, 61, 76, 77, 79, 85, 134, 158, 166, 170, 186, 200, 248, 268, 281, 281, 281, 285, 314, 315
  political 11, 209, 251, 254
physics 60, 61, 76, 77, 285, 287, 289
Platonism 76, 113
politics xi, 3, 9, 10, 17, 32, 57, 63, 67, 84, 85, 96, 111, 126, 127, 134, 201, 207, 231, 250, 251, 252, 254, 255, 261, 264, 273, 274, **281–92**, 293, 294, 299, 300, 303, 307, 308, 316
Poor Law 30
popery 2, 15, 17
property 17, 23, 121, 132, 190, **201–4**, 249, 250, 251, 252, 308, 310, 315
Protestantism/Protestants 4, 7, 17, 20, 23, 66, 225, 227, 304, 307, 308, 309, 311, 312
psychology, moral 15, 140
Puritanism/Puritans 2, 5, 11
Pyrrhonism 71, 72

Quakers 2, 226
qualities
  primary 49, **199–201**, 221, 224, 242
  secondary 49, 90, 108, **199–201**, 221, 242

rationalism 156, 289, 303, 313
recoinage 25, 29, 40, 130, 230, 274, 316
Reformation 1, 28, 210, 227, 272
religion, natural 27, 101, 135, 136, 137, 153, 271
Remonstrants 20, 65, 66, 306, 307, 309
Renaissance 9, 140, 170, 174, 282

republicanism **206–9**
République des Lettres 98, **302–13**
Restoration 2, 4, 5, 7, 13, 14, 37, 63, 81, 84, 119, 141, 208, 224, 254
Revolution 7, 9, 10, 14, 17, 18, 21, 22, 23, 24, 25, 28, 31, 32, 34, 39, 61, 101, 105, 126, 140, 206, **209–11**, 225, 246, 252, 255, 256, 289, 303, 315
  American 61, 316
  French 303
  Glorious 39, 61, 101, 105, 246, 315
Rights, Bill of 22, 23
Rome 58, 113, 114, 208, 218, 263
Royal Society 6, 37, 40, 76, 77, 179, 281, 282, 314, 315
royalists 4, 5, 13, 58, 120, 254
Rye House Plot 18, 38, 241

scepticism 2, 22, 55, 71, 90, 97, 108, 113, 115, 145, 160, 163, 186, 187, 195, 226, 227, 237, 248
scholasticism/scholastics 47, 48, 50, 185, 188, **211–13**, 238, 240, 243, 244
Scottish Succession Act 38
slavery 11, 19, 28
social contract **131–3**, 251, 310
Socinianism 26, 95, 96, 102, **213–15**, 270, 285, 316
Spain 7, 32, 87, 231
species 47, 48, 87, **122–3**, 144, 145, 159, 173, 187, 215, 217, 219, 220, 221, 224, 236, 238, 240, 243, 293

substance 27, 92, 99, 115, 116, 154, 160, 165, 178, 212, **218–24**, 229, 230, 235, 242, 243, 246, 248, 294, 295, 296

Thirty Years War 7
toleration 3, 7, 8, 10, 17, 19, 20, 21, 27, 28, 29, 42, 66, 74, 81, 105, 106, 113, 114, 121, 135, 136, 213, 214, **224–7**, 257, 258, 260, 261, 261, 264, 272, 283, 285, 294, 299, 305, 306, 309, 310, 312, 316
Toleration Act 23, 39, 225, 227, 297
Tories 16, 19, 22, 24, 29, 31, 32, 82, 254
transubstantiation 129, 248
Trinity, doctrine of the 25, 27, 95, 115, 116, 155, 270, 293, 298

Uniformity, Act of 5, 37
Unitarianism/Unitarians 95, 96, 213, 270, 271
universals **122–3**, 162
utilitarianism 157

volition **150–3**, 161

West Country 1, 2, 19, 21, 30, 31, 34
West Indies 11, 19
Westminster School 3, 37
Westphalia, Treaty of 7, 37
women, education of 73, 74